THE SYMBOLIC TURN

THE SYMBOLIC TURN

Prabhuji

The Symbolic Turn
by Prabhuji

Copyright © 2026
First edition

Printed in Round Top, New York, United States

All rights reserved. None of the information contained in this book may be reproduced, republished, or re-disseminated in any manner or form without the prior written consent of the publisher.

Published by Prabhuji Mission
Website: prabhuji.net

Avadhutashram
PO Box 900
Cairo, NY, 12413
USA

Painting on the cover by Prabhuji:
"The symbolic turn"
Acrylic on canvas, New York, USA, 2018
Canvas Size: 24"x24"

Library of Congress Control Number: 2025903444
ISBN-13: 978-1-945894-58-9

Contents

Preface.. 1
Introduction 5

Section I: Concepts, symbols, and myths

Chapter 1: The concept and the symbol according to Plato and Aristotle..17
Chapter 2: Mythology and symbols: exploring the roots of human understanding.. 27
Chapter 3: The conceptual fracture and symbolic integration 35
Chapter 4: The concept: the screen of reality 47
Chapter 5: Deciphering the enigma through concepts and symbols 55
Chapter 6: Searching for meaning in a universe of symbols.................. 67
Chapter 7: Semiotics: exploring the language of signs and symbols.......75
Bibliography section I 83

Section II: Symbols and philosophy

Chapter 8: Myths and symbols according to Friedrich Creuzer............ 87
Chapter 9: Myth and logos: the power of symbolic narrative...............103
Chapter 10: The myth transcends reason 111
Chapter 11: Concepts, symbols, and language: Kant's vision...............125
Chapter 12: Symbol: Hegel's artistic-religious approach 143
Bibliography section II...159

Section III: Symbols and religion

Chapter 13: Imagination: a bridge between myth and reality..............163
Chapter 14: The gates of myth toward the inexplicable 177
Chapter 15: The influence of concept on spirituality............................193
Chapter 16: The symbolism of religious poetry 201
Chapter 17: The symbols of Christianity... 235

Chapter 18: Christ as a living symbol according to John Damascene .. 259
Chapter 19: The symbols of *Gauḍīya* Vaishnavism 285
Chapter 20: *Mitzvot*: Symbols of the Return 337
Chapter 21: Mandalas: meetings between symbols and intuition 357
Chapter 22: The symbolism of Plato's allegory of the cave 365
Chapter 23: Symbols, myths, and self-consciousness: Ricoeur's approach 391
Bibliography section III 399

SECTION IV: SYMBOLS AND THE HUMAN BEING

Chapter 24: Myths: windows to the human psyche 403
Chapter 25: The human being: a hermeneutical and symbolic entity .. 413
Chapter 26: Symbolism and hegemony: constructing realities through discourse 425
Chapter 27: Symbolism in psychology: a path of integration 441
Chapter 28: An invitation to transcendence in Rilke's poetry 463
Chapter 29: Tracing the origins of symbolic language 479
Bibliography section IV 555

APPENDICES

About Prabhuji 561
The term *prabhuji* by Swami Ramananda 573
The term *avadhūta* 575
About the Prabhuji Mission 585
About the Avadhutashram 587
The Retroprogressive Path 589
Prabhuji today 591
Titles by Prabhuji 594

ॐ अज्ञानतिमिरान्धस्य ज्ञानाञ्जनशलाकया ।
चक्षुरुन्मीलितं येन तस्मै श्रीगुरवे नमः ॥

oṁ ajñāna-timirāndhasya
jñānāñjana-śalākayā
cakṣur unmīlitaṁ yena
tasmai śrī-gurave namaḥ

Salutations unto that holy Guru who, applying the ointment [medicine] of [spiritual] knowledge, removes the darkness of ignorance of the blinded [unenlightened] and opens their eyes.

This book is dedicated, with deep gratitude and eternal respect, to the holy lotus feet of my beloved masters His Divine Grace Bhakti-kavi Atulānanda Ācārya Mahārāja (Gurudeva) and His Divine Grace Avadhūta Śrī Brahmānanda Bābājī Mahārāja (Guru Mahārāja).

Preface

The story of my life is an odyssey from what I believed myself to be to what I truly am… an inner and outer pilgrimage. A journey from the personal to the universal, from the partial to the whole, from the illusory to the real, from the apparent to the true. A wandering flight from the human to the Divine.

Everything that awakens at dawn rests at dusk; every lit flame eventually extinguishes. Only what begins, ends; only what starts, finishes. But what dwells in the present is neither born nor dies, for that which lacks a beginning never perishes.

As a simple autobiographer and narrator of significant experiences, I share my intimate story with others. My story is not public but profoundly private and intimate. It does not belong to the turmoil of social life, but is a sigh kept in the most hidden depths of the soul.

I am a disciple of seers, enlightened beings, shadows of the universe who are nobody and walk in death. I am just a whim or perhaps a joke from the heavens and the only mistake of my beloved spiritual masters. I was initiated in my spiritual childhood by the moonlight, which showed me its light and shared its being with me. My muse was a seagull that loved to fly more than anything else in life.

In love with the impossible, I traversed the universe, obsessed with the brilliance of a star. I traveled countless paths, following the traces and vestiges of those with the vision to decipher the hidden. Like the ocean that longs for water, I sought my home within my own house.

I do not claim to be a guide, coach, teacher, instructor, educator, psychologist, enlightener, pedagogue, evangelist, rabbi, *posek halacha*, healer, therapist, satsangist, psychic, leader, medium, savior, guru, or authority of any kind, whether spiritual or material. I allow myself the audacity and daring to represent nothing and no one but myself. I am only a traveler whom you can ask for directions. With pleasure, I point you to a place where everything calms upon arrival... beyond the sun and the stars, your desires and longings, time and space, concepts and conclusions, and beyond all that you believe you are or imagine you will be.

I paint sighs, hopes, silences, aspirations, and melancholies, inner landscapes, and sunsets of the soul. I am a painter of the indescribable, inexpressible, and indefinable, and unconfessable of our depths… or maybe I just write colors and paint words. Aware of the abyss that separates revelation and works, I live in a frustrated attempt to faithfully express the mystery of the spirit.

Since childhood, little windows of paper captivated my attention; through them, I visited places, met people, and made friends. Those tiny mandalas were my true elementary school, high school, and college. Like skilled teachers, these *yantras* have guided me through contemplation, attention, concentration, observation, and meditation.

Like a physician studies the human body, or a lawyer studies laws, I have dedicated my entire life to the study of myself. I can say with certainty that I know what resides and lives in this heart.

My purpose is not to persuade others. It is not my intention to convince anyone of anything. I do not offer theology or philosophy, nor do I preach or teach, I simply think out loud. The echo of these words may lead you to the infinite space of peace, silence, love, existence, consciousness, and absolute bliss.

Do not search for me. Search for yourself. You do not need me or anyone else, because the only thing that really matters is you. What you yearn for lies within you, as what you are, here and now.

I am not a merchant of rehashed information, nor do I intend to do business with my spirituality. I do not teach beliefs or philosophies. I only speak about what I see and just share what I know.

Avoid fame, for true glory is not based on public opinion but on what you really are. What matters is not what others think of you, but your own appreciation of who you are.

Choose bliss over success, life over reputation, and wisdom over information. If you succeed, you will know not only admiration but also true envy. Jealousy is mediocrity's tribute to talent and an open acceptance of one's own inferiority.

I advise you to fly freely and never be afraid of making mistakes. Learn the art of transforming your mistakes into lessons. Never blame others for your faults: remember that taking complete responsibility for your life is a sign of maturity. Flying teaches you that what matters is not touching the sky but having the courage to spread your wings. The higher you rise, the more graciously small and insignificant the world will seem. As you walk, sooner or later you will understand that every search begins and ends in you.

Your unconditional well-wisher,

Prabhuji

Introduction

In the field of Western philosophy, the term *turn* refers to changes, more or less radical, of paradigm, which have led to significant transformations in the prevailing philosophical conceptions and practices at different moments or stages of the discipline. In this sense, the turn indicates changes in strategy, methodology, and vision that have determined how philosophy has gone about addressing and unravelling the problems and questions to which it has been responding since its origin. The different turns, at times explicit, at others implicit, which have transfigured the focus and standpoint of philosophy and its way of approaching reality, the world, and human beings over centuries and millennia, are those that have been shaping the evolution of the Western philosophical tradition. In other words, the history of Western philosophy is in part the result of the more or less radical turns that have pluralized and guided it, making it evolve.

However, the importance of the turn is not solely historical, in the sense that we may venture to define the history of philosophy as the history of its turns. Beyond that, the notion of the turn is important because it manifests profound epistemological shifts, interrogative reconfigurations and methodological reconceptualizations that define Western philosophy itself. In this sense, we might affirm that philosophy is nothing but a turn, that is, a paradigm shift whose birth in ancient Greece marked a new way of understanding the world and human existence through empirical observation, rational argumentation, and logical discourse. The emergence of this new paradigm has sometimes been poorly interpreted as if it had to do with a transitional process through which logos came to replace myth, that is, the mythical interpretations and explanations that human beings had used until then to help understand themselves in the world. But, in fact, myth is used by Plato himself on multiple occasions to explain different specific realities (the winged chariot, the myth of the cave, and so on).

As we will see later in greater detail and depth, the misinterpretation of the transition from myth to logos has had dramatic consequences. It has led to marginalizing and dismissing myth and the symbols that mythology employs to access truth and, with that, it has also ended up redrawing the parameters of human thought and imposing a new conception of reality based on a supposed pure rationality that has self-proclaimed as the only acceptable way to reach the deepest core of the human being itself.

If the supposed transition to logos introduced reason and observation as parameters to understand the world and human beings beyond mythological thought, later turns within the same Western philosophical tradition gradually went on refining and perfecting its observation and methodology. These new turns became fundamental for philosophy as a discipline and, more importantly, for the way in which human beings could rethink the world, and their own place in it. One such paradigm shift on the horizon of logos was what we know as the Enlightenment. In the field of philosophy, this 18th-century current had as one of its principal exponents the German philosopher Immanuel Kant, whose monumental work *Critique of Pure Reason* introduced us with philosophical audacity to what we now know as the "Copernican turn." The Kantian revolution resided in suggesting that mental structures and categories inherent to the cognizing entity molded our experience and wisdom, thus leaving behind the idea that knowledge is a passive reflection of the external world. Here the label "turn" suggests once again a total remodel of existing nuclear and peripheral structures that puts in a place of prominence and centrality what previously had been pushed into the margins. Prior to Kantian philosophy, the ontic, or the thing in itself, stood as the axis of philosophical reflections while knowledge circulated around. Upon the advent of Kantian thought, and its Copernican turn, the transcendental subject usurped the central position, which relegated the thing around it to a secondary orbit. That is, from Kant on, truth did not reside in the object of our observation and comprehension anymore, but rather in the structures of human thought. It could be said that the Kantian revolution represented a paradigm shift. It laid the foundations for a new philosophy that, from that moment on, would be rational and based on the transcendental subject rather than the object. However, this paradigm shift did not merely shake the foundations of the universities of philosophy, but transcended the confines of the discipline, permeating and shaping a new way of understanding reality, the world, and human beings, both philosophically but also in the fields of religion (through its theologization) and of the sciences, be they social, natural, or mathematical.

This "Copernican turn" inaugurated by Kant later gave rise to a new turn known as the "linguistic turn" or "linguistic-pragmatic turn," which established that language does not simply express thought and what is signified by it, but rather, it is thought and reality that are preceded and governed by the structures of the language.

This means that now, the cosmos is comprehensible not solely from the rational, transcendental subject, but also from and through the language of said transcendental subject. If until then, philosophical consensus in general was that language was sculpted on the basis of the objects of thought, in this post-linguistic turn era, it is those objects of thought that are the ones that acquire meaning through verbal syntax.

Reality is eminently linguistic and is and has meaning insofar as it is expressed linguistically. In the terms of the British philosopher J. L. Austin, in his work *How to do things with words*, "language creates reality." This is precisely the core of the paradigm shift of the linguistic turn; that is, that which is also known as "the performative act of language." To say something with the intention of doing something does not simply describe reality but changes it. This implies a confrontation with realism, a theory for which, on the basis of the concept of *phýsis* (that which sprouts and remains), doing does not necessarily intend to change reality, but rather simply lets things happen as they should, according to their nature, or at most, to correct that which is not *conforme natura* to bring it as close as possible to its exemplary cause. Paradoxically, this has already been explained by Hebrew wisdom in affirming that the Torah (language) was created before the world:

כַּד בָּרָא קוּדְשָׁא בְּרִיךְ הוּא עָלְמָא, אִסְתָּכַּל בָּהּ בְּאוֹרַיְיתָא, וּבָרָא עָלְמָא,
וּבְאוֹרַיְיתָא אִתְבְּרֵי עָלְמָא [...]
[...] דְּעַד אִתְבְּרֵי עָלְמָא, אַקְדִּימַת אוֹרַיְיתָא תְּרֵין אַלְפֵי שְׁנִין לְעָלְמָא, וְכַד בָּעָא
קוּדְשָׁא בְּרִיךְ הוּא לְמִבְרֵי עָלְמָא, הֲוָה מִסְתַּכָּל בָּהּ בְּאוֹרַיְיתָא, בְּכָל מִלָּה וּמִלָּה,
וְעָבִיד לָקֳבְלָהּ אוּמָנוּתָא דְּעָלְמָא.
(ספר הזוהר, פרשת תרומה, קס"א, א')

When the Holy One, blessed be He, created the world, He looked into the Torah and created the world; and thus, the world was created through the Torah.

...Before the world was created, the Torah preceded it by two thousand years. And when the Holy One, blessed be He, desired to create the world, He contemplated the Torah in every detail, and made the world correspondingly with His eternal wisdom.

(*Zohar*, "*Terumah*," 161.1)

הַתּוֹרָה אוֹמֶרֶת: אֲנִי הָיִיתִי כְּלִי אֻמְנוּתוֹ שֶׁל הַקָּדוֹשׁ בָּרוּךְ הוּא, בְּנֹהַג שֶׁבָּעוֹלָם מֶלֶךְ בָּשָׂר וָדָם בּוֹנֶה פָּלָטִין, אֵינוֹ בּוֹנֶה אוֹתָהּ מִדַּעַת עַצְמוֹ אֶלָּא מִדַּעַת אֻמָּן, וְהָאֻמָּן אֵינוֹ בּוֹנֶה אוֹתָהּ מִדַּעַת עַצְמוֹ אֶלָּא דִּפְתְּרָאוֹת וּפִנְקְסָאוֹת יֵשׁ לוֹ, לָדַעַת הֵיאךְ הוּא עוֹשֶׂה חֲדָרִים, הֵיאךְ הוּא עוֹשֶׂה פִּשְׁפְּשִׁין. כָּךְ הָיָה הַקָּדוֹשׁ בָּרוּךְ הוּא מַבִּיט בַּתּוֹרָה וּבוֹרֵא אֶת הָעוֹלָם, וְהַתּוֹרָה אָמְרָה "בְּרֵאשִׁית בָּרָא אֱלֹקִים". וְאֵין רֵאשִׁית אֶלָּא תּוֹרָה, הֵיאַךְ מָה דְּאַתְּ אָמַר (משלי ח', כ"ב): "ה' קָנָנִי רֵאשִׁית דַּרְכּוֹ".
(בראשית רבה, א', א')

The Torah says: "I was the crafting tool of the Holy One, blessed be He." The way of the world is that when a flesh-and-blood king builds a palace, he does not do it out of his mind but with the knowledge of an artisan. And the artisan does not create it from his own mind; instead, he has [plans

> and manuals written on] sheets and booklets to ascertain how he should make rooms and how to create doors. So, too, the Holy One, blessed be He, looked in the Torah and created the world. The Torah says: "In the beginning (*bereshit*) God created" (Genesis, 1:1), and beginning (*reshit*) is nothing else but the Torah, as it says: "The Lord acquired me at the beginning of His way."
>
> (*Bereshit Rabbah*, 1.1)

It is in this context of Western philosophy, marked first by the appearance of a logos that burst the seams of mythology, and then later, by the Copernican and linguistic turns, that a new turn emerges, which we call the "symbolic turn."

Like previous turns, this one also manifests a modification in perspective and in the way in which we grasp and understand phenomena and reality.

However, unlike previous turns, the symbolic turn is accompanied by a revalorization of the essentiality of symbols and signs in the creation of meanings.

Instead of being limited to a transcendental subject that ideates the world through rational and conceptual language, the symbolic turn emphasizes the immanence of the symbolic dimension in human life, which not only the linguistic and Copernican turns, but also Western philosophy in its entirety, have been veiling and ignoring to the point of placing it on the brink of oblivion, thus impoverishing any possible understanding of the human being.

The symbolic turn is a crucial shift that, by scrutinizing the depths of our thinking, modernized by the Enlightenment, will allow us to see how symbols contribute to shaping meanings and values, acting as chisels and hammers in the sculpting of our perceptions of the cosmos and in understanding our place in it. As we will see in more detail in the following chapters, symbols, as vessels laden with entangled meanings, distill effluvia from the depths and subtleties of our experience which, as such, evade the syntactic structures of the transcendental subject.

In this sense, it is worth emphasizing that the symbolic approach builds a bridge, encouraging us to embark on an exploration of the complex relationships between symbols, myths, rituals, and narratives, in order to recover the symbolic dimension of human existence that the previous turns had gradually gone burying.

As a philosophical revolution, the symbolic turn paves the way toward hermeneutics, with the aim of rethinking crucial questions such as the purpose of life, the transcendental, and the symbiotic relationship between the individual and the sacred. From the perspective of the symbolic turn, human beings transcend the bonds of the natural order, and plunge into an expansive reality that engulfs and reconfigures them. To reformulate, the human being is more than a transcendental subject capable of ideating the world rationally through syntactic and discursive structures.

Language, mythology, science, and art merge in the experience of humanity. To denigrate mythology and symbols, banishing them from true knowledge, can be considered a form of reductionism that has impoverished both knowledge itself and the philosophy that engages with it; however, to now undermine science, philosophy, and logical reason itself would be falling into the same trap.

For that reason, it is important to clarify that the symbolic turn does not seek to dig up the symbolic-mythological dimension of human thinking to simply deny rationality and to replace it. It is not about recovering myth in order to forget logos. Far from this, the objective of the symbolic turn is to allow this symbolic-mythological dimension of our being to resurface and to be considered a source of a more complete, and also more complex and enriched knowledge, which Western philosophy had previously renounced.

In this sense, the symbolic turn in philosophy marks a paradigmatic transition, underlining the importance that symbols and symbolic language systems have in the generation of meaning and, therefore, in the elucidation of reality and human experience beyond what the paradigms of previous philosophical turns had determined.

Human beings found themselves trapped in the diaphanous layers of reality, veiled by the curtain of linguistic forms, artistic images, mythical symbols, and religious rituals. That which the unveiling of the symbolic dimension shows us is that human existence is not merely a journey through a physical world, but rather it is an immersion in a realm of symbolic nature, where, without renouncing their physical dimension, human beings discover their authentic essence, beyond limits imposed by their rationality and linguisticity.

The symbolic turn offers us invaluable help in our incessant quest for self-knowledge, by allowing symbolic forms to emerge from the bosom of human consciousness so that what is genuinely human can unfold and be recognized.

In different terms, symbols emerge as the primordial expression of the human spirit. In them reside the transcendence and the inescapable relevance of its understanding. Symbols are the language of the soul or the means to communicate our innermost intimacy. The symbolic turn shows us that humans are more than "rational animals," since reason is not the essential principle driving and guiding them in their scientific as well as their religious activities.

A religion based exclusively on reason becomes a superficial experience, if it lacks the symbolic, poetic, and devotional languages, which enrich and deepen the religious experience. The stance of rationalism, which maintains that truth is exclusively the domain of reason, is not completely accurate. Our critique is not directed toward rationality *per se*, but rather toward rationalism as the doctrine, which limits truth to the realm of the rational. Reason, although fundamental, should not be considered as the sole tool to discover truth. We advocate for a balanced and reflective use of reason, avoiding the extreme of considering it as the only valid source of knowledge. This perspective allows us to embrace a broader and more nuanced understanding of truth, which integrates other forms of knowledge capable of transcending the limits of reason. That is, we promote the use but not the abuse of reason.

Ultimately, rationality constitutes only a derivative expression of more basic and fundamental principles that pervade human existence; for example, in its connatural relationship to Being. In the context of Heideggerian philosophy, especially in the work *Letter on Humanism*, a unique perspective on the essence of *Dasein* (being-there) is highlighted. Heidegger argues that what truly defines *Dasein* is not its animalistic nature or its rational capacity, but rather its relationship with Being, that is to say, *Dasein*'s inherent openness toward Being. For Heidegger, this connection with Being is far more fundamental and primordial than the characteristics of being animal or rational. This approach highlights the importance of understanding *Dasein* both in terms of its biological or cognitive attributes and its profound relationship with Being.

In its desperate aspiration to encapsulate the multifaceted essence of *Homo sapiens*, rationality exhibits its insurmountable impotence. By imprisoning the vast defining spectrum of the human being within the confined cage of rationality, the entangled and profound complexity of humanity is undermined, becoming lethargic in a single and impoverished dimension.

Moreover, the transcendental *telos*, or "purpose," of the philosophy of symbolic forms is not confined to the mere apprehension of nature, but rather delves into self-consciousness. The symbolic essence of human beings enables self-identification through various forms. It is through the symbol that humans may reveal their authentic Being. The human spirit expands itself in the infinite cultural cosmos, finding in such vastness its own mirror image and self-knowledge. As suggested by the German thinker Ernst Cassirer, it is the cultural manifestations of humanity, precisely imbued with a preponderant symbolic quality, that urge us to reevaluate human identity, advocating for a reconfiguration of *Homo sapiens* into *animal symbolicum* or "symbolic entity."

In this conceptual framework, the creative aspect is extolled, which is intrinsic to our essence, namely, the immanent aptitude that allows us to manipulate symbology, metamorphosing it into a vital utensil to forge meaning and to act as a viaduct toward interpreting our existence. *Homo sapiens* not only emerge from the mire as rational and linguistic creatures, but also, simultaneously, and through the mediation of symbols, reveal themselves as symbolic animals. This is evident with the Buddha, Muhammad, Moses, Jesus, Lao Tze, Mahāvīra, and Śrī Chaitanya Mahāprabhu. Furthermore, and as Retroprogressive Path well shows in its symbolic pirouette, the presence of the symbolic does not hang from the thread of objective reality, but rather it is the existence of entities that is the fruit of the human symbolic condition.

If the human species, with its transcendental imaginative capacity, were not to weave reality in the loom of its psyche, entities would disappear from its perception. What this indicates is that, just like Kant's Copernican turn and the later linguistic turn complementing it, the symbolic turn also constitutes an epistemological turn that places again in the center what had previously been condemned to wander the periphery, thus allowing now for the symbol to burst forth from the abysses of consciousness to open us up to a self-knowledge of greater depth, richness, and complexity.

Our objective is to address a twofold task. First, we adhere to the Western metaphysical structure in order to deepen its conception of Being. However, we will implement a symbolic turn in which the symbol will not be reduced to being a simple metaphor. Instead, we will interpret it as the essence of the same reality that the Western tradition attempts to describe. This symbolic approach allows us to have a more comprehensive and deeper understanding of the issues at hand and will move us away from superficial interpretations and toward a more holistic and meaningful vision.

Section I

Concepts, symbols, and myths

Chapter 1

The concept and the symbol according to Plato and Aristotle

The term *symbol* has been extensively discussed within the realm of classical philosophy, especially by its two pillars: Plato and Aristotle. For our analysis, we will turn to some of the quotations selected and commented upon by Iulian Butnaru in his doctoral dissertation *Nature and Scope of the Symbol.*[1] According to Aristotle, the symbol refers to the word *symbola*, which means "contract, convention, sign, or agreement." As he states in the logical treatise *On Interpretation*, more commonly known as *Peri Hermeneias* (Περὶ Ἑρμηνείας):

> Words spoken are symbols or signs of affections or impressions of the soul; written words are the signs of words spoken.[2]

The term "affections of the soul" means that within the internal realm of the human being, representations, terminologies, and connotations reside. When we say *dog*, this word affects the soul in such a way that the meaning of the word *dog* resonates in the soul of the listener, whether it be in Spanish as *perro* or in Hebrew as *kelev*. Such an expression, when vocalized, evokes pre-existing mental images and constructions intrinsic to the soul. Similarly, when the word *dog* is written down, it refers to a concrete image. But this written

---

1. Iulian Butnaru, *Nature and Scope of the Symbol* (*Naturaleza y alcance del símbolo*) (Tarragona: Universidad Rovira i Virgili, 2016).

2. Aristotle, *On Interpretation* 16a3–8, trans. Harold P. Cooke, in *Aristotle: Categories. On Interpretation. Prior Analytics*, Loeb Classical Library 325 (Cambridge, MA: Harvard University Press, 1938), 114–115.

word is not merely a graphic representation; it is also an auditory reference that, in turn, alludes to a mental construction representing a real entity. That reality imprints an image in the soul, representing content that has a meaning. This meaning, in turn, has a concept: a carnivorous mammal domesticated by humans, belonging to the canine family, characterized by its sharp sense of smell and hearing, intelligence, and loyalty to humans, who have domesticated it since prehistoric times. This definition leads to a vocal expression, which, correspondingly, leads to its written form: dog. Thus, considering the tangible dog, writing acts as a reflection of oral expression, which is the echo of the mental concept, which is finally an interpretation of the real entity. Therefore, in line with Aristotle, writing is a symbol of the voice, the voice is a symbol of the concept, and the concept is a symbol of the concrete reality.

From the Aristotelian perspective, a symbol is defined as a manifestation, whether it be the result of a convention or of nature itself. The concept, for its part, as we have just seen, is a natural symbol of reality, which, formed through the process of abstraction, finds residence in our understanding.

Let us consider an example: when observing an individual and distilling their essence, I affirm that Jaime is a rational and socio-political entity. This conceptual essence that I harbor in my consciousness is a faithful reflection of Jaime's identity. It is not an arbitrary invention, but an essence directly extracted from Jaime, an essence that he possesses. Thus, the relationship between my cognitive representation and the intrinsic essence of Jaime is direct and unmediated. From this premise, Aristotle concludes that we are dealing with a *kata physin*, or "natural symbol," meaning in harmony with nature.

In the philosophical sphere, the concept operates as the semantic reflection of the object. However, when referring to the term, the sign, or the expression *dog*, there is no suggestion of an inherent quality. In other words, the concept is a symbol of the thing, but when we say the voice, the concept, or the word *dog*, it is not natural. Aristotle says that I could mention that concept with different terms or other words. It is evident, given the profusion of languages in our world, that if words were innate, polyglotism would be a chimera. The reason we can describe reality with multiple terms is that the word is merely the sonic reflection of the concept lodged in the soul. However, this correspondence between word and concept is not innate or "by nature," but rather, in Aristotelian terms, *kata syntheken*, or "symbol by convention." It is possible to refer to the same reality with different words because the word is the symbol of the voice *dog*, and the voice *dog* is a symbol of what is in the soul, which is the concept.

Nevertheless, according to Aristotle, it is not the concept by nature but the *kata syntheken* or "by convention." This linguistic convention arises from collective agreements; therefore, naming a canine as "dog" is the result of a social consensus. On the other hand, if a different nomenclature is used in another region, it is not necessarily wrong. Aristotle does not categorize words as right or wrong; instead, he situates truth or falsity in the realm of concepts. For the Stagirite, what truly matters is the concept because it is this, and not the word, that can be true or false. For example, if we say that the dog is a living being with three legs, that would be incorrect, whereas mentioning the concept with the word *dog* cannot be either correct or incorrect, as it is merely a convention.

In Aristotelian thought, the notion of symbol presents itself as a representative figure. It is common to identify the symbol as a mere construct intended to evoke another object; this interpretation corresponds to the so-called "conventional symbol" (*kata syntheken*) in Aristotle's philosophy. However, it is crucial to discern that, for Aristotle, the "natural symbol" (*kata physin*) also prevails. In the soul dimension, this natural symbol is the notion or concept we hold of an object, while the conventional symbol manifests itself through oral and written language. Through this lens, Aristotelian symbolism differs from the common understanding of a symbol, which merges or amalgamates, though undoubtedly embodying a reality that serves as a bridge to another.

If it were not for the corresponding mental construct, we would lack the ability to conceive of the dog. This mental construct is only accessible through the internal visual representation and the linguistic denomination *dog*. Therefore, each element is intrinsically connected, evoking and leading to another. In Aristotle's worldview, a symbol is, in essence, an entity that directs toward another. From this, it follows that, for Aristotle, conceptual formation develops symbolically: words are mere representations of sounds, and these sounds reflect affections of the soul. It is fundamental to remember that, for him, what resides in the soul is a representation of objective reality. In this way, in his philosophy, the concept is the symbolic reflection of that reality. By centering his work on a philosophy based on concepts, Aristotle appreciates the conceptual from a symbolic perspective. Therefore, in his doctrine, symbolism, and philosophy are not at opposite extremes, and thus, one is not the negation of the other; rather, both belong to the same plane. This conceptual and symbolic convergence has been the core of our text, where we address the religious through symbolism and the symbolic from a conceptual perspective.

The notion of the symbol, which has gained significant importance in philosophical currents such as psychoanalysis and the hermeneutic phenomenology of Ricoeur, has a meaningful connection with Plato's understanding of the term. In *The Symposium*, a work that scholars often regard as a synthesis of his philosophy and an emblematic reflection of his time, Plato outlines the classical idea of the symbol by focusing on the discussion of love. In a contest of eloquence that gathers cultured men and critics, a dialogue takes shape that seems more like a series of speeches in honor of Eros, the deity of love. The expositions put forth by the interlocutors are not contradictory, but rather, each person presents their perspective on love so that the debate progressively expands. It is then that Socrates intervenes, dedicating himself to examining and, to some extent, correcting and dogmatizing the previous postulates.

The dialogue allows Plato to propose the idea that love represents the desire to attain what is beyond our reach and, in that sense, is a bond between the divine and the human, between the transcendental and the earthly. In essence, for Plato, love is a manifestation of the human yearning for perpetuity and immortality; it is an incessant thirst for transcendence and eternity that symbolizes the human ambition to preserve the good indefinitely and to conceive of beauty both in the bodily and spiritual realms. In this context of dialogued speeches, Plato incorporates an intervention from Aristophanes, who presents a myth in order to explain the influence of Eros on humanity, thereby providing us with a symbolic interpretation:

> First, then, human beings were formerly not divided into two sexes, male and female; there was also a third, common to both the others, the name of which remains, though the sex itself has disappeared. The androgynous sex, both in appearance and in name, was common both to male and female; its name alone remains, which labours under a reproach [...].
>
> At the period to which I refer, the form of every human being was round, the back and the sides being circularly joined, and each had four arms and as many legs; two faces fixed upon a round neck, exactly like each other; one head between the two faces ; four ears, and everything else as from such proportions it is easy to conjecture. Man walked upright as now, in whatever direction he pleased; but when he wished to go fast he made use of all his eight limbs, and proceeded in a rapid motion by rolling circularly round, — like tumblers, who, with their legs in the air, tumble round and round. We account for the production of three sexes by supposing that, at the beginning, the male was produced from the sun, the female from the earth; and that sex which participated in both sexes, from the moon, by reason of the androgynous nature of the moon. [...]
>
> They were strong also, and had aspiring thoughts. They it was who levied war against the Gods; [...] that they sought to ascend heaven and dethrone the Gods, in reality relates to this primitive people. Jupiter and the other Gods debated what was to be done in this emergency. For neither could they prevail on themselves to destroy them, as they had the giants, with thunder, so that the race should be abolished; for

> in that case they would be deprived of the honours of the sacrifices which they were in the custom of receiving from them; nor could they permit a continuance of their insolence and impiety. Jupiter, with some difficulty having desired silence, at length spoke. "I think," said he, "I have contrived a method by which we may, by rendering the human race more feeble, quell the insolence which they exercise, without proceeding to their utter destruction. I will cut each of them in half; and so they will at once be weaker and more useful on account of their numbers."[3]

In the speech presented in this work, Plato introduces the unusual and peculiar entity of the androgynous being, which is also described in the *Talmud* as follows:

> "אָחוֹר וָקֶדֶם צַרְתָּנִי" וגו' (תהילים קל"ט, ה')... אָמַר רַבִּי יִרְמְיָה בֶּן אֶלְעָזָר בְּשָׁעָה שֶׁבָּרָא הַקָּדוֹשׁ בָּרוּךְ הוּא אֶת אָדָם הָרִאשׁוֹן, אַנְדְּרוֹגִינוֹס בְּרָאוֹ, הֲדָא הוּא דִכְתִיב (בראשית ה', ב'): זָכָר וּנְקֵבָה וּנְקֵבָה בְּרָאָם. אָמַר רַבִּי שְׁמוּאֵל בַּר נַחְמָן, בְּשָׁעָה שֶׁבָּרָא הַקָּדוֹשׁ בָּרוּךְ הוּא אֶת אָדָם הָרִאשׁוֹן, דְּיוֹ פַּרְצוּפִים בְּרָאוֹ, וְנִסְרוֹ וַעֲשָׂאוֹ גַּבִּים, גַּב לְכָאן לְכָאן וְגַב לְכָאן.
>
> (בראשית רבה, ח', א')

> "You have shaped me behind and before" (Psalms, 139:5). Rabbi Yirmeyah Ben Elazar Said: "When the Holy One, blessed be He, created the first human being, He created him [as] an androgyne, as it is said, 'Male and female He created them' (Genesis, 5:2)." Rabbi Shemu'el Bar Nachman said: "When the Holy One created the first human being, He created him with two faces, then He sawed him and made for him two backs, one back to one side and one back to the other side."
>
> (*Bereshit Rabbah*, 8.1)

3. Plato, *The Banquet of Plato*, 189d–190e, trans. Percy Bysshe Shelley (Chicago: Way and Williams, 1895), 52–55.

This androgynous being displayed attributes of both the masculine and feminine genders within a single body. Its morphology was defined by a spherical silhouette, aligning its limbs and torso in a circular pattern. This shape granted it four upper and lower limbs, culminating in a bifacial countenance atop a singular neck and one head. As endowed with extraordinary strength, such beings harbored the reckless intent to confront the gods. The mythological narrative tells us that these entities conceived the daring plan to storm Mount Olympus, the abode of the gods. Zeus, in order to preserve the supremacy of the Olympians, decided to divide these beings, reducing their bipedal mobility by severing them into two, forcing them to move solely with two legs. After this division, each human fragment found itself in a relentless search for its missing counterpart. As Plato puts it, "Every one of us is thus the half of what may be properly termed a man, and like a pselta cut in two, is the imperfect portion of an entire whole."[4] Since that act of Zeus, human desire has been to reunite with its lost half.

According to the mythological tradition, an initially androgynous male and female figure emerged simultaneously. Zeus decided to divide it, resulting in independent male and female entities. From this act, the male individual yearns to reunite with his female counterpart; conversely, the female entity aspires to her male counterpart. The male finds completeness in the female, and the female in the male. In other words, the masculine and the feminine are intrinsically interconnected, suggesting that an indicator is not monolithic but dual, where each segment reflects and directs toward the other. The symbol consists of two parts, not just one, and each refers or points to the other. By its nature, a symbol requires duality to the extent that we can assert that, without the union of two parts, there would be no symbol. A genuine indicator demands the conjugation of both parts and the cohesion of these two facets.

From an analytical perspective, it is plausible to assert that the human individual operates as an indicator or a sign that tirelessly

---

4. Plato, *The Banquet of Plato* 191d–e, trans. Percy Bysshe Shelley (Chicago: Way and Williams, 1895), 57.

seeks its symbolic counterpart due to its primordial division. This means that symbolism is distinguished precisely by its referential function: it encapsulates that niche of reality situated beyond tangible barriers, whose roots do not arise from pre-established agreements but from integration processes. This implies that the symbol is characterized by reference: it brings to completion that segment of reality that lies between physical boundaries and is not established by convention but by reunification.

Analogous to the sign, the symbol is intrinsically defined by its referential nature. This axiom has solidified within philosophical discourse the concept of the symbol subsumed under the sign category, an idea evident in certain fragments of the Platonic dialogue *The Sophist*. This manuscript, one of Plato's fundamental works, emerges in his later creative phase, between 362 and 367 BCE, preceding his third visit to Sicily. The central theme of this work is the description and definition of what it means to be a sophist and how the sophist relates to epistemology, establishing a palpable contrast with the figure of the philosopher and the politician. In its development, Plato raises profound ontological questions, particularly emphasizing a critical reassessment of the theory of ideas. It is important to highlight that *The Sophist* continues *Theaetetus*, revisiting essential issues debated earlier and situating its narrative a day after the dialogue above. Throughout *The Sophist*, in addressing the topic of images reflected in mirrors and water, Plato proposes a conception of the sign that closely resembles the modern concept of the symbol:

> Stranger: "'Of the same sort'? Do you mean another real thing, or what does 'of the same sort' signify?"
> Theaetetus: "Certainly not real, but like it."
> Stranger: "Meaning by 'real' a thing that really exists."
> Theaetetus: "Yes."
> Stranger: "And by 'not real' the opposite of real?"
> Theaetetus: "Of course."
> Stranger: "Then by what is 'like' you mean what has not real existence, if you are going to call it 'not real.'"

> Theaetetus: "But it has some sort of existence."
> Stranger: "Only not real existence, according to you."
> Theaetetus: "No, except that it is really a likeness."
> Stranger: "So, not having real existence, it really is what we call a likeness?"[5]

Just as a graphic representation emulates and, at the same time, is intrinsically different from the entity it reflects, the symbol also coincides with and diverges from what it symbolizes. However, while the sign connects one thing to another through a tacit agreement, placing one element next to the other, the symbol reconstitutes the symbolized in its totality in evoking its corresponding segment. The sign points to something external to itself, whereas the symbol indicates and refers to the reality it symbolizes. In this framework, the symbol requires completeness, as in the case of the androgynous being whose halves long for reunion after their segmentation. Therefore, in the symbol, one part is not true if it lacks the other, and they are only true when united. That is, a segment lacks full authenticity without its complement, and only in their coalescence do they manage to represent a complete truth.

Individually, neither man nor woman encapsulates total truth, while they transcend the mere addition of their parts together. Therefore, as derived from Plato's dialogue, the man-woman union surpasses their individual connection, generating a higher level of reality that fits within the symbolic concept. Within the realm of symbols, the whole manifests an essence that exceeds merely the combination of its individual components, with the whole being greater than the sum of its parts, what is referred to in the West as "synergy." The Greek word speaks volumes about this: *Syn* (together) and *ergon* (action, work). The symbol combines or is a synergy of what works or acts together to manifest a higher reality.

Let us take, for example, the Star of David: when broken down, it consists of two triangles, but when united, its significance exceeds

5. Plato, *Sophist* 240a–240c, in *The Collected Dialogues of Plato*, ed. Edith Hamilton and Huntington Cairns, Bollingen Series LXXI (Princeton, NJ: Princeton University Press, 2025; originally published 1961), 983.

mere geometric superimposition. The Star of David is made of two separate triangles, but together, they are much more than two triangles. Similarly, the components of a cross are a vertical and a horizontal line; however, their fusion transcends mere linear intersections. According to Plato, human knowledge of nature is hypothetical, not due to human intellectual weakness, but because of the absence of the object's reality that must be known. One cannot know natural reality except by uniting it with an intelligible idea. In fact, the only knowledge accessible to an imperfect being is symbolic knowledge, as this type of knowledge considers the object for what it truly is, as J. Borella argues in *Criza simbolismului religios* that is, as "a symbol [...] real, an image that ontologically participates in its model."[6]

6. Jean Borella, *Criza simbolismului religios*, Editura Institutul European, Iaşi, 1995, p. 26. Translation mine.

Chapter 2

Mythology and symbols: exploring the roots of human understanding

> What we call a symbol is a term, a name, or even a picture that may be familiar in daily life, yet that possesses specific connotations in addition to its conventional and obvious meaning.[7]
>
> ~ Carl Gustav Jung

As we have just seen, the symbol is, on the one hand, what allows human beings to understand reality in a holistic, integral, and total way. It enables them to recognize diversity within unity and vice versa, which is why one should not renounce multiplicity in favor of unity nor unity in favor of multiplicity. It resolves the central problem in Plato's *Parmenides*, where he critiques his theory of Forms and problematizes the one and the many. However, the symbolic is not an epistemological methodology; instead, it is the unifying principle of reality itself, a composed, integral, and complex unity rather than a simple one. In this regard, the Greeks distinguished between *holon* (simple unity) and *panta* (composed unity), with the latter being a reality made of two parts that have been violently divided and must be reconciled and reintegrated. From this, we can say that the symbol is a composed unity, not a simple one, just like everything sacred, as seen, for example, in the Hebrew word for God, *Elohim*, where "El" is singular and "him" is plural, highlighting that the singular and plural mutually integrate into God.

---

7. Carl G. Jung, ed., *Man and His Symbols* (New York: Anchor Press/Doubleday, 1964), 20.

On the other hand, the symbol is also an auditory image charged with meaning. Although at first the expression "auditory image" might seem contradictory since, from a superficial perspective, we don't usually associate images with sound, this apparent contradiction is one of the fundamental aspects of the symbol.

> וְכָל־הָעָם רֹאִים אֶת־הַקּוֹלֹת וְאֶת־הַלַּפִּידִם וְאֵת קוֹל הַשֹּׁפָר וְאֶת־הָהָר עָשֵׁן וַיַּרְא הָעָם וַיָּנֻעוּ וַיַּעַמְדוּ מֵרָחֹק:
>
> (שמות כ', ט"ו)
>
> And all the people saw the sounds and the flames, and the sound of the horn (*shofar*), and the mountain smoking; and when the people saw it, they turned back and stood afar off.
>
> (Exodus, 20:15)

The symbol operates in a dialectic between the manifest and the unmanifest, the perceived and the imperceptible, the image and the meaning. It is precisely through this dialectical character that the symbol presents itself to us as an auditory image, meaning an image whose meaning does not lie in what it exposes or shows but in what it conceals. Since its meaning is not obvious, the only way to access it is through a narrative or story within a community. Through stories, the symbol is imbued with meaning, and this meaning acquires significance. There is always a collective behind a symbol, one that knows it, lives, experiences it, and tells its story to those who listen. This is what, in the *Bhāgavata Purana* (7.5.24), Prahlāda calls *śravaṇam*, or "hearing," and *kīrtanam*, or "speaking" about Viṣṇu. The image is observed, but its meaning is understood auditorily through the community's narration.

The symbol integrates the visual reality of the image and the auditory reality of the story, creating a brotherhood that, in turn, grants the testimony of the narrative that allows other people or congregations to understand loudly or audibly what they see in that image. It is through hearing that the community members understand what they see. This union reconciles the community with an identity in which all those contemplating the symbol and partake in its meaning become united in the image. The symbol unites, reintegrates, and reconciles what has been split and fractured, while, on the contrary, the *diábolo* divides, fragments, or dualizes. According to the discussion so far, we can affirm that the presence of a symbol is recognized when an image acquires meaning through a significant narrative for a specific brotherhood.

As we have advanced in the previous paragraph, the issue of the symbol and its true composite nature is intrinsically related to the issue of history, narrative, or storytelling, understood under the notion of myth. In short, it is precisely the narrative of the myth that allows the symbol to both conceal and simultaneously reveal its entire meaning. The Greek term *mytho*, which translates as "story" or "tale," is the genre that narrates the genesis of reality through the deeds of supernatural beings. According to Paul Ricoeur, a myth is a symbolic narrative that recounts an extraordinary event that goes back to the dawn of time.[8] These ancient symbolic narratives encapsulate the acoustic images of reality anchored in a community, society, or nation. In this sense, the myth is characterized by being an evocative oral narrative passed down from generation to generation, enriched with fabulous images of deep meaning. Mythological stories passed down over millennia are intrinsically intertwined with the essential themes of human existence and civilizations. Myths hold an unfathomable wealth of meaning that provides clues about the deepest mysteries of existence while allowing individuals to harmonize and integrate their lives with reality. However, it is crucial to understand that myths constitute true repositories of the profound experiences inherent to human existence. They represent the most hidden corners of the spirit or the literary subtleties of the soul in its tireless search for meaning. Mircea Eliade has defined the myth as follows:

> The myth, then, is the history of what took place in *illo tempore* (at that time), the recital of what the gods or the

8. Paul Ricoeur, *The Symbolism of Evil*, trans. Emerson Buchanan (New York: Harper & Row, 1967), 161–171.

> semidivine beings did at the beginning of time. To tell a myth is to proclaim what happened *ab origine* (primordial time). Once told, that is revealed, the myth becomes apodictic truth; it establishes a truth that is absolute. "It is so because it is said that it is so," the Netsilik Eskimos declare to justify the validity of their sacred history and religious traditions. The myth proclaims the appearance of a new cosmic situation or of a primordial event. Hence it is always the recital of a creation; it tells how something was accomplished, began to be.[9]

Moreover, the myth transcends the limitations of chronological time, unfolding revelations about the creative activity and the sacredness inherent in the works of these supernatural beings known for their actions in the early epochs. This implies that the myth narrates a sacred story, describing an event that happened in a primordial age, the mythical dawn of being. In other words, the myth explains how a specific reality originated through the actions of supernatural entities. This reality can encompass the entire cosmos or be limited to more specific aspects, such as an island, a plant species, a human behavior, or a social institution. In essence, the myth functions as a narrative that exposes the origins of something, explaining how it was created or began to exist. Although myths do not focus on verifiable historical events, they represent a deep truth about the world and its intrinsic nature. The myth does not speak of what has truly happened, but myths are the authentic reality of the world.

While a symbol represents an entity rich in meaning, the myth is tasked with unraveling and communicating the underlying meaning of that symbol. At the essence of the human being lies the capacity to perceive the sacred, which means that one can assign meaning and utility to nearly all aspects of the reality that surrounds them. However, for technique—understood as the practical application

9. Mircea Eliade, *The Sacred and the Profane: The Nature of Religion*, trans. Willard R. Trask (New York: Harcourt, Brace and Company, 1959), chap. "Sacred Time and Myths," 95.

of knowledge to achieve a specific end, whether for survival or the acquisition of knowledge—to fulfill its mediating function, spheres of reality must exist outside of instrumentalization. These are realities that, by their nature, elude the possibility of being used as a means to an end.

Following Plato's thought in the dialogue *Theaetetus*, it is suggested that philosophy, like religion, should be approached with a balance between serious play and playful seriousness.[10] It is essential to maintain this duality so as not to fall into the trap of taking them with extreme seriousness, which makes us forget their essentially exploratory and open nature. By taking them too seriously, we risk breaking the essence of what we seek to understand or fully experience, as rigidity distances us from the flexibility needed to play the game of life properly. Likewise, excessive lightness can lead us to lose what is valuable by failing to give it the proper importance. Similarly, taking religion with extreme seriousness, assuming that God communicates His messages exclusively to the followers of a particular current, reveals a limited and exclusionary view of spirituality. This perspective suggests that God shows preference or privilege to a specific group, forgetting the universality and accessibility of the divine to all human beings without distinction. The idea that God addresses only the adherents of a specific denomination is a simplification that ignores the complexity and richness of the human spiritual experience. Spirituality, in its essence, invites an open dialogue and a shared search beyond the borders of particular beliefs.

In contemporary times, the word *myth* is often used to refer to concepts such as "fiction," "illusion," "legends," or "traditional stories." Throughout the history of interpretation and academic analysis, the myth has frequently been misunderstood, even by scholars and experts. Its most common and superficial interpretation has often relegated it to the realm of mere narrative fiction. This limited understanding has had serious consequences, for it has contributed to a deficient understanding of the famous transition

10. Plato, *The Theaetetus of Plato*: with translation and notes, trans. Benjamin Hall Kennedy (Cambridge: Cambridge University Press, 1881), 167.

from mythos to logos. Wilhelm Nestle posited a supposed dawn of Western philosophy with Thales of Miletus in his 1940 work titled *Vom Mythos zum Logos: die Selbstentfaltung des griechischen Denkens von Homer bis auf die Sophistik und Sokrates* (*From Mythos to Logos: The Self-Unfolding of Greek Thought from Homer to Sophists and Socrates*). Contrary to reductionist interpretations, whose intentions have ultimately diminished the ontological transcendence of the myth, the myth reveals itself as a sacred narrative of a supratemporal nature, conveying archetypal events that took place in a primordial era, the mythical dawn of being. Far from being mere fanciful stories devoid of substance, the myth uses symbolic language and narrative allegory to enter reality and convey concepts beyond human understanding to reveal fundamental and universal truths. When examined from this perspective, the myth transcends its original condition as a mere prelude to logos. Logos, understood as logical and discursive rationality, has ended up violating and undermining the myth, acquiring an intrinsic quality as a form of thought and singular understanding, exalted in its own right, capable of providing a rational and verifiable truth. However, instead of conceiving the transition from myth to logos as a mere progress of substitution, as it has traditionally been understood, conceiving it as a metamorphosis in the relationship between human beings and the world is more accurate. Furthermore, we can infer that, in reality, there was never a replacement of myth by logos, but rather a coexistence; the myth has always existed and has always lived alongside the concept.

The myth refers to elements existing in the world that attest to their authenticity. If the myth speaks of the creation of the human being, here are men, women, and children as proof of its truth. From this framework, the myth unveils existential perspectives about the world and human life, acquiring a quality of truth that refers to tangible realities. If the myth narrates the creation of the heavens and the earth, both are present, supporting the truth of the mythological narrative. The notion that myth exclusively belongs to primitive thought, while philosophy is characteristic of modernity, is nothing more than a bias imposed by the Enlightenment, which leaned toward a demystification of history. Let us, if necessary, allow our study to overflow the limits and restrictions that certain aspects of conceptualization and philosophical and scientific logic have implanted, thereby impoverishing the deepest parts of the human being.

The myth narrates the manifestation of the sacred in the profane, the eruption of the supernatural in the domain of nature, and the intrusion of the absolute into the relative. In this way, the infiltration of the holy into the world is consolidated as the very foundation of its existence as we know it. In his famous *Letter on Humanism*, Martin Heidegger refers to this realm of reality with the term "the holy," describing it as a dimension of human experience that transcends any specific form of organized belief.[11] Through its relationship with the holy, the human being traces its historical trajectory, which materializes in images that unify and strengthen the identity of communities, collectives, or peoples. These stories, full of symbolism, allow communities to develop an awareness of their history and give profound meaning to their existence. The human being is distinguished by being an entity that transcends the limited sphere of animal instincts, venturing into the realm of the transcendental. The experience of the holy offers an opportunity to restore lost harmony: to reconcile with oneself, improve interpersonal relationships, reconnect with the natural environment, and open up to the transcendental dimension. In this context, the symbol acts as a means to heal such disruptions. Each social group, whether a community, collective, tribe, or people, has its own story linked to the holy, forging unique images and identities that reflect their particular relationship with the divine. In this way, holy texts are formed, which are nothing more than the crystallization of these relationships, serving as fundamental pillars in constructing identity and community sense.

Being symbolic stories, we can affirm that myths reflect the inexhaustible search for Truth throughout human history, providing guiding signals from earlier seekers. Myths are chimeras that lead us toward reality, stratagems that guide us toward authenticity, and fallacies that direct us toward truth. They represent clues or pillars

---

11. Martin Heidegger, *Letter on Humanism*, in Basic Writings, ed. David Farrell Krell (New York: Harper & Row, 1977), 218.

of our potential inherited from our ancestors, guiding us back to our source, with all its complexities and riches. We propose to resume the path of symbol and myth to embark on the search, unveiling the full meaning of our existence and our being.

Chapter 3

The conceptual fracture and symbolic integration

The evaluation of a concept requires a detailed and rigorous analysis of its meaning, origin, evolution, consistency, validity, and utility. First, one must venture into a labyrinth in search of its deepest meaning, like someone exploring a cave for treasure to understand its definition and significance. Secondly, one must also dig and tend to its roots, the origins that give life to the idea, in order to assess its relevance and appropriateness in the current context. Thirdly, we will also look at how it has evolved over time and its applications in different contexts and disciplines. Fourthly, we will proceed, as scientists do, to examine how all the pieces fit together consistently and correspond to reality. This will lead us to the fifth stage of acting as judges to evaluate its validity and determine whether it is supported by empirical evidence and whether it can be effectively applied to different contexts, which will involve reviewing the evidence supporting it and verifying if it is consistent and reliable. Finally, we will marvel at how, like a chameleon, it can change and adapt to new fields and situations, revealing its usefulness and requiring checking whether the concept is useful for understanding a specific problem. In other words, it will be a matter of determining whether the concept has relevance within the context in which it is used and if it contributes a valuable perspective to understanding the problem at hand.

In his exploration of the nature of thought, Aristotle distinguished three types of concepts through which he described the intricate intellectual taxonomy of the human being as though it were a dance of cognition and understanding traversing the cosmos of the known and the unknown. As we will see next, (1) the "attributed to the whole," (2) the "*per se*," and (3) the catholics or "integrating a multiplicity" are concepts that manifest in different ways in the matrix of reality and knowledge:

1. The principle of "attributed to the whole" unfolds before us as a representation of universal predication. In this realm, some concepts—a select set of primordial ideas—are established within the whole or totality of existence without room for exception. Take, for example, Aristotle's concept of "being." This represents an all-encompassing ideal, an imperative that imposes itself upon the entire cosmos. Every particle of existence can be ascribed under the definition of "something that is" (*tò ón*). This expression is applied in many senses (*légetai pollakhôs*) but with reference to one thing and one nature, not by mere homonymy[12]. These principles are at the peaks of intellect and are recognized as "universals," upholding all beings equally within their domain.
2. In a more restricted domain, Aristotle presents the term *kath'autó* (κατ'αὑτο), which we have translated as *per se*, a Latin expression that we can interpret as "in itself," "by itself," or "as such." Here, we encounter concepts that become inescapable when we wish to define an object or entity. Consider the tree, this natural entity, which, to conceive it in its fullness, requires including the concept of trunk or root. This essence is a *sine qua non* condition that allows us to consider something as a tree. These *per se* concepts are different from universals because they do not apply to all of existence but only to certain specific entities.[13]

12. Aristotle, *Metaphysics IV*, 2, 1003a33–34, trans. Hugh Tredennick, *Aristotle in 23 Volumes,* vol. 17 (Cambridge, MA: Harvard University Press; London: William Heinemann Ltd., 1933), 147.

13. Aristotle, *Metaphysics V*, 7, 1017a22–27, trans. Hugh Tredennick, *Aristotle in 23 Volumes,* vol. 17 (Cambridge, MA: Harvard University Press; London: William Heinemann Ltd., 1933), 237.

3. Finally, Aristotle also introduces the concept *olon to plêroma* (ὅλον τὸ πλήρωμα), which is often translated into Latin as *quoad integrum*, and which here we can translate as "integrating a multiplicity" or "relatively universal." This refers to concepts that, while not extending to all of existence, find application in a vast array of objects and entities. A representative example would be the concept of color, an attribute that can be applied to a multitude of entities: objects, plants, and animals, among others. Here, in the "catholic" realm, we find concepts that, like the *per se*, do not reach absolute universality but extend over a remarkable multiplicity of objects or entities.

The concepts "attributed to the whole" are projected as all-encompassing principles, stretching to the limits of existence, attached to the being of every entity, of everything that is. These concepts carry universality in their essence, standing as principles that apply to the entirety of existence. The *per se* concepts, on the other hand, are those that are born and consolidated as fundamental to the definition of an object or entity, granting it its intrinsic nature. They are the essential flash that shines at the core of each thing, the characteristic trait that defines and differentiates, turning the abstract into the concrete, the undefined into the defined. Finally, the catholic concepts scatter like seeds in the wind, finding residence in a multitude of objects or entities. These last concepts differ from those attributed to the whole in that they do not claim the totality of existence but coexist in various manifestations. While not assuming absolute universality, they are concepts that find their meaning in a plurality of concrete phenomena.

When we turn our gaze to objects of the phenomenal world, like a book, a dog, a parrot, or a human being, we discover a cloak of particularity that envelops them. In contrast, when these objects are the subject of our mind, the particularity dissolves, giving way to a domain of universality. Even though our words may be spoken millions of times, referring to millions of books, dogs, or human beings, each of these creatures retains its particularity intact. My canine pet is not a mere representation of the concept of a dog, nor am I a manifestation of the universal concept of a human entity. Yet, when we mentally shape reality and forge concepts, cognitive activity tends to operate in terms of universality. This is the normal condition of the conceptual process, as it involves the construction of a general framework capable of accommodating a multiplicity of particular cases.

Nevertheless, we must recognize that there are situations where the conceptualization activity takes on a more concrete and specific tone. In certain scenarios, conceptualization focuses on the singularity of the object, accounting for its uniqueness and peculiar characteristics. For example, we might consider conceptualizing a particular work of art, where the focus is on its unique style, author, historical-cultural context, and other aspects that distinguish it. Therefore, conceptualization narrows, becomes more precise, and focuses on a particular manifestation. However, even in these cases of focused attention, the activity of conceptualization is, in essence, an abstraction that attempts to capture the essential and common characteristics of the particular. Through this process, we seek to identify similarities and patterns that allow us to classify and understand different singular manifestations under the same homogenizing pattern.

Although the human mind can create conceptualizations that focus on specific cases, the fundamental nature of this activity involves generating concepts of a universal nature, encompassing and covering a multiplicity of examples and singular manifestations. The universal paradigm embodied in the term "book" exists exempt from concrete dimensions, lacking color, texture, and textual content. In contrast, in its individuality, the materialized book boasts singular attributes such as magnitude, tone, texture, and explicit content. The notion forged in the human mind is invariably a universal entity, whereas the concrete, tangible entity always resides in particularity. When intertwined with particularity, universality vanishes, just as the conceptual structure loses its meaning when confronted with empirical experience. Consequently, ideas and concepts become obsolete and irrelevant in realms outside their native habitat, that is, outside the ethereal realm of ideas where they rise and thrive. In this sense, the quiddity of the concept fades when facing the obstacle of the empirical world, as the essence of conceptual thought, in its self-sufficiency and autonomy, cannot withstand the onslaught of harsh reality. The concept is doomed to exist logically, which holds no value for the ontology of factuality, of particular things and facts. Thus, the concept stands as a monarch whose empire is confined to the realm of the ideal, within the intangible sphere of mental representations, and whose power evaporates when crossing the borders of its domain into the concrete world. What is paradoxical, however, is that the concept, which abstracts from reality and is made to know it, cannot do so. It seems that what is ontological—reality—and what is logical—its knowledge—are irreconcilably incompatible. This reminds many of St. Thomas in *De Veritate*, where the idea arises that "the individual is unknowable."

The term *tánatos* (Θάνατος) emerges from the ancient Greek lexicon, meaning "death." In that culture's mythology, Thanatos was the deity associated with death and inexorable fate. A child of the night (Nix) and twin sibling of sleep (Hypnos), Thanatos clothed death in a grim and ominous figure tasked with guiding the souls of the departed to the underworld. Art representations of this myth often depicted him carrying a scythe, an instrument associated with death used to cut down and sever. To sever the form of something is to cut away the form of the living thing. After being amputated and transformed in the mind, the mental form becomes an inert, lifeless form.

For example, the mental form of a dog does not experience hunger nor euphoria at the return of its owner, just as the mental form of a child, a friend, or a mother does not suffer, breathe, love, or live. This reveals to us that the concept consists of the mental essence of the thing, but as such, it is devoid of life. Cognition is the process through which the intentional object is presented or made present in the subject. This cognitive process that presents or brings the object into the subject involves introducing the form of the thing into the mind. However, while the form of the thing retains its vitality, in the mind, it becomes inert. In other words, conceptualization strips away life from what is being conceptualized. Unlike the *thanatic* conceptualization of reality, symbolism allows us to access something without stripping it of its vital context or, as Ortega y Gasset would say, of its circumstance.

Here lies the discrepancy between conceptualization and symbolization: the concept, in its extractive nature, divides, fractures, and fragments, whereas, as we have seen before, the symbol, in its unifying nature, joins, fuses, and integrates. While the transfiguration of myth into theology and philosophy implies the mutation of the symbol into the concept, it is only through myth that the life of Being can be preserved. Paul Ricoeur refers to this with his famous expression, "The symbol as a living metaphor."

This very cognitive process we have defined as conceptualization is also applicable to self-understanding—for the phenomenon of ego manifests through deep self-referentiality and self-conceptualization. The ego, specifically, is a conceptual representation of our inherent identity. However, experiencing existence through the prism of our mental identification implies appreciating it from a withered version of our being, a symbolic exuvia. The egoic phenomenon does not manifest our true essence but *is* simply a conceptualization, a preconceived idea of our being. The metamorphosis from what we presume to be into our true identity involves a quantum leap from the conceptual realm into the symbolic reality. Being mere conceptualization, the ego is rooted in memory, in a past already faded. This predisposition for conceptualizing is equivalent to embalming or renouncing the present. When proceeding from our embalmed version of ourselves, we detach and alienate ourselves from the now and the *continuum* of reality itself, from the vital essence. In that sense, conceptualizing is to decontextualize, and no entity is devoid of context. In philosophical exegesis, the rupture of what is perceived about oneself and the transformation into what one truly entails is a passage from the conceptual realm to the symbolic reality. As José Ortega y Gasset said, "I am myself plus my circumstance, and if I do not save it, I cannot save myself."[14]

14. José Ortega y Gasset, *Meditations on Quixote*, trans. Evelyn Rugg, Diego Marín, and Julián Marías, (University of Illinois Press, Urbana, imp. 2000), 45.

Just as it happens when we conceptualize ourselves, it also happens when we conceptualize our fellow beings, as what we are doing is immersing ourselves in the act of metaphorical "intellectual homicide" that leads us to establish relationships with "expired entities." When we "dissect" or "amputate" the intrinsic form of my aunt and transfer it into the sphere of my mind, a connection is forged with her "conceptual envelope," to the detriment of an interaction with her genuine essence. Symbolization urges us to decentralize the ego and centralize the myth from this horizon of reflection. Unlike conceptualization, symbolization allows us to understand myth as the narrative that shapes and forms the "I," rather than understanding it as a construction of the ego-idea. It would not be an ego creating a myth but a myth shaping an "I."

Just as the Zohar points out:

וְאֲנָא סִימָנָא בְּעַלְמָא.

(ספר הזוהר, בראשית, פרשת ויחי, רכ"ה, א')

And I am a mere sign in the world.

(*Zohar*, Genesis, "*Vayehi*," 225a)

The Aramaic word *alma* holds the resonance of "cosmos or space," as well as "perennity or temporality." Likewise, *he'elem* is translated from Hebrew as "evanescence or disappearance." "I am a sign in the world" suggests that the "conceptual self," the "idea-self," is nothing more than a sign, an inscription, or a symbol within the framework of time and space, which constitute the stage where the ultimate divinity fades away. Time and space, like the world (*olam*), are nothing more than the "fading" or "mask" of the ultimate deity. We are merely an emblem of consciousness concealed in space and time. What this shows us is that it will be unattainable for us to accept our true essence from a scientific conceptual perspective. To embrace love, illumination, or divinity seriously is equivalent to relating to them as a mythical truth or symbolic reality. If physics could verify divinity, that would certainly not be divinity. Science is only capable of confirming objective realities. Any god scientifically verified, that is, conceptualized, would obviously be by nature ontic; it would become another object and lose its symbolic nature.

However, and in contrast to the mere concept, the symbol takes on the enigmatic function of evoking through objects, icons, resonances, lexicons, or gestures, an essence that transcends its primal or manifest meaning. The essence of a symbol lies in its ability to serve as a messenger of a more obscure or sophisticated representation. These symbols, which indeed stand as emblems in various spheres, such as religious sacredness, the political sphere, sublime artistic expression, and rich literature, operate like the Oracle of Delphi, transmitting semantics that reach beyond the explicit. From the cross as the standard of Christ's sacrifice and resurrection to the flag as a fabric that intertwines the identity of a nation in its weave, symbols are an indelible legacy. However, adding to their multifaceted character, symbols are, like chameleons, capable of mutating in meaning depending on the cultural, historical, and social context in which they stand. Such is the case with the color white, which dresses purity and innocence in the West and, in contrast, adorns mourning and departure in certain Asian cultures.

Now, let us delve into the depths of the symbol and pay attention to its etymology. The word symbol emerges from the ashes of the Latin *symbolus*, which in turn inherited from the Greek language with *symbolon*, referring to a "sign or emblem." In ancient Hellas, *symbolon* were fragments that, when joined together, confirmed an alliance, friendship, or camaraderie between intertwined souls. Initially, this object served as an emblem of camaraderie or a secret code between individuals with hospitable inclinations. One of the hosts would break a clay tablet, keeping one portion for themselves and giving the other to the guest as a sign of hospitality. This object then became a sign of mutual recognition, a tangible symbol of the alliance established between them. In this process, as the tablet was divided, it manifested a material and symbolic metamorphosis. Thus, its form and purpose acquired a new dimension. Once divided, each portion of the clay retained the memory of its original wholeness but now carried a new symbolic burden, a testimony of generosity and hospitality, in a symbiotic dance of giving and receiving, of dividing and sharing. The portion kept by the host, a remnant of the original tablet, was a latent promise, a possibility of reunion. Its counterpart, given to the visitor, functioned as a symbolic passport, a proof of the hospitality extended, and a distinguishing sign for future encounters. In its duality, these fragments of clay represented the dialectic between belonging and otherness, familiarity and foreignness, the host and the visitor. The word *symbolus*, adopted by the Romans, refers to a badge, banner, or sign that served as a means of identification or as a formalizer of pacts. In the medieval era, the term "symbol" came to be used in the Catholic Church to refer to a sign or emblem with the power to represent an abstract notion or theological thought.

The myth, which transcends its nature as a story laden with symbolism, is in itself a symbol that has the power to bridge the visible and the unseen, the perceptible and the impalpable, the empirical and the transcendental. Its function lies in linking the relative and the absolute, the perceptible by the senses and the inaccessible to them, the evident and the authentic. As we have previously shown using *The Symposium* by Plato, specifically through the myth told by Aristophanes, the symbol alludes to "joining two parts," that is, amalgamating a duality that, as we have now seen, encloses a clay medallion that could be divided into two, becoming an emblem of camaraderie. The significance of the symbol lies in its ability to serve as a mediator between the visible and the invisible, making the incomprehensible comprehensible. The symbol grants us the opportunity to experience the texture of the intangible and unveils as evident what typically fades into the shadow of the unnoticed. Unlike the concept, which divides, fragments, and conceals the essence of reality, the symbol concretizes the abstract, granting us the key to access the veiled and the hidden. In its essence, the symbol transforms into a summoning of the absent, bearing the power to promote integration and unification in many ways:

- **Identification and a sense of belonging:** Symbols can help people identify with a group, community, or nation, which in turn creates a sense of belonging and unity among the members of that group.
- **Expression of values and beliefs:** Symbols serve as vehicles for values and beliefs shared among individuals. This contributes to the establishment of a substantial connection between individuals and the mutual dissemination of their ideals.
- **Facilitating communication:** When symbols are used as a shared language for communication, they provide a framework that favors clearer understanding and promotes cohesion between participants in the interaction.
- **Evocation of emotions:** Symbols, by stimulating emotions and feelings in people, play a fundamental role in the connection and solidarity among members of a community or group.
- **Establishment of traditions and rituals:** Symbols are often integral to traditions and rituals shared by communities. This integration helps connect individuals through a common history and culture.
- **Representation of common goals:** Symbols can be used as tools to encapsulate common objectives. Such symbolic representation fosters a sense of shared purpose, driving individuals to engage in a synergy of efforts to achieve these aims.

Therefore, symbols, at their core, are skillful tools that swiftly lift the layers of communication, unleashing a torrent of intense emotions. However, it is crucial to highlight that simultaneously, symbols are firmly rooted in the ancient pathways traced by traditions and rituals throughout history. Furthermore, symbols magnificently reflect the values, convictions, and aspirations that emanate from the community. Through the delicate intertwining of symbolic elements, a bridge is built that transcends the borders of human diversity and converges into a conceptual brotherhood.

These signs, which capture the very essence of cultural and social expression, reveal a complex dance between the symbol and the individual. Our collective identity merges visions, cultures, and experiences, and generates a symphony of shared meanings that resonates in the heart of humanity. It is through this amalgamation that symbols ignite the spark of belonging, nurture communication between diverse beings, and awaken a range of emotions that unfold across the vast panorama of human experience.

Moreover, these elements, which have the potential to unite individuals and solidify their connection with others, carry the virtue of amalgamating a multiplicity of meanings into a single visual representation. When a collective, community, or nation crystallizes a sense into a visual representation and then transfers that meaning to future generations, such a representation acquires the power to unite. The human being experiences an internal rupture, division, and isolation; however, the meaning contained in the symbol has the power to integrate and unify them.

The human being is separated from other fellow humans, from nature, and the transcendental, and it is in this context that the symbol acquires an integrative function. The symbol, in its transcendental essence, stands as a point of convergence in shared meanings. Its power lies in its ability to generate a range of emotions, trigger intricate associations, and transmit cultural values embedded in the fibers of the collective. On the other hand, crossing the boundaries of the individual, the symbol engenders a sense of belonging and cohesion in the communities it embraces.

The transmission of the symbol from generation to generation metamorphoses it into a bond that intertwines people with their history, identity, and common traditions. The use of these signs in everyday and social spheres, such as fluttering banners, proud emblems, revered insignias, sacred rituals, and solemn ceremonies, grants people the ability to identify with a community, manifest their allegiance, and contribute to the construction of a collective sense of belonging.

Symbols, as instruments of communication imbued with power, distill complex meanings into visual forms or representations with an immediacy that is recognizable and understandable to those who share a common cultural context. Symbols enable the amalgamation of individuals, chiseling a shared sense of purpose and unbreakable unity. As bearers of cultural significations, symbols are capable of overcoming individual divisions and promoting the incorporation of individuals into a collective, establishing a religious unity, that is, symbolic. Symbols become catalysts for an ineffable communion, carriers of codified wisdom that transcend the barriers of verbal language. They are heralds that unite souls, rooting their steps in the rich soil of traditions, building bridges between generations, and guiding humanity toward a shared future in which diversity and unity will walk hand in hand.

Chapter 4

The concept: the screen of reality

In this chapter, we will revisit the issue of the concept to explore it more deeply. As we mentioned earlier in an introductory context, a concept is a mental abstraction that represents objects, actions, feelings, phenomena, or other perceptible or imaginable elements. It is the idea of something, its formal grasp, and the dilution of its essence. Based on this premise, concepts serve as cognitive tools through which we seek to interpret the world around us, with the intention of classifying, categorizing, and generalizing information. Concepts arise from experience, observation, reflection, or communication. For instance, the conceptualization of "love" is an abstract construction that captures the multiplicity of a feeling experienced in our personal relationships; the notion of "justice," in turn, evokes an idea of fairness and neutral treatment within society, while the concept of a "circle" refers to a closed flat geometric figure, where all parts are equidistant from the center. Derrida, speaking of concepts, says that philosophy is the art of creating concepts, and in that case, only one who can create and manipulate concepts is truly a philosopher.

This tactic of creative reason originates from ancient Egyptian esoteric hermeticism. Within its esoteric teachings, it is held that reason has the power to shape nothingness. Only one who resides in nothingness or has the capacity to immerse themselves in it can truly create. Later, this act will be referred to in Latin as *creatio ex nihilo*, or *creation from nothing*, and it was subsequently taken up by 16th-century Italian Renaissance thinkers, as well as by idealist philosophers such as Kant and Hegel and rationalists like Descartes and Leibniz, as well as by notable scientists such as Tesla and Newton. Therefore, Derrida is actually articulating a very ancient idea.

Etymologically, the term "concept" comes from the Latin *conceptus*, derived from the verb *concipere*, and refers to something that has been shaped, erected, or conceived in the mind. It is a cognitive unit that provides meaning and is used to understand experiences derived from interaction with the environment and to express them verbally. The concept, as a definition, harbors a determined logical value that can be managed or manipulated. As such, it is acquired through the extraction of content from the perceptible reality via a process that involves appropriating the form present in an object and then incorporating it into the mind. It is acquired through the senses and attention. Nature itself is life; therefore, extraction involves capturing a fragment of vitality.

In this sense, according to José Ortega y Gasset, the concept has a dual aspect. One of them is its truthfulness, rooted in the sensible sphere, its *ad extra* face, which projects outward into the environment.[15] The other aspect is its internal logic, termed *logicity*, its *ad intra* face, confined to the mental realm and limiting its scope. Concepts, emerging as mental constructs from experience and reflection, are artifacts that enable us to decipher the world and communicate effectively. They are tools for categorizing and generalizing information. Their value lies in their ability to represent complex abstractions and facilitate the understanding of the surrounding environment.

However, to gain a more precise understanding of the extractor and delimiter nature of the concept, it is useful to return to etymology. The Greek word *horos* means "the determined" and translates into Latin as *terminus*, meaning term, which is what logical and rational thinking is conditioned by. *Horos*, however, is also related to the word "horizon," and in this sense, it implies marking limits, delimiting, determining, and cutting; that is to say, the concept's role is to delimit the object of study and pull it or extract it from its concrete and historical materiality.

Furthermore, Terminus was a god in Roman mythology who presided over boundaries and borders. He was considered the

15. José Ortega y Gasset, *Meditations on Quixote*, trans. Evelyn Rugg, Diego Marín, and Julián Marías, (University of Illinois Press, Urbana, imp. 2000), 44–45.

protector of the edges between properties, cities, and regions, and sacrifices were offered to him to maintain peace and harmony in these boundaries. *Terminus* was depicted as a headless monolith placed at the points where boundaries converged. Within Roman society, there was a deep-seated belief that any attempt to move his statue would trigger *Terminus'* relentless wrath, unleashing a Pandora's box of disputes and confrontations. *Terminus* stood apart from the myriad of Roman celestial deities as he did not have a dedicated festival. Still, his worship merged into the celebration of the Terminalia, held annually on February 23. During this event, sacrificial rites were performed at boundary markers, these territorial markers underwent purification rituals, and harmonious relations between neighboring parties were strengthened. Therefore, the word *terminus* is closely linked to the Latin word denoting limit or end. Moreover, this term originates from the Latin word *terere*, meaning "to rub" or "to wear out," referring to the boundary markers, which were often made of stone and, over time, wore down due to exposure to the elements. This connection suggests that the deity *Terminus'* association with stone relates to its role in guarding boundaries and the belief that stone was a crucial component in defining and preserving those boundaries.

Consequently, when thought becomes autonomous, it imposes its confines or demarcations, and its reflection or speculation is grounded in terms. Terms delimit the borders between objects; establishing limits means perceiving a multiplicity of different entities or things. However, it exists at a higher level than the term. It is intriguing to explore the mental process of conceptualization, which is triggered by the sensory perception of an object. The "whatness" of a table lies in those elements that specifically delineate wood as a table and not another entity. Therefore, what gives the table its status as a table is intrinsically in the table itself. The inherent form in the object is known as "essence," whereas the same form in the mind is referred to as the "concept." Hence, through the concept, the essence of the thing that resides in the object can also be found in the mind. In this way, the form of the object can coexist both in the object itself as an essence and in the mind as a concept. From this cognitive node, humanity transcends concrete reality to immerse itself in its conceptual cosmos, building relationships and exerting control, dominion, and manipulation over concepts.

In the text *De Interpretatione* or *On Interpretation*, which is part of the *Organon*, Aristotle addresses comprehensively, explicitly, and formally the nature and relationship of language with logic, thought, and reality. We read in the first chapter, titled "Writing, Voice, Thought, and Reality – The True and the False":

> Let us, first of all, define noun and verb, then explain what is meant by denial, affirmation, proposition and sentence. Words spoken are symbols or signs of affections or impressions of the soul; written words are the signs of words spoken. As writing, so also is speech not the same for all races of men. But the mental affections themselves, of which these words are primarily signs, are the same for the whole of mankind, as are also the objects of which those affections are representations or likenesses, images, copies.[16]

That is why Aristotle said in *Topics* (VI, II, 149a2) that "we must change the names according to the reason they express."[17] Instead of directly referring to the objects that occupy our reality, we find ourselves immersed in the analysis of the mental determinations associated with them. Far from residing in the things themselves, these determinations find their existence in the folds of the human intellect. Therefore, it is in the quest for precision and accuracy that the fallacy of univocity is revealed. Nevertheless, the essence of the concept is often, in most cases, ambiguous and prone to misinterpretation. Throughout generations, humanity has dedicated countless efforts to the pursuit of greater conceptual accuracy. However, in this attempt to conceptualize empirical reality, concepts have gradually become

16. Aristotle, *On Interpretation* 16a3–8, trans. Harold P. Cooke, in *Aristotle: Categories. On Interpretation.* Prior Analytics, Loeb Classical Library 325 (Cambridge, MA: Harvard University Press, 1938), 114–115.

17. Aristotle, *Topics: Book VI* 149a2, trans. and comm. Annamaria Schiaparelli (Oxford: Clarendon Press, 2024).

detached from the things they are associated with. Reality, as a polyhedral and complex phenomenon, reveals itself to be impossible to delimit with absolute precision and accuracy. Each individual is a unique subject whose subjective character conditions their perception of reality. Our insistence on grasping it in a precise and exact way leads us further away from its true essence.

Suppose we aspire to forge a clear, univocal, immutable, and precise concept of the human being, free from any imperfection or ambiguity—we should ask ourselves whether there truly exists anyone who meets such characteristics. Indeed, reality teaches us that no human being possesses absolute clarity. As the concept becomes more refined, it gradually moves further away from the reality it intends to conceptualize. That is to say, while reality is heterogeneous, multiple, mobile, contingent, material, and imperfect, the concept is one, immobile, immaterial, necessary, and perfect. It is for this reason that we say the concept and reality are inversely proportional: the more we conceptualize reality, the less we know it. Similar to the clear and univocal concept of the "human being," the circle we perceive when contemplating the moon or the sun does not possess an absolute morphology. However, when we conceptualize a circle in the depths of our mind, we construct it as an exact and perfect entity. Paradoxically, as our concepts sharpen, they gradually distance themselves from the concrete reality they aspire to represent.

Likely due to the influence of the Kantian revolution and its subsequent refinements in pursuit of rationality, the schism that conceptual thought creates between the concept and reality has ended up subverting the very cognitive process, transforming from the conceptualization of objects to the objectification of concepts. That is, instead of pursuing concepts that faithfully reflect things, that is, beings, we aspire for things to conform to concepts with increasing precision. The human intellect seeks the objects it has previously conceptualized. For centuries, humans have defined themselves as rational animals, although very few meet this description. Thus, we are compelled to find phenomena that satisfy the characteristics of our concept. Therefore, when we refer to a being, we are referring to a mental construction that has been conceptualized.

The concept itself is distinguished by being coherent with itself in its interior aspect, *ad intra*, while simultaneously conforming to the thing in its exterior aspect, *ad extra*, thereby displaying coherence and correspondence. As it progresses, thought gradually emancipates itself from the thing and metamorphoses into thought about thought. Progressively, the concept becomes independent of what is conceptualized and transforms into a conceptualization of concepts themselves. When we define a human being, we are not referring to their true essence but to our interpretation of that individual. That is why St. Thomas said that the individual is unknowable.[18]

Furthermore, if we pay attention to how we speak of things, we do not refer to the object itself. In reality, we participate in a game of mirrors with our own ideas and beliefs about that object. But, as time passes, the mind becomes serious and begins to care less about the object and more about what it thinks about the object, moving away from the real and approaching the conceived. Like a sailor at sea, the mind uses its compass of thoughts to navigate the turbulent waters of reflections and speculations on the ideas it has charted. In the discourse that addresses the essence of any physical being, it becomes imperative to point out that our words do not expose the intrinsic essence of the object but rather present our own mental constructions, beliefs, and ideals that govern our understanding of that object.

As a result, the mind progressively becomes intoxicated by the art of conceptualization, distancing itself from a direct, unmediated engagement with what was previously captured by its lobes and plunging into the meanders of speculation regarding what has been preconceived in its vast intellect. From that moment onward, we detach ourselves from concrete reality and immerse ourselves in a mental ideational dimension. Even in the domain of metaphysics, we do not refer to tangible things but to ideas and thoughts. Moreover, we conceptualize enlightenment, Truth, or God and embark on the search for what fits our concepts.

---

18. Thomas Aquinas, *Truth,* q. 4, in Disputed Questions on Truth, vol. 1, trans. Robert W. Mulligan (Chicago: Henry Regnery Company, 1952)

Faced with this scenario, in his text *Logical Investigations*, the prominent figure of Edmund Husserl proposed phenomenology as a tool to return *zu den Sachen selbst*, or "the things themselves," that is, to the object from which, as we have seen, the philosophical tradition had gradually distanced itself, especially since Kant's Copernican turn. Husserl begins his philosophical inquiry with a sharp critique of naturalism and psychologism.[19] His goal was to make philosophy a true, strict science grounded in objective principles. Returning to the things themselves responds to a search for truth. Husserl sees the reductionism of the currents he criticizes as a great problem. Phenomenology, understood as the study of the essence of things as they emerge in consciousness, starts from the very consciousness that, unlike a passive spectator sitting indifferently before the screen of a movie theater, is shown as an engaged consciousness that participates vigorously in the constitution of the movie of reality. In this framework, it is like an alchemist giving life to the inanimate. The object of consciousness, that is, the "thing-in-itself," does not have a "packaged" being within it waiting to be discovered; rather, it is consciousness, through its intentionality, that gives it form and essence. Reformulating, for Husserl, there is no object of consciousness without consciousness, just as there is only consciousness if it is conscious of something, of an object, and therefore, we can only speak of consciousness as *consciousness-of-something*. Additionally, we must add that the ontology of objects (which are always objects-of-consciousness) does not lie hermetically in itself; rather, it is consciousness that, like a goldsmith, forges its being. In a certain sense, objects are ontologically bland until consciousness constitutes them as being.

In this conjunction, intentionality emerges as the conduit through which consciousness, in an unceasing pursuit, orients itself and clings to objects, stripping them of their veils and accessing and deciphering their naked essence. We can add that this is done through the *epoché* (the suspension of judgments). It is not the place to elaborate on

---

19. Edmund Husserl, *Logical Investigations*, vol. 1, trans. J. N. Findlay, ed. Dermot Moran (London: Routledge, 2001).

concepts like *noesis*, or "the activity of consciousness," and *noema*, which is "the intentional object to which consciousness is directed." Here, intentionality stands as our link to transcend the deceptive appearance of objects and reveal their raw and naked essence, immersed in the melting pot of our subjective experience. In its ultimate essence, the manifestation of objects in the realm of consciousness and the intrinsic intentionality it entails become vital factors in understanding the phenomenal reality from the Husserlian perspective.

According to Husserl, reality is not a monolithic and impassive being waiting beyond the limits of consciousness; on the contrary, it is built in the very bowels of the interaction of consciousness with the cosmos. Thus, reality is a structure whose bricks are placed by consciousness to allow it to appear as a phenomenon in the theater of our consciousness. Moreover, Husserlian phenomenology proposes that the essence of objects is not rooted in their depths but rather springs, like a spring, from their manifestation in consciousness. Here, consciousness plays a role, not as a passive observer but rather as a dynamic architect whose intentionality captures but imbues objects with meaning, assuming a central role in their manifestation.

Despite Husserl's attempt to redraw the parameters of human knowledge in order to recover reality as it is in its essence, the problem of knowledge remains its obsession with omitting the symbol and entrusting knowledge solely to the concept. The problem with basing knowledge on concepts is that reality will always be constituted in the image and likeness of subjects and their "I," or their consciousness. This is like hiding the being of reality under the veil of a universe of concepts extended by the subject to all areas, until it generates a purely conceptual framework. With this framework, philosophy and science attempt to give meaning to human beings, sacrificing a more original reality to which only symbols, myths, and religion grant access. As long as philosophy sets aside symbols and reduces the understanding of reality to its conceptualization, it will remain anchored in the same problem: authentic Being will slip through its fingers every time it clenches its hands.

Chapter 5

Deciphering the enigma through concepts and symbols

In their endeavor to unravel the essence of being, mythology, and philosophy follow distinct paths. Mythology appeals to the power of symbols, while philosophy, as we have seen, uses concepts to think about reality. A symbol, in its essence, can be defined as an invisible image that is shown through another visible one and that acquires meaning through an audible narrative. It is an entity, whether in the form of an image, word, or action, that exceeds its superficial or literal meaning—the visible—evoking a deeper and more abstract background, that is, the invisible. As we have shown earlier, the symbol is an auditory image that conveys, through a sensible image, a suprasensible story that gives meaning from the metaphysical to the physical. The syntax of the symbol is the relationship between each element of the symbol; its semantics is the meaning it gains in light of the metaphysical path, and its pragmatics is the cultural or group context in which that semantics makes sense. The members of the group or community can fully understand the symbol because they are part of its history. Only those who belong to the group can be part of its symbol, and only those who are part of the symbol can understand it.

In other words, a symbol encapsulates abstract ideas, emotions, or values, establishing a transcendent and meaningful connection with them, creating a symbolic and profound link with the human condition. The symbol, in its primordial essence, acts as a threshold to a realm that transcends the apprehensible, lifting us toward meanings and experiences that exceed the boundaries of what is merely perceptible. Terence McKenna would say that visible reality is just the tip of the iceberg of what is really happening. Through its evocative power, the symbol awakens emotions, sensations, intuitions, and connections that link us to abstract and universal experiences. Similarly, myth immerses us in a symbolic horizon that invites us to explore existence, as well as the metaphysical folds, unfathomable in their most intimate essence.

In radical contrast to mythology, philosophy, in its perennial and tangled search for the meaning of being, according to Heidegger, has been grounded since its origins in the concept as its cornerstone. Conceptual constructions, like mental buildings, enable us to hierarchize, dissect, and grasp reality rationally and abstractly. Through conceptual assumption, philosophy pursues the intellectual and systematic conquest of phenomena and ideas. Concepts provide us with the ability to explore connections between objects and philosophical principles, thus fostering our understanding of existence. But as we have advanced earlier, while concepts cut, separate, distinguish, and differentiate, the symbol unites, rebinds, reconciles, and sutures what the concept has broken. The concept points to difference, the symbol to unity. Goethe, pointing to the same idea, would say that synthesis is the true reason.

Both myth and philosophy, immersed in the metaphysical whirlwind of the transcendental search, eagerly embark on the exploration of the existential enigma. Complexity is revealed as an enigma in perpetual becoming, only accessible to the most intrepid explorers of thought. Symbols are rooted in a specific culture or community. These symbols embody a rich history, beliefs, and values shared by those who belong to these cultural traditions. It is important to recognize that symbols have a meaning beyond the literal. They act as vehicles that connect us with abstract and universal ideas. Through them, myth immerses us in a symbolic dimension that allows us to explore and understand complex phenomena of existence and transcendental issues. Symbols unfold like encrypted treasures, entangled in the web of tradition, evoking codes that open portals to understandings beyond the superficial.

Therefore, although opposed on one hand, myth and philosophy intertwine on the other hand in the exploration of the meaning of being. Through them, we can unravel the complexity of existence and understand its profound significance. The symbolic entelechy emerges as the inscrutable mortar of the myth, fusing in its symbols the abysses of meaning and intertwining, in elliptical linkage, the finite and the transcendent. Myth, in turn, uses these symbols as transmitters of narratives that enclose arcana and universal precepts, threading the understanding of being within the vast cosmic eon. Returning to the examples mentioned earlier, the Christian cross, an emblem rooted in Christianity, and the Star of David, a vibrant icon of Judaism, emanate a profusion of narratives, beliefs, and values.

Symbols are rooted in specific cultural contexts, unlike philosophical concepts that transcend boundaries. In stark contrast to symbols—whose sacredness and meaning tend to be confined within microcosms of culture—philosophical concepts remain indifferent to such limitations. As tools, these concepts become fundamental pillars of thought, enabling scholars to reflect and speculate on their perceptions and sensations. Concepts, operating as cognitive lockpicks in the philosopher's arsenal, provide a platform for the systematic scrutiny of their environment, covering a spectrum that ranges from decoding the ontological skeleton to the epistemological foundations, ethical dilemmas, the taxonomy of justice, and even the unfathomable depths of metaphysics.

Philosophical concepts, differing radically from the fleeting nature of symbols, emerge as mental prisms of supracultural reach, meticulously carved by philosophers to unveil the most hermetic veins of reality. They address existence, pointing to the foundational pillars of reality. Symbols, on the other hand, manifest in a variety of fields, such as religion, politics, literature, and advertising. They consist of tools that, like master keys, allow access to realities that transcend the literalness of words and concrete images. With their power of evocation that transcends the superficial appearance, these emissaries of meaning leave a lasting emotional impact while simultaneously shaping the paths of cognition and behavior. They emerge as shadow catalysts that convey the transmission of abyssal ideas, encrypted values, and indecipherable emotions, transgressing the constraining limits of naked words and merely tangible images.

These polyphonic symbols permeate the spheres of consciousness, rooted in the abyssal depths of our collective unconscious, unveiling unknown domains. In the religious realm, crosses, stars, and mandalas are used to symbolize beliefs and mystical experiences. They have a strong emotional, devotional, and transcendent impact, helping the faithful connect with their faith and understand it better. In the domain of the sacred, iconography, encompassing a spectrum of emblematic artifacts, stands as the backbone in the representation of beliefs, theological theses, and metaphysical experiences. These symbols, titans of meaning, and transcendent connections build ethereal bridges between souls and their faith, opening doors to abysses of understanding and sacred experiences.

The political sphere contrasts with the above, where symbols such as banners, crests, patriotic hymns, and emblems parade as sentinels that mark and protect the cultural, political, and philosophical landscape of nations and parties. In these emblems, we find values and a sense of identity; they inspire shared goals and create a bond among citizens, generating a sense of belonging and mobilizing emotions in the citizenry. A popular proverb attributed by some to Confucius goes as follows, "Symbols are more important than words for the advancement of humanity." In the art scene, symbols carry meanings and abstractions, often more suggestive. In literature, more concretely, symbols assume nuances of meanings and abstract concepts that invite reflection.

Authors and artists play with metaphors, allegories, and visual symbols to dig into the complexity of topics, unleash emotions, and expand imaginations, generating a buffet of interpretations that enrich the experience. In advertising, symbols capture attention, creating a bond between us and brands. Symbols are emotional igniters, catalysts for imagination that, in their various forms, foster subjective hermeneutics, enhancing the aesthetic experience, instigating, and urging us to jump into reflective abysses about the quintessence of humanity.

Even in this marketing and advertising arena, there is a symbolic stratagem, as here symbols are deployed to capture attention, weave beneficial associations, and amalgamate the psyche with objects of consumption. Symbols are clever weapons that attract and bind the public to brands and products like bees and honey. Logos, slogans, and visual trademarks become potent symbols, heralds of corporate identities and values embedded in the brand and consumer aspirations. In their unique cleverness, symbols communicate and transmit meanings that transcend the prosaic lexicon and imagery. Spread across the colorful human scene; these symbols are the bread that nourishes dialogue, the wind that stirs emotions, and the chisel that shapes perceptions and actions. It will be Octavio Paz who will explain that symbols are the touchstones of our cultural identities. Symbols speak beyond words, enriching communication and evoking emotions. In essence, they unite us with something greater, they nourish us, and they make us live. Not only does man live by concepts, but by every symbol that comes from the mouth of the god. Unraveling and venerating symbology is an invitation to probe the abysses of the human experience in a tango with our innate capacity for the symbolic and the transcendent. Revealing and exalting symbology is equivalent to a descent into the caves of the human psyche, engaging in a dialogue with our symbolic and transcendental essence.

As we have previously pointed out, the symbol and the concept are related but different in their function, scope, and meaning. As posited in previous passages, both coexist in the semantic realm and although their correlation may seem inextricable, they diverge sharply in their roles and connotations. Now, focusing on the core of this presentation, we will scrutinize the fundamental discrepancies that distinguish them.

Nature

In the vast stage of human experience, symbols appear as intricate pieces of a puzzle, capable of conveying meanings beyond their physical existence. These perceptive emissaries, expressed through visual, sound, and gestural forms, acquire meaning thanks to the attributions we grant them. Symbols, in their varied range of manifestations, transcend perceptual limits. From the waving flags to the captivating logos, symbols leave traces in our memories. The letters of the alphabet are tiny pieces that come to life when combined, shaping words that express our thoughts. Numbers are numerical abstractions that provide order and structure to our quantitative conceptions. These concrete examples provide us with a view of the power and depth of symbols in our communication and understanding of the world.

On the other hand, concepts emerge as tangible representations of mental abstractions. They are cognitive tools that allow us to classify and understand specific categories of objects, events, phenomena, or relationships. Concepts provide the intellectual scaffolding necessary to organize and make sense of the vast panorama of our perceptions. Through them, we build a common and shared language, facilitating communication and the exchange of knowledge among individuals. Concepts arise as objectified manifestations of ideas. They stand as cognitive instruments that facilitate the interpretation, categorization, and understanding of our perceptions. Concepts, as intellectual pillars, provide the structure needed to organize and endow meaning to the complex panorama that surrounds us. Through them, we build a language that allows humans to experience and communicate emotions, as well as exchange ideas and knowledge. These cognitive elements form the basic foundations of human understanding and reasoning, enabling the organization and meaning-making of the environment around us.

Function

Symbols can be compared to industrious bees flying from one place to another, collecting and transporting the pollen of ideas, concepts, and meanings through the blooming field of language that we all share. But that is not all; they also have an emotional dimension as they can evoke emotions and feelings, bringing tears to our eyes or a smile to our lips. Moreover, they act as uniforms that unite a team;

they represent and strengthen the identity of a group or culture, serving as a source of pride and a reminder of what they have in common. Symbols are constituted as exalted vessels in the journey of communication, carrying ideas, conceptual constructions, and meanings through a harmonious and agreed-upon language. Additionally, they unfold as conjurers of emotions and heartbeats of the soul, and with equal mastery, they present themselves as banners that reaffirm and raise the cultural and collective identity.

For their part, concepts are like drawers that help us keep everything organized in the closet. Without them, chaos and disorder would reign. Concepts, therefore, come into action when we need to organize, categorize, and try to understand this immense and sometimes bewildering world we live in. In the field of communication, without concepts, we would only be grunting and gesticulating constantly. In the cognitive domain, concepts allow us to group similar things. For example, the concept "fruits" can refer to apples, pears, or bananas, but not to guitars.

Concreteness

Symbols, which find their home in both the tangible and the perceptible world, serve as communicative vessels to represent the vast universe of abstract concepts and ideas. Symbols disguise themselves in a wide variety of forms. An image is a portal to deeper meanings; a sound carries hidden connotations; a gesture is a term in a universal language; and a word embodies a transcendent reality. Symbols are defined as entities that carry a tangible nature or become perceptible to our senses, and they play a critical role in representing abstract or conceptual elements. They are chameleon-like in nature, and their essence can take the form of a visual construct, a sound wave, a body expression, or a sequence of immortalized characters.

A symbol is a tangible element that represents a concept or notion, while concepts are mental abstractions lacking a physical form and, therefore, defy sensory detection. Concepts are mental constructs designed to organize and make sense of information, but they need symbols as vehicles for transmission or communication.

Concepts are intangible tools forged in the forges of thought that serve as intellectual compasses for humans in their journey of interpreting their environment. Symbols, for their part, emerge as tangible beacons, carrying the weight of representing those ethereal abstractions. Like bridges, they translate abstract ideas into a language that our senses can comprehend. In other words, concepts are the architects that shape meanings and structures, while symbols are the messengers that carry these mental edifices through the waves of communication.

Contrary to what Western philosophical tradition has believed, especially since the Enlightenment, these differences in nature, function, and concreteness that distinguish the symbol from the concept do not mean that symbol and concept are incompatible. Quite the opposite, when allowed to coexist, the concept fully appropriates the symbol. Unlike the sidelining of the symbol in favor of the concept, or even the substitution of the symbol by the concept, as we have previously referred to, the proper appropriation of the symbol by the concept lies not in its displacement but in granting it space for its being. The feasibility of conceptualizing the symbol without diminishing or obliterating its nature lies in precariousness, provisionality, and freedom. Through meditative observation, a conceptualization devoid of Aristotelian abstraction emerges, and an approach to the symbol arises that does not tear it away but inserts, includes, or incorporates us into it. In our philosophical aspiration toward the study of the symbol, we cannot dismiss the value of the concept. However, we propose a mode of conceptualization that preserves the inherent depth and power of the symbol. This alternative mode of conceptualization, rooted in non-Aristotelian thought, is an analogy, and its greatest virtue is conceptualizing without killing the symbol. The concepts of analogy, univocity, and equivocity that we refer to belong to scholasticism but have their origins in Aristotle's concepts of synonymy, homonymy, and paronymy. There are three types of analogies through which it is possible to constitute or configure a concept: the analogy of intrinsic attribution, the analogy of extrinsic attribution, and the analogy of proportionality.

The analogy of intrinsic attribution

While it is true that the concepts of analogy, univocity, and equivocity are used in realistic scholasticism, we will make use of these concepts without adhering to that school. The analogy of intrinsic attribution is its logical correlate and its semantic expression. The analogy of intrinsic attribution is one in which a set of elements or entities acquire their meaning according to a primary analogate that intrinsically belongs to all of them. For example, "healthy" is a quality that intrinsically belongs to water because it preserves the health of the body. Medicine is intrinsically healthy because it heals the body. Exercise is healthy, but only if it preserves the health of the body. "Healthy" intrinsically and properly belongs to the organism because it is the one that preserves it, and it receives the cause from water, medicine, and exercise. Thus, the other elements of the analogy participate in the property that properly belongs to the organism and acquire their meaning by referring to it. This is why it is said that in this analogy, there is a primary analogate, because it is the one that possesses the meaning and grants it to the others.

The analogy of extrinsic attribution

The analogy of extrinsic attribution is one in which a property belongs intrinsically or properly to an entity and simultaneously belongs extrinsically or improperly to another. For example, in the expression "Jesus is the lion of the tribe of Judah," the attribute "lion" belongs intrinsically to the lion and extrinsically to Jesus because He is not a lion. This analogy shows that the strength of the lion is similar to that of Jesus. In fact, the analogy of extrinsic attribution is like a metaphor, in which the extrinsic attribution properly belongs to the lion but also, albeit in a very accessory way, to Jesus.

The analogy of proportionality

The statement of the analogy of proportionality, which has a *logo* or "measure" that "communicates" the four elements of the analogy, says that A is to B as C is to D; or in other words, 1 is to 2 as 3 is to 4. For example, "Plato is to Aristotle as Hegel is to Marx." If we know that Plato was Aristotle's teacher, we will understand that Hegel was Marx's teacher, and we are making a proportion. Similarly, if we say, "Bolivia is to Argentina as Canada is to the U.S.," we are stating a proportionality. In the analogy of proportionality, the visible symbol holds less hierarchy than the invisible, which is supereminent.

In all three cases of analogy, the conceptualization of the symbol is possible without killing it. In the analogy of intrinsic attribution, the visible sign participates in the invisible and derives its meaning from it. The property belongs to the invisible sign, which is the primary analogate, but secondarily also belongs to the visible, which is its expression. In the study of this analogy, we discern a common or shared essence, primarily given in the primary analogate or, depending on its magnitude, in the context of proportion. However, this framework grants us the freedom to incorporate diversity in the subsequent analogates.

In the analogy of extrinsic attribution, a metaphorical representation exists. That is, an analogy based on external attributions. For example, Jesus says that the heavenly kingdom is like a mustard seed.

> The kingdom of heaven is like a grain of mustard, which a man took and sowed in his field; which indeed is the smallest of all seeds, but when it has grown, it is the greatest of the herbs and becomes a tree, so that the birds of the air come and make nests in its branches.
>
> (Matthew, 13:31–32)

In the heavenly kingdom, there are no mustard seeds. In heaven, there is no superior and perfect version of the earthly mustard seed. However, Jesus uses a visible sign as a metaphor for the invisible.

Finally, the symbol remains alive in the analogy of proportionality, as there is one that is more and another that is less. That is, justice in the intelligible world is much fuller than justice in the perceptible world. The beauty of the intelligible reality far exceeds the beauty of the perceptible reality. The analogy of proportionality means that there is a proportion in the being that shows being but a much greater proportion in being itself.

What these three analogies reveal is that, unlike conceptualization as univocity, there is a way of conceptualizing that preserves the symbol rather than omitting it. The symbolic turn recovers the conditions that allow philosophy to think reality through concepts, but preserving the symbol.

CHAPTER 6

SEARCHING FOR MEANING IN A UNIVERSE OF SYMBOLS

Beyond the rational and linguistic faculties that, since the Enlightenment, have defined the human being, the human species is also distinguished by its symbolic nature. It is due to this symbolic nature that humanity, since its very dawn, has been generating sacred mythological narratives, which have explored the figure of a God as the origin, source, or creator of the world. The court of mythological deities and the pantheon of philosophy bow before this reality. Heidegger, navigating the turbulent waters of metaphysics, raised his banner in the search for the meaning of being.

These mythological narratives are charged with meaning, whose dual structure of form and purpose has served to provide coherence and direction to the odyssey of human existence. This means operating in the shadows like a taciturn demiurge, erecting skeletons and purposes that, with surgical mastery, stitch coherence into human experience. It is through this structure of form and purpose (*telos*) that constitutes meaning that *Homo sapiens*, now as a *Homo symbolicus*, tempestuous and multifaceted, navigate the stormy seas of its existence, immersed in a dialectic of creation and tracking of semantics, forging alchemies in the realms of the mythical and the philosophical alike. Myth emerges as a faculty of the human mind that confers order to the chaotic and grants purpose to what lacks meaning, thus channeling this configuration toward a determined direction. Both myth and concept strive to confer order. However, while myth points toward order in relation to being, the concept struggles to organize the egoistic chaos on an existential level. The human yearning to achieve happiness and fulfillment manifests as the driving axis of this configuration, and the human mind seeks comfort and meaning through its narratives, discarding those that lack transcendence. It is precisely from this perspective that it is possible to affirm that just as nothing is foreign to the realm of language, nothing is foreign to the realm of myth. Myth and language are two realms that interpenetrate and depend on each other. In fact, if myth is a narrative, and narrative is language, the human being cannot relate to the world without a meaning that gives it sense. At the same time, if meaning springs from language, and it is language that opens us to the world, or even that we inhabit the world through language, or rather, the world of language, then we must admit with Heidegger that language is the dwelling place of being and man its shepherd.

It is through language that *Homo sapiens*, the architect of its odyssey, weaves mythical narratives like scaffolds upon which to climb toward a more sublime understanding. *Homo symbolicus*, in its hermeneutic venture in the construction of mythical narratives, unfolds an expository framework that amalgamates its experience and aspires to imbue it with a subtle character in symbiosis with its axiological drive toward ontological culmination. These are attempts to conjure a coherent framework that supports the search for fulfillment. Through myth, the human cognitive framework surpasses the veil of tangible reality and delves into a dimension in which events hold a more abyssal and evocative resonance.

Myth is a telescope that allows us to look beyond the curtain of the ordinary, of the merely factual and measurable, into a cosmos where the echo of each action resounds with purpose. Such a narrative is an atlas, an ancient tome worn by use, through which we navigate in search of the essence of our humanity.

Therefore, the mythological fable acquires the stature of a *sine qua non* for exploring the human condition and approaching a more exhaustive understanding of existence. Human intellect, armed with myths as fortifications, struggles to metamorphose the incoherent into coherence and instill purpose into the random, projecting its longing for fulfillment. By embracing myth, one empowers oneself in the search for patterns within chaos, giving purpose and cohesion to the inexplicable. Many who adhere solely to a rationalist perspective, having questioned and discredited myths, experience a profound sense of disorientation and existential emptiness. They realize that their lives lack a transcendent purpose and become immersed in a context of superficial and merely transactional relationships devoid of genuine affection and commitment. This realization arises because our reality is intrinsically linked to the search for and discovery of meaning in realms that transcend the boundaries imposed by rationalism. By discarding mythological narratives, rationalism sacrifices transcendence for mere utilitarian pragmatism, denying itself the possibility of plunging into the abyss of intrinsic and indecipherable meaning and establishing connections with a higher dimension of existence. Human reason can possess two functions: to create truths or to discover them; we position ourselves alongside those who discover, not with those who manufacture them.

The rationalist turn has deprived us of access to that platform that feeds on a meaning that surpasses mere rationality and encompasses intimate and meaningful relationships with others and with the environment that surrounds us. In the absence of myth, human relationships are relegated to utilitarianism, where love, friendship, empathy, and compassion are subjected to merely pragmatic interests. This limited and narrow approach leaves an emotional void in life as the very essence of our interactions fades away, making room for depersonalization and alienation. It is in this context that the importance of myth as a vital source of meaning becomes evident.

Mortals are fractured beings and mythical symbols help them stitch these fractures in search of the primordial sacred unity called the Retroprogressive Path. Through mythology, societies have found the means to infuse meaning into their existence, explore transcendental enigmas, and establish an intimate communion with their surroundings. These societies have explored the unfathomable abysses and established a sanctified connection with the surrounding universe. By reclaiming and grasping the relevance of myth, we can restore a sense of fulfillment and transcendence, nurturing our interactions with authenticity and purpose of greater magnitude. By unraveling the symbolic significance of myth in our lives, we ignite the flame of mystical and transformative restoration, nurturing our relationships with an ontological authenticity and a purpose that is rooted in enigmatic depth.

One of the conceptual foundations in Heideggerian philosophy is based on the enigma of what in German is called *die Welt des Lebens* or *Lebenswelt*, which we can translate as "the world of life." With the "world of life," Heidegger refers to the everyday and practical context shared by human beings. However, this crucible, which encompasses the human being's apprehension of existence in their daily life, radiates upon the environment around us, the habitat in which we dwell, work, and intertwine with our fellow human beings, refers to the ontological dimension of human existence, not merely epistemological.

From the Heideggerian perspective, the cosmos of lived experience constitutes the backdrop where our concerns, latent longings, and overflowing desires germinate and bloom and where we unveil and confer meaning to our universe. According to Heidegger, this vital universe is perpetually latent in our everyday existence, although we often take it for granted and do not question it. However, when we reflect and analyze our interpretation of this vital world that beats relentlessly within us, we discover novel perspectives and fresh ways of apprehending our own existence more deeply. The interconnection that articulates our entity with the cosmos is characterized by its pragmatic nature, not theoretical. The universe of lived experience corresponds to the spectrum comprised of the totality of entities surrounding us. It is imperative to understand that not all entities that emerge in our horizon are essential components of our cosmos, but only those that reveal themselves to us as familiar and meaningful. In other words, only those entities that hold concrete and meaningful sense for us acquire the status of members of our vital world. For example, in our garden resides a toad that has managed to evade a snake. However, this drama is foreign to our world and alien to our reality. We are unaware of the existence of the toad and the snake, and therefore, this drama will not affect us, will not move or excite us, and will not modify or alter us in any way. Consequently, the world of life is composed of a set of entities that are familiar and meaningful to us because they attribute meaning to our lives. Despite coexisting as well, others remain in an ontological purgatory, external to the reality we inhabit and experience.

This fact, although it may seem trivial at first glance, is essential for understanding how we relate to the world and how we define our place within it. In this sense, it is important to emphasize that the authentic connection to the world does not rest on a theoretical or abstract relationship but on praxis and significance. Heidegger makes this explicit with a famous phrase in the work *Being and Time*: "Being is always the being of an entity."[20] Heidegger has this perspective that asking about the meaning of being is always asking about the meaning of the being of the concrete, living, historical entity. Only through the latter is it possible to establish a deep and authentic connection with the environment, providing our existence with a full and concrete sense, in no case dependent on a priori transcendental horizontals or pre-life supreme purposes.

This same aspect was forcefully addressed by Friedrich Nietzsche, who had already warned us that the belief that life harbors a prefigured purpose or meaning was nothing more than a fallacy, as, in the end, life unfolds in a chaotic and absurd order. In his work *Thus Spoke Zarathustra*, Nietzsche introduces the notion of "eternal recurrence,"[21] a term with which he suggests that everything that happens in the universe will repeat tirelessly. This enigmatic proposition undoubtedly undermines any pre-established purpose or final direction in the history of the world; that is, it discards any possibility of progress in favor of retroprogress.

Likewise, Nietzsche rejects placing meaning in a deity, proclaiming that it is up to us to build our existential meaning through the construction of our own values and goals. Nietzsche's premise suggests that life is an existence stripped of meaning, requiring the conscious creation of our goals and values to find meaning.

---

20. Martin Heidegger, *Being and Time* (New York: Harper & Row, 1962), §3, 29.
21. Friedrich Nietzsche, *Thus Spoke Zarathustra*, in The Portable Nietzsche, trans. and ed. Walter Kaufmann (New York: Penguin Books, 1977), 331–333, "The Convalescent," sec. 2.

In symmetry with this idea, Albert Camus asserts that existence stands as an absurd enigma devoid of any intrinsic goal or purpose. In the vast philosophical universe, Camus raises the flag of the futility of seeking absolute meaning in existence. The *Myth of Sisyphus* reveals the tension between the human search for meaning in an indifferent cosmos and the reality that reminds us of the lack of meaning in existence. From his unyielding stance, only those trapped in the claws of belief in a transcendental meaning rush toward suicide. In *The Myth of Sisyphus*, Camus addresses the theme of suicide. If life lacks meaning, could suicide be the answer? In one of his reflections, Camus says:

> There is but one truly serious philosophical problem, and that is suicide. Judging whether life is or is not worth living amounts to answering the fundamental question of philosophy. All the rest— whether or not the world has three dimensions, whether the mind has nine or twelve categories— comes afterwards. These are games; one must first answer.[22]

Those trapped in the nets of transcendental illusion march toward the gloomy abyss of self-destruction. While this position might seem like a discouraging echo, it also opens the doors to liberation and self-discovery. Confronted with cosmic indifference, the absence of a pre-established existential meaning offers us the opportunity to rise as architects of our own meaning, finding in the tangible a shelter of significance. In front of the impassive face of the cosmos, we can be the creators of our own sense and purpose by connecting with others and committing to causes that are aligned with our intrinsic values, discerning value in the immediate and the palpable. Through this embrace of the absurd, we shed the confusion that comes with the exhausting search for an absolute and transcendental meaning. In this way, we find instead a delight and a purpose in the actions and relationships in our daily lives. In the absurd universe painted by

---

22. Albert Camus, *The Myth of Sisyphus and Other Essays*, trans. Justin O'Brien (New York: Alfred A. Knopf, 1955), 3, chap. "An Absurd Reasoning."

Camus, meaning is not revealed but rather erected and reconfigured in every beat of existence. And it is in this act of creation that we can find a form of freedom and a purpose that, though ephemeral and contingent, can imbue our lives with value and richness.

This existentialist current with which Camus addresses the question of the meaning of life seems rooted in the ideas and works of earlier authors within the philosophical firmament, among whom we can highlight Arthur Schopenhauer and, more specifically, his magnum opus *The World as Will and Representation*.

In this philosophical journey, Schopenhauer unveils the illusion of a transcendental meaning, immersing the reader in a sea of perplexities and questions. The desperate search for an absolute purpose fades in the whirlwind of suffering and discontent that surrounds us. Schopenhauer argued that the only path to finding something akin to happiness is through the negation of desire and renunciation of worldly ambitions.[23] Drawing from his knowledge of Vedanta and Buddhism, he appeals to the denial of will and proposes avenues of escape rather than paths to happiness. In his profound reflection, renunciation of fleeting desires and contemplation of nature and art emerge as beacons of light in the dark night of understanding. In the realm of Western thought, many scholars have concluded that *Homo sapiens* is nothing more than a biological aggregation, a sum of cells destined to degrade and reintegrate into the elements, as declared in the ancient Genesis.

בְּזֵעַת אַפֶּיךָ תֹּאכַל לֶחֶם עַד שׁוּבְךָ אֶל־הָאֲדָמָה כִּי מִמֶּנָּה לֻקָּחְתָּ כִּי־עָפָר אַתָּה
וְאֶל־עָפָר תָּשׁוּב׃

(בראשית ג', י"ט)

By the sweat of your brow will you eat bread until you return to the ground, for from it you were taken. For dust you are, and to dust you will return.

(Genesis, 3:19)

23. Arthur Schopenhauer, *The World as Will and Representation*, vol. 1, trans. E. F. J. Payne (New York: Dover Publications, 1966), Sections 68–71, 379–412.

The positions of Schopenhauer and Camus, as well as those of Nietzsche and Heidegger, open a new paradigm of a hermeneutic nature in which the human being, through their cognitive apparatus, strives to give structure to the amorphous and attribute meaning to the trivial and inconsequential. This outline, comparable to a film or theatrical script, contains the anecdotes, the plot, the characters, the dialogues, and all the details necessary for its unfolding. By narrating or telling, we sculpt a stage upon which we immerse ourselves in the construction of a chronicle that transcends the mere concatenation of events, giving coherence and meaning to human vicissitude. At the threshold of this universe dictated by narrative, the individual assigns themselves a purpose and embodies a being, adopting a new identity. Thanks to the narrative, we become actors and protagonists, displaying our interpretative skills and generating meaning through the interactions and choices we make in the development of our role. This narrative process allows us to shape and structure the chaotic and disorderly aspects of reality and gives us the ability to attribute meaning and direction to them. In this way, embodying a specific character and participating in the story we have created for ourselves grants us an interpretive framework and a symbolic foundation from which we construct meaning and understand our existence. Through the activity of narration, our mind strives to confer order, meaning, and purpose through a plot that shapes the characters. By immersing ourselves in this fictional representation, we embark on a journey where we create meaning and delve into the complexity of our own existence.

Chapter 7

Semiotics: Exploring the Language of Signs and Symbols

As we mentioned earlier, the creation of meaning through mythological narratives occurs through signs and symbols, the study of which is called semiotics. This term is derived from the Greek word *sēmeiōtikós* (σημειωτικός), which in turn comes from *semeion*, meaning "symbol or sign" in English. Semiotics, or semiology depending on the academic approach, is the branch of philosophy that, with the help of components from other academic fields such as linguistics, sociology, and psychology, studies, in a scientific way, the communication through signals, indications, representations, signs, and symbols. This includes both interpretive and generative analyses of these elements. Although the discipline of semiotics itself is relatively modern, the study of signs and their meanings has ancient roots. In classical Greece, philosophers such as Plato and Aristotle had already investigated the formation and transmission of meanings through language and communication with particular interest.

Before delving into the content of this discipline, it is important to briefly distinguish between two terms that have sometimes been understood as synonyms but that involve subtle differences: semiology and semiotics. Semiotics was defined by its main precursor, Ferdinand de Saussure, in the 19th century as "a science which studies the role of signs as part of social life."[24] It could be understood as the study of symbols and signs, that is, anything that communicates a message that

24. Ferdinand de Saussure, *Course in General Linguistics*, ed. Charles Bally and Albert Sechehaye with the collaboration of Albert Riedlinger, trans. and annotated by Roy Harris (Chicago and La Salle, IL: Open Court, 1986), §3, 15.

a receiver must interpret, as well as the way humans create them. For Saussure, semiology aimed to understand the signs of communication.

On the other hand, semiotics could be understood as the discipline that seeks to understand how the processes of signification are articulated, thus leading toward two fields of knowledge: linguistics and epistemology. The American philosopher Charles Peirce (1893-1914), considered one of its founders, defined semiotics as "the quasi-necessary, or formal doctrine of signs," based on the relationship between a symbol, an object, and an interpreter.[25] In a way, similar to semiology, semiotics as a discipline would aim to study and understand how the processes of signification are articulated in all possible communication systems. Moreover, semiotics encompasses three fundamental branches: syntax, semantics, and pragmatics, which can be seen as the three central axes of discourse in relation to the sign and, consequently, the three crucial aspects of semiotic analysis. Although semiotics was initially associated solely with linguistics, recognized scholars in the field, such as the Italian Umberto Eco (1932-2016), have argued that the roots of semiotics can be found in the works of most great thinkers in the Western tradition.

In addition to semiotics and semiology, we must also mention *semiosis*, which we could define as the instance where "something acquires meaning for someone," that is, when something becomes a carrier of meaning. The term *semiosis* comes from the Greek *sēmeíōsis* (σημείωσις), derived from the verb *sēmeiô* (σημειῶ), which we could translate as "mark" and refers to the process of producing meanings from signs. This process occurs within the interpreter's mental sphere, beginning with the perception of the sign and ending with the presence of the sign in their mind.

Regarding the sign, Peirce differentiated three different types: the iconic, where the sign is similar to what it represents; the indexical, where the sign is associated with what it signifies; and the symbolic, where the sign is merely an arbitrary link. Among many other classifications, we also find denotation (the meaning of the

25. Charles Sanders Peirce, *Philosophical Writings of Peirce*, ed. Justus Buchler (New York: Dover Publications, 1955), chap. 7, "Logic as Semiotic: The Theory of Signs," 98–119.

sign), connotation (other signs associated with it), pragmatic (signs that can represent others), and syntagmatic (signs that link together in a chain). Additionally, the sign can also be studied through the three branches of semiotics, as mentioned earlier. That is, we can analyze the syntax, semantics, and pragmatics of the sign. Let us examine these three areas more closely:

The syntax of the sign analyzes the relationship between various signs or symbols. Consider, for example, the correlation between a period and a comma or the distinction between uppercase and lowercase letters. This dimension encompasses the domain of letters and numbers, examining how they interact. Thus, while "semiotics" is an appropriate arrangement of signs, "semiocita" is a syntactical error. For instance, while 1+1=2 is a correct syntactic structure, +11=2 is an error. A syntactic error occurs when a sign is not properly aligned in relation to another. In linguistics, such an error refers to deficiencies in sentence structure. Essentially, the syntax is the branch that examines how signs link, relate, and coordinate with one another.

The semantics of the sign study the relationship between a sign and what it designates, resulting in a concrete meaning. For example, a traffic light: when it illuminates green, its interpretation is "go," while its red light conveys the message "stop." In this case, the designated or referent is "stop," and the meaning is to brake or stop and not continue advancing or "prohibited to advance." Within the context of semantics, signs can be classified into three categories: natural, iconic, and conventional.

Natural: Thunder is a natural sign that signals the imminence of rainfall.

Iconic: Examples of iconic signs are the logos of well-known brands like Adidas, Coca-Cola, or Nike, as well as sports team emblems.

Conventional: Conventional or artificial signs derive their meaning from a collective agreement or social consensus. A traffic light is a classic example because it functions as an emblem of social construction and collective norms. Over time, a consensus has been established regarding the meaning of each color emitted by its lights. However, we could have agreed on a different color palette with various attributions and meanings. Nonetheless, by convention, we have agreed that the green light signals us to proceed, while red demands we stop. In this symbolic framework, what the sign denotes—whether by nature or agreement—becomes its primary meaning.

In these three types of signs, the designated meaning, whether natural or conventional, is associated with a sign. Illustratively, when a kettle releases a whistle, it tells us that the water inside has reached its boiling point.

Finally, the pragmatics of the sign examines the interaction between the sign and the context of the receiver and interpreter, which also includes aspects such as the transmitter's purpose, what is implied connotations, and actions expressed through promises, questions, or directives. This third branch of semiotics also studies the impact of historical and cultural backgrounds on the decoding of a sign. Consider, for example, the well-known Nazi salute of raising an arm. In the West, if a person extends their right arm in this way, they are immediately associated with Nazi connotations. However, replicating the same gesture before members of a Bantu tribe would make it unlikely for them to associate it with that ideology since, in this context, the historical background is irrelevant. The difference lies in the fact that in this historical context, someone does not need to deduce the meaning of the sign. Every sign acquires a specific meaning based on the context in which it appears. If a religious symbol is presented to an observer unfamiliar with that tradition, they will not recognize the sacredness of the symbol in question. If the other person lacks the appropriate cultural context, they will find it impossible to understand its meaning. Take, for instance, the example of the Cross and the evangelization of America. The efforts to communicate its meaning in the missionary work were difficult precisely due to the lack of historical background. Hence, one can observe in history crosses with indigenous elements, which would today be seen as syncretic from a Catholic perspective but which responded to the need to convey the meaning of the Cross from the indigenous observer's perspective.

Once we have examined in detail what signs are and how they operate, it is also important to recognize the essential distinction between signs and symbols. On the one hand, the sign is not limited to a mere meaning; it also evokes values and emotional connotations and can be interpreted by all human beings and even certain species of animals. Its meanings are related to a concrete situation, a specific purpose, or a particular function. The sign exhibits universality and transcends language barriers because it is understandable and decipherable beyond language, immediately, without requiring a specific context to be interpreted. It functions as a tangible representation with an unequivocal, clear, and direct interpretation. The sign is utilitarian, as its main purpose is the effective communication of data or transmission of information.

On the other hand, the symbol, imbued with a cultural nuance, is polysemic, as its meaning varies according to the receiver. No phenomenon exhausts its meaning, and therefore, it accepts a variety of interpretations. Its understanding is not universally human and completely escapes the animal sphere, given its wide, deep, and abstract nature. Every attempt to access the symbol requires a base of pre-existing knowledge, often presented in narrative form. The function of the symbol is to transmit ideas, sensations, emotions, moods, values, and ideals, and its use lacks utilitarian purpose. The symbol acts as a bridge, connecting, integrating, fusing, re-linking, and consolidating.

Just as with signs, semiotics also addresses the three dimensions of the symbol, namely its syntax, semantics, and pragmatics.

To begin with, **the syntax of the symbol** addresses the nature of the syntactic relationship between symbols. In the symbolic realm, one reality is always shown through another, never directly. A sacred reality is shown through another. The main characteristic of the symbol is the relationship or interaction that the perceived or manifested sign maintains with the imperceptible or unmanifested, that is, the link between the visible sign and the invisible. Let us use the example of how, due to existing prohibitions, early Christians secretly identified each other by adopting a fish as a secret symbol. When they met, each one would draw half, culminating in the image of the fish, recalling the story of Jonah and its parallel with the resurrection of Jesus. By using the fish as an illustration, the hidden meaning would be the resurrection of Jesus, and it is through this symbol that we come to understand this intangible concept. Therefore, a single sign acquires meaning by relating to another. Similarly, the Star of David, formed by two triangles, illustrates this concept; one points to the earthly, the other to the divine. Essentially, a symbol is the fusion of the visible and the invisible sign.

The semantics of the symbol, on the other hand, examines the connection formed in this relationship, where the perceived sign simultaneously reveals and hides the imperceptible sign. One sign reveals the other because it simultaneously points to it while concealing it; indeed, if interpreted literally, it would be impossible to access the underlying essence of the hidden sign. No wonder we find Heraclitus in his famous fragment DK B Fr. 93 asserting that "The Lord whose oracle is at Delphi neither reveals nor conceals, but gives a sign" (ὁ ἄναξ οὗ τὸ μαντεῖόν ἐστι τὸ ἐν Δελφοῖς, οὔτε λέγει οὔτε κρύπτει ἀλλὰ σημαίνει).[26] If we limit ourselves to the obvious, surface expression without delving into its deeper dimensions, it is likely that we will be unable to decipher the full scope of the imperceptible sign and its ultimate meaning. Therefore, the semantics of the symbol allow us to affirm that a symbol simultaneously reveals and hides, and it would be erroneous to assert that the symbol merely shows or simply conceals. If the symbol were only revealed, there would be no need to discern or decipher, and the necessity for interpretation would be eliminated, reducing it merely to a defined term. In other words, if it were fully displayed, it would not be a symbol but a concept. Likewise, it would not be appropriate to claim that the symbol only conceals because if that were the case, it would not be a sign, as it would fail to fulfill its function of indicating or alluding to something.

Let us explore this central aspect of the symbol's dual function of revealing and concealing by connecting it to the difference we have previously established between natural and conventional signs. As we saw earlier, the natural sign, unlike the conventional sign, does not require a historical-community context to imbue it with meaning. When we now state that the symbol constitutes a perceptible sign

26. Heraclitus, *The Texts of Early Greek Philosophy: The Complete Fragments and Selected Testimonies of the Major Presocratics*, ed. Daniel W. Graham, Part 1 (New York: Cambridge University Press, 2010), 177 (frag. 93 = DK B93).

that reveals and simultaneously hides the imperceptible, we are faced with a horizontal relationship between one sign and another, and at the same time, a vertical connection, where the tangible sign acquires its meaning by participating in the intangible sign. What this shows is that the semantics of the symbol involve a relationship based on the interdependence of both signs.

This interaction between the vertical and horizontal dimensions can be visualized as a cross. For someone unfamiliar with Western culture and Christianity, a cross is an object devoid of meaning. In order to appreciate the cross, it is essential and necessary to know something about Christianity. The historical context is what allows us to articulate these two dimensions, to the point that without such contextualization, it would be difficult to conceive the convergence between the vertical and horizontal, and ultimately, to establish the necessary participation for the perceptible to align with the imperceptible.

This can be seen in the example of the traffic light, where the visible sign is its red light, while the concept or meaning "stop" remains conceptual, intellectual, or intangible. In the vertical dimension, what we can see reveals an invisible idea; that is, the perceptible represents an abstract notion. The horizontal dimension, meanwhile, is syntactic because, as we saw earlier, signs cannot be arranged arbitrarily. For example, changing the position of elements in a sentence would alter its meaning. Similarly, in mathematics, the arrangement 1+1 differs from 11. One 1 is related to another 1 in the premise of + because if we place one 1 next to another 1, without a + or - between them, we no longer have two ones but rather an 11. This latter relationship, understandable only to those who have studied mathematics in the West, does not conceal an esoteric meaning but **is** purely conceptual, hiding the syntactic relationship in the background.

Finally, **the pragmatics of the symbol** places us in the framework of history. Every symbol has a background, a context, a collective, and a history that gives it meaning. The symbol specifically consists of the conjunction between an icon, the tangible aspect, and a myth, the hidden and imperceptible narrative. In this sense, the symbol is characterized by its ability to offer clues that invite investigation. However, the existence of a community or people is essential to narrating a story that clarifies the meaning of the visible sign. That is, the presence of a collective that articulates a narrative is necessary to provide clarity to the content of the manifest sign. As mentioned earlier, however, the symbol is also an acoustic image and, therefore, much more than a mere visual indicator. In fact, in the universe of mythological narrative, the symbol plays out in the linguistic sphere, where the leading role belongs to speakers and the signs are words. In this sense, the pragmatic dimension of the symbol is as much shaped by the intent of the speakers when communicating as by the context framing that communication. This is why we can affirm that what is visible and audible are closely connected.

On the premise that the sign and its meaning are inseparably linked, just like the two sides of a coin, Ferdinand de Saussure conducts an unprecedented examination by meticulously breaking down the structure of the linguistic sign. To begin with, the Swiss semiologist differentiates between language and speech. On the one hand, language is like an abstract scheme impervious to individual and contextual variations that gives life to a communication system. Language is more like an orchestra in perpetual motion. Understood in this way, the language system appears as the incorporeal and intangible framework of language that resides in the psyche of communicators. Speech, on the other hand, would be the embodiment of language in everyday life, rising as the pragmatic concretization of the language system within a specific context.

Crucially, it should be noted that, in Saussure's view, language firmly stands as a social framework, carefully woven through human interaction. In this endless web of signs, reality takes form. The bricks of our understanding are shaped through these interactions. We could say that it is not we who handle the words, but that the words lead us, as the stars guide the sailor. In this sense, the "I" becomes a constitution of such symbolic linguistics that could be called "myth." If we observe ourselves, we will notice that we do not speak but, rather, we are spoken.

Bibliography Section I

- Aquinas, Thomas. *Disputed Questions on Truth*. Vol. 1. Translated by Robert W. Mulligan. Chicago: Henry Regnery Company, 1952.
- Aristotle. *Metaphysics*. Translated by Hugh Tredennick. *Aristotle in 23 Volumes*, vol. 17. Cambridge, MA: Harvard University Press; London: William Heinemann Ltd., 1933.
- Aristotle. *On Interpretation*. Translated by Harold P. Cooke. In *Aristotle: Categories. On Interpretation. Prior Analytics*. Loeb Classical Library 325. Cambridge, MA: Harvard University Press, 1938.
- Aristotle. *Topics: Book VI* . Translated with an introduction and commentary by Annamaria Schiaparelli. Oxford: Clarendon Press, 2024.
- Butnaru, Iulian. *Nature and Scope of the Symbol* (*Naturaleza y alcance del símbolo*). Tarragona: Universidad Rovira i Virgili, 2016.
- Camus, Albert. *The Myth of Sisyphus and Other Essays*. Translated by Justin O'Brien. New York: Alfred A. Knopf, 1955.
- Eliade, Mircea. *The Sacred and the Profane: The Nature of Religion*. Translated by Willard R. Trask. New York: Harcourt, Brace and Company, 1959.
- Heidegger, Martin. *Being and Time*. New York: Harper & Row, 1962.
- Heidegger, Martin. *Letter on Humanism*. In *Basic Writings*, edited by David Farrell Krell. New York: Harper & Row, 1977.
- Heraclitus. *The Texts of Early Greek Philosophy: The Complete Fragments and Selected Testimonies of the Major Presocratics.* Edited by Daniel W. Graham. Part 1. New York: Cambridge University Press, 2010.
- Husserl, Edmund. *Logical Investigations*. Translated by J. N. Findlay. Vol. 1. London: Routledge & Kegan Paul, 1970.
- Husserl, Edmund. *Logical Investigations*. Vols. 1–2. Translated by J. N. Findlay. Edited with a new introduction by Dermot Moran. London: Routledge, 2001.

- Jean, Borella. *The Crisis of Religious Symbolism and Symbolism and Reality*. Translated by G. John Champoux. Brooklyn, NY: Angelico Press/Sophia Perennis, 2016.
- Jung, Carl G., ed. *Man and His Symbols*. New York: Anchor Press/Doubleday, 1964.
- Nietzsche, Friedrich. *Thus Spoke Zarathustra*. In *The Portable Nietzsche*, translated and edited by Walter Kaufmann. New York: Penguin Books, 1977.
- Ortega y Gasset, José. *Meditations on Quixote*. Translated by Evelyn Rugg, Diego Marín, and Julián Marías. Urbana: University of Illinois Press, 2000.
- Peirce, Charles Sanders. *Philosophical Writings of Peirce*. Edited by Justus Buchler. New York: Dover Publications, 1955.
- Plato. *The Banquet of Plato*. Translated by Percy Bysshe Shelley. Chicago: Way and Williams, 1895.
- Plato. *The Collected Dialogues of Plato*. Edited by Edith Hamilton and Huntington Cairns. Bollingen Series LXXI. Princeton, NJ: Princeton University Press, 2025. Originally published in 1961.
- Plato. *The Theaetetus of Plato: With Translation and Notes*. Translated by Benjamin Hall Kennedy. Cambridge: Cambridge University Press, 1881.
- Plato. *Theaetetus*. In *Plato in Twelve Volumes*, vol. 12, translated by Harold N. Fowler. Cambridge, MA: Harvard University Press; London: William Heinemann Ltd., 1921.
- Ricoeur, Paul. *The Symbolism of Evil*. Translated by Emerson Buchanan. New York: Harper & Row, 1967.
- Saussure, Ferdinand de. *Course in General Linguistics*. Edited by Charles Bally and Albert Sechehaye, with the collaboration of Albert Riedlinger. Translated and annotated by Roy Harris. Chicago and La Salle, IL: Open Court, 1986.
- Schopenhauer, Arthur. *The World as Will and Representation*. Vol. 1. Translated by E. F. J. Payne. New York: Dover Publications, 1966.

Section II

Symbols and Philosophy

Chapter 8

Myths and symbols according to Friedrich Creuzer

Friedrich Creuzer (1771–1858) was a respected German philologist and archaeologist who laid the foundations for studying comparative mythology. His perspective inaugurated a new vision that would significantly impact fields such as philosophy, anthropology, and philology. However, despite the innovative nature of his work in comparative mythology and symbolism studies, his work has not been exhaustively examined.

In this chapter, we will address his two seminal works, *Symbolism and Mythology of Ancient Peoples*, especially the Greeks, where he presents a comparative study tracing the roots of Homeric and Hesiodic mythology in the East, and on the other hand, *The Idea and Validity of Ancient Symbolism*, through which the author provides a clear and concise entry portal to his symbolic theory through four seminal aspects:

1. The comparative vision that will define his research.
2. The bifurcated approach to the symbol considers both its form and its essence or content.
3. The equivocal nature of the symbol.
4. The polar quality that distinguishes the symbol is exemplified by the figure of Silenus in the form of an enriching duality.

Creuzer's studies, which focus on the archaic stage of Eastern history corresponding to the native era of the oldest Eastern peoples, explore how, through myth and symbol, artistic development moved from East to West. For this, Creuzer focuses on the heroic period of Greek civilization, which coincides with the emergence of myth. In his work *Symbolism and Mythology*, Creuzer begins his exploration of the stationary and mute language of Eastern symbolism. As the author himself states:

> The myth, in its oldest form, through the closed brevity and the instantaneous totality of its action, still adhered faithfully to the symbol, which only gradually, as it receded, dissolved into the flow.[27]

In this quote, Creuzer explains that the myth must be understood as expressing the most original aspect of humanity, which, at that time, was capable of drawing a form that instantaneously expressed an intuitive crack in the dual platform of subject-object or space-time. This was so until, gradually, conceptualization gained ground, and the myth lost its character as an original form of expression for reasons we will explore later. This pre-conceptualizing notion of myth should not be seen as strange or foreign. On the contrary, just as a child symbolizes before conceptualizing, so too did humanity in its childhood forge the original symbols. To explain this point, the author specifically refers to Greek art's impact and influence on myth, which later "[...] came to be simply a means of entertainment." As Creuzer himself writes:

> Myth abandoned the lowest ground of reality, rose with the rhythm of poetry, and transformed into theater through ideal creations.[28]

In the ancient world to which the author refers in this work, the myths of the heroic period were stories told to entertain and amuse, but also to explain phenomena that could not otherwise be understood. Because, as Creuzer continues:

27. Friedrich Creuzer, *Simbolica e mitologia*, in *Dal simbolo al mito*, vol. II (Milan: Edizioni Spirale, 1983), 60. Translation mine.
28. Ibid., 59.

> Nature delights in expressing its visible concepts through visible symbols, just as divinity loves to show its ideas through sensible images.[29]

We propose changing the word *nature* to *Being* to convey better what the author means in this quote. The Greek *phýsis* refers to that which emerges and remains, to the force that gives life and sustains all that is visible.

Divinity, which is not an image, becomes visible through art and representations, in the same way that Being delights in expressing its concepts through visible symbols. Again, we see how the symbol manifests as a visible image loaded with an invisible meaning. The essence of the symbol consists of that which unites the visible image and the invisible meaning, the image to the eye and the word to the ear. In this sense, the symbol, manipulated by the ecclesiastical caste or organized religion, acts as the highest representation of a primordial transcendental revelation. Only those with religious access to the universe could make and manipulate the symbols, understood as the expression of the sacred origin of reality, in such a way that only a priestly caste could phenomenon a meaning through an image. A worldview and a sense of life for the people were presented through narration. Their task was to explain the transcendental mysteries that gave meaning to the empirical reality of human beings. Some archaeologists consider the burying of the dead to be a key milestone for humanity If we consider that performing an act such as this marks the beginning of humanity, it is because we understand that humans recognize themselves as beings called to transcendence and, naturally, express this through symbols, such as a funeral.

Therefore, myth, religion, and art were not separate disciplines in antiquity. Science was not either because myth, in a way, also acted as a scientific explanation of reality. As contradictory as it may seem, myth, religion, science, and art are fed into one another. There was no divorce, fragmentation, or rupture between these forms of knowledge, which created an integrated wisdom in their complicity

29. Ibid., 12.

with one another. This would explain why, in antiquity, the great religious figures were also artists. The integrity of humanity breaks when the myth is abandoned. Not only is its knowledge separated, but humanity itself is divided.

Creuzer refers more specifically to the primordial monotheistic era when the "intimate readiness of the spirit" prevailed. The profound was clearly intuited and permanently lived in that unitary revelation, which the author identifies with the term *luminosity* and defines as the "original condition of the human race" that later underwent a "gradual obscuration." Consciousness received illumination and, not being mediated by concepts, it was possible to grasp Being through the symbol intuitively and thus fully. Humans did not speculate but rather painted, danced, sang, and made the received revelation intelligible. There was no suspicion or questioning but only gratitude for what was received, expressed artistically, symbolically, or orally, as it was narrated and verbalized mythologically. The great illuminated masters spoke or painted; through their words, paintings, or drawings, they created images (symbols) that offered meanings. In this sense, the religion of antiquity was true and unfolded as such, providing access to the sacred symbolic reality through a myth that led to the image and an image that returned us to the myth. For this reason, Creuzer goes on to explain the following:

> In all of antiquity, the highest ideas of man and his most important memories were made sensible through symbolic and allegorical actions. What were the oldest celebrations, if not the periods of the year translated into actions, along with the memory of the great blessings from cultivating the land and cultures! It was a sacred year personified in a cycle of allegorical actions.[30]

Creuzer argues that, in primitive antiquity, human beings emerged from the caves and had great sacred ideas, and all of them—along with manifestations of memories—expressed sensible realities

30. Ibid., 80.

through symbologies and allegories painted in caves or written on papyri. From the beginning, humanity could only speak of the sacred through the symbolic and allegorical. Therefore, all ancient sacred books should not be read literally but artistically, as is said in the ancient scriptures of the Hebrew tradition:

> וְעַתָּה כִּתְבוּ לָכֶם אֶת הַשִּׁירָה הַזֹּאת וְלַמְּדָהּ אֶת־בְּנֵי־יִשְׂרָאֵל שִׂימָהּ בְּפִיהֶם לְמַעַן תִּהְיֶה־לִּי הַשִּׁירָה הַזֹּאת לְעֵד בִּבְנֵי יִשְׂרָאֵל.
>
> (דברים ל"א, י"ט)
>
> Now, therefore, write down this poem [or song] for yourself, and teach it to the children of Israel; put it in their mouths so that this poem may be My witness against the children of Israel.
>
> (Deuteronomy, 31:19)

It would be a great mistake to read, understand, and study the sacred scriptures exclusively as books or treatises on history or science instead of reading them fundamentally as symbolic artistic literature. This is also corroborated by the New Testament, where the Last Supper is recalled:

> While they were eating, Jesus took the bread, gave thanks to God, broke it, gave it to his disciples, and said: "Take this bread and eat it; this is my body." Then he took the cup, and after giving thanks, he gave it to them, saying: "Drink from it, all of you. This is my blood of the covenant, which is poured out for many for the forgiveness of sins. I tell you, I will not drink from this fruit of the vine from now on until that day when I drink it new with you in my Father's kingdom." When they had sung a hymn, they went out to the Mount of Olives.
>
> (Matthew, 26:26–30)

Although the Catholic Church has interpreted this metaphysical text physically and concluded that, at the supper, the diners were eating the body of Jesus, we must emphasize that the factual existence of Jesus, Buddha, Muhammad, or Mahavira would be the least significant, because, paradoxical as it may seem, the truth is precisely what is not (present). Here lies one of the essential factors of symbology and the necessity of its symbolic meaning. What the symbol entails is a dialectic between "what is" and "what is present" in which "what is present" is not and "what is" is not "present." Because, in the ontological difference, "what is present" in space and time "is not." Being "is," but it does not "exist," and from this derives the difficulty in perceiving the nonexistent. On the other hand, everything that is objective "exists" but "it is not." However, beings like Jesus, Buddha, or Chaitanya both "are" and "exist" simultaneously, unlike ordinary beings who are only conscious of their existence in space and time. In *Letter on Humanism*, Heidegger says:

> The human being is, and is human, insofar as he is the ek-sisting one. He stands out into the openness of being. Being itself, which as the throw has projected the essence of the human being into "care," is as this openness. Thrown in such fashion, the human being stands "in" the openness of being.[31]

The tree "is present," and because it "is present," it "is not"; although the tree "is present," it is not the Being, but rather, as a tree, it is an entity. Parmenides said that being is one, compact, homogeneous, and eternal, but the entity does not have these characteristics and, therefore, as an entity, it "is not." God, Being, or consciousness "is," but it "is not present"; while the human being, and what is egoic, "is present" but "is not." Enlightenment consists of being fully without the need to "be present."

In this dialectical context between "being" and "being present" that Creuzer leads us into, the essence of a symbol resides in its ability to appeal to sensitivity and simplicity; nature was established

31. Martin Heidegger, *Letter on Humanism*, trans. Frank A. Capuzzi, in Pathmarks, ed. William McNeill (Cambridge: Cambridge University Press, 1998), 266.

as the genuine teacher and guide of ancient civilizations, while priests were the guardians and vigilant shepherds of these symbolic representations captured by the senses. In the training and preparation for the ancient religion, the interpretation of symbols was central. One integral task of their functions as teachers was to construct images and give them form, and through them to point out, display, and interpret. Additionally, in ancient thinking, the auditory and visual symbols were not yet as distinguished as they are today. Instead, the image was a means of communication in the hands of the interpreters, whose mindset was that the auditory and visual were not separated but united and complemented each other, as Creuzer reminds us once again. Because, in the symbol, the ear and the eye feed each other by its nature. This would explain why we use the term *text*, which comes from *texture*, because the ancient religious masters not only read the texts but also touched and felt them. Similarly, the term *wisdom* in Greek comes from to *taste* since we approach the symbol with all the senses. Paintings were listened to, and stories were seen. Therefore, although the image is meant to be seen and the text to be heard, the enlightened masters listened to what was painted and saw in images in what was narrated. And obviously, we are not referring to ordinary sensory perception but to symbolic perception, as also referred to in the New Testament when Jesus says:

> The disciples came to him and asked, "Why do you speak to the people in parables?" He replied, "Because the knowledge of the secrets of the kingdom of heaven has been given to you, but not to them. Whoever has will be given more, and they will have an abundance. Whoever does not have, even what they have, will be taken from them. This is why I speak to them in parables: 'Though seeing, they do not see; though hearing, they do not hear or understand.' In them is fulfilled the prophecy of Isaiah: 'You will be ever hearing but never understanding; you will be ever seeing but never perceiving. For this people's heart has become calloused; they hardly hear with their ears, and they have closed their

> eyes. Otherwise, they might see with their eyes, hear with their ears, understand with their hearts, and turn, and I would heal them.' But blessed are your eyes because they see, and your ears because they hear. For truly I tell you, many prophets and righteous people longed to see what you see but did not see it, and to hear what you hear but did not hear it."
>
> (Matthew, 13:10–17)

In the preliminary preparation of ancient religions, we find the interpretations of symbols. Forging images and sculpting forms was a central aspect of their work as teachers, and through these manifestations, they pointed out, exposed, communicated, and interpreted. The sages of antiquity created images and gave them form with words. As we have said, and as Creuzer lucidly explains, ancient primordial thought did not yet distinguish, as we do today, between symbols that appeal to the ear and those that relate to the eye: the image served as discourse, it was a word, and it spoke through the interpreters. Images must be interpreted like texts, and the sacred text is a painting to be appreciated.

The direct realization of the whole is very different from how it is described. The imperceptible must be transformed into an experience to be communicated and shared. If we want to universalize the Truth, it will be necessary to conceptualize it unless we turn to art. Expression through art makes it possible to share without conceptualizing. By being conscious of itself, the root of diversity is absolute unity. When the individual tries to express it phenomenally, it creates the distinction between the visual and the auditory. It is akin to love, which, being a unified experience, must resort to poems, paintings, or songs to be shared. That is to say, while we can see or hear the expressions of love, the experience is one and the same in essence.

This leads us to understand the symbol as a "writing by images," that is, a whole that, in its origins, before the myth was conceptualized, blended, and united the visual and the auditory into one. Because in the symbol itself, everything is one. Regarding this issue, Creuzer writes again in *Symbolism and Mythology* that:

> Originally, image and word did not diverge from one another, but, having grown from a single root (which is the realization of consciousness itself), they were deeply united and interpenetrated. Whether a thought was imprinted in an image or expressed by a word this was shown in an evidently sensitive way.[32]

For this reason, Creuzer concludes by saying that "proverbs, brief and concise expressions, riddles and sayings, as the symbolic, were words of the book of nature, a character of its unchanging writing by images."

Creuzer speaks of proverbs and concise expressions, which, in Sanskrit, are called *sūtras*, that is, the maximum of wisdom encapsulated in a minimum of words. *Sūtra* means "thread or cord" and is a term used in various Eastern religions. In *Sanātana-dharma*, the *sūtras* consist of a collection of verses strung together like the beads of a necklace joined by the cord that links them. In Buddhism, a religion based on the teachings of the Buddha and whose absolute authority is based on the words of Shakyamuni, the *sūtras* are collections of his discourses or sermons. These *sūtras* were riddles and symbolic sayings. That is, words from the "book of nature" that could be understood as such because, precisely, this book lacks the term "I." It is the appearance of the egoic phenomenon and the belief in a separate "I" that creates an almost insurmountable rupture, a before and after, the leap from the symbol that is both auditory and visual at once, a whole that is one, to the symbol conceptualized and categorized from an "I" and its network of concepts that absorbs reality. The emergence of the egoic phenomenon generates a division both externally and internally; that is to say, on the one hand, it inaugurates a polarized structure between a subject-I and a nature-object separated from the former, and on the other hand, it opens a rift in the human being that begins with a process of self-conceptualization, through which the human being separates from

32. Friedrich Creuzer, *Simbolica e mitologia*, in *Dal simbolo al mito*, vol. II (Milan: Edizioni Spirale, 1983), 56–57. Translation mine.

oneself, from consciousness. This self-division leads to a search for oneself that will lead to the exertion of self-control, which, in the end, will result in a confrontation with oneself. It is from this attempt to dominate oneself that organized faith or institutionalized religion arises, which teaches and preaches a generally violent form of control. This internal conflict of the human being, however, is reflected in the loss of the ability to read that book of nature, to see, touch, and hear simultaneously, thereby generating a conflict with the surrounding reality, with the environment, with nature, giving birth to science and technology.

The self-conceptualization that arises from the egoic phenomenon leads to self-confrontation and institutionalized religion, which, along with science and technology as substitute tools for symbols, can lead the human being to its own destruction. Misunderstood religion can annihilate it from within, just as misused science can destroy it from the outside. In the face of these dangers, humanity must opt for a life less conceptualized and more symbolic. Only when it ignores the moralists and listens to nature will it be able to (re)read the book that unites the visual and the auditory. As long as it remains dissolved in its egoic formation, the preconceptualized truth of nature will remain inaccessible. In order to read the "book of nature of the Being," we must listen by seeing. Therefore, its letters are not sounds but images, charged with colors, shapes, and textures. The master is that artist who listens to what is seen and paints it so that it can be heard.

Here lies the importance of the symbol. In this context, Creuzer argues that the symbol is:

> What unexpectedly, through sight, spoke to man from the depths of nature, as a sign or warning, and imposed itself as something extraordinary; this was a *simbalon*... The relationship of these signs to the thing indicated is original and divine.[33]

33. Ibid., 27.

As this last quote clearly explains, the symbolic is that which speaks to us from the depths of our inner selves. That is to say, the human being does not invent the symbol, but stumbles upon it and finds himself seduced and captivated by it. Its voice is seen, and its image is heard from our most genuine core, from our authentic and essential nature. The symbol is a sign that warns us that the time to awaken has come, like the sound of an alarm clock. Moreover, as a sign or warning, the symbol imposes itself on us, as Creuzer says, "as something extraordinary," akin to the *ereignis*, the Heideggerian "event," or like Heraclitus' lightning, which governs everything. It is in these terms that Creuzer understands that "the relationship of these signs with the indicated thing is original and divine." A symbol unites the visible sign with the invisible reality, "original and divine." There, everything that happens merges, the substance and the origin of everything, as we can read in this Sanskrit quote:

अहं सर्वस्य प्रभवो मत्तः सर्वं प्रवर्तते ।
इति मत्वा भजन्ते मां बुधा भावसमन्विताः ॥

ahaṁ sarvasya prabhavo
mattaḥ sarvaṁ pravartate
iti matvā bhajante māṁ
budhā bhāva-samanvitāḥ

> I am the source of all; from Me everything evolves; understanding thus, the wise, endowed with meditation, worship Me.
>
> (Bhagavad Gita, 10.8)

But as we have just said, the source of the symbol is not a mere whimsical invention of the human being; instead, it is rooted in that very primitive, primordial, and original connection of signs that reveal to us the true nature of what it is. In contrast to this, we find institutionalized religions, as well as science, philosophy, and technology, whose "creationist" conception of their symbols reminds us of the maxim of Rilke: "While you do not collect what you yourself cast, everything will be just skill and insignificant loot."[34] After its birth, and over time, institutionalized religion began to adopt elements of popular ritualism, esoteric teachings, and worship of the mysteries. If it represents something of the Truth, it is because it is, in some way, connected to the ancient mystery religions. Organized faith, in and of itself, has nothing true to add but rather the opposite:

> Only what is important can become meaningful, and only what is essential can align with the dignity of the symbol. Where we present and fear what gives us much to think about, what man claims as the whole, what refers us to the mystery of our existence, what fills and moves our life, the most precious bonds and relationships, union and separation, love and renunciation [...] these are things the symbol needs and tends to unite within itself.[35]

In order to be a symbol, it must integrate the deepest realities of life that are in conflict. Without division, the symbol lacks meaning. As we have seen, the birth of the ego leads the human being to the division of oneself and a quest for self-mastery and self-control. But it is precisely in this conflict that the symbol finds its meaning, for its ultimate function is none other than to reintegrate the division in which the human being lies. We are not referring to the symbol conceptualized by religion or other disciplines. The symbol that unites what is fractured is the one intuited by the master, which manifests itself from the transcendent, both auditorily and visually, at once. Only the master knows how to interpret it artistically, unlike the human being who is subsumed and egoically dominated. Due to its conceptualizing mode of colonizing reality, the ego is incapable of stitching its own wounds, as is also understood in the *Talmud* when it says:

---

34. Rainer Maria Rilke, "Poem to Nike" (January 1922) (Translated by Walter Kaufmann).

35. Friedrich Creuzer, *Simbolica e mitologia*, in *Dal simbolo al mito*, vol. II (Milan: Edizioni Spirale, 1983), 39–40. Translation mine.

אֵין חָבוּשׁ מַתִּיר עַצְמוֹ מִבֵּית הָאֲסוּרִים.
(תלמוד בבלי, מסכת ברכות, ה', ב')

A prisoner cannot free himself from prison.
(*Talmud Bavli*, "*Beraḥot*," 5b)

No symbol manufactured by the ego will be able to take us beyond conceptualization. That is why it cannot heal its own self-fracture or denaturalization. Only myth and symbol can offer us a safe passage to access "where we present and fear what gives us much to think about, [...] what refers us to the mystery of our existence, what fills and moves our life." The terms that Creuzer uses in this quote inevitably bring to mind the words of Bertrand Russell in his famous 1916 essay, *Principles of Social Reconstruction*, where he reflects on the political landscape of the time, addressing various issues. With a broad and tolerant vision, he focuses his attention on the way individuals think:

> But if thought is to become the possession of many, not the privilege of the few, we must have done with fear. It is fear that holds men back — fear lest their cherished beliefs should prove delusions, fear lest the institutions by which they live should prove harmful, fear lest they themselves should prove less worthy, of respect than they have supposed themselves to be. Should the working man think freely about property? Then what will become of us, the rich? Should young men and young women think freely about sex? Then what will become of morality? Should soldiers think freely about war? Then what will become of military discipline? Away with thought I Back into the shades of prejudice, lest property, morals, and war should be endangered I Better men should be stupid', slothful, and oppressive than that their thoughts should be free. For if their thoughts were free they might not think as We do. And at all costs this disaster must be averted." So the opponents of thought argue in the unconscious depths

> of their souls. And so they act in their churches, their schools, and their universities.[36]

We fear that the conclusions of such thinking will function as acid, destroying and eliminating everything we believe ourselves to be and reveal what we truly are. We are terrified of discovering that, although there are thoughts, there is not truly a "thinker," and thoughts arise from pure consciousness. As Saint Augustine of Hippo, who rightfully earned the title of Doctor of the Western Church, warned:

> Warned by these writings that I must return to myself, I entered under your guidance the innermost places of my being; but only because you had become my helper was I able to do so. [...] As I first began to know you, you lifted me up and showed me that while that which I might see exists indeed, I was not yet capable of seeing it. Your rays beamed intensely upon me, beating back my feeble gaze, and I trembled with love and dread. I knew myself to be far away from you in a region of unlikeness."[37]

Saint Augustine continues:

> It is the mind (soul), and this is nothing other than my very self. What am I, then, O my God? What is my nature? It is teeming life of every conceivable kind, and exceedingly vast. See, in the measureless plains and vaults and caves of my memory, immeasurably full of countless kinds of things which are there either through their images (as with material things), or by being themselves present (as is the knowledge acquired through a liberal education), or by registering

---

36. Bertrand Russell, *Principles of Social Reconstruction* (London: George Allen & Unwin, 1916), lecture V, "Education," 166.
37. Augustine. *The Confessions*, trans. Maria Boulding, ed. John E. Rotelle, O.S.A., *The Works of Saint Augustine: A Translation for the 21st Century*, part I, vol. 1 (Hyde Park, NY: New City Press, 1997), VII.10.16, 172–73.

> themselves and making their mark in some indefinable way (as with emotional states which the memory retains even when the mind is not actually experiencing them, although whatever is in the memory must be in the mind too)—in this wide land I am made free of all of them, free to run and fly to and fro, to penetrate as deeply as I can, to collide with no boundary anywhere. So great is the faculty of memory, so great the power of life in a person whose life is tending toward death! [...] See, I am climbing through my mind to you who abide high above me; I will pass beyond even this faculty of mine which is called memory in my longing to touch you from that side whence you can be touched, and cleave to you in the way in which holding fast to you is possible.[38]

Thoughts can arise from only two sources. The first is the belief in separation, that is, the illusion of a "separate I" that thinks the thoughts. The second is consciousness itself, as an expression of its qualities. By encouraging us to think, even about the thinker, the thinking, the thought, and the thought-object, meditation will fall upon us. Along with meditation, the symbol will lead us to the realization of God.

38. Ibid., Book X, 17. 26, 254.

Chapter 9

Myth and logos: the power of symbolic narrative

From the Aristotelian perspective, a view emerges that assigns the myth a role of significant transcendence in the apprehension and elucidation of ontological reality. As explained in his monumental work *Poetics*, Aristotle firmly maintains that myths are a narrative form that reflects universal aspects inherent to the human condition and provide a symbolic appreciation of the cosmos. Aristotle calls these "topics," which point to a cosmic view of reality.

With unwavering fervor, the great philosopher from Stagira defends the idea that myths, imbued with an inalienable instructional and ethical value, unfold an educational and moral potential of unquestionable magnitude. Aristotle's magnificent exposition in *Poetics* takes flight, deconstructing the boundaries between narrative and existential becoming, revealing myths as living entities, bearers of a symbolic charge. This symbolic richness resonates in the collective psyche, unraveling the universal echoes that beat at the very essence of the human condition. In its multifaceted nature, more precisely and in detail, myth emerges as a powerful hermeneutic and pedagogical tool, capable of conveying and articulating, in an accessible and memorable way, abstract and sophisticated ideas that underlie knowledge. In contrast to the Platonic perspective, Aristotle recognizes the undeniable intrinsic usefulness of myth and its transcendental relevance in the configuration and transmission of wisdom of arcane and enigmatic character.

Unlike the traditional explanation of myth as something prior and opposed to logos, it is important to point out that the words myth (from the Greek *mythos* [μύθος]) and logos (from the Greek *lógos* [λόγος]) are synonymous terms that can be translated as "narrative." However, while myth uses the symbol as its main vehicle, logos employs logic and conceptualization. In this sense, myth (*mythos*) can be understood as a narrative that unveils psychological and spiritual realities (the Aristotelian *psyché*), while logos (*lógos*) reveals conceptual truths. In Heideggerian terms, the difference between myth and logos would be that while the former allows us to enter into Being, the latter does the diametrically opposite, distancing us from Being. Moreover, if, as Heidegger affirms, "language is the house of Being," then myth would be its most intimate private dwelling.[39]

Structurally, myth is based on the presence of a witness to an exceptional event who transmits their experience to a community that believes in what is narrated. This belief in the story allows the listener to access what was directly lived by the witness. St. Thomas Aquinas clearly establishes in his teachings that faith is the ability to see with the ears through the eyes of another. In this sense, the narrator acts as an intermediary, allowing the community to participate, through their ears, in the experience of the witness.

In ancestral communities where the relevance of myth is still preserved, a pertinent distinction is made between legends considered "authentic narratives" and tales or fables described as "false inventions."

Authentic narratives are those stories that illuminate the intricate mysteries concerning the origins of the cosmos, whose main actors are divine, supernatural, astral, or celestial entities that create a mystical and transcendental scenario, giving meaning to existence itself. Every myth is an authentic narrative, but not every authentic narrative is a myth. In these narratives, the incredible and astonishing adventures of the vernacular hero are depicted. This individual, whose origins lie in the humblest of circumstances, transforms into the savior of his community by freeing it from the clutches of monstrous creatures, overcoming hardship or calamities, or performing deeds

39. Martin Heidegger. *Pathmarks*. Translated by William McNeil. (Cambridge: Cambridge University Press, 1998), 254.

of inestimable nobility and benefit. Another type of authentic narrative is the chronicles associated with medicinal men, where theogonies are outlined, explaining how a shaman obtained their superhuman abilities or how a specific circle of shamans emerged. In contrast to authentic narratives, false inventions refer to those stories that describe feats and actions devoid of sacredness or supernatural content and lack an uplifting function.

Similar to this distinction between authentic and false narratives, for Plato, for whom there was no opposition between myth and logos since both serve to communicate the truth, there is also a difference between false myths and true myths, with false ones being those that depict carnal and lustful gods and therefore do not reflect the dignity of divinity.

In other cultural contexts, such as American Indigenous communities, numerous fables are also collected, where recurrent characters are animals like buffalo, coyote, or wolf. Though lacking the solemnity of myths, these tales also form part of the rich oral tradition of these cultures. Like Greek myth, pre-Columbian cultures' narratives also show a demarcation between "authentic stories" and "spurious tales." Both narrative variants depict a sequence of events that unfold in an arcane and wondrous past. The protagonists of the mythologies are often divine entities and metaphysical beings. At the same time, heroes or prodigious creatures populate the stories, and all of these characters converge in an essential idiosyncrasy: their otherness to everyday reality. However, the same indigenous groups discerned that these were stories of radically different nature. Everything evoked in myths concerns them directly, in contrast with tales and fables that refer to events that have triggered changes in the world, such as anatomical or physiological characteristics of certain beings, but have not transfigured the human condition per se.

The preliminary statements presented so far are sufficient to underline some cardinal characteristics of myth. According to Mircea Eliade:

> Myth narrates a sacred history; it relates an event that took place in primordial Time, the fabled time of the

> "beginnings." In other words, myth tells how, through the deeds of Supernatural Beings, a reality came into existence, be it the whole of reality, the Cosmos, or only a fragment of reality—an island, a species of plant, a particular kind of human behavior, an institution. Myth, then, is always an account of a "creation"; it relates how something was produced, began to be.[40]

In general terms, the myth, as it is lived in archaic societies, can be outlined as follows: first, the myth is sketched as a narrative reflecting the deeds of metaphysical beings through which the history of these beings and their interventions in the human theater are unraveled.

Second, the relevance assigned to myth lies in its consideration as absolute truth, conceiving it as a story that alludes to transcendental realities and possesses a sacred quality by being perceived as a direct work of metaphysical beings.

Third, the myth always touches on the concept of principles, beginnings, or origin, whether to narrate the birth of entities or to clarify the foundation of behaviors, institutions, or forms of labor. This clarifies why myths stand as paradigms for any significant human action. After these three primary characteristics, we can affirm that, in general terms, the fundamental attributes of myth pave a path toward understanding its magnitude and mission among the most archaic cultures. The *sine qua non* properties of myth foster a sharp evaluation of its significance and role within ancestral social groups. In this sense, myth nullifies the progressive sense of modernity, where everything to come is seen as superior to what has passed and revalues antiquity. In its capacity for sacred narration, myth provides an emblematic and spiritual framework, invaluable in elucidating the cosmic structure and the quintessence of human existence.

Fourth, myth is also characterized by having a scholarly domain capable of granting an understanding of the origin of entities, thereby enabling control and manipulation of them according to

40. Mircea Eliade, *Myth and Reality*, trans. Willard R. Trask (New York: Harper & Row, 1963), 5–6.

individual will. Knowledge of the myth is the key to Pandora's box, liberating the understanding of origins and granting the power to mold fate. Thanks to this, myth becomes the sword of Damocles, suspended over the origin of entities, allowing those who wield it to control them like puppet masters. This knowledge is not limited to merely external or abstract understanding but is experienced and lived ritually. Both narrating the myth ceremonially and carrying out the ritual justified by it allow for an intimate connection with that knowledge. Mircea Eliade says that the modern man, deprived of traditional rituals, finds himself naked before the cosmic reality, and this is because, according to Campbell, rituals are not simple repetitions of tradition; they are the creative act of tradition itself.

Fifth, it is crucial to highlight that myth is lived in the sense that it involves being dominated by the sacred power, which exalts the events that are remembered and reactivated. Living the myths, therefore, involves an authentically religious experience, as it is distinct from ordinary experience and everyday life. This experience is religious because fabulous, stimulating, and meaningful events are revived. We can be present in the creative works of supernatural beings, abandoning existence in the everyday world to enter into a transformed plane, resplendent and saturated with the presence of these beings.

The characteristic features we have defined allow us to affirm that myth can transport us from the ordinary to supernatural dimensions to coexist with mythological beings. It is not merely a passive commemoration of mythical events but their active reiteration. The characters and events of the myth become present, and one becomes contemporary to them. This also implies that one no longer lives in ordinary chronological time but in primordial time, when the event first occurred. Therefore, we can speak of a "strong time" of myth, a marvelous and sacred time in which something novel, powerful, and significant manifested in its full measure. Reviving that time, reintegrating it frequently, witnessing again the spectacle of the divine works, reencountering supernatural beings, and absorbing their creative lesson once more is a subtle longing that can be perceived in all ritual repetitions of myths. In short, myths reveal that the world, human beings, and life itself have an origin and a history that transcends the natural, and this history carries profound, invaluable, and exemplary meaning.

As we have already mentioned, other key elements distinguishing myth from logos include faith and belief. If the myth carries spiritual power, it is because its belief can influence the opening or closing of horizons. In other words, the door to the spiritual realm opens when we listen attentively or open ourselves to the voice of being. Similarly, Heidegger asserts that we must remain open to the voice of being; we must be in the pathos of listening because listening is trusting. It is unnecessary to ask my friends for proof of identity to verify that the names they gave me are authentic. If a relative calls me on the phone, I do not need them to send photos to confirm they are where they say they are. Friendship and familial bonds are based on mutual trust. I do not need to test whether my dear friend, who lives in New Delhi and claims to be calling me from home, is truly doing so because I give them my credibility and trust their word. Faith represents a type of knowledge acquired through others, and it is through human faith that we can access the totality of historical knowledge. Faith represents a type of knowledge acquired through others, and it is through human faith that we can access the totality of historical knowledge. Through human faith, I can understand that my hands and the objects around me, although solid, are conglomerates of constantly moving atomic particles. This implies that our conception of reality is, first and foremost, a belief based on our own interpretation of it. A scientific narrative even challenges my personal experiences. Through human faith, we embrace quantum mechanics, a field that, according to the illustrious scientists of our time, still escapes full understanding. This is why Heraclitus states, "It is wise to hearken, not to me, but to my Word (Logos), and to confess that all things are one."[41] By stating that logos must be listened to, Heraclitus underscores the importance of listening (to the logos) as a means to access the One. At the same time, despite belonging to a

41. Heraclitus, in John Burnet, *Early Greek Philosophy*, 4th ed. (London: A. & C. Black, 1920), 132 (frag. 50 = DK B50).

predominantly visual mythological tradition, he places logos within an auditory framework.

From this, it follows that, first, myth is characterized as a symbolic narrative full of meaning to be believed through listening; and second, by employing reason (logos), we always resort to faith; that is, it is thanks to our belief in the myth that we can reason it. Ultimately, logos and reason are based on faith. Mental activity is configured as an act of narration, and what we conceive as "reality" is erected as a construction emanating from that narrative because mythological existence is even revealed as more authentic than physical reality. Similarly, the existence of God acquires a dimension of greater truth in its condition as a myth than in the context of an organized religion.

It is important, however, not to confuse myth with fantasy. In order to establish an essential distinction between the two, it is crucial to consider that in the former, there was a genuine belief on the part of the people. At the same time, the latter was always recognized as a fictional and artistic manifestation. Mythology is distinguished by having been the object of genuine belief at a particular historical moment. For example, Scandinavian mythology takes on its particular mythical nuance due to the genuine belief in the existence of metaphysical entities like Thor, Odin, and Sleipnir. Similarly, Greek mythology is consolidated based on the deep conviction of the ancient Greeks regarding the presence of deities such as Zeus, Hephaestus, and Cerberus. In a diametrically opposed position, literary works such as *Snow White and the Seven Dwarfs* are classified within the domain of fantasy, as no entity truly sustains the belief in the existence of these characters. Therefore, in the collective imagination, myths hold a degree of veracity that is not attributed to fantasy tales. The latter, despite their richness and depth, do not evoke the same kind of faith or commitment that myths manage to inspire. In other words, mythical stories' dimension of reality is crucial in constructing and consolidating collective worldviews, an aspect absent in fantasy narratives.

However, as Slavoj Žižek argues, myth does not function merely to replace the objective reality sculpted by concepts with another, more real symbolic reality. According to the author, myth is not circumstantial to the human being, meaning it is not a purposeless creation that humans occasionally practice.[42] In short, human beings are perpetually constrained to create narratives and myths that give meaning to their world and their existence. In this sense, myth plays—and has always played—a central role in human development, understanding, and life. These narratives and myths that humans incessantly create resemble medicines to cope with the complexity and chaos of their surroundings, providing a sense of coherence and continuity in the dizzying whirlpool of life. However, Žižek also maintains that these myths often do not reflect reality as it is but rather are chimeras that assist us in our effort to deal with the turbulences of the world. In that sense, we tell ourselves stories to avoid seeing reality, but we believe them, hence obscuring the reality itself.

Hence, although these myths may have undeniable psychological value, they do not necessarily possess truth in the objective sense. In this context, Žižek proposes that veracity is not confined to the stories we weave around us but lies beyond them in the concrete reality of the events that cross us daily. In other words, although myths may benefit us from an emotional and existential perspective, we should not fall into the error of equating them with objective truth. In this sense, Žižek suggests questioning and surpassing the limits defined by myths in order to perceive more sharply and profoundly the reality that surrounds us and, in this way, decode reality and our human existence more authentically. However, Žižek's argument opens up the question of whether reality itself could be considered a myth, as it is constituted as a mythical-mental narrative that is an object of belief.

---

42. This idea is central to Žižek's work, particularly his engagement with Lacanian psychoanalysis and his critique of ideology. See *The Sublime Object of Ideology* (1989) and *Living in the End Times* (2010).

Chapter 10

The myth transcends reason

Myth and philosophy represent two divergent perspectives in approaching, but not in the content of, the meaning of our existence. Myth, bearer of intricate symbolism, resonates as an inexhaustible source of inspiration that elevates and strengthens the individual. On the other hand, philosophy is an inquiring discipline that seeks meaning through reason and logic (*logos*). The symbol has the power to give life and articulate it; it grants us the power of Being. Philosophy gives us power over the entity, though the entity will always be more than what is shown. While philosophy reveals, it also conceals. Therefore, it loses the power it seeks to possess. This is why we define philosophy as "a myth without power."

As we have seen so far, myth, born from the cultures and traditions of humanity, emerges as a narrative that transcends superficial appearance and delves into our symbolic dimension. In their intricate iconography, the symbols awaken vivid emotions, impart moral teachings, and establish an intimate connection between the individual and the deeper strata of their existence. In their complex semantic entanglement, they stir emotional turbulence in the psyche, instill moral precepts, and establish a transcendental communion with the unfathomable depths of human experience. Furthermore, myth transcends the constraints of reason through mythic narratives and archetypes. It delves into the recesses of the human condition, proposing a hermeneutic framework that imparts meaning to human reality. Philosophy, by contrast, rises as a discipline forged on the unshakable foundations of reason and logic, concerned with constructing concepts and logical argumentation, attempting to access conclusions that provide coherence and clarity to human experience.

Therefore, while myth emerges from its symbolic richness as an inexhaustible torrent of existential depth, philosophy immerses itself in the catacombs of logic in the search for meaning. However, despite their divergences, both approaches complement one another to bring us closer to the enigma of significance, allowing us to investigate and explore the heights of transcendence and understanding of our reality from the human perspective.

Philosophy, in one of its branches like philosophical anthropology, is like a sharp detective seeking to understand the nature of the human being. Superficial explanations do not satisfy it, and therefore, rigorous logic and deep reflection are applied to discover the answers to these fundamental questions. Like a geologist examining layers of rock, philosophy questions the layers of reality, knowledge, and morality in search of the gems of truth. It is not interested in shortcuts, predetermined answers, traditionalist interpretations, or unquestionable beliefs; it takes time to analyze and reflect, using reason as the compass for its search. Cloaked in its exploratory mantle, philosophy raises its intellectual banner in attempting to strike and decipher the ontological *ethos* of being, weaving a conceptual matrix of abstract musings. Like a cartographer of the unfathomable, it enters existence to extract answers, putting under a microscope the fortresses upon which the interstices of the human compendium stand. By formulating and analyzing theories, philosophy becomes a fascinating intellectual journey that seeks the nature of human existence, striving to discover what makes the world turn and what role the human being plays in it.

Moreover, philosophy also dives into the assumptions we take for granted and critically analyzes them. The result: solid conclusions that bring coherence. It is a discipline unafraid to challenge the established and reveal what is hidden in plain sight. By using synthesis and examination of theories as its axis, philosophy delves into the struggle to decipher the morphology of reality and the intrinsic meaning of the human journey. Like blacksmiths of the intellect, philosophers wield conceptual devices that encompass the logic and reasoning of both deductive and inductive branches to analyze abstract ideations, distill grounded and consistent conclusions. In this context, philosophy stands with a conceptual approach while also characterized by its commitment to scrutinizing the foundations and concepts that shape our understanding of the world.

The philosophical path has endless questions and answers that always seem out of reach. But by continuing to move forward, challenging the limits of understanding, new doors open. It is an enriching process that invites us to look beyond the obvious and dive into an unknown ocean. Through analytical scrutiny and critical introspection, philosophy operates in the academic realm to offer clear and grounded presentations about the teleology and ontology inherent in reality, urging intellectual rumination and the inquiry for answers that surpass the superficial threshold. It is crucial to emphasize the inextricable importance of approaching these issues with critical sharpness and epistemic rigor, as they form the foundation of the construction of knowledge.

In its quest to understand and acquire knowledge, philosophy uses the concept as a fundamental tool to unveil and master the entity. Through concepts, philosophy empowers individuals to analyze and manipulate what they seek to understand, like a detective examining evidence. Let us think of a "philosophical concept" as a mental map that traces the central features of something, such as an object, an idea, or a phenomenon. It is like having a net that captures and organizes information about something specific. With these well-crafted concepts, like lanterns in the dark, philosophy seeks to understand the fundamental bases and qualities of existence and how all these pieces fit together and relate to one another in a vast puzzle. This philosophical concept, anchored in abstraction, crystallizes the cardinal attributes of an object, notion, or phenomenon. Through the distillation of precise concepts, philosophy unfolds its momentum in unraveling both the nature and fundamental attributes of the entity and the entangled interaction that persists between them. In this pavilion of sublime abstraction, the philosophical concept appears as a mental amalgam that subsumes the archetypal traits of any entity, whether concrete or ethereal. With insight worthy of an alchemist, philosophy refines pristine concepts and, in its journey, explores the most hidden aspects of nature, unmasking the ontological properties of entities and the relationships that bind them.

For a moment, let us consider the concepts as building blocks. Philosophy is like a manual that teaches us how to use these blocks to build something meaningful. A concept in philosophy represents the critical parts of an object, idea, or phenomenon, just as a block represents a part of the built structure. By organizing these concepts precisely, philosophy gives us the skills to understand the individual parts and how they come together to form a larger whole. It is like creating a clear image from individual pieces. Furthermore, using the conceptual apparatus, philosophy provides an exegetical skeleton that enables the human entity to dive into the entity through meticulous and profound inquiry. This device of analysis and conceptual manipulation, formidable in its execution, grants the philosopher a commanding mastery over the entity, allowing them to decipher its most arcane mysteries and understand the underlying machinery of its operation.

It is imperative to emphasize that this connection between conceptual weaponry and mastery of the entity is not confined solely to the limits of philosophy. In disciplines descended from philosophy, such as science and technology, precise concepts are equally critical and allow us to unravel and model entities in countless ways, paving the way for unprecedented advances. Through concepts, we dive into the depths to uncover hidden secrets. In doing so, we embark on a journey of discovery, scrutinizing every corner in search of hidden truths. This ability to skillfully and in detail dive into the essential mechanisms empowers us in our quest for understanding. It is as if each concept were a compass pointing to a treasure of understanding.

According to Heidegger, modern society has strayed in its search for possessions and achievements, forgetting the core of its being. This is no coincidence, for as we have seen throughout these chapters, Western society has been shaped by centuries of Western thought, which, with philosophy at the forefront, has valued reason and objectivity over the inner human experience, logical reasoning over mythology, and concept over symbol. This selection, however, has created an imbalance that has had significant repercussions on the exploration of being and how the human being faces their existence. From the Heideggerian perspective, the contemporary *zeitgeist* (spirit of the time) is eminently anthropocentric, suffers from a metaphysical amnesia regarding the "being" in its essence, and is chained to the perpetual seduction of the subordination of concrete entities. Although for Heidegger philosophy can still recover the "question of Being," it is also true that, in his last stage, he resorted to poetry as a means to express what philosophy cannot reach.

That is, the prevailing worldview has transformed into the orchestration and domination of material objects and phenomena. Heidegger argued that this ontological shift arises as a consequence of a Western intellectual tradition that is rich and rooted in the concept of *orthótes* in Plato, which involves considering what appears as inaccurate until it is corrected by the subject who discovers its idea. In other words, the apparent only becomes true because the subject compares it to the non-apparent. This implies that the idea has subsumed the entity and, therefore, phenomenology has adopted the principles of metaphysics that, under the aegis of dogmatic philosophy, have exalted rationality and objectivity, relegating the preponderance of the subjective experience of the human to the margins.

With attention obsessively fixed on the orchestration and ontic domination, human beings have disconnected from the fibers that once linked them to reality. This ontic self-sufficiency arises as a rigid custodian, severing the human connection with their being and environment. In embracing the skill in manipulating entities, we have allowed our harmony with the deepest essence and the ground beneath our feet to unravel and disintegrate. It is not just a loss but an impoverishment of our relationship with the environment—a nurturing and sustaining environment that could teach if we were open to its lessons.

One of the important concepts in Heidegger's thought is *das Geviert*, or *Geviert*, translated as "the square," which responds to a deeper understanding of reality that goes beyond dualistic vision. Instead of focusing on opposites, dualism is overcome by introducing the idea of quaternity or square, which implies a more complex and dynamic structure and is used to refer to the relationships between the four aspects that make up reality: Earth, Sky, Gods, and Mortals. This theme is addressed explicitly in his work *Der Ursprung des Kunstwerkes*, or *The Origin of the Work of Art*, and it responds to a higher instance of Heideggerian thought. The use of the term *quadrature* alludes to the geometrically heuristic impulse with which Western philosophy has tried to imprison and shape reality within rigid ontological schemes as if it were a large closet where philosophy wants to store everything it knows about reality—categories here, concepts there. But Heidegger opens the closet door and shows us that it is disordered. Not only that, but he also suggests that perhaps, instead of trying to store things, we should sit and contemplate the space we have. Only then can we begin to understand our world. Heidegger argues that this rigorous stratification of reality into hierarchical concepts engenders a near-Promethean paradox. This epistemological chimera hinders the ability to approach an untainted compilation of our existence's spectrum. Heidegger understands that the square seeks control and domination of reality through its imposed conceptualization, which reduces reality to an objective world easy to classify, control, and manipulate.

In the face of such a rigid mode of thought, Heidegger proposes a new perspective with a more authentic connection based on the direct experience of being and the world. However, this will only be possible if we first relinquish our desire to label and pigeonhole reality into already-defined concepts. As a result, if human beings truly desire to approach their being and know themselves, they must first open themselves to refreshing ways of knowing and relating to the world. Inauthentic life generates existential anxiety (*angst*) that plunges us into distractions to avoid confronting our own finitude and the possibility of nothingness. In other words, we must do something akin to discarding an old pair of glasses and observing reality with a renewed vision, open to discovering and establishing relationships in ways never before considered. In direct opposition to the specified noetic articulation, Heidegger establishes his position, advocating for a more truthful symbiosis with the substratum of reality founded on immersion in *essentia* (essence) and the ontological firmament. What Heidegger proposes is a new approach to reality that subverts the hegemony of conceptual reasoning and its violent natural tendency to confine reality in a straitjacket of prefabricated concepts. Therefore, we are entrusted with the titanic task of shedding our subjugation to reality through the conceptual prism and, instead, diving into the hollows of emerging methodologies of cognition and connection with the world. This will lead to a metamorphosis in our relationship with the objective reality, allowing a plurality of understandings with the world to blossom. In this context, and according to Heidegger, the main task of philosophy is the recovery of the lost connection with being, as well as the rediscovery of the authentic meaning of human nature. Instead of attempting to dominate the world and control objective reality, philosophy must learn to live in total harmony and attunement with being. Only then will an authentic realization be possible that leads us to find the meaning of life.

This diagnosis and Heideggerian proposal are essential for the symbolic turn. As shown earlier, unlike the philosophical conceptualization of the world, which has led us to the forgetfulness of being, the symbolic myth allows and even facilitates the enveloping of being. In symbolic thought, authority and meaning emanate from the symbol, unlike Western philosophy, where the concept exerts total control over reality. Essentially, in symbolic thought, the individual is immersed in the symbol, whereas in philosophy, the concept is a tool used to control and manipulate. The manipulator of the concept moves in technique, abandoning the earth. Through the concept, we dominate, control, and manipulate things, whereas, in the symbol, we are the ones who belong to a narrative.

In Plato's dialogue The Symposium, we find a paradigmatic allegory that modern tradition has called "the game of masks."[43] In this enigmatic game, the interlocutors mask themselves by assuming different identities and adopting different roles in order to represent imaginary situations. This playful scheme, as it has been interpreted,

43. Giovanni Reale, *Eros, demonio mediador: El juego de las máscaras en el "Banquete" de Platón* [Eros, Demonic Mediator: The Game of Masks in Plato's "Symposium"], trans. Rosa Rius and Pere Salvat (Barcelona: Herder Editorial, 2004), 21. Translation mine.

had the fundamental purpose of training young people in the ability to distinguish between appearance and reality, encouraging them to unravel the truth that lies hidden behind masks and superficial representations. In this context, human beings emerge as active participants in the perpetual representation of a common narrative to which we all belong. In line with this, Heidegger, through his ontological philosophy, establishes that language constitutes the dwelling of being and that the human being acts as its shepherd so that existence and the meaning of everything precisely reside in this narrative and not the other way around. From this point of view, Heidegger conceives us as shepherds of the narrative and also as actors or characters belonging to the story. We create the illusory impression that we are the ones speaking the language and structuring the narrative when, in reality, it is the language that speaks to us and the narrative that shapes us. In this intricate game of masks, what is primary is not us but the narrative that runs through us. In this sense, we are a product of it, for there is nothing outside the myth, language, or the word that narrates the story. Therefore, it is essential to consider that philosophy, despite its noble pretensions, is also within the realm of myths, even if it lacks the power that it wields. Despite its attempts to transcend the mythological narrative, philosophy is nothing more than another character in the great drama of existence. We are all immersed in a narrative whose underlying structure dictates our scripts and determines our roles.

To say that the symbol appropriates the human being is also to say that, as part of a narrative, even philosophy is within the myth. The conceptual construct consists of a human invention, while the human being emerges from the symbolism. By overcoming our limitations, this symbolism places the myth on a higher plane than philosophy. This semiosis, rising beyond human restrictions, shows that mythological thought surpasses philosophical thought in epistemological magnitude.

Philosophy seeks to elucidate the mystery that challenges understanding, while myth is the bastion of the inherently incomprehensible. While philosophy tries to decipher the enigmatic, myth harbors that elusive core of the undecipherable. Although myth tries to clarify, it never completes its task and always leaves questions and open propositions unanswered. Since the concept is a human invention and philosophy arises from the symbol, philosophy is intrinsically linked to myth. Because power is an intrinsic part of the symbol, philosophy, by its conceptual nature, constitutes a myth lacking power or devoid of its inherent vitality. Obviously, symbols such as the Star of David, the crescent moon, the cross, Lord Chaitanya, or Jesus carry a powerful symbolic resonance. However, if I were to relegate Lord Chaitanya exclusively to a Vaishnavist organization, the cross solely to the realm of Catholicism, or the Star of David only to a specific Hasidic institution, I would be subtracting the intrinsic power of the symbol. The reason is that, in these cases, a conceptual construct would overshadow the profound reach of the symbol by appropriating it.

Heidegger addresses this issue right at the beginning of his *Being and Time*, where we find an unexpected mention of Martin Luther. Heidegger evokes him primarily for his incisive criticisms regarding the conceptual architecture of theology established in his time. We read:

> Theology is seeking a more primordial interpretation of man's Being towards God, prescribed by the meaning of faith itself and remaining within it. It is slowly beginning to understand once more Luther's insight that the "foundation" on which its system of dogma rests has not arisen from an inquiry in which faith is primary, and that conceptually this "foundation" not only is inadequate for the problematic of theology, but conceals and distorts it. Basic concepts determine the way in which we get an understanding beforehand of the area of subject-matter underlying all the objects a science takes as its theme, and all positive investigation is guided by this understanding. Only after the area itself has been explored beforehand in a corresponding manner do these concepts become genuinely demonstrated and "grounded."[44]

44. Martin Heidegger, *Being and Time*, trans. John Macquarrie and Edward Robinson (Oxford: Blackwell, 1962), §3, 30.

Luther argued that theology was supported by a conceptual structure that did not genuinely emerge from authentic experience. He claimed that the vocabulary used was unsuitable for addressing theological issues, even distorting or perverting the teachings in their purest essence. In an apparently tangential gesture to the theological core, Heidegger evokes Luther, but he does so from a decisively philosophical angle, pondering how we conceive of "being." In *Sein und Zeit*, Heidegger maintains that philosophy is not exclusive to highly erudite minds immersed in complex musings from their isolated academic chambers. Instead, it is intrinsically linked to our everyday experience. He argues that, prior to any cognitive act directed toward an object, idea, or experience, we are already imbued with a conceptual or affective prelude regarding that object. Before conceptualizing an object or experience, we already harbor preconceived feelings or perceptions about it. In all reflection or analysis, there is an underlying structure of innate understanding, a background always present that allows us to comprehend the thing even when it is not consciously thought about. In short, if we closely observe the scientific domain, we will see that its building is not exclusively erected upon the cornerstone of empirical observations, data, or experimental evidence. Preceding any scientific investigation, there is a preexisting notion or experience. There is always prior experience before any scientific investigation because it is unfeasible to approach a topic of study without at least a basic or rudimentary idea about it. There is always a foundation, a prior groundwork, before embarking on a study or acquiring additional knowledge. There is always something or someone that we already know before investigating or learning about it. That is why, for Heidegger, knowing is consubstantial with our nature and existence.

Luther disagreed with how religion was taught, arguing that excessive conceptualization distorted its real essence and altered its true meaning. According to Heidegger, something similar happens in our attempt to theoretically define the world and life, making the mistake of reducing the essence of existence to mere conceptual structures.

We agree with Hans-Georg Gadamer in emphasizing that Heidegger's recognition of Luther's perspective in *Being and time* is unrelated to confessional matters. Heidegger is interested in Luther's discovery of how a dogmatic framework, in which concepts crystallize into unmovable theories, can divert our understanding of secular or religious reality. Heidegger saw in Luther a figure who recognized that religion had shifted from being an existential event to a mere doctrinal construct. Luther prioritized religious experience over any manual or prescriptive guide that dictated our religious and spiritual experience. The intrinsically authentic experience sheds theoretical-philosophical conceptual superstructures; its essence does not lie in the normative projection or expectation of reality but in its naked and genuine manifestation. The genuine experience presents itself without the veil of theoretical interpretations. It is not seen from the perspective of what it should be or what is anticipated but from reality as it is. Inspired by Luther, Heidegger can see a certain similarity with the situation of an excessively complicated philosophy, lost in convoluted terminologies and obscure jargon. With a critical gaze, Heidegger advocates for a return to the essence of phenomena as they emerge in pure perception. This return, as we have indicated before, involves bypassing the conceptual through which the philosophical tradition has factualized reality and, in doing so, obscured its most essential Being. This is what Heidegger calls *destruction* which he describes as a process of returning to the original, consisting in ridding oneself of preconceived concepts and ideas. Heidegger refers thereby to a philosophical exercise that demands the deconstruction of sedimented conceptual structures in order to renew the connection with what is primordial. As he writes:

> If the question of Being is to have its own history made transparent, then this hardened tradition must be loosened up, and the concealments which it has brought about must be dissolved. We understand this task as one in which by taking the question of Being as our clue, we are to. destroy the traditional content of ancient ontology until we arrive at those primordial experiences in which we achieved our first

> ways of determining the nature of Being-the ways which have guided us ever since.[45]

It is necessary to reorient ourselves toward the authenticity of the primordial before it is darkened or obscured by conceptual structures and their respective theoretical elaborations. It is imperative to reconnect with the freshness of the primordial and the original essence before theoretical abstractions and their intricate postulations overshadow it. There is an urgent need to divert the course of theoretical dialogues that are alienated from tangible existence and make philosophy regain its intrinsic liveliness and epistemological relevance. It intends to cease theoretical debates disconnected from real life and restore philosophy's meaningful vitality.

> But this destruction is just as far from having the negative sense of shaking off the ontological tradition. We must, on the contrary, stake out the positive possibilities of that tradition, and this always means keeping it within its limits; these in turn are given factically in the way the question is formulated at the time, and in the way the possible field for investigation is thus bounded off. On its negative side, this destruction does not relate itself towards the past; its criticism is aimed at "today" and at the prevalent way of treating the history of ontology, whether it is headed towards doxography, towards intellectual history, or towards a history of problems.[46]

Therefore, Martin Heidegger, inspired by Luther, emphasizes the return to the essence of philosophy: focusing on what is truly important, vital, and significant, thereby avoiding getting trapped in trivialities, details, and theories that obscure more than they clarify. Although philosophical jargon may appear profound, it often lacks tangibility in the face of concrete lived reality. Sophisticated discursivities, in their striving for erudition, paradoxically obscure our

45. Martin Heidegger, *Being and Time*, trans. John Macquarrie and Edward Robinson (Oxford: Blackwell, 1962), §6, 44.
46. Ibid.

connection to the real. In their longing for illustration and scholarly depth, the paradoxes of discourse distort and distance us from our connection with the underlying reality because the experience with being is theoretical and pre-ontological. Heidegger, in his perennial evolution, reflects a transition to post-metaphysical thought. In order to overcome the limits of philosophy, a fundamentally philosophical approach is required, a fact made palpable in his *Letter on Humanism*, where he writes:

> It is time to break the habit of overestimating philosophy and of thereby asking too much of it. What is needed in the present world crisis is less philosophy, but more attentiveness in thinking; less literature, but more cultivation of the letter. The thinking that is to come is no longer philosophy, because it thinks more originally than metaphysics—a name identical to philosophy. However, the thinking that is to come can no longer, as Hegel demanded, set aside the name "love of wisdom" and become wisdom itself in the form of absolute knowledge. Thinking is on the descent to the poverty of its provisional essence. Thinking gathers language into simple saying. In this way language is the language of being, as clouds are the clouds of the sky. With its saying, thinking lays inconspicuous furrows in language. They are still more inconspicuous than the furrows that the farmer, slow of step, draws through the field.[47]

The understanding that mere concepts cannot fully capture life is fundamental to authentic metaphysics. Paradoxically, the genuine metaphysical approach emerges by understanding that our task is not essentially metaphysical. Valuing concepts requires understanding their insufficiency in the face of life, as existence escapes rigid conceptual structures. Concepts only acquire value in life when we realize that these same concepts have no value for life, because existence always eludes conceptual structures.

47. Martin Heidegger, *Letter on Humanism*, in Basic Writings, ed. David Farrell Krell (New York: Harper & Row, 1977), 265.

Chapter 11

Concepts, symbols, and language: Kant's vision

The Greek notion of knowledge encompasses three possible dimensions. On the one hand, *aisthèsis*, which is often translated as "aesthetics," denotes the apprehension or grasping of an object through sensory experience. As such, it requires the intervention of at least one of the five senses, namely sight, hearing, smell, taste, or touch, to see, hear, smell, taste, or feel. Secondly, knowledge is also given through the *nous*, which we can define as the understanding of the intellect or mind, reflecting the capacity of reason to intuit mentally in an immediate way. In this sense, it is an intuitive and direct knowledge of what surrounds us, sometimes similar to the "common sense" to which Aristotle refers or even to the direct and immediate apprehension of ideas in the case of Plato. Thirdly, knowledge also proceeds through *diànoia*, that is, through a discursive use of reason that allows us to obtain knowledge by using a chain of premises that ultimately leads us to a conclusion. The word *diànoia*, or "reason," contains the term *dia*, which means "through" in Greek. In turn, the word "discourse" is composed of *dia* and *cursus*, which comes from the Latin *currus* and means "chariot," allowing us to translate the expression "discursive reason" as something like "riding in a chariot."

Therefore, it is not by chance that Parmenides found himself in a winged chariot when he began his discourse. Riding in a chariot lends itself to giving a discourse, that is, reasoning being. This metaphor suggests a path of thought through which reason discursively elaborates a process that also grasps the thing, but always through the use of principles and premises that later lead us to knowledge. In this sense, the difference between understanding (*nous*) and discursive reasoning (*diànoia*) is that the former consists in the immediate apprehension of the idea of a thing, while the latter refers to a non-immediate, and therefore mediated, knowledge through (*dia-*) premises and principles that lead us to a conclusion. For example, the idea of a "table" is that of a horizontal surface with a type of support. But if we want to reason in order to know the table, we must begin by saying that any horizontal surface supported by some base is a table.

Kant divides his famous work *Critique of Pure Reason* into three major chapters: *Transcendental Aesthetics*, *Transcendental Analytic*, and *Transcendental Dialectic*. What the three chapters have in common is, at first glance, that Kant's approach to aesthetics, analysis, and dialectic is purely transcendental and, therefore, by default, not empirical as such. Kant himself defines the term transcendental as follows: "I call all cognition transcendental that is occupied not so much with objects but rather with our mode of cognition of objects insofar as this is to be possible a priori."[48] In other words, Kant's approach to knowledge does not begin with things; that is, it does not ask what things are in themselves but how we come to know them. Kant makes an epistemic turn. He shifts from the question of the thing itself (the substance) to the question of the human capacity to know. Essentially, it is an anthropological turn, which inquires more about humans than about reality. To do this, he must deny the thing in itself and focus on the phenomenon, which is ultimately what we know. This, if observed carefully, has a creative aim but is greatly limited. On the one hand, Kant has, in the transcendental subject and in the a priori categories, the possibility of knowledge that, in its union, somehow generates a knowable reality. However, denying the thing in itself is a limitation of reality, which only exists insofar as it is knowable by man, which is very poor. Reality can never be limited by human beings and their capacity for knowledge or creation.

48. Immanuel Kant. *Critique of Pure Reason* (The Cambridge Edition of the Works of Immanuel Kant). Translated and edited by Paul Guyer and Allen W. Wood. (Cambridge University Press, 1998), 149 (A12).

Therefore, for Kant, metaphysics (the study of being and immutable principles, for example, "the whole is greater than the part") does not conform to his model. On the other hand, metaphysics, in realism, is the highest degree of knowledge after empirical knowledge (physics, biology) and knowledge of ideal beings and their laws (mathematics).

It is important to point out against which type of philosophy Kant is reacting: against empiricism on one side and against rationalism on the other. Against empiricism, he insists on the importance of a priori elements in the formation of knowledge, and against rationalism, he points out that these a priori elements are not innate ideas but forms of the mind that make experience possible. His transcendental philosophy seeks to reconcile the apparent tensions between empiricism and rationalism. If you want to know a philosopher's philosophy, ask yourself who they are criticizing. From there, the philosopher from Königsberg embarks on a deep study to answer the question of how knowledge is possible, which will later give rise to and be baptized as the "Copernican revolution."

Kant's study begins with *aisthèsis* or "sensory perception," he asserts that all knowledge always and effectively begins with sensory experience. However, he quickly conceives that what we perceive is the phenomenon, that is, not the object in its supposed pure state, but the object as it appears or is presented to us sensorially. This difference between the object in its pure state, or thing in itself (*noumenon*), and the object as it appears to us (*phenomenon*) will be fundamental to understanding the rest of Kant's investigation. Let us take the example of a bottle. When we look at it, we do not see the bottle entirely, in its wholeness and fullness, all at once, but we must turn it, rotate it, and wait for all its aspects to present themselves to the senses gradually. Objects, therefore, always present themselves to us first at the level of "sensory perception" (*aisthèsis*), filtered through what Kant will call the two pure forms of sensibility, that is, space and time, which we can define with Kant as follows: space, on the one hand, is a pure form of sensory intuition that shapes our perception of objects' extension and location. However, it is not an external characteristic of the human being but rather a subjective a priori structure that underlies our experience. Kant holds that space is three-dimensional and that all our perceptions are inserted and intertwined within this spatial framework. It is our way of knowing several entities simultaneously through coexistence.

On the other hand, time reveals itself as the other pure form of sensory intuition that determines the sequence and duration of events. It is a subjective a priori structure that allows us to experience and organize our perceptions in a temporal succession. Time unfolds as a linear dimension, and all our experiences are arranged and connected in this continuous temporal flow. It is our way of knowing the same entity in or through several moments.

After seeing how Kant understands space and time as pure forms of sensory experience, we can return to the example of the bottle to show that it only appears to us gradually (temporally) in some place or space (spatially). However, the space and time through which the bottle appears to us do not lie in the thing itself but, instead, in the very appearance of the thing, that is, in the sensory experience itself, which Kant places in the realm of the transcendental subject, not the empirical object. This leads Kant to affirm that the pure forms of sensibility are fundamental and innate structures of our faculty of perceiving and experiencing the sensible world. These pure forms precede any empirical experience and establish the a priori framework through which we gain knowledge of phenomena. In other words, space and time are not inherent properties of objects but necessary conditions, that is, a priori, for perception and understanding of phenomena in all our sensory experiences. Or, put another way, within the Kantian perspective, there are no phenomena without a subject.

Inspired by Kant's worldview, we recognize that it is through corporeal and sensory manifestation that we have receptivity to the tangible entities that surround us. This sensory knowledge (*aisthèsis*) is the horizon in which all knowledge is possible. Specifically, it is from sensory experience that the subject can think and understand phenomena. At this point, Kant introduces the understanding (*nous*) as that intrinsic and essential faculty of our being through which we discern and categorize the concepts that give structure and order to our perception of the world. The senses provide us with knowledge of particular, contingent, and mobile realities, while the categories of understanding grant these realities a universal, necessary, and immutable unity that Kant calls "synthetic a priori judgment." Put differently, understanding takes the matter (phenomena) and gives it form. To know sensible things, Kant argues that understanding (*nous*) produces and uses what he calls "categories," applying them to the data of sensibility.

These categories are of a fundamental nature and shape the conceptual framework required for perceiving phenomena. They are, so to speak, mental molds that process the sensory information presented through intuition. Regarding the categories, their status as universal and necessary entities is the catalyst that organizes the spectrum of experiences into a cohesive and discernible system. Think of them as conceptual tools we equip ourselves to distill and taxonomize our mundane experiences.

Kant specifically proposed the categories of unity, plurality, and totality (as categories of quantity); reality, negation, and limitation (as categories of quality); inherence and subsistence (substance and accident); causality and dependence (cause and effect), and community (interaction between agent and patient); and possibility-impossibility, existence-nonexistence, and necessity-contingency (as categories of modality). What is important here, beyond the categories themselves, is the fact that Kant understands them as pure a priori concepts that allow us to classify any other concept as a posteriori. In this sense, the "categories" are products of the same faculty of understanding, revealed as a *sine qua non* condition for thinking and comprehending the world and what exists within it.

The production of categories by the understanding (*nous*) should not be understood as if they were Platonic or Cartesian innate ideas with a life of their own in an ideal world. On the contrary, Kant argues that understanding produces them within the process of sensible experience, and therefore, in Kant's own words, "they have no life outside the understanding of the phenomenon." Categories can be seen as our way of understanding or thinking about objects as they affect us, are given to us, and, during the period in which they affect us, appear to us as phenomena of experience. As human beings, Kant would argue, we have no other way of understanding the world around us and in which we live. We understand only what we can understand and how we can understand it.

Thus, for example, if we take the example of a wooden table, we could say that, at first, the senses provide us with the object as it appears to us, in this case, by sight. The object appears to us in space and time, that is, gradually and in a specific space and position. In its appearance to the mind through the senses, however, the understanding immediately applies the categories of unity, totality, difference, causality, and others to all the sensible data that make up the "table" as it appears to us *qua* phenomenon. Applying categories, that is, conceptualizing is a process of synthesis that occurs through division and fragmentation. For example, high is different from low, good is the opposite of bad, beautiful is different from ugly, intelligent is different from fool, and brave is the opposite of coward. That is, one is understood in opposition to the other. The categories are ordered, one below and the other above, creating dichotomies that exclude each other. This is why Kant will say that understanding determines the sensible thing according to a concept that determines it and distinguishes it from the opposite and the contrary. Only from these purely formal concepts can we then apply other concepts a posteriori, such as size, wood, leg, surface, and others. Knowledge is produced precisely by performing this synthesis between categories and sensory data.

From this perspective, knowledge is a hylomorphic entity composed of content (matter) and form. Objects, through sensible certainty, provide us with content through the recognition of the pure forms of sensitivity. At this stage, we acquire knowledge of the sensory properties of objects, such as color, taste, magnitude, smell, texture, shape, sound, and other aspects. However, each sensory experience is contingent, singular, and unique.

The objective apprehension of entities with various physical and aesthetic characteristics shapes our experiences. A repeated experience leads us to a conclusion. For example, suppose we repeatedly observe that a fragment of metal expands when exposed to heat; in that case, we use the category of totality to infer that all metals expand at high temperatures. Therefore, we transform a series of particular experiences into a universal concept. Consequently, according to Kant, knowledge acquires a scientific nature when applying theories to reality. We use the category of particularity by affirming that a specific metal expands with heat. Similarly, by asserting that all metals expand in the presence of heat, we resort to the category of universality.

Likewise, we can affirm, deny, and maintain that no metal fails to expand when exposed to high temperatures, using the categories of totality and negativity. Despite the apparent epistemological emptiness of negation, the categories confer necessity to knowledge devoid of such a quality. They establish laws and a conceptual framework that provide intelligibility and epistemic value to seemingly irrelevant sensory data. In this way, knowledge takes on a scientific hue by subjecting the theory to the scrutiny of reality. As a result, the category plays a crucial role in establishing the conceptual framework in which sensible experience becomes an intelligible phenomenon.

For its part, Kantian understanding operates through two essential faculties: synthesis and judgment. Synthesis encompasses the amalgamation of sensory diversity into concepts, representing the task of unifying data into a coherent experience. Judgment, on the other hand, involves the application of categories to the synthesis of intuition, generating statements about the objects of experience. Therefore, while the categories are the fundamental concepts we use to organize and comprehend sensible experience, the understanding is the cognitive faculty that employs these categories to process and generate knowledge about the phenomenal world. In this way, the categories and understanding allow the human mind to organize, interpret, and construct knowledge from sensory information.

Therefore, the Kantian cognitive process is configured as an intricate network of synthesis and judgment, a constant interplay of interpretation and construction that enables the human mind to transcend mere sensory experience and venture into the realms of formal and abstract knowledge. Without the understanding, the world would "appear" to us as chaos, an explosion of images, smells, sounds, and scratches through which we would wander timid, violated, and directionless. The cognitive process organizes the world as it appears to us, *qua* phenomenal, and not as it supposedly is in itself. This is an important detail to consider within the Kantian philosophical universe.

Understanding only has access to the *phenomenon*, which is the object as it is presented to us through sensible experience. In contrast, we do not have access to the *noumenon*, which is the object as it is in itself. For example, the empirical object in itself (noumenon) would be the rainbow as a collection of droplets with specific dimensions, shapes, and arrangements; on the other hand, the phenomenon, which is the appearance of the noumenon through experience, would be the band of colors we see in the sky. According to Kant, human beings cannot access the noumenon through understanding or pure reason.

That being said, it is important to clarify that the phenomenon is not an imperfect, false, or deficient noumenon. According to Kant, phenomena should not be understood as illusions but as objects as they appear to us and are understood, filtered by the forms of sensitivity (space and time) and categories. Moreover, phenomena are not inferred creations of our mind, whose existence is dispensable. On the contrary, phenomena should be considered external realities that exist in the space and time of our experience. Phenomena are things that are shown to us; things in themselves, which are distinct from the phenomena, are not shown to us and, moreover, could never be perceived through phenomenal representations, although things must be considered as external objects to us and, therefore, must be presented in empirical intuition."[49]

Furthermore, phenomena are indispensable because in order to be a self-conscious I, objects must exist outside of me and be given to me in space/time. When I am conscious of myself, I am only so insofar as I am aware of these objects. That is, there is no self-knowledge without knowing something that is not "myself."

49. Immanuel Kant. *Critique of Pure Reason* (The Cambridge Edition of the Works of Immanuel Kant). Translated and edited by Paul Guyer and Allen W. Wood. (Cambridge University Press, 1998), 426 (A 369/B 396).

It has sometimes been argued that the noumenon (the object in itself) and the phenomenon (the object as experienced) are different objects, one that exists in the space and time of human experience (phenomenon) and is thus an object of understanding, and another (the noumenon) that exists outside of these coordinates, and therefore beyond our access to it through experience and understanding. However, for Kant, the phenomenon and the noumenon are not two different real objects belonging to two parallel worlds, one within the reach of our senses and the pure forms of intuition (space and time) and the other outside of us and our faculties of access to it. On the contrary, according to Kant, there is only one object (in itself), but it appears to us as a phenomenon filtered through our sensitivity and understanding, and it could not be given to us in any other way because these are our human faculties.

The Kantian schema, however, is not reduced to *aisthèsis* (sensible knowledge or perception) and *nous* (understanding) but also integrates reason (*diànoia*), thereby replicating the classical structure of knowledge as outlined by the Greek philosophy of *lógos*. If, on the one hand, understanding is the faculty of producing concepts and relating them through judgments, human reason, on the other hand, is responsible for linking these judgments through reasoning and producing transcendental ideas that, although in themselves, do not serve to increase knowledge of objects, fulfill a "regulatory" function. If, as we have seen earlier, understanding deals directly with phenomena and unifies them into judgments, reason is the faculty that unifies judgments in light of a higher principle, always attempting to seek a greater synthesis of knowledge, following a natural tendency toward the unconditioned.

Kant distinguishes between a logical and a pure use of reason. The former consists of employing it in the formal realm as the faculty of making inferences or reasoning, while the latter would be the one that aims to discover the totality of the conditions, that is, to complete the unity of the categories. It is precisely from this pure use that transcendental ideas emerge. Thus, while on the one hand, ideas regulate, give unity, and systematize knowledge from understanding, on the other hand, reason is the faculty of producing and applying categories, laws, and general principles (through these transcendental ideas) to what we experience through the senses and understanding. However, unlike Plato's eidetic world, and as with the categories, ideas—as Kant conceives them—also have no life beyond the very process of thought but are the limits that regulate concepts and that, therefore, these cannot transgress.

The three transcendental ideas by which reason unifies life's great experiences are those of world, soul, and God. According to Kant, we cannot have a valid concept of these ideas. They are, however, as natural to reason as the categories are to understanding, with the difference that while the latter leads us to truth, that is, to the concordance of our concepts with their objects, transcendental ideas produce a simple illusion that, despite being an illusion, is irresistible and hard to combat. Let us take a closer look at these three ideas:

The World: We experience things like hardness, smell, taste, texture, shape, sound, color, and temperature, which are individual physical aspects. However, it is impossible to experience all the physical aspects in their totality. No one can claim to have experienced all that is physical, as human experience is limited to particularity or singularity, not totality. When we speak of the totality of physical aspects, we call it the "world." For humans, all physical aspects occur within this "world," even though we do not experience the world in its entirety. Therefore, the world is a postulate of reason. Reason creates the idea of the world to articulate physical phenomena, an articulation that it calls the "antinomy of reason." The term antinomy means "a law that is in front." In this case, humans place the "law of reason" before them, without which they could not unify the physical phenomena they collectively call "the world."

The Soul: We also possess experiences of psychic phenomena. Humans know that they think, desire, love, feel, remember, and so on. All these are particular psychic phenomena, whether an idea, an emotion, a sensation, or a reflection. However, we lack experience in the totality of psychic phenomena. This totality is called the "soul." Kant will say that we possess the experience of feeling and thinking but lack the experience of our souls. If, in this context, we engage in philosophy based on the concept of the soul, we would be using what he calls the "paralogism of reason," understanding paralogism as 'a logos parallel to another.' Just as we articulate the law of the world, we also articulate the law of the soul.

God: We now suppose that the world and the soul are encompassed by an idea of absolute totality that articulates all physical and psychic phenomena. This idea is called "God." Therefore, God is the ideal of reason. Kant will say that God is the absolute symbol because He allows us to unite the totality of phenomena. The greatness of Kant's thought is that reason synthesizes all experiences, which is the value he gives to metaphysics. These ideas differ from the pure concepts of understanding, such as substance, cause and effect, relation, possibility, and others. The latter are seemingly distant from empirical sensible intuition and only make sense in relation to spatiality and temporality. This does not happen with the ideas of God, the soul, and the world, which would only make sense in relation to the absolute totality in each field.

Although, as we have previously mentioned, Kant is the greatest exponent of the Enlightenment and the Copernican turn, with which the philosophical tradition refines its logocentrism at the expense of symbolic thought, Kant's own philosophy opens, perhaps more unnoticed than knowingly, interesting doors for the recovery of the importance of the symbol in thought. To demonstrate that this is the case, we will refer to a brief excerpt from the third chapter of Cirilo Flórez Miguel's work *Dialectics and Symbolism in Kant*, where we read the following:

> The objectivity of the ideas Kant speaks of should not be sought in the world of objects, which is the realm of understanding, but rather in the world of language, the world of the subject, from which a "distension of unity" is possible, allowing us to make an analogical reference to the supersensible while avoiding illusions. And therein lies precisely the task of Kantian dialectics, which is critical of illusion and legitimizes the correct use of ideas, which is a

> symbolic use that never forgets that reason is the reason of a finite subject [...].[50]

Kant argues that true objectivity does not primarily reside in the object itself but in the linguistic sphere of the subject and its capacity to emit judgments through understanding. It is within this linguistic realm where the object acquires universality, as Heidegger would later argue when referring to language as the dwelling place of being and humans as its shepherd.

In this context, Kant strongly criticizes the position that considers our sensible perceptions as indisputable sources of knowledge, labeling as dogmatic anyone who confidently trusts the validity of sensible perceptions as the only source of knowledge. Although, as we saw earlier, he does not reject the importance of sensible perception, even recognizing it as the origin of all knowledge, he asserts that knowledge is not reducible solely to what is experienced through the senses. For Kant, in contrast to Hume, true knowledge transcends mere experiences of seeing, hearing, touching, smelling, or tasting. If we accept that understanding occurs within the confines of what we perceive, we would admit that perceived objects possess an intrinsic existence and meaning independent of our experience and processing of them through our cognitive faculties and language.

This is why, in opposition to dogmatism, Kant proposes a critical stance toward the idea that reality is merely as we perceive it through our senses. Kant intends to justify and validate our experiences, recognizing that their validity does not come solely from perception but from the subject who perceives and interprets what is perceived through language. Consequently, our perception of the world is not inherently valid but to the extent that we can articulate this perception through language. As Cirilo Flórez Miguel explains:

50. Cirilo Flórez Miguel, "Dialectic and Symbolism in Kant [Dialéctica y simbolismo en Kant]," Azafea. Revista de Filosofía 3 (January 1990): 87. Translation mine.

> The distinction between illusion (what our eyes see) and phenomenon (the synthesis between what our eyes see and what we add as subjects) leads us to the topic of objectivity in the Critique of Pure Reason. This notion of objectivity is one of the core concepts of the entire Critique (both in his first Critique, Critique of Pure Reason, as well as in the second and third critiques, that is, the Critique of Practical Reason and the Critique of Judgment). It is the result of a constitutive process of synthesis carried out by the aprioric dynamism of the subject.[51]

As we have already mentioned, Kant calls transcendental all cognition "that is occupied not so much with objects but rather with our mode of cognition of objects insofar as this is to be possible a priori."[52] Thus, he emphasizes that his philosophical interest lies in exploring our way of apprehending and knowing things and not in their intrinsic nature. Objectivity arises from the joint work of what sensitivity and understanding contribute in order to artistically construct the object that presents itself to consciousness in the form of a concept.

In this sense, and insofar as this object does not conform to the characteristics of a merely empirical object but rather is an artistic production, we can understand this object as a symbol. For, although we grasp objects, what we truly perceive is the way they manifest as phenomena influenced by our senses and filtered through space and time. Humans do not apprehend the object itself or the noumenon in its pure essence, but our understanding has categories that, when incorporating sensory perception, generate the symbol, which ultimately is what we know. Therefore, the subject does not grasp the world but the symbol it forms from the world; it does not know reality but the symbol it shapes from it.

---

51. Ibid., 92. Translation mine.
52. Immanuel Kant. *Critique of Pure Reason* (The Cambridge Edition of the Works of Immanuel Kant). Translated and edited by Paul Guyer and Allen W. Wood. (Cambridge University Press, 1998), 149 (A12).

Although we contemplate a tree, this tree that we appreciate consists of a representation generated from our perception. Similarly, in the realm of self-perception, the image we discern is only a symbol of what I am, shaped from the perceived that we call "I." Alberto Vanzo says:

> We see that a tree has leaves, we can hypothesize that all trees have leaves, or the second tree has leaves, the third has leaves, and so on. To verify these hypotheses, we need to represent them: they must be our thoughts. To have a thought, we need concepts because thinking is representing something through concepts.[53]

Therefore, unlike Aristotle, concepts are symbols for Kant. This reflection brings us to a question that links the aesthetic dimension with morality and the rational faculty. As has been analyzed, reason is what applies categories to the objective manifestations or phenomena perceived sensitively. As Kant states in the *Critique of Judgment*:

> But, by an aesthetic idea (a term that comes from the Greek αἰσθητική [*aisthetikḗ*], the feminine form of the adjective αἰσθητικός, in Latin *aesthetica*, which means being endowed with perception or sensitivity, perceptive, sensitive) I mean that representation of the imagination that occasions much thought without any determinate thought, i.e. concept, being adequate to it, and which language, consequently, can never quite fully capture or render completely intelligible.[54]

Kant asserts that aesthetic perception escapes the limits of rationality due to the impossibility of being justified, demonstrated, or validated by it. Under this lens, the notion appears as a subjective processing and formulation. From this, Kant argues:

---

53. Alberto Vanzo, *Kant e la formazione dei concetti* [Kant and the Formation of Concepts] (Trento: Verifiche, 2012), 21–22. Translation mine.

54. Immanuel Kant, *Critique of the Power of Judgment*, ed. Paul Guyer, trad. Paul Guyer y Eric Matthews (Cambridge: Cambridge University Press, 2000), §49, 142.

> Now, I say, the beautiful is the symbol of the morally good, and only in this light (a point of view natural to everyone, and one which everyone demands from others as a duty) does it give us pleasure with an attendant claim to the agreement of everyone else, whereupon the mind becomes conscious of a certain ennoblement and elevation above mere sensibility to pleasure from impressions of the senses, and also appraises the worth of others on the score of a like maxim of their judgement.[55]

Aesthetic morality holds that what we consider beautiful is intrinsically related to our notion of what is morally good. What is aesthetically correct awakens a positive appreciation in us; the good pleases us, as if morality possesses an inherent pleasurable quality, and the spirit feels ennobled by the beauty of the object. This convergence of morality and beauty elevates us to a transcendence beyond mere sensory perception. The human being judges and values through this lens, postulating that for the human mind, beauty is inherently good, as Nietzsche said that in art and aesthetics, goodness is a consequence of beauty. In this structure, the concept articulated by the individual is the bridge that connects our essence with the cosmos; it is the symbol that integrates our soul and the world. This link between the human psyche and the universe is established through the concept that the subject places and serves as a link. The human soul and the world reconcile through this symbol, which is the concept facilitated by language. Without language, no conceptualization would be possible. Wittgenstein said: "The limits of my language mean the limits of my world."[56]

Based on what has been said so far, it is possible to assert that the seed of the symbolic turn is implicit in Kant's Copernican turn itself since, according to him, reality occurs in language, through which the concept to which categories elevate the object acquires the

55. Ibid., §59, 180.

56. Ludwig Wittgenstein, *Tractatus Logico-Philosophicus*, trans. D. F. Pears and B. F. McGuinness, with an introduction by Bertrand Russell (London: Routledge Classics, 2001), 5.6, 68.

qualities of a symbol, as Kant himself has shown. However, Kant's notion of language here is of special interest.

As we have seen, Kant developed the idealist theory of categories. The category, a term derived from the Greek *katêgoria*, which can be translated as predicate or attribute, is an abstract and general notion that enables recognition, differentiation, and classification of entities. Or, to illustrate it another way, categories are the essential concepts with which the subject groups and organizes the surrounding world. As we have likewise shown earlier, these categories or concepts are a priori, as they are produced by understanding when it engages with the phenomenon in space and time. As such, categories are spontaneous and do not arise from or depend on sensory experience. This leads us first to assert that understanding produces categories through language and, consequently, that the transcendental conditions of all knowledge are expressed through judgments with which we speak of reality.

Being possessors of language, humans emit judgments. A judgment is an affirmative or negative proposition that attributes a property to an entity. One judgment may say, "This table is round." Another may say, "Some tables are white." Another may say, "All tables are things." In terms of quantity, announcing the proposition according to "these," "some," or "all" refers to quantity: "these" corresponds to the category of singularity (this S is P), "some" to particularity (some S is P), and "all" to totality (all S is P). Singularity, particularity, and totality are categories. We deduce categories from ways of speaking, judgments, or language. If we discover three ways of speaking about things, it is because there are three quantity judgments.

If we say, "The sky is beautiful," the quality will be affirmative (S is P). If we later say, "The earth is not damp," the quality of this judgment will be negation (S is not P). And if we say "man is not God," it will be infinitive (S is not P). Therefore, we have three categories: affirmation, negation, and infinitive, which depend on three different ways of speaking. What this indicates is that the transcendental deduction of categories depends on the transcendental deduction of judgments, which is why the being of things depends on our way of speaking about things. Or, expressed otherwise, being depends on the language. Sensible impressions represent images that, as they are constructed by the subject as a result of their perception, awaken thought. In similar ways, Flórez Miguel has expressed it when he says:

> Kant is concerned with the communication of our sensations, knowledge, feelings, and thoughts and tries to find an explanation for the issue of communication within the general framework of his philosophy. In sensible intuition, direct communication is possible because there is a direct and clear reference between our intuition and the thing that can be shown. In the case of our thoughts, their communication can only be indirect through symbols, which allow the words of our language not only to show the world of things but also to express our experience of the world through analogies that, thanks to the creative power of imagination, transcend the limits of sensible experience.[57]

Kant's primary concern was to clarify how humans communicate their thoughts, whether through words, concepts, or symbols. According to him, we are ignorant of what we perceive, for we perceive only sensations and not the true essence of the object itself. There is a transcendent reality, a noumenon, to which we cannot access through our senses nor reasoning. Immanuel Kant was very close to discovering that our reality comprises only thoughts, emotions, and perceptions.

57. C. Flórez Miguel, "*Poiesis* y *mimesis* en la experiencia estética kantiana" [Poiesis and *Mimesis* in the Kantian Aesthetic Experience], in *En la cumbre del criticismo: Simposio sobre la «Crítica del juicio» de Kant*, ed. A. R. Rodríguez and G. Villar (Barcelona: Anthropos, 1992), 107–121, p, 110. Translation mine.

CHAPTER 12

SYMBOL: HEGEL'S ARTISTIC-RELIGIOUS APPROACH

The seed of symbolic thought that Kant himself timidly brought to light within his philosophical revolution will manifest more clearly in the philosophy of Hegel, who granted the symbol the weight it holds in human thought within the realms of art and religion as higher states of existence. However, this evolution from Kant to Hegel arises from certain convergences, parallels, and divergences.

On the one hand, Kant and Hegel converge in their postulates about the use of concepts by the understanding. In trying to grasp and comprehend reality within the framework of transcendental analysis, Kant tends to solidify it, trapping it in formal categories that are expressly static and binary. Such an approach, inherent to the understanding, reflects an intrinsic dualism that surfaces, for example, when he posits that life can only be understood in opposition to death, that the notion of low only makes sense in relation to high that light has no meaning without darkness, and so on.

For his part, Hegel, while not denying categories as a way of conceptualizing reality, significantly distances himself from Kant's postulates and challenges his categories as mere static and universal concepts applied to sensory experience. This critique stems from the fact that, for Hegel, Kant's categories are "too a priori," which, within Hegel's thought, means they are ahistorical. That is, Hegel believes it is impossible to claim that categories are a priori while simultaneously asserting that they have no life prior to understanding. Therefore, Hegel sees them as excessively static. On the other hand, Kant might have thought that if he had made them more dynamic, they would lose their "formal" and normative character, which would have returned him to Hume. For Hegel, truth is not the static position of one category above another but the process through which categories collide, opening the way for a much broader and transcendental unity, breaking the boundaries that limit them to particularity. Hegel emphatically argues that categories, constrained and sedentary, are not competent to capture the opulence and tangled nature of a reality that is always mutable and, consequently, offers a philosophical paradigm in which categories are transformative and elevated through the dialectic of contradiction and negation.

Both philosophers also converge regarding reason. Kant situates understanding as the instrument for achieving knowledge and reason as a faculty operating in unknown territories, stimulating the intellect. When certainty is established, thought settles, as thinking is only required when what is known is no longer useful. In this sense, thought moves toward the unknown that affects us (the phenomenon). For his part, Hegel holds that reason itself, in its dialectical unfolding, generates and overcomes categories in its process of apprehending reality.

If, for Kant, reason integrates through paralogisms, antinomies, or the ideal of reason, for Hegel, reason integrates concepts through history, and it is based on this that he will claim that *diànoia*, "reason," is a historical reason. That is, a reason that synthesizes the moments of understanding or *nous*. To exemplify the issue, understanding might determine that a particular religion is superior but later assert that the same religion is obsolete or inferior to another. At some point in history, understanding may determine that the body and matter should be denied, only to assert later that they must be affirmed. Therefore, understanding proceeds as affirmation, negation, and synthesis: thinking "this is good," then asserting "this is bad," only to later proceed to a synthesis, thinking "it is neither so good nor so bad." Reason, for its part, rises as a perpetual movement of thought that encompasses all dimensions of experience, synthesizing them into a more vast totality. This dialectical dance, later choreographed by Marx with the terms thesis, antithesis, and synthesis, is the key to a more comprehensive and vivid view of reality.

Hegel argues that, while the concept resides in the realm of understanding, thought exists in the realm of the symbolic, which he defines as a form of knowledge that transcends mere binary categorization and penetrates into abstract and integrative realms. Reason is not conceptual but symbolic, an instance that encompasses multiple meanings and fullness. In the realm of reason, concepts do not stagnate in perpetual immobility but succeed one another in a constant flow, in a becoming where they are incessantly negated and affirmed, as in an eternal dialectical movement. This process culminates in a synthesis in which the original dichotomies, far from persisting, vanish, giving way to a new, enriching unity. Therefore, in the domain of reason, duality does not unfold but a dialectical unity that transcends fragmentation and conceptual polarization. In the concept resides truth, while in the symbol, truth is irrelevant. Truth consists in the adequacy of thought to the thing, but things exist only in objects, and objects exist only in concepts. In the symbol, truth transcends objectivity.

Each moment of understanding reveals itself as an instance through which reason unfolds in order to know itself. However, according to Hegel, this reason is not merely a human faculty, as Kant would have said, but is absolute, spiritual, and, as such, transcends humanity, revealing and knowing itself through the history of philosophy. Hegel identifies the absolute with history and makes divinity something immanent to the world. By conceiving the absolute as something that, in its self-unfolding, realizes itself, he eliminates all possibility of thinking of a transcendent God because that absolute, outside of its self-realization in the moments of history, is nothing, and as such is an absolute immanent to time.

This is Kierkegaard's great critique of Hegel's thought: Hegel turns everything possible into a necessity, once it has been, eliminating contingency and submitting even God himself to becoming. This is why Kierkegaard responds with the purest existentialism, of contingency, of anguish. This Absolute Spirit, which we can understand as God, knows itself and makes use of those who, with their reflective activity, allow the mediation through which Being thinks itself, as Heidegger later also suggested, so that humans are

Dasein, being-there in the world, the there (*da*) of Being (*Sein*), the place where the question of being and by being is posed.

In the reason of God, of this Absolute Spirit, the most perfect union that exists takes place. God is the symbol that unites being and thinking. Thought is the true being, and being is thought. But not human thought, but that of being which uses the human without being human. It is not human consciousness but divine, the Absolute, which thinks itself through the human being. Therefore, the Hegelian Spirit, which we take here as God, affirms itself in the history of philosophy, only to later negate itself and thereafter synthesize itself, again and again, in a retroprogressive process of self-consciousness that leads it to absolute self-consciousness. This self-consciousness, or Truth, is the Bacchic delirium in which all those moments are integrated into a single absolute knowledge. The symbol in Hegel will be the sacred union of being and thinking, through which God, the Absolute Spirit, recovers its identity.

The *Phenomenology of Spirit* is surely Hegel's most important work and has had the greatest impact on philosophy and other disciplines and knowledge areas.[58] The entire work is dedicated to illustrating precisely what the title itself indicates: the detailed process through which Spirit manifests itself. Toward the conclusion of the text, Hegel makes a direct reference to art; specifically, to the relationship between Spirit and aesthetic religion, through which he introduces us to his concept of art understood as a creation of Spirit, rather than as the product of an individual artist. According to Hegel, art is an intuitive impulse that emerges as the manifestation of a Spirit or consciousness in its search for self-consciousness, and as the vehicle through which this consciousness affirms and evolves in the world.

In his view, Spirit becomes the "artist," that is, the one who intertwines the innately organic with the strange constructions of thought, transcending the mere task of amalgamating or synthesizing the visual with the hidden. In this process, Spirit itself transforms into a spiritual craftsman, a demiurge of symbolism. However, what art

58. Robert Stern. *Routledge Philosophy GuideBook to Hegel and the Phenomenology of Spirit* (London: Routledge, 2002), 2.

unveils in this process of self-manifestation or self-consciousness of Spirit in the world is, according to Hegel himself, the ethical Spirit. To put it another way, the "seed" or the genuine spirit of artistic religion is the universal substance, the essence of each individual, and the one capable of transcending art. Within this vision, Hegel affirms that:

> Later on, Spirit transcends art in order to gain a higher representation of itself, viz. to be not merely the substance born of the self, but to be, in its representation as object, this self not only to give birth to itself from its Notion, but to have its very Notion for its shape, so that the Notion and the work of art produced know each other as one and the same.[59]

The Spirit in Hegel's philosophy does not refer to individual human essence but to a transcendental entity that contains everything and everyone within itself. It is the being or supra-human consciousness in which all human beings participate, the Universal Spirit, and the Totality that holds particularity in its highest form. This consciousness evolves progressively through various means, such as science, philosophy, and art, until it approaches the point of culmination or fullness of its beingness, which is none other than religion, the sublime dimension of the Absolute Spirit. This allows us to simultaneously understand history as the path of Spirit toward its full self-realization, *itinerarium ad menti Deum* or "the itinerary of the mind toward God."

In Chapter Six of the *Phenomenology of Spirit*, Hegel describes the Spirit as an artist who, beyond merely synthesizing, fuses the natural with the peculiar structures of thought. In this process, the Spirit adopts a new form, becoming a spiritual potter, a worker of the immaterial realm. The Spirit reveals itself through a perceptible representation, unfolding or communicating its unmanifest essence.

59. G. W. F. Hegel, *Phenomenology of Spirit*, trans. A. V. Miller, with analysis and foreword by J. N. Findlay (Delhi: Motilal Banarsidass, 1998), chap. VII "Religion," sec. B "Religion in the Form of Art," §702, 426.

Hence, its symbolism is precisely through the perceptible image that it emits an imperceptible meaning. Therefore, the exposition in the *Phenomenology of Spirit* deals with absolute knowledge in its transformation, or the transition from one state to another, through which the Absolute Spirit comes to know itself through the history of philosophy and culture.

However, artistic religion is not the end of the historical process; instead, it serves as the means through which the Spirit manifests itself as ethical Spirit, where being reconciles with itself. That is to say, what benefits humanity is what the Spirit accomplishes with itself, and we only need the required sensitivity to perceive this spiritual movement. The Spirit is the universal substance that lies within everything and everyone, meaning it is where we realize our own individuality. In other words, our authenticity is not inherently within us but in the ability to connect with that universal essence, which is Being. By connecting with this universal essence, we discover our true nature: to be part of it.

This symbolic process we are defining involves accessing this universal essence to discover our reality or, equivalently, to reconcile with Being. We find our beingness by interacting with the universal essence of Spirit through the symbol. This task of reconciliation through the symbolic originates from the Spirit, not from the individual, emanating from the transcendental and not from empirically human. This is why Heidegger, in his *Letter on Humanism*, maintains that in the relationship between *Sein* (Being) and *Dasein* (Being-there), *Sein* takes precedence.

The reconciliation of the Absolute Spirit we have referred to manifests in a process through which the Spirit passes through the artistic and religious stages. According to the thought of William Blake (1757–1827), the great British poet, painter, and engraver, recently considered by *The Guardian* as "the greatest artist Britain has produced," Christianity manifests as art, while Jesus Christ, as its highest exponent, functions as the source and paradigm of artistic activity. These conceptions constitute the cornerstone of both his religious and artistic perspective, materializing in many ways throughout his career. This is evident from his early narratives on poetic genius in *All Religions Are One* to his later aphorisms in *Laocoön*. On one occasion, the renowned artist stated, "Religion is art, not a means to enrich oneself." Only a mystical poet of the stature of William Blake could have expressed such a profound postulate.

The term "art" itself has its roots in the Latin word *ars, artis*, which conveys the idea of an activity laden with creativity. Its Greek equivalent is *τέχνη* (*téchne*), which translates as "technique." This explains its use in earlier times to designate both crafts that required specific manual skills, such as metal forging, and areas recognized today as artistic, such as literature, dance, poetry, painting, or music. In other words, art is related to the way certain activities are executed.

Religion, like art, consists of a way of doing, loving, seeing, speaking, living, and existing. Religion consists in being participants with God in His act of creation, that is, living as collaborators of God in His creative act and, therefore, being co-creators. Although art is not religion, it is undoubtedly a vector that offers us signs toward ourselves; a path or direction toward the sacred, in which beauty expresses the good, as Hegel already suggested. This became evident in the Middle Ages, with the cathedrals pointing toward the sky, with spectacular monuments full of sacred art. To appreciate this, one only needs to visit cathedrals, churches, synagogues, and mosques.

The artist undoubtedly experiences an approach to the sacred, even though society generally does not regard him as such. One of the great difficulties of Prakāśānanda Sarasvatī in recognizing Lord Chaitanya Mahāprabhu as a wise, enlightened saint was precisely that he saw him as an artist who sang and danced. For Prakāśānanda Sarasvatī, the activities of Lord Chaitanya were art, but not religion. Society, in general, does not link art with religion. A priest, a *brāhmaṇa*, or a rabbi will be accepted as religious but not as poets, singers, painters, or sculptors. On the other hand, it is undeniable that the artist is known through his artistic labor, just as the religious is also an artist who makes and knows himself through his labor. In religion, God is the artist from whom art emerges, through which He knows. God is aware of Himself through the artist's and religious work, whether it be the tales of Rabbi Nachman of Breslov or the dance and poems of Lord Chaitanya. It is already stated in Exodus (31:1–5) that Bezalel, an artist and creator of culture, was the first person to be "filled with the Spirit of God."

> וַיֹּאמֶר דָּוִיד לְשָׂרֵי הַלְוִיִּם לְהַעֲמִיד אֶת־אֲחֵיהֶם הַמְשֹׁרְרִים בִּכְלֵי־שִׁיר נְבָלִים
> וְכִנֹּרוֹת וּמְצִלְתָּיִם מַשְׁמִיעִים לְהָרִים־בְּקוֹל לְשִׂמְחָה:
> (דברי הימים א', ט"ו, ט"ז)
>
> And David spoke to the chiefs of the Levites to appoint their brethren to be the singers with instruments of music, lutes and lyres and cymbals, playing loudly to raise sounds of joy.
> (I Chronicles, 15:16)

Artistic morality does not draw from regulations, laws, or conventional principles dictated by something or someone. What guides the artistic is its aesthetic intuition, meaning that it would be impossible for the artist to harm others because it would be an aesthetically repulsive act. The artist's measure is harmony, order, and beauty. As we mentioned earlier, when we said that the artistic culminates in the religious, art leads to religion, which, ultimately, is where Spirit can manifest its "ethicality" or "ethical order" (*sittlichkeit*).

The famous Italian artist Jean Albert Carlotti precisely expressed his perspective on beauty. While observing his wife clean and organize his studio, he declared, "Beauty is the atoms and molecules working together in harmony and peace; nothing needs to be subtracted or added; only patience is needed to see it in its entirety and purity. That is you. You are beautiful." His moved wife responded, "Thank you for showing me what beauty truly is!"

Beauty can be interpreted in many ways, but all interpretations converge in the notion of order and unity, which are fundamental for the creation of form. The French composer André Jolivet said, "Beauty is the object of intelligence or intuitive knowledge, in that it results from conditions that are only accessible to intelligence. These conditions are the integrity of the object, the proportion or unity in variety, and the clarity or splendor of intelligibility. This puts the senses in a state of well-being and satisfaction."[60]

As long as human beings do not live as "creators," it will be absolutely impossible for them to approach, understand, or comprehend the true creator. Saying that God knows Himself through the concrete works of artists and religious beings brings us back to Hegel, who argues that Being manifests objectively through art (which is somewhat similar to what Vedanta calls Īśvara), as it is in this relationship that it can gain "a higher representation of itself, viz. to be not merely the substance born of the self," meaning not only substance created from the human but also "its representation as object." The process of self-knowledge and full manifestation of Being has a double meaning, as Hegel continues: "this self not only to give birth to itself from its Notion, but to have its very Notion for its shape, so that the Notion and the work of art produced know each other as one and the same."

What Hegel is saying here is that the idea of the artwork, the artwork itself, and the object represented in the symbol are one and the same. Only Spirit can realize this absolute reconciliation through the symbolic, which fuses being and thought and whose union is the symbol. Although the symbol transcends the concept, human beings understand it through the symbol. Therefore, the symbol becomes a representation of the concept. This is precisely what allows Hegel to affirm:

> Now these ideas in their universality and essential implicit character art concentrates again into a picture for contemplation by direct consciousness and sets them out

60. Caroline Rae, ed., André Jolivet: *Music, Art and Literature* (Routledge, 2020). Juan Granados Valdez, "The Thomistic Aesthetics of Jolivet, Nédoncelle, Pieper, and Pareyson" ["La estética tomista de Jolivet, Nédoncelle, Pieper y Pareyson"], Konvergencias: Philosophy and Cultures in Dialogue, no. 33 (October 2021), Buenos Aires. Translation mine.

> for the spirit in the objective form of a picture. This is the beginning of art.[61]

In his particular skill, the artist encapsulates the universal essence of Being in his own essential being, transferring it to a tangible representation through his intuition, for it is intuitively that he perceives the immediate consciousness of Being. The artist does not clearly digest this immediate perception of consciousness until the work is completed. The artist lacks the ability to theoretically formulate existence before having created the work. Once the work is finished, the artist can understand, elaborate, and conceptualize the consciousness. After it is finished, the work can objectify that image through conceptualization. In other words, the artist intuits nature without being able to conceptualize it until it is artistically expressed. Therefore, the artist enjoys an immediate perception of consciousness or of Being, transcribing it through painting, dance, singing, or writing. This artistic process of manifesting the essence of reality through immediate intuition, prior to its conceptualization, happens through the symbol. In this regard, we can quote Paul de Man when he states:

> The symbol is the mediation between the mind and the physical world of which art manifestly partakes, be it as stone, as color, as sound, or as language. Hegel says so in no uncertain terms in the section on symbolic art.[62]

In the symbol, the human being accesses the reconciliation of the manifested and the unmanifested, the perceptible reality and the imperceptible, the visible world and the invisible. We perceive the manifested when we listen to a melody, read a poem, or see a painting.

---

61. G. W. F. Hegel, *Aesthetics: Lectures on Fine Art*, vol. 1, trans. T. M. Knox (Oxford: Clarendon Press, 1975; repr., 1988), in Part II: "Development of the Ideal into the Particular Forms of Art," "Section I: The Symbolic Form of Art," subsection "Introduction—The Symbol in general," 279–80.
62. Paul de Man, "Sign and Symbol in Hegel's Aesthetics," Critical Inquiry 8, no. 4 (1982): 761–75, at 763.

However, we access the imperceptible reality through the conceptual explanation of the meaning of the artwork. Therefore, painting pertains to the sense of sight as well as to the sense of hearing, with its meaning not being exclusively visual but also auditory. The meaning of painting resides not only in what it shows but in what it says. Painting is not only looked at but also heard. A symbolic painting, therefore, must be both seen and heard. A work of art is a true symbol if it must be seen and heard together so that all the truth it contains may be revealed.

> וְכָל־הָעָם רֹאִים אֶת־הַקּוֹלֹת וְאֶת־הַלַּפִּידִם וְאֵת קוֹל הַשֹּׁפָר וְאֶת־הָהָר עָשֵׁן וַיַּרְא הָעָם וַיָּנֻעוּ וַיַּעַמְדוּ מֵרָחֹק:
>
> (שמות כ', ט"ו)

> And all the people saw the sounds and the flames, and the sound of the horn (*shofar*), and the mountain smoking; and when the people saw it, they turned back and stood afar off.
>
> (Exodus, 20:15)

> "וְכָל־הָעָם רֹאִים אֶת־הַקּוֹלֹת". וּכְבָר פֵּרַשְׁתִּי טַעַם "רוֹאִים אֶת־הַקּוֹלוֹת". כִּי כָּל הַהַרְגָּשׁוֹת מִתְחַבְּרוֹת אֶל מָקוֹם אֶחָד.
>
> (פירוש אבן עזרא לשמות כ', ט"ו)

> "All the people saw the sounds." I have already explained the meaning of "saw the sounds," that all the senses are connected to one place.
>
> (*Commentary on Exodus* by Ibn Ezra, 20:15)

As we saw at the beginning of this chapter, art is part of the historical process through which Spirit manifests in its complete fullness. It also means that artistic evolution corresponds to the reflection of spiritual development. In this sense, the evolution of art parallels that of spirit: it begins with abstract and unique artistic expressions, evolves through the development of self-consciousness, and culminates in the emancipation of objectivity. For this reason, we can affirm that art is not a mere discipline or technique that

Spirit could do without. Far from it, art, or more precisely the artistic religiosity that Hegel formulates, reveals itself as essential and indispensable in the unfolding of Spirit in which the human being reconciles with themselves as what they truly are.

At the same time, art can be so important because its symbolic nature allows it to manifest Spirit in the form of Absolute Consciousness or Being. Hegel himself explains this in *The Phenomenology of Spirit*, saying, "Through the raising of the whole into the pure Notion, the shape acquires its pure, spiritually appropriate form."[63]

If this adequacy is possible, that is, if Spirit can manifest and be understood in the artwork, it is because Spirit finds a way to reveal itself in the artwork itself, and in doing so, the work attains its purest form. This leads us to say that art is the objectification of an absolute "I."

But for this to be possible and for art to play the role it does, we must understand art as symbolic. Hegel primarily addresses the symbol in relation to art, which is particularly relevant when he focuses on artistic beauty, representing the highest expression of the Absolute Spirit. This is why Hegel asserts that symbolic art unfolds where:

> The Idea still *seeks* its genuine expression in art, because in itself it is still abstract and indeterminate and therefore does not have its adequate manifestation on and in itself, but finds itself confronted by what is external to itself, external things in nature and human affairs.[64]

In other words, it is precisely the symbol that allows the artwork to reflect the Absolute Spirit and, at the same time, thanks to this, acquire its purest form. Furthermore, Being does not intend to limit itself solely to conceptualization but likewise seeks to be artistically expressed. Understood within the historical process of the unfolding

---

63. G. W. F. Hegel, *Phenomenology of Spirit*, trans. A. V. Miller, with analysis of the text and foreword by J. N. Findlay (Oxford: Oxford University Press, 1977), §706.

64. G. W. F. Hegel, *Aesthetics: Lectures on Fine Art*, vol. 1, trans. T. M. Knox (Oxford: Clarendon Press, 1975), 300, in Part II: "Development of the Ideal into the Particular Forms of Art," 300.

of Being as Absolute Spirit, we can assert that the conceptualization of Being is only possible through its prior manifestation as symbolic art. The symbolic reconciliation is proper to religious art, and for Being to be conceptualized, it must also be danced, sung, written, sculpted, carved, painted, and expressed in works of art.

Being evolves in its self-consciousness, but it cannot know itself only through philosophical ideas. Although consciousness, or the Absolute Spirit, aspires to its self-realization, this is immediately denied, with the symbolic nature of artistic religion facilitating the process of self-manifestation and self-revelation. This is why the penultimate chapter of *The Phenomenology of Spirit* deals with religion and absolute knowledge.

The concept and art are steps of the process that are intrinsically connected to one another. In a certain sense, it is possible to say that the self-comprehension of Spirit begins with the empirical-scientific conceptualization of nature. This scientific understanding transcends itself, evolving into philosophical conceptualization, but this, too, cannot alone show the full depth of the Absolute Spirit and must transcend itself and mutate into artistic expression or religiosity. Due to its symbolic nature, Spirit unfolds its own full divinity in artistic religiosity, allowing human beings to reconcile with their innermost and most authentic being. There lies the importance of the symbol.

From this perspective, Hegel defines the symbol as:

> Symbol as such is an external existent given or immediately present to contemplation, which yet is to be understood not simply as it confronts us immediately on its own account, but in a wider and more universal sense. Thus at once there are two distinctions to make in the symbol: (i) the meaning, and (ii) the expression thereof. The first is an idea or topic, no matter what its content, the second is a sensuous existent or a picture of some kind or other.[65]

65. Ibid., 303–4.

Hegel interprets the symbol as a sensible image, an external existence that is not a product of human invention but a manifestation of Spirit. Although human beings may believe they are the author of the work, the true creator is Spirit through the individual who gives form and meaning to the artwork; that is, it is the universal that creates, acting through the individual. In this sense, the artistic work is present intuitively in the artist in an immediate way. Although the artist is not fully aware of the conceptualization and meaning enclosed within, they intuit it because the true source lies in Spirit. As we mentioned earlier, it is only once the work is finished and the artist has intuitively shaped it that the full "meaning and expression" of the work allows the artist and the observer to understand it and come to self-understanding through the work itself.

Hegel defines the symbol as composed of two aspects: the meaning (auditory) and the expression (visual). The meaning of the symbol is auditory and is based on the narration of a community or the description of an artist. The artistic expression can be perceived visually but lacks meaning without the artist's explanation. The symbol is the union of the visual expression of the painting with the auditory explanation of the artist. The visual expression is related to a sensible manifestation, while the meaning is its mental representation. Therefore, the meaning of the artwork lies in how it manifests in a more extensive and universal sense.

Hegel attributes to the symbol a property of ambiguity, a detail that has captured the attention of many experts in symbolism. Hegel's speculative philosophy identifies a dialectic between the universal and the specific, the general and the particular, between the interior and the exterior, between the sign and its meaning, between the indicator and the indicated. "The concrete" or "the specific" would be the image, and "the universal" or "the general" would refer to the words used to describe it. For example, I called one of my paintings *Dasein*; the visualization of this painting is the specific aspect, but its interpretation is universal. The painting is an external representation, while its interpretation is internal; if the painting is the indicator, the words used to explain it constitute its interpretation.

Nevertheless, Hegel himself clarifies in *Aesthetics* that "such dubiety disappears only when each of the two sides, the meaning and its shape, are expressly named and thereby their relation is enunciated at once."[66] For example, consider the similarity between the displayed painting and the explanation that accompanies it about *Dasein*. In this case, the visual and auditory expressions are simultaneous because I painted what *Dasein* is for me. When both sides of an idea are revealed and related, duality or ambiguity yields and the symbol also arises. The artwork becomes a symbol along with the fusion between the explanation of *Dasein* and the visual presentation of the painting. In a symbol, the author allows and facilitates that union between the verbalized and the illustrated.

As Hegel himself notes, the universal representation (the meaning) and its tangible figure (the sign) come face to face in the symbol. As we have seen in previous chapters, symbols are intrinsically linked to myths, as they contain a direct union between both facets of reality and are considered complete in their representations, images, and deities. The symbol exists due to the discrepancy between the sign and the meaning, which is not evident or verifiable in myth. For this reason, Hegel asserts that "mythology must be understood symbolically." By "symbolically," he means that myths "embrace within them meanings about the nature of God, as products of Spirit." In this sense, we also see in Hegel the integration of myth as a symbolic narrative, being a union of a visual representation with an auditory one. The integration and inseparability of the auditory and visual aspects of the symbol allow Spirit to unveil itself in all its fullness.

The process of self-realization or self-comprehension of the Being that we are would be a journey beyond ourselves in search of Being, only to discover that we were always immersed in Being. This process of self-comprehension implies renouncing our ideas or beliefs about who we are in order to awaken our true identity;

66. G. W. F. Hegel, *Aesthetics: Lectures on Fine Art*, vol. 1, trans. T. M. Knox (Oxford: Clarendon Press, 1975; repr., 1988), in Part II: "Development of the Ideal into the Particular Forms of Art," "Section I: The Symbolic Form of Art," subsection "Introduction—The Symbol in general," 306.

it is about putting aside our apparent essence to discover, accept, and reconcile with our genuine nature. Hegel affirms that by going beyond art, when in this artistic work man accesses the universal substance of Being, he will realize that the artwork ends in religion. That is, every symbol is sacred.

Bibliography section II

- Augustine. *The Confessions*. Translated by Maria Boulding. Edited by John E. Rotelle, O.S.A. *The Works of Saint Augustine: A Translation for the 21st Century*, Part I, Vol. 1. Hyde Park, NY: New City Press, 1997.
- Burnet, John. *Early Greek Philosophy*. 4th ed. London: A. & C. Black, 1920.
- Butnaru, Iulian. *Naturaleza y alcance del símbolo* [*Nature and Scope of the Symbol*]. PhD diss., Universitat Rovira i Virgili, 2014.
- Creuzer, Friedrich. *Simbolica e mitologia*. In *Dal simbolo al mito*, Vol. II. Milan: Edizioni Spirale, 1983.
- De Man, Paul. "Sign and Symbol in Hegel's Aesthetics." *Critical Inquiry* 8, no. 4 (1982): 761–75.
- Eliade, Mircea. *Myth and Reality*. Translated by Willard R. Trask. New York: Harper & Row, 1963.
- Flórez Miguel, Cirilo. "Dialectic and Symbolism in Kant" ["Dialéctica y simbolismo en Kant"]. *Azafea. Revista de Filosofía* 3 (January 1990): 87. License CC BY-NC-ND 4.0.
- Flórez Miguel, Cirilo. "Poiesis y mimesis en la experiencia estética kantiana" ["Poiesis and Mimesis in the Kantian Aesthetic Experience"]. In *En la cumbre del criticismo: Simposio sobre la «Crítica del juicio» de Kant*, edited by A. R. Rodríguez and G. Villar, 107–21. Barcelona: Anthropos, 1992.
- Granados Valdez, Juan. "The Thomistic Aesthetics of Jolivet, Nédoncelle, Pieper, and Pareyson" ["La estética tomista de Jolivet, Nédoncelle, Pieper y Pareyson"]. *Konvergencias: Philosophy and Cultures in Dialogue*, no. 33 (October 2021). Buenos Aires.
- Hegel, Georg Wilhelm Friedrich. *Aesthetics: Lectures on Fine Art*. Vol. 1. Translated by T. M. Knox. Oxford: Clarendon Press, 1975. Reprint, 1988.

- Hegel, Georg Wilhelm Friedrich. *Phenomenology of Spirit*. Translated by A. V. Miller. With an analysis of the text and foreword by J. N. Findlay. Delhi: Motilal Banarsidass, 1998.
- Hegel, Georg Wilhelm Friedrich. *Phenomenology of Spirit*. Translated by A. V. Miller. With analysis and foreword by J. N. Findlay. Oxford: Oxford University Press, 1977.
- Heidegger, Martin. *Being and Time*. Translated by John Macquarrie and Edward Robinson. Oxford: Blackwell, 1962.
- Heidegger, Martin. *Letter on "Humanism."* Translated by Frank A. Capuzzi. In *Pathmarks*, edited by William McNeill, 239–76. Cambridge: Cambridge University Press, 1998.
- Kant, Immanuel. *Critique of the Power of Judgment*. Edited by Paul Guyer. Translated by Paul Guyer and Eric Matthews. Cambridge: Cambridge University Press, 2000.
- Kant, Immanuel. *Critique of Pure Reason*. Edited and translated by Paul Guyer and Allen W. Wood. *The Cambridge Edition of the Works of Immanuel Kant*. Cambridge: Cambridge University Press, 1998.
- Reale, Giovanni. *Eros, demonio mediador: El juego de las máscaras en el Banquete de Platón* [*Eros, Demonic Mediator: The Game of Masks in Plato's Symposium*]. Translated by Rosa Rius and Pere Salvat. Barcelona: Herder Editorial, 2004.
- Russell, Bertrand. *Principles of Social Reconstruction*. London: George Allen & Unwin, 1916.
- Stern, Robert. *Routledge Philosophy Guide Book to Hegel and the Phenomenology of Spirit*. London: Routledge, 2002.
- Vanzo, Alberto. *Kant e la formazione dei concetti* [*Kant and the Formation of Concepts*]. Trento: Verifiche, 2012.
- Wittgenstein, Ludwig. *Tractatus Logico-Philosophicus*. Translated by D. F. Pears and B. F. McGuinness. With an introduction by Bertrand Russell. London: Routledge Classics, 2001.
- Žižek, Slavoj. *The Sublime Object of Ideology*. London: Verso, 1989.
- Žižek, Slavoj. *Living in the End Times*. London: Verso, 2010.

SECTION III

SYMBOLS AND RELIGION

Chapter 13

Imagination: A Bridge Between Myth and Reality

> Imagination is more important than knowledge. Knowledge is limited to what we know and understand, while imagination embraces the entire world.
>
> ~ Albert Einstein

The term "imagination" comes from the Latin *imaginatio* (representation, image, or illusion), which in turn comes from the word *imago* (portrait, likeness, or appearance). We understand imagination as a multidimensional capacity, present in countless aspects of human life, ranging from artistic invention to scientific exploration. It is a talent that overflows the confines of ordinary reasoning and, as such, has been scrutinized by various disciplines. It has also fascinated thinkers from antiquity and has become a point of heated discussions within the philosophical tradition, where many prestigious philosophers have addressed it differently.

In classical Greece, Plato conceived imagination as a deceptive phenomenon that distances us from true knowledge. For him, imagination consisted of imitating reality that produced second-hand copies of the true world of ideas or forms. Plato did not distinguish imagination, or *eikasía* (εικασία) in Greek, from sensation or knowledge through images, and understood it as a supposition, considering it the first degree of sensible knowledge in his metaphor of the line. Unlike Plato, Aristotle gave imagination a positive role within the process of knowledge and reasoning. Aristotle called it *phantasía* (φαντασία) and not only distinguished it from both sensation and discursive thought (*diánoia*) but also assigned it the necessary role of accompanying all knowledge. However, he also considered it capable of error. According to the Stagirite, imagination helps conceptualize sensory information. Aristotle defined imagination as "the faculty of forming sensible images." In his work *De Anima*, Aristotle argued that imagination is a cognitive function that lies between perception and thought. In his *Poetics*, he considered it essential for poetry and, in rhetoric, important for persuasion. As Jolivet says, imagination is the faculty of preserving, reproducing, and combining the images of sensible things. Its object is everything received by the senses.

Imagination associates, dissociates, and combines to create images. These could be considered its main methods. The need for imagination to understand abstract ideas is central. On the brink of modernity, René Descartes understood imagination as a form of thinking that required a mental effort greater than simple understanding.[67] However, without completely rejecting the usefulness of imagination, he did not see it as indispensable for rationally understanding reality.

For David Hume, on the other hand, it is through imagination that we grasp reality from our sensory perceptions. Imagination is the mechanism that allows us to integrate separate sensory impressions into a coherent perception of the world. According to Hume, imagination can separate ideas and then unite them in the way it sees fit. Furthermore, he recognized that imagination transcends notions, and that the combination of ideas would not be possible without imagination. In this sense, imagination manifests at a mental level what is absent in sensitive intuition or direct perception through the senses.

For Immanuel Kant, imagination is a basic faculty that performs a crucial function in perception and knowledge. According to him, it enables humans to integrate sensory impressions into a coherent experience. In his *Critique of Pure Reason*, Kant offers an excellent definition of imagination: "Imagination is the faculty for representing

67. René Descartes, *Meditations on First Philosophy: With Selections from the Objections and Replies*, trans. Michael Moriarty (Oxford: Oxford University Press, 2008), Sixth meditation, 52 (margin ref. 73).

an object even without its presence in intuition."[68] That is to say, it is the ability to formulate representations or mental impressions that may or may not have a direct relationship with reality. This productive faculty also manifests as the artistic ability to express what has never been seen. It is a mental and creative process that fabricates representations of what has or has not been perceived through our senses, even in the absence of concrete external stimuli. For example, we could form a mental image of the ocean without actually seeing the sea. Therefore, imagination is still directly linked to memory because, in general, what we imagine is connected to a prior reality. In this sense, imagination can be seen as a tool for deciphering reality, allowing the construction of various theories.

For Hegel, imagination is an active and creative work. It is a mental capacity of the human being applicable to any discipline, essentially consisting of thinking with images. In general, imagination differs from representation and memory, although it is related to both. It is intimately related to representation because imagination arises from combining elements that were sensory representations in the past. However, it is also connected to memory because imagining would be impossible without the ability to remember those representations. Etymologically, imagination is a new representation of images without which knowledge would be impossible.

According to Jean-Paul Sartre, imagination emerges as a luminary of consciousness that dispels the mists of tangible reality and projects beams of light toward future possibilities. Immersed in the depths of Husserl's phenomenology, he advocates for imagination as a bastion between perception and thought. His works *The Imagination* (1936) and *The Imaginary* (1940) promote this premise. Here, the "imaginary" emerges as a parallel dimension, inhabited by objects arising from "imaginative consciousness," capable of invoking the presence of the absent and creating fictitious objects and an alternate reality, an "anti-world," which denies reality itself and, in contrast, exalts the freedom of consciousness. From his perspective, imagination

68. Immanuel Kant, *Critique of Pure Reason*, trans. and ed. Paul Guyer and Allen W. Wood (Cambridge: Cambridge University Press, 1998), 256 (§24 [B151]).

consists of an act of freedom that challenges given reality. Sartre stands among the defenders of imagination, firmly rejecting its underestimation. However, it was not until the 20th century that it was examined from a scientific approach, specifically through neurology and psychology.

Despite philosophical and later scientific studies, imagination has commonly been condemned and devalued. Upon hearing the word *imagination*, we often think of something useless, devoid of value, because no one seeks imaginary achievements but real ones. However, human beings have a powerful capacity to imagine, which can be used to destroy and create. George Bernard Shaw says: "Imagination is the beginning of creation. You imagine what you desire, you will what you imagine and at last you create what you will."[69] Everything positive and negative, creative and destructive, good and bad, beautiful and ugly in the world has come through imagination. Both art and war are products of imagination, as are major scientific discoveries. It is a very powerful capacity that can lead us to paradise or hell, depending on how it is used. If used incorrectly, it can even destroy us or drive us mad.

Let us imagine a spiritual power flowing like a mighty river both inside and outside our body. Let us imagine that this flow is present in the furniture, the walls, the floor, and every object in our home. Let us also imagine that slowly, the entire planet and the entire cosmos have been spiritualized by this flow and that the whole universe has been completely dematerialized and spiritualized. Through the capacity of consciously imagining, we begin to eliminate mental patterns because when imagining that everything is only consciousness, concepts like interior and exterior, inside and outside, evaporate. Imagination allows us, thus, to dissolve all limits and boundaries. Under the auspices of pure imagination, everything that exists is an infinite and unlimited ocean of pure consciousness. However, what really happens is not that we are creating an image foreign to reality out of nothing, but instead, imagination is what allows us to access

69. George Bernard Shaw, *Back to Methuselah: A Metabiological Pentateuch* (London: Constable and Company, 1921), Preface.

reality itself by dissolving the limits that allow us to penetrate it. It is impossible to access reality or recognize consciousness without transcending our own mental conditioning. As conditioned beings, we only have access to our own musings about reality. Reality is what is transcendental to all conditioning. In this sense, and as an example, the ability to imagine would be like the acid capable of dissolving accumulated intellectual conditioning.

Imagination is intrinsically linked to symbolization. In the symbolic act, the image adopts a duality of meanings, and it does so through two types of imagination: a receptive and passive one and another active and creative. Receptive and passive imagination is the one that receives the sacred influence of the symbol. On the one hand, this imagination passively accepts the spiritual sign, which, as such, is imperceptible to the senses because it does not manifest as an image. At the same time, the same sign must transform into an image through active or creative imagination in order to be comprehensible.

As an illustration, let us take the case of God, who, although cannot be visually perceived, becomes visible through Jesus Christ in Christianity, thus making Jesus Christ the image of God. That is why, according to the New Testament, Jesus proclaims, "He who has seen me has seen the Father," or *ego sum imago Dei*, a concept clarified at the Second Council of Nicaea. At this council, the Eucharistic Christ is discussed; therefore, Jesus is the image of the Father, and the Eucharist is the image of Jesus.

This argument about imagination allows us to establish that, in essence, the symbol is imperceptible, but it becomes concrete in the visible realm through the human being in order to be understood. However, it is important to explain that it is not the human who generates this image; instead, it emerges from the symbol itself when it is revealed to our faculties. The symbol exists independently of the human, becoming a sensory image to be understood. There is an active aspect; as the person receives the stimulus, the influence of this revelation shapes the image. And although the author of such an image is the person themselves, it always draws inspiration from the divine.

The deity of Kṛṣṇa installed in the temple, for example, is a human creation, but its inspiration does not come from the human but from the sacred. Therefore, the symbol acts as the efficient cause, and the human as the instrumental cause. However, it should be noted that, in religions like Catholicism, the human is not the cause but rather the occasion for the fulfillment of divine will. In one way or another, all religions are the consequence of a process in which "nothing" becomes "something" through someone to be perceived by all.

Imagination acts as the receiver of the conceptual influence of the sacred, generating a sensible image that serves as an indication of an invisible reality. Maimonides explains:

> הִנֵּה כָּל כְּלִי גַּשְׁמִי שֶׁתִּמְצָאֵהוּ בְּכָל סִפְרֵי הַנְּבוּאָה, הוּא אִם כְּלִי תְּנוּעָה מְקוֹמִית לְהוֹרוֹת עַל הַחַיִּים, אוֹ כְּלִי הַרְגָּשָׁה לְהוֹרוֹת עַל הַהַשָּׂגָה, אוֹ כְּלִי הַמִּשּׁוּשׁ לְהוֹרוֹת עַל הַפְּעֻלָּה, אוֹ כְּלִי הַדִּבּוּר לְהוֹרוֹת עַל הַשְׁפָּעַת הַשְּׂכָלִים עַל הַנְּבִיאִים, כְּמוֹ שֶׁיִּתְבָּאֵר.
>
> הִנֵּה תִּהְיֶה הַיְשָׁרַת הַהַשְׁאָלוֹת הָהֵם כֻּלָּם – לְיַשֵּׁב לָנוּ שֶׁיֵּשׁ נִמְצָא חַי פּוֹעֵל לְכָל מָה שֶׁזּוּלָתוֹ מַשִּׂיג לְפָעֳלוֹ גַּם כֵּן. וְהִנֵּה נְבָאֵר כְּשֶׁנַּתְחִיל בְּהַרְחָקַת הַתְּאָרִים, אֵיךְ יָשׁוּב זֶה כֻּלּוֹ לְעִנְיָן אֶחָד וְהוּא עַצְמוֹ יִתְבָּרַךְ לְבַד; כִּי אֵין כַּוָּנַת זֶה הַפֶּרֶק אֶלָּא לְבָאֵר עִנְיַן אֵלּוּ הַכֵּלִים הַגַּשְׁמִיִּים הַמְּיֻחָסִים לוֹ – יִתְעַלֶּה מִכָּל חִסָּרוֹן – וְשֶׁהֵם כֻּלָּם – לְהוֹרוֹת עַל פְּעֻלּוֹת הַכֵּלִים הָהֵם אֲשֶׁר הַפְּעֻלּוֹת הָהֵם – שְׁלֵמוּת אֶצְלֵנוּ בַּעֲבוּר שֶׁנּוֹרֶה עַל הֱיוֹתוֹ שָׁלֵם בְּכָל מִינֵי הַשְּׁלֵמוּת כְּמוֹ שֶׁהֶעִירוּנוּ בְּאָמְרָם "דִּבְּרָה תּוֹרָה כִּלְשׁוֹן בְּנֵי אָדָם".
>
> אָמְנָם כְּלֵי הַתְּנוּעָה הַמְּקוֹמִית הַמְּיֻחָסִים לוֹ יִתְעַלֶּה, בְּאָמְרוֹ: "הֲדֹם רַגְלָי" (ישעיהו ס"ו, א'), "וְאֶת־מְקוֹם כַּפּוֹת רַגְלַי" (יחזקאל מ"ג, ז'); וְאָמְנָם כְּלֵי הַמִּשּׁוּשׁ הַמְּיֻחָסִים לוֹ יִתְעַלֶּה, בְּאָמְרוֹ: "יַד־ה'" (שמות ט', ג'), "בְּאֶצְבַּע אֱלֹקִים" (שמות ל"א, י"ח), "מַעֲשֵׂה אֶצְבְּעוֹתֶיךָ" (תהילים ח', ד') כוזה, "וַתָּשֶׁת עָלַי כַּפֶּכָה" (תהילים קל"ט, ה'), "וּזְרוֹעַ ה'" (ישעיהו נ"ג, א'), "יְמִינְךָ ה'" (שמות ט"ו, ו'); וְאָמְנָם כְּלֵי הַדִּבּוּר הַמְּיֻחָסִים לוֹ: "פִּי ה' דִּבֵּר" (ישעיהו א', כ'), "וְיִפְתַּח שְׂפָתָיו עִמָּךְ" (איוב י"א, ה'), "קוֹל ה' בַּכֹּחַ" (תהילים כ"ט, ד'), "וּלְשׁוֹנוֹ כְּאֵשׁ אֹכָלֶת" (ישעיהו ל', כ"ז); וְאָמְנָם כְּלֵי הַהַרְגָּשָׁה הַמְּיֻחָסִים לוֹ: "עֵינָיו יֶחֱזוּ עַפְעַפָּיו יִבְחֲנוּ" (תהילים י"א, ד'), "עֵינֵי ה' הֵמָּה מְשׁוֹטְטִים" (זכריה ד', י'), "הַטֵּה אֱלֹקַי אָזְנְךָ וּשְׁמָע" (דניאל ט', י"ח), "קְדַחְתֶּם בְּאַפִּי" (ירמיהו י"ז, ד').
>
> (רמב"ם, מורה הנבוכים, תרגום אבן תיבון, חלק א', פרק מ"ו)

Now, all the physical organs which you will find [attributed to God] in the writings of the prophets are either organs of locomotion, indicating life; or organs of sensation, indicating perception; or organs of touch, indicating action; or organs of speech, indicating the overflow of the intellects toward the prophets, as will be explained.

Now, the object of all these figurative indications is to establish for us that there is a living existence, the maker of all else, and is also conscious of all that He created. We shall explain, when we speak of the inadmissibility of the divine attributes, that all these various attributes convey exclusively one notion, namely, the essence of God, may He be exalted. For the sole object of this chapter is to explain in what sense these physical organs are attributed to Him, the most perfect Being, namely, that they are mere indications of the actions performed by these organs. Such actions, which are considered by us as perfections [since we need them to carry out our imperfections], are attributed to God, because we wish to express that He is the most perfect in all respects, as we remarked above in explaining the rabbinic phrase, "The Torah speaks in the language of man."

The organs of locomotion which are attributed to Him, may He be exalted, occur in verses such as: "My footstool" (Isaiah, 66:1); "the place of the soles of my feet" (Ezekiel, 43:7). Organs of touch are ascribed to Him, may He be exalted, in such instances as: "the hand of the Lord" (Exodus, 9:3); "with the finger of God" (Exodus, 31:18); "the work of Thy fingers" (Psalms, 8:4), "and Thou hast laid Thy hand upon me" (Psalms, 139:5); "the arm of the Lord" (Isaiah, 53:1); "Thy right hand, O Lord" (Exodus, 15:6). The organs of speech are attributed to him in such cases as the following: "The mouth of the Lord has spoken" (Isaiah, 1:20); "And He would open His lips against you" (Job, 11:5); "The voice of the Lord is mighty" (Psalms, 29:4); "And His tongue like devouring fire" (Isaiah, 30:27). Organs of sensation are attributed to him in the following instances: "His eyes

> behold, his eyelids try" (Psalms, 11:4); "The eyes of the Lord that run to and from" (Zechariah, 4:10); "Incline your ear unto me and hear" (Daniel, 9:18); "Thou hast kindled a fire in my nostril" (Jeremiah, 17:5).
>
> (Maimonides, *Guide for the Perplexed*, 1.46)

In this context, we can recognize different types of symbols: natural, conventional, iconic, and supernatural. The supernatural symbol is the transmutation of nothing into something through someone. Since the phenomenon or entity actually hides or obscures its foundation, we have a variety of symbols, such as the metaphorical one. Jesus compares the heavenly kingdom to a mustard seed, which, as such, does not exist in the transcendental realm, as its presence is limited to the sensible world and, therefore, is a metaphor for the intelligible universe.

From a metaphysical point of view, the cause is superior to the effect. However, if we approach the matter from a fundamentally logical perspective, we can conclude that the effect inherits the perfection of its cause, with that perfection being more accentuated in the cause than in the resulting effect. If we question which has a higher temperature, would it be the fire that heats the iron or the iron itself that the fire has heated? The answer to this question is quite obvious. Thus, if we consider that the transcendental reality is the fundamental cause of the tangible universe, we can infer that the superior reality is the generator of our perceptible platform. Through direct and intuitive perception, the visionary can understand the supersensible reality by forming a representation in their imagination, which can be proportional if the attribute in question has a presence in the perceptible world, or metaphorical if that quality is not found in the sensible universe. We observe perfections in this life, such as existence, consciousness, or bliss. And it is assumed that these perfections are much more superlative in transcendental reality. In this sense, there is a proportionality when the perfection exists both in the intelligible and sensible universes, as happens with existence, consciousness, or bliss, and there is a correlation between the two. What some philosophies call "participation."

Although Jesus is an incarnation in human form, his true nature is eternal, beyond time. Similarly, Lord Chaitanya Mahāprabhu is the universal consciousness, or God Himself, manifesting in the form of a devotee. In a certain sense, we are all reflections of this consciousness, as our true essence is eternal. The separation between beings like us and beings like Jesus or Lord Chaitanya happens at the level of consciousness: Jesus is a son of God, just like us, but with the distinction of being fully conscious of this fact. Lord Chaitanya is a personification of God, like each of us, but He is aware of it. Just as both the police officer and the drug detection dog are members of the police force, the main difference is that the officer fully understands this.

In a way, imagination resembles a mirror capable of reflecting the intelligible reality. Hegel would say that it is a mirror because, through speculation or the mirror, being knows itself, and through the sensible image, it can acquire something of its essence. Being knows itself through the being. Revelation consists of a giving in images and words. Our imagination must, therefore, serve as a lighthouse that gives meaning to the vast cosmos, not as a curtain behind which we hide.

When venturing into the religious path, it is essential to keep in mind that the mythical figures populating it are, in essence, entities of a symbolic nature. Although they are imbued with meaning, they provide cohesion and externalize deep aspects of the human condition while lacking objective, palpable existence in the physical realm. As long as we maintain this transcendent distinction, the divinities can be experienced in a transcendental way in our existence, providing us with invaluable support and assistance. However, if corporeality is ascribed to them and they are turned into "idols," the divinities become obstacles, leading us into a fictitious and unreal universe of alienation. It is imperative that tangible objective reality does not negate or annihilate the intrinsically subjective. Let us keep our inner cosmos vivid but without merging both dimensions.

Let us take, by way of illustration, the *Śiva-liṅga* from the Hindu worldview, embraced by a myriad of symbolisms, interpretations, and meanings. Within the mythology of India, the generative force inherent in this symbol is closely intertwined with Śiva, the transcendental divinity. The *liṅgam,* a word that in Sanskrit means "sign, symbol, or mark," represents an abstract or iconic image of Śiva, a primary deity in Shaivism. Śiva, whose name means "the auspicious one," symbolizes the purity and untouched innocence of our consciousness, the most refined aspect of our being that remains immaculate. This icon is commonly the central figure of worship in temples dedicated to Śiva. However, it can also be found in smaller shrines or natural forms that are considered divine manifestations in themselves. Traditionally, the *liṅgam* rests on a disc-shaped base known as the *yoni*, symbolizing the feminine principle, in contrast to the verticality of the *liṅgam* that represents the masculine principle. This ensemble symbolizes the union of the feminine and masculine aspects of the universe, and the ongoing process of creation and regeneration, reflecting the interconnection between the microcosm and the macrocosm.

The concept of *liṅgam* as a "sign" extends to its spiritual interpretation in ancient texts such as the *Śvetāśvatara Upanishad*, where it is stated that Śiva, the Supreme Lord, is beyond any *liṅgam*, understanding this to mean that He transcends any distinctive characteristic, including gender signs. This characteristic underscores the transcendental nature of Śiva, considered the supreme symbol of "formless Reality." In this context, the *liṅga* symbolizes the union of matter, or Prakṛti, with pure consciousness, or Puruṣa, emphasizing the conception of an ultimate reality that merges primordial essence with transcendental spirit.

For some, it embodies sexuality and the very matrix of vital energy, while for others, it symbolizes purity, freshness, and regeneration. In the *Liṅga Purana,* the primordial *Liṅga* is outlined as an ontological manifestation, stripped of sensory attributes such as smell, color, or taste. It represents the generative power and the conjunction of masculine and feminine principles in the engendering of creation. In the sacred Hindu tradition, the *liṅga* is intrinsically interwoven with the concept of the cosmic egg, an archetype that personifies cosmic totality and infinity itself. It is viewed as a mirror of absolute truth, an inexhaustible source of knowledge, and an emblem of the limitless.

This symbolism reflects a profound understanding of creation, offering humanity an object of veneration that, in turn, acts as a reminder that it is merely a symbol of the unmanifested consciousness that Śiva embodies. The question then arises: how to venerate this omnipresent, omnipotent, all-pervading divinity? The human mind needs a focal point to direct its prayers and offerings. That is why all the world's religious traditions designate an object or symbol to which prayers are directed, even those that renounce the worship of any physical form of divinity, such as in the Sikh tradition with its scriptures or in Islam with the Kaaba. Aware of the nature of the human mind, the ancient Vedic *ṛṣis* granted the freedom to worship the supreme divinity in any form deemed appropriate. Therefore, even a simple stone can serve to remind the faithful that it is only a symbol, representing the omnipresent consciousness that transcends all names and forms.

It is crucial to emphasize that the hermeneutics of the aforementioned symbols and enigmatic visions, unraveled in the context of meditation, embrace a profoundly intimate and subjective nature. The spectrum of experiences and understandings, inevitably unique, finds its roots in the spiritual, emotional, and cultural path that is inalienable to each being. In such a scenario, symbols and visions become primordial tools that enable a deeper exploration into the depths of individual consciousness, exploring the dark depths of the unconscious and accessing the inner and abyssal layers of the psyche. Through this introspective journey, one can aspire to a deeper apprehension and a fuller acceptance of one's own identity, translating into an increase in internal balance and harmony. The intrinsic symbolism of the multiple deities populating the Hindu pantheon resides in the mythical domain. In objective rigor, these entities lack palpable corporeality in our existential realm. Thus, the existence of mythological gods stands as a primarily subjective reality.

In human society, we are accustomed to allowing the objective to bury the subjective or to project an illusion onto the objective reality, rendering it ethereal, which is why Husserl insists that there is no *cogito* without *cogitatum*. To avoid falling into this error, we must see the parity between both components of the relationship. On one extreme stand the symbolic and conceptual dimensions, myth, and logos. On the other, philosophy and theology. Scientific conceptualization persists in denying subjective realities, while theology obstinately opposes science. Here lies the paradox, as it is known in the West. Historical discipline, in its essence, faces inherent limitations in capturing and recording truth in all its fullness. Historiography primarily focuses on the accumulation and scrutiny of objective facts, neglecting aspects of deeper and symbolic nature.

In the context of India, two dissimilar epistemological mechanisms emerge: the first, known as history, is dedicated to the meticulous documentation of events that occurred in time; in contrast, the second, called *purāṇa*, or "mythology," undertakes the titanic task of recording and perpetuating the primordial Truth. The latter approach, distant from orthodox historiography, adopts a more encompassing and integrative perspective, transcending the limits of objectivity and venturing into the realm of the fundamental and timeless. Here, truth is more than a chain of events; it manifests as universal principles and laws that capture the essence of existence. In this way, the division between history and *purāṇa* illustrates the tension between objectuality and subjectuality, material reality versus the immaterial, and the contrast between the transient and the eternal. This tension escapes any resolution and, therefore, endures. It emphasizes the paradox inherent in humanity's search for Truth.

It is of utmost importance to underline that in the Indian subcontinent, the practice of recording conventional narratives about revered spiritual figures such as Buddha, Mahavira, or Kṛṣṇa has not been embraced. This decision stems from the desire to preserve the pristine depth of their teachings, thus avoiding their distortion by reducing them to mere historical events within the narrow human perception. These personifications embody immeasurable wisdom and beauty, transcending the confines of collective consciousness. Reducing them to the realm of nebulous unconsciousness would constitute a transcendental loss for humanity. The East, wisely, has chosen not to document historical narratives about masters, sages, and enlightened saints. Instead, it has shaped myths that encapsulate their sublime essence and eternal legacy.

A myth stands as a symbolic narrative that points to an elusive truth that is nonexistent only in a manner that does not provide precise information about it. It is like a finger that, in silence, points to the moon. Eastern deities do not embody historical stories or tangible individuals. They are sacred idols that evoke meditative states and shape inner elements, such as inner serenity. They represent the visible of the invisible, the palpable of the intangible, and the objective manifestations of the subjective. They are the iconophanic expressions of the enigmatic and the aniconic founding phenomena of a groundless foundation, *Abgrund*.

Therefore, the East ventures into a divergent epistemological paradigm, one that transcends conventional objectivity and embraces a deeper and more holistic dimension of reality. When contemplating the deities in deep silence, entering a receptive state, we are astonished by the effects that emerge in our internal landscape, generating effects that surprise us. Something in the statue, in its objective artistic manifestation, resonates with our inner disposition. By presenting ourselves before the statues of Buddha, Śiva, or Kṛṣṇa, not as active agents but as silent witnesses, we can appreciate their symbolic magnitude. Then, the authentic meaning of mythology can be unraveled. Appreciating facts or truths lies in the perspective from which we observe them. We look at our surroundings, glimpsing a sequence of ordinary events. However, only a meditative gaze grants us the possibility of delving into the reality of transcendental events, into a reality beyond the empirical and measurable. Only eyes imbued with genuine love can perceive the true meaning of a grain of sand or a galaxy.

We observe and see a botanical flower composed of sepals, petals, androecium, and gynoecium. However, meditative eyes are needed to apprehend the reality of a flower as a smile emanating from the very earth. While one aspect of the flower is physical, its reality far exceeds that realm. Only when we perceive a flower as a manifestation of the divine will we enter into communion with the ultimate Truth. Reality can only be apprehended through a meditative vision that transports us beyond empirical and mundane limitations. From an ordinary perspective, existence is woven with mere tasteless events, lifeless facts, disconnected occurrences, fortuitous and accidental episodes. When contemplating reality with meditative eyes, everything harmonizes, and we glimpse its genuine meaning. Then, we realize that living at the boundaries of events, occurrences, incidents, or historical episodes is an existence devoid of meaning and transcendence.

The vastness and omnipotence of human imagination would warn us of the inevitable possibility of being seduced by our own convictions. However, in the absence of such precious discernment, we risk succumbing to the insidious attraction of our own fantasy, embracing purely imaginary constructions as tangible realities. It is worth stressing, insistently, that while our imagination can be a formidable tool, it should not become a crutch urging us to escape from harsh reality. It is of vital importance that we firmly commit to resisting the seduction of turning imagination into an architect of parallel universes, a captivating refuge designed to evade the challenges that saturate our daily existence. Instead, I would suggest that we use our imagination to deepen our connection with reality, adopting it as a resource to decipher and appreciate the magnitude of the world around us. The Retroprogressive Path, in its wisdom, preserves the objective in its original state, allowing the subjective, the symbolic, and the mythical to persist in their essence. Let us maintain a perfect balance between the two, without falling into confusion, so that we preserve ourselves as religious beings but equally as clear-minded and healthy minds.

Chapter 14

The gates of myth toward the inexplicable

Myth, metaphor, and legend, entangled in the dense fabric of narrative and the imaginative sphere, are often confused due to their inherent connection. However, each holds a particular connotation and application. The myth, wrapped in its tale, seeks to unravel the intricacies of phenomena and events through the presence of transcendent or divine elements. Its dissemination, mostly oral in nature, stands as an instrument of transmission of values, social norms, and beliefs rooted in a specific culture. The metaphor, a rhetorical figure of distinguished lineage, establishes links of similarity between two entities, even if they do not literally resemble each other. Its purpose lies in figuratively describing something or someone, generating more vivid mental images or those imbued with a poetic imprint. Finally, the legend stands as a narrative grounded in historical or real elements, which has evolved over time by incorporating imaginative and fantastic elements. It is often used as a vehicle to transmit values and morals, though it can also serve as a source of entertainment. Thus, while the myth unveils divine events, the metaphor poetically connects elements, and the legend amplifies historical events.

The cardinal attribute that distinguishes the human species lies in its clear aptitude to challenge the corporeal confines and delve into the metaphysical dimension. In his work *Metaphysics*, Aristotle posits a fundamental premise: "All men, by nature, desire to know."[70] This idea, also shared by Plato, establishes the desire for knowledge as an innate inclination in human beings. Both philosophers conceive this yearning for understanding as the foundation of philosophy. This desire is stimulated by a sense of wonder and curiosity in the face of natural phenomena, driving humans to investigate and understand the world around them. Achieving such a feat requires the establishment of a renewed *ethos*, an ethical and moral framework that enables the individual to access the essence of their existence. Therefore, a range of worldviews emerges, which, through symbolic structures, metamorphose into mythologies and religious creeds, granting humanity the fortune of a reunion with itself and the attainment of a state of sublimity. Science empowers us to dominate nature but does not provide life meaning. In contrast, the myth removes that power and returns it to Being, creating the abode that allows us to dwell in sublimity.

Ernst Cassirer, a distinguished philosopher of the German tradition, marked a milestone in thought with his masterpiece *Philosophical Anthropology*, which offers a sophisticated analysis of the human condition and its position within the cosmic framework. The text pays special attention to aspects such as human nature, the culture that envelops us, linguistics, and freedom, which he understands as pieces of a puzzle. In this study, Cassirer particularly ventures into the waters of mythology and religion, finding similarities and connections but also significant differences regarding their approaches, functions, forms of practice, and transmission over time. Cassirer begins by defining mythology as an attempt to explain the uncontrollable, while religion seeks a connection with the divine. Therefore, according to Cassirer, mythology focuses on the study and explanation of myths, which vary widely depending on their origin, such as the Greeks and Romans, constituting a vast collection of tales involving supernatural beings, with the purpose of providing meaning to various aspects of the world. On the other hand, he also

70. Aristotle, *Metaphysics*, Book A, in vol. 1, ed. and trans. W. D. Ross (Oxford: Clarendon Press, 1924), 980a21.

defines religion as a set of beliefs in deities, mostly honored through prayer, but which becomes a construct of interpretation aimed at unraveling the essence of the universe and the foundation of reality.

One notable difference between religion and mythology is that, while in religions, it is common to find followers who profess faith in one or more specific gods, in mythology, the presence of followers or believers is not as deeply rooted. As a result, the myth is always subject to the interpretation of each individual, while religion manifests as a collective phenomenon, which includes rituals where the faithful gather to live their relationship with the god they worship.

Despite these differences, there is also a close interrelationship between mythology and religion, which lies in their implication of trust and attribution of power to non-terrestrial entities, that is, to deities. This has led some scholars to even argue that mythology can be considered a form of religion since in the myths, the characters believe in and have faith in immortal deities to whom they grant absolute power.

To now delve into the matter of myth and religion, as well as their relevance, we must first address certain terms and issues that will allow us to contextualize them as phenomena in our study. Let us begin, then, by saying that, according to all that has been argued in these chapters, the human being has revealed itself, in its nature as a self-determined entity, as a being confronted with a perception of disconnection from the natural environment, marked by a feeling of detachment from its peers and by internal dissonance with its essence, leading it to live in a hiatus regarding the supramaterial. It is in this context that we must understand the work of myth and religion as bearers of the conception of the divine, that is, of a transcendental entity devoid of discernible attributes that persist and sustain itself solely in its symbolic codification. As we will see in the following paragraphs, neither religion nor myth could be what they are without the symbolic.

With intellectual delight, one could meticulously approach the term *exist*, whose etymological roots are firmly anchored in the Latin verb *existere*, a result of the amalgamation of *ex*, which symbolizes "the notion of coming out or being outside," and *sistere*, which translates as "to maintain an upright posture." In the days of ancient Rome, the word *existere* was invoked to characterize the irruption or revelation of something in the sphere of the phenomenal, implying a corporeal and evident manifestation. Over time, *existere* acquired a nuance that referred to the presence and reality of human beings, that is, to their existence in the world. Therefore, the manifestation of God outside of His unmanifest state is realized exclusively through His symbolism. Symbols are masks of God. In Kantian terms, they are the phenomenon of the noumenon since all religions are phenomenal as they are an expression of divinity, but they are not divinity. As the *Śrīmad-bhāgavatam* states:

मायाजवनिकाच्छन्नमज्ञाधोक्षजमव्ययम् ।
न लक्ष्यसे मूढदृशा नटो नाट्यधरो यथा ॥

māyā-javanikācchannam
ajñādhokṣajam avyayam
na laksyase mūḍha-dṛśā
naṭo nātyadharo yathā

> Being beyond the range of limited sense perception, You are the eternally irreproachable factor covered by the curtain of deluding energy. You are invisible to the foolish observer, exactly as an actor dressed as a player is not recognized.
> (*Śrīmad-bhāgavatam*, 1.8.19)

Understood in this way, and recalling what Cassirer said earlier, religion is established as such through its social, collective dimension, in which a human being, uprooted from nature and themselves, seeks and sees in the symbolic as a mask of the divine, the essence of their reality and the universe. The issue of collectivity is important for understanding the significance of religion and the divine in all societies.

Human collectivities and communities, consciously or unconsciously, focus their emotions and attention on certain interests. In this sense, the term *egregor* represents the unified thought of a community or collectivity that, through an image, provides a historical and unifying sense to the life of that group. An *egregor* is a concentration of energy that resides in the astral plane and is linked to a particular concept, archetype, emotion, or mode of thinking. There are *egregors* composed of positive energies and negative *egregors* associated with unhelpful and unfavorable emotions. The *egregor* is the psychic counterpart of a human collective. When a considerable number of individuals focus their attention on the same issue with similar intensity, a collective energy is generated. We are all familiar with this revitalizing effect, which we experience when collaborating on an exciting project or during a vibrant moment. The concentration of activities blends the intentions of each participant into a collective consciousness that seems to propel the whole. Therefore, a series of ordered processes develops among the participants beyond individual perception. The specific intentions of a collective provide the particular characteristics to the entity known as an *egregor*, while emotions provide the energy. Attention gives direction and form, while emotion supplies the material. The word *egregor*, which some interpret as a "collective entity," is actually a misinterpretation of the Greek term *egrégoros* (ἐγρήγορος), which simply means "watchful."

It is true that any collective can be seen as possessing a subtle force formed by the contributions of all its past and present members. This power is, therefore, more considerable and can generate stronger effects as the older the group is and the larger the number of individuals that comprise it. The power and influence of an *egregor* are proportional to the number of human beings who forge and maintain it through their attention and emotions. Every *egregor* is an intelligent entity capable of learning, developing, and evolving, and it resists any threat against its existence or the existence of its creators, who, whenever invoked, will come to the aid of the one who nourishes them with emotion, attention, and intention. The unmanifested and intangible nature, along with its concrete and tangible power, give this energetic entity a sacred dimension.

There are several occult schools and esoteric traditions in which the *egregor* occupies a central place in their rituals. The pioneers who explored its properties were the Masonic lodges, united by their enigmatic codes and initiations. Different occult schools also use the *egregor* as a prophetic tool, while shamanism, for its part, creates a way to access cosmic energy through trance and group ceremonies.

Another important concept is that of *tulpa*, which refers to an entity created through mental faculties. In the various traditions of Western occultism, this notion is evoked to characterize what could be conceived as an imaginary figure but endowed with its own will, reasoning, and vision, possessing a certain autonomy. Although in the West, many proponents of mysticism believe the term *tulpa* comes from Buddhism, the truth is that it is an elaboration of Theosophy that merges various Buddhist concepts. Buddhist scholars combined the Buddhist concept of emanation *tulku* with a similar Theosophical concept, giving rise to the word *tulpa*, which supposedly means "ghost that emanates." However, it is worth noting that in the Tibetan language, *tulpa* does not have representation; the term *sprul-pa* is used instead, which describes a malevolent entity created by a magician that materializes by inhabiting a living being. Although there are events similar to the modern definition of tulpa in Buddhism, they are not exactly the same. An example might be the miracle of Shravasti, where it is said that the historical Buddha multiplied his form to demonstrate the truth of his *dharma pratītyasamutpāda*. However, it is important to clarify that in Buddhism, it is believed that the Buddha Shakyamuni could perform such miracles because of his state of enlightenment. The supernatural phenomena, or *iddhi* in Pali, attributed to the Buddha during his earthly journey are manifestations of a heightened and full consciousness.

The concepts we have just presented, belonging to different traditions and cultures, allow us to show what we had previously advanced—that the divine manifests itself through the symbols and myths to human beings. These symbolic and mythical forms act as a bridge that connects the human with the divine, the apparent with the real, since the human being places their faith and devotion in the symbol. The manifestation of the unmanifested divinity occurs exclusively through symbology. The symbol, like a magnifying glass concentrating scattered sunlight to achieve combustion, has the ability to reunify and strengthen.

Furthermore, the symbol facilitates the convergence of beliefs, convictions, creeds, and superstitions, which, once amalgamated, are directed toward the symbol as the object of faith. Likewise, the symbol fosters the integration of scattered feelings and emotions, which, when unified, can be consciously directed toward the symbol as an act of devotion, as we have seen with the concepts of *egregor* and *tulpa*. The power attributed to figures such as Moses, Jesus, Muhammad, Buddha, Shankara, or Lord Chaitanya is not of a personal nature but instead possesses a symbolic dimension. The power of the master or guru is more related to the symbol than to the individual. To be a symbol means to be an image endowed with profound meaning. The symbol can take the form of Mount Sinai, and this symbolic image will be imbued with meanings such as freedom, liberation, love, peace, future, hope, unity, and camaraderie. Whenever the community evokes Mount Sinai, it immerses itself in these meanings. While each individual may interpret Mount Sinai personally, all will experience brotherhood in relation to that symbol. My personal interpretation, or yours, of the resurrection of Jesus, as well as our perspectives on the lives of Mahavira, Buddha, Muhammad, or Chaitanya, are completely irrelevant. What matters is that we safeguard ourselves, come together, and strengthen ourselves through the symbol that represents God.

In the vast chronology of history, some beings have held the status of human emblems. The array of illustrations is overwhelming, embodied by great men, social crusaders, historical luminaries, or beings invested with a superior aura, whose actions and existence have forged a place in the pantheon of symbolism associated with certain values, ideals, or crusades. Mahatma Gandhi stands as an emblematic case, metamorphosing into a bulwark of peaceful resistance in the pursuit of liberation and justice in India, and his designation and iconography have resonated globally in the representation of such principles. Likewise, individuals such as Martin Luther King Jr., Nelson Mandela, Che Guevara, and others have been elevated to symbolic immortality in the realm of specific political and social struggles. It is interesting that myth, in these cases of the political and social sphere, can never be alive; rather, it becomes myth after death, or even the way in which they died is what made them myths.

This metamorphosis of an individual into a symbol occurs when their existence and actions are imbued with connotations of magnitude and transcendence that surpass their mere entity and temporal era—that is, when their image or name embodies something that goes beyond their intrinsic personality and their own historical individuality. It is conceived as an incontrovertible certainty that illuminated figures have been carved in time as icons; their lives and doctrines, and the legacies they perpetuated, have attained a depth and relevance that go beyond being mere characters in a page of history. In this regard, the process of symbolization rests on the premise of recognizing and attributing symbolic value to a being. This happens when the actions and experiences of that being acquire a relevance that transcends the merely factual. The apprehension of a deeper and more meaningful sense in their legacy resonates in the beliefs, aspirations, and longings of future generations. Through imparting knowledge and the lived example, the enlightened beings have managed to inspire and transcend the space-time limitations of their era. In their legacy, we find a treasure of values that speak to us, regardless of where we are from or what language we speak. Something amazing happens when we talk about love and kindness, insight, and spiritual inquiry. Like waves in an infinite ocean, these words move through time, and in the process, they help shape how we think about life, what is right, and what is beyond the mundane.

More than simple names, Jesus, Buddha, and Muhammad are symbols, but this does not mean an indiscriminate cult or a monolithic adoption of their doctrines. Instead, they serve as maps, filled with routes and paths we can take in our own search for understanding and growth. Their emblematic quality generates a spectrum of perspectives and a diversity of appropriations among different collectives and sacred traditions. Every human being can glimpse in them a pattern for their own spiritual and moral self-discovery, adjusting and recontextualizing their legacy according to their own context and personal background. The metamorphosis of a human being into a symbol occurs when their life trajectory and acts become an entity of such transcendence that it surpasses their own historical individuality. In other words, when their image and name embody something of a magnitude greater than themselves, their teachings and legacies resonate within humanity, acquiring an archetypal representativeness of universal values essential to the human condition. Symbolization encompasses a diverse range of interpretations and appropriations, sharpening insight and spiritual flourishing in different temporal and cultural frameworks.

This would be the iconic case of Jesus of Nazareth, whose existence and precepts have deeply impacted the psyche of countless souls, rising as a symbol of charity, compassion, and renewal.

In a parallel context, Buddha emerges as the personification of spiritual enlightenment and the emancipation from suffering in Buddhism, while the life and teachings of Muhammad, the Islamic prophet and forerunner, stand as a venerable beacon for multitudes of Muslim communities. It is pertinent to note that the halo of prominence and magnetism surrounding these prophetic figures in the journey of my being is not based on scientific discoveries or archaeological evidence, nor is it anchored in ancient relics, sacred writings, or manuscripts.

The symbolic power lies in them as transcendent archetypes of existence, the unconscious, and the most exquisite manifestation of human potential. They personify the supreme values of life, such as love, compassion, and bliss. Jesus did not penetrate the depths of the soul because of the Christian narrative. Christ is not part of our collective unconscious because he existed but because he exists as an archetype for all of humanity.

Just as the scientific corpus enables access to knowledge, technique, controlled manipulation of objects, and machination mastery, so too can the symbol provide meaning to existence. In its attempt to engulf human beings in ignorance of their own self, science leads them inexorably toward the conquest of objects and even toward their own objectification, turning them into a mere factual object, both physiologically and psychologically. Technique and machination, in turn, pull us away from our innermost essence, plunging us into a desperate search for control and possession, where what one possesses is overvalued at the expense of what one is.

Likewise, the transformation of the symbol into concept, myth into philosophy, and religion into theology turns its intrinsic evocative power into a technical domain, replacing its capacity to articulate differences with a monogamous conceptuality. When this happens, it is the concept that absorbs the symbol and dominates it. While the symbol itself holds power in the symbolic realm, in the conceptual domain, the subject controls the symbol and shapes it according to their own image and likeness. To some extent, this would be the superior stage of the domination of technique that Heidegger denounces.

This metamorphosis disconnects human beings from their reality, plunging them into the inherent emptiness of the concept, subjugated to the control of others, manipulated by nature, and dominated by God. Just as human beings surrender to the God of religion, the God of theology becomes a God subjected to the yoke of the concept. For there is always more we do not know about God than what we do know. The God of theology will always be a partialized God. Each theological deity rises as an idol subjugated to human dominion, inert in the face of the possibility of transcending conceptual barriers. By crystallizing divine revelation within a conceptual framework, it metamorphoses into a law that constrains the behavior of God itself. With this conceptualization, the divine being is locked within a rigorously determined structure, barred from any expression beyond the predetermined limits.

From this, specific theological structures emerge that vary according to different cultures. It is difficult for a devout follower of Kṛṣṇa to accept that the Supreme Personality of God would impose edicts on the people of Israel. Similarly, an Orthodox Jew cannot conceive of the "God of hosts" dancing among humble shepherdesses and cattle. Jews await the arrival of the Messiah, while Christians await the second coming of Jesus. An Orthodox Jew would identify the Messiah through his scholarship in the corners of the *Talmud,* an aspect that a Christian could not accept. In his second coming, a Christian could not conceive of Jesus engaging in meditation beneath a tree, similar to Buddha, or dancing in the streets like Lord Chaitanya. Orthodox Jews could not reconcile the acceptance of a Messiah who would captivate the audience through the rapture. God cannot, by virtue of the concept, transcend the boundaries that have been erected and constrain Him. As a result, a transcendental shift is observed in the conception of God: His role evolves from being perceived as the supreme ruler of the cosmos to an entity that, for the first time, finds itself in a position subordinate to human beings. This profound yet clear shift, resulting from the conceptualization of the symbol, the "philosophization" of the myth, and ultimately the "theologization" of religion, recalibrates our understanding of the relationship between divinity and humanity:

> כִּי לַה' הַמְּלוּכָה וּמֹשֵׁל בַּגּוֹיִם:
>
> (תהלים כ"ב, כ"ט)
>
> For the kingship is the Lord's, and He rules over the nations.
>
> (Psalms, 22:29)

On the religious path, we are compelled to abandon the use of veridical and deceitful language as it is conceived in the scientific sphere. Following the theory of correspondence, outlined by prominent thinkers such as Aristotle, Thomas Aquinas, and, more recently, Bertrand Russell, a statement achieves the status of truth when it meticulously aligns with objective reality. In other words, from a scientific perspective, truth lies in the precise concordance between verbal discourse and the object to which it refers. However, since God cannot be reduced to the status of a mere object, these principles are inapplicable to His transcendent Being.

The efficacy of the symbol, for its part, lies in its ability to provide strength and integration. If the symbol connects us with love, respect, compassion, devotion, meaning, surrender, and joy, it stands as something sacred, detached from the confines of scientific perspective. A life clinging to the conceptual domain and distanced from the realm of myth unfolds without experiencing the inherent sacredness, for in the conceptual domain, the transcendent is oppressed by the realm of technical arts exercised by human beings. Submerged in the jaws of a conceptual existence, humans become trapped by their own machinations and slaves to their own control. On the other hand, the symbol operates as an emancipatory agent by endowing the human being with a symbolism capable of transcending the limits of their limited conceptualization. A life oriented toward the concept and distant from myth is lived without experiencing the sacred, for in the conceptual realm, the transcendent is subjected to the domain of human technique. In its intrinsic essence, the ineffable symbol exceeds the ontological limitations of language and human understanding, standing as an object of a qualitative nature that accommodates the inexplicable and the ambiguous. The symbol is the witness to the attribute-less, which encompasses a dimension of inherent unknowability. As a manifest and perceptible entity, the symbol embodies the capacity to evoke the absent and the imperceptible and, in a paradoxical simultaneity, makes the ineffable speak. In this sense, the symbol constitutes the iconophanic expression of an aniconic mystery, the visual testimony of a sphere of the enigma that resists any form of an icon or visual representation.

The term *iconophanic*, rooted in the Greek word εικονοφάνεια (*eikonofaneia*), refers to the aversion to religious images and their veneration. The historical foundations of its use are situated in the Byzantine era, where the well-known iconoclastic controversy emerged; essentially, a confrontation that proscribed the use of graphic representations with religious connotations in cultic practices. On the other hand, the term aniconic refers to those objects or phenomena that lack visual representation or oppose it through images. Originating in the Greek *άνικονος* (*anikonos*), the term *aniconic* denotes what is devoid of images. Therefore, the symbol is configured as the visual epitome of what has been rendered invisible, the perceptible incarnation of what transcends sensory experience, thereby perpetuating the paradox of its own existence. Thus, the symbol consists of the visual expression of the invisible, the sensible manifestation of what transcends sensory experience.

In the heart of Hellenic cosmogony, Dionysus revered as one of the august Olympian gods, occupies a place of privilege, displaying his divinity in the realm of fertility and intoxicating nectar. He is the inducer of ritual mania and ecstasy, a model of creative impulse that enlightens both agricultural fields and theatrical stages. His lineage connects him to Zeus and Semele, making him the grandson of Harmony and great-grandson of the gods Aphrodite and Ares. However, other mythological variants suggest his origin as the offspring of Zeus and Persephone. Carrying his royal banner, the Epiphany is erected in his honor, and this feast is the privileged stage where masks acquire a leading role in the dramatic representations that intertwine with the festivity. The once-god consecrated to theater infused life into tragedies and comedies during the festivity, granting characters a facial garment in the form of masks. Furthermore, these masks held a ritualistic background within the solemnity of the Epiphany, as these artifacts were believed to possess a sort of magical spell that allowed actors to make direct contact with the divine Dionysus, transforming into his earthly avatars. By virtue of this conception, the masks were erected as sacred objects, endowed with the gift of respect and carrying a transcendental meaning in the religious ceremonies that adorned the celebration.

Likewise, during the joyous festival of *Purim*, the Jewish people dress up and wear masks that enrich the celebration. One must delve into its origin to understand the intimate connection between the masks and *Purim*. The reading of the *Megilat Esther* recited during this festivity, evokes the symbolism of the masks, for Queen Esther is the name of the heroine in the story, a word derived from the Hebrew verb *lehastir*, which means "to conceal or to hide." Before entering the palace, her name was Hadassah, which means "star" in Hebrew, but she was compelled to veil her Jewish identity. In Jewish teachings, Esther is known as *Hester Panim*, which carries the idea of "facial concealment." It is noteworthy that the word *panim* can also be translated as "inner" (*pnim*), suggesting that by masking her face, God covers her inner essence to manifest in her external and superficial aspect.

אֶסְתֵּר מִן הַתּוֹרָה מִנַּיִן? "וְאָנֹכִי הַסְתֵּר הַסְתֵּר אַסְתִּיר" (דברים ל"א, י"ח)
(תלמוד בבלי, מסכת חולין, קל"ט, ב')

Where Esther [can be found] in the Torah? "And I will surely hide [*haster astir*] My face" (Deuteronomy, 31:17–18).
(*Talmud Bavli*, "*Chullin*," 139b)

Both in the Epiphany and in Purim, a suggestion proposes the possibility that the divine, in its magnificence, may choose to manifest itself in a way accessible to humanity through an image. This is how the Supreme Being decides to reveal itself to mortals by enveloping itself in a mask and adopting the names of Adonai, Jehovah, Father, Allah, Kṛṣṇa, Govinda, Śiva, Brahman, Shangdi, Shen, Zhù, Bhagavān, Īśvara, Akal Purakh, Aten, and Mitra, among others.

From a mythological perspective, Judaism presents itself as a coherent and continuous chronicle passed down through generations. These narratives are a compendium of the feats and experiences of the Hebrew people. At the core of these stories, we find key episodes such as the appearance of the God worshiped by Abraham, Isaac, and Jacob. Furthermore, the liberation of the people from servitude in Egypt, their passage through the Red Sea, and the divine revelation on Mount Sinai are documented. The outcome culminates with the arrival of the Hebrew people to the land that was promised to them. All of this forms a rich and multifaceted historical plot. For each Jew, this Hebrew myth takes on a profound significance.

However, it is essential to emphasize that while Jacob, Mount Sinai, and the Red Sea have substantial and symbolic relevance for Jews, they hold no significance for cultures such as Korean, Thai, or Congolese. For the Jewish people, what stands as a sacred mountain for a member of the Mapuche ethnic group holds no special connotation. This discernment highlights the contextual nature of myths and their meaning. Due to its history, beliefs, and collective experiences, each culture develops a unique mythology that resonates deeply within its identity. At the center of a particular community, myths emerge as entities charged with symbolic power, embedding themselves in the traditional legacy and shaping their understanding of the cosmos.

Therefore, it becomes indisputable that the significance inherent in these myths does not boast of universality or objectivity but is part of the cultural perspective and the subjective perceptions of the individual and their environment. Hence, certain precepts that might be elevated to the pantheon of the sacred by some appear as mere trivialities to others. It is crucial to recognize that cultural diversity and the multiplicity of perspectives call us to understand and honor the different ways in which the world and myths are conceived in various communities and traditions. In this sense, Judaism, similar to any mythological system, displays an opulent symbolic endowment that provides meaning and cohesion to Hebrew identity. Symbols do not exist because there is a Jewish people; there is a Jewish people because symbols exist.

However, when the human being attempts to appropriate or control this image, the divine becomes veiled, leaving only its powerful resonance behind. This resonance, emanating from the hiddenness of the divine, arises as a result of manipulation and technique. By tuning into this resonance, the human being establishes an authentic connection with life and comes to understand, as well as their relationship with Being itself. Although Being remains reluctant to technology, it does not withdraw entirely; but manifests as an ontological presence in the world through its captivating resonance. However, when the symbol metamorphoses into a concept, its interpretation is restricted to a single perspective. One who dares to interpret it divergently will be labeled as deceitful, false, erroneous, idolatrous, or heretical. Exclusive interpretation becomes the only truth, raising its banner as an unshakable dogma. When the symbol is conceptualized, it is no longer evaluated for its intrinsic qualities but by its criterion of truth or falsity.

Unlike the various theological disciplines that proclaim themselves as liberating and redeeming for the human being, the Retroprogressive Path stands as a paradigm that seeks to emancipate God from the yokes imposed by metaphysics and concept, advocating for the propagation of a symbolic God in which the human being finds an inexhaustible source of hope and meaning.

Chapter 15

The influence of concept on spirituality

As we have seen earlier, unlike the concept, which manifests its power in the political, social, economic, and philosophical spheres, symbolic power is of a psychological and spiritual nature. That said, the symbol can, however, also acquire a conceptual character when its diversity of meanings is conceptualized. In this process, the symbol transforms into a concept that replaces the original image of the thing, thereby relinquishing its significant richness in favor of conceptual structuring. By undergoing this metamorphosis, the symbol broadens its understanding but limits its scope; it gains truthfulness but sacrifices its universality by becoming immersed in the play of truth and falsehood.

This conceptualization of the symbol is a process that turns its polysemic meaning into a univocal one. As a result, and as we have already noted, the symbol loses its significant richness, obtaining a closed and impoverished conceptual structure. Although, upon conceptualizing it, the symbol acquires a clearer and deeper understanding, this conceptualization submerges it in a duality of truth-falsehood that restricts its reach. By replacing the image, the concept weakens its power and vitality, as it imposes limitations and restricts its potential, resulting in an exchange that Paul Ricoeur calls "the living metaphor," in which the symbol is exchanged for the death of the idea.

To allow a thing to remain alive, we must see it in its context rather than considering it in isolation. This is of particular relevance when thinking about the human being. Let us suppose we are facing Peter and Paul, whom we wish to know, and with that purpose, we define the first as a rational and political animal. We then also define Paul as a rational and political animal. If this definition applies to both, it will mean that there are one or more essential qualities that belong to both. That is, Peter's substantial essence is exactly the same as that of Paul. In that case, studying either of them or anyone else would be completely irrelevant if the knowledge I gain from them is formal knowledge in which their individuality and history hold no meaning. If both definitions are exactly the same, it would make no sense to talk about Peter or Paul. Similarly, if we study the formal similarities between A and B, we will not truly know A or B, but rather a third entity that is the similarity between the two. This means that, to know A or B, we must know what is proper to each one. Instead of limiting ourselves to the similarities between them, we must see the differences. In this sense, and as Aristotle rightly points out, the concept only allows us to know the similarity since "art is born when from many experimental observations a universal notion arises about similar cases" (*Alpha of Metaphysics,* Chapter 1); that is, from many particular knowledges, a universal idea arises through similarity. It is precisely this similarity that gives rise to the conceptualization of the thing and, with it, to its very death, as that similarity, that conceptualization, separates the thing from its concrete materiality, emptying it of its most inherent meaning or truth.

Similarly, if I define a human being as a rational and political animal but exclude their biography, history, talents, and character, I will not be able to know them beyond the mental image I may create of their formal dimension. In this case, I will not know the person, and I will simply be relating to the mental image I have created of them. By likening the thing, what conceptualization does is formalize it, demarcate it, and outline its boundaries while renouncing its being, which is what makes it truly what it is. Duns Scotus opposed analogy, that is, similarity, in support of univocity or *hecceity*. In short, it is only in the symbol that it is possible to know what is properly a reality in its unity, since the unity that the concept seeks is logical, whereas reality is ontological. That is why we say that the symbol is not an idea but pure reality. When Heidegger introduces the term *Dasein*, that is, "being-there," he never posits a being separate from the "there," but precisely the opposite, as being is, *per se*, being-there. What Heidegger is saying is that it is not possible to think of being outside of the there of being. To think of being is to think of being-there as its only mode of being, which suggests a thinking liberated from conceptualization.

As we have seen earlier, the word *symbol* means "to unite or to reconcile." Life is related to union, while death is associated with fracture, division, and duality. In short, the rival of *sim-bolon* is *di-bolon*, a term meaning "to disunite, separate, or divide," which we usually translate as "devil." By virtue of this etymology, it follows that while philosophy kills, religion grants life because it unites and integrates. The symbol seeks integration and restores religious unity, while the devil is concerned with separation, division, fracture, and fragmentation.

Myth and religion are symbolic, while philosophy and science are conceptual. Through the symbol and myth, religion unites what is fractured. Through the concept, however, philosophy and science fracture, divide, or separate, extracting the concrete reality of the thing. Symbolism consists precisely in allowing the thing to be what it is, in its own being, without being mentalized or conceptualized, but integrated with its own existence, life, and individuation.

In contrast, conceptualization, in its tangled development, engenders the blasphemy of idolatry, where the word *idol* emerged from the dark abyss of *idōlum* and *eidōlon* in Latin and Greek, connoting an "image" or "representation." Initially, *eidōlon* (idol) was used to refer to images or statues of deities venerated in the ancient polytheistic religions. The Greek *eidōlon*, however, is also the origin of the verb *eido* (εἴδω), which whispers "I saw," from which the word *idea* has evolved, expressing "form, appearance, aspect, or mental image." While "idol" refers to a physical image, *idea* refers to a conceptual image; both terms share the grim sense of representation, whether physical or mental. Idolatry has been unanimously repudiated by institutional faith based on the interpretations of certain passages from the scriptures:

אַל־תִּפְנוּ אֶל־הָאֱלִילִם וֵאלֹהֵי מַסֵּכָה לֹא תַעֲשׂוּ לָכֶם אֲנִי ה' אֱלֹהֵיכֶם:
(ויקרא י"ט, ד')

> Do not turn to idols, neither make for yourselves molten gods, I am the Lord, your God.
>
> (Leviticus, 19:4)

Nevertheless, it is essential to highlight the existence of synagogues adorned with exquisite Torah scrolls, safeguarded in the epicenter of the synagogue within a sacred ark called in Hebrew an *aron hakodesh*. According to Ashkenazi tradition, the Torah scroll is wrapped in a refined cloth called *vimpel.* On the other hand, in Sephardic tradition, it is placed in a vertical chest with a pointed silhouette called *tik*. For their part, Christian churches are adorned with sculpted representations of saints, the Virgin Mary, and Jesus. This issue has been a source of debate within the context of the early church, as a large number of Christians, known as "iconoclasts," believed that any visual representation was a form of idolatry. We read:

> Nevertheless, already in the Old Testament, God ordained or permitted the making of images that pointed symbolically toward salvation by the incarnate Word: so it was with the bronze serpent, the ark of the covenant, and the cherubim.[71]

As mentioned, the Second Ecumenical Council of Nicaea (787) justified the veneration of icons of Christ, but also of the Mother of God, the angels, and all the saints. By becoming incarnate, the Son of God introduced a new "economy of images" (CCC 2131). Since then, the teachings of the Catholic Church have been:

> The Christian veneration of images is not contrary to the first commandment which proscribes idols. Indeed, "the

71. Catechism of the Catholic Church, 2nd ed. (Vatican City: Libreria Editrice Vaticana, 1997), 516 (§2130).

> honor rendered to an image passes to its prototype," and "whoever venerates an image venerates the person portrayed in it." The honor paid to sacred images is a "respectful veneration," not the adoration due to God alone.[72]

As we have said, the death of the thing in the idea occurs in the conceptualization because conceptualizing involves tearing or extracting the thing, dividing matter and form. It is no coincidence that the word *death* comes from the Greek *thanatos*, which means "to separate," in this case, the soul from the body.

If in hylomorphism both matter and form are united, in conceptualization, the form is torn and separated from the matter, being introduced into the intellect, but disembodied, giving birth to the concept. That is why we can affirm that conceptualizing corresponds to taking the form out of the matter and adding it disembodied to the intellect. By separating the matter from the form, we snatch the life from the hylomorphic. When the concept is born, the human being stops relating to the hylomorphic to relate exclusively to the form. That is, as we mentioned earlier, the birth of the concept implies the death of the thing.

Moreover, when we create a conceptualized idea, we turn it into an idol. To idolize means to worship a mental image instead of the thing itself. The conceptualization of the myth immerses us in a reality where only idols remain, but worship fades away. However, in the symbolic myth, the idol becomes a mere accessory, while worship occupies a place of paramount importance. The idol becomes a tool, an instrument, or an excuse for those who lack knowledge in the art of worship.

For the human mind, it is arduous to relate to the formless, as revealed in the Bhagavad Gita:

> क्लेशोऽधिकतरस्तेषामव्यक्तासक्तचेतसाम् ।
> अव्यक्ता हि गतिर्दुःखं देहवद्भिरवाप्यते ॥

72. Ibid., 517 (§2132).

kleśo 'dhikataras teṣām
avyaktāsakta-cetasām
avyaktā hi gatir duḥkhaṁ
dehavadbhir avāpyate

Great is the difficulty for those whose minds are set on the unmanifested (Nirguṇa-brahman), because the unmanifested is difficult for embodied beings to achieve.

(Bhagavad Gita, 12.5)

In their penetrating retroprogression, the enlightened sages perceive that the vast majority of human beings require an idol as an accessory. The boundless transcendence of the formless demands a point of support in the journey of the mind. Undoubtedly, this resting point must be inspiring, integrative, and used with wisdom. There is no religious tradition that has not made use of idols in its practice to a greater or lesser extent. When the symbol is subjected to conceptual conversion and the myth is transmuted into theology, idols are emptied and reduced to mere stones and lifeless metals, before which no person endowed with even minimal discernment would bow. The concept demystifies the idol, leaving only statues of stone, marble, or metal empty and purified of the idea. Conceptualization creates idols made purely of form, of idea, concealing the original symbol without understanding its essence. The original symbol is not reducible to the concept and can only be understood by the heart. This reminds us of the words of Blaise Pascal when he says: "The heart has its reasons, which reason does not know."[73] The heart... that mystery that dictates our lives, that heart that drives a variety of sometimes contradictory emotions. It makes us say things we would never have revealed or do things we never thought we would... The reasons of the heart are not always rational; desires and wants, reason ignores them.

73. Blaise Pascal, *Pensées*, trans. W. F. Trotter, Section I: Thoughts on Mind and on Style (1660), fragment 277.

In our time, we witness how the public kneels before the cross and statues of the Virgin Mary, kisses the *mezuzahs* and Torah scrolls, offers incense and lights to the divinities, but without an integral participation of their hearts. We find ourselves in the presence of idols but in the absence of genuine worship, and therefore we kneel before symbols devoid of veneration. Idolatry emerges when idols gain superiority over the act of worship itself. It is crucial to keep in mind that idols can take on both physical and mental or conceptual forms. When there is no "full participation of the heart," there can be many forms of idolatry.

Although God cannot be conceptualized, He can be symbolized. Everything that exalts, inspires, and integrates us, infusing us with a deep sense, embodies the divine. On the other hand, any force that fractures, breaks, or splits the pleromatic (fullness) unity of the symbol, becomes diabolical. If we find inspiration in a poem, that poem becomes a symbol of God. If we are elevated by contemplating a sunset, that sunset becomes a divine symbol. However, if it persists in a conceptual existence, the human being inevitably dwells in the emptiness of forms without essence. Only by living symbolically can one integrate the various aspects in constant conflict.

Just as poetry aims to move our hearts rather than recount historical events, the symbol seeks integration rather than conveying scientific discoveries. The concept itself cannot transcend the truth understood as the perfect correspondence between the object and the mind-sense. However, the symbol, due to its significant charge, surpasses mere sensory perception and has the capacity to unite the rational with the suprarational, the mind with the supramental.

The Retroprogressive Path refers to the practice of worship in which symbols or idols become stages along the path of whose vocabulary the terms "truth" and "falsehood," as well as the concepts of "error" and "falsity," have been removed. This path does not present a new truth or an additional truth but consists of freeing religion from the exclusive domain of the concept and emancipating spirituality from both truth and falsehood.

Chapter 16

The symbolism of religious poetry

The Vedas, sacred guardians of erudition in the Vedic legacy of India, stand as a literary monument that has been rising since time immemorial. These writings are composed in the form of poetic hymns that date back to ancient eras. As one of the most primitive and revered collections of sacred texts in India's Vedic heritage, the Vedas reflect a sublime blend of the lyrical and the introspective. Rooted in the shadow of antiquity, these texts, written in Sanskrit, address a vast array of themes, from cosmology and the natural world to spirituality and ethics, reflecting the variety of the human experience. Vedic lyricism is a garden of symbolism, where each petal is a metaphor, and the scent it emanates is knowledge and wisdom that transcend the ages. The Vedic lyricism unfolds with symbolic opulence. Its hymns, recited in rituals and ceremonies, stand as an ephemeral yet powerful conduit to establish communication with the divine realms. Such sacred verses consist of praises and prayers directed at the deities, expressing an unshakable reverence for nature and the cosmos. In other words, the sacred Vedas contain praises and prayers directed at the deities and resemble a vault that houses the principles for a virtuous existence in balance with the cosmic order. Through Vedic poetry, with its metrical structure and melodic tone, the aim was to catalyze a transcendental experience at the emotional and cognitive core of the participants. Its main text is the *Bhagavad Gita*, whose title could be translated as "The Song of the Lord." As the Hindu philosopher Rabindranath Tagore says: "India is the song of poetry. India is the poet."

Moreover, the *Brāhmaṇas* and Upanishads emerge with their compendium of prose and verse. These manuscripts delve into the intricate matrix of mysticism, shedding light on the nature of the spacetime continuum, the ontological essence of being, and spiritual sublimation. The Vedas house hymns that are channels of erudition and devotion through which a profound connection is forged between the human experience and the divine; they bring together cognitive tribute and piety, fostering a synergy between the human and the celestial, forged in an ancestral dialect and a literary aesthetic of magnificence.

The forging of sacred texts in poetic molds is a widespread practice across various religious traditions. Concerning the Bible, there are numerous books that fall into the poetic category due to their unique stylistic and lyrical content, including Psalms, Proverbs, the Book of Job, and the Song of Songs. Psalms are a treasure trove encompassing 150 hymns and poetic fragments, indispensable elements in the worship practices and liturgy of ancient Israel. The Psalms traverse a heterogeneous thematic spectrum, including praises to the deity, supplicatory invocations, testimonies of gratitude, laments, wisdom, and meditations. On the other hand, the Proverbs offer a collection of aphorisms, maxims, and adages aimed at providing pragmatic discernment so that life may unfold under the banners of wisdom. These proverbs are meticulously constructed in verse and make use of rhetorical figures such as metaphor and visual representation to convey their implicit message.

The Book of Job, for its part, stands as a poetic narrative that meticulously scrutinizes the cardinal themes related to human suffering and divine justice. Through a succession of dialogues and speeches, the Book of Job questions the usual stances surrounding retribution and divine discernment. Lastly, the Song of Songs, also known as the Oda of Solomon, unfolds as a lyrical poem that exalts love and romantic passion between two human entities. This work employs imagery and poetic metaphors to portray love through the lens of natural beauty and vehement desire.

Together, these poetic books of the Bible reflect the plurality of expression and spiritual depth embedded in the Judeo-Christian tradition. Through their use of poetry, these texts convey messages of worship, wisdom, spiritual reflection, and devotional expression.

The Quran, the supreme sacred text of the Islamic faith, is not constituted by poetry or verses in the classical, conventional sense. This singular volume stands as an exceptional literary creation with its unparalleled style and content. It is written in melodic prose and employs a form of poetic language known as *madian* prose. Although the Quran's style inherently possesses a poetic quality, it does not adhere to the formal structures of classical Arabic poetry, such as the metrical patterns and rhymes typical of pre-Islamic poetry. Instead, it is distinguished by its use of repetition, parallelisms, and melodic rhythm that contribute to its unique cadence. The Quran inexorably serves as the vehicle for divine revelations through the Prophet Muhammad. As a religious and normative compendium, it reflects on a broad spectrum of themes, from the ontogenesis of the cosmos and piety before the sacred to the dynamics between the divine and mortals, including ethics and justice. The language and aesthetics of the Quran have been exalted for their elegance and intoxicating dialectic, thus carving a lasting groove in the Arabic literary tradition.

In the Buddhist framework, we find a collection of literary creations that, although imbued with lyrical elements, resist classification as poetic texts in the orthodox sense. These manuscripts are essentially compendiums, verses, doctrines, and literature originating from revered Buddhist masters, who imbue their works with a poetic touch in structure and language. A paradigmatic example is the *Dhammapada*, a collection of verses attributed to Siddhartha Gautama who is honored as the Buddha. Essentially, the *Dhammapada* contains the core teachings of Buddhism, navigating through wisdom, morality, contemplation, and the odyssey toward emancipation from the clutches of suffering.

On the threshold of Buddhism, a literary collection of vast dimension unveils fragments imbued with lyrical symbolism. Literary liturgies belonging to the Buddhist pantheon form a liturgical, scholarly ensemble sheltered by lyrical manifestations that nevertheless avoid the categorization of poeticity in its most orthodox appearance. In the Buddhist worldview, numerous sagacious and eloquent scriptures are imbued with lyrical elements, even though they refrain from embracing the traditional poetic taxonomy.

Simultaneously, we find *sūtras*, manuscripts, and postulates of Buddhist ascetics, whose lexical channels employ a taciturn lyricism to unravel a transcendental philosophical complexity. The *sūtras* and legacies of poets and scholars, such as the Zen ascetic Ikkyū Sojun, utilize lyricism to articulate transcendental experiences. In its pragmatism and empirical experience, Buddhism forges these texts as dialectical swords in the struggle toward enlightenment. By employing lyrical language, this collection of writings becomes a provocative agent that distills the essence of reality's inquiry. With its emphasis on the primacy of lived experience, Buddhism uses its literary corpus intertwined with poetry as a multifaceted tool for transmitting and deepening its teachings.

On the other hand, Jainism, sculpted in the vast temporal expanse of ancient India, presents a transcendent literary legacy. With a profuse literary range, Jainism encompasses sacred writings, often including poetic verses that serve as vehicles for transmitting this ancient religious tradition's fundamental values and teachings. Although prose predominates, the existence of texts employing lyrical vestments to address more sublime dimensions of existence cannot be overlooked. Among canonical literature, the *āgamas* stand out, texts wrapped in poetry, rhyme, and rhythm containing the sermons and teachings of the *Tīrthaṅkaras*, the enlightened beings in the Jain worldview. Crafted in harmonious verse structures, they are considered the bulwarks and foundations of Jain doctrine and application, the ontological and axiological pillars of Jainism. The *āgamas*, emblems of literary refinement, venture into spheres of non-violence (*ahimsā*), renunciation, compassion, and metaphysical emancipation. These are accompanied by works such as the *Pravachanasara* and *Niyamasara* by Kundakunda, which reveals the intrinsic nature of Jainism. These versified texts are revered tools to foster immersion in Jain principles and establish a sacred connection with them.

Meanwhile, Sikhism, inspired by Guru Nanak in the 15th century, holds its literary treasures in the *Guru Granth Sahib*, a compendium that transcends temporal boundaries. The *Guru Granth Sahib* is a crucible of poetry and hymns and is considered the eleventh and final perpetual Guru of the Sikh faith. The manuscripts in question are in Gurmukhi, a script specific to Sikhism. The *Guru Granth Sahib*, exalted as the eternal word of the supreme deity, operates in duality: as a metaphysical guide and a venerable sacred source for Sikh followers. The hymns and elegies, with their dazzling metric and stylistic diversity, radiate doctrines of love, balance, equity, and unity across a spectrum of perplexities. Music is central to Sikhism; chanting these lyrical verses in *kīrtana*, with particular harmonies, is imperative.

Immersed in the Japanese sphere, Shintoism, a spiritual lineage of ancient roots, harbors an eternal zeal for the exaltation of the *kami*, deities incarnated in the essence of nature. As reflected in the *Kojiki* or *Furukotofumi*, "Record of Ancient Things": "The *kami* wove creation with divine threads." Lacking a literary systematization and a range of texts analogous to other religious matrices, Shinto sacred literature contains lyrical compositions that stand as fundamental pillars of the Shinto ethos. While Shinto sacred literature does not possess the structure and extent comparable to those of other religious traditions, there are certain poetic compositions and texts considered integral parts of the Shinto corpus. Majestic among these, the *Kojiki*, with poise and reverence, can be interpreted as a "Record of Arcane Events." This book, compiled in the 8th century, contains a conglomeration of myths, tales, and genealogical stories linked to the origins of Japan and its deities. Although the *Kojiki* is not strictly composed poetically, it employs symbolic language to describe the actions and divine characters.

Another work of profound significance is the *Nihon Shoki*, or "Chronicles of Japan." Parallel to the *Kojiki*, the *Nihon Shoki* constitutes a historiographical and mythological amalgamation, incorporating epics related to Japan's deities and primordial foundations. This document, rich in a plurality of narratives and legends, meticulously assembles myths and historical events that endure as an essential compendium for the exegesis of Japanese identity and cultural heritage. Although it cannot be considered entirely poetic literature, it incorporates poetic elements in its narrative style. In addition to these texts, there are collections of poems called *waka*, written in later periods, which reflect the religious and aesthetic sensitivity of Shintoism. These poems are typically related to nature, the *kami*, and spiritual experiences. *Waka* are traditional Japanese poetic forms that have been passed down through the centuries.

As we have seen throughout this compendium of religious literature belonging to a wide variety of traditions and cultures, due to its unparalleled ability to communicate the ethereal and subtle, poetry stands as the ideal literary medium for articulating the sacred, in contrast to prose, which often suffers from a certain dryness in this realm. At its peak, Lyric meter plunges into the unfathomable depths of the transcendental experience, capturing with refined eloquence the magnificence of beauty and the transcendent in carefully chosen terms. Sacred poetry, inherently linked to the divine and the human, uses symbolism and metaphors to communicate truths that transcend the confines of reasoning. Lyrical hymns, charged with devotion, infuse a sense of reverence and unfold a portal to a meditative state that unravels beyond ordinary perception, offering the reader a passage to the mystical experience that transcends the bounds of conventional knowledge.

Through sacred poetry, one aspires to transcend the limitations of vernacular communication and penetrate a deeper dimension of our reality, embarking on an odyssey to cross the threshold of mundane communication and immerse oneself in the abysses of enigmatic silence. The verses, imbued with a nearly tangible semantic density, summon meditation and convergence toward the superhuman, narrowing the gap between the tangible and the transcendental. They vehemently provoke meditative introspection and a confluence with the numinous, erecting an invisible architecture that links the human realms with the metaphysically unreachable. The incorporation of poetry into sacred writings embraces the mission of projecting the sacred with greater fervor and evocation. The intertwining of poetry in sacred literature is not accidental but rather a meticulous calculation to invigorate the representation of the sacred, acting as a catalyst for transcendental particles. Poetry stands as a chisel in the sculptor's hand, decoding the mysteries that lie in consciousness and restoring the lost connection with the supramundane. In the realm of poetry, one perceives a lexical arabesque, erudite, and multifaceted that embraces the ineffable and the delicate, vigorously establishing the ancestral connection with the supernatural realms beyond our phenomenological perception.

> וְכָל מַחֲלֹקֶת הַתַּנָּאִים וְהָאֲמוֹרָאִים, וְהַגְּאוֹנִים וְהַפּוֹסְקִים בֶּאֱמֶת, לַמֵּבִין דָּבָר לַאֲשׁוּרוֹ – דִּבְרֵי אֱלֹקִים חַיִּים הֵמָּה, וּלְכֻלָּם יֵשׁ פָּנִים בַּהֲלָכָה. וְאַדְרַבָּה: זֹאת הִיא תִּפְאֶרֶת תּוֹרָתֵנוּ הַקְּדוֹשָׁה וְהַטְּהוֹרָה. וְכָל הַתּוֹרָה כֻּלָּהּ נִקְרֵאת "שִׁירָה", וְתִפְאֶרֶת הַשִּׁיר הִיא כְּשֶׁהַקּוֹלוֹת מְשֻׁנִּים זֶה מִזֶּה, וְזֶהוּ עִקַּר הַנְּעִימוּת. וּמִי שֶׁמְּשׁוֹטֵט בְּיַם הַתַּלְמוּד – יִרְאֶה נְעִימוֹת מְשֻׁנּוֹת בְּכָל הַקּוֹלוֹת הַמְשֻׁנּוֹת זֶה מִזֶּה.
> (הרב יחיאל מיכל הלוי אפשטין, הקדמה לספר ערוך השלחן)

> And all the disputes of the *Tanna'im*, *Amora'im*, *Ge'onim*, and *Poskim* (different generations of *Talmudic* and post-*Talmudic* Hebrew saints), in reality, to whom who understands the essence of things, are all—"living words of the living God," and all are valid aspects of the *Halachah* [or "The way of walking"] (the divine law). Moreover, this is the glory of our holy and pure Torah: The entire Torah is called *shirah* (a poem or a song), and the greatness of a song is when the voices differ, which is the essence of all melodies. He who travels the "sea of *Talmud*" will witness diverse melodies in many different voices.
>
> (Rabbi Yechiel Michel HaLevi Epstein,
> introduction to the book *Aruch HaShulchan)*

In light of what has been presented in this chapter, mythology is revealed to us as a poetic form whose language allows us to glimpse flashes of the transcendent. For example, in the *Śrī Caitanya-caritāmṛta*, it is said that:

> গচ্ছন্ বৃন্দাবনং গৌরো ব্যাঘ্রেভৈণখগান্ বনে ।
> প্রেমোন্মত্তান্ সহোন্নৃত্যান্ বিদধে কৃষ্ণজল্পিনঃ ॥

gacchan vṛndāvanaṁ gauro
vyāghrebhaiṇa-khagān van
premonmattān sahonnṛtyān
vidadhe kṛṣṇa-jalpinaḥ

> On the way to Vṛndāvana, Lord Śrī Caitanya Mahāprabhu passed through the forest of Jhārikhaṇḍa and made all the tigers, elephants, deer, and birds chant the *Hare Kṛṣṇa mahā-mantra* and dance. Thus, all those animals were overwhelmed with ecstatic love.
>
> (*Śrī Caitanya-caritāmṛta*, "*Madhya-līlā*," 17.1)

It is necessary to apply philological scrutiny to discern that the text in question is imbued, like dye on parchment, with poetry in its purest and pristine form. It is precisely at the intersection of linguistics and epistemology that virtue lies. Far from being a factual narrative, it is a poetic proposition that distills a deeper meaning that is impossible to convey otherwise. This verse suggests that instinctual nature is transcended and surpassed by interacting directly with an enlightened being. In the presence of the divine, the animal instinctual propensity is elevated beyond human romantic attachment, entering the sacred realm of devotion. This is not an ordinary event but a rich metaphor that represents the profound transformation that can take place under the guidance of an enlightened spiritual master. In its elevated expression, poetry allows us to glimpse these unfathomable mysteries of spiritual experience.

In the intricate byways of the hadiths that make up the Islamic tradition, a narrative is told in which the prophet Muhammad, while tending a flock of sheep, was visited by two individuals wearing immaculate white robes, carrying a golden vessel that contained the white purity of snow. These figures rushed toward him, pinning him to the ground. With deliberate movements, they inserted their hand into the prophet's chest and extracted his heart. From this cardinal organ, a drop of liquid with deep blackness was taken, subjected to a purification process through ablution in the snow, and then carefully reintegrated to its original place before these ethereal beings vanished. Following the model of the childhood narratives found in the Gospels, these stories do not aim to achieve historical veracity but unfold as living metaphors that shed light on the enigma of prophetic experience. This symbolic narrative explicitly refers to the process of internal purification, inescapable on the path of retroprogressive evolution, in the spiritual transmutation that underlies the journey from the mundane to the sacred. A similar revelation appears in the New Testament (John 20:1–18), where we read:

> On the first day of the week, very early, while it was still dark, Mary Magdalene went to the tomb and saw that the stone had been removed from the entrance. So she ran to Simon Peter and the other disciple, the one whom Jesus loved, and said to them:
>
> "They have taken the Lord out of the tomb, and we do not know where they have put him!"
>
> Peter and the other disciples started for the tomb. Both were running, but the other disciple outran Peter and reached the tomb first. He bent over and looked in at the strips of linen lying there but did not go in. Then Simon Peter came along behind him and went straight into the tomb. He saw the strips of linen lying there, as well as the cloth that had been wrapped around Jesus' head. The cloth was still lying in its place, separate from the linen. Finally, the other disciple, who had reached the tomb first, also went inside. He saw and believed.
>
> (They still did not understand from Scripture that Jesus had to rise from the dead.)
>
> Jesus Appears to Mary Magdalene
>
> Then the disciples went back to where they were staying. But Mary stood outside the tomb crying. As she wept, she

bent over to look into the tomb and saw two angels in white, seated where Jesus' body had been, one at the head and the other at the foot.

They asked her, "Woman, why are you crying?"

"They have taken my Lord away," she said, "and I don't know where they have put him."

At this, she turned around and saw Jesus standing there, but she did not realize that it was Jesus.

He asked her, "Woman, why are you crying? Who is it you are looking for?"

Thinking he was the gardener, she said, "Sir, if you have carried him away, tell me where you have put him, and I will get him."

Jesus said to her, "Mary."

She turned toward him and cried out in Aramaic, "Rabboni!" (which means "Teacher").

Jesus said, "Do not hold on to me, for I have not yet ascended to the Father. Go instead to my brothers and tell them, 'I am ascending to my Father and your Father, to my God and your God.'"

Mary Magdalene went to the disciples with the news: "I have seen the Lord!" And she told them that he had said these things to her.

The death of Jesus through crucifixion and his subsequent resurrection after three days is presented not as a historical chronicle but as a poetic metaphor. Here, a symbolic truth is revealed, claiming that one who expires in God conquers immortality by reviving in another dimension of existence. Those who leave behind the physical body in a higher plane of consciousness abandon the earthly to ascend to the celestial; that is, they die to the constraints of time and space to be reborn in eternity.

It seems that all religions, once institutionalized, have tried, with obsessive dedication, to validate that this symbolic, mythological, poetic literature refers to historical or scientific events as if its value had to be measured by its degree of veracity. More than anything, these maneuvers reveal their lack of understanding since these sacred writings refer to symbolic realities and truths. To claim that a poem is false would be as absurd and senseless as to propose that a song is good simply because it is true. The symbolic does not lend itself to the game of truth as adequacy or science but to the game of functionality and experience. There are no reprobates or heretics in the symbolic, only people living the symbol.

Poems and songs cannot be categorized as true or false, for their value lies in their ability—or sometimes inability—to move. When evaluating a poem, various elements must be considered, with one of the most notable being the poet's skill in using words and creating an environment that evokes emotions in the reader, as well as the emotional or intellectual impact the poem has after reading it.

Just as with poems, symbols also cannot be judged as true or false. Poetry is not critically evaluated in terms of its truthfulness, just as symbols and myths cannot be valued based on parameters of truth or falsehood. It is impossible to ignore that the fulcrum of its importance lies in the ability to transmute meaning and symbolic density into a compendium, allowing us to wander through experiences. Regardless of their degree of accuracy, these components function as catalysts, inciting reflection and meditation, facilitating the connection with the most abysmal dimensions of human existence. Poetry, as an artistic manifesto, transcends mere words. We find supplication, devotion, meditation, and deep perplexity in its encompassing spectrum. Poetry holds a religious dimension, for it leads us toward a communion with the whole, surpassing conceptual reasoning and allowing us to venture beyond the mental perception of the factual reality of events.

In this sense, poetry reveals itself as an astonishing phenomenon, with the ability to divide the waters that cover the depths of our being, granting us the opportunity to move from the mind to a supramental stratum. Thanks to this ability, poetry becomes a path to connection with the divine and the transcendental. It is academically essential to assimilate that poetry is not restricted to the realms of literary luminaries such as William Shakespeare, Homer, Dante Alighieri, Rabindranath Tagore, Pablo Neruda, and Emily Dickinson, to name just a few. Through empirical and erudite inquiry, one should discern with clarity that poetry, that vast linguistic and cultural edifice, is not restricted solely to the pantheon of the famous William Wordsworth or Johann Wolfgang von Goethe. Quite the contrary, poetry, as rooted in the essence of being human, unfolds its wings in a multifaceted thematic arc that spans the most sublime and obscure strata of human cognition. All of the aforementioned poets have experienced flashes of poetry, being touched by fleeting lightning bolts of mystery. One single flash can catalyze the blooming of a great poet. However, without the recognition of consciousness, great artists remain in the shadows of ignorance. In the presence of authentic enlightened masters, such as Moses, the prophets, Jesus, Muhammad, Mahavira, Buddha, Shankara, Lao Tzu, or the Baal Shem Tov, the previously mentioned artists are relegated to the category of mere versifiers. Poets can reach remarkable heights, but enlightened beings have wings that allow them to fly in absolute freedom. Poetry flows fluidly, constantly, and fully through the enlightened masters of all times and places.

Everything presented so far in this chapter shows that the totality of sacred literature from all religious traditions should not be approached as a newspaper, a book of history, or a book of physics but as a compendium of poems. It is absurd to approach religion from an exclusively conceptual perspective, as religion is based on symbolic narratives endowed with profound significance.

Regardless of their origin, time, or lineage, the wise did not merely experience fleeting flashes of consciousness but were consumed by it, transmuting into poetic entities themselves. From the lineage of the enlightened masters arises poetry with vigorous vitality. Something unusual happens with the words of a Buddha: the heart trembles, and emotions bloom, for poetry becomes a sublimating process that refines humanity toward the divine. From the luminous abysses of consciousness, poetry emerges a tide that reverberates and dissolves the strong defenses of the heart. But this sea is not merely a storm of emotion; instead, it is an alchemist that forges the human soul toward a divine zenith through the weight of its tools, verses, and symbols, which are not mere whirlpools in the river of imagination. On the contrary, verses and symbols are more like the tentacles of a kraken that submerge the navigator in the depths of their being to discover buried treasures in the catacombs of consciousness. Poetry and symbol should not be viewed solely as artistic expressions or products of the imagination but as tools endowed with a profound power to awaken our original state. As an example, we can mention Kabir, St. John of the Cross, Fray Luis de León, Farid al-Din, Hildegard of Bingen, Rumi, St. Francis of Assisi, Mīrābāī, Buleh Shah, Sahajo, Nanak, Rab Solomon Ibn Gabirol, Rab Yehuda Ha'Levi, or Rab Israel Najara. We share here some of their poems, starting with Rumi:

Stay close, my heart

Stay close, my heart, to the one who knows your ways;
Come into the shade of the tree that always has fresh flowers.
Don't stroll idly through the bazaar of the perfume-markers:
Stay in the shop of the sugar-seller.
If you don't find true balance, anyone can deceive you;
Anyone can trick out of a thing of straw,
And make you take it for gold.
Don't squat with a bowl before every boiling pot;
In each pot on the fire you find very different things.
Not all sugarcanes have sugar, not all abysses a peak;
Not all eyes possess vision, not every sea is full of pearls.
O nightingale, with your voice of dark honey! Go on lamenting!
Only your drunken ecstasy can pierce the rock's hard heart!
Surrender yourself, and if you cannot be welcomes by the Friend,

Know that you are rebelling inwardly like a thread
That doesn't want to go through the needle's eye!
The awakened heart is a lamp; protect it by the hem of your robe!
Hurry and get out of this wind, for the weather is bad.
And when you've left this storm, you will come to a fountain;
You'll find a Friend there who will always nourish your soul.
And with your soul always green, you'll grow into a tall tree
Flowering always with sweet light-fruit, whose growth is interior.

The Awakening

In the early dawn of happiness
you gave me three kisses
so that I would wake up
to this moment of love
I tried to remember in my heart
what I'd dreamt about
during the night
before I became aware
of this moving
of life
I found my dreams
but the moon took me away
It lifted me up to the firmament
and suspended me there
I saw how my heart had fallen
on your path
singing a song
Between my love and my heart
things were happening which
slowly slowly
made me recall everything
You amuse me with your touch
although I can't see your hands.

You have kissed me with tenderness
although I haven't seen your lips
You are hidden from me.
But it is you who keeps me alive
Perhaps the time will come
when you will tire of kisses
I shall be happy
even for insults from you
I only ask that you
keep some attention on me.

Next, a wonderful poem by St. Francis of Assisi:

Canticle of the Creatures

Most High, all-powerful, good Lord,
Yours are the praises, the glory, and the honor, and all blessing.
To You alone, Most High, do they belong,
and no human is worthy to mention Your name.
Praised be You, my Lord, with all Your creatures,
especially Sir Brother Sun,
Who is the day and through whom You give us light.
And he is beautiful and radiant with great splendor;
and bears a likeness of You, Most High One.
Praised be You, my Lord, through Sister Moon and the stars,
in heaven You formed them clear and precious and beautiful.

Praised be You, my Lord, through Brother Wind,
and through the air, cloudy and serene, and every kind of weather,
through whom You give sustenance to Your creatures.
Praised be You, my Lord, through Sister Water,
who is very useful and humble and precious and chaste.
Praised be You, my Lord, through Brother Fire,
through whom You light the night,

and he is beautiful and playful and robust and strong.
Praised be You, my Lord, through our Sister Mother Earth,
who sustains and governs us,
and who produces various fruit with colored flowers and herbs.

Praised be You, my Lord,
through those who give pardon for Your love,
and bear infirmity and tribulation.
Blessed are those who endure in peace
for by You, Most High, shall they be crowned.

Praised be You, my Lord, through our Sister Bodily Death,
from whom no one living can escape.
Woe to those who die in mortal sin.
Blessed are those whom death will find in Your most holy will,
for the second death shall do them no harm.

Praise and bless my Lord and give Him thanks
and serve Him with great humility.

A poem by Saint Teresa of Avila:

I live without living in me

I live without living in me,
and I expect a life so high,
that I die because I do not die.
I live already beside myself
since I am dying of love;
because I live in Him,
who wanted me for Himself:
when I gave my heart to Him
He placed this sign in it,
that I die because I do not die.

This divine prison,
the love in which I'm living,
has made God my captive,
and my heart free;
causing in me such passion,
to see God, my prisoner,
That I die because I do not die.
Oh, how long is this life!
How hard this exile,
this prison, these chains
which my soul has entered!
Just waiting to get free
causes me so much fierce pain,
that I die because I do not die.
Ah! so much bitterness in this life
without God as my lover!
Because if to be in love is sweet,
to wait so long is not:
take this burden God,
heavier than steel,
that I die because I do not die.
Trusting in You alone, I only live
because I know I'll die
because in death I know
that I will live;
death, where I'll find life
do not be slow, it is you I wait for,
that I die because I do not die.
You see how strong love is;
life, do not hinder me,
you see, all I need do to gain you
is to lose you.
Come on already sweet death
come quickly death
that I die because I do not die.
That life above,

that is the true life,
until this life dies
nothing can be enjoyed in living
death, don't be coy;
let me live by dying first,
that I die because I do not die.
Life, what can I give
to my God who lives in me?
In losing you,
then I am worthy of gaining Him.
I want to reach Him by dying,
Since I love my lover so,
that I die because I do not die.

The following poems are by Rabbi Solomon ibn Gabirol:

Ecstasy

שְׁאָלוּנִי שְׂעִפַּי הַתְּמֵהִים:
לְמִי תָרוּץ כְּגַלְגַּלֵּי גְבֹהִים?
לְאֵל חַיַּי תְּשׁוּקַת מַאֲוַיַּי
וְנַפְשִׁי עִם בְּשָׂרִי לוֹ כְמֵהִים!
מְשׂוֹשִׂי גַּם מְנָת כּוֹסִי וְעוֹשִׂי
אֲשֶׁר עֵת אֶזְכְּרָה אוֹתוֹ וְאָהִים –
הֲיִנְעַם טוּב לְנִשְׁמָתִי עֲדֵי כִי
תְּבָרֵךְ שֵׁם אֲדֹנָי הָאֱלֹהִים!

My thoughts, in awe
they asked me why,
to the spinning wheels high above I flew,
in ecstasy I run without ceasing,
the living God is my longing,
takes me on wings of fire to fly,
body and soul want to reach Him.

The living God is my joy and my happening,
This yearning in me He brought forth,
At the thought of Him, I palpitate with pleasure.
Will the song, with all its beauty,
to immerse my soul in happiness with certainty
before the God of Gods, in his greatness?

Before my King

שְׁעָלַי אֶפְרְשָׂה תָּמִיד לְמַלְכִּי / וְאֶקֹּד לוֹ עֲלֵי אַפִּי וּבִרְכִּי
לְפָנָיו אֶעֱרֹךְ לִבִּי כְּקָרְבָּן / וְדִמְעִי אֶשְׁפְּכָה נֶגְדּוֹ כְּנִסְכִּי
מְיַחֵל כָּלְתָה נַפְשִׁי לְחַסְדּוֹ / כְּתוֹחַלְתִּי לְאוֹר בֹּקֶר בְּחָשְׁכִּי

הֲלֹא פָּנָיו אֲשַׁחֵר אִם יְאַחֵר / וְיָדַעְתִּי אֱמֶת כִּי יַעֲנֶה כִּי
וְלִבִּי מַר יְשִׂיחֵנִי בְּמַאְמַר / זְכַרְיָה כִּי מְאֹד מָתוֹק לְחִכִּי
וְנִשְׁמָתִי תְּדַבֵּר עַל לְבָבָהּ / דְּעִי כִּי לֶאֱלֹהַּ חַי תְּחַכִּי.

In prayer prone before my King,
I bend to Him my face and knee,
My heart His sacrifice shall be,
My tear His liquid offering.

In waiting for the sun's caress,
In watching for the morning light
To scatter all my godless night,
My soul consumes in weariness.

Though He delays, shall I not start

To seek His face? Nay, of a sooth
I yet shall find His word of ruth
Bring comfort to my bitter heart.

The promise Zechariah gave,
How sweet it tastes in this our woe!
My soul shall bid my heart to know
I trust the living God to save.

Mīrābāī composed nectareous devotional poems:

It is true I went to the market

My friend, I went to the market and bought the Dark One.
You claim by night, I claim by day.
Actually I was beating a drum all the time I was buying him.
You say I gave too much; I say too little.
Actually, I put him on a scale before I bought him.
What I paid was my social body, my town body, my family body,
and all my inherited jewels.
Mīrābāī says: The Dark One is my husband now.
Be with me when I lie down; you promised me this in an earlier life.

Don't go, don't go

Don't go, don't go. I touch your feet. I am sold to you.
No one knows where to find the bhakti path;
teach me where I should go.
I wish my body would become a pile of incense and sandalwood,
and that you would set a torch to it.
When it has fallen to gray ashes, scatter me over
your shoulders and chest.
Mīrā says: You raise the mountains; I have a little light,
I want to mix it with yours.

My eyes

My eyes are thirsty for you.
All day
I look at the road,
my aching eyes.
The bird on the branch sings,
also painful for me.
People speak
and laugh at me.
But Mīrā is sold to Hari.
She is his slave for many lifetimes.

My love is my house

My love is in my house,
I watched the road for years
but never saw him.
I put out the worship plate,
gave away gems.
After this, he sent word.
My dark lover has come,
joy is on my limbs.
Hari is an ocean,
my eyes touch him.
Mīrā is an ocean of joy.
She takes him inside.

Let me see you

Grant me Your grace
In the hot weather of late May

The land is desiccated, the birds suffer
As May gives way to June,
The peacock cries out piteously
And the cuckoo wails for the clouds
When the rains set in,
The women observe the Tīj festival
In the month of Bhādon
The rivers swirl—
No one absents themselves then
In the month of Kwār,
The oyster-shells hanker for rain
In the month of Kārttik
People worship in the temple,
But in my case,
Thou art my only divinity
Cold are the days of Mārgaśīrṣ,
So come quickly to protect me
In the month of Pauś
The earth is covered with thick frost,
Come Yourself to see it
In the month of Māgh
They celebrate Vasant-pañcamī
In Phālgun they sing songs
They celebrate Holi With mirth and games
And burn whole woods In bonfires
In the month of Caitra
Longing rises in the heart—
Grant me Thy sight
In the month of Vaiśākh
The trees burst into blossom,
And the cuckoo sings his plaintive song
The day has passed In driving off crows
And I have also consulted the astrologers
Mirā is abandoned and miserable
When will she have His sight?

My pitcher breaks

My pitcher breaks against the ground.
I am overwhelmed.
His beauty drives me mad. Father, mother, brother, and sister
all speak kind words. Come home, forget it.
But the dark dancer inhabits me.
His love is light throughout my body.
Let them say I am lost.
The secret. Giridhār knows.

Storm

Thick above my head
the monsoon clouds,
a delight for this fevered heart.
Rainy season,
season of uncontrolled sighs—
The Dark One returns!
Ah, inflamed heart,
Ah, sky bordered with humidity,
the tongue of lightning first
and then thunder,
convulsive rains spat out
and then the wind, chasing the heat of summer.
Mīrā says: Dark One, I have waited
it's time to bring my songs to the streets.

I want to share this wonderful poem composed by Śrīlā Bhaktivinoda Ṭhākura in Jagannātha Purī on 18th July, 1871 and translated to English by Swami B.V. Giri.

Vṛndāvana

(1)

My treasure, Śrī Kṛṣṇa, always sports in the eternal abode of Vṛndāvana. He resides in its forest-bowers that are full of divine knowledge, that are decorated with spiritual creepers and buds of love divine.

(2)

The purest type of worship is exhibited on the banks of the Kālindī and is eternally found in the hearts of the devotees there. The topmost *bhava* acquired by the *jīvas* is manifest at Govardhāna, where there are animals such as cows reside.

(3)

There, the eternal disposition is in the mood of the *sakhīs* as well as brotherly affection, and bliss is the only commodity. There is no lust, envy etc. or anything of that type and only mellows of divine love are performed.

(4)

That realm is full of the *rasas* of servitude, friendship, parental affection, and amorous love. Indeed, Vraja-dhāma is the home of love divine. There, the *jīvas* do not experience birth, death, endurance or disease. They take shelter of the nectar of *prema*.

(5)

That land, which is most dear to Kṛṣṇa, is beyond matter and all mundane sense-perception. It eternally transcends time and space. One who has a material body and whose mind is attached to matter can never reach it.

(6)

Those *jīvas* who have discovered the happy shelter of Śrī Guru and Kṛṣṇa are most fortunate. They transcend the mental and physical bodies, and attain that abode of bliss.

(7)

They attain a divine form, enter Vraja, and take refuge at the feet of the *sakhīs*. They find happiness serving Rādhā-Kṛṣṇa, leave behind all miseries, and rise the stage of *mahā-bhāva*.

(8)

Therefore, O friends, let us go to Vṛndāvana! That land is not very far away. Control your senses, enter within, and finally you will attain *samādhi*.

(9)

For a while, our experience of material time and space may remain, but the *ātmā's* intimate connection with that land will eventually develop. O *sādhus*! Know that the land of Vṛndāvana is where you will eventually behold Rādhā-Govinda.

(10)

There, you will enter the Yamunā's waters with great ecstasy and play with the *sakhīs* while serving Śrī Rādhikā. Rādhikā, the Mistress of the *jīvas*, who is Kṛṣṇa's dearmost, the Goddess of all, will speak words of love unto you.

(11)

You will hear the sound of Govinda's flute, which pierces the heart of the *jīva* and makes the world go mad. It will forcibly take you to the base of a blossoming *Kadamba* tree and you will be drowned in the nectar of love divine.

(12)

Entering the waters of the Yamunā, the fire of *prema* will burn even stronger and your heart will begin to palpitate. Returning to the riverbank, you will see the form of Kṛṣṇa and suddenly you will become unconscious.

(13)

Śrī Vṛndāvana-dhāma brings delight to all *jīvas*. There is no fool greater than one who leaves Vṛndāvana and goes elsewhere. O brother, think about it! You will never find divine love anywhere else.

(14)

Living with women, jokes, stories, bottles of wine, ornaments etc. are the root cause of all miseries. It is a mistake on your part to consider them to be happiness. You must understand this very clearly.

(15)

Fever will enter your body and make you shiver. Your throat will become filled with mucus. Your ears will be unable to hear, your nose will be unable to smell, and your eyes will stop working.

(16)

Those whom you think are your dearest friends will become like strangers. Your family members will shun you. They will stop you at the door like a gatekeeper and their children will poke fun at you.

(17)

All of your former lovers will hate you. Alcohol will no longer give you any happiness. The bones you chew on and enjoy will now cause you untold misery, as you will become toothless.

(18)

Wearing ornaments will not make you look more attractive, and your body will look like a monkey. Where have your grand mirror and decorations gone? Think about this and become detached.

(19)

Therefore, brother, let us now go to Vṛndāvana! You will find everlasting happiness there. Divine love for Kṛṣṇa is eternal and never causes any misery. With that you will become faultless.

(20)

You will attain a divine form and a residence in Vṛndāvana. Your mundane body will remain in the material world. When you die, your body comprised of the five elements, will remain here, but you will never leave Vraja.

(21)

Thus, Kedarnātha Datta describes the truth about Vṛndāvana. My guru is Chaitanya Gosāi. When you take the association of His servants, your mind will never drift towards matter. O brother, take shelter of Śrī Chaitanya!

Śrīlā Bhaktivinoda Ṭhākura composed the following poem in in Jagannātha Purī on 13th July 1891. It was published in The Gauḍīya, Volume 18 on July 1940.

Upadeśa

(1)

O dear friends, kindly hear my plea, if you desire everlasting
bliss. Do not accept happiness in material things. Try to
understand that which is of a transcendental nature.
Relish the essence of those things.

(2)

The delight found in drinking alcohol and eating meat is totally
miserable. It is all merely an illusion of happiness. Pleasure gained
from the senses may seem to be happiness, but eternal bliss cannot
be found in them.

(3)

Why do you continuously roam around, bound by hopes on all
sides and associating with your *anarthas*? There is no end to our
desires, just like a deer who always remains thirsty. The only result
will be an ocean of misery.

(4)

Even when we inhabit the form of a tree, and the bird-
like *jīva* departs from it, what will be the use of any
sense gratification? At that time, the moon, sun, wind, and
water may show their strength, but they will not be able
to invite you back (for you have already departed and
left that form of a tree).

(5)

(At the time of death) Your dear ones will cry piteously, and your mind will burn with great lamentation and angst—will all these things be able to awaken you? Falling under such a great spell, you will roll around and finally you will be transformed into ashes, worm stool etc.

(6)

You have affection for this body which has forced you to wander through so many lands, but it will eventually be eaten by dogs and jackals. No matter how much you may take care of it, the terrible claws of time will never let go of this body. Alas!

(7)

Therefore, give up your wandering and strive to attain the highest goal. Worship Kṛṣṇa and absorb yourself in thoughts of Him. Piercing through the physical plane and the vast expanse of the mental sphere, let us go to Vṛndāvana.

(8)

Dressed as a cowherd, the color of a raincloud, youthful, effulgent, and peaceful, He takes shelter under a beautiful desire tree. The sound of His extraordinary flute maddens all the *jīvas*–in this way, Śyāma is the Lord of the heart.

(9)

The cow-like *jīvas* belong to Him. Though He has unlimited opulence, still His sweetness (*mādhurya*) is most prominent. Sitting under a *Kadamba* tree, the power of His flute is blissfully attracting. He captures the minds and hearts of the *sādhakas*.

(10)

Through detachment you will extinguish all your attachment to material things. By proper knowledge you will destroy ignorance. By sprinkling water in the form of hearing and chanting, the wonderful creeper of *prema* will manifest.

(11)

If you wish to be close to Kṛṣṇa, always take the association of *sadhus* and shun bad company. Kṛṣṇa is not very far away. Kṛṣṇa will become your very life if you drink the nectar of love divine.

(12)

All types of *yajña*, *homa*, fruitive activities, philosophies such as *Advaitavāda*, and the intoxicating wine of *jñāna*–know all these to be your enemies. As a *jīva*, you are a servant of Kṛṣṇa. *Jñāna* and karma are your fetters, and *prema* alone is your real wealth.

(13)

The material body, mind etc. are your enemies. You should keep them all firmly underfoot! See to it that they do not rebel and hurl you into the realm of material enjoyment under the guise of karma, *jñāna*, yoga, and dharma.

(14)

By the strength of *prema* keep them subservient to *sevā*. Engage them in activities born out of *kṛṣṇa–prema*, then these adversaries will become your friends. They will not be able to bind you to material objects.

(15)

Always chant, "Hari! Hari!" fix your mind, and surrender your body to Kṛṣṇa. Do not let your mind dwell on other thoughts or desires. In this way, perform *sādhana*.

(16)

With intense internal hankering, allow *kṛṣṇa-tattva* to penetrate your mind. Then enter deep into the pastures of your heart. Gaze there at that form of divine knowledge, who spiritedly manifests in Vṛndāvana as that Divine Youth (Navīna-Kiśora).

(17)

Body, mind, friends, home, pets, food, wealth–all these things will become obscure to you. You will seem to become totally insane and so many people will throw dirt at you, but the wealth of *prema* will remain with you.

(18)

The wealth and assets of Brahmā, the eighteen mystical perfections, enjoyment and liberation etc. become as insignificant as a piece of straw. Due to the influence of *prema*, all these things will fear you and run away.

(19)

Alas, what value does all the land in the world have compared to the wealth you will acquire? You will attain Kṛṣṇa, who is the crest-jewel of sweetness and the opulence of the wealthiest.

(20)

You are a *jīva* endowed with transcendental knowledge, and you are not meant for such fleeting happiness. The bliss of Kṛṣṇa is your dearmost treasure. The tongue, eyes, ears, and nose are all trying to satiate your thirst, but they cannot do so even for a moment.

(21)

The shelter of the lotus feet of Śrī Chaitanya is my very life. Kedāra says, "O Brothers, please listen! He is the helmsman who will help us cross over this world of birth and death. There is none else other than Him."

The poem *Mārkine Bhāgavata-dharma* was written by H.D.G. A.C. Bhaktivedānta Svāmī Prabhupāda upon his arrival in Boston.

> My dear Lord Kṛṣṇa, You are so kind upon this useless soul, but I do not know why You have brought me here. Now You can do whatever You like with me.
>
> But I guess You have some business here, otherwise why would You bring me to this terrible place?
>
> Most of the population here is covered by the material modes of ignorance and passion. Absorbed in material life, they think themselves very happy and satisfied, and therefore they have no taste for the transcendental message of Vāsudeva. I do not know how they will be able to understand it.
>
> But I know Your causeless mercy can make everything possible, because You are the most expert mystic.
>
> How will they understand the mellows of devotional service? O Lord, I am simply praying for Your mercy so that I will be able to convince them about Your message.

All living entities have come under the control of the illusory energy by Your will, and therefore, if You like, by Your will they can also be released from the clutches of illusion.

I wish that You may deliver them. Therefore if You so desire their deliverance, then only will they be able to understand Your message.

The words of *Śrīmad-bhāgavatam* are Your incarnation, and if a sober person repeatedly receives it with submissive aural reception, then he will be able to understand Your message.

He will become liberated from the influence of the modes of ignorance and passion and thus all inauspicious things accumulated in the core of the heart will disappear.

How will I make them understand this message of Kṛṣṇa consciousness? I am very unfortunate, unqualified, and the most fallen. Therefore, I am seeking Your benediction so that I can convince them, for I am powerless to do so on my own.

Somehow or other, O Lord, You have brought me here to speak about You. Now, my Lord, it is up to You to make me a success or failure, as You like.

O spiritual master of all the worlds! I can simply repeat Your message, so if You like You can make my power of speaking suitable for their understanding.

Only by Your causeless mercy will my words become pure. I am sure that when this transcendental message penetrates their hearts, they will certainly feel engladdened and thus become liberated from all unhappy conditions of life.

O Lord, I am just like a puppet in Your hands. So, if You have brought me here to dance, then make me dance, make me dance, O Lord, make me dance as You like.

I have no devotion, nor do I have any knowledge, but I have strong faith in the Holy Name of Kṛṣṇa. I have been designated as Bhakti-vedānta, and now, if You like, You can fulfill the real purport of Bhakti-vedānta.

Signed – the most unfortunate, insignificant beggar A. C. Bhakti-vedānta Svāmī on board the ship Jaladuta, Commonwealth Pier, Boston, Massachusetts, U.S.A. dated 18th of September, 1965

Finally, this is a poem I wrote several years ago:

I dreamt that I wasn't

I dreamt that I wasn't...
That I had never been born...
I dreamt that I was an eternity...
Only an eternity... that I do not live
What a vivid and clear dream
The presence of nothingness
Losing itself in the void
So free... nothing to stop or prevent it
Is it that... perhaps
I am nothing more than that... the other... the one in the dream
Who dreams the existence of his forgetfulness...
And perhaps...
I am nothing more than a dream...
Only a lost dream...

Chapter 17

The symbols of Christianity

While Jesus stands out as the inspiring icon, the foundation, and the basis of Christian history, the key figure in his narrative is Saint Paul, whose role in Christianity is the subject of intense debates. Bearing the title "Apostle of the Gentiles," Paul dedicated himself to spreading the faith among all people without distinction. While many praised him, the Jews viewed him differently. From the perspective of some, Paul was like a deserter, straying from the established beliefs and bringing something new to the table: a variant that, they argued, was based on the teachings of Jesus of Nazareth but resembled heresy to them. The duality of the situation is interesting. While some elevate him to the status of a hero, others label him as a heretic. Beliefs and the lenses through which one views them play a crucial role in this division. Such is the nature of human perception and how individual values can cast shadows or bathe the figure of a single person in light.

Saint Paul's role in Christianity bears a certain similarity to that of Prometheus, whose actions angered Zeus to the point of letting his fury take control and taking severe measures against both Prometheus and humans for having been deceived. In a fit of rage, Zeus observed how humans began to behave boldly, burning bones in sacrifice and delighting in the meat. For Zeus, this was unacceptable, and so he made a drastic decision: he would take away fire from them. He thought this would teach them a lesson for their audacious behavior. But this is where Prometheus' cunning comes into play, for he was not willing to stand idly by while Zeus imposed his will. So, he devised a daring plan: he would steal the fire that Zeus kept so jealously. Prometheus embarked on this mission with intelligence and courage, willing to face the risks and consequences. He made the bold decision to climb Mount Olympus to take the fire. We do not know exactly where this fire was kept; some say it might have been in Hephaestus' forge or in Helios' chariot. What we do know is that Prometheus was intelligent and skilled, which allowed him to sneak into Mount Olympus and steal the fire without the gods noticing. By the time the gods realized the fire was missing, it was too late: humans had it in their possession. Prometheus used the stalk of a plant called *canaheja* to carry the fire. It turns out this plant burns very slowly, which allowed the fire to last longer, providing warmth to humans until it was completely consumed.

We carry a divine spark in our hands as if we are holding the flames that Prometheus boldly stole from Zeus. That was a challenge to divine powers. Saint Paul's actions have a certain resemblance. Imagine the God of the Jews, with his sacred riches, and Saint Paul, with his audacity, taking those spiritual treasures when forming Christianity and generously extending them among the people. Here we have, in two stories, bravery and generosity united.

Jesus of Nazareth, commonly referred to as Jesus Christ, was born in a place called Bethlehem. Considered by his followers as the Son of God, he is the central pillar of Christianity. The name Christ comes from the Greek and means "the anointed," which is similar to the title of Messiah. There are texts called gospels, written by the early Christians, that tell the story of Jesus.

The story of Christ unfolds before us in a fascinating historical setting. Although his birth has become the anchor point of the modern calendar, he actually made his debut in history a few years earlier, specifically in the time of Herod, who left this world in 4 BCE. The shadow of Herod was ominous, so Jesus' family decided that safety lay in distance, making Egypt their temporary refuge. After Herod ceased to be a threat, the family returned, establishing their home in Nazareth. It was in this environment that Jesus, the enigmatic young man, embraced his father's trade and began to carve wood as a carpenter. Although the word used in the Bible is *tekton*, which refers to a craftsman. It is commonly translated as "carpenter," but it could be understood as a builder, someone with multiple skills who could perform various manual jobs, such as blacksmithing, carpentry, masonry, and others. This was in line with the trades of the time. This laid the foundation for a life that would later take a more transcendental and spiritual turn.

At the age of thirty, Jesus took on a mantle of solemnity and began his ministry. He established ties with his cousin, John, who had become known for his strong condemnations and convictions. One key day was when Jesus, in an act of humility, allowed John to baptize him in the Jordan River. John, with serious solemnity during this event, recognized Jesus as the prophesied Messiah. John also preached that he was the one preparing the way for the Messiah. He preached conversion and repentance. He did this by the Jordan River, the place through which the Jewish people had entered Canaan, that is, the place of entry. Why? Because symbolically, to enter the kingdom, one must purify oneself, which is why he baptized and called for repentance, to enter the promised land. It is also worth noting that John, by condemning the marriage of Herodias to Herod Antipas, sealed his fate, being captured and subsequently decapitated at the instigation of Herodias and Salome.

After being baptized, Jesus spent forty days in solitude, and upon finishing, he began his mission to preach, leading him to travel across Palestine. It is no surprise that his words attracted many. But among the crowd, twelve individuals stood out from the rest, becoming his apostles. Jesus spoke of profound topics and questioned Hebrew tradition. He emphasized the importance of love for others, detachment from wealth, forgiveness, and the idea of life beyond the earthly. One of his best-known speeches is the Sermon on the Mount, where he eloquently outlined the central principles of his teachings. Additionally, he had a particular way to teach, using parables that seemed simple on the surface but with layers of meaning waiting to be discovered by those willing to delve deeper. Also noteworthy is the issue of miracles. Some say he performed supernatural feats, which only added to his growing reputation. The Pharisees, bewildered by Jesus' audacity, felt threatened and labeled him as subversive, claiming that he had proclaimed himself king of the Jews, which led to him being judged by Pilate, the Roman governor of the province of Judea.

However, it must be understood that when Jesus spoke of the "kingdom of God," he was not making a political campaign. His message was deeper and spiritual. Knowing that the forthcoming events were inevitable, Jesus decided to go to Jerusalem just as Passover was approaching. Upon his arrival, an excited crowd welcomed him with open arms. But there was something that disturbed him: the Temple had become a marketplace. This enraged him, and with determination, he drove out the merchants who were there. He could not stand by while the sacred place was so disrespected. During these events, Jesus shared a meal with his disciples as a form of farewell. That same night, while Jesus prayed on the Mount of Olives, lost in thought, he was captured. Judas, one of his own, had betrayed him by revealing information to the religious leaders. And thus began what is known as the "Passion of Christ": a period of intense suffering that ended with his death. With his sacrifice for his convictions, Jesus pointed to his followers a path that many of them would choose to follow, enduring hostility and martyrdom. According to the New Testament accounts, while Jesus endured torture under his custody, Pilate chose to disengage from the incident, leaving the religious leaders to determine Jesus' fate, which they ultimately decided would be crucifixion.

The cross, once simply used to cause pain, became the heart of what Christianity represents. Here is the twist: It is said that Jesus resurrected three days after his death. Not only that, but he appeared to his disciples and, according to the account, gave them an important mission: they must spread the faith. After about forty days of appearing to various followers, Jesus ascended to heaven. This is documented in a book of the Bible called the *Acts of the Apostles*. Tragically, Judas could not bear the guilt of what he had done and took his own life. Meanwhile, the apostles, filled with determination, scattered across the Mediterranean area to share the teachings that Jesus had left them. Contemporary exegesis has distilled a fascinating revelation that Jesus of Nazareth, that iconic figure, might not have sought the mantle of divinity. The source of this deification was Paul, a master player in the theological board, who, with audacity, moved Christianity away from its Hebrew roots. This process by which Jesus' disciples try to clothe him with a divine halo of extraordinary supernaturalism is what the theologian Rudolf Bultmann called "mythologization" in his book *History of the Synoptic Tradition.*

Friedrich Nietzsche, that enigmatic intellectual, found an affinity with this perspective, elevating Jesus while savagely tearing apart Paul, even calling him the "genius of hate" in his incendiary work *The Antichrist.* In *Thus Spoke Zarathustra*, there is a phrase that, we might say, suggests some admiration: "The very word *Christianity* is a misunderstanding—at bottom there was only one Christian, and he died on the cross.[74] Numerous interpretations have surrounded Jesus and Paul over the centuries. Paul's role is a catalyst for debates: as we have said before, some praise him as the beacon that illuminated the Christian message, while others see him as the destroyer of the Jewish link. Analyzing the scriptures and thoughts of Paul of Tarsus, it becomes clear that he was not a great admirer of the Hebrew Torah. Although undoubtedly, before his conversion, Paul was a great exponent of Pharisaism, according to Philippians 3:5, "circumcised on the eighth day, of the stock of Israel, of the tribe of Benjamin, Hebrew of Hebrews; as touching the law, a Pharisee." Some think that precisely because of this, he was chosen as Apostle. Because of his perfect Pharisaism, which arose as a disciple of Gamaliel (Acts, 22:3). In fact, he seemed inclined to adopt a pagan perspective, which is evident in how he attributed divine characteristics to Jesus. Moreover, in his writings, we find that Paul had no problem with slavery and firmly believed that women should be submissive to their husbands. Paul's thought borrowed from different realms and adapted the figure of Jesus to a new set of beliefs. It is quite reasonable to call Paul of Tarsus a kind of architect of Christianity. With a firm hand and a determined vision, he laid the foundations for this religion. His main contribution was to expand it, not only among the Jews but also among the non-Jews, the Gentiles. So, if we trace his work, we will see that his impact was profound and lasting.

74. Friedrich Wilhelm Nietzsche, *The Antichrist*, trans. H.L. Mencken (New York: Alfred A. Knopf, 1920), sec. 39, 111.

However, there is an intriguing detail in how he approached the message of Jesus. Originally, Jesus' teaching focused on God, his Father. Paul, however, changed the game and, with a skillful twist, repositioned Christianity to revolve around Jesus himself. This was no small adjustment. It was, in many ways, a refoundation of the vision and core values of the faith. This is affirmed by the Protestant theologian N. T. Wright: "[...] through the symbols of creation, of bread and wine, we are invited to become part of Jesus's story—of the event of new creation itself—and thus become the chalices and bearers of God's new world and of the saving events that enable us to share it."[75]

Yet when a story rich in symbolism—originally bearing deep significance for a specific community—crosses borders and attains global reach, its transformation becomes inevitable. Wright himself maintains that historical events become theology when we uncover their deeper meaning, such that the birth of Jesus is both a historical fact and a symbol of redemption.

However, when a story full of symbolism, which originally had very special meaning for a specific group of people, crosses borders and becomes something global, it is inevitable that it will transform. This is evidenced, for example, by what the Protestant theologian N. T. Wright says: "Historical events become theology when we discover their deeper meaning. The birth of Jesus is both a fact and a symbol of redemption." This redemption is, for Paul's message, a universal redemption. It adjusts, redefines itself, and, in the process, adopts new nuances. It is like a river that flows, changing its course with the land it traverses. Essentially, it is being recontextualized and adapted to resonate with a broader audience. Thus, what was originally revered and unique for a minority is now spreading and forming connections with a wide range of cultures and perspectives.

Catholic, a word derived from the ancient Greek expression *katholikos*, *kata hólon*, *kata holou*, *katolou*, meaning "according to the

75. N. T. Wright, *Surprised by Hope: Rethinking Heaven, the Resurrection, and the Mission of the Church* [*Sorprendidos por la esperanza: Repensando el cielo, la resurrección y la vida eterna*], trans. (Barcelona: Editorial CLIE, 2014), 254.

whole," translates as "universal" and "of total reach." In the context of ancient Greece, this expression had no connection to faith but was instead a term used by citizens when coming together to discuss issues of collective importance. But then, like a chameleon changing color, this word metamorphosed. Early Christians, in a clever move, embraced the term *catholic* to represent the nature of the Church in its mission to reach hearts and minds in all corners of the world. The first person to link the term *catholic* to the Church was Saint Ignatius of Antioch: "Where the bishop appears, there the community is gathered, just as where Christ is, there is the Catholic Church" (*Epistle to the Smyrnaeans*, 8, 2). Christianity turned the symbol of a particular nation, like Judaism and its history, into proselytism and universal myth. However, since myth cannot be universal, it had to become philosophy, and just as religion made philosophy could not remain myth, it became theology. The Church Fathers turned the Christian myth into a conceptual theology of universal scope, dismantled the symbol of a nation into universal concepts, and transformed the particular history into general metaphysics.

Therefore, what once resonated in the Greek Agoras with one meaning later found a new home in the sermons and songs of a growing faith. This exposition, however, places us before an essential question: the idea of a truly universal symbol is, to some extent, an illusion. As we saw in the earlier chapters of this book, any symbol, no matter how many meanings it may have, is irrevocably intertwined with the history of a specific community. Let us take Mount Sinai as a case in point: its symbolism runs deep in the identity of the Jewish people, and moving it from that context makes that connection vanish. Religion, in its essence, is an experience that transcends the everyday, emerging from the depths of human existence. And this is where theology makes its appearance, with a mandate of global reach. When an attempt is made to give the Christian message a global scope, a metamorphosis emerges: symbols mutate into ideas, religion is reconfigured as theology, and myth is refined into philosophy.

Let us consider the shift from focusing on Jesus to developing Christianity: this represents a transition from the realm of legends to the territory of logic and from symbolic representation to conceptual clarity. When symbols are subjected to cold logic, an entire dimension of the symbol is lost. Heidegger clearly saw this when he stated that strict analyses do not do justice to symbols. It is like trying to describe a sunset in terms of physics; it simply does not capture the beauty. Symbols are powerful, bringing nuances, emotions, and perspectives that logic cannot touch. The mystery and the symbol have a very special connection. The symbolic, without mystery, makes no sense because it becomes conceptual since everything is understandable if there is no mystery. When the mystery is present and recognized, the symbolic gains strength and becomes true. Let us remember this. It is an unfortunate fact that when the symbol is forced through the filter of conceptualization, its multifaceted ability to be interpreted weakens, and its potential to invoke the enigmatic and the accessible is reduced. In essence, it's like a mistreatment.

> In the beginning was the logos, and the logos was with God, and the logos was God.
>
> (John, 1:1)

We are witnesses to a long process of theologizing the symbolic from and through a diversity of intellectual positions and debates. First, Paul stands out, followed by St. Augustine and St. Thomas, among others, as architects of this conceptualization, thanks to which it has also been possible to create a "church" as an institution or an organized faith. Therefore, we have moved from myth, symbol, and religion to theologization or conceptualization and finally to its institutionalization, with all the attenuating factors, including political and economic power relations. Mircea Eliade was already aware of the risks, although he considered the path necessary; in his words: "The transition from symbol to conceptual theology is a necessary but risky journey. Let us not lose the symbolic richness in the search for doctrinal clarity."

This transformation that Christianity has experienced over time has involved the intellectual clarification and consolidation of its principles, which has greatly impacted how it has spread and the essence of its symbols. Paul of Tarsus was a key figure in this process, overcoming cultural barriers and expanding the number of followers. However, it is important to note that this has not been an easy path. Paul left behind a diverse set of interpretations and a complex legacy that still generates debates. By dedicating time and effort to studying Christianity and the changes it has undergone, one can understand its evolution, the associated symbols, and the beliefs that sustain it. A meticulous analysis of this process has allowed us to acquire the ability to appreciate and understand the historical trajectory and teachings of Christianity insightfully so that we can later reflect deeply on the situation and challenges Christianity faces today.

At the beginning of this religion, Jesus' followers experienced a period of theological flourishing. But not everything was easy: there were ongoing debates and discussions about Jesus' teachings. In this historical context, significant theological and philosophical dilemmas arose that required well-thought-out and measured responses for those just entering the faith. Understanding the triad: God the Father, Jesus Christ, and the Holy Spirit represented a complex challenge. A heterogeneous contingent of believers embarked on the mission to amalgamate faith in a supreme being whose core vibrated with pure love, with the cruel reality of human pain and injustice. An imposing enigma unfolded: Is there a link that intertwines God's omnipotence and benevolence with the harsh landscape of human suffering? With internal maps and compasses, they set sail on a spiritual journey, digging for answers, trying to unveil the enigma of human sin and unravel the path to salvation. In that search, they encountered the intricate task of harmonizing the freedom of choice with ethical responsibility, inquiring how humanity, imprisoned by its own faults, could be emancipated under the mantle of divine grace. This question led to a range of theories and viewpoints that intertwined in the depths of early Christianity. Church leaders, supported by theologians and philosophers, laid out their reasoning and provided clarity to the emerging doctrines and theological foundations. Augustine, for example, stood out for his insightful thinking. Then came Scholasticism in the Middle

Ages, with its sophisticated intellectualism. Before us unfolds a vast horizon of spiritual inquiry, focused tenaciously on forging a corpus of theological doctrines of almost enigmatic depth.

Over time, scholars with an unquenchable thirst for knowledge took the lead in this colossal endeavor to subject the crucial challenges in Christian theology to conceptual scrutiny. At each step, an unceasing dedication was distilled. They ventured determinedly on an intellectual journey that led them to the deepest foundations of the Church. Their mission was to give meaning and clarity to aspects that, although fundamental, often seemed unattainable. These intellectuals sought to build a solid understanding with dedication and rigor, connecting the dots of centuries of religious wisdom. They embarked on a journey to concretely shape what is fundamentally symbolic, as well as to find logical solutions to questions rooted in myths. This has generated a change: what was symbolic has evolved into something more defined and religion now encompasses a wide range of doctrines.

Christianity in its early days showed greater unification, while today it has diversified into Catholicism, Greek Orthodox Church, Eastern Orthodox Church, Church of the East, and Protestantism. It is like an extensive mural of theological approaches, where each has its own character and background, evidencing a process of conceptualization that continues to diversify. An effort has been made to evolve the initial experience of Christianity through the objectification of ideas. Symbolic elements have become concepts in this process, and religion has acquired philosophical and theological dimensions. Facing questions of great magnitude and significance, scholars dedicated their intellects to building sophisticated theological systems based on meticulous interpretations of sacred texts. With effort and dedication, experts contributed to a more detailed understanding of the faith. The resulting doctrines, firmly rooted in these interpretations, have shaped the beliefs of countless people over the centuries.

During the early development of Christianity, prominent thinkers such as St. Augustine of Hippo and St. Thomas Aquinas were crucial in the creation of the Christian theological framework.

St. Thomas, known for his insight, wisely leveraged Aristotle's teachings. On the other hand, St. Augustine was heavily influenced by Platonic and Neoplatonic thought. There is a book that explains this well: *Determination of the Neoplatonic Influence on the Formation of St. Augustine's Thought* by Octavio Derisi. St. Augustine mentions in his *Confessions* that he had in his hands "books of the Platonists," where he discovered an intelligible world above the material world of the Manichaeans, a world of ideas or intelligible truths, which he later identified with the mind of the Word. Both, with their respective inspirations, were key in the fabric of Christian theology.

Throughout history, Christian theology has followed a path of change and growth, absorbing elements from philosophy, science, and culture. Today, it stands out as a solid field of study. Seminaries and universities approach it with seriousness, offering a space to analyze and reflect on its aspects. Let us take, for example, the doctrine of the Trinity. It is fascinating how this teaching, which articulates the union of three distinct entities or persons within a divinity, was shaped according to Christian theology. Imagine the halls filled with passionate scholars debating and analyzing the scriptures with magnifying glasses. After these effervescent discussions, in the year 325, the First Council of Nicaea was the crucible where this doctrine finally took its definitive form. It is also important to highlight that there are groups called "non-Trinitarians" who do not subscribe to the idea of the Trinity and who depart from different interpretations of the elements that make it up. This shows that Christian theology is not a simple field; on the contrary, it is quite convoluted. Discrepancies in the belief of something as central as the Trinity are a testament to that.

The process of conceptualization of Jesus

It is important to distinguish between two concepts: "absolute inclusivism" and "absolute exclusivism." Absolute inclusivism can be compared to a speaker proclaiming a message to an entire audience without exception. The problem is that, by addressing everyone, the message becomes diluted and fails to truly connect with anyone, making it ineffective. On the other hand, a speaker follows absolute exclusivism when speaking in a closed room, only to a very specific group of believers who share the same interpretation of their faith. Here, the message is very focused but excludes many. In summary, absolute inclusivism is like casting a net into the sea, while absolute exclusivism is like fishing in a fishbowl. Both approaches have their limitations, highlighting that extreme discourse does not serve as a bridge between humans and that balance is key when communicating.

Let us think of the shrewd speaker as a tightrope walker, walking the fine line between inclusion and exclusion. Jesus, as a master communicator, did not speak to a hermetic group but to one that was permeable and dynamic. The crowd was his audience, to whom he addressed enigmatic parables, while his disciples received plain explanations in intimacy. Discipleship brings with it privileged access. Jesus was extremely balanced in his teachings. The master calibrated the depth and accessibility to connect with a diverse audience, not leaving anyone forgotten but offering additional layers of understanding to his disciples who sought them eagerly.

The disciples of the apostles, including those of Paul, insisted on transforming a message from a Jewish sect into a doctrine with a global reach, where Jesus would be relevant to all. To this end, they used tactics to universalize this message rooted in symbolism. Symbolism carries with it a rich history, but if it is stripped of its historical context, it loses its essence, and its meaning becomes diluted. Therefore, their approach included what was necessary for the message to spread and resonate with a wider audience. It is important to note that when a story has roots in a specific culture, it is primarily that community that can grasp its essence. Imagine there is a message with symbolic weight in a religion. If someone unfamiliar with the traditions and history behind it is able to easily understand it, then we are no longer talking about symbolism. In that case, it is more accurate to say the message is conceptual because it does not require prior cultural knowledge to be understood. The statement "a straight line is the shortest path between two points" implies a concept anyone can understand. However, symbolic messages like *Hare Kṛṣṇa* or *Jaya Śrī Rādhe* are not obvious or self-evident and cannot be deciphered by just anyone; they are complex and require a deeper understanding to be grasped, but for that reason, they do not jump out immediately; they are discovered through a story or narration.

Generally, behind a symbolic message stands a people or community. Because the symbol, generation after generation, develops a tradition or school of thought where interpretations of the masters' teachings are passed down. However, when a particular reading of the master's tradition is canonized over the others, it ceases to be a tradition. This happens when the symbol is conceptualized, creating a single possible true interpretation of the symbol. Therefore, while the symbol par excellence calls for and reconciles a variety of interpretations, its conceptualization prevents this richness, making polysemy turn into orthodoxy. This moment, when polysemy becomes orthodoxy, is marked by the difference in approach to the symbol. In the eyes of religion, the symbol enjoyed an immense wealth of possible meanings. However, the philosophization and theologization of religion conceptualizes the symbol and gives birth to orthodoxy. *Orthodoxy* is a Greek term composed of *doxa* (faith) and *ortho* (correct), thus meaning "the correct faith."

The term, introduced by Plato as *orthótes*, which we translate as "correction of religion," establishes the existence of an authentic faith that the leaders of a particular religion and their immediate followers preach and teach, demarcating boundaries beyond which "heresy" is born. Heretics are those who do not accept that single interpretation and therefore remain outside of orthodoxy, relegated to followers of the incorrect. Therefore, anyone who interprets the sacred book in any way other than that which adheres to the "correct faith" will be cursed, cut off, anathematized, or excommunicated from the religion because they are breaking away from it. Therefore, conceptualization not only creates orthodoxy but also gives birth to the anathematized, that is, heresy, which excludes or marginalizes those who interpret or think about the symbol differently. In short, orthodoxy increases heresy because it requires its existence;

the orthodox seeks and pursues the heretic until they find and excommunicate them, and even in the case that they cannot find one, or if one does not exist, they create one to justify their own existence. This is why the term *heresy* only exists within the context of conceptual religion.

By conceptualizing their symbols, a specific type of congregation is produced. Therefore, those with different interpretations can continue to be part of an open congregation that accepts that its symbol is polysemous. Conceptual religion, on the other hand, by creating a structure based on orthodoxy and heresy, ends up giving rise to a closed congregation that only accepts those who interpret the symbol in one way. The preservation of the symbol and its safeguarding against the concept is ultimately what marks the difference between two different articulations of religion, with all that it entails. For while the symbol has something in common that can unite everyone, the concept disaggregates, discriminates, and excludes.

This congregation articulated around orthodoxy and heresy is also established in terms of power. In short, its sole "correct faith" becomes power by imposing itself forcibly over other interpretations as the only canonical or valid one. By conceptualizing, the symbol loses its congregational power and, therefore, its meaning, as the term "symbol" precisely means "to gather, to unite, or to reconcile" a multitude of different interpretations. Then, the Christianity of Jesus stops being a symbolic religion to become a conceptual philosophy and religion.

The symbol lost its richness when it was directed only to sect members and became absolute exclusivism. Jesus shared his teachings from an intermediate position between absolute exclusivism, or the sectarian spirit, and absolute inclusivism, which addresses all people in any way. Wisdom lies in finding the balance between these two extremes. The process of conceptualization of Jesus that began with Paul and his disciples later spread to the Fathers of the Church in Alexandria, who began to increase their use of Western philosophy, which transcended the religious realm to even interfere in the social and political spheres, as clearly demonstrated by the theologizing philosophy of Saint Augustine in *The City of God* (*De Civitate Dei*). It is also interesting to note that to belong to the Roman Empire, one had to belong to the Christian Church, as this meant being baptized and becoming "civilized." Otherwise, one was considered a barbarian if they held the faith of the rural areas, i.e., if they were from the countryside. Conversely, to be considered civilized, one had to belong to the city, to *civitas* or Rome, which could only be entered through baptism. By aligning the church with political power, it transformed into the religious institution that maintained that power, which, for its legitimization, needed the support of a universal power. And to achieve that, nothing is better than to have God's backing.

Unlike the Christian conception, the Hebrew tradition is a culture of the ear, as can be seen in the *Shema Israel* or "Hear, O Israel" because, for this tradition, faith is based on what one hears. The most important thing is what parents transmit through testimony in the form of a story, not so much what each individual can see. The story is transmitted by a people, whereas truth is an individual matter in Greek culture and later in Christianity. Thomas tells the apostles that he will not believe until he sees Jesus and places his finger in the wound, to which Jesus replies, "Blessed are those who have not seen and yet have believed" (John, 20:29). For Jesus, faith is not about seeing but believing in the testimony of someone who narrates. Truth lies in the story or narration; therefore, faith moves in a dimension that transcends the visual verification of the truth or falsity of the stories. Later, the Fathers of the Church and Saint Augustine, under the influence of Greek philosophy, introduced the matter of sight, that is, of the understanding of the idea or concept.

As we argued earlier, the image is the visible idea of the thing, and the concept is its invisible image, which means that both theology and idolatry, filtered through Greek philosophy and the "philosophical turn" itself, start with sight as the metaphor for truth, because according to Greek philosophy, truth resides in what can be seen, whether with the eyes or with the mind. It is precisely this that iconoclasts called *concupiscencia ad oculus*.

This new approach brought about a profound change because it was no longer about the resonance of the Hebrew symbol that is heard but about a search for the Truth in the Hellenic style of what can be seen. This is a significant shift because, until now, the focus had been on the congruence between what we say and what we observe; from now on, the validity of the narrative would depend on our ability to conceptualize its truth.

It is precisely within this new context that "the true religion," the exact interpretation or orthodoxy of the symbol, will occupy a central place. Saint Augustine wrote a book titled *The True Religion*, an eminently philosophical text that speaks extensively about Plato. This particular text is one of the foundations of this renaissance of Christianity because it is through this Greek-Platonic vision of Saint Augustine that Christianity merges with Greek philosophical mythology, shedding its Hebrew symbolic essence in the process. This is where we can talk about a mythologization of Christianity or, equivalently, a Hellenization of what, in its beginnings, was essentially a branch of Judaism. This Hellenization was not only due to Greek philosophy, particularly Platonism, which impregnated Christianity but also due to the colonialist drive of the Greeks to spread their beliefs. The Hebrews, on the other hand, never entered the race to gain converts because, for them, the more exclusive, the more powerful their faith was. The Sinai revelation was for a chosen people, without the need for anyone to join them. Jesus did not appear on the scene with the idea of founding a new religious "ism" but was faithful to his ancestral roots.

From Jesus as a symbol to conceptual Christianity

In the process of transforming early Christianity into the various organized doctrines we know today, we clearly see how elements of the legend were distilled and refined. Focusing on the figure of Jesus, we find a story imbued with symbolic meaning. After the theological interpretation of a prominent Christian thinker like Paul, Jesus becomes the Logos, or the fundamental principle, in this new perspective. Similar to how the mythical Prometheus defied the gods by stealing fire and giving it to humanity, Paul works to elevate the narrative of Jesus beyond the realm of myths, providing renewed purpose and meaning to the followers of the faith. In his effort to universalize a myth born within a community or nation, its abstraction becomes unavoidable, thereby transforming it into theology. When constructing a theological building, ideas converge toward a single direction, a singular hermeneutic or conceptual narrative. Every theology that becomes conceptualized ceases to be a symbolic narrative rooted in a community, conglomerate, or lineage, instead acquiring a universal character in its message.

Abstracting the myth implies annihilating its meaning. Consequently, universalizing Hebrew symbolism inevitably leads to the conceptualization of figures like Abraham, Isaac, and Jacob, the revelation on Mount Sinai, and the figure of Moses. The sacred chronicle, upon abstraction, is stripped of its original authentic meaning, not merely for the Hebrew nation but for humanity as a whole. Indeed, the result of any attempt to universalize a symbolic narrative culminates in a gain in comprehensive transparency at the cost of the potency of its meaning. Meaning does not always coexist harmoniously with reasoning, logic, and understanding. Like in love, the conviction that the person I love is the most beautiful on Earth may lack rational sense but be full of meaning.

When the Pauline Jesus directs his disciples toward universal proclamation, a legitimate transition from myth to the Logos occurs, giving rise to Christianity. From this cardinal moment, it is impossible to conceive an orthodox Christianity stripped of theology. In Paul's particular case, it is fitting to accept that he does not adhere to a radical approach to the existence and message of Jesus but embarks on a process of conceptualizing his doctrines. However, it is important to highlight that this is not a creation of his genius but a liberation from the restrictions imposed by the Jewish framework, expanding it into the Hellenistic cultural landscape, which, as a result, grants it a cosmopolitan perspective, emphasizing the liberation and freedom Jesus offers:

> For Christ has set us free. Stand firm, then, and do not let yourselves be burdened again by a yoke of slavery… There is neither Jew nor Gentile, neither slave nor free, neither male nor female, for you are all one in Christ.
>
> (Paul's Letter to the Galatians 5:1; 3:28)

Judaism, on the other hand, expresses reluctance toward propagation and dissemination, as it guards and defends the Hebrew myth, upholding the inaccessibility of the symbol. The Jesus outlined by Paul dilutes the original Hebrew myth by broadening the narrow entrance through which only a small minority could pass, but by expanding it, no one can cross. Consequently, it is essential for Christianity to incorporate and maintain Hebrew symbolism; its absence would be unsustainable for the integrity of the doctrine. In other words, Christianity maintains a Hellenized or colonized Hebrew symbolism. In contrast, Judaism holds a divergent perspective. A prominent scholar, Yeshayahu Leibowitz (1903-1994), strongly asserted that the New Testament holds no significant relevance within the Jewish worldview. It becomes paramount to understand that any assertion made by a religious entity regarding Jesus is destined to fail. Thus, any theology born from the womb of systematized faith cannot be either truthful or authentic. In reality, there is no divergence between those who worship Jesus and those who persecuted him. The priestly caste, instigators of his demise, has merely mutated in denomination and appearance, but in spirit, it is exactly the same. The relevance of institutions, whether Jewish, Catholic, Hindu, or Buddhist, dissipates, as all display a similar methodical operation.

Our acquisitions in the Christian discipline are tributaries of texts, courses, and lectures, but my vision of Jesus is a direct child of meditation. Only one who has unveiled the truth of his essence can truly embrace the understanding of Jesus. In the depths of meditation, the true encounter with all the enlightened masters of history occurs. The discrepancies between them are nothing more than superficial cultural or intellectual adornments. By transcending the realm of thought, we find ourselves beyond the dialectic of differences as mutually exclusive interpretations. Embodied faith fervently holds that Jesus represents the only way to salvation. However, the essence of reality is revealed in the light that each enlightened master embodies a unique path, as the routes to Truth are as innumerable as the stars in the night sky.

Religions unite in the symbol

As a result of orthodoxy, which generates the conceptualization of the symbol, the preacher, with his ceremonial habit, does not seek Truth in its pure form but aims to build an empire around it. In this paradoxical scenario, the clergyman emerges not as a guide but as the sole architect of the concept of sin, merely in order to trade the offer of redemption. From his commercial standpoint, backed by a conceptual interpretation of religiosity, he is compelled to assert vehemently that his path is the only legitimate one and that any other path is riddled with errors. In his calculation, what he seeks are not genuine believers but convinced individuals; he does not pursue followers or faithful disciples but a clientele that consumes his dogmas. For this very reason, all organized religions proclaim tenaciously to be the only way to salvation, condemning us if we venture onto other paths. It becomes a conspicuous paradox that the ecclesiastical guild, that institutionalized network that with its actions favored the eradication of luminous beings like Jesus, paradoxically rises as the architects of the canons of their sacred scriptures, as well as assuming the role of authorized interpreters of their vital lessons. Nevertheless, the genuine assimilation of the essence of Jesus' teachings proves practically unattainable through the mediation of the ecclesiastical guild. The essence of Jesus' message is discovered, not in the dogmas dictated from pulpits, but in introspection, in the profound depths of our inner being. This sacred sanctuary is not attained by sermon orators but by visionary mystics.

For countless centuries, institutionalized religion has strived to keep humanity in a state of perpetual immaturity, fearing that, upon achieving full maturity, its members will no longer be susceptible to childish manipulation. It is of vital importance to internalize that the need for salvation is an invention, and that in fact, we are participants and products of nature itself. By stigmatizing the natural essence of being, we generate feelings of guilt, a powerful tool in the hands of the priestly caste to orchestrate their commercial trickery. For this reason, Swiss psychologist Carl Jung maintained that Jesus is not a historical person but an archetype of the collective unconscious. He does not speak of Christ but of the "Christic."

It is immensely difficult to conceive that Jesus proclaimed his crucifixion as the redemptive sacrifice for sinful humanity rather than opting for a more plausible reading that this sacrifice is but the fruit of a doctrine imposed by the priestly lineage upon the sacred texts. After all, the earliest gospels were written at least a century after Jesus' death. There is no need for priests or any redemption. What is truly essential is the liberation from guilt and the sinful self-perception. However, the priestly caste obstructs this. The essence lies in the recognition of consciousness. We speak of the pre-Pauline Jesus, that is, conceptualized and transformed into Christ, the symbol of Christianity. The same happens with Muhammad and Islam, Buddha and Buddhism, Mahavira and Jainism, Lord Chaitanya and *Gauḍīya* Vaishnavism. The inner experience of enlightened masters challenges all institutionalization, yet when attempting to organize the master's teachings, their essence is murdered, leaving only a dead idol, incapable of transformation.

We can consider ourselves followers of Jesus but without the need to harbor sympathy for any Christianity. In fact, to truly connect with Jesus, it is vital to transcend all Christianity. The churches obstruct the understanding of Jesus' authentic teachings. The enigma of Jesus' identity lies at the heart of history. Many have dared to question, and others have answered, though only in fragments. Both the question and its echo resonate clothed with deep prejudices. Those who question rebel against his divinity; those who answer remain blind to his humanity. Both inquisitors and responders are willing to accept a half-Jesus. The Jews lean toward his humanity but deny his divine aspect. The Christians, eager to believe in a divine Jesus, renounce his humanity. Those who refuse to recognize him as a being of flesh and bone, alongside humanity, are called Docetists.

Others, the Arians, do not consent to see him as divine. This mystery is not exclusive to Jesus but pertains to all enlightened masters. Both Jesus and any enlightened sage can only plunge into the abyss of our soul when embraced entirely as a living lighthouse.

This debate about the humanity or divinity of Jesus, which has pervaded the history of Christianity, is anchored in another historical dilemma revolving around whether Jesus was the son of man or the son of God. Both debates are mere products of the conceptualization and theologization we have described so far, which have nothing to do with the symbolic perspective from which humanity-divinity and being the son of man or God pose no contradiction whatsoever. The conflict does not reside in Jesus but in our incessant battles to cage him in concepts. Jesus stands as a symbolic bridge between the relative and the absolute, the manifest and the hidden, the ephemeral and the eternal, the human and the divine. Every interaction between polarities resonates with an ineffable ecstasy, a dance of complementary powers. The burning whisper of the meeting between the masculine and the feminine unfolds in an ecstatic dance. And at the heart of such dynamics, we find the figure of Jesus, the sublime meeting of the deepest polarities: the human and the divine, converging in one vibrant entity. Similarly, the figure of Lord Chaitanya Mahāprabhu resonates as a deep echo of the apparent divine duality, for he personifies the intoxicating encounter between the most sacred polarities of lover and beloved, merging into one being in a perpetual dance of mutual adoration. Every question or echo arising from the religious conceptual sphere about the humanity or divinity of Jesus is inexorably at odds with the Truth, for such inquiries or answers only achieve genuineness when emanating from the source of symbolic innocence.

The distinction between Jesus and the vastness of humanity does not lie in **what he is** but in **the consciousness of what he is**. Jesus is the son of God, just as we are; the divergence lies in the fact that, unlike the rest of us, he knows it and is fully conscious of it. There is a possibility that someone has bestowed upon us a fortune of millions of dollars, but in our ignorance, we remain nothing more than peasants. We will emerge as an opulent being only when the

Truth is revealed to us. We are all as much children of God as he is, but human ignorance constructs the vast disparity. Jesus is the "only" son of God, for he is the only one fully awakened to that reality. Jesus is as human as any one of us, and we are as divine as he is, knowing Jesus is discovering our true essence. The humanity in Jesus or in us are not two disparate manifestations, for the human is a reflection of the divine, and the divine is the essence of the human. Understanding Jesus involves entering that sublime encounter between the human and the divine in the starry night.

Inherent in each of us lies a divine spark, a celestial shoot of the Supreme Architect, hidden in the dark cave of our interior. Absorbed, we find ourselves more fascinated by the vanity of possessions than by the essence of our being. What requires revelation is nothing but our undeniable divine nature, hidden beneath the surface like consciousness. Our Heavenly Progenitor, undisputed sovereign of the infinite cosmos, languishes in the oblivion of our memory. Neither Jesus nor any enlightened master possesses exclusive privileges over us. Nothing would justify divine preference, for it would imply supreme injustice. Every being is endowed with identical powers. On the divine platform, we all share an undeniable common ground. Inequality is a human invention, a specter of our creation. Through the divine lens, every soul is equivalent, with no distinctions between one and the entire cosmos. Jesus, a genuine embodiment of humanity, fervently embraced earthly existence, being an example of authenticity. Despite his commitment to the fullness of the human experience, his simultaneous divinity cannot be denied.

Nonetheless, a contingent of skeptics persists, arguing that entities like Jesus or Lord Chaitanya cannot be divine, for a Supreme Being cannot be confined to a spatiotemporal framework. They argue that infinity cannot be restricted to finitude, nor the unlimited bound to the limited. It is inexplicable to them how eternity can materialize in the temporal realm or how the infinitude of consciousness can be embodied in such a limited vessel. It seems absurd to them to think of divinity given to street dances and songs or teaching publicly.

अवजानन्ति मां मूढा मानुषीं तनुमाश्रितम् ।
परं भावमजानन्तो मम भूतमहेश्वरम्

avajānanti māṁ mūḍhā
mānuṣīṁ tanum āśritam
paraṁ bhāvam ajānanto
mama bhūta-maheśvaram

Fools mock me when I descend in human form. They do not know my transcendental nature as the Supreme Lord of all that exists.

(Bhagavad Gita, 9.11)

The deepest veil of reality reveals the divine incarnation in every tiny creature: God unfolds in every baby. Arising with grace, flowers become divine effigies, and in puppies, God reveals Himself in their innocence. In every sprout of promise, a sacred reflection emerges. In the vastness of an ordinary cosmos, a human has the power to plant enough seeds to fill a neighborhood with their progeny. Therefore, to think that the Supreme Architect of Existence, the Ineffable Father, is limited to a single son is an assumption that borders on the absurd.

If we perceive Jesus as a symbol, rather than distancing ourselves from figures like Buddha, Muhammad, Moses, or Lao Tzu, we are brought closer and invited to brotherhood. However, when the symbol petrifies into a concept, the reality it symbolizes becomes distorted, and the discord of heresy arises. Heresy, as we have seen, is the bitter fruit of conceptualization, the rigidity of a truth that forgets its origin in symbolism. A spiritual symbol is true when it unites us with all religions, when it builds bridges to all beliefs, and not when it erects walls. When it mutates into concepts, religion transforms into theology, the abode of heretics, gentiles, apostates, and pagans. This conceptualization movement is what prevents humans from discovering in the symbol the authentic underlying unity of all humanity. In its essence, the symbol unifies, integrates, and gathers the fragments. Its nature lies in the interpretation that unites us all on spiritual paths, on all paths to divinity. The represented reality becomes blurred in the ethereal dance of symbols, facilitating communion between all beliefs.

No theological volume can unravel the true figure of Jesus; only through the arc of intense meditation can we touch upon his essence. In the tender nest of thoughts, built with delicate twigs of devotion during meditation, we contemplate the newborn Christ, pacified by the dove of our inner peace. The arrival of the new Christic Consciousness in the village of our meditation will be an ineffably captivating, strengthening, and expansive spectacle for our soul. One must prepare for the coming of Christ, adorning the Christmas tree of their meditative consciousness with sparkling perceptions of the divine Christ, stars of wisdom that eternally shine and lotus buds of divine love.

Chapter 18

Christ as a living symbol according to John Damascene

A devout Christian of Arab descent, Saint John Mansur (675-749 CE), nicknamed Damascene for being born in Damascus, Syria, was the precursor of the tradition of Christian Aristotelians and is also recognized as one of the two great poets of the Eastern Church. During the second half of the 7th century CE, Syria, like Palestine, was under Muslim rule. In the early stage of the occupation, the Muslims maintained a certain degree of tolerance toward Christians. John's father, Sergio Mansur, was a man of resources and a tax collector of the caliphate for the Christians, a position that did not prevent him from being a fervent Catholic and assisting his fellow Christians. John and his family lived under Islamic governance, which later created the unusual situation of him being a Father of the Christian Church, openly living his Christian faith at the caliph's court, protected from the reprisals of a Christian emperor whom he criticized without restraint for his heresies.

As a philosopher and theological author, John never sought originality. His work consisted of organizing and compiling the writings of his predecessors. Saint John Damascene received solid training in theology, philosophy, music, and astronomy during his youth. He was inspired by his tutor, Cosmas, a monk of great knowledge who had come to the city as a Christian prisoner and whom John's father, Sergio, bought his freedom to assign him as the tutor of his children. John Damascene was a polemicist and author of *Disputations of Christians and Saracens*, one of the first in the genre. His greatest work was *The Fountain of Knowledge*, written around 743 CE.

Despite his training in his youth, John was inclined to follow in his father's footsteps as head of the tax collection department, a position he eventually inherited and performed with integrity and efficiency, earning the admiration of the city's prominent Muslim leaders. Around 700 CE, after several years in the role, he decided to dedicate himself to the ascetic life and live the gospel radically. John distributed all his belongings and wealth among the poor, freed his servants, and embarked on a pilgrimage to Palestine. Along with his brother, who would later become the bishop of Maiouna, they gave themselves to the monastic path. John was honored with ordination as a priest and entrusted with the duty of preaching at the Basilica of the Holy Sepulchre in Jerusalem. In this sacred environment, John dedicated most of his time to prayer and the contemplative analysis of the Holy Scriptures. Later, he entered the Monastery of Saint Sabas, located between Jerusalem and Bethlehem, where he began writing his first works against the iconoclasts and composing hymns and poems until his death at an advanced age.

When John Mansur arrived at the Monastery of Saint Sabas, he was given the following rules: "Never attempt to impose your will. Learn to die to yourself so that you achieve complete renunciation of all creatures. Dedicate your actions, sufferings, and prayers to God. Do not take pride in your knowledge or anything else; instead, convince yourself more and more of your ignorance and weakness. Abandon vanity, distrust your own judgments, and do not covet extraordinary heavenly appearances and privileges. Expel from your memory everything that binds you to the world. Faithfully adhere to silence and understand that it is easy to fall into sin by doing only good."

Following these guidelines to the letter, Saint John Damascene quickly reached a high level of spiritual excellence. He never left the monastery except to evangelize in Jerusalem. His transcribed homilies spread like a valuable treasure, propagating throughout the East. One of his most renowned sermons was on the Transfiguration, where he reflects on his favorite theme: the duality of Christ's nature. He cites fundamental texts of the Scriptures to support the primacy of Saint Peter and defends the Catholic doctrine of sacramental Confession, attributing various graces to the intercession of the Virgin Mary.

The second of his three sermons on the Assumption is especially noteworthy for its detailed description of the ascension of the Virgin Mary's body to heaven, a story, he clarifies, based on the oldest and most reliable tradition. The dogma of the Assumption of the Virgin Mary into Heaven would be proclaimed many centuries later. Both the rules John received when entering the monastery and his later sermons and homilies are significant as they frame his position in the debate known as the Iconoclastic Crisis.

At that time, Constantinople was immersed in a deep ecclesiastical storm whose epicenter could be formulated as follows: is it permissible within the Catholic Church to depict sacred figures such as Christ, the Virgin Mary, and the saints? This storm began in 730, when Leo III, the Byzantine emperor of the time, decided to issue an edict eradicating the cult of images. This edict was confirmed in 754 CE through the Council of Hiereia. This imperial move was not arbitrary but rather a response to practices already rooted at the beginning of the 8th century among Christians, who tended to illustrate the walls of their churches with frescoes and create wooden icons to decorate their homes and to display during processions in the streets of Constantinople.

In reality, this conflict, which stretched over a century, was permeated with overwhelming violence. It carved a deep division in the Church, with both factions alternatively bearing the weight of anathemas. It also caused a relentless persecution of monks who defended icons, resulting in the destruction of most works from before this period. Therefore, the oldest icons from the 6th century that have survived come from regions considerably distant from the Byzantine capital, particularly from the Monastery of Saint Catherine in Sinai. From the iconoclasts' perspective, the veneration of images was interpreted as idolatry and a direct confrontation with Moses' edicts. This position was joined by the growing influence of Islam at the time, a faith that categorically rejects the depiction of icons, and it was further compounded by the fact that the veneration of these representations occurred primarily in the private sphere, suggesting that it was a custom predominantly feminine.

John Damascene openly took sides in the debate, being one of the most solid and fervent defenders of the cult of sacred images during the bitter period of controversy with the iconoclasts, who advocated for their destruction. In fact, exasperated by the writings of Saint John Damascene, the Byzantine emperor devised a plan to harm him. He managed to seize a manuscript of the saint, who, remember, lived as a subject of a foreign power. He designed a false letter through expert scribes in which John allegedly committed to delivering Damascus to the monarch. With such a letter in hand, Leo III warned the caliph of Damascus, "as a faithful ally," about the existence of a traitor among them. Although Saint John proclaimed his innocence, the caliph assumed the letter's authenticity and ordered the amputation of his right hand. However, according to the saint's earliest biographer, that hand was supernaturally reattached to the arm by the intervention of the Virgin Mary. The caliph acknowledged Saint John's innocence due to the miracle and reinstated him in his position. By then, however, the saint had become disillusioned with the world and decided to withdraw to the Monastery of Saint Sabas in Palestine, where, around 749 CE, at nearly 100 years old, he bade farewell to the earthly world.

Due to his profound knowledge and great erudition in theology and other secular subjects, John was nicknamed "the Saint Thomas of the East." So much so that Leo XIII named him a Doctor of the Church in 1890 due to his significant contribution to the theology and liturgy of the Eastern Church; he is known for his three *Discourses Against Those Who Defame Sacred Images*. He left an important doctrinal legacy with his work *De Fide Orthodoxa*, which provides an original synthesis of Greek Patristic thought and the doctrinal decisions of the Councils of his time and continues to be an essential reference for both Catholic and Orthodox theology. He also wrote *De Haeresibus*, on the most widespread Christian heresies of his time. His postulates and those of Saint Germanus of Constantinople were confirmed during the Second Council of Nicaea, even after his death. His great work, *The Fountain of Knowledge*, is the first theological summa in history. This work is divided into three parts:

1. Dialectics: A philosophical part that presents essential concepts of Aristotelian-Porphyrian logic (concepts like synonymy, homonymy, paronymy, etc.). It also addresses themes of the Trinitarian nature (concepts like person and hypostasis). Why is the *Isagoge* (an introduction to Aristotle's categories by Porphyry, which was the standard logic manual of the time) related to the Trinity? Because they are useful given the genus, species, specific difference, species or individual framework, which easily fits with essence, relations of origin, and hypostasis.
2. A Repertoire of Heresies: *De Haeresibus*, as previously mentioned. It is a repertoire modeled after *Panarion* by Epiphanius of Salamis, except for heresy 100 (Monothelitism: the heresy that claims Christ had two natures but only one divine will, condemned at the Third Council of Constantinople) and issues with Islam.
3. A Set of 100 Theological Chapters: Titled *The Orthodox Faith*. This part has a plan divided into four parts: *De Deo Uno* (On the One God), Creation, History of Salvation, and Various Issues. The History of Salvation corresponds to Christology and constitutes the historical core of theological summas in Latin. It is one of the main sources for medieval theology. It is credited with the theory of divine names, which distinguishes between negative names (what God is not) and positive names (what is fitting to God's nature but does not signify His nature itself).

His pure devotion through his literary work greatly enriched the liturgy of the Eastern Church. The writings of John Damascene in favor of the cult of images emerged at a specific historical period when the practice of venerating sacred images among Christians was virtually nonexistent. This situation originated from a tradition that discouraged it, based on interpretations of biblical passages like

"You shall not make for yourselves a graven image, or any likeness of anything that is in the heaven above, or on the earth below, or in the waters beneath the earth. You shall not bow down to them or serve them" (Exodus 20:4–5); "Nor shall you set up for yourselves a sacred pillar, which the Lord your God hates" (Deuteronomy 16:22); and "You shall not make idols for yourselves, nor shall you set up a carved image or a sacred pillar, nor shall you place a stone image in your land to bow down to it, for I am the Lord your God" (Leviticus 26:1).

Against the strict campaign that the Byzantine emperor Leo the Isaurian had unleashed against the veneration of sacred images, John, at the request of Pope Gregory III, took on the role of tireless defender of these images throughout his life, employing several strategies to challenge the iconoclastic mindset. John's position was based on an interpretation of the sacred scriptures, with his main argument being the central event of the Christian faith, namely, the Incarnation of the Word of God: if the Son of God had presented Himself as a man and had transitioned from being invisible to visible and tangible, then Jesus was the divine image symbolizing and materializing the invisible God:

> He is the image of the invisible God, the firstborn of all creation.
>
> (Colossians, 1:15)

By studying the decrees of the Second Council of Nicaea, convened as a result of the internal conflict in the Catholic Church known as Iconoclasm, it is possible to understand the intricacy of the dilemma. The word iconoclasm comes from the Greek *eikon*, meaning "image," and *klastes*, meaning "destroyer," indicating that the term iconoclasm is closely tied to the demolition or destruction of images. The iconoclasts, including ecclesiastical figures like Saint Augustine and Saint Ambrose, were theologians and Christian leaders who argued that Christianity, following the writings of the Old Testament, should not retain or venerate images. According to their perspective, graphic representations should not be held because God is incomprehensible. Creating a tangible representation of the intangible God would be a form of idolatry. In contrast, defenders of these representations, particularly Saint John Damascene, argued that Christ is the representation of God the Father and that we are the reflection of Christ. Just as the Father becomes visible in the Son, the Son becomes visible in the images, which are windows to heaven. The Father is the authority of Christ, and Christ is our authority; therefore, whoever observes us sees Christ, and whoever sees Christ sees the Father. Therefore, we access the Father through the Son.

The enigma posed by the iconoclasts transcended the realm of Christian art and called into question the Christian conception as a whole. The stance of the defenders of images was unequivocal. According to an aphorism by St. Germanus, Patriarch of Constantinople and victim of the iconoclastic heresy, what was being questioned was the entirety of divine economy in its human manifestation since contemplating the human face of the Son of God is seeing a reflection of the invisible God.

> And the Word was made flesh and dwelt among us [and we beheld his glory, the glory as of the only begotten of the Father], full of grace and truth.
>
> (John, 1:14)

Under this premise, the representation of the human face of the Son of God could be considered a visible representation of the invisible God.

Pope John Paul II himself, in his apostolic letter to the bishops of the Catholic Church on the twelfth centenary of the Second Council of Nicaea (787 CE), wrote the following:

> Therefore, art can represent the form, the effigy of God's human face and lead the one who contemplates it to the ineffable mystery of God made man for our salvation. Thus, Pope Hadrian could write: "By means of a visible face, our spirit will be carried by a spiritual attraction towards the invisible majesty of the divinity through the contemplation of the image where is represented the flesh that the Son of

> God deigned to take for our salvation. May we thus adore and praise him together while glorifying in spirit this same Redeemer for, as it is written, 'God is Spirit,' and that is why we spiritually adore his divinity."[76]

Furthermore, in his catechesis to the general audience on May 6, 2009, Pope Benedict XVI reminded that:

John Damascene was also among the first to distinguish, in the cult, both public and private, of the Christians, between worship (*latreia*), and veneration (*proskynesis*): the first can only be offered to God, spiritual above all else, the second, on the other hand, can make use of an image to address the one whom the image represents.[77] Obviously, the saint can in no case be identified with the material of which the image is made. This distinction is very important in responding in a Christian way to those who sought to view the strict prohibition in the Old Testament of using images in worship as universal and eternal. This was also a great debate in the Islamic world, which accepts this Jewish tradition of the total exclusion of images. St. John Damascene articulates his apologetics through two fundamental categories: image and veneration. We rely on trustworthy sources such as the famous work *On Holy Images*, composed of three discourses that progressively clarify and add new developments to the previous one. In the first part of the book, called *Against Those Who Decry Holy Images*, he says as follows:

> Of old, God the incorporeal and uncircumscribed was never depicted. Now, however, when God is seen clothed in flesh, and conversing with men, I make an image of the God whom I see. I do not worship matter, I worship the God of matter, who became matter for my sake, and deigned to

76. John Paul II, *Apostolic Letter Duodecimum Saeculum*, to the Episcopate of the Catholic Church on the occasion of the 1200th anniversary of the Second Council of Nicaea, (December 4, 1987), III, 9. Citing the Letter of Hadrian I to the Emperors, in Mansi XI, 1062AB.

77. Benedict XVI, General Audience, Saint Peter's Square, May 6, 2009, https://www.vatican.va

> inhabit matter, who worked out my salvation through matter. I will not cease from honouring that matter which works my salvation. I venerate it, though not as God. How could God be born out of lifeless things? And if God's body is God by union (καθ' ὑπόστασιν), it is immutable. The nature of God remains the same as before, the flesh created in time is quickened by a logical and reasoning soul. I honour all matter besides, and venerate it. Through it, filled, as it were, with a divine power and grace, my salvation has come to me. Was not the thrice happy and thrice blessed wood of the Cross matter? Was not the sacred and holy mountain of Calvary matter? What of the life-giving rock, the Holy Sepulchre, the source of our resurrection: was it not matter? Is not the most holy book of the Gospels matter? Is not the blessed table matter which gives us the Bread of Life? Are not the gold and silver matter, out of which crosses and altar-plate and chalices are made? And before all these things, is not the body and blood of our Lord matter? Either do away with the veneration and worship due to all these things, or submit to the tradition of the Church in the worship of images, honouring God and His friends, and following in this the grace of the Holy Spirit. Do not despise matter, for it is not despicable. Nothing is that which God has made.[78]

Because of the incarnation, matter appears as divinized. This is a new vision of the world and of material realities. God has become flesh, and the flesh has truly become the dwelling of God, whose glory shines in the human face of Christ. Without a doubt, Damascene perceived a certain Docetism in the iconoclasts. Therefore, the invitations of the eastern Doctor are still highly relevant, considering the immense dignity that matter received in the Incarnation, as by faith, it could become an effective sign and sacrament of the encounter between man and God.

78. St. John Damascene, *On Holy Images*, trans. Mary H. Allies (London: Thomas Baker, 1898), 15–17.

Therefore, St. John Damascene is a privileged witness to the veneration of images, which has been one of the characteristic aspects of Eastern theology and spirituality up until today. However, it is a form of veneration that simply belongs to the Christian faith, the faith in the God who became flesh and visible. St. John Damascene's doctrine thus fits into the tradition of the universal Church, whose sacramental doctrine foresees that material elements taken from nature can be instruments of grace by virtue of the invocation (epiclesis) of the Holy Spirit, accompanied by the confession of the true faith.

His approach adopts a conventional structure that, while presenting certain specificities, remains anchored in the meticulous study of the definition, justifications, and various forms of these two key ideas. To begin, his analysis of the image is organized as follows.

Initially, Damascene focuses his attention on the idea of the image. According to him, it refers to "a likeness, a model, and a reproduction of something that shows in itself what is represented," that is, a correspondence, a pattern, and a representation of something that projects in itself what it is representing. Therefore, the image entails a direct relationship with what it symbolizes while simultaneously differing significantly, as it cannot reflect all aspects of the original model. Or, as in the case of Jesus as the Son, who, although being the image of the Father, has differences because the Son is not the Father. We read:

> Πρῶτον, τί ἐστιν εἰκών; Εἰκὼν μὲν οὖν ἐστιν ὁμοίωμα καὶ παράδειγμα καὶ ἐκτύπωμά τινος ἐν ἑαυτῷ δεικνύον τὸ εἰκονιζόμενον, πάντως δὲ οὐ κατὰ πάντα ἔοικεν ἡ εἰκὼν τῷ πρωτοτύπῳ τουτέστι τῷ εἰκονιζομένῳ –ἄλλο γάρ ἐστιν ἡ εἰκὼν καὶ ἄλλο τὸ εἰκονιζόμενον– καὶ πάντως ὁρᾶται ἐν αὐτοῖς διαφορά, ἐπεὶ οὐκ ἄλλο τοῦτο καὶ ἄλλο ἐκεῖνο. Οἷόν τι λέγω· Ἡ εἰκὼν τοῦ ἀνθρώπου, εἰ καὶ τὸν χαρακτῆρα ἐκτυποῖ τοῦ σώματος, ἀλλὰ τὰς ψυχικὰς δυνάμεις οὐκ ἔχει· οὔτε γὰρ ζῇ οὔτε λογίζεται οὔτε φθέγγεται οὔτε αἰσθάνεται οὔτε μέλος κινεῖ. Καὶ ὁ υἱὸς εἰκὼν φυσικὴ ὢν τοῦ πατρὸς ἔχει τι παρηλλαγμένον πρὸς αὐτόν· υἱὸς γάρ ἐστι καὶ οὐ πατήρ.

> Firstly, what is an image? An image is a likeness and representation of some one, containing in itself the person who is imaged. The image is not wont to be an exact reproduction of the original. The image is one thing, the person represented another; a difference is generally perceptible, because the subject of each is the same. For instance, the image of a man may give his bodily form, but not his mental powers. It has no life, nor does it speak or feel or move. A son being the natural image of his father is somewhat different from him, for he is a son, not a father.[79]

In a second approach, Damascene addresses the issue of the origin of the image, arguing that its reason for existence lies in its ability to illustrate and reveal what is hidden. We read:

> Δεύτερον, τίνος χάριν ἐστὶν ἡ εἰκών; Πᾶσα εἰκὼν ἐκφαντορικὴ τοῦ κρυφίου ἐστὶ καὶ δεικτική. Οἷόν τι λέγω· Ἐπειδὴ ὁ ἄνθρωπος οὔτε τοῦ ἀοράτου γυμνὴν ἔχει τὴν γνῶσιν σώματι καλυπτομένης τῆς ψυχῆς οὔτε τῶν μετ' αὐτὸν ἐσομένων οὔτε τῶν τόπῳ διεστηκότων καὶ ἀπεχόντων ὡς τόπῳ καὶ χρόνῳ περιγραφόμενος, πρὸς ὁδηγίαν γνώσεως καὶ φανέρωσιν καὶ δημοσίευσιν τῶν κεκρυμμένων ἐπενοήθη ἡ εἰκών, πάντως δὲ πρὸς ὠφέλειαν καὶ εὐεργεσίαν καὶ σωτηρίαν, ὅπως στηλιτευομένων καὶ θριαμβευομένων τῶν πραγμάτων διαγνῶμεν τὰ κεκρυμμένα καὶ τὰ μὲν καλὰ ποθήσωμεν καὶ ζηλώσωμεν, τὰ δὲ ἐναντία τουτέστι τὰ κακὰ ἀποστραφῶμεν καὶ μισήσωμεν.

> Secondly, For what purpose the Image is made. Every image is a revelation and representation of something hidden. For instance, man has not a clear knowledge of what is invisible, the spirit being veiled to the body, nor of future things, nor of things apart and distant, because he is circumscribed by place and time. The image was devised for greater knowledge, and

79. Ibid., 92.

> for the manifestation and popularising of secret things, as a pure benefit and help to salvation, so that by showing things and making them known, we may arrive at the hidden ones, desire and emulate what is good, shun and hate what is evil.[80]

In a third phase, Damascene points out that not all images are identical and proposes a classification into categories. He begins with the natural image, a category he uses to distinguish what is by nature from what exists in a circumstantial and imitative manner. An example of this image would be the Son, as a natural and exact reflection of the Father, since "the Son is the natural image of the Father, identical and similar in all respects to the Father, except in the absence of generation and paternity" (Damascene, §18). This type of image is also applied to the Spirit in relation to the Son, with the only difference being the origin, as the latter is begotten, not proceeding from the former.

The second category of images refers to those elements that were conceived from eternity by the immutable will of the Father and which appear at the moment He has determined, "It happens that they are images and models of things that will come to be by His intervention" (Damascene, §19), and which will manifest at specific moments in history.

The third mode of visual representation is linked to the human being, emerging as an imitation since the created being cannot share the same nature with its Creator. From his concrete existence, man exercises dominion over creation, as described in Genesis. In relation to this, the fourth mode refers specifically to the Holy Scriptures, which symbolize elements, configurations, and archetypes of incorporeal and invisible entities that take on a tangible form to facilitate an approximate understanding of God and the angels:

> Τέταρτος τρόπος εἰκόνος τῆς γραφῆς σχήματα καὶ μορφὰς καὶ τύπους ἀναπλαττούσης τῶν ἀοράτων καὶ ἀσωμάτων σωματικῶς τυπουμένων πρὸς ἀμυδρὰν κατανόησιν θεοῦ

80. Ibid., 92–93.

τε καὶ ἀγγέλων διὰ τὸ μὴ δύνασθαι ἡμᾶς τὰ ἀσώματα ἄνευ σχημάτων ἀναλογούντων ἡμῖν θεωρεῖν, καθώς φησιν ὁ πολὺς τὰ θεῖα Διονύσιος ὁ Ἀρεοπαγίτης. Ὅτι μὲν γὰρ εἰκότως προβέβληνται τῶν ἀτυπώτων οἱ τύποι καὶ τὰ σχήματα τῶν ἀσχηματίστων, οὐ μόνην αἰτίαν φαίη τις εἶναι τὴν καθ' ἡμᾶς ἀναλογίαν ἀδυνατοῦσαν ἀμέσως ἐπὶ τὰς νοητὰς ἀνατείνεσθαι θεωρίας καὶ δεομένην οἰκείων καὶ συμφυῶν ἀναγωγῶν. Εἰ τοίνυν τῆς ἡμῶν προνοῶν ἀναλογίας ὁ θεῖος λόγος, πάντοθεν τὸ ἀνατατικὸν ἡμῖνποριζόμενος, καὶ τοῖς ἁπλοῖς καὶ ἀμορφώτοις τύπους τινὰς περιτίθησι, πῶς μὴ εἰκονίσει τὰ σχήμασι μεμορφωμένα κατὰ τὴν οἰκείαν φύσιν καὶ ποθούμενα μέν, διὰ δὲ τὸ μὴ παρεῖναι ὁρᾶσθαι μὴ δυνάμενα; Φησὶ γοῦν ὁ θεορήμων Γρηγόριος, ὅτι πολλὰ κάμνων ὁ νοῦς ἐκβῆναι τὰ σωματικὰ πάντη ἀδυνατεῖ· «Ἀλλὰ καὶ τὰ ἀόρατα τοῦ θεοῦ ἀπὸ κτίσεως κόσμου τοῖς ποιήμασι νοούμενα καθορᾶται.» Ὁρῶμεν δὲ καὶ ἐν τοῖς κτίσμασιν εἰκόνας μηνυούσας ἡμῖν ἀμυδρῶς "Ποιήσωμεν ἄνθρωπον κατ' εἰκόνα ἡμετέρανκαὶ καθ' ὁμοίωσιν", καὶ εὐθέως ἐπήγαγε· "Καὶἀρχέτωσαν τῶν ἰχθύων τῆς θαλάσσης καὶ τῶνπετεινῶν τοῦ οὐρανοῦ", καὶ πάλιν "καὶ ἄρχετετῶν ἰχθύων τῆς θαλάσσης καὶ τῶν πετεινῶν τοῦοὐρανοῦ καὶ πάσης τῆς γῆς καὶ κατακυριεύσατεαὐτῆς."

The fourth kind of image are the figures and types set forth by Scripture of invisible and immaterial things in bodily form, for a clearer apprehension of God and the angels, through our incapacity of perceiving immaterial things unless clothed in analogical material form, as Dionysius the Areopagite says, a man skilled in divine things. Anyone would say that our incapacity for reaching the contemplation of intellectual things, and our need of familiar and cognate mediums, make it necessary that immaterial things should be clothed in form and shape. If, then, Holy Scripture adapts itself to us in seeking to elevate us above sense, does it not make images of what it clothes in our own medium, and bring within our reach that which we desire but are unable to see? The

> spiritual writer, Gregory, says that the mind striving to banish corporeal images reduces itself to incapability. But from the creation of the world the invisible things of God are made clear by the visible creation. We see images in created things, which remind us faintly of divine tokens. For instance, sun and light and brightness, the running waters of a perennial fountain, our own mind and language and spirit, the sweet fragrance of a flowering rose-tree, are images of the Holy and Eternal Trinity. For God says: "Let us make man in our image and likeness," and immediately adds: "And let [them] rule over the fish of the sea and the birds of the air," and again "and rule over the fish of the sea and the birds of the air and over all the earth and subdue it." (Genesis 1:26-28).[81]

This means that the Holy Scriptures enable the definition of images that perform a function similar to divine realities, contributing to a gradual and careful contemplation of aspects that, otherwise, would be incomprehensible.

The fifth categorization focuses on images in theological discourse that anticipate or symbolize future events. One example is the burning bush, representing the divine presence, or water as a metaphor for baptism (Exodus, 3:2 and Exodus, 16:33).

Next, the sixth categorization centers on images that serve as reminders of wondrous events or as warnings of censurable actions, intending to influence and modify future behavior. This category has two dimensions: one is reflected in key elements of Scripture, such as the tablets of the law (Deuteronomy, 5:22), a tangible image; the other in specific representations of the history of the people of Israel, such as the Ark or the twelve stones of the Jordan River (Exodus, 16:33 and Exodus, 28:9–12). This classification allows him to conclude:

> Ἕκτος τρόπος εἰκόνος ὁ πρὸς μνήμην τῶν γεγονότων ἢ θαύματος ἢ ἀρετῆς πρὸς δόξαν καὶ τιμὴν καὶ στηλογραφίαν

81. Ibid., 95–96.

τῶν ἀριστευσάντων καὶ ἐν ἀρετῇ διαπρεψάντων ἢ κακίας πρὸς θρίαμβον καὶ αἰσχύνην τῶν κακίστων ἀνδρῶν, πρὸς τὴν εἰς ὕστερον τῶν θεωμένων ὠφέλειαν, ὡς ἂν τὰ μὲν κακὰ φύγωμεν, τὰς δὲ ἀρετὰς ζηλώσωμεν. Διπλῆ δὲ αὕτη· διά τε λόγου ταῖς βίβλοις ἐγγραφομένου – εἰκονίζει γὰρ τὸ γράμμα τὸν λόγον, ὡς ὁ θεὸς τὸν νόμον ταῖς πλαξὶν ἐνεκόλαψε καὶ τοὺς τῶν θεοφιλῶν ἀνδρῶν βίους ἀναγράπτους γενέσθαι προσέταξε – καὶ διὰ θεωρίας αἰσθητῆς, ὡς τὴν στάμνον καὶ τὴν ῥάβδον ἐν τῇ κιβωτῷ τεθῆναι προσέταξεν εἰς μνημόσυνον αἰώνιον καὶ ὡς τὰ ὀνόματα τῶν φυλῶν ἐγκολαφθῆναι τοῖς λίθοις τῆς ἐπωμίδος ἐκέλευσεν, οὐ μὴν ἀλλὰ καὶ τοὺς δώδεκα λίθους ἀρθῆναι ἐκ τοῦ Ἰορδάνου εἰς τύπον τῶν ἱερέων – βαβαὶ τοῦ μυστηρίου, ὡς μέγιστον τοῖς πιστοῖς ἐν ἀληθείᾳ – τῶν αἰρόντων τὴν κιβωτὸν καὶ τῆς τοῦ ὕδατος ἐκλείψεως. Οὕτω καὶ νῦν τὰς εἰκόνας τῶν γεγονότων ἐναρέτων ἀνδρῶν πρὸς ζῆλον καὶ μνήμην καὶ ζῆλον ἡμῶν πόθῳ ἀναγράφομεν. Ἢ τοίνυν πᾶσαν εἰκόνα ἄνελε καὶ ἀντινομοθέτει τῷ ταῦτα προστάξαντι γίνεσθαι ἢ ἑκάστην δέχου κατὰ τὸν ἑκάστῃ πρέποντα λόγον καὶ τρόπον.

The sixth kind of image is for a remembrance of past events, of a miracle or a good deed, for the honour and glory and abiding memory of the most virtuous, or for the shame and terror of the wicked, for the benefit of succeeding generations who contemplate it, so that we may shun evil and do good. This image is of two kinds, either through the written word in books, for the word represents the thing, as when God ordered the law to be written on tablets, and the lives of God-fearing men to be recorded, or through a visible object, as when He commanded the urn and rod to be placed in the ark for a lasting memory, and the names of the tribes to be engraved on the stones of the humeral. And also He commanded the twelve stones to be taken from the Jordan as a sacred token. Consider the prodigy, the greatest which befell the faithful people, the taking of the ark, and the parting of the waters. So now we set up the images of

> valiant men for an example and a remembrance to ourselves. Therefore, either reject all images, and be in opposition to Him who ordered these things, or receive each and all with becoming greeting and manner.[82]

Once he has meticulously defined the image, John Damascene builds an argument in defense of the image around two fundamental pillars. First, the intimate connection of man with God is articulated in the incarnation of Christ.

> Τίς πρῶτος ἐποίησεν εἰκόνα; Αὐτὸς ὁ θεὸς πρῶτος ἐγέννησε τὸν μονογενῆ υἱὸν καὶ λόγον αὐτοῦ, εἰκόνα αὐτοῦ ζῶσαν, φυσικήν, ἀπαράλλακτον χαρακτῆρα τῆς αὐτοῦ ἀιδιότητος, ἐποίησέ τε τὸν ἄνθρωπον κατ' εἰκόνα αὐτοῦ καὶ καθ' ὁμοίωσιν. Καὶ Ἀδὰμ εἶδε θεὸν καὶ ἤκουσε τῆς φωνῆς τῶν ποδῶν αὐτοῦ περιπατοῦντος τὸ δειλινὸν καὶ ἐκρύβη ἐν τῷ παραδείσῳ, καὶ 'Ιακὼβεἶδε καὶ ἐπάλαισε μετὰ τοῦ θεοῦ – δῆλον δέ, ὅτι ὡς ἄνθρωπος ἐφάνη αὐτῷ ὁ θεός –, καὶ Μωσῆς ὡς ὀπίσθια ἀνθρώπου εἶδε, καὶ Ἡσαΐας ὡς ἄνθρωπον εἶδε καθήμενον ἐπὶ θρόνου, καὶ Δανιὴλ ὁμοίωμα ἀνθρώπου εἶδε καὶ ὡς υἱὸν ἀνθρώπου ἐλθόντα ἐπὶ τὸν παλαιὸν τῶν ἡμερῶν. Καὶ οὐ φύσιν θεοῦ εἶδέ τις, ἀλλὰ τὸν τύπον καὶ τὴν εἰκόνα τοῦ μέλλοντος ἔσεσθαι· ἔμελλε γὰρ ὁ υἱὸς καὶ λόγος τοῦ θεοῦ ὁ ἀόρατος ἄνθρωπος γίνεσθαι ἐν ἀληθείᾳ, ἵν' ἑνωθῇ τῇ φύσει ἡμῶν καὶ ὁραθῇ ἐπὶ γῆς. Προσεκύνησαν οὖν πάντες οἱ ἰδόντες τὸν τύπον καὶ τὴν εἰκόνα τοῦ μέλλοντος, καθὼς Παῦλός φησιν ὁ ἀπόστολος ἐν τῇ πρὸς Ἑβραίους ἐπιστολῇ· "Κατὰ πίστιν ἀπέθανον οὗτοι πάντες μὴ κομισάμενοι τὰς εὐαγγελίας, ἀλλὰ πόρρωθεν αὐτὰς ἰδόντες καὶ ἀσπασάμενοι." 'Εγὼ οὖν οὐ μὴ ποιήσω εἰκόνα τοῦ δι' ἐμὲ ὀφθέντος σαρκὸς φύσει καὶ προσκυνήσω καὶ τιμήσω αὐτὸν διὰ τῆς εἰς τὴν εἰκόνα αὐτοῦ τιμῆς καὶ προσκυνήσεως; Εἶδεν Ἀβραὰμ οὐ φύσιν θεοῦ ("θεὸν γὰρ οὐδεὶς ἑώρακε πώποτε"), ἀλλ' εἰκόνα θεοῦ καὶ πεσὼν προσεκύνησεν. Εἶδεν 'Ιησοῦς ὁ τοῦ Ναυῆ οὐ

82. Ibid., 97–98.

φύσιν ἀγγέλου, ἀλλ' εἰκόνα (φύσις γὰρ ἀγγέλου σωματικοῖς οὐχ ὁρᾶται ὀφθαλμοῖς) καὶ πεσὼν προσεκύνησεν, ὁμοίως καὶ Δανιήλ (ἄγγελος δὲ οὐ θεός, ἀλλὰ κτίσμα καὶ δοῦλος θεοῦ καὶ παραστάτης), προσεκύνησε δὲ οὐχ ὡς θεῷ, ἀλλ' ὡς θεοῦ παραστάτῃ καὶ λειτουργῷ. Κἀγὼ μὴ ποιήσω εἰκόνα τῶν φίλων τοῦ Χριστοῦ καὶ μὴ προσκυνήσω οὐχ ὡς θεοῖς, ἀλλ' ὡς εἰκόσι φίλων θεοῦ; Οὔτε γὰρ Ἰησοῦς οὔτε Δανιὴλ ὡς θεοῖς προσεκύνησαν τοῖς ὀφθεῖσιν ἀγγέλοις, οὐδὲ ἐγὼ ὡς θεῷ προσκυνῶ τῇ εἰκόνι, ἀλλὰ διὰ τῆς εἰκόνος καὶ τῶν ἁγίων τῷ θεῷ προσάγω τὴν προσκύνησιν καὶ τὴν τιμήν, δι' ὃν καὶ τοὺς αὐτοῦ φίλους σέβω καὶ δι' αἰδοῦς ἄγω. Οὐχ ἡνώθη φύσει ἀγγέλων ὁ θεός, ἡνώθη δὲφύσει ἀνθρώπων. Οὐκ ἐγένετο ὁ θεὸς ἄγγελος, ἐγένετο δὲ ὁ θεὸς φύσει καὶ ἀληθείᾳ ἄνθρωπος. "Οὐ γὰρ δή που ἀγγέλων ἐπιλαμβάνεται, ἀλλὰ σπέρματος Ἀβραὰμ ἐπιλαμβάνεται." Οὐκ ἐγένετο φύσις ἀγγέλων υἱὸς θεοῦ καθ' ὑπόστασιν, ἐγένετο δὲ φύσις ἀνθρώπου υἱὸς θεοῦ καθ' ὑπόστασιν. Οὐ μετέσχον ἄγγελοι οὐδὲ ἐγένοντο θείας κοινωνοὶ φύσεως, ἀλλ' ἐνεργείας καὶ χάριτος, ἄνθρωποι δὲ μετέχουσι καὶ κοινωνοὶ θείας φύσεως γίνονται, ὅσοι μεταλαμβάνουσι τὸ σῶμα τοῦ Χριστοῦ τὸ ἅγιον καὶ πίνουσι τὸ αἷμα αὐτοῦ τὸ τίμιον· θεότητι γὰρ καθ' ὑπόστασιν ἥνωται καὶ δύο φύσεις ἐν τῷ μεταλαμβανομένῳ ὑφ' ἡμῶν σώματι τοῦ Χριστοῦ ἡνωμέναι καθ' ὑπόστασίν εἰσιν ἀδιασπάστως καὶ τῶν δύο φύσεων μετέχομεν, τοῦ σώματος σωματικῶς, τῆς θεότητος πνευματικῶς, μᾶλλον δὲ ἀμφοῖν κατ' ἄμφω, οὐ καθ' ὑπόστασιν ταυτιζόμενοι (ὑφιστάμεθα γὰρ πρῶτον καὶ τότε ἑνούμεθα), ἀλλὰ κατὰ συνανάκρασιν τοῦ σώματος καὶ α ἵματος. Καὶ πῶς οὐ μείζονες ἀγγέλων οἱ φυλάττοντες διὰ τῆς τηρήσεως τῶν ἐντολῶν εἰλικρινῆ τὴν ἕνωσιν; Ἡ μὲν φύσις ἡμῶν βραχύ τι παρ' ἀγγέλους ἠλαττωμένη διὰ τὸν θάνατον καὶ τὴν τοῦ σώματος παχύτητα, ἀλλ' εὐδοκίᾳ καὶ συναφείᾳ θεοῦ γέγονεν ἀγγέλων μείζων· παρίστανται γὰρ αὐτῇ μετὰ φόβου καὶ τρόμου ἄγγελοι καθημένῃ ἐπὶ τοῦ θρόνου τῆς δόξης ἐν τῷ Χριστῷ καὶ παραστήσονται ἔντρομοι ἐν τῇ κρίσει· οὐ συγκαθεύδοντες οὐδὲ κοινωνοὶ τῆς θείας δόξης ὑπὸ τῆς γραφῆς ἐρρήθησαν ("εἰσὶ γὰρ πάντες λειτουργικὰ πνεύματα, εἰς διακονίαν ἀποστελλόμενα διὰ τοὺς μέλλοντας κληρονομεῖν σωτηρίαν") οὐδ' ὅτι συμβασιλεύσουσιν οὐδ' ὅτι συνδοξασθήσονται οὐδ' ὅτι ἐπὶ τῆς τραπέζης τοῦ πατρὸς καθίσουσιν, οἱ δὲ ἅγιοι υἱοὶ θεοῦ, υἱοὶ τῆς βασιλείας καὶ κληρονόμοι θεοῦ καὶ συγκληρονόμοι Χριστοῦ. Τιμῶ οὖν τοὺς ἁγίους καὶ συνδοξάζωτοὺς δούλους καὶ φίλους καὶ συγκληρονόμους Χριστοῦ, τοὺς δούλους ἐκ φύσεως καὶ φίλους ἐκ προαιρέσεως καὶ υἱοὺς καὶ κληρονόμους ἐκ θείας χάριτος, ὥς φησιν ὁ κύριος πρὸς τὸν πατέρα. Εἰπόντες τοίνυν περὶ εἰκόνος εἴπωμεν καὶ περὶ προσκυνήσεως, καὶ πρῶτον, τί ἐστι προσκύνησις.

In the beginning God begot His only begotten Son, His word, the living image of Himself, the natural and unchangeable image of His eternity. And He made man after His own image and likeness. And Adam saw God, and heard the sound of His feet as He walked at even, and he hid in paradise. And Jacob saw and struggled with God. It is evident that God appeared to him in the form of a man. And Moses saw Him, and Isaias saw as it were the back of a man, and as a man seated on a throne. And Daniel saw the likeness of a man, and as the Son of Man coming to the ancient of days. No one saw the nature of God, but the type and image of what was to be. For the Son and Word of the invisible God, was to become man in truth, that He might be united to our nature, and be seen upon earth. Now all who looked upon the type and image of the future, worshipped it, as St Paul says in his epistle to the Hebrews: "All these died according to faith, not having received the promises, but beholding them afar off, and saluting them." Shall I not make an image of Him who took the nature of flesh for me? Shall I not reverence and worship Him, through the honour and worship of His image? Abraham saw not the nature of God, for no man ever saw God, but the image of God, and falling down he adored. Josue saw the image of an angel, not as he is, for an angel is not visible to bodily eyes, and falling down he adored, and so did Daniel. Yet an angel is a creature, and servant, and minister of God, not God. And he worshipped the angel not as God, but as God's ministering spirit. And shall not I make images of Christ's friends? And shall I not worship them as the images of God's friends, not as gods? Neither Josue nor Daniel worshipped the angels they saw as gods. Neither do I worship the image as God, but through the image of the saints too, show my worship to God, because I honour His friends, and do them reverence. God did not unite Himself to the angelic nature, but to the human. He did not become an angel: He became a man in nature, and in truth. It is indeed Abraham's seed which He embraces, not the angel's.

The Son of God in person did not take the nature of the angels: He took the nature of man. The angels did not participate in the divine nature, but in working and in grace. Now, men *do* participate, and become partakers of the divine nature when they receive the holy Body of Christ and drink His Blood. For He is united in person to the Godhead, and two natures in the Body of Christ shared by us are united indissolubly in person, and we partake of the two natures, of the body bodily, and of the Godhead in spirit, or, rather, of each in both. We are made one, not in person, for first we have a person and then we are united by blending together the body and the blood. How are we not greater than the angels, if through fidelity to the commandments we keep this perfect union? In itself our nature is far removed from the angels, on account of death and the heaviness of the body, but through God's goodness and its union with Him it has become higher than the angels. For angels stand by that nature with fear and trembling, as, in the person of Christ, it sits upon a throne of glory, and they will stand by in trembling at the judgment. According to Scripture they are not partakers of the divine glory. For they are all ministering spirits, being sent to minister because of those who are to be heirs of salvation, not that they shall reign together, nor

> that they shall be together glorified, nor that they shall sit at the table of the Father. The saints, on the contrary, are the children of God, the children of the kingdom, heirs of God, and co-heirs of Christ. Therefore, I honour the saints, and glorify the servants and friends and co-heirs of Christ: servants by nature, friends by their choice: friends and co-heirs by divine grace, as our Lord said in speaking to the Father. As we are speaking of images, let us speak of worship also, and in the first place determine what it is.[83]

Christ fully assumes humanity, and it is stated, as we have read: "Shall I not make an image of the one who has been seen for my sake in a nature of flesh, and venerate and honor it through the honor and reverence due to its image?" There are examples in the Scriptures where figures like Joshua (Joshua, 5:14) and Daniel (Daniel, 8:17) venerate an image of God without fear.

The second pillar focuses on the veneration due to those who have had a singular and intimate relationship with the Creator. As we read in the previous citation, Damascene affirms: "And I, will I not make an image of the friends of Christ and venerate it, not as gods but as images of the friends of God? [...] Nor do I worship the image as God, but through the image and the saints, I present my veneration to God and offer Him honor, by which I also revere His friends and treat them with respect." What Damascene emphasizes here is that veneration is not directed at the image itself, but at what it represents.

Images are pillars for us to ascend to the sacred, visible symbols of the invisible reality. According to Damascene, the function of the image is epistemological, for it guides knowledge in situations where human understanding is limited. For example, when attempting to comprehend the imperceptible, the course of future events, or in situations where the person is absent and restricted by space and time limitations. Damascene's argument suggests, therefore, that the image was designed as a resource to allow human beings to

83. Ibid., 100–104.

approach what would otherwise be incomprehensible, making the inaccessible accessible to the senses, and it is precisely in this way that human beings can distinguish between right and wrong, between good and evil.

Based on what has been argued so far, Saint John Damascene also addresses the veneration of images and relics of the saints, convinced that Christian saints, having been made partakers of Christ's resurrection, cannot be considered merely "dead." Listing, for example, those whose relics or images are worthy of veneration, Saint John says in his third discourse:

> Πρῶτον μέν, ἐφ' οἷς ἀναπέπαυται ὁ θεὸς ὁ μόνος ἅγιος καὶ «ἐν ἁγίοις ἀναπαυόμενος» ὡς τῇ ἁγίᾳ θεοτόκῳ καὶ πᾶσι τοῖς ἁγίοις. Οὗτοι δέ εἰσιν οἱ κατὰ τὸ δυνατὸν ὁμοιωθέντες θεῷ ἔκ τε τῆς ἑαυτῶν προαιρέσεως καὶ τῆς θεοῦ ἐνοικήσεως καὶ συνεργίας, οἵτινες καὶ θεοὶ λέγονται ἀληθῶς, οὐ φύσει, ἀλλὰ θέσει, ὡς πῦρ λέγεται ὁ πεπυρακτωμένος σίδηρος, οὐφύσει, ἀλλὰ θέσει καὶ μεθέξει πυρός · φησὶ γάρ · "Ἅγιοι ἔσεσθε, ὅτι ἐγὼ ἅγιός εἰμι."

> First, those places in which God, who alone is holy, has rested, and His resting-place in the saints, as in the holy Mother of God and in all the saints. These are they who are made like to God as far as possible, of their own free will, and by God's indwelling, and by His abiding grace. They are truly called gods, not by nature, but by participation; just as red-hot iron is called fire, not by nature, but by participation in the fire's action. He says: "Be ye holy because I am holy."[84]

Therefore, after a series of such references, Saint John Damascene calmly concluded:

> God, who is good, and greater than any goodness, was not content with the contemplation of himself, but desired that there should be beings benefited by him, who might share in

84. Ibid., 106–107.

> his goodness: therefore he created from nothing all things, visible and invisible, including man, a reality visible and invisible. And he created him envisaging him and creating him as a being capable of thought (*ennoema ergon*), enriched with the word (*logo[i] sympleroumenon*), and orientated towards the spirit (*pneumati teleioumenon*).[85]

And to further clarify his thought, he adds, somewhat following Plato's idea that all philosophy begins with wonder, that our faith also begins with awe at creation, at the beauty of God made visible:

> We must allow ourselves to be filled with wonder (*thaumazein*) at all the works of Providence (*tes pronoias erga*), to accept and praise them all, overcoming any temptation to identify in them aspects which to many may seem unjust or iniquitous, (*adika*), and admitting instead that the project of God (pronoia) goes beyond man's capacity to know or to understand (*agnoston kai akatalepton*), while on the contrary only he may know our thoughts, our actions, and even our future.[86]

Furthermore, Damascene specifies that we must not confuse adoration with *doulia*, that is, conscious veneration, from which it follows that the image is a window to heaven for the human and a mirror for the divine that is reflected in it, as John himself debates:

> Given this state of affairs and stepping out as though on the royal highway, following as we are the God-spoken teaching of our holy fathers and the tradition of the catholic church —for we recognize that this tradition comes from the holy Spirit who dwells in her—we decree with full precision and care that, like the figure of the honoured and life-giving cross, the revered and holy images, whether painted or made of mosaic or of other suitable material, are to be exposed in the

85. Benedict XVI, General Audience, Saint Peter's Square, May 6, 2009, https://www.vatican.va. *Contra imaginum calumniatores* II, 2 (PG 94, col. 865A).
86. Ibid., PG 94, col. 865A.

> holy churches of God, on sacred instruments and vestments, on walls and panels, in houses and by public ways, these are the images of our Lord, God and saviour, Jesus Christ, and of our Lady without blemish, the holy God-bearer, and of the revered angels and of any of the saintly holy men. The more frequently they are seen in representational art, the more are those who see them drawn to remember and long for those who serve as models, and to pay these images the tribute of salutation and respectful veneration. Certainly this is not the full adoration (*latria*) in accordance with our faith, which is properly paid only to the divine nature, but it resembles that given to the figure of the honoured and life-giving cross, and also to the holy books of the gospels and to other sacred cult objects. Further, people are drawn to honour these images with the offering of incense and lights, as was piously established by ancient custom. Indeed, the honour paid to an image traverses it, reaching the model, and he who venerates the image, venerates the person represented in that image.[87]

As we also see in the New Testament where it is said that:

> God, who at various times and in various ways spoke in time past to the fathers by the prophets, has in these last days spoken to us by His Son, whom He has appointed heir of all things, through whom also He made the worlds, who being the brightness of His glory and the express image of His person, and upholding all things by the word of His power, when He had by Himself purged our sins, sat down on the right hand of the Majesty on high, being made so much better than the angels, as He has by inheritance obtained a more excellent name than they.
>
> (Hebrews, 1:1–4)

87. Second Council of Nicaea, "Council Fathers – 787 A.D.," Papal Encyclicals Online, https://www.papalencyclicals.net.

The importance of St. John Damascene in relation to the issue at hand can be summarized in his central argument regarding the incarnation of Christ: “Today, since God has appeared in the flesh and has lived among men, I make a representation of what is visible in God.” At the same time, and to clear any hint of idolatry, John Damascene asserts that veneration of icons was not worship but reverence while proclaiming the dignity of matter: “I do not bow before the matter, but before the creator of it,” “the honor granted to the image is transferred to its prototype,” he affirmed.

Finally, St. John Damascene also saw in the image a pedagogical potential, for example, in the symbolism of the Virgin of Guadalupe for the indigenous people, which has been a path of conversion for thousands of them. The image saved words, and they understood the message despite the cultural shock of such magnitude. Aware of the stream of pilgrims flowing to Jerusalem, he highlighted the usefulness of images to educate the masses and move their hearts: just as sacred places and relics are tangible proof of the coming of Christ.

The crisis for and against the use of images faded with Emperor Theophilus's death (842 A.D.). His spouse, Saint Theodora, propelled the icon defenders, restored peace, and proclaimed the “triumph of orthodoxy” (843 CE). Never had the icon held such preeminence. It would be found at the epicenter of the liturgy and would become a powerful tool for the evangelization during the next century.

There are three basic positions reflecting the current situation. These positions are referred to as “the Catholic,” “the Orthodox,” and “the Protestant-inspired.” The latter refers to the following of the postulates of the 16th-century reformers, who consider the image unnecessary for Christian life. Christians who use images in places of worship are considered idolaters.

The Catholic and Orthodox positions share several points in common: the communicative value of the image and the recognition of the Christological foundation, also widely explained and with a perfect conclusion. But there is an interesting difference to highlight. When speaking of the status of the image in relation to revelation, both doctrines affirm that they belong to the deposit of faith, transmitted through tradition. However, the valuation is different.

The Orthodox affirm that images, being present from the origin of Christianity, are an essential element of Christian revelation and possess the same dignity as scripture. They reveal and make God present. They have a sacramental character. But for Catholics, they are not an essential element of revelation. They are accessories and lack sacramental character.

Jesus is the symbol of the Father, and his role is to unite the perceptible with the imperceptible. Jesus has an invisible and a visible dimension, so he is the link that unites physical substance and spirit, the ephemeral and the eternal, the human and the divine, since in him, both realities converge.

Chapter 19

The symbols of *Gauḍīya* Vaishnavism

On March 7, 1486, during the full moon night of the month of Phālguṇa, in the region of Bengal, a momentous event of significant importance occurred: the advent of Śrī Chaitanya Mahāprabhu. His birth took place in an India that, under the reign of logic and Islamic rule, was in desperate need of profound change—socially, intellectually, morally, politically, and spiritually. Based on the Vedic scriptures, great sages had prophesied this event as the earthly manifestation of divine love. Chaitanya emerged in a Brahmin family in the city of Navadwip, in present-day West Bengal, India, located approximately seventy-five miles north of the bustling city of Kolkata. On the banks of the Ganges, the vibrant city of Navadwip stretched in both directions along the sacred river.

Throughout his life, Śrī Chaitanya was known and revered under various names. He was called Śacīnandana in honor of his mother, Śacī. Due to his birth under a neem tree, he was affectionately nicknamed Nimai during his childhood and youth. The local population identified him as Gaurāṅga due to his golden, fair skin and remarkable physical beauty. In a later stage of his life, when he embraced the path of renunciation, or *sannyāsa*, he formally adopted the name Chaitanya. As his reputation grew as a devoted saint and enlightened master, he was honored with the title Mahāprabhu, which translates as "great master" or "great lord."

Chaitanya's ancestors hailed from Sylhet in eastern Bengal. They had left their ancestral home and settled in Navadwip, a prominent center of learning at the time. The family's new residence was established near the Ganges River, the birthplace of Chaitanya's father, Jagannātha Miśra. Chaitanya's mother was Śacī-devī, the eldest daughter of Nīlāmbara Cakravartī, a scholarly astrologer from Navadwip. She faced the tragedy of losing eight daughters consecutively during childbirth. In her ninth pregnancy, she gave birth to her son Viśvarūpa and twelve years later to Śrī Chaitanya.

The appearance of Śrī Chaitanya coincided with the celebration of *Dolā-yātrā*, the spring festival dedicated to Lord Kṛṣṇa, which traditionally occurs during the full moon of the months of February or March. This is not merely an anecdotal fact in *Vaiṣṇava* theological studies; it holds profound spiritual significance. It is interpreted that Kṛṣṇa, perpetually immersed in love for his beloved *gopīs*, adopted the emotional disposition and radiant golden hue of Śrīmatī Rādhārāṇī. In the rich mythology of Hinduism, Rādhā emerges as a central figure. This *gopī*, or "cowherd girl," transcended her everyday role to become Kṛṣṇa's most beloved consort during his time in Vrindavan, a period when Kṛṣṇa shared his existence with the *gopīs*. Despite being the legitimate wife of another *gopa*, or "cowherd boy," Rādhā stood out as the most loved among Kṛṣṇa's lovers, intimately accompanying him. Within the framework of the bhakti movement, a devotional stream of Vaiṣṇavism, Rādhā is often interpreted, in her feminine form, as embodying the human soul, while in her masculine form, she represents the supreme divinity. This symbolism reflects a profound allegory about the union of humans with the divine, a recurring theme in various philosophical and spiritual traditions. In the *Gauḍīya Vaiṣṇava* theology, Rādhā is considered the internal energy of Kṛṣṇa, or *hlādinī-śakti*. That is, Rādhā and Kṛṣṇa are viewed as two aspects of the same entity.

রাধাকৃষ্ণ এক আত্মা, দুই দেহ ধরি' ।
অন্যোন্যে বিলসে রস আস্বাদন করি' ॥
সেই দুই এক এবে চৈতন্য গোসাঞি ।
রস আস্বাদিতে দোঁহে হৈলা একঠাঁই ॥

rādhā-kṛṣṇa eka ātmā, dui deha dhari'
anyonye vilase rasa āsvādana kari'
sei dui eka ebe caitanya gosāñi
rasa āsvādite doṅhe hailā eka-ṭhāṅi

> Rādhā and Kṛṣṇa are one and the same, but They have assumed two bodies. Thus They enjoy each other, tasting the mellows of love.
> Now, to enjoy *rasa*, They have appeared in one body as Lord Caitanya Mahāprabhu.
> (*Śrī Caitanya-caritāmṛta*, "*Ādi-līlā*," 4.56–57)

In this way, Kṛṣṇa left his revered Vrindavan to manifest in his sacred and hidden abode of Navadwip, considered the hidden Vrindavan. In his incarnation as Śrī Chaitanya, it is believed that he poured out a torrent of divine love over the lands of Bengal.

নমো মহাবদান্যায় কৃষ্ণপ্রেমপ্রদায় তে ।
কৃষ্ণায় কৃষ্ণচৈতন্যনাম্নে গৌরত্বিষে নমঃ ॥

namo mahā-vadānyāya
kṛṣṇa-prema-pradāya te
kṛṣṇāya kṛṣṇa-caitanya-
nāmne gaura-tviṣe namaḥ

> O most munificent incarnation! You are Kṛṣṇa Himself appearing as Śrī Kṛṣṇa Caitanya Mahāprabhu. You have assumed the golden color of Śrīmatī Rādhārāṇī, and You are widely distributing pure love of Kṛṣṇa. We offer our respectful obeisances unto You.
> (*Śrī Caitanya-caritāmṛta*, "*Ādi-līlā*," 19.53)

Chaitanya Mahāprabhu's mission was to bestow *vraja-prema*, with a particular emphasis on *gopī-prema*. This message is crucial for those who have not yet understood the Bhagavad Gita from its devotional symbolic perspective. Today, many devotees in the West are showing an increasing interest in deepening their understanding of what Mahāprabhu came to reveal, expressed in the mantra:

অনর্পিতচরীং অনর্পিতচরীং চিরাৎ করুণয়াবতীর্ণঃ কলৌ
সমর্পয়িতুমুন্নতোজ্জ্বলরসাং স্বভক্তিশ্রিয়ম্ ।

হরিঃ পুরটসুন্দরদ্যুতিকদম্বসন্দীপিতঃ
সদা হৃদয়কন্দরে স্ফুরতু স্ফুরতু বঃ শচীনন্দনঃ ॥

anarpita-carīṁ cirāt karuṇayāvatīrṇaḥ kalau
samarpayitum unnatojjvala-rasāṁ sva-bhakti-śriyam
hariḥ puraṭa-sundara-dyuti-kadamba-sandīpitaḥ
sadā hṛdaya-kandare sphuratu vaḥ śacī-nandanaḥ

May the Supreme Lord, who is known as the son of Śrīmatī Śacī-devī, be transcendentally situated in the inmost chambers of your heart. Resplendent with the brilliance of molten gold, He has appeared in the age of Kali, by His causeless mercy, to bestow what no incarnation had ever offered before: the most sublime and radiant mellow of devotional service, the mellow of conjugal love.

(*Śrī Caitanya-caritāmṛta*, "*Ādi-līlā*," 1.4)

Both in India and the West, there is a similar yearning to understand the essence of the Śrīmad-bhāgavatam, which focuses on *gopī-prema*. Devotional evolution is not static; bhakti is a constantly flowing current. It begins with *sādhana-bhakti*, evolves into *bhāva-bhakti*, ascends to *prema-bhakti*, and ultimately reaches the higher stages of *vraja-bhakti* and *gopī-bhakti*. This path culminates in the bhakti that Śrīmatī Rādhikā feels for Kṛṣṇa. Therefore, it is essential to understand the true reason for the coming of Śrī Chaitanya Mahāprabhu. His purpose was not limited to the spread of the *nama*; it went far beyond that. The supreme fruit of the Holy Name is the realization of Kṛṣṇa, the ocean of *rasa*, or "nectar."

Throughout history, eminent devotees of Śrī Chaitanya, including figures such as Śrīla Vṛndāvana dāsa Ṭhākura, Śrī Locana dāsa Ṭhākura, and Śrīla Kṛṣṇadāsa Kavirāja Gosvāmī, among others, have left behind a rich literary heritage. This tradition, enriched in the last two hundred years by luminaries such as Śrī Viśvanātha Cakravartī and Śrī Bhaktisiddhānta Sarasvatī Ṭhākura, is characterized by its deep roots in the revered *śāstras*—Vedas, Puranas, Upanishads, as well as the *Rāmāyaṇa* and the *Mahābhārata*.

These works, the result of meticulous study and unwavering devotion, stand out for their unique composition and exceptional presentation. They are an inexhaustible source of transcendental knowledge, testimony to an erudite tradition that has managed to perpetuate itself through the centuries. Śrīla Murāri Gupta, a contemporary physician and devotee of Śrī Chaitanya, meticulously documented the early years of his life. Moreover, the final stage of the Lord's life was faithfully recorded by his private secretary, Śrī Dāmodara Gosvāmī, also known as Śrīla Svarūpa Dāmodara. His constant presence alongside Śrī Chaitanya in Purī allowed for detailed and profound observation. These records, captured in *kaḍacās*, or "notebooks," formed the foundation upon which later literary works detailing the life and teachings of the Lord were built. These texts, the result of exhaustive and devotional documentation, have become fundamental pillars for the study and understanding of the life of Śrī Chaitanya Mahāprabhu. His presence was not a manifestation of divinity but also a catalyst for profound changes in the political, judicial, and social structure of the region. It is believed that Śrī Chaitanya, in addition to breathing a renewed religious and devotional spirit, established a new order, marking a turning point in the history and culture of Bengal.

The full moon bathes the nights of the world with its soft, silvery rays. Śrī Chaitanya was born on the night of a full moon eclipse, as if nature itself were proclaiming the rise of a different moon, one of a unique and divine nature. Following tradition, the vast majority of the inhabitants of Navadwip were gathered by the sacred Ganges River, chanting the Holy Names of the Lord in order to counteract the potential negative influences of the eclipse. This new moon symbolized fullness, purity, freshness, gentleness, generosity, and poetic beauty, eclipsing the ordinary moon and any other source of earthly joy.

At that time, in the spring, the bare trees were adorned with fresh buds and copper-colored shoots. The mango buds attracted swarms of buzzing bees in search of nectar, while floral bushes and vines waved their branches and spread their fragrance in the wind. It seemed as if the very goddess of nature, dressed as a bride, was anticipating the arrival of her consort, the Lord of infinite worlds, adorning herself with all her beauty for the imminent sacred union. The transformation of nature into such splendor suggested that it was the day destined for the meeting of the Creator with his creation.

The women of the city blew conch shells, creating an auspicious vibration that filled the earth and the sky. Peace reigned in all directions; the waters of the rivers flowed calmly, and even the most common plants and creatures appeared to be brimming with joy. The name of the Supreme Lord resonated on the lips of all, and every heart overflowed with happiness. It was as if everyone held their breath, awaiting the appearance of Nimai, the son of Śacī.

জগৎ ভরিয়া লোক বলে–'হরি' 'হরি' ।
সেইক্ষণে গৌরকৃষ্ণ ভূমে অবতরি ॥

jagat bhariyā loka bale - 'hari' 'hari' 'hari'
sei-kṣaṇe gaurakṛṣṇa bhūme avatari

When the whole world was thus chanting the Holy Name of the Supreme Personality of Godhead, Kṛṣṇa in the form of Gaurahari advented Himself on the earth.

(*Śrī Caitanya-caritāmṛta*, "*Ādi-līlā*," 13.94)

কলিকালে নামরূপে কৃষ্ণ-অবতার ।
নাম হৈতে হয় সর্বজগৎ-নিস্তার ॥

kali-kāle nāma-rūpe kṛṣṇa-avatāra
nāma haite haya sarva-jagat-nistāra

In this Age of Kali, the Holy Name of the Lord, the Hare Kṛṣṇa *mahā-mantra*, is the incarnation of Lord Kṛṣṇa. Simply by chanting the Holy Name, one associates with the Lord directly. Anyone who does this is certainly liberated.

(*Śrī Caitanya-caritāmṛta*, "*Ādi-līlā*," 17.22)

আপনি শ্রীকৃষ্ণ যদি করেন অবতার ।
আপনে আচরি' ভক্তি করেন প্রচার ॥

āpani śrī-kṛṣṇa yadi karena avatāra
āpane ācari' bhakti karena pracāra

[Advaita Ācārya thought:] "If Śrī Kṛṣṇa were to appear as an incarnation, He Himself could preach devotion by His personal example."
(*Śrī Caitanya-caritāmṛta*, "*Ādi-līlā*," 3.99)

নাম বিনা কলিকালে নাহি আর ধর্ম ।
সর্বমন্ত্রসার নাম, এই শাস্ত্রমর্ম ॥

nāma vinu kali-kāle nāhi āra dharma
sarva-mantra-sāra nāma, ei śāstra-marma

In this Age of Kali there is no religious principle other than the chanting of the Holy Name, which is the essence of all Vedic hymns. This is the purport of all scriptures.
(*Śrī Caitanya-caritāmṛta*, "*Ādi-līlā*," 7.74)

After the birth of Lord Chaitanya, the wise astrologers gathered to conduct a detailed analysis of his birth chart, an essential step before proceeding with the naming ceremony, a ritual deeply rooted in Vedic traditions. After an exhaustive and thorough study of the celestial configurations, they reached the unanimous conclusion that the name Viśvambhara would be the most suitable for the newborn. This name, filled with meaning, translates as "the sustainer, nourisher, and protector of the universe" (*bhara* means "to sustain, nourish, or support," and *viśvam* means "universe").

Despite the importance and depth of this name, which reflects a cosmic role and intrinsic spiritual connection, the people of his community continued to address him by the nickname Nimai, an affectionate term evoking his birth under a neem tree. This duality in Chaitanya's designation, between a name symbolizing his divine role and a nickname reflecting his humanity, closeness, and intimacy, illustrates the complex interaction between his transcendental identity and his connection to the community.

From his earliest childhood, Śrī Chaitanya Mahāprabhu showed signs of his divine mission. At the *anna-prāśana* ceremony, at the age of six months, coins and the *Śrīmad-bhāgavatam* were presented to him, and he chose the latter, foreshadowing his future spiritual devotion. This symbolic choice marked the beginning of a path filled with revelations and teachings.

In his childhood, Śrī Chaitanya interacted with a serpent, an event that astonished those present but was resolved without incident. On another occasion, a thief attempted to kidnap him with the intent to rob him, but, ironically, he returned him to his home, leaving the thief confused and the child unharmed. These episodes illustrate the exceptional nature of his early years.

Lord Chaitanya also manifested when a traveling *brāhmaṇa* visited his home. In an act of childhood disobedience, he repeatedly consumed the offerings meant for the deity, forcing the *brāhmaṇa* to cook repeatedly. Finally, he revealed his divine identity to the *brāhmaṇa*, a transcendental moment that underscores his connection to the divine from an early age.

During his childhood, Nimai experienced a significant change in his family environment when his brother Viśvarūpa, motivated by his intense religious vocation, renounced his home to take up the life of a wandering monk. This event deeply affected their parents, who, fearing Nimai would follow a similar path, were hesitant to begin his formal education. They worried that extensive instruction might lead him to detach from worldly affairs and leave home.

In this situation, Nimai demonstrated precocious intelligence and a unique ability to influence his parents' decisions. On one occasion, after being scolded by Śacī-mātā for childish mischief, Nimai responded by sitting in a pile of garbage, causing his mother distress. When questioned about his behavior, Nimai replied with insightful logic: he argued that, as a *brāhmaṇa*, it was expected that he acquires knowledge and discernment; however, without education, it would be impossible for him to distinguish right from wrong or pure from impure. In his view, the lack of instruction placed him in a position of ignorance, where he could not tell a clean place from a dirty one.

This episode, documented in the *Ādī Khaṇḍa* of the *Caitanya-bhāgavata* by Śrīla Vṛndāvana Dāsa Ṭhakura, illustrates Nimai's intellectual sharpness from an early age and his ability to use logical argumentation and rhetoric to achieve his goals, even in the familial realm. His capacity to confront and overcome obstacles in his quest for knowledge reveals crucial aspects of his character and foreshadows his later influence as a saintly spiritual leader.

After witnessing the eloquence and cunning with which Nimai argued, Jagannātha Miśra recognized the futility of restricting his access to formal education. Consequently, he enrolled Nimai in the prestigious academy of Gaṅga Dāsa Paṇḍita. In an astonishingly short period, Nimai mastered Sanskrit grammar and delved into more complex disciplines. His skill was such that, when encountering scholars in the streets, he often challenged them with intricate questions about grammar and logic, leaving them perplexed and embarrassed by their inability to answer. This method can be compared to Socratic maieutics, which often ended in bewilderment and the impossibility of answering—a necessary step to bring forth the truth. These scholars even began avoiding him by crossing the street when they saw him approaching. However, through these interactions, Chaitanya was actually imparting a lesson on the true purpose of learning. He expressed this purpose in the *Caitanya-bhāgavata* (1.12.49), where he posed the fundamental question: "What is the purpose of learning? It is to know devotion to Kṛṣṇa. If one does not learn this, what is the point of being educated?" In other words, the ultimate cause of learning is spiritual.

কেহ কেহ সাক্ষাতে ও প্রভু দেখি' বোলে "কি কার্যে গোঙাও কাল তুমি বিদ্যা-ভোলে?" ॥
কেহ বোলে,–"হের দেখ, নিমাঞি-পণ্ডিত! বিদ্যায কি লাভ?–কৃষ্ণ ভজহ ত্বরিত ॥
পড়ে কেনে লোক?–কৃষ্ণ-ভক্তি জানিবারে সে যদি নহিল, তবে বিদ্যায কি করে?" ॥

keha keha sākṣāte o prabhu dekhi' bole
"ki kārye goṅāo kāla tumi vidyā-bhole?"
keha bole,-"hera dekha, nimāñi-paṇḍita!
vidyāya ki lābha?-kṛṣṇa bhajaha tvarita
paḍe kene loka?-kṛṣṇa-bhakti jānibāre
se yadi nahila, tabe vidyāya ki kare?"

Someone also directly told Nimāi, "Why are You wasting Your time with mundane education?"
Another person said, "Look, Nimāi, what do You gain from studying? Just worship Kṛṣṇa.
Why do people study? Education is only for understanding devotional service of Lord Kṛṣṇa. If that purpose is not served, then what is the use of Your education?
(*Caitanya-bhāgavata*, "*Ādi-khaṇḍa*," 12.47–49)

In *Śrī Caitanya-caritāmṛta*, it is stated:

প্রভু কহে, – "কোন্ বিদ্যা বিদ্যা-মধ্যে সার?"
রায় কহে, – "কৃষ্ণভক্তি বিনা বিদ্যা নাহি আর" ॥

prabhu kahe, - "kon vidyā vidyā-madhye sāra?"
rāya kahe, - "kṛṣṇa-bhakti vinā vidyā nāhi āra"

On one occasion the Lord inquired, "Of all types of education, which is the most important?" Rāmānanda Rāya replied, "No education is important other than the transcendental devotional service of Kṛṣṇa."
(*Śrī Caitanya-caritāmṛta*, "*Madhya-līlā*," 8.245)

This perspective highlights the primacy of spiritual devotion over mere academic knowledge. Unfortunately, Jagannātha Miśra passed away before Nimai finished his studies. Nimai faithfully observed the funeral rites and honored his father's memory before resuming his education. Soon, his reputation as a brilliant student spread, allowing him to eventually open his own school and attract many students eager to learn from his vast knowledge and devotional approach.

During his adolescence, Śrī Chaitanya displayed a playful character, often teasing the local *brāhmaṇas* and the young girls performing rituals on the Ganges. These interactions, though mischievous, reflect a deep understanding of the customs and beliefs of his time and highlight his ability to communicate and affect people in meaningful and sometimes surprising ways.

In the time of Śrī Chaitanya Mahāprabhu, Bengal was a hotbed of dialectic and argumentation. Navadwip, the place where Śrī Chaitanya was born and raised, stood as the hub of instruction and logical thought across all of India. The *Navya-nyāya* school was prominent. *Navya-nyāya*, also known as the *darśana* of Indian Neological Logic and Philosophy, emerged in the 13th century CE through the efforts of the eminent philosopher Gaṅgeśa Upādhyāya of Mithilā. This new approach was based on the foundations of the classical *Nyāya darśana* and continued through the contributions of Raghunātha Śiromaṇi of Navadwip. However, to fully understand the development of *Navya-nyāya*, it is also crucial to recognize the significant influences of earlier prominent thinkers such as Vācaspati Miśra and Udayana.

Navya-nyāya flourished over the centuries and remained active in India until the 18th century CE. In a time of intense intellectual fervor, scholars from this school made considerable advances in the fields of logic and Indian philosophy, solidifying the position of *Navya-nyāya* as a respected lineage in the intellectual context of the nation. The school left an indelible mark on the development of philosophical thought in India, and its legacy has endured to the present day as a subject of study and admiration.

Navadwip emerged as the most relevant epicenter for logical studies of the time, and its reputation was such that very few dared to challenge a scholar from there. Scholars trained in Navadwip were considered invincible in debate. The study centers, and schools were filled with students from all over India, and anyone who could refute a scholar from Navadwip instantly gained fame across the subcontinent. Navadwip was the nerve center of Indian scholars, and it was home to some of the most prominent names in logic. Śrī Chaitanya Mahāprabhu, who is credited with an exceptional mastery of logic, became the most famous scholar in the region and, even in his youth, demonstrated intellectual feats, debating and triumphing over intellectual luminaries.

At that time, Navadwip received the visit of Keśava Kāśmīrī, a renowned scholar who traveled and debated with other academics. The *paṇḍitas* of Navadwip, aware of their prestige and fearful of being overshadowed in an intellectual confrontation, faced a dilemma. Concerned for their city's reputation as a center of wisdom, they decided to appoint Nimai as their champion. They reasoned that if Nimai, who was still very young, were defeated, Navadwip's prestige would remain intact. On the other hand, a victory would elevate the honor of the entire community.

When Nimai and Keśava Kāśmīrī faced off in their intellectual debate, the Kashmiri *paṇḍita* showcased his skill by composing one hundred improvised verses in praise of the Ganges. Nimai, with his sharp insight, perfectly recalled all the verses and pointed out several grammatical, metrical, lexical, and rhetorical errors. This intervention overshadowed Keśava Kāśmīrī's performance, and the spectators hailed Nimai's victory. After the debate, Keśava Kāśmīrī, an expert in the sciences, was left bewildered by the unexpected reality of being corrected by a young grammar apprentice. This event led him to a deep introspection in the solitude of his dwelling. In the stillness of the night, a dreamlike vision appeared to him: Sarasvatī, the revered goddess of knowledge, imparted a transcendental directive: to surrender to the will of the Lord. This revelation marked a turning point in the life of the Kāśmīrī Paṇḍita, who, under divine guidance, found his spiritual path as a disciple of Śrī Chaitanya. This turn of events underscores the confluence between academic knowledge and spiritual wisdom, a recurring theme in the philosophical exploration of the relationship between human knowledge and the divine.

Shortly thereafter, Nimai married Lakṣmī Devī, the daughter of Vallabhācārya. A few months later, he embarked on a journey to East Bengal, present-day Bangladesh, to impart teachings and earn a living. During his absence, Lakṣmī Devī passed away due to a snake bite. Upon his return, Nimai found his mother in despair and offered her words of comfort, which are recorded in the *Caitanya-bhāgavata:*

লোকানুকরণ-দুঃখ ক্ষনেক করিযা কহিতে লাগিলা নিজে ধীর-চিত্ত হৈযা ॥
কস্য কে পতি-পুত্রাদ্যা মোহ এব হি কারণম্ ॥
প্রভু বলে,–"মাতা, দুঃখ ভাব' কি-কারণে? ভবিতব্য যে আছে, সে খণ্ডিবে কেমনে? ॥
এই-মত কাল-গতি, কেহ কা'রো নহে অতএব, 'সংসার অনিত্য' বেদে কহে ঈশ্বরের অধীন সে সকল-সংসার সংযোগ-বিযোগ কে করিতে পারে আর? ॥
অতএব যে হৈল ঈশ্বর-ইচ্ছায হৈল সে কার্য, আর দুঃখ কেনে তায? ॥
স্বামীর অগ্রেতে গঙ্গা পায যে সুকৃতি তা'র বড আর কে বা আছে ভাগ্যবতী?" ॥

lokānukaraṇa-duḥkha kṣaneka kariyā
kahite lāgilā nije dhīra-citta haiyā.
kasya ke pati-putrādyā moha eva hi kāraṇam.
prabhu bale,-"mātā, duḥkha bhāva' ki-kāraṇe?
bhavitavya ye āche, se khaṇḍibe kemane?
ei-mata kāla-gati, keha kā'ro nahe ataeva, 'saṁsāra anitya' vede kahe īśvarera
adhīna se sakala-saṁsāra saṁyoga-viyoga ke karite pāre āra?
ataeva ye haila īśvara-icchāya
haila se kārya, āra duḥkha kene tāya?
svāmīra agrete gaṅgā pāya ye sukṛti
tā'ra baḍa āra ke vā āche bhāgyavatī?"

After He lamented as an ordinary man for some time, He began to speak with patience.
Who in this material world is the husband, son, or friend of whom? Actually no one is related with anyone. Nescience alone is the cause of this misunderstanding.
The Lord said, "O mother, why are you feeling so sad? Who can check what is destined to happen?"
Such is the current of time. No one is related to anyone else, therefore the Vedas declare that this material world is temporary. All universes are under the control of the

> Supreme Lord. Who other than the Supreme Lord can unite or separate people?
> Therefore, whatever has happened by the desire of the Supreme Lord was destined. Why should you lament?
> Who is more fortunate and pious than a woman who leaves her body before her husband dies?
> (*Caitanya-bhāgavata*, "*Ādi-khaṇḍa*," 14.181–187)

Lord Chaitanya expressed that both life and death are governed by divine will and that the premature death of a wife, leaving her husband a widower, is considered fortunate. The following year, Nimai continued his teaching work at the home of Mukunda Sañjaya. His days were spent teaching his students intensively from dawn until noon, dedicating the afternoons and nights to deepening his own studies. During this time, Śacī Devī, deeply longing to see her son settled in a new marriage, began to make arrangements for it. She entrusted Kāśīnātha Paṇḍita with the responsibility of managing the matrimonial negotiations for Nimai with Viṣṇupriyā, the devout daughter of Sanātana Miśra.

Sanātana Miśra, a *brāhmaṇa* of impeccable reputation and a fervent devotee of Viṣṇu was recognized for his many virtues. His character was distinguished by charity, hospitality, truthfulness, and self-control. Additionally, his position as a scholar in the royal court afforded him considerable wealth. In this context, Buddhimanta Khān, another wealthy citizen of the town, volunteered to cover the wedding expenses. When the astrologically auspicious time for the ceremony was identified, Nimai led a grand and festive wedding procession to the residence of Sanātana Miśra. There, the traditional rituals were performed, culminating in the marriage of Nimai and Viṣṇupriyā.

Despite being married to Viṣṇupriyā, a wife both beautiful and virtuous, Chaitanya Mahāprabhu began to experience a growing disinterest in the pleasures and responsibilities of married life. In 1509, when he was approaching twenty-three years of age, he set out on a journey to Gayā. His goal was to perform offering rituals, known as oblations, at the revered Brahma-kuṇḍa to honor the memory and facilitate the spiritual transition of his late father.

After immersing himself in the purifying waters of Brahma-kuṇḍa and completing these sacred rituals, Mahāprabhu visited Cakraberia Tīrtha, the site of the famous temple that houses the footprints of Lord Viṣṇu. During his meditation at this holy place, Mahāprabhu heard the recitation of divine glories from the scriptures, which triggered a torrent of ecstatic transcendental symptoms within him, manifested in an incessant flow of tears comparable to the current of the Ganges River.

It was in this elevated state of consciousness that Mahāprabhu encountered Īśvara Purī, who was destined to become his master. Their meeting was marked by a surge of ecstatic love for Kṛṣṇa, flooding their hearts. Mahāprabhu revealed to Īśvara Purī that the deepest purpose of his journey to Gayā had, in fact, been this divine encounter.

প্রভু বলে,–“গযা-যাত্রা সফল আমার যত-ক্ষণে দেখিলাঙ চরণ তোমার ॥
তীর্থে পিণ্ড দিলে সে নিস্তরে পিতৃ-গণ সেহ,–যারে পিণ্ড দেয, তরে’ সেই
জন তোমা’ দেখিলেই মাত্র কোটি-পিতৃ-গণ সেই-ক্ষণে সর্ব-বন্ধ পায
বিমোচন ॥
অতএব তীর্থ নহে তোমার সমান তীর্থের্ ও পরম তুমি মঙ্গল প্রধান ॥
সংসার-সমুদ্র হৈতে উদ্ধারহ মোরে এই আমি দেহ সমর্পিলাঙ তোমারে ॥
‘কৃষ্ণ-পাদ-পদ্মের অমৃত-রস পান আমারে করাও তুমি’–এই চাহি দান” ॥

prabhu bale,—"gayā-yātrā saphala āmāra
yata-kṣaṇe dekhilāṅa caraṇa tomāra
tīrthe piṇḍa dile se nistare pitṛ-gaṇa
seha,—yāre piṇḍa deya, tare' sei jana
tomā' dekhilei mātra koṭi-pitṛ-gaṇa
sei-kṣaṇe sarva-bandha pāya vimocana
ataeva tīrtha nahe tomāra samāna
tīrther o parama tumi maṅgala pradhāna
saṁsāra-samudra haite uddhāraha more
ei āmi deha samarpilāṅa tomāre
kṛṣṇa-pāda-padmera amṛta-rasa pāna
āmāre karāo tumi'—ei cāhi dāna"

> The Lord said, "My journey to Gayā has become successful the moment I was able to see your lotus feet. If one offers oblations to the forefathers in a holy place, then the forefathers are delivered. But one delivers only he to whom the oblation was offered. By seeing you, however, millions of forefathers are immediately freed from material bondage. Therefore, holy places are not equal to you, for you purify even the holy places. Please deliver Me from the ocean of material existence. I surrender Myself unto you. I beg that you make Me drink the nectar of Kṛṣṇa's lotus feet."
>
> (*Caitanya-bhāgavata*, "*Ādi-khaṇḍa*," 17.50–55)

Chaitanya Mahāprabhu emphatically emphasized that the true value of visiting holy places lies in the meeting and association with saintly sages and realized masters who reside there. Pilgrimage to sacred sites constitutes a means or instrument for a higher purpose. Therefore, it is a mistake to assume that merely visiting a place of pilgrimage guarantees contact with an authentic saint or enlightened master. The role of the master is transcendental, as they possess the ability to instill in others the longing for devotional service to Kṛṣṇa, the supreme goal of life according to Mahāprabhu's teachings.

According to the *Gauḍīya Vaiṣṇava* tradition, Śrī Chaitanya Mahāprabhu, in his role as a devotee and universal master, is the incarnation of Kṛṣṇa, who takes the form of His own devotee in the emotional state of Rādhārāṇī, in order to impart the means to attain divine love. However, to highlight the importance of receiving initiation from a genuine master, Mahāprabhu exhibited the pastime of accepting the ten-syllable Kṛṣṇa mantra from Īśvara Purī.

After this initiation, Nimai became a being completely intoxicated with devotion to Kṛṣṇa. Śrī Gaurāṅga underwent a profound devotional transformation. The initiation into the *mahā-mantra* by Īśvara Purī radically transformed his very essence. Upon returning to Navadwip, he distanced himself from his previous identity as an intellectual, scholar, academic, and expert. Renouncing all his prior concerns, including his family and professional life, he abandoned teaching, closed his school, and dedicated his existence to the search for Kṛṣṇa, invoking His name with intense emotion and experiencing episodes of fainting from the anguish of separation.

From that moment on, Śrī Chaitanya's existence underwent a drastic turn, leading him to abandon the conceptual, rational, and logical dimension on which he had based his knowledge and in which he had excelled. Instead, he turned toward the symbolic, spiritual, devotional, and supramental, experiencing a shift that took him from the conceptual mind to the devotional heart. Lord Chaitanya perplexed the world, abandoning conceptualization to dance and sing the Holy Names of God in public, proclaiming that the unity and diversity of the divine are beyond human comprehension, a remarkable statement coming from someone who had dedicated his life to conceptualization, speculation, and logic. This powerful expression of the divine's ineffable nature profoundly impacted those who heard it. For Śrī Chaitanya, the highest form of worship was not through rationalizing the divine, but through participating in the sound-symbol of the *mahā-mantra.*

हरेः शक्तेः सर्वं चिदचिदखिलं स्यात्परिनतिः ।
विवर्तं नो सत्यं श्रुतिमतविरुद्धं कलिमलम् ॥
हरेर्भेदाभेदौ श्रुतिविहिततत्त्वं सुविमलं ।
ततः प्रेम्णः सिद्धिर्भवति नितरां नित्यविषये ॥

hareḥ śakteḥ sarvaṁ cid-acid-akhilaṁ syāt parinatiḥ
vivartaṁ no satyaṁ śruti-mata-viruddhaṁ kali-malam
harer bhedābhedau śruti-vihita-tattvaṁ suvimalaṁ
tataḥ premṇaḥ siddhir bhavati nitarāṁ nitya-viṣaye

In their entirety, the material and spiritual worlds are the transformations of the energies of Lord Hari, the Supreme Lord. *Vivarta-vāda*, the impersonal theory of illusory transformation of Brahman, is false. It is venomous contamination in this age of Kali and is contradictory to the conclusions of the Vedas. The philosophy of *acintya-bhedābheda-tattva*, the doctrine of inconceivable oneness and difference simultaneously, is the only true essence of the Vedas. The practice of this philosophy promotes a person to the perfectional stage of developing divine transcendental love for Śrī Hari, the absolute eternal Truth.

(Śrīla Bhaktivinoda Ṭhākura, *Gaurāṅga-līlā-smaraṇa-maṅgala Stotra*, verse 83)

Within Vaishnavism, there are four schools, or *sampradāyas*, accepted as authorized:

- *Brahma-madhva-sampradāya* represented by Śrī Madhvācārya.
- *Lakṣmī sampradāya* represented by Śrī Rāmānujācārya.
- *Śiva sampradāya* represented by Śrīpāda Viṣṇusvāmī.
- *Kumāra sampradāya* represented by Śrī Nimbārkācārya.

Lord Chaitanya Mahāprabhu accepted the doctrine of Śrī Madhvācārya while simultaneously recognizing certain important aspects contained in the *tattvas* of the other three *Vaiṣṇava sampradāyas*. In the exact words of Lord Chaitanya, cited by Śrī Jīva Gosvāmī:

মধ্ব হৈতে সার-দ্বয় করিব গ্রহণ ।
এক হয় কেবলাদ্বৈত নিরসন নিরসন ॥
কৃষ্ণ-মুর্তি নিত্য জানি' তা হার সেবন ।
সেই ত' দ্বিতীয় সার জান মহাজন ॥
রামানুজ হৈতে আমি লৈ দুই সার ।
অনন্য-ভকতি, ভক্ত-জন-সেবা আর ॥
বিষ্ণু হৈতে দুই সার করিব স্বীকার ।
ত্বদীয়-সর্বস্ব-ভাব, রাগ-মার্গ আর ॥
তোমা হৈতে লব আমি দুই মহা-সার ।
একান্ত-রাধিকাশ্রয়, গোপী-ভাব আর ॥

madhva haite sāra-dvaya kariba grahaṇa
eka haya kevalādvaita nirasana
kṛṣṇa-mūrti nitya jāni' tāṅhāra sevana
sei ta' dvitīya sāra jāna mahājana
rāmānuja haite āmi lai dui sāra

ananya-bhakati, bhakta-jana-sevā āra
viṣṇu haite dui sāra kariba svīkāra
tvadīya-sarvasva-bhāva, rāga-mārga āra
tomā haite laba āmi dui mahā-sāra
ekānta-rādhikāśraya, gopī-bhāva āra

O great personality, from the *Madhva-sampradāya* I will accept two essential principles: the refutation of *kevalādvaita* (exclusive monism) and service to Śrī Kṛṣṇa's deity form, having accepted this form as eternal. From Śrī Rāmānuja I will accept exclusive devotion (*ananya-bhakti*) and service to the devotees. From Śrī Viṣṇusvāmī I will accept the sentiment that Bhagavān Śrī Kṛṣṇa alone is my everything (*tvadīya-sarvasva-bhāva*) and the path of spontaneous devotion (*rāga-mārga*). From your *sampradāya* [the line of Śrī Nimbāditya, or Nimbārka] I will accept two supremely essential principles: to exclusively take shelter of the lotus feet of Śrīmatī Rādhikā (*ekānta-rādhikāśraya*) and the sentiments of the *gopīs*.

(Śrīla Bhaktivinoda Ṭhakura, *Śrī Navadvīpa-dhāma-māhātmya*, "*Parikramā-khaṇḍa*," 16.52–56)

When a scholar of logic at the level of Nimai Paṇḍit proposes that the transcendent is *acintya-bhedābheda*, or "inconceivable oneness and difference," he is promoting a shift from the conceptual to the symbolic. The term *cintya* means "thinkable," referring to a "concept," and the opposite is *acintya*, or "non-conceptual." *Bheda* is translated as "difference," and the opposite is *abheda*, or "non-difference." The theological view of *bhedābheda-tattva* asserts that God is "simultaneously one with His creation and different from it." No school, no matter how inconceivable Brahman, God, or the Ultimate Truth may be, labels it as "inconceivable." It is absurd to define something as indefinable (*acintya*). Obviously, this is not a conceptual definition but a shift from the conceptual realm to the symbolic because, through concepts, there is no access to the transcendent. The symbol and the myth allow the possibility of immersing oneself in the unfathomable, in the exultation, madness, and immaculate naivety of primordial innocence. Remember that a symbol, in its essence, can be defined as an invisible image that is shown through another visible one and gains meaning through an audible narrative. It is an entity that has a visible and an invisible aspect, an image, word, or action that exceeds its superficial or literal meaning, evoking a deeper and more abstract background. The symbol is an auditory image that conveys, through a sensible image, a supersensible story that gives meaning to the physical through the metaphysical. The syntax of the symbol is the relationship each element of the symbol has. The semantics of the symbol is the meaning it acquires in the light of the metaphysical path. And the pragmatics of the symbol is the cultural or group context in which this semantics makes sense. The members of the group can fully understand it because they are part of its history. Only someone who belongs to the group can be part of its symbol, and only someone who is part of the symbol can understand it. Therefore, it is necessary to clearly understand the profound shift that the term *acintya* entails within this context.

Subsequently, Nimai began actively participating in *kīrtanas*, ecstatic celebrations of singing and dancing the sacred names of Kṛṣṇa, held at the residence of Śrīvāsa Paṇḍita, a venerable neighboring *Vaiṣṇava* devotee. Today, Śrīvāsa's dwelling is known as Saṅkīrtana Rāsa Sthalī, evoking the place where Kṛṣṇa performed His *rāsa* dance with the *gopīs*. Just as those pastimes of Kṛṣṇa are considered the most outstanding, *saṅkīrtana* embodies the most significant pastime of Śrī Gaurāṅga. Furthermore, Śrī Chaitanya occasionally led *kīrtanas* at the house of Candraśekhara Ācārya.

The resonances of Śrī Chaitanya Mahāprabhu's *kīrtana* spread to Śāntipura, where they resonated among his closest associates: Nityānanda Prabhu, Advaita Prabhu, Hari Dāsa Ṭhākura, Gadādhara Paṇḍita, Śrīvāsa Paṇḍita, and other distinguished devotees like Puṇḍarika Vidyānidhi, Murāri Gupta, and Buddhimanta Khān. This event marked the beginning of the *saṅkīrtana* movement, evoking the image of an ecstasy of divine love, which seemed to descend from the spiritual realm to seize the hearts of the faithful, manifesting His presence through the recitation of Kṛṣṇa's sacred name.

The atheists, those whose perception is limited to the materiality of the body and the tangible world, were unable to comprehend the transformation experienced by Mahāprabhu, much like how a barren woman cannot comprehend motherhood. The *pāṣāṇḍīs*, or "heretics" of Navadwip, absorbed in worldliness and oblivious to divine love, expressed various opinions about Mahāprabhu's *kīrtanas*, all of them adverse. Some criticized them for disturbing the peace and public order with their apparent incoherent uproar; others dismissed them, calling them mere drunken feasts. Despite the criticism and condemnation from the *pāṣāṇḍīs*, each based on their limited understanding, the devotees remained unwavering, fully dedicating themselves to chanting the Holy Names alongside Nimai. While chanting the mantra, Śrī Gaurāṅga danced, possessed by a divine, nectarean madness that infected everyone around him, making them dance and chant with him. Quickly, Śrī Chaitanya became the undisputed leader of Kṛṣṇa's devotees in Nadia. However, his popularity soon sparked jealousy among some *brāhmaṇas* who tried to impede the *saṅkīrtana* movement. When the envious opponents realized the futility of their efforts to suppress the *kīrtana* through their adverse rhetoric, they decided to raise their complaints to the Kazi, the magistrate Nawab Hussain Shah, the local Muslim authority in Bengal. The magistrate was the authority in a Bengal dominated by Islamic followers at the time. In an attempt to quell the dissent, he issued a ban on the *kīrtana*. He even personally went to a house where a *kīrtana* was taking place and furiously broke a *mṛdanga* drum. However, Nimai, vehemently rejecting such interference, defied the order with unshakable firmness. He proclaimed: "In this age of Kali, no mortal has the authority to silence the sacred chanting of the Holy Names." Nimai, in an act of open defiance, urged his followers: "Continue with the *kīrtana*." The devotees continued their chanting for some time, but they could not do so freely. Fearing the Kazi, Nimai said to his followers: "Tonight, we will illuminate Navadwip with the light of our devotion. Will the Kazi dare to interrupt such a divine manifestation? If necessary, we will show our resolve, even before the monarch." His words resonated with a steadfast determination, an invitation to challenge the established conventions in the name of transcendental love for Kṛṣṇa.

Nimai's response was to call for a massive demonstration, a procession of *Vaiṣṇavas* and sympathizers that stretched through the streets of Navadwip, bravely directed toward the residence of the Kazi. The crowd, inflamed by revolutionary fervor, quickly wreaked havoc around the Kazi's house, destroying gardens and orchards. The few soldiers at the Kazi's disposal were insufficient against the overwhelming number of demonstrators, united in their support for Nimai.

The Kazi, overwhelmed by fear in the face of Nimai's imposing figure, chose to retreat to his home, refusing all encounters. Nimai, confronted with the Kazi's refusal, expressed his indignation firmly and clearly, demonstrating the depth of his commitment to the *Vaiṣṇava* cause and the freedom of religious expression.

ক্রোধে বলে প্রভু–"আরে কাজী বেটা কোথা ঝাট আন' ধরিয়া কাটিয়া
ফেল মাথা ॥
পুড়িয়া মরুক সব-গণের সহিতে সর্ব বাড়ী বেড়ি' অগ্নি দেহ' চারি-ভিতে ॥
সঙ্কীর্তন-আরম্ভে মোহার অবতার কীর্তন-বিরোধী পাপী করিমু সংহার...

krodhe bale prabhu-"āre kājī beṭā kothā
jhāṭa āna' dhariyā kāṭiyā phela māthā
puḍiyā maruka saba-gaṇera sahite
sarva bāḍī veḍi' agni deha' cāri-bhite
saṅkīrtana-ārambhe mohāra avatāra
kīrtana-virodhī pāpī karimu saṃhāra"

In that angry state, the Lord said: "Where is that fellow Kazi? Bring him here quickly, and I'll cut off his head. Let the Kazi burn to death along with his associates. Surround the house and set it on fire from all sides. I have incarnated to inaugurate the *saṅkīrtana* movement. I will destroy those sinners who are inimical to *kīrtana*."

(*Caitanya-bhāgavata*, "*Madhya-khaṇḍa*," 23.388, 399, 402)

Upon perceiving the imminent threat of the approaching crowd carrying blazing torches, the Kazi realized that his situation was untenable. In the meantime, some devotees, concerned by Mahāprabhu's visible anger, made efforts to calm him down. Their efforts were successful: Chaitanya regained his composure, and the destructive fury that had taken hold of him dissipated. In front of the main entrance of the Kazi's residence, Nimai and his followers sat down. Nimai entrusted a distinguished citizen of Navadwip with the task of entering and delivering his demands to the Kazi. Upon being informed that Nimai did not seek to harm him, the Kazi felt relieved and agreed to receive him. The meeting between the Kazi and Nimai Paṇḍita unfolded in an atmosphere of mutual courtesy, a proper deference given the Kazi's position of authority.

A bond of familiarity arose between them when the Kazi addressed Nimai as his nephew, and Nimai reciprocated by calling him uncle (*māmā*). This connection was rooted in the Bengali tradition of village relationships, which established affectionate bonds beyond direct family ties. Since the Kazi shared a common origin with Nimai's mother, Śacī, he was considered her village brother and, by extension, Nimai's uncle, despite the differences in social class.

In that historical context, the interaction between *brāhmaṇas* and Muslims was strongly restricted; even indirect contact with the shadow of a Muslim would require a *brāhmaṇa* to undergo a purifying bath in the Ganges. Therefore, the direct and close dialogue between Nimai, a high-caste *brāhmaṇa*, and the Kazi, a Muslim magistrate, broke established conventions and marked a significant milestone in the intercultural relations of the time.

The congregation of countless citizens who had followed Nimai formed a circle around him and the Muslim magistrate, paying meticulous attention to their conversation. Nimai began the discussion with a profound reflection on the Quran and Muslims' practice of the slaughtering of cows.

Nimai, with his serene presence and melodic voice, expressed his ideas with irrefutable logic and captivating eloquence. This combination of humility, sweetness in speech, and lucid argumentation left a lasting impression on the Kazi.

Then, the Kazi told Nimai how a fearsome lion with a human body (Lord Nṛsiṁhadeva) had appeared to him. Piercing his chest with its claws, the lion warned him to stop opposing the chanting of the Holy Name, or he would lose his life.

এত বলি' কাজী নিজ-বুক দেখাইল ।
শুনি' দেখি' সর্বলোক আশ্চর্য মানিল ॥

eta bali' kājī nija-buka dekhāila
śuni' dekhi' sarva-loka āścarya mānila

After this description, the Kazi showed his chest. Having heard him and seen the marks, all the people there accepted the wonderful incident.

(*Śrī Caitanya-caritāmṛta*, "*Ādi-līlā*," 17.187)

Then, the Kazi described how different groups of Muslims and Hindus approached him, asking him to stop the *saṅkīrtana* movement. He then concluded his words with the following statement.

হিন্দুর ঈশ্বর বড় যেই নারায়ণ ।
সেই তুমি হও,—হেন লয় মোর মন ॥
এত শুনি' মহাপ্রভু হাসিয়া হাসিয়া ।
কহিতে লাগিলা কিছু কাজিরে ছুঁইয়া ॥
তোমার মুখে কৃষ্ণনাম,—এ বড় বিচিত্র ।
পাপক্ষয় গেল, হৈলা পরম পবিত্র ॥
'হরি' 'কৃষ্ণ' 'নারায়ণ'—লৈলে তিন নাম ।
বড় ভাগ্যবান্ তুমি, বড় পুণ্যবান্ ॥

eta śuni' mahāprabhu hāsiyā hāsiyā
hindura īśvara baḍa yei nārāyaṇa
sei tumi hao, — hena laya mora mana
kahite lāgilā kichu kājire chuṅiyā
tomāra mukhe kṛṣṇa-nāma, — e baḍa vicitra
pāpa-kṣaya gela, hailā parama pavitra
'hari' 'kṛṣṇa' 'nārāyaṇa' — laile tina nāma
baḍa bhāgyavān tumi, baḍa puṇyavān

> I know that Nārāyaṇa is the Supreme God of the Hindus, and I think that You are the same Nārāyaṇa. This I feel within my mind. After hearing the Kazi speak so nicely, Śrī Chaitanya Mahāprabhu touched him and smilingly spoke as follows. "The chanting of the Holy Name of Kṛṣṇa from your mouth has performed a wonder — it has nullified the reactions of all your sinful activities. Now you have become supremely pure. Because you have chanted three Holy Names of the Lord — Hari, Kṛṣṇa and Nārāyaṇa — you are undoubtedly the most fortunate and pious."
>
> (*Śrī Caitanya-caritāmṛta*, "*Ādi-līlā*," 17.215–218)

In this exceptional circumstance, the Kazi's behavior, stripped of the usual protocol rigidity, revealed a bewildering familiarity toward an ordinary citizen like Nimai. Immersed in the intensity of the moment, the Kazi seemed to have completely shed the etiquettes dictated by his social rank. His gaze clouded with tears, was fixed on Nimai's serene face, captured by a mix of reverence and admiration. Mentally, he surrendered at the lotus feet of Nimai, a gesture of submission and devotion. With humility and sincere pleading, he begged for divine grace, longing for the precious gift of pure devotion to God, a state of spiritual ecstasy that transcended the conventions and social distinctions of his time.

এত শুনি' কাজীর দুই চক্ষে পড়ে পানি ।
প্রভুর চরণ ছুঁই' বলে প্রিয়বাণী ॥
তোমার প্রসাদে মোর ঘুচিল কুমতি ।
এই কৃপা কর,–যেন তোমাতে রহু ভক্তি ॥

eta śuni' kājīra dui cakṣe paḍe pāni
prabhura caraṇa chuṅi' bale priya-vāṇī
tomāra prasāde mora ghucila kumati
ei kṛpā kara, — yena tomāte rahu bhakti

After the Kazi heard this, tears flowed down from his eyes. He immediately touched the lotus feet of the Lord and spoke the following sweet words. "Only by Your mercy have my bad intentions vanished. Kindly favor me so that my devotion may always be fixed upon You."

(*Śrī Caitanya-caritāmṛta*, "*Ādi-līlā*," 17.219b–220)

Although initially, the Kazi ordered the cessation of the *saṅkīrtana* movement of Chaitanya, after a personal conversation with Gaurāṅga, the Kazi completely changed his mind and became his devotee. With the resolution of the conflict over the *kīrtana*, the schemes of the *pāṣāṇḍīs* proved futile. The tomb of Chand Kazi, located in the village of Bamanpukur near Navadwip, became a place of respect for both Hindus and Muslims. Some historians point to this event led by Nimai as the dawn of the Indian struggle for freedom.

Freed from the restrictions imposed by the Kazi, Nimai promoted *kīrtana* in various places, fostering a significant change in those previously hostile to this practice. Among the most notable converts were Jagāi and Mādhāi, two brothers whose life of depravity seemed boundless.

Despite their countless faults, they had refrained from blaspheming against the devotees, which proved their salvation. Kṛṣṇa, in His incarnation as the son of Śacī, sent Nityānanda Prabhu and Hari Dāsa Ṭhākura to spread the Holy Names, and it was in this mission that they encountered the infamous brothers.

On one occasion, while Nityānanda Prabhu and Śrīla Haridāsa Ṭhākura were walking down a main street, they came across a tumultuous crowd. Inquiring among the people present, they discovered that the source of the commotion was the two brothers, Jagāi and Mādhāi, whose scandalous behavior was exacerbated by drunkenness. Despite being born into a respectable *brāhmaṇa* family, these brothers had fallen into disgrace due to bad influences, sinking into vices and reprehensible conduct.

Moved by compassion, Nityānanda Prabhu decided to intervene, considering that the redemption of such fallen souls would be a glorious act that would exalt the name of Lord Chaitanya. Despite the obscenities and hostility they faced, Nityānanda and Haridāsa continued their mission of urging the brothers to chant the Holy Name of Hari.

The following day, in a subsequent encounter, Nityānanda Prabhu, known as an *avadhūta* and beyond social conventions, was attacked by Mādhāi. However, instead of becoming angry, Nityānanda responded with extraordinary patience and kindness, once again urging the brothers to devotion. This attitude awakened a change in Jagāi, who, impressed by Nityānanda's magnanimity, repented and pleaded for mercy for his brother.

This incident culminated in the furious arrival of Lord Chaitanya, who was ready to punish the transgressors. However, Nityānanda intervened, reminding Chaitanya of His mission to save the lost souls of this age. Chaitanya, moved by the brothers' plea and repentance, agreed to forgive them on the condition that they renounce their sinful ways.

This story highlights the unconditional compassion and steadfastness in the spiritual mission of Nityānanda Prabhu and Śrī Chaitanya Mahāprabhu, which transcends the barriers of conduct and social status, emphasizing the importance of inner transformation and genuine redemption.

After receiving the blessing of Nityānanda Prabhu, Jagāi and Mādhāi experienced deep remorse for their past transgressions. They immersed themselves in the devotional community, adopting rigorous practices of prayer and contemplation. Their sinful paths were left behind, and their past gradually faded into oblivion. Transformed, they rose to the position of exemplary devotees, and Mahāprabhu instructed His disciples not to judge them for their former faults.

Nityānanda Prabhu entrusted Mādhāi with the mission of incessantly chanting the name of Kṛṣṇa and dedicating himself to the service of the Ganges, meticulously cleaning the steps of the *ghāt*. This act of humility and penance, offering reverence to each bather, transformed Mādhāi Ghāt. Today, the place known as Mādhāi Ghat remains a testament to his redemption.

The story of Jagāi and Mādhāi profoundly illustrates the teachings of Chaitanya Mahāprabhu on the spiritual path. He, a high-caste *brāhmaṇa*, along with Hari Dāsa Ṭhākura, from a Muslim background, and Nityānanda Prabhu, an *avadhūta* outside the caste system, demonstrated that spiritual truth transcends human barriers of caste, class, or religion. Mahāprabhu emphasized that the promotion of chanting the Holy Names and the teachings of Kṛṣṇa should never be motivated by material interests. Treating religion as a means of material gain constitutes a serious offense.

In this pastime, an esoteric secret is also revealed: anger, an emotion typically seen as negative, can be channeled into service to Kṛṣṇa. Narottama Dās Ṭhākura expressed this in his teaching to direct anger against those who oppose Kṛṣṇa. Thus, in exceptional cases, anger does not contradict spiritual growth, as exemplified by Hanumān in the Rāmāyaṇa, where his fury against Rāvaṇa was an expression of his devotion to Lord Rāmacandra.

In the foundational year of the *saṅkīrtana* movement in Navadwip, Mahāprabhu orchestrated a series of pastimes, each a microcosm of divinity. These acts displayed the six divine attributes enshrined in Vedic literature: wealth, bravery, fame, beauty, wisdom, and detachment. One particular incident stood out, marking a turning point in his life. In his abode, Mahāprabhu immersed himself in the melancholy of a *gopī*, grieving over Kṛṣṇa's apparent indifference. Lost in this trance, he repeatedly cried out "*gopī, gopī.*" A student, confused and critical, asked Mahāprabhu, "Why do you chant the name of the cowherd girls and not that of Kṛṣṇa? What do you accomplish by this?" Mahāprabhu, still absorbed in his role as the aggrieved *gopī*, responded with anger. He accused Kṛṣṇa of being unfaithful and of betraying His love. The student, unable to decipher the deep meaning of his words, was scandalized, viewing it as blasphemy. Mahāprabhu, exacerbated, chased the student with a stick, causing him to flee in terror.

The incident with the student caused consternation among the local *brāhmaṇas*. They conspired to have thugs punish Mahāprabhu, beating him up. The misunderstanding and hostility from the brahmin community plunged him into deep sorrow. In response to this conflict, Mahāprabhu uttered a riddle, an enigmatic reply to the censure and misunderstanding he faced.

"করিল পিপ্পলিখণ্ড কফ নিবারিতে উলটিয়া আরো কফ বাড়িল দেহেতে" ॥

karila pippali-khanda kapha nivarite
ulatiya aro kapha badila dehete

I made the medicine *pippalikhaṇḍa* to clear excess mucus, but instead of clearing the mucus in the body, it created more.
(*Caitanya-bhāgavata*, "*Madhya-khaṇḍa*," 26.121)

In other words: "I have shown so many wonderful pastimes to teach these people spiritual life, but they have been unable to understand anything. In fact, they are becoming hostile to pure devotion." He concluded that he had to take extraordinary measures to remedy the problem and save them.

অতএব অবশ্য আমি সন্ন্যাস করিব ।
সন্ন্যাসি-বুদ্ধ্যে মোরে প্রণত হইব ॥

ataeva avaśya āmi sannyāsa kariba
sannyāsi-buddhye more praṇata ha-iba

I shall accept the *sannyāsa* order of life, for thus people will offer Me their obeisances, thinking of Me as a member of the renounced order.
(*Śrī Caitanya-caritāmṛta*, "*Ādi-līlā*," 17.265)

At a crucial juncture, Mahāprabhu chose the ascetic life of a *sannyāsī*. Kaśava Bhāratī, on his way to Katwa, crossed paths with Mahāprabhu in Navadwip. To him, Mahāprabhu entrusted his purpose, a secret shared only with five close associates: His mother Śacī Devī, Gadādhara Paṇḍita, Candraśekhara, Mukunda, and Brahmānanda. However, the news spread quickly throughout the town, except to Viṣṇupriyā Devī, his wife, who remained unaware.

Viṣṇupriyā, the daughter of Sanātana Miśra, had entered Mahāprabhu's life with the hope of a happy marriage. But despite her hopes, tranquility always eluded her, tormented by her husband's growing spiritual devotion and the lingering fear of being abandoned.

On the eve of his departure, Mahāprabhu immersed himself in a *kīrtana* with his followers, silently bidding them farewell. At dusk, he returned home, where Śacī Mātā and Viṣṇupriyā were waiting for him. Viṣṇupriyā, adhering to tradition, washed Mahāprabhu's feet. That night, he fulfilled his household duties, praying and dining in the company of his mother before retiring to his room.

The room was filled with palpable tension, marked by the imminent separation. Viṣṇupriyā's anguished questions resonated with a heart-wrenching urgency. In the dim light, Viṣṇupriyā's tears shone, reflecting the pain of a broken heart. In this emotional scene, Mahāprabhu's resolve wavered. Moved by love and compassion, he embraced Viṣṇupriyā, seeking to ease her distress. He spoke words of comfort and affection in that embrace, striving to calm her troubled spirit.

In those moments, Nimai and Viṣṇupriyā enacted scenes that poets have fervently described: a lover and his beloved on the threshold of union. Nimai, with care and tenderness, helped Viṣṇupriyā adorn herself with her finest sari and golden jewelry. Their room, bathed in the light of pure love and devoid of lust, became a refuge of intimacy and affection. However, at the end of the night, with Viṣṇupriyā deep in sleep, Nimai broke the bonds of affection and silently departed for Katwa.

At dawn, accompanied by Nityānanda Prabhu, Candraśekhara Ācārya, and Mukunda Datta, Nimai began his journey toward a new life as a *sannyāsī*. After crossing the Nirdayā Ghat on the Ganges, whose name evokes the absence of piety in his departure, he reached Katwa. There, at the ashram of Keśava Bhāratī, Mahāprabhu requested *sannyāsa*. His friends, immersed in *saṅkīrtana*, waited as a barber shaved Mahāprabhu's head, an act that filled everyone present with sorrow.

In an unexpected gesture, Mahāprabhu whispered a mantra into Keśava Bhāratī's ear and asked him to repeat it, thereby reversing the traditional master-disciple relationship. Keśava Bhāratī, following Mahāprabhu's wish, gave him the name Kṛṣṇa Chaitanya. In his saffron robes, Mahāprabhu radiated exceptional beauty.

Meanwhile, in Navadwip, the news of his departure and his conversion to *sannyāsī* caused deep sorrow. Śacī Devī and Viṣṇupriyā, immersed in mourning, faced an unfathomable emptiness. Viṣṇupriyā, still young, watched as her world crumbled, lost in overwhelming solitude, with the hope of future happiness fading like an unattainable dream. Her love in separation became a paradigm of devotion and sacrifice.

The entire town resonated with the lamentations of the devotees, an echo of sadness that endures to this day. In the collective memory, the words of Govinda Ghosh revive that feeling of loss and longing, keeping alive the story of Mahāprabhu and his impact on the hearts of his followers.

হেদে রে নদীয়া বাসি করাও মুখ চাও ।
বহু পাসারিয়া গোড়া চাঁদেরে ফিরাও ॥

hede re nadiya vasi kara-o mukha cao
bahu pasariya gora candere phirao

> O citizens of Nadia! To whom will you now turn? Raise your arms to the heavens and pray for our golden moon to come home!
>
> (From a poem written by Govinda Ghosh)

After his initiation as a *sannyāsī*, Mahāprabhu left Katwa and headed toward Śāntipura. A messenger, hurriedly walking, made his way to Navadwip to inform Śacī Devī, his mother. She, distressed but determined, traveled to Śāntipura to meet her son. In an emotionally charged dialogue, Śacī Devī begged Mahāprabhu to change his initial plans to go to Vrindavan. Instead, she urged him to settle in Jagannātha Purī, thus making it easier for her to receive news about him.

Upon arriving in Puri in March of 1510, Mahāprabhu went directly to the Jagannātha temple. The majestic presence of the deity plunged Mahāprabhu into a deep ecstasy, causing him to faint on the temple floor. Sārvabhauma Bhaṭṭācārya, a renowned scholar of Vedanta and a witness to this extraordinary event, was deeply moved. He took Mahāprabhu to his home, where the devotees, by his side, woke him up by chanting the Holy Names of Kṛṣṇa.

Once his consciousness was restored, Sārvabhauma, intending to impart his knowledge, offered to teach Mahāprabhu the perspective of Advaita Vedanta. Mahāprabhu accepted and patiently listened for seven days to Sārvabhauma's explanations of the *Vedānta-sūtra* based on Śaṅkara's commentary. However, Mahāprabhu's prolonged silence began to trouble Sārvabhauma, who asked him if he had any doubts. Mahāprabhu then expressed his view: although he found Vyāsa Deva's aphorisms clear, their interpretations by others obscured their meaning, diverting them from their true purpose.

প্রভু কহে, – "সূত্রের অর্থ বুঝিয়ে নির্মল ।
তোমার ব্যাখ্যা শুনি' মন হয় ত' বিকল ॥

prabhu kahe, — "sūtrera artha bujhiye nirmala
tomāra vyākhyā śuni' mana haya ta' vikala"

Śrī Caitanya Mahāprabhu then revealed His mind, saying, "I can understand the meaning of each *sūtra* very clearly, but your explanations have simply agitated My mind."

(*Śrī Caitanya-caritāmṛta*, "*Madhya-līlā*," 6.130)

According to Mahāprabhu, the true understanding of Vedanta resided in the doctrine of *acintya-bhedābheda-tattva*, or "the inconceivable simultaneous unity and difference." In an enlightening debate, Mahāprabhu demonstrated his mastery of the scriptures to convince Sārvabhauma Bhaṭṭācārya of his spiritual perspectives. Then, intrigued, Bhaṭṭācārya requested Mahāprabhu to interpret the verse *ātmārāmāś ca munayaḥ* from the *Śrīmad-bhāgavatam* (1.7.10). First, Bhaṭṭācārya presented nine interpretations, showcasing his scholarship. However, Mahāprabhu, without referring to Bhaṭṭācārya's explanations, revealed eighteen distinct interpretations, leaving the scholar astounded. This revelation led Sārvabhauma to surrender to Mahāprabhu, who, in return, showed him his divine forms and enlightened him with a profound understanding of the divine truth.

It was later revealed that Sārvabhauma Bhaṭṭācārya, prominent in his field, had his roots in Navadwip. This connection became evident when it was discovered that his father and Nīlāmbara Cakravartī, the maternal grandfather of Śrī Chaitanya Mahāprabhu, had been studying companions. This historical link instilled in Bhaṭṭācārya a paternal affection toward the young *sannyāsī*, Śrī Chaitanya.

Bhaṭṭācārya, a renowned scholar and master of several *sannyāsīs* from the Śaṅkarācārya *sampradāya* tradition, had a deep interest in sharing the teachings of Vedanta with Śrī Chaitanya. His own affiliation with this philosophical current motivated him to wish for the young *sannyāsī* to also be enriched with this knowledge. This aspiration reflected a bridge between generations and traditions, symbolizing a crossroads between the past and present, between the academic and the spiritual.

One month later, in April 1510, Mahāprabhu embarked on a pilgrimage to South India. At the urging of Nityānanda Prabhu, he accepted the company of Kṛṣṇa Dāsa, a *brāhmaṇa*, as his servant. Before his departure, Sārvabhauma offered Mahāprabhu some clothes and suggested meeting Rāmānanda Rāya near the Godāvarī River. Accompanied by Nityānanda and other devotees, Mahāprabhu was escorted to Ālālanātha, where they bid farewell.

During his journey, Lord Chaitanya, immersed in the nectarean state of a *gopī* separated from Kṛṣṇa, chanted the Holy Name, turning all he met into devotees. His compassion and generosity blossomed even more in the South than in Navadwip. In Kurmasthan, Mahāprabhu visited the temple of Kūrma Deva and stayed with a local *brāhmaṇa*. Vāsudeva Vipra, a *brāhmaṇa* afflicted with leprosy, sought his mercy there. In a gesture of compassion, Mahāprabhu embraced him, instantly curing his physical and spiritual afflictions, and named him Vāsudevāmṛta-prada, the giver of immortality.

Continuing his journey toward the Godāvarī, Mahāprabhu met Rāmānanda Rāya, an encounter foretold by Sārvabhauma. Rāmānanda, impressed by Mahāprabhu's presence, prostrated before him. After Rāmānanda's insistence, Mahāprabhu agreed to stay for a week to discuss Kṛṣṇa. In the nightly conversations, Mahāprabhu challenged Rāmānanda to explain the purpose of life and the means to achieve it. Rāmānanda's initial responses, although wise, did not satisfy Mahāprabhu, who considered them superficial. Finally, Rāmānanda concluded that ecstatic love for Kṛṣṇa represents the pinnacle of spiritual devotion. Mahāprabhu, pleased with this answer, encouraged Rāmānanda to delve even deeper. Rāmānanda then revealed that transcendental romantic love for Kṛṣṇa, particularly that of the *gopīs* of Vrindavan, is the highest form of devotion, a love that in our material world becomes a source of disillusionment and suffering, being a perverted reflection of its transcendental counterpart. In the realm of *Vaiṣṇava* devotion, Mahāprabhu recognized the love for Kṛṣṇa, as experienced by the *gopīs*, as the zenith and paradigm of spiritual devotion. This recognition led Rāmānanda to exalt Śrīmatī Rādhārāṇī, who is considered the most exalted among Kṛṣṇa's consorts.

According to the Nārada Pañcarātra, a text of deep relevance in the Vaiṣṇava tradition, Rādhārāṇī is distinguished as the sovereign of the *rāsa* dance, a divine act of love and surrender. In this dance, the loving interaction between Kṛṣṇa and the *gopīs* reaches its climax, symbolizing a mystical union. This narrative highlights the importance of Rādhārāṇī in the devotional context and provides a window into understanding the complex dynamic between the divine and the human in the realm of Hindu spirituality. Śrīmatī Rādhārāṇī stands as the incarnation of *hlādinī-śakti*, the energy of pleasure that Kṛṣṇa experiences. She represents the essence of pure and selfless devotion toward Lord Kṛṣṇa, being the primordial source of unmotivated service to the divine. As the monarch of the realm of perfect love, Rādhārāṇī symbolizes the core of divine affection. In this realm, everything that exists is imbued with intense and varied feelings of love for God, a manifestation that is nourished and expanded through Śrīmatī Rādhārāṇī.

হ্লাদিনী করায় কৃষ্ণে আনন্দাস্বাদন ।
হ্লাদিনীর দ্বারা করে ভক্তের পোষণ ॥

hlādinī karāya kṛṣṇe ānandāsvādana
hlādinīra dvārā kare bhaktera poṣaṇa

That *hlādinī* energy gives pleasure to Kṛṣṇa and nourishes His devotees.

(*Śrī Caitanya-caritāmṛta*, "*Ādi-līlā*," 4.60)

एवं विश्वस्य नान्यत्वं तत्स्थायीश्वर दृश्यते।
ह्लादिनी सन्धिनी साम्बत् त्वय्येका सर्वसंस्थितौ ॥

evaṁ viśvasya nānyatvaṁ
tat-sthāyīśvara dṛśyate
hlādinī sandhinī sāmbat
tvayyekā sarva-saṁsthitau

O Lord! You sustain everything. The three attributes *hlādinī*, *sandhinī*, and *samvit* exist in You as a single spiritual energy. But the material modes, which cause bliss, misery and amalgamation of the two, do not exist in You, because You have no material qualities.

(*Viṣṇu Purana*, 1.12.69)

According to *Gauḍīya* Krishnaism, the depth of the ecstasy experienced by Rādhārāṇī in her devotional service was a mystery even to Lord Kṛṣṇa. In an attempt to understand and experience this supreme bliss, Kṛṣṇa assumed the emotional perspective of Rādhārāṇī, manifesting as Lord Chaitanya Mahāprabhu. This incarnation was none other than Kṛṣṇa imbued with Rādhā's feelings.

During his earthly existence, Lord Chaitanya Mahāprabhu progressively revealed the highest essence of love for Kṛṣṇa, especially in the later stages of his earthly pastimes. His experience mirrored that of the *gopīs* of Vrindavan, who endured intense separation when Kṛṣṇa left for Mathurā, a farewell without return. In a similar state of longing and desolation, Lord Chaitanya wandered through Jagannātha Purī, overwhelmed by the absence of Kṛṣṇa. This state of devotion, known as *vipralambha-seva*, or "service in a state of separation," allowed Lord Chaitanya to savor the ecstasy of devotion that Rādhārāṇī felt deeply. His experience illustrates a crucial aspect of *Vaiṣṇava* devotion: the intensity of spiritual love is magnified in separation, a paradox that underscores the dynamism and depth of divine emotions.

After delving deeply into the subject of supreme devotion, Śrī Chaitanya inquired of Rāmānanda about the possibility of an ordinary person attaining such a state. Rāmānanda, with wisdom, indicated that imitating the ways of the *gopīs* is the essential path to reaching the pinnacle of devotional service, representing the highest achievement in human existence. This exchange profoundly enriched Lord Gaurāṅga, who found great satisfaction in Rāmānanda's words.

Subsequently, Rāmānanda made a transcendental decision: he renounced his government position and, with the king's approval, moved to Puri to enjoy the constant association of Śrī Chaitanya. This move marked a turning point in their lives and the dynamics of Puri's spiritual community.

Later, Mahāprabhu continued his pilgrimage through South India. Upon returning to Puri, he settled in the residence of Kaśi Miśra, a renowned spiritual master of the king. In a strategic and visionary act, Mahāprabhu instructed Nityānanda Prabhu to return to Bengal. His mission was to galvanize and organize the devotees in spreading the divine message and glorifying the Holy Names. This direction marked a new phase in the dissemination of Mahāprabhu's spiritual message, extending his influence beyond the borders of Puri.

At that time, the kingdom of Orissa was under the rule of Pratāparudra, whose chief advisor was Sārvabhauma Bhaṭṭācārya. The latter longed for Mahāprabhu to meet the monarch, although Mahāprabhu was reluctant, adhering to the strict codes governing the life of a renunciant, who must avoid contact with figures involved in materialism, a category that a ruler inherently fell into by definition. Mahāprabhu's refusal remained firm despite Sārvabhauma's efforts.

The arrival of Rāmānanda Rāya in Puri, after leaving his governmental duties with the approval and support of the king, partially shifted Mahāprabhu's perspective. Still, he remained unyielding in his *sannyāsī* principles. With the arrival of the *Snāna-yātrā*, Mahāprabhu left Puri, unable to bear the temporary absence of the deity of Lord Jagannātha, and only returned for the *Ratha-yātrā*.

King Pratāparudra, in a gesture of deference and hospitality, made sure that the *Vaiṣṇavas* from Bengal were well taken care of, which led Nityānanda Prabhu and others to urge Mahāprabhu to grant him an audience. However, Mahāprabhu remained firm in his decision, leading Nityānanda to offer the king a garment Mahāprabhu wore as a consolation. In a carefully arranged plan by Rāmānanda, Mahāprabhu agreed to meet with the king's son, a young prince and blessed him with an embrace.

During the *Ratha-yātrā*, King Pratāparudra demonstrated his humility by sweeping the path of the Lord Jagannātha's chariot, an act that deeply impressed Mahāprabhu. At a pause during the festival, while Mahāprabhu rested in a garden, the king, disguised as a *Vaiṣṇava*, approached and began massaging his feet. While doing so, he recited soulful verses from the *Śrīmad-bhāgavatam*, thus capturing Mahāprabhu's attention and heart.

The following verse from the *Śrīmad-bhāgavatam* is especially dear to Śrī Chaitanya:

तव कथामृतं तप्तजीवनं
कविभिरीडितं कल्मषापहम् ।
श्रवणमङ्गलं श्रीमदाततं
भुवि गृणन्ति ये भूरिदा जनाः ॥

tava kathāmṛtaṁ tapta-jīvanaṁ
kavibhir īḍitaṁ kalmaṣāpaham
śravaṇa-maṅgalaṁ śrīmad ātataṁ
bhuvi gṛṇanti ye bhūri-dā janāḥ

The nectar of Your words and the descriptions of Your activities are the life and soul of those suffering in this material world. These narrations, transmitted by learned sages, eradicate one's sinful reactions and bestow good fortune upon whoever hears them. These narrations are broadcast all over the world and are filled with spiritual power. Certainly, those who spread the message of Godhead are most munificent.

(*Śrīmad-bhāgavatam*, 10.31.9)

"ভূরিদা' 'ভূরিদা' বলি' করে আলিঙ্গন ।
ইঁহো নাহি জানে, ইহোঁ হয় কোন্ জন ॥

'bhūridā' 'bhūridā' bali' kare āliṅgana
iṅho nāhi jāne, - ihoṅ haya kon jana

> After reciting this verse, Śrī Caitanya Mahāprabhu immediately embraced the King and cried, "You are the most munificent! You are the most munificent!" At this point Śrī Caitanya Mahāprabhu did not know who the King was.
> (*Śrī Caitanya-caritāmṛta*, "*Madhya-līlā*," 14.14)

Upon hearing this verse, Śrī Chaitanya embraced King Pratāparudra, recognizing him not as a mundane person, but as a genuine *Vaiṣṇava*, humble and devoted. This event marked a turning point in Śrī Chaitanya's perception of the monarch.

Soon after, Śrī Chaitanya embarked on a pilgrimage to Vrindavan, choosing a route along the Ganges. According to certain narratives, Śrī Chaitanya stopped in Śāntipura, where he may have seen his mother for the last time, as he would never return to his homeland. In Rāmakeli, near the capital, Śrī Chaitanya met Rūpa and Sanātana, important officials in Hussein Shah's government. Under their influence, these brothers renounced their ministerial positions and embraced a life of renunciation.

Upon returning from Vrindavan, Śrī Chaitanya met Rūpa Gosvāmī in Prayāg and later Sanātana in Benares. He imparted teachings to both on devotional practices and philosophies. He instructed Rūpa and Sanātana to rescue the forgotten holy places where Kṛṣṇa had performed His divine pastimes, to write books on devotion, and to establish temples where the deity of Śrī Chaitanya could be worshipped, thus laying the foundation for the *Gaudiya Vaiṣṇava* tradition.

After visiting sacred places like Vrindavan, Mathura, Prayāga, and Benares, Mahāprabhu returned to Puri around the year 1515, where he remained until his departure in 1533. In Puri, he lived in a hut known as Gambhīra, built on the land of Kāśi Miśra, the spiritual master of King Pratāparudra. Over time, his interest in worldly affairs diminished considerably. He was surrounded by close devotees like Svarūpa Dāmodara, Rāmānanda Rāya, and Paramānanda Purī, but his awareness of the outside world gradually faded.

Extraordinary ecstatic symptoms manifested in Mahāprabhu. At times, in a state of divine madness, he would run to the Jagannātha temple and fall unconscious at its entrance. On other occasions, Mahāprabhu would lose himself in the sand dunes of the beach, mistaking them for the hill of Govardhana in Vrindavan or diving into the ocean, believing it to be the Yamunā River. One full moon night, while walking through the flower gardens chanting verses from the Śrīmad-bhāgavatam about the *rāsa-līlā*, Mahāprabhu was drawn to the silvery reflection of the moon on the ocean. Mistaking the sea for the Yamunā, he plunged into the water in a trance, imagining himself as a servant of the gopīs in Kṛṣṇa's water sports. His body was carried by the tide toward Konark.

On that fateful night, while Śrī Chaitanya was submerged in the depths of the ocean, his devotees, led by Svarūpa Dāmodara, embarked on a frantic search along the shore. Desperation overtook them, fearing that Gaurāṅga had perished in the relentless waves. Amidst their lamentations, an unusual figure caught their attention: a fisherman wandering along the shore, overwhelmed by an inexplicable ecstasy, repeatedly chanting the names of Kṛṣṇa.

Moved by intuition, Svarūpa Dāmodara approached the fisherman and inquired about the cause of his trance. The fisherman, still immersed in his state of spiritual intoxication, revealed that during his nighttime fishing, something colossal had gotten caught in his net. Upon drawing it from the sea, what he had initially thought to be a corpse turned out to be the source of his inexplicable ecstasy. Terrified at first, he believed he had encountered some mystical being or specter.

Upon hearing this account, a spark of hope ignited in the hearts of the devotees. Svarūpa Dāmodara and the others realized that the supposed corpse in the fisherman's story was none other than Śrī Chaitanya Mahāprabhu. With words of encouragement, they persuaded the fisherman to guide them to the location of the discovery. Upon finding Śrī Chaitanya, they clothed him in dry garments. As he regained consciousness, Gaurāṅga shared the mystical visions he had experienced: "I found myself in Vrindavan, watching Kṛṣṇa with the *gopīs*, playing in the waters of the Yamunā, splashing and hiding from each other. From the shore, I, like one of the *gopīs*, watched their water sports."

Every year, Gaurāṅga would send a messenger to Bengal to reassure his mother, Śacī Devī, the epitome of maternal love. On one occasion, he entrusted this mission to Jagadānanda Paṇḍita, who carried the comforting message of Mahāprabhu and, fulfilling a request from Paramānanda Purī, brought with him a garment worn by Mahāprabhu and *prasāda* from the deity of Jagannātha. During his stay in Bengal, Jagannātha Paṇḍita visited both Navadwip and Śāntipura before beginning his return journey to Puri. On this occasion, Advaita Prabhu sent a message to Mahāprabhu, presented in the form of an enigmatic riddle. The message was as follows:

বাউলকে কহিহ, – লোক হ-ইল বাউল ।
বাউলকে কহিহ, – হাটে না বিকায় চাউল ॥
বাউলকে কহিহ, – কায়ে নাহিক আউল ।
বাউলকে কহিহ, – ইহা কহিয়াছে বাউল ॥

bāulake kahiha, - loka ha-ila bāula
bāulake kahiha, - hāṭe nā vikāya cāula
bāulake kahiha, - kāye nāhika āula
bāulake kahiha, - ihā kahiyāche bāula

Please inform Śrī Caitanya Mahāprabhu, who is acting like a madman, that everyone here has become mad like Him. Inform Him also that in the marketplace rice is no longer in demand.

Further tell Him that those now mad in ecstatic love are no longer interested in the material world. Also tell Śrī Caitanya Mahāprabhu that one who has also become a madman in ecstatic love [Advaita Prabhu] has spoken these words.

(*Śrī Caitanya-caritāmṛta*, "*Antya-līlā*,"19.20–21)

The interpretation of the riddle posed by Advaita Prabhu eluded the understanding of many, generating a diversity of exegeses. The essence of the enigma pointed to a saturation in the "market" of the Holy Name, a metaphor suggesting such a widespread diffusion of love for Kṛṣṇa that the physical presence of Mahāprabhu in this world would no longer be essential. Mahāprabhu's concise and serene response was "Let it be so," reflecting his acceptance of Advaita's veiled proposition. This symbolic exchange marked the prelude to the final act of Mahāprabhu's earthly existence.

In the final years of Mahāprabhu, his ecstatic divine madness intensified. One night, his face frantically rubbed against the walls of Gambhīra as if trying to pass through them to reunite with Kṛṣṇa. Svarūpa Dāmodara and Rāmānanda, in an attempt to soothe his spiritual torment, sang melodies from devotional poets like Daṇḍi Dāsa, Vidyāpati, and Jayadeva. These last twelve years of Mahāprabhu's life were a continuous intertwining of wakefulness and sleep, both indistinguishable in his profound spiritual ecstasy.

Regarding the mystery surrounding Mahāprabhu's disappearance, there is a notable silence in the writings of most of his biographers, such as Murāri Gupta, Kavi Karṇapūra, Vrindāvana Dāsa, and Kṛṣṇa Dāsa Kavirāja. Only Locana Dāsa addresses this topic in his chronicles, though with a caution that suggests more mystery than clarity. This enigma, rooted in the heart of the *Gauḍīya Vaiṣṇava* tradition, has fascinated and confused devotees and scholars alike, keeping the flame of mystery surrounding the life and work of Chaitanya Mahāprabhu alive. Locana Dāsa writes:

তৃতীয় প্রহর বেলা রবিবার দিনে ।
জগন্নথে লীন প্রভু হইলা আপনে ॥

tṛtīya prahara velā ravivāra dine
jagannāthe līna prabhu ha ilā āpane

In the third watch on a Sunday, Mahāprabhu disappeared into Lord Jagannātha's body.

(*Caitanya-maṅgala*, 4.1.24)

According to this chronicle, on a Sunday twilight, Mahāprabhu merged in an embrace with the divine image of Lord Jagannātha inside the sacred precincts of Guṇḍicā. Śrīvāsa Paṇḍita, Mukunda Datta, Govinda, Kaśi Miśra, and several other devotees were witnesses to this scene. They saw Mahāprabhu enter the sanctuary; however, his prolonged absence beyond the temple's thresholds unleashed a wave of consternation. The search for Mahāprabhu spread throughout the temple, but their efforts proved unsuccessful. Uncertainty and anxiety gripped the hearts of the devotees, who began to consider the possibility that Mahāprabhu had transcended the material plane, leaving behind His visible form. This event, shrouded in mystery and reverence, marked a crucial point in the *Vaiṣṇava* tradition, symbolizing Mahāprabhu's mystical and final union with the divinity, an episode that continues to be the subject of deep contemplation and study among followers and scholars of this spiritual tradition.

They asked the *pūjārī* of the Guṇḍicā temple to open the temple doors, but he responded:

ভক্ত আৰ্ত্তি দেখি পণ্ডিছাকহয়ে কথন ।
গুঞ্জাবাড়ূর মধ্যে প্রভুর হৈল অদর্শন ॥
সাক্ষাতে দেখিল গৌর প্রভুর মিলন ।
নিশ্চয় করিয়া কহি শুন সর্বজন ॥

bhakta ārtti dekhi paṇḍichākahaye kathana
guñjābāḍūra madhye prabhura haila adarśana
sākṣāte dekhila gaura prabhura milana
niścaya kariyā kahi–śuna sarvajana

Mahāprabhu has disappeared inside the Guṇḍicā temple. I saw him enter Jagannātha with my own eyes, so I can tell you this with all certainty.

(*Caitanya-maṅgala*, 4.1.27–28)

There are alternative versions regarding the earthly end of Mahāprabhu, according to which, in a moment of divine ecstasy, he left his mortal form in front of Gadādhara Paṇḍita, one of his closest and most devoted friends. According to this narrative, the revered remains of Mahāprabhu would rest in the sacred precincts of the Ṭoṭā-gopīnātha temple. These accounts, imbued with deep mysticism, present questions that challenge our conventional understanding. In the Vedic scriptures, episodes are narrated of illustrious saints like Dhruva and divine avatars such as Rāmacandra, who ascended to the spiritual realms in their corporeal forms. So, is it implausible to think that Mahāprabhu, whose life was filled with the supernatural, transcended in a similar manner, either merging with the divinity of Jagannātha or Ṭoṭā-gopīnātha?

The existence of Chaitanya Mahāprabhu, marked by symbolic events, offers a spiritual richness of incalculable value to those seeking to delve deeper into his history. The legendary legacy of Śrī Chaitanya lies in the fact that symbols acquire meaning through the renunciation of the concept, just as non-conceptualized and, therefore, non-institutionalized religion acquires meaning through the abandonment of theology. With his devotional guidance, Śrī Chaitanya conveyed to the world that mythology is restored with the transition from the conceptual to the symbolic. Immersing oneself in ecstasy, dance, and music is only possible by transcending logic. Lord Chaitanya deserted conceptualization and fully embraced the sonic symbol of the Holy Names. In the specific case of Śrī Chaitanya Mahāprabhu, this conversion took place when he encountered a manifestation of symbolic nature and far-reaching impact in the *mahā-mantra*, through whose sacred syllables his soul was profoundly affected, reaching the point of detecting the unmistakable presence of the divine.

It is important to highlight once again that this affectation and subsequent detection are possible thanks to the symbol, which, at its core, reveals itself as an intelligible means providing us with a glimpse of a reality that is ontologically transcendent and stands as unattainable for our pedestrian understanding. While unveiling truths manifestly, it allows for a multitude of interpretations and meanings, enabling the observer to add novel elements to discover broader contexts. The symbol, bearer of autonomous life, becomes a vehicle for the expression of ideas and directions.

Being a synthetic element, it has the ability to encapsulate, in a single word, phrase, or image, a universe of teachings. Thus, the threshold to the symbolic dimension is not reached through rational discourse but requires intuitive grasping, a flash that eludes standard logic. The symbol urges us to surpass the boundaries of what is known, immersing us in the vastness of the unknown. The devotional praxis of Chaitanya Mahāprabhu illustrates this intricate symbolic journey, in which the *mahā-mantra* stands as a threshold to divinity in its transcendental form, embodied by Lord Kṛṣṇa.

This "awakening," if we can call it that, has, in the case of Śrī Chaitanya, a strong connection with enlightenment, which, in its purest beauty, arises from the poignant encounter between antagonistic polarities. In their habitual lethargy, the average human dwells under a veil of ignorance about their true essence. It is only in the recognition of the latent divinity within that ecstasy unfolds. This joy originates from the venerable conjunction between the earthly and the supraterrestrial, the material and the transcendental, the fleshly envelope, and the incorporeal soul. In the void of the sacred, humanity plunges into an unrelenting search for the divine, a longing that perpetually eludes satisfaction. However, it is imperative to note that, in the divine, there also resides a longing for the human. Consequently, the amalgamation of the human and the divine generates a joy that resonates in the infinite cosmos, an ecstatic bliss that surpasses the limits of imagination.

Only by freeing ourselves from the conception of ourselves as insular and circumscribed entities can we disintegrate the dichotomy that separates the human from the divine. In transcending all limitations, the eternal filters through and permeates our temporal reality. The shadowy dimness that darkens our inner being is flooded with divine brilliance. Neither we nor God will ever be the same, although, in essence, we persist in our original identity, for when the human and the divine merge, neither the human nor the divine exist. This transformation is profound and transcendental, leaving an indelible mark on the texture of what we once were and what God was before this encounter. A drop of water will not change the ocean, but the ocean would not be the same without that drop.

The encounter of the drop with the sea implies a simultaneous transformation of both parts. In enlightenment, we cease to be limited beings, and God ceases to be an impersonal energy. Both are reborn as a fullness flowing freely.

In the chapter dedicated to Christianity, we have seen how the messianic figure of Jesus, as conceived and theologized by Saint Paul, spread among all nations, becoming organized conceptual religiosity. Likewise, the teachings of Lord Chaitanya, based on the renunciation of the concept and the surrender to the symbolic power of sound, underwent a gradual conceptual transformation until it forged what we now know as *Gauḍīya Vaiṣṇavism*. Three centuries after Śrī Chaitanya Mahāprabhu left this earthly plane, the *Gauḍīya Vaiṣṇava* tradition did not remain stagnant but advanced. In the early years, the followers of Nityānanda Prabhu and Advaita Ācārya, contemporaries of Chaitanya, taught and initiated individuals scattered across Bengal. The six *Gosvāmīs* of Vrindavan, distinguished disciples with pen in hand and clear minds, gave written form to a theology of bhakti. This theology is aligned with the ecstasy of Śrī Chaitanya and focuses on the devotional relationship with Rādhā and Kṛṣṇa, attributing to Chaitanya a status of a combined incarnation, although he did not endorse such a claim.

Jīva Gosvāmī, a prominent member of the six *Gosvāmīs* of Vrindavan, left an indelible mark as a theologian in the *Gauḍīya Vaiṣṇava* tradition. He approached *Gauḍīya Vaiṣṇava* theology with impressive rigor in his *Ṣaṭ Sandarbhas*, treatises covering a broad spectrum: spiritual reality, the soul-God relationship, devotional surrender, and the affirmation of Kṛṣṇa as the supreme manifestation of the divine. Rūpa Gosvāmī, his counterpart, is acclaimed for his *Śrī Bhakti-rasāmṛta-sindhu*, an exquisitely systematic treatise that unravels the nuances of love and devotion to God. Sanātana Gosvāmī, another of the six, gives us the *Hari-bhakti-vilāsa*, a meticulous work on bhakti centered on the pragmatic: rituals, norms, and disciplines. In the constellation of scholars of the *Gauḍīya Vaiṣṇava* tradition, Viśvanātha Cakravartī Ṭhākura shines for his contributions, who wrote *Śrī Camatkāra-candrikā*, a work that unravels devotional love to Kṛṣṇa. Baladeva Vidyābhūṣaṇa, though not one of the six *Gosvāmīs*, carved out a niche with *Govinda-bhāṣya*, a masterful commentary on the *Vedānta-sūtra* that defended *Gauḍīya Vaiṣṇava* theology and established the preeminence of Kṛṣṇa. In the generational succession, Narottama, Śrīnivasa, and Śyāmānanda, disciples of Jīva Gosvāmī and crucial drivers in the propagation of theology in Bengal and Orissa, emerged. The religious conclave of Kheturi, held around the year 1574, was presided over by Jahnava Ṭhākurāṇī, consort of Nityānanda Rāma. This sacred event allowed the *Gauḍīya Vaiṣṇava* tradition to be organized and systematized more efficiently as its members became familiar with the various branches and their respective theologies and practices. Although it remains a pluralistic tradition without a central authority overseeing its matters, this festival allowed members of the tradition to connect with each other and understand their shared beliefs. This contributed to the cohesion of this branch of *Vaiṣṇava* theology as a distinct entity. The process of conceptualization that begins with the departure of Lord Chaitanya, his associates, and the six *Gosvāmīs* is evident. His disciples codified most of his message as theology and philosophy.

Śrī Chaitanya Mahāprabhu left behind as a written legacy only eight *ślokas*, collectively known as the *Śikṣāṣṭaka*. The *Śikṣāṣṭakam* is cited in the *Śrī Caitanya-caritāmṛta*, the biography of Chaitanya Mahāprabhu written in Bengali by Kṛṣṇadāsa Kavirāja Gosvāmī. The name of the prayer comes from the Sanskrit words *Śikṣā*, which means "instruction," and *aṣṭaka*, which means "consisting of eight parts," meaning, stanzas. These verses encompass the essence of the entire message of bhakti yoga within the *Gauḍīya* tradition:

(1)

चेतोदर्पणमार्जनं भवमहादावाग्निनिर्वापणं
श्रेयः कैरवचन्द्रिकावितरणं विद्यावधूजीवनम् ।
आनन्दाम्बुधिवर्धनं प्रतिपदं पूर्णामृतास्वादनं
सर्वात्मस्नपनं परं विजयते श्रीकृष्ण संकीर्तनम् ॥

ceto-darpaṇa-mārjanaṁ bhava-mahā-dāvāgni-nirvāpaṇaṁ
śreyaḥ-kairava-candrikā-vitaraṇaṁ vidyā-vadhū-jīvanam

ānandāmbudhi-vardhanaṁ prati-padaṁ pūrṇāmṛtāsvādanaṁ
sarvātma-snapanaṁ paraṁ vijayate śrī-kṛṣṇa-saṅkīrtanam

Glory be to the *saṅkīrtana* of Śrī Kṛṣṇa that cleanses the mirror of the heart of all the dust accumulated for years and extinguishes the fire of the conditioned life of repeated births and deaths. This movement of *saṅkīrtana* is the chief blessing for all mankind for it diffuses the rays of the moon of bliss, is the life of all transcendental knowledge, increases the ocean of transcendental bliss and enables us to taste the nectar for which we are ever eager.

(2)

नाम्नामकारि बहुधा निजसर्वशक्ति-
स्तत्रार्पिता नियमितः स्मरणे न कालः।
एतादृशी तव कृपा भगवन्ममापि
दुर्दैवमीदृशमिहाजनि नानुरागः॥

nāmnām akāri bahudhā nija-sarva-śaktis
tatrārpitā niyamitaḥ smaraṇe na kālaḥ
etādṛśī tava kṛpā bhagavan mamāpi
dur-daivam īdṛśam ihājani nānurāgaḥ.

O my Lord! Only Your Holy Name can bestow all kinds of benedictions on living beings; and therefore You have hundreds and millions of names, such as Kṛṣṇa and Govinda, in these transcendental names You have invested all Your transcendental energies, and there are not even strict and difficult rules for chanting these names. Oh, my Lord! You are so kind that You have allowed us to approach You easily by chanting Your Holy Names, but I am so unfortunate that I do not feel attraction for them.

(3)

तृणादपि सुनीचेन तरोरपि सहिष्णुना ।
अमानिना मानदेन कीर्तनीयः सदा हरिः ॥

tṛṇād api sunīcena
taror api sahiṣṇunā
amāninā mānadena
kīrtanīyaḥ sadā hariḥ

One should chant the Holy Name of the Lord in a humble state of mind considering oneself lower than the litter of the street, one should be more tolerant than a tree, be devoid of all feelings of vanity and be willing to offer full respect to others. In such a state of mind one chants the Holy Name of the Lord constantly.

(4)

न धनं न जनं न सुन्दरीं कवितां वा जगदीश कामये।
मम जन्मनि जन्मनीश्वरे भवताद्भक्तिरहैतुकी त्वयि॥

na dhanaṁ na janaṁ na sundarīṁ
kavitāṁ vā jagad-īśa kāmaye
mama janmani janmanīśvare
bhavatād bhaktir ahaitukī tvayi

O my Lord, I have no desire to accumulate wealth, nor do I desire followers, nor beautiful woman nor flowery language. All I want is Your causeless devotional service, birth after birth.

(5)

अयि नन्दतनुज किङ्करं , पतितं मां विषमे भवाम्बुधौ ।
कृपया तव पादपंकज- स्थितधूलीसदृशं विचिन्तय ॥

ayi nanda-tanuja kiṅkaraṁ
patitaṁ māṁ viṣame bhavāmbudhau
kṛpayā tava pāda-paṅkaja-
sthita-dhūlī-sadṛśaṁ vicintaya

O son of Mahārāja Nanda, I am Your eternal servant, but somehow or other I have fallen into the ocean of birth and death. Please take me out of this ocean of death and place me as one of the atoms of Your lotus feet.

(6)

नयनं गलदश्रुधारया वदनं गद्गदरुद्धया गिरा ।
पुलकैर्निचितं वपुः कदा तव नामग्रहणे भविष्यति ॥

nayanaṁ galad-aśru-dhārayā
vadanaṁ gadgada-ruddhayā girā
pulakair nicitaṁ vapuḥ kadā
tava nāma-grahaṇe bhavisyati

O my Lord, when will my eyes be adorned with tears of love flowing constantly as I chant your Holy Name? When will my voice be choked and the hairs of my body stand on end as I recite your name?

(7)

युगायितं निमेषेण चक्षुषा प्रावृषायितम् ।
शून्यायितं जगत् सर्वं गोविन्दविरहेण मे ॥

yugāyitaṁ nimeṣeṇa
cakṣuṣā prāvṛṣāyitam
śūnyāyitaṁ jagat sarvaṁ
govinda-viraheṇa me

> Oh Govinda! Feeling your separation I consider a moment as twelve years or more, tears flow from my eyes like torrents of rain and in your absence I feel all alone in the world.

(8)

आश्लिष्य वा पादरतां पिनष्टु पिनष्टु मामदर्शनान्मर्म हतां करोतु वा ।
यथा तथा वा विदधातु लम्पटो मत्प्राणनाथस्तु स एव नापरः ॥

āśliṣya vā pāda-ratāṁ pinaṣṭu mām
adarśanān marma-hatāṁ karotu vā
yathā tathā vā vidadhātu lampaṭo
mat-prāṇa-nāthas tu sa eva nāparaḥ

> I know no one but Kṛṣṇa as my Lord and He will remain so, even if He mistreats me with His embrace or tears my heart apart by not being present before me. He is completely free to do as He wishes with me for He is always my worshipful Lord without any conditions.

In the *Śrī Caitanya-caritāmṛta*, these eight verses are followed by this beautiful verse:

এইমত হঞা যেই কৃষ্ণনাম লয় ।
শ্রীকৃষ্ণচরণে তাংর প্রেম উপজয় ॥

ei-mata hañā yei kṛṣṇa-nāma laya
śrī-kṛṣṇa-caraṇe tāṅra prema upajaya

> If one chants the Holy Name of Lord Kṛṣṇa in this manner, he will certainly awaken his dormant love for Kṛṣṇa's lotus feet.
>
> (*Śrī Caitanya-caritāmṛta*, "*Antya-līlā*," 20.26)

Lord Chaitanya Mahāprabhu is considered an incarnation or *avatāra* of Lord Kṛṣṇa, undoubtedly a symbolic entity who distributes divine love in and through humanity. As we have seen, the figures of Jesus and Śrī Chaitanya have experienced similar fates. Their own followers have attempted to spread the original voice of the master through generations.

In both contexts, the proselytizing impulse has led to a paradoxical evolution: the gradual conceptualization and, at the same time, desymbolization of their teachings. Followers of later generations, especially in the tradition arising from the second case, driven by the desire to spread their beliefs "in every city and town," were forced to forge a detailed theology. It is ironic that a tradition initiated by Śrī Chaitanya Mahāprabhu, who rejected conceptual structures in favor of immersion in the symbolic sound of the *mahā-mantra*, ultimately culminates in a return to its original form as a conceptually structured theology. After a period of symbolic emphasis, this cycle of returning to conceptual principles reflects an intricate dynamic in the evolution of institutionalized religiosity.

Chapter 20

Mitzvot: Symbols of the Return

The Hebrew term *mitzvah* is usually translated as "precept, ordinance, or commandment." The *mitzvot* are the 613 sacred precepts found in the Torah. The Sinaitic revelation is not a mere compendium of dogmas and theological conceptions. It is a guide that permeates every aspect of human life and prescribes a wide spectrum of norms and daily behaviors. These guidelines dictate the way everything in creation is dealt with: the choice and processing of food, effective time management, and different types of relationships such as commercial, academic, or social. Even trivial everyday acts, such as night's rest, are not excluded from these regulations, which have precise instructions on how to carry them out. This collection of regulations and practices is called *halachah* in Hebrew. Although it is often translated as "Jewish law," is better understood as "the path one walks, one's journey or road of life."

> וְעַתָּה יִשְׂרָאֵל מָה ה' אֱלֹהֶיךָ שֹׁאֵל מֵעִמָּךְ כִּי אִם־לְיִרְאָה אֶת־ה' אֱלֹהֶיךָ לָלֶכֶת
> בְּכָל־דְּרָכָיו וּלְאַהֲבָה אֹתוֹ וְלַעֲבֹד אֶת־ה' אֱלֹהֶיךָ בְּכָל־לְבָבְךָ וּבְכָל־נַפְשֶׁךָ:
> לִשְׁמֹר אֶת־מִצְוֹת ה' וְאֶת־חֻקֹּתָיו אֲשֶׁר אָנֹכִי מְצַוְּךָ הַיּוֹם לְטוֹב לָךְ:
> (דברים י', י"ב–י"ג)

> And now, O Israel, what does the Lord, your God, ask of you? but to fear the Lord, your God, to walk in all His ways, and to love Him, and to serve the Lord, your God, with all your heart and with all your soul; to keep the Lord's commandments, and His statutes, which I enjoin upon you today, for your good.
>
> (Deuteronomy, 10:12–13)

The verb root of *halachah* includes the Hebrew letters *Hei*, *Lamed*, *Kaf*, which means “to walk or go.”

> אִם בְּחֻקֹּתַי תֵּלֵכוּ וְאֶת מִצְוֹתַי תִּשְׁמְרוּ וַעֲשִׂיתֶם אֹתָם:
> (ויקרא כ"ו, ג')
>
> If you walk in My statutes and keep My commandments and do them.
>
> (Leviticus, 26:3)

Hence *halachah* is the method and means of navigating the ocean of existence in pursuit of reconnecting with the Divine. The Hebrew term *teshuvah*, on the other hand, is generally translated as “repentance,” although it encompasses a wider range of meanings.

> וְשַׁבְתָּ עַד ה' אֱלֹהֶיךָ וְשָׁמַעְתָּ בְקֹלוֹ כְּכֹל אֲשֶׁר אָנֹכִי מְצַוְּךָ הַיּוֹם אַתָּה וּבָנֶיךָ בְּכָל לְבָבְךָ וּבְכָל נַפְשֶׁךָ:
> (דברים ל', ב')
>
> And you shall return unto the Lord, your God, and hearken to His voice according to all that I enjoin upon you this day, you and your children, with all your heart and with all your soul.
>
> (Deuteronomy, 30:2)

The Hebrew letters *Taf*, *Shin*, *Vav*, and *Bet* form the word *tashuv*, or “will return,” which alongside *hei* (ה'), which symbolizes HaShem or the Lord, indicate a return to our divine origin. One who successfully walks the path of *teshuvah* is called *ba’al teshuvah* (בעל תשובה), or “master of return.”

> אָמַר רַבִּי אֲבָהוּ: "מָקוֹם שֶׁבַּעֲלֵי תְשׁוּבָה עוֹמְדִין – צַדִּיקִים גְּמוּרִים אֵינָם עוֹמְדִין, שֶׁנֶּאֱמַר: 'שָׁלוֹם שָׁלוֹם לָרָחוֹק וְלַקָּרוֹב' (ישעיהו נ"ז, י"ט). 'לָרָחוֹק' בְּרֵישָׁא, וַהֲדַר 'לַקָּרוֹב'".
> (תלמוד בבלי, מסכת ברכות, ל"ד, ב')

> Rabbi Abbahu said: “In the place where *ba’alei teshuvah* (masters of the return) stand, even the full-fledged righteous do not stand, as it is stated: ‘Peace, peace upon the one who is far and the one who is near.’ Peace is extended first to the one who is far [the master of the return], and only thereafter is peace extended to the one who is near [the full-fledged righteous].”
>
> (*Babylonian Talmud*, “*Berachot*,” 34b)

When *teshuvah* is used in the sense of “repentance,” it alludes to a process of recognizing shortcomings. Through observation and introspection, individuals identify their weaknesses and return to their primordial essence. *Lashuv* also means rotation, “to turn,” which refers to the existence of a pivotal field or space of adaptability that enables the necessary modifications to return to our divine source. In this framework, *halachah* refers to a retroprogressive walk along the path on which moving forward returns us to our primordial source. It is a retroprogressive process because instead of distancing us from our roots, it brings us closer to them.

> עַל־יְדֵי הַתְּשׁוּבָה הַכֹּל שָׁב לָאֱלוֹהוּת, עַל־יְדֵי מְצִיאוּת כֹּחַ הַתְּשׁוּבָה, הַשּׁוֹרֵר בָּעוֹלָמִים כֻּלָּם, שָׁב הַכֹּל וּמִתְקַשֵּׁר בִּמְצִיאוּת הַשְּׁלֵמוּת הָאֱלֹהִית, וְעַל־יְדֵי הָרַעֲיוֹנוֹת שֶׁל הַתְּשׁוּבָה, דֵּעוֹתֶיהָ וְהַרְגָּשׁוֹתֶיהָ, כָּל הַמַּחֲשָׁבוֹת, הָרַעֲיוֹנוֹת וְהַדֵּעוֹת, הָרְצוֹנוֹת וְהָרְגָשׁוֹת, מִתְהַפְּכִים וְשָׁבִים לְהִקָּבַע בְּעֶצֶם תְּכוּנָתָם בְּתֹכֶן הַקֹּדֶשׁ הָאֱלֹהִי.
>
> (הראי"ה קוק, אורות התשובה, ד', ב')

> Through the *teshuvah* (repentance, return, going back), everything returns to divinity. Through the existence of the power of *teshuvah*, which reigns in all worlds, everything goes back and reconnects with the reality of divine Wholeness. And through the ideas of *teshuvah*, its thoughts and emotions, all thoughts, ideas, opinions, desires, and emotions are transformed and go back to be anchored in their essential quality in the essence of the Divine *kodesh* (holiness).
>
> (Rabbi Avraham Isaac HaCohen Kook, *Orot HaTeshuvah*, 4.2)

Halachah offers a manual, a detailed guide to direct each step. It is not merely a religious practice, rather, it is an expression of an inherent nature for maneuvering through life.

וּכְמוֹ שֶׁבְּאִילָן הוֹצָאַת הָעֲנָפִים וְהַפֵּרוֹת שֶׁלּוֹ לְצָרֵף אֶת טִבְעוֹ כַּאֲשֶׁר רָאוּי, וְאִם לֹא הָיָה מוֹצִיא הָעֲנָפִים וְהֶעָלִין וְצוּרַת הַפְּרִי, בְּוַדַּאי הָיָה מְקֻלְקָל, כַּאֲשֶׁר רָאִינוּ שֶׁאֵינוֹ מוֹצִיא שְׁלֵמוּת שֶׁלּוֹ אֶל הַפֹּעַל. כָּךְ הוּא דָּבָר זֶה: אִם לֹא הָיָה מוֹצִיא פְּעֻלַּת הַמִּצְווֹת אֶל הַפֹּעַל, הָיָה נִשְׁאָר בְּכֹחַ מֻטְבָּע בְּחֹמֶר, וְדָבָר זֶה – קִלְקוּל אֵלָיו, כַּאֲשֶׁר נַפְשׁוֹ מִלְמַעְלָה וְהִיא מֻטְבַּע בַּגּוּף. אִם כֵּן הַנֶּפֶשׁ הִיא נִשְׁאַר בְּכֹחַ, וְצָרִיךְ שֶׁתֵּצֵא נַפְשׁוֹ אֶל הַפֹּעַל מִן הַחָמְרִית, וְאֵין זֶה רַק עַל יְדֵי מִצְווֹת אֱלוֹהִיּוֹת. כְּמוֹ שֶׁיֵּצֵא לַפֹּעַל זֶרַע הַנָּטוּעַ בָּאָרֶץ. וְדָבָר זֶה צֵרוּף נַפְשׁוֹ כַּאֲשֶׁר יוֹצֵאת לַפֹּעַל. [...] לְפִיכָךְ מִצְווֹת הַתּוֹרָה אֲשֶׁר נִתַּן לָאָדָם כְּנֶגֶד הָאָדָם וְעוֹלָמוֹ אֲשֶׁר דָּר בּוֹ הָאָדָם וְהוּא מְקוֹמוֹ. וְהָאָדָם בְּעַצְמוֹ יֵשׁ לוֹ רמ"ח אֵבָרִים שֶׁהֵם שְׁלֵמוּת הָאָדָם, וּכְנֶגֶד זֶה נִתַּן לוֹ רמ"ח מִצְווֹת עֲשֵׂה שֶׁהֵם שְׁלֵמוּת הָאָדָם, וְיֵשׁ לוֹ מָקוֹם אֲשֶׁר הוּא בּוֹ, אֲשֶׁר הַמָּקוֹם מַגְבִּיל הַדָּבָר שֶׁלֹּא יֵצֵא. וּכְבָר אָמַרְנוּ כִּי מְקוֹמוֹ שֶׁל אָדָם הוּא תַּחַת הַחַמָּה, וְכָךְ נִתַּן לָאָדָם שס"ה מִצְווֹת לֹא תַעֲשֶׂה כְּנֶגֶד הַחַמָּה שֶׁיֵּשׁ לָהּ שס"ה יָמִים. וְאֵלּוּ שס"ה מִצְווֹת מַגְבִּילִין אֶת הָאָדָם שֶׁלֹּא יֵצֵא חוּצָה וְיַעֲבֹר אֵלּוּ שס"ה מִצְווֹת, וְהֵם מְקוֹמוֹ, כְּמוֹ שֶׁהַחַמָּה שס"ה יָמִים, שָׁנָה, הוּא מְקוֹמוֹ שֶׁל אָדָם.

(מהר"ל, תפארת ישראל, פרק ז')

In the same way that for the tree bringing forth branches and fruits is the refinement of its proper nature, to be as it should be, and if it would not be producing branches, leaves, and fruits, it would be certain that something is not functioning well, as clearly, it is not expressing its full potential. So it is here: If [a person] would not bring the *mitzvot* into action, that person would remain as potential, embedded into matter. And this is considered a malfunctioning, when the person's soul is elevated and yet embedded into the body, for in this way, the soul remains as a mere potential, while it should actualize itself out of matter. This [actualization] is possible only through divine *mitzvot*, in the same way, that the seed is actualizing its potential when planted in the ground. And when the soul is actualizing its potential, it is being refined....

Therefore, The Torah's *mitzvot*, which were given to human beings, correspond to human beings, and to the world, which is their place of residence. Humans have 248 limbs and corresponding to that, they received 248 positive *mitzvot* [actions to be performed], which are their perfection. This human being has also a place, and a place implies boundaries, which are not to be crossed. We already mentioned that the place of the human being is under the sun, and therefore, the human being received 365 negative *mitzvot* [actions to be avoided] corresponding to the sun that has 365 days [in its cycle]. These 365 *mitzvot* place boundaries on human beings not to go out and transgress them, and therefore they are their place, in the same way that the sun, the year of 365 days, is the place of human beings.

(Maharal, *Tif'eret Israel*, Chapter 7)

In the Bhagavad Gita, the legendary warrior Arjuna asked Kṛṣṇa:

अर्जुन उवाच -
स्थितप्रज्ञस्य का भाषा समाधिस्थस्य केशव ।
स्थितधीः किं प्रभाषेत किमासीत व्रजेत किम् ॥

arjuna uvāca -
sthita-prajñasya kā bhāṣā
samādhi-sthasya keśava
sthita-dhīḥ kiṁ prabhāṣeta
kim āsīta vrajeta kim

Arjuna said: "O Kṛṣṇa, what are the symptoms of one whose consciousness is thus merged in transcendence? How does he speak, and what is his language? How does he sit, and how does he walk?"

(Bhagavad Gita, 2.54)

The behavior of human beings reflects their level of consciousness. While ordinary beings perform mere activities, sages immerse themselves in actions. Action and activity may seem synonymous, but they are radically different.

> אָמַר רַבָּה בַּר בַּר חָנָה אָמַר רַבִּי יוֹחָנָן: "מַאי דִּכְתִיב: 'כִּי יְשָׁרִים דַּרְכֵי ה׳ וְצַדִּקִים יֵלְכוּ בָם וּפֹשְׁעִים יִכָּשְׁלוּ בָם' (הושע י"ה, י') – מָשָׁל לִשְׁנֵי בְּנֵי אָדָם שֶׁצָּלוּ אֶת פִּסְחֵיהֶן, אֶחָד אֲכָלוֹ לְשׁוּם מִצְוָה, וְאֶחָד אֲכָלוֹ לְשׁוּם אֲכִילָה גַּסָּה. זֶה שֶׁאֲכָלוֹ לְשׁוּם מִצְוָה – 'וְצַדִּקִים יֵלְכוּ בָם'. וְזֶה שֶׁאֲכָלוֹ לְשׁוּם אֲכִילָה גַּסָּה – 'וּפֹשְׁעִים יִכָּשְׁלוּ בָם'".
>
> (תלמוד בבלי, מסכת נזיר, כ"ג, א')

> Rabba bar bar Ḥanna said in the name of Rabbi Yoḥanan: "What is the meaning of: 'For the paths of the Lord are straight, and the righteous shall walk in them, while the transgressors stumble in them (Hosea, 14:10)?' How can the same path lead to such different outcomes? This is comparable to two people who roasted their *pesach* offerings [on Passover eve]. One ate it for the sake of *mitzvah*, and one ate it gluttonously. The one who ate it for the sake of *mitzvah*, has fulfilled the first part of the verse: 'And the righteous shall walk in them,' while the other, who ate it gluttonously, is described by the end of the verse: 'But transgressors stumble over them'."
>
> (*Babylonian Talmud*, "*Nazir*," 23a)

Action arises at the right moment, responding to the needs of the present, while activity is driven by past experiences. Action emerges as an organic response to the immediate demands of the environment and life itself. Activity, on the other hand, arises from our anxieties and uses circumstances as mere pretexts to express these anxieties. Hence instead of responding to an existential requirement of the present, activity is a stress release, an outlet for accumulated anxieties from the past that are expressed in the present. The origin of action is serenity. Activities reflect our agitated and altered mental state, revealing restlessness and nervousness. Action flourishes at the right moment; activity is characterized by its irrelevance and insignificance. Action springs from the now; activity is rooted in memory, in the past.

Activity's goal resides in the future and thus belongs intrinsically to a past projected onto tomorrow, that is, a memory looking at the next moment. The only framework that existence acknowledges is the here and now. By engaging in activity, we are absent from the present reality. Genuine *mitzvah* action does not project onto future expectations nor does it harbor underlying goals or ulterior motives.

אָמַר רַב נַחְמָן בַּר יִצְחָק: גְּדוֹלָה עֲבֵרָה לִשְׁמָהּ מִמִּצְוָה שֶׁלֹּא לִשְׁמָהּ.
(תלמוד בבלי, מסכת נזיר, כ"ג, ב')

Rav Naḥman bar Yitzḥak said: "A transgression (*aveirah*) committed for its own sake, is better than a *mitzvah* performed not for its own sake."

(*Babylonian Talmud*, "*Nazir*," 23b)

Action emerges as a spontaneous and direct response to an immediate situation in the present context without selfish motives. Through superficial occupations, or what Heidegger calls "busywork," we squander our energy and vitality. Only those who maintain serenity and relaxation preserve the essential energy needed to channel it into action. Mere activity arises from ignorance and lack of discernment, whereas action emerges from cognitive luminosity or complete clarity. Immersed in action, laborious tasks become delightful, effort becomes play, burdens become happiness, and heaviness becomes joy.

מִצְוֹות צְרִיכוֹת כַּוָּנָה.
(תלמוד בבלי, מסכת ברכות, י"ג, א')

Mitzvot require intent.

(*Babylonian Talmud*, "*Berachot*," 13a)

Activity is so automatic and unconscious that those doing it are not even aware of their own behavior. Examples of activities include nail biting, overeating, substance abuse, excessive talking, and smoking. By aligning ourselves with the framework dictated by the *halachah*, we make our existence sacred, so even the simplest and most trivial actions become transcendental. The intention is not to infuse a superficial touch of religiosity or spirituality into our days through sentimentality, but to enrich our lives with a solid and tangible sacred structure.

> וְכִי מָה אִכְפַּת לוֹ לְהַקָּדוֹשׁ־בָּרוּךְ־הוּא, בֵּין שֶׁשּׁוֹחֵט אֶת הַבְּהֵמָה וְאוֹכֵל אוֹ אִם נוֹחֵר וְאוֹכֵל? כְּלוּם אַתָּה מוֹעִילוֹ אוֹ כְּלוּם אַתָּה מַזִּיקוֹ? אוֹ מָה אִכְפַּת לוֹ, בֵּין אוֹכֵל טְהוֹרוֹת לְאוֹכֵל נְבֵלוֹת? אָמַר שְׁלֹמֹה, 'אִם חָכַמְתָּ – חָכַמְתָּ לָּךְ' וגו' (משלי ט', י"ב). הָא לֹא נִתְּנוּ הַמִּצְוֹת אֶלָּא לְצָרֵף בָּהֶן אֶת הַבְּרִיּוֹת וְיִשְׂרָאֵל, שֶׁנֶּאֱמַר: 'אִמְרַת־ה' צְרוּפָה' (תהילים י"ח, ל"א). לָמָּה? שֶׁיְּהֵא מָגֵן עָלֶיךָ, שֶׁנֶּאֱמַר: 'מָגֵן הוּא לְכָל הַחוֹסִים בּוֹ' (תהילים י"ח, ל"א).
>
> (מדרש תנחומא, פרשת שמיני, סימן ח')

> And what does the Holy One, Blessed be He, care whether one ritually slaughters cattle and eats [the meat] or slaughters it by stabbing and eats it? Will such thing benefit Him [the Holy One, blessed be He,] or will it harm Him? Or what does He care whether one eats carcasses or eats ritually slaughtered animals? Solomon said [about this] (in Proverbs, 9:12), "If you gained wisdom, you gained wisdom for yourself". Thus, the commandments were given only to refine humans and the people of Israel through them, as stated (Psalms, 18:31), "the word of the Lord is refined." Why? So that He might be a shield over you, [as stated] (ibid., cont.), "He is a shield for all who take refuge in Him."
>
> (*Midrash Tanḥuma*, "*Shemini*," 8)

In this sense, the Hebrew revelation offers a profound and enduring way to connect and reintegrate the human and the Divine.

> "הָאֵל תָּמִים דַּרְכּוֹ אִמְרַת־ה' צְרוּפָה מָגֵן הוּא לְכֹל הַחֹסִים בּוֹ" (תהילים י"ח, ל"א). אִם דְּרָכָיו תְּמִימִים, הוּא – עַל אַחַת כַּמָּה וְכַמָּה. רַב אָמַר: "לֹא נִתְּנוּ הַמִּצְוֹת אֶלָּא לְצָרֵף בָּהֶן אֶת הַבְּרִיּוֹת. וְכִי מָה אִכְפַּת לֵיהּ לְהַקָּדוֹשׁ בָּרוּךְ הוּא לְמִי שֶׁשּׁוֹחֵט מִן הַצַּוָּאר אוֹ מִי שֶׁשּׁוֹחֵט מִן הָעֹרֶף? הֱוֵי – לֹא נִתְּנוּ הַמִּצְוֹת אֶלָּא לְצָרֵף בָּהֶם אֶת הַבְּרִיּוֹת".
>
> (בראשית רבה, מ"ד, א')

> "As for God, His way is perfect; the word of the Lord is refined, He is a shield for all who take refuge in Him." (Psalms 18:31) If His way is perfect, how much more is He Himself! Rav said: "The *mitzvot* were given so that man might be refined by them. Do you really think that The Holy One, Blessed be He, cares if an animal is slaughtered by the front or by the back of the neck? Therefore, *mitzvot* were given only to refine humans."
>
> (*Bereshit Rabbah*, 44.1)

Mitzvot are not merely tools, instruments, or mechanisms that facilitate our relationship with the transcendent; they are the very process of aligning with divinity. The term *mitzvah*, translated as "precept," is intimately related to the word *tzavta* (צוותא), which means "connection or bond." Thus, each biblical precept is as a symbol that merges the individual and the Divine.

> וְגַם אֶת־שַׁבְּתוֹתַי נָתַתִּי לָהֶם לִהְיוֹת לְאוֹת בֵּינִי וּבֵינֵיהֶם לָדַעַת כִּי אֲנִי ה' מְקַדְּשָׁם:
> (יחזקאל כ', י"ב)
>
> Moreover, I gave them My *sabbaths* to serve as a symbol between Me and them, that they might know that it is I, the Lord, who sanctifies them.
>
> (Ezekiel, 20:12)

In numerous verses and passages of the Torah, *mitzvot* are referred to as symbols.

> וּקְשַׁרְתָּם לְאוֹת עַל־יָדֶךָ וְהָיוּ לְטֹטָפֹת בֵּין עֵינֶיךָ:
> (דברים ו', ח')
>
> Bind them [the *tefillin*] as a symbol on your hand and let them serve as *totafot* (frontlets) on your forehead.
>
> (Deuteronomy, 6:8)

The enlightened sages of antiquity point out a parallel between *mitzvot* and the physical structure of the human being.

דָּרַשׁ רַבִּי שִׂמְלַאי: "שֵׁשׁ מֵאוֹת וּשְׁלֹשׁ עֶשְׂרֵה מִצְווֹת נֶאֶמְרוּ לוֹ לְמשֶׁה, שְׁלֹשׁ מֵאוֹת וְשִׁשִּׁים וְחָמֵשׁ לָאוִין כְּמִנְיַן יְמוֹת הַחַמָּה, וּמָאתַיִם וְאַרְבָּעִים וּשְׁמוֹנָה עֲשֵׂה כְּנֶגֶד אֵיבָרָיו שֶׁל אָדָם".

(תלמוד בבלי, מסכת מכות, כ"ג, ב')

Rabbi Simlai expounded: "There were 613 *mitzvot* stated to Moses in the Torah, consisting of 365 prohibitions corresponding to the number of days in the solar year, and 248 positive *mitzvot* corresponding to the number of a person's limbs."

(*Babylonian Talmud*, "*Makkot*," 23b)

בְּגִין דְּאִית בְּבַר־נָשׁ רמ"ח שַׁיְפִין, לָקֳבֵל רמ"ח פִּקּוּדִין דְּאוֹרַיְיתָא דְּאִינּוּן לְמֶעְבַּד אִתְיְהִיבוּ, וְלָקֳבֵל רמ"ח מַלְאָכִין דְּאִתְלַבְּשַׁת בְּהוֹן שְׁכִינְתָּא וּשְׁמָא דִּלְהוֹן כִּשְׁמָא דְּמָארֵיהוֹן, וְאִית בְּבַר־נָשׁ שס"ה גִּידִין, וְלָקֳבְלֵהוֹן שס"ה פִּקּוּדִין דְּלָאו אִינּוּן אִתְיְהִיבוּ לְמֶעְבַּד, וְלָקֳבֵל שס"ה יוֹמֵי שַׁתָּא.

(ספר הזוהר, פרשת וישלח, ז')

Because there are 248 limbs in a person, corresponding to the 248 mitzvot of the Torah that were given to be done (positive *mitzvot*) and to the 248 angels that the *Shechinaḥ* (God's presence) is enclothed within them and their name is like that of their Lord. And there are 365 sinews in a person – they correspond to 365 *mitzvot* that were given to not do (negative *mitzvot*); they also correspond to the 365 days of the year.

(*Zohar*, "*Vayishlaḥ*," 7)

This passage says that the 248 positive precepts correspond to the 248 limbs of the human body. Likewise, the 365 prohibitive precepts are equated with the 365 ligaments in human anatomy.

The objective world is constantly present as what is perceived. Senses such as sight, touch, and smell allow for direct sensory experience. Through our actions, we directly connect to this platform. While we can experience tangible reality through actions such as walking, dancing, painting, eating, writing, and speaking, it is impossible to process or understand it through thought alone. Unlike actions, thought lacks direct and immediate access to reality. When we engage in mental conceptualization, our access to reality is obstructed by abstract ideas. Thought entails a certain alienation because we interact with reality conceptually. The act of thinking does not establish a direct link to life nor is it sufficient to fully process it. On the contrary, by its inherent nature, it instills a demarcation, a separation, a distance. In this same sense, Hans-Georg Gadamer maintains that Truth implies a belonging and an approximation to the Self, while methods impose distance and separation. Therefore, if we want to access authentic and genuine Truth, we must dispense with methods.

By subjecting reality to analysis or deduction, we inevitably distance ourselves from it. When we reflect "on" it or reason "about" it, we erect an unbridgeable gap. "On" or "about" suggests a mediated link or an indirect relationship; they denote that we do not experience or interact with things in the present. Such prepositions prevent a genuine connection with trees, flowers, and so on.

Discourse "on" or "about" reality dissociates us, separates us, and intrinsically excludes us from it. Intellectuals, no matter how eminent, distance themselves from action because thought is inherently indirect and mediated, while action can only be direct and immediate. In fact, thinking renders acting impracticable and unattainable. Unlike thinkers, genuine artists achieve a direct and unconceptualized relationship with the world.

In the world we inhabit, many people use their cognitive abilities to speculate and ruminate but lack the energy to make their ideas concrete and accomplish something tangible with their lives. Conversely, many unreflective individuals possess considerable vigor and impetus to do things. Though they do not pause to think and evaluate, their desires drive them to do a lot. Unfortunately, many of these unthoughtful but strong-willed beings have generated considerable conflict and devastation, causing painful disasters and havoc throughout history. Only genuine inquiry into reality will interrupt the vicious cycle of mental chatter. When conceptual activity ceases, consciousness awakens. Then, the cognitive faculty metamorphoses and manifests itself as greater mental clarity. The energy that fuels thought is reformulated and becomes lucid.

The purification process begins when mental activity ceases; however, this does not mean suspending consciousness. On the contrary, consciousness persists, gaining greater clarity and lucidity leading us to action. Moving closer to reality, to the essence of things as they are, requires a balanced combination of action and consciousness.

> וַיִּקַּח סֵפֶר הַבְּרִית וַיִּקְרָא בְּאָזְנֵי הָעָם וַיֹּאמְרוּ כֹּל אֲשֶׁר־דִּבֶּר ה' נַעֲשֶׂה וְנִשְׁמָע:
> (שמות כ"ד, ז')
>
> Then he took the book of the covenant and read it in the hearing of the people. And they said: "All that the Lord has spoken we will do (*na'ase*) and hear (*nishma*)."
>
> (Exodus, 24:7)

In Hebrew, *shema* means "hear or listen," but can also mean "pay attention," which is the active aspect of consciousness, like when a teacher asks students to focus their awareness. *Shema* is more than a request to listen, since it urges focus. The main mantra of the Hebrew tradition, "*shema* Israel," is an intimate exhortation to the people of Israel to not only listen but pay attention. When we say *shema*, we are asking people to both listen and be aware, so it is clear that the word *shema* evokes awareness.

Based on this reading, the expression *na'ase venishma* (נַעֲשֶׂה וְנִשְׁמָע), or "we will do and we will listen," closely related to *mitzvot*, refers to action and consciousness. Hence a deeper contemplation of *na'ase venishma* reveals that it is a dual call to action and conscious observation. It not only represents the dimension of acting but also of remaining attentive during the action, in what is termed "meditative action."

However, there are those who misunderstand this notion of remaining attentive during action, associating it with the need for isolation. This is evident in Patañjali's well-known statement in his *Yoga Sūtra*:

योगश्चित्तवृत्तिनिरोधः।

yogaś citta-vṛtti-nirodhaḥ

Yoga is the cessation of mental activity.

(*Yoga Sūtra*, 1.2)

If these wise words are understood incorrectly, they can lead us to conclude that the key to appeasing the mind lies in isolation from society. It is a grave mistake to believe that abstaining from worldly activities guarantees true peace. Cloistering oneself in monasteries while retaining the same mental turmoil can only lead to a disconnection from reality. As Kant would say, authentic faith belongs to practical reason, not theoretical reason.

וְעַתָּה יִשְׂרָאֵל שְׁמַע אֶל הַחֻקִּים וְאֶל הַמִּשְׁפָּטִים אֲשֶׁר אָנֹכִי מְלַמֵּד אֶתְכֶם לַעֲשׂוֹת לְמַעַן תִּחְיוּ וּבָאתֶם וִירִשְׁתֶּם אֶת הָאָרֶץ אֲשֶׁר ה' אֱלֹהֵי אֲבֹתֵיכֶם נֹתֵן לָכֶם: לֹא תֹסִפוּ עַל הַדָּבָר אֲשֶׁר אָנֹכִי מְצַוֶּה אֶתְכֶם וְלֹא תִגְרְעוּ מִמֶּנּוּ לִשְׁמֹר אֶת מִצְוֹת ה' אֱלֹהֵיכֶם אֲשֶׁר אָנֹכִי מְצַוֶּה אֶתְכֶם: [...] וְאַתֶּם הַדְּבֵקִים בַּה' אֱלֹהֵיכֶם חַיִּים כֻּלְּכֶם הַיּוֹם:

(דברים ד', א', ב', ד')

And now, O Israel, *shema* (hearken) unto the statutes and unto the ordinances that I am teaching you to perform, so that you may live and come and inherit the land which the Lord, the God of your fathers, is giving you. You shall not add anything to what I command you or take anything away from it, but keep the *mitzvot* of the Lord, your God, that I enjoin upon you. [...] But you, who held fast to the Lord, your God, are all alive today.

(Deuteronomy, 4:1,2,4)

The millennia-old Hebrew revelation does not require renouncing action to access reality. On the contrary, it affirms that action is a path to Truth. Halachic actions, performed with full awareness, act as a bridge between what is apparent and what is real, leading us from the relative to the absolute. The biblical precepts have a symbolic character, since they reintegrate us with our original source. The term *symbol* derives from the Greek *sýmbolon* (σύμβολον), which in turn is composed of *sýn* (σύν), meaning "together," and *bállō* (βάλλω), which is "to throw or to cast." Originally, the verb *symbállo* meant "to gather, to bring together, or to unite." In many spiritual traditions, symbols are considered mediators between visible and invisible worlds. Thus, the symbolism in *mitzvot* reconnects us with our absolute dimension, elevating us to meanings and experiences that transcend what is perceptible. Precepts allow for the divinization of the human through conscious action. *Mitzvot* allow humanity to enter divinity and divinity to enter humanity.

Na'ase venishma (נַעֲשֶׂה וְנִשְׁמָע) meaning "we will do consciously or attentively," does not emerge from a limited mind, but is an expression of pure consciousness. It means surrendering to action without concepts intervening, as the mind disconnects us from praxis, from what is factual or real, and plunges us into the theoretical realm of ideas, opinions, and conclusions. According to the Sinaitic revelation, the sacred transcends mere conceptualization by manifesting in the many facets of our daily lives. God is present in the water we drink, the food we eat, the music we listen to, the clothes we wear, and in our interactions with family and friends.

Those who immerse themselves exclusively in reflections and speculations become merely thinking entities, confined to a cosmos of theories, postulates, notions, abstractions, inferences, deductions, concepts, and conclusions. However, they should not inhibit reasoning because their intellectual acuity may atrophy. It is best to not evade action but to endow it with greater lucidity and presence, infusing it with more consciousness and clarity, thus merging action and consciousness.

Na'ase venishma encapsulates the essence of meditation. It hints at the transition from the mind to lucidity, the withdrawal of thought, and the revival of consciousness. The secret lies in immersing oneself in action, allowing the mind to flow freely like a river taking its natural course without resistance. By transcending the mind, the potency of thought is redirected toward its origin: pure, genuine consciousness. As mental activity dims and thoughts fade away, we evolve toward a lucid and deeply conscious existence. In this state of mental stillness, no thoughts prevail, regardless of their nature or attributes. Although the mind may fluctuate, knowingness persists, constant and unaffected. It is still possible to perform everyday actions such as walking, talking, smelling, working, eating, or sleeping while remaining fully aware.

The inherent transparency of consciousness transcends and far surpasses mental capacities. Even when ideational, notional, and conceptual entities emerge in the cognitive panorama, attentive observation remains independent. Eventually, mental activity is eclipsed by the radiating lumen of consciousness. This luminescence dispels darkness as mental silhouettes gradually fade and disappear, yielding to the preeminence of ascending consciousness.

Gradually, we enter a process of metamorphosis, transmuting from thinking beings to conscious beings. Upon realizing the crystalline consciousness, our mental constructs vanish like shadows in radiant light. The vigorous lucidity of observation sharpens perception and intensifies acoustic and olfactory sensitivity. Although the actions themselves remain unchanged, they undoubtedly acquire a uniquely renewed attribute. These manifested actions are elevated to the realm of the sacred, aligning with the inherent transcendence of *mitzvot*.

Ordinary people live fragmented lives, with a separation between their words and actions, between their steps and intentions. In contrast, every word spoken by a being fully present in each syllable holds a unique essence, an innate singularity. In the daily behavior of most people, we observe a clear automatism, as they act out of mere habit, disconnected from their activities. However, when someone who is just a shadow of existence acts, every glance, word, gesture, and movement is a full extension of their presence. The average human lives oblivious of their own visual perception, but when someone who is no one looks at us, we feel pierced, as if the entire cosmos is focusing its attention on us through those penetrating eyes.

At the core of symbolic beings there is no fragmentation, dissociation, division, disjunction, or fracture but an absolute integrative cohesion that eliminates any distinction between themselves and their actions. Being the Self, they become the pure manifestation of their actions. The *mitzvot* aspire, in essence, to unite action and consciousness into a coherent and indivisible whole.

The word *experience* originates from the Latin term composed of three parts: the prefix *ex*, meaning "separation"; the verbal root *peri*, which can be translated as "to try"; and the suffix *entia*, which means *qualitas agentis*, or "quality of an agent." An experience consists of witnessing, perceiving, feeling, or knowing something. Accordingly, we can affirm that the term *experience* refers to events, interactions, or perceptions involving a subject and an object—that is, the experiencing subject and the experienced object. Drinking is an experience that involves the interaction between a subject—the one who drinks—and an object, such as a glass of water.

We also have mental and emotional experiences. The entirety of human diegesis can be conceived as a continuous sequence of experiences. At first glance, each experience implies an interaction involving the subject, object, and knowingness. Knowingness apprehends experiences but, paradoxically, is not an experience itself. Objective reality, with its inherent duality and relativity, is an illusory construct with only four components: thoughts, emotions, sensations, and perceptions. Only knowingness, or pure consciousness, is truly real and ontologically immutable, thus identified with the Absolute or divinity. Each *mitzvah* is a symbol that melds the human and the Divine, uniting the relative and the Absolute, the apparent and the real. The purpose of these precepts is to build a home for consciousness in the tangible dimension, within the realm of experiences. *Mitzvot* allow us to create a space for consciousness in the phenomenological sphere, within the orbit of everyday human experiences.

"בָּאתִי לְגַנִּי אֲחוֹתִי כַלָּה" (שיר־השירים ה', א'). אָמַר רַבִּי שְׁמוּאֵל בַּר נַחְמָן: "בְּשָׁעָה שֶׁבָּרָא הַקָּדוֹשׁ־בָּרוּךְ־הוּא אֶת הָעוֹלָם, נִתְאַוָּה שֶׁיְּהֵא לוֹ דִּירָה בַּתַּחְתּוֹנִים כְּמוֹ שֶׁיֵּשׁ בָּעֶלְיוֹנִים. בָּרָא אֶת הָאָדָם וְצִוָּה אוֹתוֹ וְאָמַר לוֹ: 'מִכָּל עֵץ הַגַּן אָכֹל תֹּאכֵל, וּמֵעֵץ הַדַּעַת טוֹב וָרַע לֹא תֹאכַל מִמֶּנּוּ' (בראשית ב', ט"ז–י"ז) וְעָבַר עַל צִוּוּיוֹ. אָמַר לֵיהּ הַקָּדוֹשׁ־בָּרוּךְ־הוּא, 'כָּךְ הָיִיתִי מִתְאַוֶּה שֶׁיְּהֵא לִי דִּירָה בַּתַּחְתּוֹנִים כְּמוֹ שֶׁיֵּשׁ לִי בָּעֶלְיוֹנִים, וְדָבָר אֶחָד צִוִּיתִי אוֹתְךָ וְלֹא שָׁמַרְתָּ אוֹתוֹ'. מִיַּד סִלֵּק הַקָּדוֹשׁ בָּרוּךְ הוּא שְׁכִינָתוֹ לָרָקִיעַ הָרִאשׁוֹן. מִנַּיִן? דִּכְתִיב (שם ג', ח'): 'וַיִּשְׁמְעוּ

אֶת קוֹל ה' אֱלֹקִים מִתְהַלֵּךְ בַּגָּן'. כֵּיוָן שֶׁעָבְרוּ עַל הַצִּוּוּי, סִלֵּק שְׁכִינָתוֹ לָרָקִיעַ הָרִאשׁוֹן. עָמַד קַיִן וְהָרַג לְהֶבֶל, מִיַּד סִלֵּק שְׁכִינָתוֹ לְרָקִיעַ שֵׁנִי כוּ'. אָמַר הַקָּדוֹשׁ־בָּרוּךְ־הוּא: 'שִׁבְעָה רְקִיעִים בָּרָאתִי, וְעַד עַכְשָׁו יֵשׁ רְשָׁעִים לַעֲמֹד בָּהּ'. מֶה עָשָׂה? קִפֵּל אֶת כָּל הַדּוֹרוֹת הָרִאשׁוֹנִים הָרְשָׁעִים וְהֶעֱמִיד אַבְרָהָם. כֵּיוָן שֶׁהֶעֱמִיד אַבְרָהָם, סִגֵּל מַעֲשִׂים טוֹבִים, יָרַד הַקָּדוֹשׁ־בָּרוּךְ־הוּא מִן רָקִיעַ שְׁבִיעִי לְשִׁשִּׁי. עָמַד יִצְחָק וּפָשַׁט צַוָּארוֹ עַל גַּבֵּי הַמִּזְבֵּחַ, יָרַד מִשִּׁשִּׁי לַחֲמִישִׁי כוּ'. עָמַד מֹשֶׁה וְהוֹרִידָהּ לָאָרֶץ, שֶׁנֶּאֱמַר: 'וַיֵּרֶד ה' עַל הַר סִינַי' (שמות י"ט, כ') וּכְתִיב (שיר־השירים ה', א'): 'בָּאתִי לְגַנִּי אֲחוֹתִי כַלָּה'. אֵימָתַי? כְּשֶׁהוּקַם הַמִּשְׁכָּן".

(מדרש תנחומא, פרשת נשא, ט"ז)

"I have come into my garden, my sister, O bride" (Song of songs, 5:1). Rabbi Samuel bar Naḥman said: "When the Holy One, Blessed be He, created the world, He longed to have an abode in the lower worlds just as He has in the higher worlds. [For this end] He created Adam, commanded him and said to him (Genesis, 2:16–17): 'You may freely eat of any tree in the garden; But as for the tree of the knowledge of good and evil, you may not eat of it.' Then he [Adam] transgressed against His commandment. The Holy One, Blessed be He, said this to him: 'This is what I longed for, that just as I have a dwelling on high, I would likewise have one below. Now when I have given you one command, you have not kept it. Immediately the Holy One, Blessed be He, removed His divine Presence [up] to the first firmament. Where is it shown? Where it is stated (Genesis, 3:8): 'Then they heard the voice of the Lord God moving about in the garden.' Since they transgressed the commandment, He removed His divine presence to the first firmament [and therefore they could only **hear** God]. [When] Cain arose and killed Abel, He immediately removed His divine Presence [from the first firmament] to the second firmament etc. The Holy One, Blessed be He, said: 'I created seven firmaments, and up to now there are wicked ones [still] arising upon [the world].' What did He do? He folded away all the generations of the wicked and raised up Abraham. When Abraham arose and performed good works, the Holy One, Blessed be He, immediately descended from the seventh firmament to the sixth. [Then] Isaac arose and stretched out his neck upon the altar, He descended from the sixth firmament to the fifth, etc. [Then] Moses arose, he brought it [the divine Presence] down to earth, as stated (Exodus, 19:20): 'And the Lord descended onto Mount Sinai.' And it is written (Song of songs, 5:1): "I have come into my garden, my sister, O bride." When? When the Tabernacle was set up.

(*Midrash Tanḥuma*, "*Naso*," 16)

Each *mitzvah* reveals the knowingness that has been subsumed in the background of everyday life, bringing it to a central position in the theater of our experiences. Without being an experience itself, consciousness becomes visible, unveiling itself as the foundation of all experiences. In *Pirkei Avot*, we read about the reward for fulfilling *mitzvot*:

בֶּן עַזַּאי אוֹמֵר, הֱוֵי רָץ לְמִצְוָה קַלָּה כְּבַחֲמוּרָה, וּבוֹרֵחַ מִן הָעֲבֵרָה. שֶׁמִּצְוָה גוֹרֶרֶת מִצְוָה, וַעֲבֵרָה גוֹרֶרֶת עֲבֵרָה. שֶׁשְּׂכַר מִצְוָה, מִצְוָה. וּשְׂכַר עֲבֵרָה, עֲבֵרָה.
(פרקי אבות ד', ב')

Ben Azzai says: "Run to perform a 'light' (minor) *mitzvah* as to a 'heavy' (major) one and flee from an *averah* (transgression); for a *mitzvah* begets a *mitzvah*, and an *averah* begets an *averah*; For the reward of a *mitzvah* is a *mitzvah* and the reward of an *averah* is an *averah*."

(*Pirkei Avot*, 4.2)

For someone who has strayed from their authenticity, *mitzvot* seem to be forced and imposed activities. However, they are spontaneous and natural actions for those who have realized their true nature. The practiced *mitzvah* reveals the inherent *mitzvah*, as its practical application paves the way to its intrinsic essence. In other words, natural *mitzvot* are deciphered through practiced *mitzvot*, as Rabbi Yehuda HaLevi describes:

אָמַר הֶחָבֵר: "אֲבָל יִעוּדֵנוּ – הִדַּבְּקֵנוּ בָּעִנְיָן הָאֱלֹהִי בַּנְּבוּאָה, וּמָה שֶׁהוּא קָרוֹב לָהּ, וְהִתְחַבֵּר הָעִנְיָן הָאֱלֹהִי בָּנוּ בַּגְּדֻלָּה וּבַכָּבוֹד וּבַמּוֹפְתִים. וְעַל כֵּן אֵינֶנּוּ אוֹמֵר בַּתּוֹרָה, כִּי אִם תַּעֲשׂוּ הַמִּצְוָה הַזֹּאת, אֲבִיאֲכֶם אַחֲרֵי הַמָּוֶת אֶל גַּנּוֹת וַהֲנָאוֹת, אֲבָל הוּא אוֹמֵר: וְאַתֶּם תִּהְיוּ לִי לְעָם וַאֲנִי אֶהְיֶה לָכֶם לֵאלֹהִים מַנְהִיג אֶתְכֶם, וִיהְיֶה מִכֶּם מִי שֶׁיַּעֲמֹד לְפָנַי וּמִי שֶׁיַּעֲלֶה לַשָּׁמַיִם כַּאֲשֶׁר הָיוּ הוֹלְכִים בֵּין הַמַּלְאָכִים, וְיִהְיוּ גַּם כֵּן מַלְאָכַי הוֹלְכִים בֵּינֵיכֶם בָּאָרֶץ וְתִרְאוּ אוֹתָם יְחִידִים וְרַבִּים, שׁוֹמְרִים אֶתְכֶם וְנִלְחָמִים לָכֶם, וְתַתְמִידוּ בָּאָרֶץ אֲשֶׁר הִיא עוֹזֶרֶת עַל הַמַּעֲלָה הַזֹּאת, וְהִיא אַדְמַת הַקֹּדֶשׁ, וְיִהְיֶה שָׂבְעָהּ וְרַעֲבוֹנָהּ וְטוֹבָתָהּ וְרָעָתָהּ – בָּעִנְיָן הָאֱלֹקִי כְּפִי מַעֲשֵׂיכֶם וְיִהְיֶה נוֹהֵג כָּל הָעוֹלָם עַל הַמִּנְהָג הַטִּבְעִי – זוּלַתְכֶם. [...] וְהָיָה כָּל זֶה וְהַתּוֹרָה הַזֹּאת וְכָל יִעוּדֶיהָ מֻבְטָחִים, לֹא יִפֹּל מֵהֶם דָּבָר; וְיִעוּדֶיהָ כֻּלָּם כּוֹלֵל אוֹתָם שֹׁרֶשׁ אֶחָד וְהוּא יִחוּל קִרְבַת אֱלֹהִים וּמַלְאָכָיו".

(ספר הכוזרי, חלק א', ק"ט)

The *chaver* ("Rabbi", "holy," or "righteous") said: "Now our purpose is that we shall adhere with the Divine Nature by means of prophecy, and everything that is annexed to it, and the Divine Nature connected with us through grand and awe-inspiring miracles. For this reason, we do not find in the Torah statements such as: 'If you keep this *mitzvah*, I will bring you after death into beautiful gardens and great pleasures.' But instead, we find statements like: 'You shall be my nation, and I will be a God unto you, who will guide you. There will be those of you who will stand before me, and who will ascend to heaven, as those who mingle among the angels, and also my angels shall mingle among you on earth. You shall see them singly or in hosts, watching over you and fighting for you. You shall always remain in the land which forms a stepping-stone to this high level, viz. the Holy Land. Its fertility or barrenness, its happiness or misfortune, depend upon the divine influence which your conduct will merit, whilst the rest of the world would continue its natural course […]. All this and this Torah and its purposes are promised, nothing will remain unfulfilled. All these purposes have one basis, viz. the anticipation of the proximity of God and His hosts."

(Rabbi Yehuda HaLevi, *The Kuzari*, 1.99)

Consequently, through the meticulous observance of the precepts as symbolic acts, we align ourselves with the divine character or consciousness. The Hebrew revelation has various interpretive facets, from *pshat* (simple) to *sod* (secret). Each *mitzvah* unveils the secret that our intrinsic nature is divine. The precepts are not mere decrees or laws; they restore individuals fractured by concepts to their primordial symbolic essence. They are links that reintegrate what we think we are with what we truly are.

Chapter 21

Mandalas: meetings between symbols and intuition

The term *intuition* is often understood as a form of discernment or immediate apprehension characterized by the object of perception being made present without the involvement of logical reasoning or deduction. With the inexorable advance of time and the progressive evolution of philosophy, intuition has been the subject of innumerable reinterpretations, all of which depend on both the philosopher who addresses it and the philosophical context in which it is framed. Let us briefly review the different interpretations of the term made by some of the philosophers we have discussed so far in these reflections.

Among the most notable interpretations, we find that of Plato, for whom intuition emerges as an innate and direct knowledge of the "Forms" or "Ideas"; it is the knowledge of the perennial and unchanging realities that constitute the substrate of the temporal manifestations of the physical world. Aristotle also spoke of intuition in the context of direct intellectual understanding. However, for Aristotle, intuition was more connected to experience and sensory perception than it was for Plato. Thomas Aquinas, for example, considered intuition to be a form of direct knowledge of God and eternal truths. Later, and according to the proponents of modern rationalism, such as Descartes and Spinoza, intuition consists of a form of evident and immediate knowledge. Specifically, for Descartes, intuition is a "mental vision," clear and distinct, which serves as the foundation for deductive reasoning. Kant, on the other hand, proposes conceptualizing intuition. According to him, our experiences are made possible through the a priori forms of intuition, specifically space and time, which structure sensory perceptions.

In contemporary thought, intuition is typically defined as a "feeling of certainty" experienced when confronted with a proposition prior to its justification through logic. Through the lens of phenomenology formulated by Husserl, intuition is conceived as a type of "immediate perception" or "sudden recognition of the essence inherent in an event." Later, Heidegger would define intuition as the direct apprehension "of what is given corporeally as it itself appears." These different interpretations are not necessarily mutually exclusive, as they can be interpreted as facets of a broader concept of intuition. However, in all of these cases, intuition is independent of the logical or discursive reasoning that operates through inference and deduction.

In contrast to this reading of intuition as a kind of rational faculty, we will define intuition as the immediate apprehension of the essence of something without the mediation of reasoning. In this ability for silent wisdom, intuition reveals itself to us as the privileged access to the multiple layers of meaning that reside in the symbol. Its nature eludes the powers of reason but is, instead, accessible through an immediate apprehension that does not require concepts. In this sense, intuition would be the indispensable resource in the process of unveiling the varied manifestations of the symbol and the entangled structure that characterizes it.

As we have seen earlier, the symbol plays the role of a link, bridging the gap between what is discernible and what is inscrutable, between the evident and the enigmatic, facilitating access to spheres usually closed off. Indeed, symbols function as gateways that introduce us to renewed modes of understanding and perception of the reality that surrounds us. Asserting that symbols can be understood exclusively through rational approaches or argumentative structures is ignoring their broad spectrum and essence. Independently of logical reasoning, concepts, and categories, intuition provides us with a tool to examine in its totality the different levels of the symbol, which often remain inaccessible to analytical thought. It is through intuition, as the clear and immediate vision of what is, that the symbol can reveal itself to us in its entirety, facilitating our entry and inviting us on a journey of self-exploration and understanding beyond the limitations of unidirectional thought. The term "integrity" is important here, as while the concept captures by section and dissection, intuition captures the symbol as a whole.

When exploring the lives and teachings of prominent masters and enlightened sages within the *Sanātana-dharma*, one might encounter some confusion regarding the phenomenon of divine contemplation. Let us highlight Rāmakṛṣṇa Paramahaṃsa, who contemplated the Mother Kālī, or even Lord Chaitanya, whose experience with Kṛṣṇa was analogous. Countless yogis of elevated spiritual stature testify to visualizations of their deities during their meditations. Many find the relationship of the devotees of *Sanātana-dharma* with the *devas*, or "gods," enigmatic, whether is with Kṛṣṇa, Śiva, Ganeṣa, Kālī, Durgā, or Umā. Questions often arise as to whether their existence is considered real or merely symbolic. Although, truly, the phenomenon in question is not a monopoly of Hinduism but permeates all spiritual traditions, it is precisely in Hinduism that this issue becomes especially evident.

Hindu mythological entities embody external manifestations of the internal states of the human being. By immersing oneself in certain states of consciousness, whether emotional or spiritual, access to symbolic visions of these deities unfolds. Even though these visions may fluctuate in minute details due to their respective cultural origins and traditions, a notable congruence is unveiled at their essence. Each of these deities is a crucible of specific qualities and emotions. By entering into the abysmal web of wisdom, the pilgrim unveils the most hidden meanings guarded by their *Iṣṭadeva*, or "favorite deity," and strives to incorporate these attributes. Thus, one crosses the threshold toward deeper connections with the inscrutable, clearing a path that is oriented toward the divine essence residing within the individual. This, in turn, empowers one to transcend the limits of the mundane and enter, with calculated urgency, into the realm of the sacred.

To discern the nature of this phenomenon, it is essential to understand that mythology, contrary to conceptual thought, is not anchored in the objective physical reality. While myth unfolds in relation to reality, its connection does not lie in the physical plane of occurrence but in the psychological domain of existence. Therefore, it is crucial to understand that myth holds an unparalleled utility as an entity of the psychological domain. The *devas* do not embody tangible physical entities but are symbols with genuine resonance in the human psyche. They constitute archetypes that reside in the collective unconscious, in accordance with Carl Jung's postulation, whose influence and reality must not be dismissed. Although we are confronted with a reality of a supernatural nature, impervious to the ordinary epistemological avenues of perception, through the channel of devotion, this sublimity can fervently fill individual consciousness.

Carl Gustav Jung was a Swiss thinker and a stellar figure and bastion in the fields of psychiatry and psychology. His contribution to analytical psychology is undeniable. He masterfully outlined the psychological odyssey of the differentiation of the self through the temporality of existence, skillfully merging conscious and unconscious elements into individual identity.[88] Jung articulated that differentiation constituted the crux of human development. It is worth noting that he was the driving force behind world-renowned psychological concepts such as synchronicity, archetypes, the collective unconscious, psychological complexes, and the dimensions of extraversion and introversion. Delving into symbolism, he ventured into collaboration with patients suffering from mental health conditions, urging them to, with pen or brush in hand, free themselves from chains and let their thoughts flow. A thorough analysis of the human psyche led Jung to recognize certain parallels in the behavioral patterns of individuals diagnosed with schizophrenia. He was astonished and puzzled to observe how, as patients overcame the painful fragmentation of their mental state and reintegrated into a state of unity, the pictorial representations of their patients began to adopt circular forms. This crucial observation led him to discover that the reunified mind manifested through the symbol of the

88. C. G. Jung, *Psychological Types*, Bollingen Series XX, vol. 6, trans. H. G. Baynes, rev. R. F. C. Hull (Princeton: Princeton University Press, 1971).

mandala. With the following sentence, he summarized his thoughts on the intersection between psychology and culture: "Individual psychology is partly innate and partly acquired. The acquired part is the set of ancestral images of human experience." Hence, the importance of culture and the aforementioned terms.

The notion of *maṇḍala* is a term carved in the Sanskrit language, which can be interpreted as "circle or disk." This geometric figure embodies a profound meaning reflecting totality, integrity, and unity. Its structure suggests a sacred and symbolic space, a circle nested within a square form, a worldview encapsulated in a simple and intricate design. Their circular shape and symmetrical layout characterizes the manifestations of mandalas. These visual arrangements, whose aesthetic appeal is indisputable, are composed of figures and repetitive patterns arranged around a central axis.

The radial morphology of mandalas illustrates an expansive phenomenon of consciousness flowing from the epicenter of the being to the edges of the universe. Mandalas carry with them the heritage of eons and have been revered instruments in a variety of cultures and traditions, such as Hindu, Buddhist, and Tibetan currents, among others. However, their influence is not limited to Eastern or pre-Columbian cultures, such as the *chacanas* in Andean cosmogony or the patterns of the Pueblo natives and others; it has even had an impact in the West, specifically through the mandorla in medieval Christian art, labyrinths in Gothic period churches, and rose windows in cathedrals, thus certifying the universality of this symbol.

The circle-mandala is divided into internal compartments by cardinal axes, resonating with the individual's orientation in the cosmos. This circular pattern, emblematic of the life wheel and the cyclical repetition of cosmic phenomena, helps guide human beings on their journey toward understanding the totality of their existence and their position in the universe. Mandalas, with their omnipresent feature of concentric shapes, evoke perfection, symbolizing uniform distances from a central core. Moreover, the circumference alludes to perpetual cycles, reminiscent of the Hellenistic ouroboros; although, in contrast to these serpents that bite their tails, Buddhist mandalas tend to be more descriptive, illustrating scenes from the life and teachings of the Buddha.

Especially in Eastern cultures, the purpose of these structures is both spiritual and therapeutic, serving as prisms that channel attention, promote internal reflection, and nurture mental symmetry, facilitating concentration, calm, and connection with the "self," which, in turn, allows for the expression and self-exploration aimed at promoting emotional well-being. In Hindu doctrines, *yantras* adopt a linear design, forming energetic patterns whose purpose lies in facilitating meditative practice and concentration. Based on these foundations, I have outlined the method known as Meditative Philately. As a manifestation of an internal subjective reality, the emblem can serve as an invaluable tool for delving deeper into our self-understanding.

The act of coloring mandalas is valued as a creative and relaxing exercise, benefiting concentration and inner peace. The meticulous and extensive engagement with the mandala grants us a path toward the most hidden corners of our mental and emotional activity. In this way, this symbol rises as a device to achieve an incisive vision of our inner reality. This symbol provides a vantage point that assists us in unraveling the mysteries of our unconscious and the depths of our spirit.

Similarly, in the magical ceremonies of Western occult traditions, we glimpse the trace of a sacred space, set apart from the profane, for which magical circles are invoked, performing functions analogous to Eastern mandalas, creating a safeguarded space where magical operations take place, and spiritual energies are summoned.

Jung distinguished that, in a state of disintegration of the self, the mandala did not appear in the paintings of the patients, whereas it did appear in the reintegration of the subject with their mental state. This crucial observation demonstrated a deep correlation between the mandala and the subject's internal process. The psyche manifests particular symbols in specific states, and these manifestations transmute in parallel with internal transformations. Jung posited that the mandala constituted a representation of the reintegrated inner perimeter of the individual, transforming into a powerful emblem that reflected the subject's healing process. His work with the psyche and symbols constitutes a notable contribution to the field of psychiatry.

Through his discoveries, he opened virgin paths in the realm of examining and understanding mental disorders, as well as in healing mechanisms. The adoption of a symbolic approach provided a refreshing lens to probe the secrets of the human mind. Significantly, this allowed psychiatry to transcend its traditional focus on pathology and encompass the symbolic and spiritual dimension within human experience. What is important and underlying in Jung's work, but also in mandalas as a way of accessing the interior of the human soul, is precisely the intuition as the apprehension of what lies within the psyche and which, time and again, resists the reasoned processes of the human mind. Symbolic thinking is intuitive thinking, through which the symbol reveals a truth that does not need to be filtered through the mesh of reason. Symbols and their meanings are not mere products of the discursive thought of reason; they are the innermost being that lies behind the door that only intuition opens for us.

Chapter 22

The symbolism of Plato's allegory of the cave

In these last chapters, we have seen that intuition reveals itself as the non-conceptual and direct vision or knowledge that characterizes symbolic thinking. In other words, intuition is what captures the symbol as a means of penetrating the most unfathomable being of reality, to which discursive reasoning has no access. In this context, we can now define mythology as a corpus of symbols whose nature transcends the literal limits to appeal to a particular sensitivity and foster a characteristic process of information and thought. The effects of this process are reflected in the feedback of such information or language.

We can state that the human condition is intrinsically marked by the inescapable need to achieve integral completeness, an aspiration that can be interpreted as a powerful metaphor and symbol. This search for wholeness transcends the limits of the merely individual, encompassing existential, psychological, and social aspects. Such a yearning for completeness manifests in multiple dimensions of human life, driving individuals to explore and develop their potential in various realms. Ultimately, this metaphor and symbol of completeness can be understood as a fundamental force that drives action and evolution in the human condition. This aspiration to reach completeness originates from our ignorance of our own nature.

The primary impulse that *Homo sapiens* feel to embark on the quest for self-knowledge is a universally known theme. The ancient words γνῶθι σεαυτόν (*gnōthi seautón*) from Greek and their Latin counterpart *nosce te ipsum* reach us, resonating as a fundamental call to introspection. What makes these commands so powerful? The phrase, inscribed in the pronaos of the Temple of Apollo in Delphi, Greece, corresponds to a Delphic maxim, making it part of divine wisdom. Throughout human history, many authors and movements, such as Epictetus, Confucius, Jung, Hermeticism, and Existentialism, to name a few, have embraced and elaborated on it. Its resonance across various philosophical movements and cultures highlights its universality and continued relevance. Its power lies in the ability to spark within us the urge to investigate our being and delve into our hidden capacities through metaphor, symbolism, and refined language as vehicles to approach the intricate web that constitutes human existence.

When modes of expression that exceed the merely logical and literal are adopted, a bridge is built toward the discovery of what is hidden and the unveiling of truths rooted in existence, which remain obscure in everyday language. By embracing such a stance, the doors are opened to a deeper and more comprehensive understanding of what surrounds us and what lies within us, simultaneously sharpening our abilities for self-scrutiny and personal evolution. The two cornerstones that embody this intersection are mythology and sacred geometry, supreme entities within the constellation of symbolic thought.

Within the realm of sacred geometry, we find intertwined philosophy and mystical dimensions that address numerology, aligning with the legacy of the Pythagorean school. Mythology, on the other hand, stands as a less arcane ally to delve into the symbolic jungle. It is in this maelstrom of symbology that the imposing "Allegory of the Cave" by the esteemed Plato (428–347 BCE) emerges, written with a colossal narrative that exposes human essence, from the shadowy chains of ignorance to the brilliant clarity of erudition. The *Book VII* of *The Republic*, written around 380 BCE, is the custodian of this masterful allegory, and its original text goes as follows:

"Next, then," I said, "make an image of our nature in its education and want of education, likening it to a condition of the following kind. See human beings as though they were in an underground cavelike dwelling with its entrance, a long one, open to the light across the whole width of the cave. They are in it from childhood with their legs and necks in bonds so that they are fixed, seeing only in front of them, unable because of the bond to turn their heads all the way around. Their light is from a fire burning far above and behind them. Between the fire and the prisoners there is a road above, along which see a wall, built like the partitions puppet-handlers set in front of the human beings and over which they show the puppets."

"I see," he said.

"Then also see along this wall human beings carrying all sorts of artifacts, which project above the wall, and statues of men and other animals wrought from stone, wood, and every kind of material; as is to be expected, some of the carriers utter sounds while others are silent."

"It's a strange image," he said, "and strange prisoners you're telling of."

"They're like us," I said. "For in the first place, do you suppose such men would have seen anything of themselves and one another other than the shadows cast by the fire on the side of the cave facing them?"

"How could they," he said, "if they had been compelled to keep their heads motionless throughout life?"

"And what about the things that are carried by? Isn't it the same with them?"

"Of course."

"If they were able to discuss things with one another, don't you believe they would hold that they are naming these things going by before them that they see?"

"Necessarily."

"And what if the prison also had an echo from the side facing them? Whenever one of the men passing by happens to utter a sound, do you suppose they would believe that anything other than the passing shadow was uttering the sound?"

"No, by Zeus," he said. "I don't."

"Then most certainly," I said, "such men would hold that the truth is nothing other than the shadows of artificial things."

"Most necessarily," he said.

"Now consider," I said, "what their release and healing from bonds and folly would be like if something of this sort were by nature to happen to them. Take a man who is released and suddenly compelled to stand up, to turn his neck around, to walk and look up toward the light; and who, moreover, in doing all this is in pain, and, because he is dazzled, is unable to make out those things whose shadows he saw before. What do you suppose he'd say if someone were to tell him that before he saw silly nothings, while now, because he is somewhat nearer to what is and more turned toward beings, he sees more correctly; and, in particular, showing him each of the things that pass by, were to compel the man to answer his questions about where they are? Don't you suppose he'd be at a loss and believe that what was seen before is truer than what is now shown?"

"Yes," he said, "by far."

"And, if he compelled him to look at the light itself, would his eyes hurt and would he flee, turning away to those things that he is able to make out and hold them to be really clearer than what is being shown?"

"So he would," he said.

"And if," I said, "someone dragged him away from there by force along the rough, steep, upward way and didn't let him go before he had dragged him out into the light of the sun, wouldn't he be distressed and annoyed at being so dragged? And when he came to the light, wouldn't he have his eyes full of its beam and be unable to see even one of the things now said to be true?"

"No, he wouldn't," he said, "at least not right away."

"Then I suppose he'd have to get accustomed, if he were

going to see what's up above. At first he'd most easily make out the shadows; and after that the phantoms of the human beings and the other things in water; and, later, the things themselves. And from there he could turn to beholding the things in heaven and heaven itself, more easily at night—looking at the light of the stars and the moon—than by day—looking at the sun and sunlight."

"Of course."

"Then finally I suppose he would be able to make out the sun—not its appearances in water or some alien place, but the sun itself by itself in its own region—and see what it's like."

"Necessarily," he said.

"And after that he would already be in a position to conclude about it that this is the source of the seasons and the years, and is the steward of all things in the visible place, and is in a certain way the cause of all those things he and his companions had been seeing."

"Its plain," he said, "that this would be his next step."

"What then? When he recalled his first home and the wisdom there, and his fellow prisoners in that time, don't you suppose he would consider himself happy for the change and pity the others?"

"Quite so."

"And if in that time there were among them any honors, praises, and prizes for the man who is sharpest at making out the things that go by, and most remembers which of them are accustomed to pass before, which after, and which at the same time as others, and who is thereby most able to divine what is going to come, in your opinion would he be desirous of them and envy those who are honored and hold power among these men? Or, rather, would he be affected as Homer says and want very much 'to be on the soil, a serf to another man, to a portionless man," and to undergo anything whatsoever rather than to opine those things and live that way?"

"Yes," he said, "I suppose he would prefer to undergo everything rather than live that way."

"Now reflect on this too," I said. "If such a man were to come down again and sit in the same seat, on coming suddenly from the sun wouldn't his eyes get infected with darkness?"

"Very much so," he said.

"And if he once more had to compete with those perpetual prisoners in forming judgments about those shadows while his vision was still dim, before his eyes had recovered, and if the time needed for getting accustomed were not at all short, wouldn't he be the source of laughter, and wouldn't it be said of him that he went up and came back with his eyes corrupted, and that it's not even worth trying to go up? And if they were somehow able to get their hands on and kill the man who attempts to release and lead up, wouldn't they kill him?"

"No doubt about it," he said.

"Well, then, my dear Glaucon," I said, "this image as a whole must be connected with what was said before. Liken the domain revealed through sight to the prison home, and the light of the fire in it to the sun's power; and, in applying the going up and the seeing of what's above to the soul's journey up to the intelligible place, you'll not mistake my expectation, since you desire to hear it. A god doubtless knows if it happens to be true. At all events, this is the way the phenomena look to me: in the knowable the last thing to be seen, and that with considerable effort, is the idea of the good; but once seen, it must be concluded that this is in fact the cause of all that is right and fair in everything—in the visible it gave birth to light and its sovereign; in the intelligible, itself sovereign, it provided truth and intelligence—and that the man who is going to act prudently in private or in public must see it."

> "I, too, join you in supposing that," he said, "at least in the way I can."[89]

The emblematic "Allegory of the Cave" exceeds the mere epistemological realm, connecting closely with the vast domain of symbolic thought. This story, saturated with allegories, stands as a significant philosophical tool that reveals the essence of the human being when submerged in ignorance and restricted perception. Its rich symbolism extends beyond elementary cognition, showing how the *Homo sapiens* has the capacity to surpass sensory limits and carve a path toward a sharper interpretation of the cosmos. Therefore, it invades the domain of symbolism, underscoring human skill in unveiling mysteries and ascending beyond the merely apparent.

With a sharp pen and narrative mastery, Plato guides us through a symbolic universe that challenges us to think carefully. Albert Camus argues that "Myths are made for the imagination to breathe life into them."[90] He suggests that myths must be thought, not believed since they awaken the mind, but they do not dominate it. The myth itself presents a cave in which human beings are chained to the wall, restricted in their limbs and necks, so their vision is limited to the dark wall of the cave. In the complexity of this situation, the prisoners have no direct access to the truth. They perceive only the shadows projected on the wall, a product of the light coming from a fire placed behind them. These shadows, deceptive illusions, become their only perception of the world. Incorrectly believing that they constitute reality, the shadows are illusionary, or *māyā*. They create a fictitious reality where there is only a stage set, or as Schopenhauer said, "a world that is the representation of a will."

At the same time, there are other figures in the cave, such as human beings carrying objects and making comments. When illuminated by the fire, these objects cast shadows on the wall. Upon observing these constantly moving shadows, the prisoners attribute

89. Plato, *The Republic*, Book VII, 514a–517d, trans. Allan Bloom, 2nd ed. (New York: Basic Books, 1968), 176–179.

90. Albert Camus, The Myth of Sisyphus and Other Essays, trans. Justin O'Brien (New York: Alfred A. Knopf, 1955), 89.

an autonomous existence to the objects and give them voices that communicate with each other.

In their captivity, the prisoners become mere spectators, passively contemplating the shadows that repeatedly unfold before them as a fictional spectacle. This leads them to believe that the shadows constitute the totality of reality, that is, the truth. This deception is perpetuated due to the lack of a broader perspective, a vision that would allow them to detach themselves from the sensory prison and discover the authentic reality.

Plato immerses us in the desolate landscape of the cave but also presents an exit from this prison of ignorance. Through the ascending route, one of the chained individuals is freed and embarks on a difficult journey to the realm outside their confinement, toward the brilliance of sunlight. This journey symbolizes a metamorphosis both in spatial and cognitive terms, suggesting the movement from a state of limitation to one of expansion and understanding. Or, in other words:

असतो मा सद्गमय ।
तमसो मा ज्योतिर्गमय ।
मृत्योर्माऽमृतं गमय ॥
ॐ शान्तिः शान्तिः शान्तिः ॥

oṁ asato mā sad gamaya
tamaso mā jyotir gamaya
mṛtyor mā amṛtaṁ gamaya
oṁ śāntiḥ śāntiḥ śāntiḥ

Lead me from the unreal to the real,
Lead me from darkness to light,
Lead me from death to immortality.
Oṁ, peace, peace, peace.

(*Bṛhad-āraṇyaka Upanishad*, 1.3.28)

This emblematic journey corresponds to the search for Truth and the acquisition of knowledge that surpasses the limitations of the cave. Truth is not something we possess, but something we move towards Truth is like an engine driving our upward journey because every search for truth is an ascending journey. Truth generates attraction toward itself, but since it implies difficulty, it simultaneously grants the means to overcome it. The transition of the captive from the shadow toward the sunlight involves an awakening that brings him closer to reality in its essence. It is crucial to focus on this milestone, for here lies the crux of the journey: the metamorphosis from ignorance to understanding. This passage from captivity to freedom implies a radical change of perspective. It is interesting to highlight that, paradoxically, the liberation from the chains does not bring immediate peace but marks the beginning of a series of challenges and difficulties. The act of freeing oneself from these chains involves a break with the comfort of ignorance, a departure from the familiarity experienced in the dim light of the cave. Very often, what is known is no longer hostile to us, whereas it is the unknown that can liberate us. Or, as Holderlin said "Most kind is; but no one by himself can grasp God. But where danger threatens That which saves from it also grows."[91]

The emancipation from these bindings places the human being in the urgent need to rise and begin walking. This symbolic action evokes the command that Jesus gave to Lazarus to rise and leave the tomb, thus marking a process of resurrection and rebirth: "Rise, take up your bed and walk" (John, 5:8). Similarly, when shedding the bonds of ignorance, the individual begins a process of search and transformation that symbolically leads to authentic and full life.

However, this transition is not a bed of roses. As we rise to seek the Truth, we encounter obstacles and challenges that demand the strength of our character. The encounter with the sunlight, which represents Truth and absolute knowledge, can be disorienting for those who have been immersed in darkness. Acclimating to this renewed reality is not a simple task; on the contrary, it requires

91. Friedrich Hölderlin, *Poems and Fragments*, trans. Michael Hamburger (Ann Arbor: University of Michigan Press, 1980), Poem: Patmos, 479.

continuous introspection and a reevaluation of our convictions. It is imperative that the person, once liberated from their bonds, scrutinizes everything they held as true, thus challenging the mental structures that previously confined them. In this context, the breaking of the chains announces the beginning of an unceasing path of learning and discovery. The person ventures into an unknown realm where doubt and ambiguity become constant companions. However, it is exactly in this process of confronting and overcoming barriers that the possibility of personal growth and expansion of consciousness emerges. This shedding of chains becomes an invitation to exploration and transcendence. The person embarks on a journey of self-exploration, gradually freeing themselves from the limitations imposed by the cave to immerse themselves in a universe of endless possibilities.

After reading and analyzing this myth, we can affirm that there is a similarity to our own situation. For if we were not liberated, we would never have approached this book. The mere act of acquiring such a text is, in itself, an irrefutable testimony that we have emancipated ourselves. Consequently, we notice that, upon freeing ourselves from the chains, the real and difficult problems to face emerge. At the moment of emancipation, the individual turns around the wall and perceives that those dark projections were nothing but mere deceptive appearances. In that moment, the person undergoing liberation understands that the shadows on the wall bear a striking resemblance to the objects the subjects carry, as they are simply projections on the wall created by the presence of the fire. The objects, illuminated by the flames, obstruct the passage of light. Understanding this phenomenon reveals the very nature of illusion and the deceptive appearance surrounding us. The shadow, far from being a concrete entity, is the manifestation of the deprivation of light, the lack of a luminous and real being. Instead of constituting an entity in itself, the shadow is the antithesis of the luminous fullness located behind the wall.

This perspective invites reflection on the notion of reality, intrinsically linked to presence and absence. What we interpret as tangible reality on the wall is not an active generation. It is the absence of light that hinders the genuine manifestation of what is real. The figures appearing on the wall are the result of an obstacle that prevents the path of light, distorting our perception. In the plot of existence, we find an intricate interplay between presence and absence, clarity and obstruction. The shadow unmasks the negative dimension of reality, arising from the interaction between light and matter. This interaction reveals the duality between light and darkness, between presence and absence. The eminent figures in wisdom from multiple traditions have called us to overcome illusion, known as *māyā* in Sanskrit, which resides in the shadows, and encourage us to direct our focus toward the preeminent light, the origin, and matrix of all manifestations. Beyond the deceptive projections lies the consummated Truth, which unveils the unity and completeness residing in the essence of the universe. By identifying the fallacious nature of the shadows and their association with the lack of light, we cultivate in ourselves the willingness to appreciate reality in its purest and most sublime form.

The East has asserted for millennia that God does not create the universe through the creation of an otherness with the purpose of acting. Both Advaita Vedanta and Buddhism reject the creationist notion as it is understood in Western theologies. The existence of the world resides as the very shadow of the immaculate radiance, which is *māyā*. From the light of divinity, the reality of the world arises naturally and spontaneously as its shadow. Although the shadow lacks substantial reality, it persists in being; although it lacks genuine existence, **it is**, walking when we walk, advancing when we advance, stopping when we stop, following us wherever we go, always in rhythm with our movement. Just as nothing can exist without its shadow, so too does absolute reality, or consciousness, conceive its shadow. Therefore, the reality we perceive as the world is nothing but the shadow of absolute reality.

According to this ancient conception, an intricate relationship between the manifest and its reflection in illusion is established. The shadow is not simply the absence of light; rather, it is a manifestation projected by the primal reality. It is the obvious and inevitable result of the presence of an entity. Just as a person stands in their splendor, their shadow emerges spontaneously. In this way, the phenomenal world that surrounds us, with its multiplicity of forms and appearances, stands as an emanation of the cosmic shadow. In this context, *māyā* is understood as a cosmic illusion that generates an apparent reality. Like a mysterious and transcendental game, illusion offers a diverse, multiple, and complex experience. However, it is important to emphasize that this illusion lacks substantial reality and, instead, is a veil that obscures the true nature of being. It is a deceptive reflection that captivates us in its web of appearances and illusory perceptions. The shadow of Brahman materializes as *māyā*, an antithetical entity.

On the human scale, the shadow of *māyā* is individual ignorance. Ignorance is our small portion of *māyā* assigned, our personal illusion. The unfathomable *māyā* consists of a source of misery and anguish, and for this reason, we yearn to abolish it. Ignorance surrounds us and coexists with the human condition. If even Supreme Existence cannot rid itself of illusion, it is absurd for human beings to attempt to free themselves from it. If ignorance is intrinsic to the universe, where opposites are inexorably present, and it is impossible for Brahman to free itself from *māyā*, then all human effort is meaningless. The eradication of ignorance requires the will to dissolve into nothingness. Persisting in being prevents its disappearance and perpetuates duality. Both ignorance and being subsist or dissolve together. The latter will persist as a shadow by affirming the desire to persist and longing for the destruction of ignorance. It is analogous to the unattainable desire to want to remain while one's own shadow disappears. There is no way possible for us, being, to free ourselves from our shadow. The only path lies in self-dissolution so that the shadow fades away, which is why I emphasize the dissolution of the ego. It is in the dissolution of the egoic entity into Brahman that ignorance fades in *māyā*. Because in every creation, ontic reality arises from Brahman, while ignorance arises from *māyā*. As I dissolve, my shadow dissolves and I converge in union with Brahman, not as an "I" but as emptiness.

The work of Jung, the psychologist referred to earlier, covered an extensive and profound study of this reality from a singular perspective, revealing that at the deepest level of every human being lies an existence in the shadows, a veiled personality. This idea, deeply rooted in the matrix of the human psyche, prompts an absorbing examination of the veiled layers of our identity and the impact they have on our individual and collective experiences. In his effort to decipher the intricacies of the human psyche, Jung explored the vast realm of shadows, a domain where the hidden traits of our character dwell. He detected that these shadowy entities emerge as a product of everything that is obstructed or denied. These are neglected fragments, suppressed desires, and silenced fears. However, these entities possess a potency that yearns to express itself. They are like seeds waiting for germination. Under certain circumstances, when our barriers give way, these shadowy entities rise from the depths and demand prominence.

The phenomenology of these shadowy personalities takes on various manifestations in daily life. One example that stands out in psychological literature is the so-called "dissociative identity disorder," a pathological condition that has captured the attention and scrutiny of many in the field of psychology. In extreme scenarios, the individual becomes immersed in a state of fragmentation of their identity that culminates in the manifestation of independent personalities living within the same human entity. In such circumstances, there is a lack of coherence and coordination in the individual's thoughts, emotions, and actions, revealing the presence and influence of these shadowy personalities. However, we all harbor dark and unknown aspects of ourselves that may manifest in more subtle forms in our daily lives. It may be the sudden emergence of anger in response to a seemingly trivial situation, the expression of a repressed desire in a moment of vulnerability, or the emergence of contradictory and bewildering behavioral patterns. These manifestations can leave the individual perplexed, questioning their own integrity and the coherence of their identity. When they manifest, the shadowy personalities compel us to confront the intricate nature inherent in our being and encourage us to delve into the winding labyrinth of our minds.

In the Allegory of the Cave, the captive, at some point, perceives the possibility of emancipating themselves from the cave's bonds and prepares to delve into deeper realms of scholarship. Their awakening occurs when they realize that the fire in the cave is not the supreme source of light but that a more powerful, transcendental, and ultimate light exists: the Sun. In this discovery, the prisoner glimpses the existence of two sources of light: the internal one, represented by the fire in the cave, and the external one, personified by the radiant solar presence. The importance of the first source of light, the fire within the cave, lies in its ability to reveal the functioning of the illusion of the shadows on the wall. Through this light, the prisoner understands how the projected shadows deceive their senses and distort their perception of reality. The fire's light, therefore, becomes their initial guide, indicating the path to emancipate from the cave and transcend the limitations imposed by the shadows. However, the prisoner's liberation process is not free from difficulties. With determination and meticulousness, Plato emphasizes that the prisoner faces numerous obstacles in adjusting to the sunlight. The sudden exposure to a completely different, dazzling, and unfamiliar reality is overwhelming for the prisoner, who is unaccustomed to the intensity and clarity of the sun. This transition from darkness to light demands a great effort of adaptation and a profound transformation in the perception and understanding of the world; it is precisely this that Heidegger calls care or cure, using the German word *Sorge*, meaning "to care for" and "to watch over," referring to the care of things and the care for others. Furthermore, it means "worry, concern, and alarm;" in the broader sense, it is a vigil for "oneself," to assume destiny as an existential interest. As we read in the Allegory of the Cave:

> No, he wouldn't," he said, "at least not right away." "Then I suppose he'd have to get accustomed, if he were going to see what's up above. At first he'd most easily make out the shadows; and after that the phantoms of the human beings and the other things in water; and, later, the things themselves. And from there he could turn to beholding the

> things in heaven and heaven itself, more easily at night—looking at the light of the stars and the moon—than by day—looking at the sun and sunlight.[92]

In the beginning of their adaptive process, people would prostrate before the shadows, only to then plunge into the reality reverberating upon the watery mirror. They would keep their gaze absorbed in those reflections until reaching a degree of familiarity that would allow them to raise their eyes toward the stars, the moon—whose luminosity is but an echo of the sun—and, finally, toward the solar light itself. For those who have languished in twilight, light is not a beacon of clarity; it does not unveil but rather dazzles and blinds.

However, the story does not end here, in the cognitive domain, but also inevitably brings forth the realm of morals and ethics. After the arduous journey from darkness to light, it is imperative not to fix the gaze on the self but to extend consideration toward others in their entirety. This process evokes the *bodhisattva*'s vow in the Buddhist tradition, a testament to the *bodhisattva*'s commitment to enlightenment, but not for his own well-being, instead for the benefit of all sentient beings, at the risk that, upon returning, the one who is no longer a prisoner of the cave may be attacked, as the allegory itself reveals:

> Wouldn't it be said of him that he went up and came back with his eyes corrupted, and that it's not even worth trying to go up? And if they were somehow able to get their hands on and kill the man who attempts to release and lead up, wouldn't they kill him?"
> "No doubt about it," he said.[93]

92. Plato, *The Republic*, Book VII, 514a–517d, trans. Allan Bloom, 2nd ed. (New York: Basic Books, 1968), 176–179.
93. Ibid.

This fragment evokes the beautiful prayer of this *śanti-mantra*:

ॐ सह नाववतु ।
सह नौ भुनक्तु ।
सह वीर्यं करवावहै ।
तेजस्विनावधीतमस्तु मा विद्विषावहै ।
ॐ शान्तिः शान्तिः शान्तिः ॥

oṁ saha nāvavatu
saha nau bhunaktu
saha vīryaṁ karavāvahai
tejasvināvadhītamastu
mā vidviṣāvahai
oṁ śāntiḥ śāntiḥ śāntiḥ

May we (master and students) be protected
May we be nurtured
May we work together with energy and vigor.
May our study be enlightening
May there be no animosity between us.
Oṁ, peace, peace, peace.
(*Śānti-mantra* of *Taittirīyopanishad*, *Kaṭhopanishad*, and *Śvetaśvataropanishad*)

In it, we precisely find a very strange prayer that also refers to the issue of animosity: "Let there be no animosity between us" (*mā vidviṣāvahai*). The acceptance of the potential belligerence between disciple and master represents an intrinsic challenge to the sacred *guru-śisya*, or "master-disciple," relationship. This dilemma arises when the master takes on the task of assisting the disciple in their retroprogressive pilgrimage of metamorphosis and decides to intervene actively in the disciple's journey toward transformation. At the moment when the master asks disciples to renounce their precious egoic toys, an emotional cyclone is triggered in their psyche. These objects are the most treasured jewels of the learner, imbued with an unfathomable emotional and psychological value. They represent the guardians of their dreams, fantasies, and illusions, the most intimate and valuable fragments of their being. From the egoic perspective, the disciple comes to see the master as a genuine enemy, a being conspiring to strip them of their identity and immerse them in the vortex of total annihilation.

In this situation, the transformation process becomes a challenge for both figures involved. Masters, imbued with wisdom and compassion, dedicate themselves to the mission of assisting the disciple in transcending their egoic attachments and awakening to a greater reality. However, from the limited perspective of the disciple, this invitation to detach from their most valuable possessions may be perceived as an act of psychic violence. Resistance and rejection emerge as defensive reactions of the wounded ego, which feels threatened in its own existence.

This process of metamorphosis, with its intrinsic complexity, charts a path full of challenges. As the master delves deeper into guiding the disciple, the possibility of conflicts and hostilities increases, awakening a deep dissatisfaction and animosity in the disciple toward the master due to the proposed renunciation of their egoic attachments. From their wise perspective, the master understands that removing these attachments is an essential step for the disciple's spiritual evolution, but the disciple's ego may reject this perspective.

It is important to highlight that this dynamic of conflict does not arise inevitably or intrinsically in the master-disciple relationship. Instead, it is an indirect consequence of the master's commitment to the disciple's transformation. In the nobility inherent in their guiding function, the master does not shy away from the possibility of being misunderstood or encountering resistance. This sacrifice, far from being an obstacle, forms part of the core of their vocation. The cardinal purpose of the master is to assist the disciple in their emancipation from the restrictions imposed by the ego and to pave the way for an existence in which a greater consciousness and fulfillment prevail.

Even the illustrious Plato faced this dilemma explicitly and directly. The freed prisoner who returns to the cave to describe reality to the remaining slave companions risks being considered insane. That is why we say that it is with the master but without the master; it is with the father but without the father. If the master is an opportunity, they must die; if they do not, they become the master, and the disciple becomes the slave. Only by symbolically killing the master can the disciple immortalize them, as was already hinted at in the First Letter of Paul to the Corinthians in the New Testament, where it says:

> For the word of the cross is to those who are perishing foolishness; but to us who are being saved, it is the power of God.
>
> (1 Corinthians, 1:18)

Plato's allegory of the cave provides a harrowing vision of the human condition and the potentially lethal consequences of challenging the cognitive *status quo*. In it, Plato introduces the notion that wisdom and enlightenment are not always welcomed by those who remain in ignorance. The remaining prisoners, still chained to their illusory perceptions, violently resist the claims of the one who has seen reality. Their knowledge, which challenges the established reality, is seen as a threat to the comfort of their ignorance. In a surprising twist, Plato suggests that overwhelmed by terror and confusion, the prisoners, trapped in their ignorant state, might conspire and, in effect, eliminate the freed prisoner if circumstances allowed. Within the framework of the allegory proposed by Plato, this cunningly highlights the bitter irony of enlightenment: those who have reached the heights of erudition are often met with disdain, ridicule, and, in some cases, the threat of death from those whose limitations they attempt to eradicate. Through the lens of this allegory, one can identify a veiled yet sharp critique of Athenian society and its treatment of Socrates, Plato's revered guide, who was sentenced to death under accusations of corrupting the youth and disrespecting Athenian deities.

However, when observed from a broader perspective, the allegory of the cave sheds light on human resistance to modification and examination of deeply rooted concepts. This resistance can reach such severe levels that those who venture to challenge the conventional may be doomed to a fatal fate, both literally and allegorically. What lies before us unfolds as a metaphor filled with symbolism. Symbols manifest as the shadows projected onto the wall of the cave by the chained beings. These shadows are nothing more than the spectral manifestations resulting from the artifacts presented by a group of individuals before the flicker of a flame. It is worth noting that the artifacts are not innate to the cave but have been introduced from an external space. Thus, the path to follow involves a diligent and methodical pursuit of the visions, which become increasingly authentic and tangible, leading to luminosity as the primordial principle and undeniable origin of all that exists.

In this framework, a symbol is conceived as an entity that can take the form of a word, a story, an image, or a sensory representation, such as those we perceive daily. Its essential function lies in its ability to establish a connection with an alternate reality. The charm of symbolic language lies in its capacity to operate as a link between the sensory and immaterial domains, merging spheres and bringing to light deeper truths that are hidden behind the facade of external reality.

Siddhartha Gautama, the young prince who would transcend to become known as the Buddha, defied his father's attempts to protect him from the ravages of disease, aging, and suffering. Despite his father's efforts to keep his aristocratic purity intact, the future Sakya Muni chose to relinquish the palace comforts and venture into the reality of those who were his subjects. During this inaugural journey, he encountered an elderly man. His charioteer, Channa, explained to him that aging was a universal human condition, a revelation that urged Gautama to continue his explorations beyond the palace walls. In his subsequent travels, Gautama came across a sick man, a decaying corpse, and an ascetic. These "four encounters" profoundly shook Siddhartha Gautama's psyche, prompting him to commit himself to the metaphysical conquest of aging, disease, and death through ascetic life. This narrative seems to be an adaptation of the older story found in the *Digha Nikaya* (DN 14.2), where the youth of a previous Buddha, Vipassi, is portrayed. Accompanied by his faithful charioteer and riding his horse Kantaka, Gautama decided to renounce his life as a member of royalty to embark on the search for the Truth. It is said that, in order to prevent the palace guards from detecting his departure, the gods muffled the sound of the horse's hooves.

The four symbolic encounters experienced by the young Buddha—a man of advanced age, a sick person, a corpse, and a renunciant—represent more than mere interactions with individuals. When Buddha first encountered the elderly man, he did not simply see an old person but a mirror of his own inevitable fate: aging. Upon encountering a sick person, he glimpsed his own susceptibility to disease. Before a corpse, Buddha did not merely see a deceased person but his own mortality. Finally, through a symbolic perspective, he arrived at a broader truth, a realization of the misery inherent in human existence. Buddha interpreted aging, illness, and death as the inexorable fate, not only of himself but of all human beings. In this symbolic vision, the individuals he encountered became bridges to greater realities.

At its innermost core, a symbol stands as a kind of gate. It leads us to a wealth of information intrinsically related to the different spheres in which our existence manifests. Additionally, symbols embrace elements whose magnitude exceeds superficial dressings, articulating concepts that slip into the most profound reaches of the human intellect, leaving behind the realm of simple metaphor. The final order of existence, metaphorically represented by the sun in the philosophical domain, is entirely metaphysical and ineffable. Its intrinsic nature defies verbal or conceptual explanation. This plane belongs to the experience of a transcendental order, a domain that escapes the constraints of description and definition, of adjective and verb, situated in a space that is simultaneously unfathomable and ineffable, resistant to the inherent limitations of human language.

Plato has shown us with this myth, among other things, that a symbol establishes a connection with the transcendental sphere, generating a multiplicity of interpretations that extend to infinity, as it would be impossible to apprehend it in its entirety. The apprehension of the symbol is not merely limited to its study and assimilation but involves an intimate coexistence or symbiosis with its essence, in which the very symbol becomes a constant companion. In that relationship, the symbol is constantly actualized, reviving physical, emotional, mental, and spiritual information. The apprehension of the symbol does not respond to a mere subject-object structure in which the first absorbs and devours the second but rather involves coexistence, a Heideggerian cure, which opens the door to symbolic thought beyond the darkness imposed by logical-conceptual thinking.

In Plato's Allegory of the Cave, we encounter a story that simultaneously serves as a metaphor for his epistemological thought and as an allegory addressing symbolic thought, among other profound themes. What makes this myth so special? To begin with, it is fertile ground for an endless array of interpretations. Each interpretation, like a rough diamond, unveils unique facets of its semantics. It offers us a valuable treasure of limitless exegesis, contributing to a richer and more nuanced appreciation of the elusive and heterogeneous nature of reality. Finally, after transcending the limits of perception and experiencing the sublimity of light, the moment of reversal is established. To return, metaphorically evoking the reunion with the primordial essence, with the initial dwelling, becomes indispensable, for without a proper synchronization of our inner cosmos with the radiant reality in which we find ourselves immersed, all attempts will be in vain.

We have resided for extended periods in the twilight, confusing simple sensory perception with authentic reality. Our neurobiological system, our encephalic core, each microscopic unit of our being, has almost reflexively grown accustomed to this distorted interpretation of the world. After the revelation of light, it is imperative to undergo a process of realignment, adjusting all the hidden facets of our existence to fit the newly discovered reality to which we have awakened. In the deepest and darkest recesses of our being, each of us harbors different aspects of our own identity, encapsulated fragments that still react to shadows as if they were tangible manifestations of the real. The act of returning to the gloomy spaces within to liberate these enslaved facets becomes indispensable, as it is intrinsically linked to our total adaptation to the reality that emerges after awakening.

The sign constitutes a transcendental encapsulated artery, a microcosm of liberation. Each symbolic figure, whether a cross, the Star of David, the crescent moon, or the mystical *Oṁ*, projects mere shadowy murals. In a state of servitude or captivity, the shadows would remain as such. However, it is possible to shed the bonds and relegate the fascination with the shadows, orienting ourselves toward *die kehre*, or "the Heideggerian turn." He who directs his gaze toward the very origin of these shadowy projections is engulfed in a profound revelation upon realizing that, despite his capacity for vision, he has been looking in the wrong direction. Only by understanding the causes that have impressed these shadows on the wall will he discern that the sign transcends the mere wall shadow, referring to an artifact. But even after awakening, these signs will persist as specters representing the path previously traveled.

Unfortunately, a significant multitude remains entrenched and exalted in the veneration of trinkets and artifacts through successive existences. Numerous individuals transfer their infatuation with the shadows to the artifacts and subsequently to the flame. The perception that the shadow is linked to a substantial object constitutes one of the crucial steps in the symbolic experience. The journey toward awakening continues when we gather our preconceptions and, from the twilight, focus our cognition on the artifacts. The transit from the symbol to the symbolized leads us to the inevitable inspection of the artifact, questioning its provenance and genesis. It is only at this crossroads that we distinguish between a candle and the sun. The candle, a human product, is light manifested by an individual who, in some way, has embarked on the task of illuminating the interior of a dark cave. Indeed, there is nothing harmful in the cave, in the shadows, in the artifacts, or in the glow of the fire; what is truly harmful is remaining in captivity, considering the shadows as unquestionable truths and the symbols as the authentic reality. The harm lies in our interpretations, which result from our limitations.

However, what extends from the chains to ascend from the deepest to the highest, from the darkness to the light, is entirely beneficial as part of the transcendent path. Therefore, even the small candle deserves our respect and veneration. For if, at first, we conceive that the shadows on the wall are there because of the artifacts, we later realize it is thanks to the fire. The glow, in its representation, is that primordial luminosity carried by deeply inspired human entities who have been a metaphor for the light itself. The fiery element stands as the banner of the great initiates, prophets, and mentors who, from their intrinsic humanity, spread clarity to illuminate certain aspects of reality, transforming it into shadowy allegories.

Nevertheless, we must not root ourselves in the fire, for the enlightened one is a tiny flame but not the conclusion of the path. True masters are those who, upon witnessing how the captives break free from their chains and pivot toward them, emphatically declares that they are not the end and urge them to continue in pursuit of what transcends them. The master will always argue that he has only taken a glimpse of the arcane fire of the gods, just as the legend of Prometheus tells us, the Greek myth that narrates how this titan stole the fire from the gods to give it to humanity. Here, we certainly refer to the fire of the spirit. Once the human who is capable of illuminating the cave is transcended, the captive may embark on his journey toward the indescribable realization of the sunlight.

Therefore, the symbols rise as shadowy blessings filled with hidden meanings. These shadows whisper to us the reality of our servitude, inviting us to inquire about their origin. Simultaneously, they act as an invitation to decipher the murmurs of those entities who, behind us, manipulate the artifacts. Despite their invisibility, these figures offer crucial guidance and information. If the daring to know what is authentically real awakens, we will strive to reveal the source of these shadows. The *kehre* will place us before the artifacts that the Lord of the Fire has arranged to allow us to contemplate the shadow. Finally, after offering our respectful reverence to the Lord of the Fire, we embark on our journey directly out of the cave toward the light.

In the retroevolutionary process of self-knowledge, the path leading to the light is intricate but essential. It is through symbolic thought, that innate and complex ability of our cognition, that we can reunite with the internal solar light. However, it is not enough to approach symbols only from an intellectual perspective. Symbols, in their essence, resist being reduced to mere concepts and, therefore, require a deeper interpretation, a discernment that goes beyond mere cognition and delves into the depths of feeling and being. Dictionaries of symbols, as well as various theologies, offer different murmurs from those who handle the artifacts, explaining what each shadow means. They constitute echoes of the shadows, mere approximations that, while useful, do not capture the totality of what symbols represent.

Unfortunately, many are content with these murmurs as explanations of the symbolic. They are satisfied with superficial interpretation without diving into the deep waters of symbolism, where truth is revealed not to the mind but to the soul. They accept the projected shadows as reality, unaware that these are mere silhouettes of a more complex, richer, and, above all, more enlightening reality. Thus, it is warned in the Allegory:

> "Necessarily."
> "And what if the prison also had an echo from the side facing them? Whenever one of the men passing by happens to utter a sound, do you suppose they would believe that anything other than the passing shadow was uttering the sound?"
> "No, by Zeus," he said. "I don't."[94]

The comments mentioned constitute an invitation extended to the slaves for a conceptualization of the shadows or symbols. A scenario is established in which words and concepts usurp the place of direct existential experiences of the transcendent, a dislocation of the truth that resides in direct experience and not in abstraction. For many, this discourse gives them a sense of knowing, a false security that allows them to remain at ease in their place, firmly believing that they have accessed the truth about the artifacts and the sun. They make the mistake of confusing knowledge and information with wisdom,

94. Ibid.

failing to realize that true wisdom transcends mere accumulation of data and enters the realm of direct and existential experience. The slave, who is bound or chained, justifies his immobility because, limited by his shackles, he has no alternatives; he does not feel captive. But if one is free, if one has broken the chains, then he must be utterly obtuse to remain there, sitting, satisfied with those explanations about those shadows. Let us not fall into the delusion of confusing the echo with the voice, the representation with the represented, or the map with the territory.

From all that has been said so far regarding the myths, it follows that there are two types of myths: those that facilitate our integration into the whole and those that strengthen our egoic personality. If the first are the myths that merge us into the unity of being, those of the second type are the ones that reinforce our individuality and fragment us. This is why Plato argues that it is essential to choose wisely the myths we transmit to the youth. The myths we choose to instill in young minds have a profound impact, shaping the way individuals interact with the world and understand their place within it.

The exegesis of the symbolic myth, or what we might alternatively call the hermeneutics of the sign, is in fact an allegorical interpretation of any spiritual path. This process stands as a vademecum for the champions in the search for our intrinsic genuineness, a compass for those aspiring to the great epiphany of consciousness. It is a metaphysical cartogram that points to the path of return to that timeless space, a sort of essential Ithaca, a *locus amoenus* that we have never truly abandoned despite the apparent existential paradoxes. Therefore, it materializes as an intricate map of ontological coordinates that guides us back to what we have always been, but which it seemed we had relegated to the shadows of forgetfulness in the enigma of our temporality. It is an enigmatic and sublime map that points the way back to the primordial space that we have never truly vacated in the grand theater of existence.

Chapter 23

Symbols, myths, and self-consciousness: Ricoeur's approach

One of the authors who has most effectively addressed the issue of myth and symbol within Western philosophy is Paul Ricoeur, a French philosopher born in 1913 and passed away in 2005, whose work left an indelible mark on 20th-century thought.

From the perspective of Western philosophy and Christianity, Ricoeur addresses the theme of symbolic thought and self-knowledge of that deeper self that languishes in the shadows through the issue of confession, a phenomenon he unravels through an analysis of language, particularly symbolic language. As his work clearly demonstrates, any philosophical perspective that aims to integrate confession into the understanding of self-perception must construct an interpretive paradigm that allows for the decoding of symbols, even if in rudimentary terms. As Paul Ricoeur states: "I wager that shall have a better understanding of man and of the bond between the being of man and the being of all beings if I follow the indication of symbolic thought."[95]

In this regard, Ricoeur posits that it is impossible to fully grasp the reflective and introspective use of symbolism without referring to its most fundamental forms. In this stratum, self-consciousness, typically in a privileged position, is eclipsed by the cosmic magnitude of the sacred. In every authentic symbol, we observe the fusion of three domains: the cosmic, the dreamlike, and the poetic. Only

95. Paul Ricœur, *The Symbolism of Evil*, trans. Emerson Buchanan (Boston: Beacon Press, 1967), 355.

within the context of these three functionalities of the symbol can we discern its fullness and richness.

On the one hand, Ricoeur links the concepts of confession and self-consciousness to the essential problem of evil, a dichotomy he understands as an ambivalent manifestation in human beings. This duality has the potential to make the individual perceive themselves both as guilty and as a victim, generating a fracture in their being. This dichotomy suggests that evil has two faces: a passive one, representing the suffering one experiences, which we call "pain," and an active one reflecting the harm one can inflict, which we call "guilt," the case presented to us in the Scriptures through Adam and Eve, who stand as both actors and affected by evil. Evil, when interpreted as guilt, drags us into past memories, while that related to pain and fear projects us toward the unknown of the future. Thus, guilt anchors us to the shadows of what was, and anguish confronts us with the inevitable abyss of what is to come, symbolized by death. The notions of guilt and pain are determinant in the internal fragmentation of the human being. The issue of evil plays a fundamental role in generating an urgent need to strip ourselves of traumatic episodes like guilt and pain. It is in this endeavor to overcome these tragedies that man plunges into religion, seeking relief and forgetfulness. As Marx himself argued, religion is nothing but the "opium" that serves as a means to mitigate pain.

The greatest evil this individual faces is the inescapable death, a constant that, by nature, tends to be evaded. This is why, as Heidegger suggested, human beings are a *Sein Zum Tode*, or "being-toward-death," something that humans try imperiously to forget, alienating themselves from themselves and devoting their time to dwell in culture. This awareness of finitude is often marginalized by human beings, who, immersed in the cultural and social maelstrom, seek to avoid reflecting on their finitude. In this process of distraction, through which daily life is filled—from art to daily labor—human beings get alienated, distancing from the essential truth of their finite existence. Such alienation is but a vain attempt to escape the inexorable mortal destiny that awaits us all. To escape this certainty, man immerses himself in the cultural realm, where he can temporarily overlook his finitude. It is within this context of evil and death, and of guilt and pain, that Ricoeur, as a Christian, places the symbol—in this case, of the cross—as a means of confronting and reconciling with guilt and pain. According to him, this fracture in which the human being lives can only be mended again through symbolism or, in other words, through symbolic thinking grounded in intuition, which, as such, allows the human being to reunite with themselves.

The connection between evil, guilt, and pain, on the one hand, and symbolic thought, on the other, inevitably raises the issue of the sacred. From the human perspective, this question is evident through various elements or aspects of the world we inhabit. Spoken symbolism leads us to manifestations in which the sacred makes its appearance in a fragment of the cosmos. At the same time, symbolic language acts as a guide, leading us to the discoveries of the sacred, known as hierophanies. It is within the framework of these revelations where the individual, in their search for internal cohesion, clings to restorative symbols that facilitate a reunion with themselves, such as the tree of life or mountains adorned with sanctity. These emblems give the individual a sense of divine proximity. It is vital for man to perceive this celestial alliance to appease both their internal anxieties and guilt.

Therefore, the first symbolic representations emerge linked to cosmic phenomena. The act of symbolizing these realities is equivalent to condensing into a single conglomerate various intentions laden with meaning that invite discourse. According to Paul Ricoeur, the concept "makes one think," while the symbol "makes one speak." Symbolic manifestation is the matrix of significations in the form of words. Ricoeur firmly establishes this when he argues that symbolizing these realities is similar to bringing together a large number of meaningful purposes that motivate communication in a single visible set. Before stimulating contemplation, and therefore intuition, the symbol makes one speak. From here, Paul Ricoeur asks whether the symbol precedes or even distinguishes itself from verbal language, given its cosmic connotation.

The symbolic representation, understood as a unity, operates as the substrate from which the symbolic exegeses articulated in the lexicon emerge, constituting the root of the symbolic interpretations expressed in words. The discourse on the sky and its interpretation into verbal structures never ends, as Mircea Eliade illustrates in his comparative study of phenomenology. In other words, the dialogue about the divine never concludes because the sacred is inexhaustible. Precisely, the sacred is characterized by its rejection to be encapsulated by a final definition; no one can have the last word. Whoever claims that their perspective on the symbol is conclusive is simply exhausting the richness of the symbol, or worse, conceptualizing it. Practically all traditions continue writing and commenting.

Another theme Ricoeur addresses in this context is that of sin. To understand in detail the symbolic nature of sin, it is imperative to examine the symbolism associated with the notion of impurity and contamination. According to Ricoeur, the fear of contamination is deeply rooted in our emotions, permeating our perspective and behavior concerning guilt. With this touch of guilt, we venture into the "territory of fear," and we ask ourselves: Can we truly understand and update the full connotation of this stain?

To address this matter, we will make use of the vast symbolism that encompasses this experience of guilt. It is thanks to its ability to generate symbols indefinitely that we remain closely tied to guilt and pain. We see the stain as a stage already overcome in the consciousness of individual guilt, both from an objective and subjective perspective. Ricoeur posits that when an interaction is established, this contamination possesses an intrinsic capacity for transmission and corruption, emerging as an active and dominant principle. It is imperative to recognize that our interpretations of impurity and stain should primarily focus on their symbolic dimension rather than their literal character.

Nevertheless, a primordial interpretation still suggests a preeminent value of impurity and an unfavorable perception of purity. The symbolism of sin detaches itself from the symbolism of the stain, but from the same perspective, it intersects again with the primordial intention of the symbolism of impurity. This duality grants sin a concrete dimension, attributing it with genuine existence. What we mean is that the symbol of impurity does not exist because there is sin, but rather, we speak of sin because within man resides the symbol of impurity. It is the symbol that creates the reality of guilt, not the other way around. Therefore, we must approach both the promotion of a new symbolism and the revision and reconstruction of the old one under the influence of the new paradigm.

The rupture with the symbolism of the stain and its subsequent restoration on a different plane becomes even more striking when considering the inclusion of the symbolism of redemption, for it is impossible to comprehend one without the other. According to Ricoeur, as we delve into the exploration of the symbolism of evil, it is crucial to focus our attention on the symbolism inherent in sin itself. It is imperative to consider this symbolism not in isolation but in conjunction with the conception of redemption, as the two have an antagonistic interaction. While the symbolism of sin denotes the dissolution of a relationship, the disappearance of an ontological status, that of redemption, evokes the central idea of a "reunion" or "reconciliation." As we have already seen, while the rupture is *day-bolon*, or "separation," reconciliation is *sim-bolon*, or "union."

Therefore, Ricoeur proposes to reconsider the interpretation of these symbols, revealing that, within the symbolic framework, sin is clearly distinguished from the concept of impurity. Fault, infraction, deviation, rebellion, and loss are postulated as symbols that denote a disturbed correlation.

In the collective consciousness, we create a culture where we relegate those primordial experiences and that original moment, which is guilt and suffering. Neurosis is the forgetting of tragedy, while culture consolidates this forgetfulness process. This cultural construct, inherently rooted in our being, generates discomfort, a feeling of dissolution in an anonymous mass, reflecting what Heidegger articulates as the phenomenon of the "it is said." We are immersed in this collective anonymity: we adopt the words that "are said," reflect thoughts that "are thought," dress as "it is dressed," say what "is spoken," and follow norms that "are established." Despite the dissolution of the individual in the collective, this homogenization offers a sense of belonging and an identity that provides purpose to human existence. This process of anonymization, where the individual dissolves and converges with the collective, operates as a support that, paradoxically, enables the individual to identify as an essential component of the social structure and acquire a defined identity that gives meaning to their life. In this dynamic, the symbol emerges as a mechanism by which the human being elevates and transforms their pain, as it is imbued with a redemptive connotation.

Christian doctrine suggests that through pain, the expiation of transgressions and the absolution of guilt are achieved. The human being channels this suffering through the symbol, visualizing their participation in the Christic sacrifice and assuming pain as a valuable instrument for the purification and absolution of their guilt. Therefore, suffering, far from being mere affliction, is elevated and metamorphosed through the intervention of the religious symbol. In this framework, the individual formulates a symbolic representation of evil, articulated in terms of guilt and fear, a foundational notion for Christian symbolism. Religion, from this perspective, provides a structure that enables man to navigate the turbulent waters of pain and guilt with steadfastness. For those wishing to gain a more exhaustive understanding of this phenomenon, it is imperative to turn to the emblematic work of Paul Ricoeur titled *Finitude and Guilt*.

At this point in the debate, Ricoeur himself links myth to gnosis, proposing the symbol's function as a key to understanding or a hermeneutic tool. His argument is to demonstrate how myth becomes a secondary function of primary symbols. Diving deeper, Ricoeur delves into the dialectic of discerning why a myth, in its narrative essence, carries a symbolic value rather than having a causal origin. To approach this matter, it is essential to resort to the analysis of mythical consciousness as configured by religious phenomenology, supported by theorists of the caliber of Van der Leeuw, Leenhardt, and Mircea Eliade. At first glance, this interpretation seems to dissolve the narrative myth into an indivisible consciousness that, rather than desiring to tell anecdotes, aspires to connect affectively and practically with the totality of the cosmos.

In opposition to religious phenomenologists, who attempt to trace the narrative to the pre-narrative roots of myth, Ricoeur embarks on the opposite route, following the path from pre-narrative consciousness to the mythical narrative, a transition in which precisely the mystery inherent to the symbolic function of the myth resides. From this base, the intrinsic duality of the myth is deduced: on the one hand, it is translated into words; on the other, in the myth, the symbol takes the form of a story, a narrative. In the first stage of Ricoeur's thought, the notion of the symbol plays a fundamental role, that is, the possibility of interrogating and interpreting the myth, which is given by the symbol's capacity to liberate meaning, which "makes one think."

According to religious phenomenology, the narrative myth is simply the verbal expression of an ethos or a way of life that was experienced and perceived before being articulated in its beginnings. Religious phenomenology re-evaluates the essence of myth by focusing on its underlying mythical structure, which acts as a matrix for specific figures and narratives in each mythological tradition. From this phenomenological perspective, a link is identified between this structure and the essential categories of myth, emphasizing the connection with the sacred.

Myths, in their seemingly chaotic and arbitrary nature, emerge from the dichotomy between a rich symbolism and the limited experiential capabilities of the human being, which provide us with mere allusions to the transcendental reality they attempt to portray. Therefore, we turn to narratives and rituals to delineate and honor the manifestations of the divine, such as certain sites or artifacts imbued with sanctity.

The dichotomy observed between the global architecture of the myth and its individual expressions is fundamentally a symbolic reflection of the desire to encapsulate an essence that, by nature, is both vast and whole. Since the concept of the sacred is not experienced in its pure form but is represented symbolically, it gives rise to a multiplicity of myths. In this way, the structure and specific episodes of the myth arise both from the attempt to show circumstantial representations of an inherently symbolic divine event and from the evolutionary and episodic nature of time itself.

Bibliography section III

- Aristotle. *Metaphysics*. Vol. 1. Edited and translated by W. D. Ross. Oxford: Clarendon Press, 1924. Benedict XVI. *General Audience.* Saint Peter's Square, May 6, 2009. https://www.vatican.va.
- Camus, Albert. *The Myth of Sisyphus and Other Essays.* Translated by Justin O'Brien. New York: Alfred A. Knopf, 1955.
- Catechism of the Catholic Church. *Second Edition* Vatican City: Libreria Editrice Vaticana, 1997.
- Catechism of the Catholic Church. *Second Edition, revised in accordance with the official Latin text promulgated by Pope John Paul II.* Washington, D.C.: United States Catholic Conference, 1997.
- Damascene, St. John. *On Holy Images.* Translated by Mary H. Allies. London: Thomas Baker, 1898.
- Damascene, St. John. *Apologia of St. John Damascene Against Those Who Decry Holy Images, Part 1.* Translated by F. H. Chase. New York: The Macmillan Company, 1929.
- Descartes, René. *Meditations on First Philosophy: With Selections from the Objections and Replies.* Translated by Michael Moriarty. Oxford: Oxford University Press, 2008.
- Friedrich, Wilhelm Nietzsche. *The Antichrist.* Translated by H. L. Mencken. New York: Alfred A. Knopf, 1920.
- Hölderlin, Friedrich. *Poems and Fragments.* Translated by Michael Hamburger. Ann Arbor: University of Michigan Press, 1980.
- John Paul II. *Apostolic Letter Duodecimum Saeculum to the Episcopate of the Catholic Church on the Occasion of the 1200th Anniversary of the Second Council of Nicaea.* December 4, 1987.
- Jung, C. G. *Psychological Types.* Bollingen Series XX, vol. 6. Translated by H. G. Baynes. Revised by R. F. C. Hull. Princeton: Princeton University Press, 1971.
- Kant, Immanuel. *Critique of Pure Reason.* Translated and edited by Paul Guyer and Allen W. Wood. Cambridge: Cambridge University Press, 1998.

- Pascal, Blaise. *Pensées.* Translated by W. F. Trotter. Section I: "Thoughts on Mind and on Style." 1660.
- Plato. *The Republic.* Translated by Allan Bloom. 2nd ed. New York: Basic Books, 1968.
- Ricœur, Paul. *The Symbolism of Evil.* Translated by Emerson Buchanan. Boston: Beacon Press, 1967.
- Second Council of Nicaea. "Council Fathers – 787 A.D." *Papal Encyclicals Online.* https://www.papalencyclicals.net.
- Shaw, George Bernard. *Back to Methuselah: A Metabiological Pentateuch.* London: Constable and Company, 1921.
- Wright, N. T. *Surprised by Hope: Rethinking Heaven, the Resurrection, and the Mission of the Church.* Translated edition [*Sorprendidos por la esperanza: Repensando el cielo, la resurrección y la vida eterna*]. Barcelona: Editorial CLIE, 2014.

Section IV

Symbols and the Human Being

Chapter 24

Myths: windows to the human psyche

In his famous work dedicated to Freud, Paul Ricoeur says:

> I contend that the psychoanalyst is a leading participant in any general discussion about language. To start with, psychoanalysis belongs to our time by virtue of Freud's written work; through this medium psychoanalysis addresses itself to those who are not analysts and who have not been analyzed. I am well aware that without actual practice a reading of Freud is truncated and runs the risk of embracing only a fetish. But if the textual approach to psychoanalysis has limits which practice alone can remove, still it has the advantage of focusing attention upon an entire aspect of Freud's work that may be hidden by practice or overlooked by a science whose sole concern is to account for what goes on in the analytic relationship. A meditation on Freud's work has the advantage of revealing that work's broadest aim: not only the renovation of psychiatry, but a reinterpretation of all psychical productions pertaining to culture, from dreams, through art and morality, to religion. This is how psychoanalysis belongs to modern culture. By interpreting culture it modifies it; by giving it an instrument of reflection it stamps it with a lasting mark. The fluctuation in Freud's writings between medical investigation and a theory of culture bears witness to the scope of the Freudian project. True, the major texts on culture are to be found in the last part of Freud's work. However, psychoanalysis should not be regarded as a

form of individual psychology, tardily transposed into a sociology of culture. A summary glance at the Freudian bibliography shows that the first texts on art, morality, and religion follow shortly upon The *Interpretation of Dreams* and are then developed alongside the great doctrinal texts that constitute the "*Papers on Metapsychology*" (1913–17), *Beyond the Pleasure Principle* (1920), and *The Ego and the Id* (1923). In fact, to grasp how the theory of culture is related to the theory of dreams and the neuroses, it is necessary to go back to The Interpretation of Dreams of 1900, for it is here that the connection with mythology and literature was first established. Ever since 1900 the *Traumdeutung* had proposed that dreams are the dreamer's private mythology and myths the waking dreams of peoples, that Sophocles' *Oedipus* and Shakespeare's *Hamlet* are to be interpreted in the same way as dreams. We shall see that this proposal presents a problem. Whatever the outcome of this difficulty, the entrance of psychoanalysis into the general contemporary discussion about language is not due solely to its interpretation of culture. By making dreams not only the first object of his investigation but a model (in what sense we will discuss below) of all the disguised, substitutive, and fictive expressions of human wishing or desire, Freud invites us to look to dreams themselves for the various relations between desire and language. First, it is not the dream as dreamed that can be interpreted, but rather the text of the dream account; analysis attempts to substitute for this text another text that could be called the primitive speech of desire. Thus analysis moves from one meaning to another meaning; it is not desires as such that are placed at the center of the analysis, but rather their language.[96]

96. Paul Ricœur, *Freud and Philosophy: An Essay on Interpretation*, trans. Denis Savage (New Haven: Yale University Press, 1970), 4–6.

In this chapter, without leaving Paul Ricoeur's perspective, we embark on a fascinating journey where language and interpretation reveal themselves as protagonists of psychoanalysis. He does not see this discipline as a therapy performed by a doctor in a white coat, but as a cultural archaeology that goes beyond medical therapy and dives into an ocean of culture, exploring from art to religion, dreams, and myths. From this perspective, a study of Freud's work will allow us to delve into the relationship between dreams and myth and then outline with greater precision and acuity everything that surrounds and defines myth as such in the human psyche. Let us now examine these issues more closely.

Scientific inquiry into the dream sphere gained prominence in 1899 with the advent of *The Interpretation of Dreams* by Sigmund Freud, whose original title *Die Traumdeutung* could perhaps have been better translated as "hermeneutics of dreams," in honor of Hermes, the messenger of Zeus, and the fact that, as the text itself proposes, dreams are messengers of the unconscious that demand to be interpreted. This monumental text, a gem in the legacy of its author, stood out for its profound impact and for being the dawn of a new academic branch that influenced many other disciplines within the social sciences and philosophy itself. Prior to the Freudian revolution, dreams were mainly the focus of shamans and astrologers, who offered explanations shrouded in mysticism or religiosity.

Some 19th-century thinkers also speculated on the meaning of dreams, considering them incoherent biological residues or manifestations of the emancipated soul. In his scholarship, Freud postulated with conviction that, given the complexity of the psyche, dreams must contain discernible meaning and offer crucial clues for understanding and helping patients. For Freud, the dream acted as a conduit between the conscious and unconscious mind. Unraveling dreams, Freud believed, provides greater introspective clarity, fosters personal development, and reveals the mysteries of the mind.

Within the framework of his work, Freud paved the way for the study of dream content as a mechanism for accessing the patient's unconscious. The approach he developed was based on interpreting dreams as the symbolic manifestation of hidden desires. Expressed in a wide mosaic of signs and metaphors, dreams, in Freud's conception, act as openings in the walls of the psyche, allowing us to glimpse the latent aspects that the conscious mind strives to ignore. In this context, Freud argued that the origin of our psychological constitution lies in the early years of life, with each initial experience contributing to shaping the configuration of the adult self. He also postulated that what is experienced during this stage, particularly repressed desires and traumas, significantly impacted the dreams of adulthood. Freud conceived the dream as a tool used by the organism to transfer to conscious memory what is hidden and censored in the unconscious. Within Freud's extensive discourse, three categories of dreams of unfathomable complexity are clarified:

First, there are the wish-fulfillment dreams, which reflect conscious and unmet desires that, unfortunately, have not been fulfilled in the realm of reality. They are marvels of waking life that externalize wishes, presenting content that seems to be what one, in their passionate existence, longs to experience.

Second, there are dreams of latent content, which are dream manifestations that allegorize repressed desires and deep psychological conflicts. Their content, at first glance, seems confusing, absurd, and indistinct; therefore, they require astute interpretation to unveil their encrypted meaning and uncover the internal conflicts symbolically manifested in such dreams.

Lastly, there are dreams of manifest content, which directly carry repressed desires or those wrapped in a minimal symbolic veil. In contrast to dreams of latent content, the message of such profound fantasies becomes clearer and does not require a layered interpretation to grasp the revealed repressed desires.

It is important to note that, according to Freud's conception, dreams are often intricately cryptic, permeated by symbolic elements and encrypted representations that demand a thorough analysis and interpretation in order to unveil their true meaning and uncover the subconscious drives that propel them. The hermeneutic exegesis of these symbolic mysteries and fleeting visions, on the threshold of introspection and subjective experience, inevitably fluctuates according to the beliefs, traditions, and individual perspectives embedded in the innermost being of each person. These images and symbols stand as polysemous vessels, imbued with multiple meanings and various personal resonances.

It is in this precise sense that, as Freud first suggests and later Ricoeur reminds us, we can think of dreams as if they were our personal collection of myths, and myths as the dreams shared by society.

In this context, Ricoeur conceives psychoanalysis as a fruitful tool to ponder and reformulate culture through interpretation. However, Freud's assertion that dreams are the private mythology of the individual and that myths are the waking dreams of communities involves considering both as externalizations of human longing, structured and mediated by language. Myth and dream are, in essence, narratives susceptible to interpretation in order to reveal underlying desires. Hence, language and interpretation become indispensable for the psychoanalyst.[97] Ricoeur concludes that psychoanalysis does not focus on desire *per se* but on its lexicon, interpreting texts to uncover the desires they contain or conceal, thus actively participating in the contemporary dialogue surrounding language.

Understanding myths as the dreams of a collective psyche is equivalent to saying that, in their majestic abstraction, myths embody the historicity of a conglomerate, whether it is a village, a town, or a nation. In essence, their purpose is to provide an enlightened reasoning through their symbolic reading. As mirrors of the human psyche, myths display subtle realities that materialize within the subconscious, revealing an authenticity superior to the intrinsic nature of tangible, corporeal elements. Thus, mythical existence becomes the bearer of what is truly real, materializing in its symbolic narratives the realities that emerge from the abyss of the psyche, surpassing in authenticity the material manifestations.

A profound immersion in the mythical ocean inevitably requires the echo of the voices of scholars who, with lucidity and rigor, have explored its abysses: Jung, Eliade, Campbell, Ricoeur, Freud, and

97. Ibid., 7.

Nietzsche. The traces of their intellectual pilgrimages have left an unquestionable legacy that has facilitated a panoramic and deep vision of the mythical phenomenon. With a keen eye and meticulous examination, they unravel the veil of myths, showing that at its core lies a guide for humanity in its cultural journey. These texts provide keys that open doors. Equipped with the critical and analytical thinking they provide, we can unravel the messages of myths and, in doing so, enrich and contextualize our existence.

Through the rigorous lens of their questions, the multifaceted aspects of myths have been uncovered, thus revealing their capacity to encapsulate unfathomable meanings and offer humanity, as well as the forging of cultural identities, an exegetical scheme of incalculable wealth. Consequently, by diving into their writings, the reader is equipped with an esoteric key that unlocks the gates of a mythological realm. These texts provide scholars with an arsenal of conceptual and analytical tools to unveil the encrypted manuscripts within myths and to astutely calibrate their applicability in heterogeneous cultural contexts. Through the sharp lens they place on their object of study, the intricate layers of myths emerge into the light, enclosing vast meanings that provide our life and culture with a framework that makes sense of the unfathomable.

In this sense, myths are like safes that treasure profound meanings, offering our lives and identities a richer context. Sacred writings are like master keys to access a mythical dimension and, as such, deliver tools that allow us to analyze and understand the messages they contain, helping us better understand our cultures.

The traces of humanity's traumatic vicissitudes are permanently etched in the abyss of the collective unconscious. Just as individual traumas refract in intimate dreams, collective scars are inscribed in the mythical canvas conjured by society. In the dimness of slumber, the collective consciousness acts as the hand that shapes these myths, projecting onto them the traumatic impressions rooted in the unconscious. Similar to how personal traumas are sketched as dreamlike images, social conflicts manifest through mythical imagery. The dream, a faithful testimony of the truths we avoid, those that our consciousness fears to acknowledge, becomes the darkroom that projects individual traumas, just as collective experiences are inscribed in the communal dream. Society configures its myth during this slumber, transforming the unconscious traumas into narrative artifacts.

Mythological narratives, inherited through the generational thread, contain at their core the conflicts, fears, and challenges that have marked the historical plot of a society. Through these symbolic tales, humanity explores and perpetuates its collective experiences, allowing for the reflection and understanding of the traumatic events that have shaped the historical path and molded the identity of a collective. The analysis and mythical research offer a stained-glass window to history, an intensified introspection into the psychosocial and cultural dynamics that guide the vital pulse of communities. The veil of ancient wisdom is lifted through the interpretation of symbols and significations hidden within the mythical fabric, and the collective process of metamorphosis and healing is illuminated.

Through its symbolic essence, myth provides a cohesive function, amalgamating experiences linked to a particular reality, yet not manifesting it in a journalistic or literal manner but through symbolic communication. In the human psyche, the symbolic acquires a deeper resonance than the merely factual, which helps explain why a nation's identity affects us more by what it represents than by its objective reality. Similarly, our loyalty to a sports club is not rooted in its tangible reality but in what it symbolically represents in our personal universe.

From this perspective, we propose that myth reveals the reality dreamed by communities during their waking hours. The myth, in its role, symbolically addresses situations or conditions that impact a collective. If a myth, for example, tells of the daily threat of a colossal lion seeking to devour a country at a specific hour, it would be inappropriate to focus on the bodily characteristics of the feline; it would be inept to focus on the pigmentation of its skin rather than addressing the fears and anxieties of the population. Myth, through its allegories and symbolic narrative, provides a more sophisticated introspection of the emotional, psychological, and social dimensions that permeate the existence of a community, allowing for the exploration and assignment of meaning to collective experiences and directing the fears, desires, and ambitions of the people toward a symbolic manifestation. Against this backdrop, literal or decontextualized answers are not sought; rather, the appropriate focus lies in decoding and understanding the meaning and purpose that underlie the mythical images and symbols. Thus, a more fruitful understanding of human reality is accessed, erecting a bridge between the everyday banality and the transcendental essence. It is not merely a technique of interpretation, but a gateway to transcendence.

As we just mentioned, myth is relevant because it allows us to transcend factual and literal reality, opening us to a horizon of meaning much deeper and more relevant to the human being. This transcendence of the factual should also be seen as going beyond the historical accuracy of the events that myths recount. It does not matter whether Moses crossed the Red Sea, whether Jesus rose from the dead, or whether Lord Chaitanya merged with the deities of Śrī Jagannātha. In fact, myths encapsulate the historical pulses of a people and acquire value as an expression of these. Their significance and meaning, however, do not reside in their historical truth. In fact, Buddha or Jesus are not symbols of the spirit for existing as beings, but for being symbolically within the essence of Being. Who would want a god who is limited by space and time? The historical existence of figures such as Abraham, Isaac, Jacob, Jesus, Muhammad, Buddha, Lao Tzu, Mahavira, Shankara, Lord Chaitanya, or Rabbi Nachman does not add relevance to their status as religious icons. Their symbolic status is not rooted in their historical existence. Although society tends to interact with the Hebrew myths as if they were scientific facts, and to interpret Greek mythology as apocryphal tales spun by old women, we must assert that the truth of myth does not depend on or derive from the factual, literal, or historical truth of the events it narrates. On the contrary, myths, those ancient tales, carry an astonishing power far more relevant than the factual or historical events they recount—namely, they illuminate the path toward knowledge, hide treasures of meaning, and unfold truths that leap beyond facts. They are like master keys, opening doors to the deepest part of the human soul. They ask who we are, intertwine with our comings and goings, and build bridges to the sacred. Myths are like ancient masters. They are stories, yes, but they contain profound lessons. They carry within them wisdom, rich meanings, and truths that do not concern themselves with dates and places. They take us by the hand and guide us through the mysteries of the human condition in our relationships and, why not, in our searches for the spirit.

At the pinnacle of mythological scholarship lies the intrinsic value of myths, which serve as an effective vehicle for transmitting teachings, unraveling abyssal meanings, and conveying axioms that transcend mere historical chronicles. Myths, thus forged, serve as epistemological tools, enabling a venture into the depths of human ontology, elucidating both collective dialectics and transcendent spiritual longings. It is not merely a matter of receiving them as literal narratives but of immersing oneself in their symbolism and exploring the multiple layers of meaning they safeguard. In this exercise, we can appreciate the cultural and spiritual wealth that myths contribute to humanity and their potential to resonate with us personally and collectively.

Chapter 25

The human being: a hermeneutical and symbolic entity

The relationship between dream and myth has helped us outline the function that myth has in human societies, in the collective psyche of a nation, people, or congregation. It has also allowed us to see how language and interpretation play an essential role that we must now pay special attention to. To do so, we will delve into the matter of hermeneutics. Hermeneutics is the illustrious philosophical discipline that studies our ways of interpreting texts, discourses, symbols, and signs, all framed within various cultural and social landscapes. Far from stopping there, its true mission is to reveal the hidden: the meaning and intent that lie dormant in messages. Although as an interpretive art, it uncovers a world with multiple layers and paths—literature, art, religion, law, science—hermeneutics has no limits. Interpretation is not a simple black-and-white photograph; rather, it is a painting whose brushstrokes are given by history, culture, and the dance between the text and the reader. In other words, hermeneutics aims to merge the horizons of the creator and the receiver, establishing an interpretive dialogue that enriches and expands the understanding of the message.

From a Heideggerian perspective, hermeneutics is not presented as a mere external instrument but as an intrinsic property of our existence. Hence, from a perspective diametrically opposed to Cartesian transparency, Heidegger describes a human being who stands as a riddle, whose essence unfolds through the very act of interpretation. Human beings and interpretation are, therefore, inextricably intertwined. On the one hand, the human being is, in its essence, an enigma in search of a solution; on the other, interpretation acts as the key to uncover hidden truths. In this sense, Heidegger maintains that humans must be interpreted, that is, they are texts to be deciphered.

"Interpret" has the prefix "inter," which signals that its mission is to discover internal or hidden meanings that do not present themselves in an evident manner. Let us momentarily consider the realities that are transparent and precise but, due to their self-evident nature, do not call for interpretation. On the contrary, there are other realities that do not reveal themselves to a fleeting glance but require interpretation through careful examination. Consider, for example, the statement made by Aristotle in *Nicomachean Ethics* when he says, "The beginning is admittedly more than half of the whole."[98] Here, the meaning is enigmatic, and its understanding requires an interpretive act. This is not a reality that unfolds before our eyes with crystalline transparency, as might be the case with the mathematical statement 2+2=4. Therefore, it demands an interpretive process that sheds light on its intricate corners. Hermeneutics has another boundary: the type of message, as we see the different levels of reality. Some are clearer and more precise, and others are more obscure. Descartes wanted to make reality mathematical, hence his desire for clear and distinct precision. We can understand that reality has various facets, from the simplest to the most complex. But hermeneutics is designed for that fundamental facet of human life, which is precisely unclear or distinct.

Building on what was said in the previous paragraph, it is relevant to highlight that the reality of the human being, due to its cryptic nature, far from being explicit, calls to be interpreted. In the breadth of its existence, human reality manifests as an entity imbued with hermeneutics. Its meaning seems to elude immediate understanding, and for this reason, self-understanding involves a constant challenge. The symbol exhibits a peculiar duality, a double play of concealment and revelation. At the same time that it reveals, it also conceals. As

98. Aristotle, *Nicomachean Ethics*, trans. H. Rackham, vol. 19 of *Aristotle*, ed. H. Rackham, Loeb Classical Library (Cambridge, MA: Harvard University Press, 1934), 1098b23.

Heraclitus mentioned, the oracle of Delphi "neither shows nor hides, it only points." In the human being, their being-there manifests, while the meaning of that being remains veiled. The ontological difference lies in the relationship between being and its meaning. In its symbolic condition, the human being simultaneously reveals and conceals its fundamental reality. Reality emerges, veiled in enigmas, as a cryptic text calling for the lucid exegesis of a skilled decipherer. Within the convoluted hallways of philosophical hermeneutics, a mystery weaves its web, awaiting to be unraveled. Or, in other words, the symbol needs to be interpreted for its meaning to come to light.

Ernst Cassirer, a scholar whose pen charted paths in 20th-century German philosophy, speaks precisely of a symbolic human being, one who inhabits a clear network of symbolic representations. What is surprising here is the idea that our experience of the world is not direct; rather, we are navigators in an ocean of symbols. Moreover, Cassirer boldly claims that our hand does not touch objective reality in its purest form. According to him, our interaction with the world is articulated through symbolic capacities, with language and the creation and use of images and signs as its cornerstones. These symbols are the bricks with which we build a reality that frames and gives meaning to our experiences. The significant point here is that this reality emerges and evolves in a dance with history and culture.

Cassirer, with analytical rigor, presents a cardinal perspective: the human being does not play a merely receptive role with regard to the information coming from the environment; on the contrary, as human beings, we are engaged in an active construction of reality, utilizing a diverse set of symbols that manifest in areas such as art, religion, science, and language. "Rather, it is not only looking, but doing, that forms the center from which the spiritual organization of reality begins for man."[99] Cassirer makes doing central to humanity. Unlike Kant, it is not an abstract faculty of knowledge that provides the basis for our relationship with the world, but the active orientation in the world, for the human being has always been in a world, and

99. Ernst Cassirer, *The Philosophy of Symbolic Forms, Volume 1: Language*, trans. Ralph Manheim (New Haven: Yale University Press, 1955).

every form of reference to the world depends on symbolization. In Cassirer's framework, language stands as a fundamental resource that facilitates communication between individuals but whose reach is deeper, allowing for the conceptualization and representation of our world. Therefore, for Cassirer, language is the scaffolding upon which we construct categories and concepts that are fundamental to understanding reality. Furthermore, language acts as a guardian of wisdom, preserving and transmitting historical knowledge. Nevertheless, the human symbolic repertoire extends beyond words. We humans are also masters in the creation of symbols and visual images, which can manifest in works of art, photographs, films, and more, providing us with additional avenues to explore and articulate what our being feels.

Cassirer's thesis reveals a telling premise by understanding humans as intrinsically symbolic beings. Images and symbols surround our existence, and it is through these that we give meaning and interpretation to the world. Moreover, and here lies the radicality of his stance, humans cannot inhabit the world without interpreting it, and more importantly, we cannot interpret it without symbols. Therefore, our ability to forge and employ symbols is the catalyst, with language and visual representations as key players in this process. Cassirer's theory, then, illuminates the critical role of symbolic interaction in the conception of our reality and the assimilation of the environment in which we coexist.

In relation to what Cassirer proposed, Jacques Lacan, a prominent figure whose influence spread across the 20th century in psychoanalysis and philosophy, points us toward a territory where humans find themselves immersed in a symbolic universe. Let us imagine for a moment that cultural codes bind us, and our interpretations of the world are puppets whose strings are manipulated by language and symbols. This image is based on Freudian foundations but with a twist: the unconscious is like an ancient tongue that, from the abysmal depths, navigates the seas of our psyche, subtly modulating currents of thoughts and emotions.

According to Lacan, language and symbols act as the foundations of the human mind upon which the unconscious and our subjectivity are built. The individual is caught in a dilemma: on one hand, the desire that wells up in the heart; on the other, the norms that society imposes. Where is this battle fought? In the realm of language and symbols. As we grow, we absorb language and adopt cultural codes, which, on the one hand, provide us with tools to interact and position ourselves in society but, on the other, are chains that limit our expression.

As a result of this battle, the identity of the individual, more than an immutable rock, emerges like a flowing river, with language and symbols being the currents that guide it, to the point of asserting that—according to Lacan—humans do not speak a language; rather, it is the language that speaks through us. Through social interaction and the absorption of cultural significations, individuals configure the landscape of the reality in which they live and self-portraits based on language and social expectations. This, it is worth noting, can trigger dissonances, as the molded image often deviates from our more essential internal experiences, which Lacan refers to as the "true I." In an interesting turn, Lacan emphasizes the transcendence of language in psychoanalysis, viewing this field of psychology as a dialogue in which language acts as a scalpel, unraveling the unconscious through dreams and lapses in speech. It is under this premise that Lacan can advance the thesis that humans are symbolic entities, immersed in an extensive web of language and symbols in which, on the one hand, symbols act as pillars in shaping our identity and managing the tensions between our aspirations and societal expectations, and on the other, language, through firmly rooted systems of meaning in culture, acts as the prism through which we perceive and understand the world around us.

As we have seen before, psychoanalysis dives into the deep waters of the unconscious to try to understand how this hidden ocean shapes our everyday existence. Lacan takes a step further in this horizon of language and symbols by postulating, intriguingly, that humans do not suffer because of events themselves, but because of the mental representations we create. In other words, pain does not arise from paternal repression but from the interpretation and mental image we create of our father. Likewise, it is not the criticism from our partner that disturbs us but our mental representation. Therefore, we predominantly inhabit a domain of representations and symbolic images in which our existence is essentially hermeneutic.

With all this, Lacan is saying that our world is not a world whose horizon and meaning precede us, but the world that we ourselves have sculpted in our consciousness. This represented world, however, is not a false world. In fact, the mental image we have of our parents may be as true, if not truer, than their physical presence. The psychological repercussions and traumas that arose in our childhood can persist throughout our existence, even if the figures who caused them are no longer present. In a symbolic sense, our father is more real than the concrete father figure. Similarly, the mental representation we have of our mother can be more effective than tangible reality. The same goes for our very "I."

This position, however, opens the door to reading this representative and creative faculty as one in which we tend to understand and communicate only the aspects of ourselves that we find pleasing, making it especially difficult to face and understand the facets of our personality that we dislike. Honest self-reflection becomes arduous when it comes to the darker or less appreciated edges of our identity. Therefore, we tend to project and share with others only those traits that validate a positive image of ourselves, relegating to the shadows those aspects that we judge less worthy or problematic. We lean toward selective communication with the social diaspora, privileging those traits that we find in line with our preferences while subconsciously evading those vectors of our identity that we consider discordant or refractory to the idealized image we long to project.

Lacan's stance leads us to assert that humans do not interact directly with the world as it is, but through the images we have of it and the meaning we assign to it. This same idea will appear in Jung's work. According to him, the represented or symbolic reality with which we interact consists of symbols that, however, should not be understood as mere random inventions but rather as "the expression of something that cannot be characterized better." According to Jung, the symbol stands as the manifestation of a concept that eludes more precise definitions and will retain its relevance and vitality as long as it remains pregnant with meaning, that is, as long as it holds interpretative significance. The symbolic is not a lie but rather the opposite. In fact, everything is real in the symbolic because, as Cassirer says, humans are symbolic animals because we relate to the world through symbols. According to him, although we consider ourselves rational beings and enjoy the idea that we always act logically, human nature is not strictly rational and logical but eminently symbolic. Our apprehension of reality cannot always be rational due to the various ways of understanding it. Our interpretations construct the reality of our will and our will construct the representation of our world. This is precisely why we can say that, in the symbolic, everything is real. The following anecdote serves to illustrate this point: it is said that while Jung was attending to a neurotic patient who told him that he traveled to Mars daily, his secretary said to him:

> Doctor, why do you agree with the patient, confirming that he travels to Mars every day? Can you really cure him by lying or deceiving him?" To which Jung responded: "Sorry, but where did you get the idea that I am lying to my patient? Who told you that he does not travel to Mars every day?

In a way, both Cassirer's and Jung's positions lead us to maintain that human beings only represent what they want and how they want it. The will is the representation of our world because we only desire what we understand of the world, and we only represent what we want from it. Our will is a mirror of our understanding of the world because we only wish for what we have come to understand. Furthermore, our interpretation of the world is filtered through our desires, because we only form a mental image of those aspects that have sparked our interest. In this context, we can say that there is a mutual influence between our feelings and thoughts, which neuroscience even supports. We cannot desire what we do not understand, just as we cannot understand what we do not desire.

The human being is a symbolic being who creates symbols of reality with which they interact and coexist as their true reality.

This argument was already present in Nietzsche's philosophy when he proposed the fundamental premise that human experience is inextricably linked to the creative impulse and the use of symbols to give meaning to our existence. Let us begin by noting that Nietzsche calls into question the classical demarcation that separates the aesthetic from the cognitive or rational. His argument goes further, as he asserts that aesthetics (*aisthèsis*) is not merely a domain reserved for art or beauty but a prism through which we experience our entire existential totality. This perspective allows him to propose that our perceptions and understandings of the world are intertwined with our ability to symbolize. In other words, symbols are, in Nietzsche's view, vehicles of representation that help interpret reality. They abound in various forms, including language, myths, metaphors, and beliefs deeply rooted in culture. Through the application of symbols, we forge a symbolic cosmos in which we live and establish relationships with our fellow humans. This leads him to claim that this aesthetic and symbolic realm is a replica of the turbulent and unpredictable nature of reality. In other words, symbols act as tools that impose structure and order in the world; they are, in another way, the architects of meanings and valuations that guide us. In this context, we can affirm that the invention and use of symbols is an intrinsically human manifestation that allows us to reclaim our subjectivity and forge our own cosmogonies.

Nietzsche also identifies aesthetic creativity as a means of self-overcoming and transcending human tragedy. With art and symbolic synthesis as our copilots, we rise from the plain of the ordinary, entering the stratosphere of new possibilities and paradigms. These symbols allow us to decipher and weave meanings into a reality in which we are both actors and spectators. This was well understood by Nazism, making its grandiose aesthetic a symbol of its self-perceived predestination as the Chosen Nation.

One could argue that aesthetic creativity serves as a tool of liberation, allowing us to transcend the barriers of the ordinary and delve into the exploration of deeper meanings. For Nietzsche, the abode of the human being is an aesthetic cosmos, an illusion formed by images that enable us to exist beyond the harsh and often unbearable reality. It is not truth, but beauty and aesthetics, that the constitution of man is designed to endure. The raw and unfiltered truth is too heavy a burden for human fragility, which is why we opt for the construction of images of the world that allow us to veil the harshness of the real. Humans are not prepared for unbearable truths, so they sublimate those tragic truths through art. They inhabit art to avoid succumbing to truth, that is, to tragedy.

Heidegger takes up this point, arguing that metaphysics has created an image of the world to protect human beings from the devastating impact of truth: here lies the inherent tragedy of human existence. Without this veil, man would face the threat of madness, the unfathomable abyss of a reality too raw to be contemplated without mediation. Interpretation reveals itself as a survival strategy, a defense mechanism against the unbearable lightness of being. In this sense, Heidegger firmly asserts that traditional metaphysics has designed a construct, a representation of the world that masks the tragic essence of human existence. He claims that metaphysics has sought to find certainties and security in an objective and rationalized order, an initiative that, while comfortable, has led to the alienation of authentic human experience and the misunderstanding of the genuine and tragic truth of life. Heidegger delivers a scathing critique of Western philosophical tradition for its excessive focus on representation and objectivity. He argues that metaphysics has perpetuated a conception of the human being as a knowing subject standing before the world, representing it objectively. This metaphysical methodology has resulted in a distancing between the individual and their cosmos, reducing human experience to a mere cognitive link. In contrast, Heidegger invites us to examine a richer and deeper perspective of human life, one that integrates and recognizes its inherent tragic nature.

In his seminal work *Being and Time*, Heidegger argues that the primordial truth of human existence is its being-toward-death. This means that mortality and finitude are constituent elements of our existence, confronting us with the possibility of our own annihilation. Furthermore, and in parallel with psychoanalytic diagnoses related to neurosis and other conditions, Heidegger's philosophical diagnosis postulates anxiety. Anxiety emerges as the non-being that removes manifest meaning from us. Anxiety exposes us to the reality that there is a meaning of life delineated by nothingness or death that most human beings remain unaware of. Death, understood as the absence of existence or the nothingness of existence, becomes the hidden meaning of life, which, as such, is distressing to the human being. It is this anxiety that has led us to create a metaphysical representation of the world.

However, Heidegger critiques traditional metaphysics for having forged an image of the world that is nothing more than a simple construct seeking certainty and security in a rational and objective order. He also asserts that the consequence of this has been the denial of authentic human experience and the truth of our finitude. In response, Heidegger proposes overcoming this philosophical-metaphysical image of the world and opening ourselves to a more authentic understanding that recognizes contingency and finitude as fundamental aspects of our existence.

In other words, Heidegger helps us return to Nietzsche and to a whole thread of thought that advocates for symbolic thinking that transcends rational, discursive thought, which, since the very birth of Western philosophy in ancient Greece, has populated our human psyche with empirical and objective truths that today prove insufficient to unveil and interpret the shadows where the deep meanings of the human soul lie.

The authors mentioned in this chapter, specifically Nietzsche and Heidegger, are important because they help us redraw a reality that traditional metaphysical philosophy has ultimately hidden. Heidegger's critique, more specifically, is accompanied by another critique of technique. According to the author, metaphysical thought has given rise to technique, understood as the instrumentalizing practice of reality. While technique, like art or politics, is also a way of understanding the world, its metaphysical roots lead it to become a practice that uses and controls everything around us. It generates an anthropocentric worldview where all is degraded to an instrument ready to be exploited and controlled by human beings who have become masters and rulers. This diagnosis, while certainly innovative, has already appeared in earlier moments of Western tradition, giving rise to philosophical turns that have sought to guide us toward dimensions of our existence that had until then been hidden and thus foreign to our interpretation. The importance of these turns, such as the Copernican or linguistic turn, is that they showed where the problem lay and offer a path capable of guiding us to dimensions of our being that we ourselves, through philosophy and science, had buried. With the current "symbolic turn," based on the theses of Cassirer, Freud, Jung, Lacan, Nietzsche, and Heidegger, among others, we aim to present the human being not just as the maker of symbols but, above all, as the receiver of them.

Chapter 26

Symbolism and hegemony: constructing realities through discourse

The invitation to the symbolic turn, with which, hand in hand with Nietzsche and Heidegger, we have closed the previous chapter, should be understood as a need to recover or rescue a dimension of the human being that Western metaphysical-philosophical thought has been gradually eroding. Despite being considered rational and logical, human beings are also influenced by hidden impulses and underlying motivations. As the field of psychoanalysis has taught us, from Freud to Jung through Lacan, human behavior contains an amalgam of propensities and passions hidden in the shadows of consciousness. Therefore, human conduct is influenced not only by pure reasoning, but also by those unresolved questions and enigmas that remain indelible. Thus, human beings are driven by what they know and understand but also by the mysteries they have not yet deciphered.

Two aspects motivate humans. One is the knowledge they have and the other is what they know, but do not know that they know. Therefore, not all their decisions can be explained by reason. Their behavior oscillates between thought and emotion, their duties and their desires. Therefore, the human psyche is immersed in a bifurcated dynamic, a tension between two poles of the same hydraulics—that is, between the rational and the emotional, the explicit and the hidden, the unconscious and the conscious. Although humans predominantly operate in the realm of consciousness, they are often unable to discern the underlying forces that determine their behavior and decipher their own conduct. This same tension, and specifically the pole of the emotional, the hidden, and the unconscious, plays a central role in human creativity, as described by Nietzsche in the previous chapter. That is, if we have the ability to create symbols that allow us to understand reality in one way or another, it is not solely due to our rational ability but to this other subconscious face of the human being that hides behind reason itself.

As human beings, in our daily lives, there are moments when we express sympathies or antipathies or feel attraction or aversion without fully understanding the causes, roots, or origins. Our responses and reactions frequently originate in subconscious processes that evade our conscious understanding. Human consciousness is saturated with icons and images loaded with obvious meanings, universal signs bearing clear and patent meanings. For instance, take the symbol "no smoking," where we see a cigarette crossed by a red line indicating that smoking is not allowed in that area. Or consider the symbol for electrical danger, represented by a lightning bolt that warns us of the risk of electrocution. These examples have an explicit component, the graphic representation and an underlying semantic component. The symbol is precisely the synthetic unit of meaning between a phenomenal polarity that contains both the perceptible and the imperceptible, the manifested and the hidden, simultaneously the obvious or evident and the mysterious or enigmatic.

The symbol that arises from human creativity is, in essence, an amalgamation of meaning that reconciles the tangible and the intangible, intertwining the evident and the latent, the explicit and the underlying implicit. Consider, for example, the sculptural representation of Buddha, the revered figure of Kṛṣṇa, the emblematic Jewish hexagram, or the Christian crucifix. All of these present an identifiable form at first glance, but their meaning may elude immediate comprehension. While their form is clearly apprehensible, the multitude of meanings they contain remains on a more elusive plane. The symbol integrates both the concrete and discernible aspects, as well as the abstruse and hidden: the form is its external manifestation, while its meaningful essence operates on a more concealed register.

Within the realm of human consciousness, however, we find signs that express meanings that can be both conscious and unconscious, indicators carrying both denotations, tangible and intangible. In many circumstances, humans remain in a state of partial ignorance regarding the totality of the meanings transmitted by signs. In fact, a considerable proportion of these meanings operate from the depths of the subconscious, silently exerting their influence on our behavior. Specifically, we are referring to those signs that, passing through the subliminal (*sub*: "what is given beneath" *lumen*: "the light of consciousness"), impact our lives, referring to all that information that merges with our cognition without our being aware of it. On the other hand, a symbol encompasses more than just an image; it is an auditory resonance laden with a meaning originating from extraordinary narratives shared and perpetuated within communities. These narratives can manifest and persist both through oral tradition and pictorial representations. In the context of a symbol, the graphic representation acquires meaning through words that, consciously or unconsciously, are associated with it.

The symbol is configured as a predominantly auditory entity within the semiotic framework. While objects like a bottle are universally recognized, the statue of Buddha does not share that immediacy of recognition. Similarly, while a knife is a tool for immediate discernment, figures like Dattātreya or Kārttikeya require a higher degree of erudition for comprehension. It is not possible to decipher the meaning of the figure of Buddha with certainty if we lack prior explanation of who this character is and what their story is. Therefore, the symbol is an auditory entity because it only makes sense when complemented with a narrative. It is an entity whose essence and purpose become clear only in the context of the story that contextualizes it.

According to Lacan, and as we have already advanced in the previous chapter, the spheres of the imaginary and the symbolic are nothing but intentional projections of the real, of that which intrinsically belongs to the tangible domain. The imaginary, framed within a specific psychological structure, stands as the means by which the real is apprehended, that physical dimension that surrounds us. Lacan argues that human beings access the real through two fundamental avenues: the imaginary, with its catalogue of images, and the symbolic, articulated in language. The real unfolds through visual constellations and verbal codifications, placing reality itself in a realm of logical inaccessibility.

The sensory perceptions we can process are incorporated into the conscious domain and stored in our consciousness. However, there are representations that, despite affecting our perception, reside without being understood, finding their dwelling in the unconscious depths, which is what we call "the imaginary." Within the sphere of the imaginary, once incorporated and metabolized into our cognitive structure, it emerges as an essential common space for interpreting, weighing, and discerning the tangible reality of our cosmos. It is precisely these images that structure and dimension our perception of the real, mediating our understanding of existence. Therefore, it is through these images, whether of a conscious or unconscious nature, that human beings grant meaning to the vast universe that envelops us.

Simultaneously with the imaginary, the symbolic, perceived as a sequence of meanings, facilitates the formulation of laws that, when specific to a given human set, become the reference for evaluating each action according to the rewards or sanctions entailed by the adherence to culturally established rules. What is important about this, however, is that it reveals to us that the individual, through language, constructs a mesh of interpretations that outlines our existential purpose. Through the use of words, the human being gives meaning to life. Directives, legislations, rituals, habits, and cultural inheritances shape our lives. They determine what is right or wrong, beautiful or grotesque, useful or harmful, permitted or forbidden, attractive or repulsive. In this way, our cosmos is built on these conceptions and articulations.

That is, a symbol, in its nature, imparts an understanding that shapes our identity, and this, in turn, imparts value. Therefore, a symbol is never impartial or neutral in moral terms. This is the case, for example, with the emblem of the cross, which encloses a profound manifestation of values ranging from surrender to the acknowledgment of suffering, sacrifice, affliction, and pain. The very word *sacrifice* comes from the Latin *sacro* and *facere*, meaning "to make things sacred," thus suggesting the action of consecrating or elevating something to the divine. We said that the symbol conveys meaning, meaning possesses identity, and identity conveys value. In the context of the cross, it evokes the notion of sacrifice as a noble act, assigning it a positive valuation.

As we have seen, reality does not present itself to us immediately; rather, we interpret it through symbolic structures that are not only laden with meaning and value but are also eminently linguistic. When we claim that a symbol operates as an auditory image, what we are saying is that this manifestation is intrinsically linked to linguistic discourse. The symbol consists of an auditory image because it emerges and manifests itself in language. Therefore, just as we said, that reality presents itself to us through symbols, and since these are linguistic, we must also say that it is precisely through language that we structure and outline our existence.

However, and paradoxically, although language is our tool for imparting meaning to existence, the words we use already come with a pre-existing semantic load. In this sense, Wittgenstein asserts that "The limits of my language mean the limits of my world,"[100] or as Nietzsche had already warned "facts are precisely what is lacking, all that exists consists of interpretations"[101]. This statement precisely addresses what has been called the "linguistic turn," an expression that conveys the idea that, as human beings residing in Being, we ultimately think the world with and in language, as the second Heidegger will say.

The topic of language, however, involves certain problems and contradictions. First, we have seen that language manifests itself in our lives as a constant pre-definition or even an imposition instead of a freely chosen tool. The terms we use to fill the world with meaning are given to us and imposed on us. Thus, we use words without being aware of their meanings. We use language without

100. Ludwig Wittgenstein, *Tractatus Logico-Philosophicus*, trans. D. F. Pears and B. F. McGuinness, with an introduction by Bertrand Russell (London: Routledge Classics, 2001), 5.6, 68.

101. Friedrich Nietzsche, *The Will to Power*, trans. Walter Kaufmann and R.J. Hollingdale (New York: Vintage Books, 1968), §481, 13.

full discernment of the semantic essences of its components, often without questioning the inherent connotations of its terms. The linguistic constructs, their words, the narratives, and discourses with which we tell the world are, in reality, not ours but others. The foreign discourse inhabits our unconscious in an unnoticed manner, saturating it with expressions and conceptions that, imperceptibly, have nested in our identity, infiltrating our being. Unbeknownst to us, we not only integrate words and external narratives into our thoughts but, more alarmingly, remain ignorant that we have internalized them.

Lacan posits that this alienation emerges precisely because an individual's actions are inexorably tied to those of others, which hinders the "individual's" possibility of accessing desire as a manifestation of potential autonomy. That is, every human action gains meaning only in relation to other actions, thus establishing the individual as an entity capable of acting, thinking, desiring, and longing. However, when an individual's decisions and actions are conditioned by another's, the former becomes trapped in a relationship of subordination. When, on the other hand, the operation of the human being is knotted or linked to that of another, the former loses their freedom and becomes the subordinate, while the other becomes the master and can relate to the slave in countless ways. This asymmetric relationship can manifest in various forms.

For example, if someone hears an argument condemning a certain ideology and, as a result, ends a friendship because their friend supports it, they have lost autonomy and become a subordinate of the one who spread the argument. That is, we have a discourse and two subjects, where the discourse of one becomes the discourse of the other as well: the first becomes the master, and the second becomes the slave. In the discursive dynamic, two entities interact: when one party adopts the rhetoric of the other as their own, a hierarchy is established. In this scenario, the first emerges as dominant, while the second assumes a subordinate position. From this argument, it follows that the creation of symbols, being of a linguistic structure, is a creation that must be understood as belonging to a cultural context that dictates the meanings of the terms we use. The symbolic creation with which we engage to understand reality is a process that originates from a discursive dynamic rooted in alienation.

This relationship of alienation and the imposition of wills directly leads us to the issue of untimeliness. In his work *On the Use and Disadvantages of History for Life*, also known as *The Second Untimely Meditation*, Nietzsche argues that the authentic freedom of the will is revealed historically only when it manifests in an untimely manner. This untimeliness occurs when the will frees itself from the temporal restrictions that condition it because, as Nietzsche himself says, "these thoughts are "out of season," because I am trying to represent something of which the age is rightly proud—its historical culture—as a fault and a defect in our time, believing as I do that we are all suffering from a malignant historical fever and should at least recognize the fact."[102] Thus, Nietzsche argues that we are captives of the trends of our time, trapped by the dominant and prevailing discourses, and that only when a person manages to distance themselves from these prevailing paradigms—that is, from the conventional and the hegemonic—can they taste true freedom.

Nietzsche understands this distancing as a kind of temporal dissociation and discrepancy, a disconnection and a misalignment from contemporary discourses.

In fact, Nietzsche himself argues that, paradoxically, individuals who are not fully synchronized with their time truly belong to their era. Those who do not blindly follow current trends can acquire a more appropriate vision of the present. In other words, only by positioning ourselves beyond what is strictly contemporary can we be authentic contemporaries; if we are not prisoners of fashion, we can access a proper perspective on what is happening. The condition of being contemporary implies a unique position: to stand above the current era.

In contrast, historicism relegates us to a subordinate role, making us mere products of our era, or in other words, children of our time. Being truly contemporary goes beyond merely being aligned

102. Friedrich Nietzsche, *The Use and Abuse of History for Life*, trans. Adrian Collins, 2nd rev. ed. (Indianapolis: The Bobbs-Merrill Company, 1957), 4.

with the present era; it implies being a precursor, an architect of the future age. In this sense, contemporaneity is not a mere chronological coincidence with the present, but a proactive and visionary attitude. It involves a deep understanding of current patterns and the ability to influence and shape what is to come. It is not just about experiencing the present, but also actively participating in the creation of the future. To be contemporary is to be a father and creator of the future, not a mere passive observer of the ongoing history. As Giorgio Agamben expressed:

> Contemporariness is a singular relationship with one's own time, which adheres to it and, at the same time, keeps a distance from it. More precisely, it is that relationship with time that adheres to it through a disjunction and an anachronism. Leaning beyond the beast, the contemporary is the one who detaches himself from his time, in order to stare the time directly in the eyes.[103]

According to Lacan, these hegemonic discourses in which we constantly find ourselves trapped and which, as we have said before, we have adopted and assimilated into the deepest parts of our psyche, are reflections of the very historical period in which they arise, acting as representatives of the symbolic in human relations. The term *hegemonic* originates in the concept of hegemony proposed by the Italian philosopher Antonio Gramsci, who argued that power and control in society are based on coercion and force, as well as on the ability of a dominant class to establish their worldview as the commonly accepted view by all. For example, in Nazi Germany, the Jew was symbolized as greedy and evil, while the Aryan was portrayed as the victim. From that symbolism, the hegemonic discourse was born that legitimized such symbolism.

Following that same pattern, today, feminism has become an ideology with a hegemonic discourse that symbolizes the man as

103. Giorgio Agamben, *What Is the Contemporary?*, in *What Is an Apparatus? and Other Essays*, trans. David Kishik and Stefan Pedatella (Stanford, CA: Stanford University Press, 2009), 39.

the oppressor and the woman as the oppressed. This symbolization has given rise to a feminism that, like all ideological constructs, often presents a partial and even misleading truth. We know that half-truths are always the most dangerous. For in clinging to the fragment of truth they contain, we risk embracing without question the entire system that surrounds it. Before the creation of feminism as such, we gradually devalued sexuality, responsibility, partnership, and family. After dismantling all those relationships, we then needed a new discourse or narrative to validate that disconnection or rupture. If a society has an imaginary in which women must stay at home raising their children and taking care of domestic chores, a narrative or discourse will be needed to legitimize that role. That legitimation came for a long time from organized religion. However, when the imaginary changed, the narrative also shifted, and another discourse became necessary to justify a new role, in which our society invented feminism as we understand it today. According to this new discourse, women must now join the workforce to, paradoxically, support and contribute to the development of capitalism.

The feminist discourse expresses a set of relationships between men and women that essentially replicates the Marxist narrative about a society based on the dialectic between oppressors and the oppressed. If, according to classical Marxism, the oppressor was the bourgeois and the oppressed was the proletariat, in the interpretation of contemporary feminism, the man replaces the bourgeois, and the woman takes the place of the proletariat. This interpretation has further created and consolidated an image of man as a violent, aggressive, unjust, authoritarian, misogynistic, paternalistic, and dominant being, while painting the female figure as subdued, oppressed, victimized, vulnerable, and fragile. It is no coincidence that Friedrich Engels said, "Within the family he is the bourgeois and the wife represents the proletariat."[104] In this context, feminism, as a hegemonic discourse, has emerged to collect and enunciate that set of interactions that already manifested in society.

104. Frederick Engels, *Origin of the Family, Private Property, and the State*, trans. Alick West (Leopard Books India, 2015), 96.

Women, marginalized, abused, exploited, and fragile, have to must free themselves from men, who are guilty, violent, powerful, and dishonest. Every hegemonic discourse uses a pattern of thought to generate an intellectual reality. It creates an icon that operates in society, regardless of the circumstances. As a result, real facts are gradually interpreted in accordance with that discourse.

Other examples of this are the symbols of the master and the disciple. In the East, for many generations, the master was presented as the beacon that dispelled the darkness and guided the disciple toward the Truth. The glorious disciple, in turn, represented surrender, passion for the Truth, loyalty, and devotion. This symbolism has gone hand in hand for centuries with its corresponding discourse. With the spread of Eastern religions in the West, the symbolism of the master-disciple relationship has been transformed under the prism of Western mentality and its own discursive patterns, capitalized in the 20th century by the dialectical reading with which Marxism has interpreted society and the world, always in the image and likeness of the West. From this point of view, imagination has now created a photograph in which the guru is portrayed as authoritarian, a charlatan, opportunistic, and manipulative—and equivalent to the bourgeois man—and the disciple as a fool, naïve, unwitting, defenseless, and a victim whose brain has been washed—equivalent to the proletariat and the woman, giving rise to the predominant anti-cult discourse.

This highlights the importance of conscious and deliberate commitment, the conscious surrender of the disciple to their master. Because if one surrenders to their guru without realizing that they are surrendering, they will be becoming their slave, and the relationship will be one of alienation rather than liberation.

What all these examples of hegemonic discourse confirm is that they are mere fruits of a preponderant discursive structure that ends up internalizing and resonating in the thoughts of individuals within a society. In all these cases, whether anti-Semitism, feminism, or the sectorization of religions, they are expressions of the same fixed Marxist-dialectical pattern, which stipulates that, as Marx himself stated in the *Communist Manifesto*: "The history of all hitherto existing society is the history of class struggles. Freeman and slave, patrician and plebeian, lord and serf, guild-master and journeyman, in a word, oppressor and oppressed, stood in constant opposition to one another, carried on an uninterrupted."[105] Conditioned by an a priori discursive pattern that determines that all social reality is dialectical, we are blinded to the actual behavior of individuals. Under this view, the man will always be seen as evil and the woman as a victim; the guru as a manipulator and exploiter, and the disciple as a fool or naïve; the businessman as an exploiter and the proletariat as an exploited mass.

The problem here is twofold. On the one hand, they all end up reduced to mere representations of a prior categorization that disregards whether the individual in question is honorable, honest, or sincere. On the other hand, this a priori structure is what we have assimilated into our psyches, which makes us think that the world is a certain way without even being aware of it. Hegemonic discourse seems to stipulate and repeat the same dialectical pattern, with which it tries to explain reality and its supposed advances, thus submitting all thought and reality to its own structures. It is in this context that Nietzschean untimeliness reveals itself as necessary to promote a symbolic turn that allows us to deconceptualize the symbol, liberating it from discursive reason, to unveil the being that today lies dormant in the dungeons of a collective psyche in which only a mesh of conceptualized symbolism seems to pulse, with which we imagine and represent the world.

To understand this notion of the deconceptualization of the symbol, we must first return to the issue of the symbol and resume our study from where we left off in the previous chapters. As we have seen, the symbol is an image that spreads through a discourse generated by a subject who hegemonizes the meaning of that image through its discursive interpretation. By imposing their own interpretation of the image as the only valid one, they take ownership of the symbol, creating a hegemonic discourse that colonizes the

105. Karl Marx and Friedrich Engels, *The Communist Manifesto,* trans. Samuel Moore, intro. David Harvey (London: Pluto Press, 2008), 33.

subjectivity of the receiver. The latter accepts this discourse as the only valid interpretation of the image, leading to alienation, since by accepting the hegemonic discourse, they cease to be themselves, becoming a "being for another." The hegemonic discourse colonizes and dominates other possible interpretations and all other potential interpreters of the image. In this process, the symbol becomes a concept, the concept turns into a mental construct, and this construct becomes subjective power that subjects the individual.

All of this leads us to say that every mental purpose is, ultimately, the product of a symbolic network whose power can, as such, foster the implantation of a negative stimulus in the mental space of another individual, pushing them to perform actions they are not fully aware of. Everything we desire as human beings is already mediated by the world we inhabit in our minds, and it could lead us to accept or reject something and then influence another to reject the same thing as we do. Because even though I am unaware of the reasons for my preferences or aversions, I have the ability to make others despise the same things. In this sense, the power of the symbolic network that lies in our subconscious increases through each of us as we perpetuate, expand and strengthen it. This can be considered a continuous feedback loop. When the symbolic network influences us, and we make it grow and strengthen, this stronger network, in turn, influences us much more. This process is an inertial cycle, where both the network and its members grow through cross-feeding.

The solution to this type of cycle is untimeliness. Let us suppose that I insistently and passionately adopt the conviction that "X is condemnable." I will tirelessly work to cement and consolidate this thought until it materializes into tangible actions, and I will try to convince others of this statement, instilling my truth into them. Imagine that X is the figure of a Jew, and "condemnable" is their attribute. Thus, we obtain a sign, a representation filled with meaning. If this representation hides its potential to convey values, it becomes an unconscious symbol.

In this context, Nietzschean untimeliness invites us to analyze which discourses interpellated, confine, and imprison us. Only then can we free ourselves from those narratives and conceptions and, more essentially, from the "symbolic-imaginary-real other" of our time. Distancing ourselves from our era and its prevailing discourses implies, above all, as psychoanalysis shows, unmasking ourselves. This requires detaching from the conceptualized "I," as it is the one that has internalized and assimilated the discourses of our time. Because that "I" we conceptualize as our essence is nothing more than a set of postulates and external perspectives on our identity. This self-concept is merely the crystallization of foreign evaluations that shape our identity, perpetuated through interactions with parents, educators, peers, and superiors throughout our life. Considering this, the act of emancipation, both for the individual and for collectives, lies in the deconstruction and critical questioning of the narratives imposed on us. True freedom is evading the traps of the external discourse that we have internalized and assimilated as our own, avoiding being subjugated to preconceived ideas without rigorous examination.

It is evident that the individual is in a constant state of conditioning by structures like politics or religion. Generally, our identification as Jewish, Hindu, Christian, or atheist comes from a series of concepts transmitted at moments of little critical awareness. Much of our identity emerges from principles embedded in our psyche before we can question them. This process, however, seems inevitable.

In fact, despite the different contexts in which one may develop in the world, every individual is subject to some form of influence or encoding to a greater or lesser extent. This influence or programming is, in fact, intrinsic to the very educational system, even when it is adorned with aspirations of emancipation. People are condition-able, and the more inauthentic and less untimely their life is, the more conditioned it will be. Hypothetically, if we were raised in the depths of the jungle, the wild creatures living there would instill their own structures of understanding in us. Inevitably, the guardian of an infant shapes their perception, often without conscious intent. The act of educating inherently carries an inevitable process of conditioning.

Ironically, any attempt at deprogramming will lead to another form of conditioning. Every human relationship is established through thought and articulated by language. Deprogramming with the same tools will be another form of external imposition. For this reason, the "symbolic turn" understood as the recovery of the symbol stripped of conceptualization, becomes necessary to transcend the boundaries and limits of discursive-conceptual thinking. Therefore, symbolic thought must be understood as a thinking that does not start from the conceptualized "I," but from a deeper dimension from which the symbolic meaning of Being can be revealed in all its richness.

Language forges our understanding of the world and chisels the perception we have of ourselves. In the face of the alienation inherent in human nature, meditation emerges as the only process of deconditioning. It is by meditation alone that thought completely disintegrates and human beings are freed from their bondage to words. When words vanish, it is possible to experience reality in its pure state. Unmediated by thought, one lives in a state of pure being.

The animal kingdom lies below this linguistic stratum, while the transcendental realm of the divine extends above the language boundary. We humans reside between these two realities. We are, so to speak, inhabitants of an intersection, a liminal zone between two essential domains. The human mind is shaped and structured through words that constitute the raw material of our thinking and act as the foundations of mental construction. Our domain is saturated with words, philosophies, narratives, stories, writings, discourses, theories, and ideologies. But true religion is not a matter of study and can neither be learned nor taught. It is imperative, therefore, that we gradually divest ourselves of words to dive into the depths of silence.

Whenever I am asked about the practice of meditation, my answer does not meet expectations. Rather than investing in the method or technique for meditating, it is essential to understand how to embrace inactivity, because meditation, in its essence, emerges spontaneously. The central core of meditation is to find serenity in non-doing. In this state of non-action, or passivity according to Jean Luc Marion, meditation arises and develops naturally. This orientation goes against the tendency to seek active techniques and concrete methods, and stresses the importance of mental tranquility and non-intervention as precursors to a genuine meditative state.

This process, far from being a difficult and complicated task, is made easier by the mere attempt. Just by trying, it simply happens, because the path is made by walking, as Antonio Machado would say.

Deep introspection leads to an inner silence where mental activity ceases and linguistic constructions, to which we grant unquestionable authority, dissipate. It is simply a matter of relaxing within ourselves until we fall into the depths of our own silence. To establish ourselves there where there is not even the slightest residue of mental activity and, therefore, where the structures of linguistic discourse that we usually accept as given vanish.

Pure reality manifests when the mind is not obstructed by clouds of thoughts, but there is only a state of conscious, limpid, and clear attention. In the absence of thoughts, the self reaches a state of undisturbed stillness. In this stillness, one gains access to reality, a terrain that is not suitable for thought. It can be observed, but not conceptualized, since the act of thinking distorts it, distancing us from its essence. Instead of thinking, simply be. Because learning is apprehending.

Normally, our consciousness is saturated with superfluous thoughts, like a mirror fogged with steam. The mind, in its usual state, resembles a roadway filled with constant traffic: thoughts and narratives flow incessantly. Day after day, this mental activity persists, even at night. While we sleep, the mind is still active, dreaming, thinking, and worrying about what is to come.

In contrast, meditation represents the absence of this mental traffic. It consists of a state of pure consciousness without mental interference and exempt from content. When thoughts cease, when there are no desires arising, a state of total silence is reached. This silence is the essence of meditation and where truth is revealed. Meditation is therefore transcendental to the mind or a non-mental state. The mind cannot lead us to meditation, for its tendency is to perpetuate itself. Meditation is only found by abandoning or renouncing the mind, by maintaining calmness, indifference, observing the passing of thoughts without identifying with them. Meditation implies the recognition that "I am not the mind." Meditation is not action but passion; it is not governance but freedom.

When contemplating the moon, the mind intervenes, labeling it as "beautiful" and thus triggering a succession of associations that take us away from the moon and its true nature. Lost in a sea of thoughts, we forget the starry night. Watching the moon reflecting in a peaceful lake, just be with it; do not transfer it to your mind, let it be an observed moon and not a thought moon. Keep words from interfering with your encounter with it, just observe its being. No thought could capture its essence. In that attentive and conscious observation, leaving aside all thoughts or ideas, the moon will reveal to you the mystery of its reality. Do not put words over it. Do not wrap it with concepts that make it darker. Let it be, while being you with it. In those moments, you are meditating on the full moon. You can meditate on a flower, the sea, a cloud, a seagull, or a friend. Simply observing, allow your gaze to be steady, intense, penetrating, without allowing thoughts to interfere. Gradually, silent pauses will develop, bringing with them a deep, fresh peace.

As the consciousness goes deeper or internalizes, moments of silence emerge, pure spaces, instances of transparency, where nothing moves, and everything is still. Beyond the mental barriers, previous attachments are dismantled, and genuine freedom can be accessed. There is no other effective way to transcend all conditioning or programming. In that stillness, it is possible to recognize our true identity and begin to decipher its mystery.

CHAPTER 27

SYMBOLISM IN PSYCHOLOGY: A PATH OF INTEGRATION

In order to approach this notion of meditation, which we also call "inner intuition," we will turn to the work of Carl Jung, whose autobiography begins as follows:

> My life is a story of the self-realization of the unconscious. Everything in the unconscious seeks outward manifestation, and the personality too desires to evolve out of its unconscious conditions and to experience itself as a whole. I cannot employ the language of science to trace this process of growth in myself, for I cannot experience myself as a scientific problem. What we are to our inward vision, and what man appears to be *sub specie aeternitatis* (from the perspective of eternity), can only be expressed by way of myth. Myth is more individual and expresses life more precisely than does science. Science works with concepts of averages which are far too general to do justice to the subjective variety of an individual life.[106]

As psychoanalysis has well pointed out, within the unconscious is stored everything that has been repressed, even though this process of repression is not carried out consciously. Each individual has a conscious "I" and an unconscious "I." Jung sought to unify these two facets of reality into one. His goal was to unravel what lies in

106. C. G. Jung, *Memories, Dreams, Reflections*, recorded and edited by Aniela Jaffé, translated by Richard and Clara Winston, revised ed. (New York: Vintage Books, 1989), 3.

the unconscious and bring it to the light of consciousness, that is, to make the unconscious conscious through symbols. In dreams, images appear that one can express through art or describe verbally, thus allowing them to pass from the unconscious state to integrate into the conscious state. Jung described this integration of the unconscious with the conscious using the term "self."

> When we now speak of man we mean the indefinable whole of him, an ineffable totality, which can only be formulated symbolically. I have chosen the term "self" to designate the totality of man, the sum total of his conscious and unconscious contents.[107]

The Self refers to the fundamental epicenter of our psychic system, serving as an organizing center from which regulation originates. The primary function of this core lies in integrating or amalgamating both conscious and unconscious dimensions of the being. Therefore, it consists of a synthesis of contradictions; that is, it fuses opposite poles, which gives it a mysterious and inscrutable character. This reminds us of Hegel and his dialectic. Hegel's dialectic is a philosophical methodology that develops through a thesis, antithesis, and synthesis process. Hegel conceives change and development in terms of the constant interaction between opposites, which leads to an advancement or progression in understanding and reality. Thesis is an initial assertion or idea. Antithesis is the negation or contradiction of the thesis. Synthesis is the reconciliation of the thesis and antithesis into a new state that preserves and transcends the previous contradictions.

This dialectical process repeats continuously: each synthesis becomes a new thesis that generates a new antithesis, leading to continuous development. I would say that Hegel is the philosopher of the conflict between life and death and a dreamer of transcendence, not of this world. In his phenomenology, Hegel speaks of being, the

107. C. G. Jung, *Collected Works of C. G. Jung*, vol. 11, *Psychology and Religion: West and East*, trans. R. F. C. Hull, 2nd ed., Bollingen Series XX (Princeton, NJ: Princeton University Press, 1969), 140.

positive life. But that is constantly and permanently confronted with non-being, the negative, and death. In that dynamic clash appears the "overcoming of the conflict" (*aufhebung*). But this overcoming is momentary because the dialectic continues its movement. For Hegel, reality is not a substance or a set of substances but a set of relations, a continuous network of interactions with moments identified as substances. And this is precisely what the analyzed phrase says. The synthesis of contradictions can only be a mystery because the overcoming of death can only be made possible by life. But that new life, that synthesis between life and death, but no longer on the same plane. Death is assumed by life. For example, when individuals question their intellectual capacity, whether they are dull or sharp, the conscious part may lean toward reaffirming their sharpness. However, their unconscious side may bring up memories of times when they felt inept, mediocre, useless, or even foolish. In *Discourse on the Method*, Descartes says that all men believe they possess good sense, even those who are unsatisfied with everything else. In the self, both realities are synthesized. The reality in which one perceives oneself as intelligent and the repressed reality that resides deep within the psyche must be synthesized.

Stated another way, the self is the construct in which the individual's conscious and unconscious realities merge, uniting the approval of the individual's consciousness with the disapproval of the individual's unconscious. Thus, the individual's consciousness approves of me, the individual's unconscious disapproves of me, and I can synthesize the individual's consciousness and unconscious in the self. Therefore, in the self exists yin and yang, integration, and synthesis, which is the space where opposites amalgamate and find balance. However, this integration of the conscious and unconscious is not immediate. On the contrary, according to Jung, balance occurs when a person can sincerely recognize that they are neither a genius nor an ignorant, that they are neither a saint nor a villain. It is in this gradual process of recognition and acceptance that conscious and unconscious life begin to integrate and coexist in harmony. The self, according to Jung, acts as the matrix and architect of our dream experiences and is considered the complete encapsulation of the psyche. This concept is clearly distinguished from the ego, which only occupies a tiny fraction of our psychological totality.

Within this vastness that is the self, we find an authentic identity that encompasses both the "individual consciousness"—an aspect of our identity that sometimes feels distant from its true essence—and the "individual unconscious"—considered a part of the broader "collective unconscious." In his 1916 essay *The Structure of the Unconscious*, Jung makes a meticulous distinction between the Freudian "personal unconscious," which is imbued with repressed impulses and erotic fantasies, and the "collective unconscious," understood as a kind of universal reservoir of the human psyche. From the beginnings of his theoretical reflection, Jung postulated that the "collective unconscious" serves as an explanatory matrix to discern the consonance of psychological patterns between individuals from different cultural lineages. However, he believed that the self is inaccessible in a direct manner and can only be understood through symbols, which, as Mircea Eliade later explained, cannot be the object of mere cognitive knowledge that operates through logical-conceptual systems.

> Symbolic thinking is not the exclusive privilege of the child, of the poet or of the unbalanced mind: it is consubstantial with human existence, it comes before language and discursive reason. The symbol reveals certain aspects of reality—the deepest aspects—which defy any other means of knowledge. Images, symbols and myths are not irresponsible creations of the psyche; they respond to a need and fulfil a function, that of bringing to light the most hidden modalities of being. Consequently, the study of them enables us to reach a better understanding of man [...].[108]

The viability of symbolic thinking lies in that it is not exclusively confined to the linguistic framework when interpreting reality.

108. Mircea Eliade, *Images and Symbols: Studies in Religious Symbolism*, trans. Philip Mairet (London: Harvill Press, 1961), 12.

Consider the case of an infant in the early stages of their cognitive development. Their understanding is not yet fine-tuned to discern beings in their objective authenticity. Instead, their perception is shaped by personal representations and inferences that lead them to live in a world molded by their own images and interpretations. By using the term "daddy," the infant is not referring to the literal figure of a male parent but rather evoking the semblance of an unbreakable entity, the image of an invincible hero. It is an inherent predisposition of the human being to build these subjective perceptions before reaching the fullness of linguistic mastery and structured logical reasoning. In this way, before an infant can coherently articulate their thoughts, they have already conceived in their psyche that daddy is an extremely powerful figure and mommy a symbol of benevolence and absolute care.

In this sense, a symbol does not provide us with instructions on how to prepare coffee or how to feed ourselves, but instead, it unveils intrinsic aspects of the human being that are of such depth and magnitude that they transcend the limitations inherent in the descriptive capacity of concepts. The symbol, which acts as a window, we are allowed access to the hidden and enigmatic dimensions of the psyche. It should be noted that the human unconscious, in its vastness and complexity, primarily communicates through a repertoire of symbols and dream manifestations. Therefore, when studying the dynamics between humans and symbols, we immerse ourselves in analyzing and exploring their connection to the deepest regions of the unconscious. In this context, Jung postulated that the unconscious does not stand as a hostile entity but as "the great friend, the counselor and guide of consciousness." In contrast to symbolic thinking, Jung explains:

> It is on such evidence that psychologists assume the existence of an unconscious psyche— though many scientists and philosophers deny its existence. [...] Our psyche is part of

> nature, and its enigma is as limitless. Thus we cannot define either the psyche or nature.[109]

From this perspective, through the lens of psychology, the study and analysis of symbols—especially in psychoanalysis—requires an interest in humanity and its psychological, moral, and spiritual dilemmas. From ancient times, humans have intuitively felt the existence of an inner core, an inner center. The term self, employed by Jung, refers to the unique archetype of each individual, to the quintessence of the human being, whose psyche we can access through the use of symbols. For example, Jung, following his own theory of individuation, turned to art, specifically painting, as a means to explore and understand his own psychology. He painted and then conceptually studied the paintings, which were symbols. His canvases depicted a variety of symbols that, for him, acted as a kind of decompression, releasing and exposing unconscious content. Through careful observation and interpretation of these artistic manifestations, Jung was able to delve deeper into his own psychological universe. For Jung, painting was what cleansed the chimney of the unconscious and expressed the symbols, and by studying these paintings, he delved into the depths of his psyche. A parallel can be drawn here with Hindu yogis, who became laboratories for their own experiments.

The process of studying and unveiling our own psyche does not adhere to the patterns of scientific thinking because, as Jung himself explained:

> In the living psychic structure, nothing takes place in a merely mechanical fashion; everything fits into the economy of the whole, relates to the whole. That is to say, it is all purposeful and has meaning. But because consciousness never has a view of the whole, it usually cannot understand this meaning. We must therefore content ourselves for the

109. Carl G. Jung, ed., *Man and His Symbols* (New York: Anchor Press/Doubleday, 1964), 23.

> time being with noting the phenomenon and hoping that the future, or further investigation, will reveal the significance of this clash with the shadow of the self.[110]

In this Jungian context, the economy is intrinsically intertwined with the concept of administration, a process that unfolds progressively or sequentially, but always keeping in mind that it is an indivisible totality, a unified whole, whose structure must be understood as a holistic entity. In parallel with Jung's conception, the Gestalt school, emerging in the early decades of the 20th century in Germany under the influence of prominent figures such as Max Wertheimer, Wolfgang Köhler, Kurt Koffka, and Kurt Lewin, asserts that, regarding perception and other psychological functions, the global conglomerate exceeds the mere addition of its components. This implies that a complete system can manifest properties not present in its parts when considered individually. This approach also impacts how humans process information and experience the environment, focusing on patterns and contexts rather than isolated elements. Thus, according to Gestalt, human cognition operates mainly in terms of totality.

In the realm of philosophy, Theodor W. Adorno argues that totality is the non-truth. Humanity tends to think in integrated structures, in which each part is relevant to the whole and vice versa. This is because we have a natural inclination to conceptualize in terms of cohesive systems, where each component holds significance intricately tied to the global system. In the human mind, the concept of totality is intrinsic: each factor influences and is influenced by the rest. We think in structures related to the whole, and the whole relates to everything because everything affects everything. Within this theoretical framework, it is essential to discern the influence of the unconscious, as it constitutes a vital segment of our totality, playing a determining role in our essential constitution. The unconscious, as an integrative part of the whole, also determines and shapes us.

110. C. G. Jung, *Memories, Dreams, Reflections*, recorded and edited by Aniela Jaffé, trans. Richard and Clara Winston, rev. ed. (New York: Vintage Books, 1989), 246.

Humanity does not compartmentalize its experience into airtight sections; instead, everything is in constant interaction; that is, the human being does everything with everything. In its quest for understanding, it does not segment its experience into rigid categories; instead, it perceives everything as an interconnected flow. There are no separate areas of our life that belong exclusively to archetypes, concepts, or the physical realm. On the contrary, everything is integral and interconnected: archetypes manifest in the body, and in turn, the body is a vessel for archetypes. That is, each aspect is connected to the rest, and everything we do involves the totality of our being. Therefore, spiritual, material, symbolic, and cognitive dimensions are not perceived in isolation but are integrated and converged in our everyday reality. Our lives include all these components, without sharp divisions or well-defined barriers. This is why symbolic thinking neither proceeds nor addresses its objects in the same way as scientific thinking because, as Jung himself asserts, the human mind cannot obtain a complete and total scientific vision of the psyche, being limited to acquiring only a partial and fragmented understanding, since an integral vision would equate to a total perspective of our psychology. We are in the presence of an integral view of the human being, but no longer in the Aristotelian manner, but from the symbolic turn. Instead of emphasizing the delimitation of the parts, as the Stagirite does, we focus on the relationships and their integration. Only the symbol can access totality, for that implies gaining access to the dark aspect of the individual. As we have mentioned several times in this book, while concepts separate and dissect, the symbol unifies and totals. Jung himself states:

> But if the individuation process is made conscious, consciousness must confront the unconscious and a balance between the opposites must be found. As this is not possible through logic, one is dependent on symbols which make the irrational union of opposites possible.[111]

111. C. G. Jung, *Psychology and Religion: West and East*, trans. R. F. C. Hull, The Collected Works of C. G. Jung, vol. 11 (Princeton, NJ: Princeton University Press, 1958), 755.

Human beings live immersed in a holistic world composed of opposites, such as beauty and ugliness, height and brevity, obesity and thinness, and depth and superficiality. While these polarities are constructs of our conscious mind, in the recesses of the collective unconscious, these dualities merge, revealing to us that what we consider ugly may hold traces of beauty, and, conversely, the beautiful may contain less attractive nuances. In this sense, the symbol presents itself as a means through which it is possible to reconcile these contradictions, thus allowing us to see the whole in all its plurality and richness. While the individual conscious mind, the source of segmentation, cannot synthesize them, the symbol, by its integrative nature, is capable of amalgamating disparities. As Jung continues to explain:

> Thus a word or an image is symbolic when it implies something more than its obvious and immediate meaning. It has a wider "unconscious" aspect that is never precisely defined or fully explained. Nor can one hope to define or explain it. As the mind explores the symbol, it is led to ideas that lie beyond the grasp of reason.[112]

In the realm of human thought, it is only through the use of the symbol, and not the concept, that we can articulate those dimensions that transcend rationality. The symbol acts as a cohesive force, consolidating and harmonizing that which seems dissimilar. When we attempt to understand certain realities through the conceptual prism, we encounter insurmountable obstacles, for concepts present reality through aspects that are incongruent with one another. When we categorize reality, it appears to us through concepts that seem mutually exclusive or become incompatible and, therefore, cannot be reconciled through the conceptual lens. Conceptualization always returns a fragmented reality in pieces, represented through individualized categories and ideas, which,

112. Carl G. Jung, *Man and His Symbols*, ed. M.-L. von Franz (New York: Anchor Press/Doubleday, 1964), 20–21.

ultimately and paradoxically, makes it truly incomprehensible. This problem is not only of a strictly epistemological nature, but it affects our entire reality. For example, while the scientific mind of humans has always insisted on the separation between the sacred and the profane, non-institutionalized religion has always subverted this scheme. This is evidenced by the figure of Jesus, who, though considered divine, did not hesitate to commune with those labeled as transgressors or sinners, thus dissolving the boundaries between seemingly mutually exclusive polarities. “It is not the healthy who need a doctor, but the sick. I have not come to call the righteous, but sinners” (Mark, 2:17). Similarly, we could also conceive of the divinity and its devotee as completely different entities. However, and paradoxically, Lord Chaitanya embodies the divinity manifested in the likeness of his faithful servant and perfect devotee, a notion that, at first glance, challenges common discernment.

It is in this context of opposites, that Jung introduces dreams and symbols as a way to access an integrated reality of the human being, as he himself states when he says:

> But to know and understand the psychic life-process of an individual’s whole personality, it is important to realize that his dreams and their symbolic images have a much more important role to play.[113]

That is to say, for Jung, dreams constitute a vast repository, an inexhaustible storehouse of symbolisms. Those who manage to decode what these symbols are trying to communicate in their inherent messages will receive a valuable tool, the master key that opens the gate to access their unconscious sphere. Decoding or deciphering these symbols provides a sharp understanding of the underlying dynamics of our psyche, which manifests intrinsically symbolically. The most faithful and truthful way to know the essence of an individual lies in the scrutiny of their dream visions. We approach their genuine personality if we uncover the veil of their

113. Ibid., 28–29.

collective unconscious. However, if we only know their conscious sphere, our understanding will be merely superficial, partial, and incomplete. There is a marked disparity between knowing a person through symbolic revelations and merely through their own statements. If we know an individual only by what they say about themselves, we are likely to be influenced by their qualities, merits, and virtues. As René Descartes expressed:

> Good sense is the most evenly distributed thing in the world; for everyone believes himself to be so well provided with it that even those who are the hardest to please in every other way do not usually want more of it than they already have.[114]

Unlike Freud, Jung views dreams as a symbolic mine that exposes the essence of humanity. That is why he writes:

> I was never able to agree with Freud that the dream is a "facade" behind which its meaning lies hidden a meaning already known but maliciously, so to speak, withheld from consciousness. To me dreams are a part of nature, which harbors no intention to deceive, but expresses something as best it can, just as a plant grows or an animal seeks its food as best it can.[115]

According to this citation, Freud postulates that dreams constitute unconscious desires and wishes, thoughts, wish fulfillment, and motivations, with human behavior driven by suppressed desires and underlying wishes lying in the unconscious, especially emphasizing aggressive instincts of a sexual nature. Under his view, the dream acts as a prism that distorts the psyche, revealing murky aspects of the human soul and exposing the negative shadows inherent in the individual. On the other hand, Jung considers the unconscious as a

114. René Descartes, *A Discourse on the Method*, trans. Ian Maclean (Oxford: Oxford University Press, 2006), Part 1.

115. C. G. Jung, *Memories, Dreams, Reflections*, ed. Aniela Jaffé, trans. Richard and Clara Winston (London: Collins and Routledge & Kegan Paul, 1963), 157.

guide and, therefore, believes it is imperative to attend to it without repressing it, as it provides indications and signals regarding the right direction in life. Far from being an adversary or a hostile entity, the unconscious emerges as a mentor, counselor, companion, friend, and ally in the human journey. As Jung says:

> A symbol always presupposes that the chosen expression is the best possible description or formulation of relatively unknown fact, which is none the less known to exist or is postulated as existing.[116]

It is important not to confuse the symbol with the sign here. As L. Pinkus states:

> From the outset, Jung clarifies the conceptual definition of the term "symbol", distinguishing it from signs, indicating (with the latter) meanings of realities known through immediate reflection on significant objects, while clearly explaining the nature of the symbol as an expression of human creativity.[117]

From Jung's perspective, the sign refers to a tangible entity, while the symbol acts as an indicator of a structure inherent in the psychic realm. Even the transcendent or God appears in the symbol through the human being's imagination. This manifestation finds its parallel in the Christian tradition under the name "divine inspiration."

> So long as a symbol is a living thing, it is an expression for something that cannot be characterized in any other or better way. The symbol is alive only so long as it is pregnant with meaning. But once its meaning has been born out of it, once that expression is found which formulates the thing sought, expected, or divined even better than the hitherto

116. C. G. Jung, *Psychological Types*, vol. 6 of *Collected Works of C. G. Jung*, rev. R. F. C. Hull, trans. H. G. Baynes (Princeton, NJ: Princeton University Press, 1971), 814.
117. Pinkus L., *La dimensione simbolica: aspetti psicodinamici* en *Studia Anselmiana* 64 (1974), 11-28, p. 16. Translation mine.

> accepted symbol, then the symbol is dead, i.e., it possesses only an historical significance.[118]

By concretizing and delimiting a symbol in explicit and univocal terms, we subject it to a conceptual transformation. That is, if we convert the symbol into something intelligible and univocal and exhaust its meaning, we are conceptualizing it. This metamorphosis eliminates the symbol, stripping it of its rich ambiguity, potential, polysemy, and multifaceted essence. In the realm of institutionalized, conceptualized, and dogmatic religion, an attempt is made to achieve homogeneity and unity in thought, relegating dissent to the margins, labeled as heterodoxy or even heresy. On the other hand, a religion grounded in symbolism favors a broad spectrum of understandings and exegeses, allowing polysemy or a wide variety of comprehensions and interpretations. The emergence of symbols in various scenarios of human life provides the individual with a bridge over the abyss of materialism, protecting them from getting trapped in the pragmatism of tangible signs and helping them transcend the limitations of their condition.

Jung and analytical psychology assert that no symbol arises by chance but originates in a context determined by nature, and its purpose is to transcend it. The symbol is not imposed by force but through its essence and undeniable clarity. Jung reveals an inherent simplicity in the intuition: "Whether a thing is a symbol or not depends chiefly on the attitude (q.v.) of the observing consciousness."[119] According to Jung, symbols have an inherent vitality because they act and communicate deeply inspiring intuitions, foreshadowing unknown phenomena. Dreams, symbols, and archetypes are recurring elements in his work, converging intimately and systematically, maintaining a close relationship with each other. For the famous Swiss psychologist, symbols were not mere static representations but possessed a dynamism that made them capable of evoking sublime intuitions and foreshadowing

118. C. G. Jung, *Psychological Types*, vol. 6 of *Collected Works of C. G. Jung*, rev. R. F. C. Hull, trans. H. G. Baynes (Princeton, NJ: Princeton University Press, 1971), 816.
119. Ibid., 818.

realities yet to be discovered. Although Jung associated symbols with archetypal images, he did not limit them solely to such images, as the symbol is structured with a multiplicity of components.

From a philosophical standpoint, the symbol is understood from a perspective of dualities, in the exchange and dialectic between the conscious and the unconscious, in a synthesis that does not even aim to exhaust comprehension or define its limits. This inherent tension, intrinsic to human existence, finds its resolution in symbolic production and creativity.

> From the opposing archetypal tensions arises the demand for an element of coincidence, a synthesis that includes the opposing aspects of the archetype-existential solicitation, expresses both, allowing psychic energy to move from unreflective expression to more creative modalities... which transforms the very instinct, channeling it toward specifically human and creative goals, initiating the history of mankind.[120]

Jung's theoretical stance on the integration of dichotomies, particularly between the realms of the conscious and the unconscious, finds its echo in the Eastern axiom of yin and yang. This premise highlights the coexistence of two entities that, despite appearing diametrically opposed, interrelate in a complementary manner, constituting a fundamental pillar in the cosmic conception. Yin is related to the feminine, darkness, inactivity, passivity, and the earth. On the other hand, yang is associated with the masculine, light, activity, and the sky. According to this Chinese philosophy, both powers are indispensable for the maintenance of cosmic balance. This vision originates from the Yin Yang school, which was part of the well-known "100 schools of thought," a group of philosophical and spiritual currents that emerged in China between 770 BCE and 221 CE.

---

120. Pinkus L., *La dimensione simbolica: aspetti psicodinamici* in *Studia Anselmiana* 64 (1974), 11-28, p. 17–18. Translation mine.

Later, Taoism incorporated the principles of the Yin Yang school to propose that everything existing has a necessary complement for its existence. The idea of the unalterable, the immobile, is denied, and it is proposed that everything is in permanent transformation, in an incessant flow, harmonious and balanced by the forces of yin and yang. According to Taoism, yin and yang respond to certain universal principles that can be summarized as follows:

- Yin and yang are opposites, but they are not absolute, as in this philosophy, everything is relative in existence.
- Yin resides in yang, just as yang resides in yin, a principle that supports the previous one by stating that in each force resides its counterpart, even in potential, which reaffirms that they are not absolute.
- The two forces create and exhaust each other: an increase in yin energy leads to a reduction in yang energy, but this phenomenon is not considered an imbalance, rather part of the life cycle.
- Yin and yang can be subdivided and metamorphosed infinitely: yang energy can fragment to generate both yin and yang energy (and vice versa). Similarly, one of the forces can transmute into its opposite.
- Yin and yang are interdependent: each of these energies requires the other for its existence.

In other words, we find the coincidence in yin and yang, meaning that black is not entirely black, just as white is not entirely white.

This theory of opposites is not foreign to the issue of creativity and art as symbolic. As already mentioned, creativity and art play a fundamental role in Jung's psychology. By generating symbols from their imagination, human beings pave the way to the essence of being. However, the generation of symbols occurs through artistic creativity, which, according to Jung, serves as the foundation for all epistemic attitudes. From this, it follows that art emerges as a vehicle to understand the essence. If to know is to create, art is, without a doubt, a way of knowing the being. It is no coincidence that both Heidegger and Jung accord an elevated distinction to art: the former does so with oratory or poetry, and the latter with visual representation or painting. Both assign art special value because they both conceived that art, in its symbolic nature, transcends mere conceptualization in the search for essential understanding.

In painting, an act of creation is established, for the act of painting itself is a foundational act. By undertaking the pictorial act, one gives rise to an unprecedented and unrepeatable entity. The intrinsic process of painting can be equated with the act of erecting the primordial foundations of a structure or conceiving an idea from its nascent nonexistence. Therefore, each intervention on the canvas is but a testimony to the generation of a fully unprecedented and authentic entity. However, this manifestation is not governed by whims or subjectivities; it is, in fact, a luminous revelation of the sacred, providing representations of realities that would otherwise remain inaccessible. Precisely for this reason, Jung argues that the true knowledge of being is obtained through this imaginative and creative faculty, in which the dichotomies that make up our psyche are amalgamated, thereby enabling access to the self, that coherent, integrated, and unbroken "I" that eludes understanding through concepts. Thus, creativity is considered the portal that leads to the self because art acts as the crucible where the reflective and unreflective, the deliberate and spontaneous converge. Artwork is the medium in which the rational, irrational, intellectual, and instinctive are synthesized. And this imaginative faculty, which Jung exalts, has its foundations in transcendental thought, specifically in the transcendental imagination articulated by Kant.

In a manner similar to Jung, but now expressed through Heidegger, the relevance of art and creativity lies in the fact that the symbol, or that which unveils to us the quintessence of reality by invoking the notion of Being, emerges from the constitutive faculty of the human being through art.

Symbols do not emerge intrinsically with individual existence but are sculpted within the psychic framework. Shaped by a heterogeneous range of stimuli, these elements, in their transformation, acquire a form and communicative capacity.

> In this respect, dream symbols are the essential message carriers from the instinctive to the rational parts of the human mind, and their interpretation enriches the poverty of consciousness so that it learns to understand again the forgotten language of the instincts. No dream symbol can be separated from the individual who dreams it, and there is no definite or straightforward interpretation of any dream. Each individual varies so much in the way that his unconscious complements or compensates his conscious mind that it is impossible to be sure how far dreams and their symbols can be classified at all.[121]

Every dream is inherently linked to the individual who experiences it, mirroring the ontological uniqueness of their being. Psychoanalysis firmly opposes the path to abstraction, for it would lead it to be a mere philosophical construct. Attempting to dissociate the dream from the tangible context of the dreamer would result in a conceptual error, guiding us toward an imprecise generalization. Similarly, the symbol must be understood in the context of what it symbolizes. Its decoding must be inherent to its semantic sphere, avoiding its uprooting or amalgamation with external entities without extracting it from that framework or merging it with other notions. Maintaining the integrity of the symbol and the symbolized is crucial for discerning the message and its meaning from the dreamer's perspective.

Two key aspects reemerge at this point. The first is the luminosity of Being, and the other is symbolic language:

> A synthesis between the conscious and the unconscious... something truly real that transcends conceptual understanding... laden with an energy of its own that is called (by Rudolf Otto) "numinosity." It is a symbol in that it suggests and stimulates human beings to realize the

121. Carl G. Jung, *Man and His Symbols*, ed. M.-L. von Franz (New York: Anchor Press/Doubleday, 1964), 52–53.

> possibilities that would be denied if one only followed pure rationality and conscious logic.[122]

As we have seen throughout the second part of this text, the conceptualization of symbols and the use of formal language have deprived the human being of access to the deeper and numinous levels of reality that rest in the very essence of being. Symbolic thought is not, in itself, an innovation, so to speak. On the contrary, what these reflections have aimed to show is that, originally, human beings have always thought symbolically, using mythology and other forms of expression to explain and understand the essence of being, of their own being. That is, humanity has employed symbolic language to express supreme realities that, though perceptible, challenge direct articulation and resist being articulated in prosaic terms. We can say that the symbol is consubstantial with the human being. However, with the birth of Western philosophy and later of science, conceptual thought has gradually colonized the forms of life through which human beings relate to the world, to their history, and to their being. This colonization has been carried out linguistically. Western philosophy is distinguished by its assumption that reality exists within its linguistic expression. This thought, characterized by a logical-formal nature, has only constructed a reality based on ontic dimensions, without managing to decipher the essence of life.

Philosophy, in its intrinsic nature, lacks the ability to probe this dimension of being that only expresses itself symbolically. This, however, does not demand the end of philosophy as such and its overcoming through symbolic thought. Quite the opposite, the symbolic turn should not be understood as the end or overcoming of any other turn, but rather as a need to unveil the buried symbolic dimension of the human being so that we may approach the deepest core of our being. What this expresses, put another way, is the need for Western philosophy to merge with meditative and symbolic reflection in order to achieve a holistic vision.

---

122. Pinkus L., *La dimensione simbolica: aspetti psicodinamici* in *Studia Anselmiana* 64 (1974), 11-28, p. 18. Translation mine.

This request or requirement already appears in certain authors, such as Paul Ricoeur, in his first work on symbolism, titled *The Symbolism of Evil*, where he argues that certain fundamental experiences, like evil, elude mere conceptual understanding and require the mediation of symbols and myths. Cardinal dimensions and other fundamental aspects of life are symbolic. Addressing these realities through the symbol allows a holistic apprehension of their nature. The revelations obtained through symbolism can then be subjected to philosophical reflection. Thus, symbolic thought and conceptual thought do not exclude one another; rather, both are needed. Weaving symbolic thought with conceptual thought implies bridging the divine and the earthly.

The symbol, therefore, reveals itself as the essence for accessing human life in its deepest becoming. Since the dawn of humanity, the symbol has served as a bridge to the transcendent, the ineffable, which the human being gradually transformed into an instrument for transmitting acquired truths. In some cases, these symbolic forms were directly taken from their environment, from nature itself; in others, they were human creations or even received through revelation. While their original purpose was eminently extraordinary, their application diluted toward more mundane spheres of existence over time and became a means for ordinary life.

To understand the importance of the symbol as such, let us consider, for example, the cross: its sacred meaning did not emerge until Jesus was crucified on it. A similar reasoning applies to the chalice Jesus used and the garments he wore, given their symbolic interaction. Likewise, 500 years ago, during his journey from Navadvipa to Puri, Śrī Chaitanya Mahāprabhu spent the night in Bhadrak, on the banks of the sacred Salandi River. He slept in an ancient temple of Śrī Śrī Rādhā Madana Mohana, located in the village of Santhiya. Before departing for Puri, he blessed the temple *pūjari* by giving him his personal blanket. This blanket has been venerated for the last 500 years by the descendants of the original priest. The blanket remains hidden in the temple throughout the year, but once a year, on the anniversary of Śrī Chaitanya Mahāprabhu's visit to Bhadrak, it is displayed to the public and a great festival is celebrated. The sacredness of the blanket did not emerge until Lord Chaitanya had used it. In this sense, it is noteworthy that certain visionaries, such as prophets, lived the symbol not only as a representation but as an authentic epiphany. Mircea Eliade, a leading authority in the study of religious thought, asserts that the symbol expands the dialectic of hierophany, the phenomenon through which the sacred reveals itself in the profane context: "Everything that is not directly consecrated by a hierophany becomes sacred by the fact of participating in a symbol."[123] The sacred manifests symbolically, and an object or concept can acquire this sacredness by participating in the symbol.

Similar to linguistic structures like parables or metaphors, the symbol's mission is to communicate a vision of the cosmos and reality. This vision, though it may manifest in various forms, retains an immutable essence in the consciousness of different cultures and eras. Therefore, the history of religions provides us with a valuable testimony, as it has played a crucial role in the revaluation and understanding of the function and efficacy of symbols. Consequently, the analysis of these symbolic representations merits rigorous and specialized scrutiny. In his work *Images and Symbols*, Mircea Eliade posits that "symbolic thinking 'breaks open' the immediate reality without any minimizing or undervaluing of it: in such a perspective this is not a closed Universe, no object exists for itself in isolation'."[124]

Ricoeur quotes Eliade, who affirms that that a symbol possesses multiple interpretations and is not limited to a single meaning. That is, the symbolic richness is polysemic, not unisemic, referring to the multiplicity of interpretations. In the epistemological framework, a symbol is not confined to one connotation but holds a vast spectrum of interpretations. Confining meanings to a single definition is indeed to undermine its richness, as it would lead to its conceptual encapsulation. Thus, positing that "it is not isolated" suggests recognizing its integral nature, hinting at its reference to a totality.

123. Mircea Eliade, *Tratado de historia de las religiones* [*Treatise on the History of Religions*] (Madrid: Ediciones Cristiandad, 1974), vol. 2, 235. Translation mine.
124. Mircea Eliade, *Images and Symbols: Studies in Religious Symbolism* (London: Harvill Press, 1958), 178.

Symbolic representations offer the human being a pathway to access the most hidden dimensions of universal truths. Within this latent dimension, Truth emerges in its essence as an unaltered constant, though susceptible to varied configurations, expressions, and projections. Despite the apparent divergences and phenomenal variability in myths, poems, and religious systems, all converge on a common core of understanding. This is why a diversity of religions that employ these symbolic and mythological forms, despite their particular manifestations, convey teachings that are essentially analogous. While logical reasoning deals with the surface of being, the symbols, myths, and religions probe the depths of human consciousness.

Chapter 28

An invitation to transcendence in Rilke's poetry

Let us carefully read the words of wisdom in this poem by R. M. Rilke:

> Catch only what you've thrown yourself, all is
> mere skill and little gain;
> but when you're suddenly the catcher of a ball
> thrown by an eternal partner
> with accurate and measured swing
> towards you, to your center, in an arch
> from the great bridgebuilding of God:
> why catching then becomes a power-
> not yours, a world's.[125]

The poem focuses on self-knowledge as an opening to something broader and more meaningful than our separate I.

"Catch only what you've thrown yourself"

This maxim suggests that when we live focused on the strictly personal, existence unfolds in a narrowly limited dimension. The one who only collects what they themselves have thrown remains trapped within the sphere of machination, under the yoke of technical skill

125. Rainer Maria Rilke, "Poem to Nike" (January 1922) (Translated by Walter Kaufmann).

and control. Living only for and from our autonomous ego translates into a life centered on limitation.

In this framework, our desires are subordinated to what our mind craves, and we are incapable of transcending the boundaries of what we can conceptualize. We do not seek to achieve true bliss but; our own ideas about it. Erroneously believing that happiness resides in the objective plane, we dedicate our lives to attaining tangible goals. By conceptualizing, we objectify paradise, God, or enlightenment, which leads us to live pursuing our notions of what we conceptualized.

When analyzing the etymology of *idol*, we find that it can be understood as a "conceptual image." It comes from Late Latin *idolus*, derived from Greek *éidolon* (image). Its root *eidon* means "crafted work" and is related to *eidos* (idea or form). The idol is not a reality in itself, but a projection of our desires and expectations. The idol is always a replacement for the foundation. We become idolaters when, from our egoic limitation, we substitute that foundation with images and concepts. But this means something important: man does not live without a foundation. This is why idolatry is so common. Either we rest in the Divine or we create an idol according to our own projection. Ultimately, if we establish the foundation, we fulfill the desire to be like gods. It consists of the incarnation of desires, a figure created in our image and egoic likeness. This image keeps us trapped in the conceptual sphere, hindering a deeper perception of our existence. This same idea appears in the Scriptures; in this case, it is linked to "evil."

לֹא יִהְיֶה בְךָ אֵל זָר וְלֹא תִשְׁתַּחֲוֶה לְאֵל נֵכָר:

(תהילים פ"א, י')

There should not be any alien god within you; and do not bow down to any foreign god.

(Psalms, 81:10)

אָמַר רַבִּי אָבִין: [...] "לֹא יִהְיֶה בְךָ אֵל זָר וְלֹא תִשְׁתַּחֲוֶה לְאֵל נֵכָר", אֵיזֶהוּ אֵל זָר שֶׁיֵּשׁ בְּגוּפוֹ שֶׁל אָדָם? הֱוֵי אוֹמֵר, זֶה יֵצֶר הָרָע.

(תלמוד בבלי, מסכת שבת, ק"ה, ב')

> Rabbi Avin said: [...] "There should not be any alien god within you; and do not bow down to any foreign god" (Psalms, 81:10). What is the strange god that exists within a person's body? One could say that it is the evil inclination.
>
> (*Talmud Bavli*, "*Shabbat*," 105b)

"all is mere skill and little gain"

Skill, when applied to the acquisition of ideas and concepts, yields nothing but an empty result, a perpetual dissatisfaction. Technique grants us skill but not mastery; it gives us loot, that fruit of plundering or undeserved profit, yet falls short when it attempts to provide true compensation, reward, or just retribution. Technique stands as the mechanism by which the human being is manipulated; it is the alchemy that generates the entity from the mere concept. Technique allows us to tear, extract, and detach ourselves from what is given without necessarily having earned what is obtained. This is "little gain," an object devoid of meaning and transcendence, the fruit of our own creations. Transcending ourselves through technique is a chimera. There is no action within our power to transcend our own conceptualization. No technique has the ability to take us beyond what we think we are or the conceptualization we have sketched of ourselves. Truth lies in a transcendental realm, inaccessible to any method. No meditation technique can confer enlightenment upon us, as the ego's effort cannot take us beyond itself. It is absurd to try to lift ourselves by pulling on our shoelaces or the belt of our pants. Ascension is not achieved through our own effort, but through the abandonment of technique and an opening toward the transcendental.

"but when you're suddenly the catcher of a ball thrown by an eternal partner"

Genuine inquiry is centered on that which surpasses us, that which transcends us as mere ideas. Specifically, *Homo sapiens* are commonly motivated by three fundamental reasons: fear, retribution, or inspiration. The majority act out of panic or some form of monetary or symbolic retribution. Only those who struggle for a goal that exceeds their individuality act under the guidance of inspiration. We become "hunters of the ball" at the precise moment when we abandon the search for what we have generated ourselves and choose to accept the spherical nature of existence that our eternal companion throws at us.

This "eternal partner," immutable and constant, who never abandons us even for an instant, is consciousness. Only that which has the capacity to know and record each of our experiences can be called by this name. We refer to this as "knowingness" or "knowability," an eternal presence that has accompanied our journey from the beginning but goes unnoticed because of our insatiable desire to gather, fascinated, what we ourselves scatter.

"with accurate and measured swing towards you"

This line suggests that there is a deep and predestined connection with this "eternal partner," a profoundly rooted bond that seems to be an integral part of our very identity. Our eternal consort will begin to propel the ball of existence toward us the moment we cease the act of collecting what we have self-generated, redirecting us through a meticulously known impulse toward our half, a guiding force that leads us to integration and union with our eternal consort.

"to your center"

As we mentioned, Aristotle states that *arjé hemisus panton*, or "The beginning is admittedly more than half of the whole."[126] However, this statement holds a dilemma, for that beginning, the primordial foundation that constitutes half of the totality, does not fall under our control, leading this assertion to a deep abyss of reflection. Jean-Paul Sartre, in his seminal work *Existentialism is a Humanism*, argues

126. Aristotle, *Nicomachean Ethics*, trans. H. Rackham, vol. 19 of Aristotle, ed. H. Rackham, Loeb Classical Library (Cambridge, MA: Harvard University Press, 1934), 1098b23.

that "man is nothing other than what he makes himself."[127] In this framework, Sartre maintains that human beings lack a preconceived essential nature or predetermined purpose and are, therefore, free to shape their own lives and give them meaning. However, he also acknowledges that a series of external factors, such as culture, society, and education shape individual existence. At the crossroads of these two assertions emerges a conclusion: the beginning, that origin that is half of the whole, is not inherent to us.

Aristotle argues that the **first nature** is the unalterable and immovable identity. According to Heidegger, this essence is the *existentiale* he calls "the clearing," or "the state of openness," in which human beings, in their consciousness, are open to being. However, the **second nature** is that which concerns us and which we can modify. For this reason, we can choose to be either authentic or inauthentic beings. In the poem, the first "half" refers to the relationship with being, and "your half" refers to our choice between an authentic or inauthentic relationship.

The primacy, the inaugural half, is the exclusive domain of the gods. Mythological-symbolic thinking is a thinking not anchored in an ego that is the origin and end of everything, as in philosophical-conceptual thinking, where gathering what we have thrown ourselves inevitably leads us to the phenomenon of the ego, which tries to seize that first half that is not its own through the concept. In the role of technician, the human being becomes the controller of the beginning and end of everything, a demiurge of their own reality. Conceptualization, by gathering our own creations, develops skill and ability, but only yields a fleeting and irrelevant loot due to its superficiality.

"in an arch from the great bridgebuilding of God"

God's bridge is found in *Likutei Moharan*:

---

127. Jean-Paul Sartre, *Existentialism Is a Humanism*, trans. Carol Macomber, ed. John Kulka (New Haven: Yale University Press, 2007), 22.

וְדַע, שֶׁהָאָדָם צָרִיךְ לַעֲבֹר עַל גֶּשֶׁר צַר מְאֹד מְאֹד, וְהַכְּלָל וְהָעִקָּר - שֶׁלֹּא יִתְפַּחֵד כְּלָל.
(ליקוטי מוהר"ן, תנינא, מ"ח, ב', ז')

> And know, that a person must cross a very narrow bridge, and the main thing is not to be afraid at all.
> (*Likutei Moharan*, *Tneina*, 48.2.7)

This "bridgebuilding of God" appears in the canonical texts as the narrow gate or the narrow path proposed by Jesus (Matthew, 7:13), referring to the delicate and tortuous framework that connects the relative and the absolute, the ephemeral and the eternal, the conceptualization of being and the essence of being itself, the human and the divine, consciousness and that which transcends it. With our perception distorted by the sense of an isolated "I," we interpret ourselves as entities independent of the cosmos as a whole. But our true essence is inescapably an indivisible part of a much broader and more meaningful matrix than the limited perspective of our egoic life. Intercepting that celestial ball, which has been thrown by our eternal companion toward our own half, is to enter the realm of grace, openness, or what Heidegger calls *ereignis*. This term, which translates as "event, occurrence, or becoming," refers to the manifestation of Being in itself and through humanity. It is the unfolding of Being in time and space, allowing human consciousness to witness that unfolding. For Heidegger, *ereignis* is fundamental to the harmonious relationship of human beings with their own existence and with reality. This leads him to affirm that the vast majority of people live trapped in an everyday existence, in the habitual, prisoners of trivial concerns and oblivious to the experience of *ereignis*. The donation is the opening of Being, while reception is what phenomenology has called "the intentionality of consciousness"; when both horizons merge, *ereignis* occurs. Access to an authentic existence is precisely what allows establishing a genuine relationship with Being and with one's own being-in-the-world, or *Dasein*. In *Being and Time*, Heidegger delves into the concept of "authentic existence," which involves openness to *ereignis*, that is, to the unfolding of Being. *Ereignis* represents a possibility to overcome the forgetfulness of the question of Being.

"why catching then becomes a power-not yours, a world's."

The lyricist concludes by postulating that, in conjunction with the discovery and restoration of the bonds with our eternal companion, the transcendent consciousness, the faculty called "catching" metamorphoses, ascending to a more powerful and transcendental stature, shedding its mere character of individual skill or expertise.

It is necessary to pause at the origin of the expression "accept," which dates back to the classical languages, specifically Latin *acceptāre*, the root of terms such as *acceptatio*, translatable as "acceptance." Formed from the prefixes *ad-* (toward) and *capere* (to take, to catch), its semantics unfold into the idea of "approving," as well as of "receiving." In its embryonic state, this word was used to express "to take something toward oneself" or "to receive something offered." In this sense, to know how to take or catch is inseparably linked to the act of knowing how to accept. The wisdom needed to appropriate an event involves mastery in accepting what our eternal companion throws at us. Thus, "catching" manifests as "knowing how to receive or accept." Acceptance stands as a fundamental requirement for being able to grasp what life offers us. The ball that our eternal companion throws toward our half is not caught with the purpose of acquiring it, but of accepting it. In contrast to philosophical thought, which, as we have seen, creates reality in the image and likeness of its own concepts from a position of absolute dominance, mythological thought is a thought of openness and acceptance of that which transcends us, that is, of the divine. While the former ontologizes reality and prevents it from being shown in its mode of being, the latter accepts Being without exerting any violence upon it. This mythological-symbolic thought, however, is much more than a mere technique or epistemological method designed to know things and accumulate knowledge of empirical facts. To accept and receive is a mode of being and revealing that requires a certain attitude.

We could say that this is true realism, to allow reality to be without invading or ontologizing it.

Unconditional acceptance of reality in its entirety is projected as the primordial essential step toward authentic transformation. The denial or repression of our emotions, whether negative or positive, only leads us down the path of suffering. If we are unable to accept the first half of our past, with its pleasant aspect and its unpleasant counterpart, it will be impossible to fully inhabit the present.

To exist completely in the now, it is crucial to be able to accept both the pleasant and unpleasant aspects of our past. Self-acceptance, with all our beautiful qualities and our imperfections, stands as a *sine qua non* condition for finding the longed-for inner peace. Similarly, in order to establish meaningful relationships, it is necessary to accept others as they are, without judgment or attempts to change them. In the same sense, in order to establish cardinally important connections, it becomes essential to accept human figures in their most authentic and indomitable essence, without exercising critical judgment or desiring to alter their intrinsic nature. It is of vital interest to understand that our happiness, a subjective and multifaceted phenomenon, does not gravitate around external actors but emanates from the epicenter of our own being.

Here, we are faced with a concept of holistic and unconditional acceptance, an embrace of the totality of life's manifestations, grounded in an unshakable faith in the fabric of existence. This posture of unrestricted acceptance symbolizes the culmination of the meditative art, as it exceeds our inclinations and repulsions toward the becoming of life. When we reach the capacity to accept life in its entirety, it becomes possible to be serene witnesses or observers of the events unfolding in our proximity. Acceptance of the abyssal depths of reality, the authentic self, and human entities grant us the ability to experience an inner metamorphosis and access a more evolved state of tranquility. Along with the renunciation of resistance and prejudice, we surrender to the fullness of the present moment, allowing life to flow with the naturalness of a mighty river.

אָז אָמַרְתִּי הִנֵּה־בָאתִי בִּמְגִלַּת־סֵפֶר כָּתוּב עָלָי:
לַעֲשׂוֹת־רְצוֹנְךָ אֱלֹהַי חָפָצְתִּי וְתוֹרָתְךָ בְּתוֹךְ מֵעָי:
(תהלים מ', ח'-ט')

Then I said: "See, I will bring a scroll recounting what befell me. O my God, I desired to do Your will and [to have] Your law within my innards."

(Psalms, 40:8–9)

וְהוּא בְאֶחָד וּמִי יְשִׁיבֶנּוּ וְנַפְשׁוֹ אִוְּתָה וַיָּעַשׂ: כִּי יַשְׁלִים חֻקִּי וְכָהֵנָּה רַבּוֹת עִמּוֹ:
(איוב כ"ג, י"ג-י"ד)

But he is unchangeable, and who can turn him? and what his soul desires, even that he does. For He will complete my sentence and there are many such things with Him.

(Job, 23:13–14)

The penetrating understanding that the supreme divinity is the only true demiurge, acting from its unfading perfection and untouched by any external energy, leads the devotee to dwell in a state of profound acceptance. From this perspective, the deity is recognized as a personification of unconditional love. Therefore, unwavering trust is placed in the premise that all of its actions are the optimal equation for our existence.

The recognition of the absolute supremacy of the deity and its omnipotent calls us to dissolve any resistance or attempt to impose our autonomous volition on the course of circumstances. Instead, we surrender to divine wisdom and love, trusting that all the experiences and situations that emerge on our path have a purpose and meaning that transcends our limited understanding. The act of humility involved in postponing the machinations about being, in order to liberate it, suggests the possibility of allowing Being to reveal itself without weaving the premises with which it must appear, not subsuming Being to the ought-to-be prescribed by individual consciousness.

This attitude of receptivity toward Divinity implies a surrender to its providential guidance and an unwavering trust that its designs are always imbued with benevolence, allowing us to recognize that divine love surrounds us at every moment of existence, even when we face challenges or difficulties that seem insurmountable. In this state of deep acceptance, we open ourselves to the grace and peace that spring from the connection with the divine. We find refuge in complete trust and unconditional surrender by recognizing that only the deity is the true craftsman and accepting its will as the best path for our existence. Living in harmony with divine love, we experience a profound acceptance that allows us to discover meaning and peace in every facet of our existence.

> I am crucified with Christ: nevertheless I live; yet not I, but Christ liveth in me: and the life which I now live in the flesh, I live by the faith of the Son of God, who loved me, and gave himself for me.
>
> (Galatians, 2:20)

My life no longer belongs to me; it has already been given to the Lord, and therefore He can do with it as He wishes.

आश्लिष्य वा पादरतां पिनष्टु मामदर्शनान्मर्महतां करोतु वा ।
यथा तथा वा विदधातु लम्पटो मत्प्राणनाथस्तु स एव नापरः ॥

āślisya vā pāda-ratāṁ pinaṣṭu mām
adarśanān marma-hatāṁ karotu vā
yathā tathā vā vidadhātu lampaṭo
mat-prāṇa-nāthas tu sa eva nāparaḥ

> I know no one but Kṛṣṇa as my Lord, and He shall remain so even if He handles me roughly by His embrace or makes me brokenhearted by not being present before me. He is completely free to do anything and everything, for He is always my worshipful Lord, unconditionally.
>
> (*Śikṣāṣṭakam*, 8)

In his sacred communion of prayers, the genuine devotee does not beg for what is pleasing to his senses, but instead, he fervently pursues the devotion and dedication necessary to accept and pay tribute to what the divinity assigns him. This stance of receptivity and gratitude implies having the disposition to embrace and welcome all that life has in store for us, even when it is tinged with pain or does not align with our preferences. Devotees place their trust in the premise that, although in the present moment, it may seem incomprehensible, what is given to them is optimal for their own evolution.

This prism implies recognizing that we do not always have the capacity to fully unravel the purpose hidden behind the circumstances we face. Despite the veil of uncertainty, the devotee maintains the certainty that every experience, even those considered uncomfortable or unpleasant, is precisely what is required for his development journey. Through such experiences, we are granted opportunities to learn, fortify ourselves, grow, and progress on our path to fulfillment.

The ability to welcome and accept whatever is unfolded in life with appreciation and humility is crucial for the retroprogressive process. By shedding our own expectations and preferences, we open ourselves to receive the gifts and teachings that are presented to us in every fleeting moment. This receptivity allows us to flow with greater harmony and confidence through the course of existence, knowing that we are in loving and wise hands. It is imperative to be capable of welcoming and accepting with gratitude whatever life offers us, even when it manifests as a hard obstacle or an unyielding challenge; this is an inherent trait of the true devotee. This disposition enables us to trust in divine wisdom and receive exactly what we need for our growth and spiritual awakening. Only then will we be capable of knowing how to take, knowing how to accept.

Clearly, acceptance does not imply complacency in the face of situations with negative connotations or harmful to the development of existence. Thus, for example, when we find ourselves entangled in a toxic relationship or working in an unsatisfactory job environment, acceptance does not mean a resigned submission to these pernicious circumstances. In such scenarios, adopting decisive actions to alter or improve the pre-existing situation is crucial. Therapy involves a good diagnosis, and the diagnosis examines the symptom without denying it.

The concept of acceptance is more appropriately applied in the context of the ethereal present, focusing on the recognition of reality in its rawest and most authentic form, as it presents itself in the current moment. It becomes crucial not to fall into our negative mental narratives that label us in a derogatory manner as failures or losers. Recognition implies freeing ourselves from these self-destructive thoughts that erode our inner being.

Acceptance is exercised in a selective and conscious manner, weighing the need to make healthy and constructive decisions in situations of marked disadvantage. It is not about adopting a passive stance toward any negative circumstance, but about fostering an attitude of understanding and acceptance of the present while diligently seeking to grow and improve our quality of life. Acceptance is exclusively applied to the present moment and does not encompass the entirety of a situation over the course of existence.

It becomes essential to understand that no one aspires to remain in a harmful situation for the long term. However, in the present, we can embrace reality without generating resistance, admitting the presence of discomfort or unease. Consider the example of being caught in the rain without an umbrella. Although the situation may be unpleasant, it is illogical to increase suffering by complaining about the weather. Acceptance in this scenario means adapting to the present moment and avoiding any unnecessary resistance. However, accepting does not mean remaining passive under the rain. We can seek shelter or an umbrella.

Acceptance can easily be confused with passive resignation, so it is important to identify the first as an open attitude that serves as a healthy foundation for making conscious and constructive decisions. It facilitates adaptation to present circumstances and acts as a catalyst capable of generating significant changes in our lives. Acceptance consists of abandoning our attachment to desired outcomes, as well as renouncing our escape from undesirable experiences. Full acceptance of *what is* lays the foundation for authentic transformation. It is a conscious and deliberate choice to relate to reality free from judgments and resistances.

Letting go of our expectations frees us from the heavy emotional burden that accompanies resistance, allowing an opening to a variety of perspectives and unexplored possibilities. The recognition and assimilation of the reality of our existence, in all its facets, constitutes the boldest act that an individual can undertake. Such acceptance forges in us a strength that opens the doors to the unknown. It is through this courage that we are equipped to venture into the vast sea of the unexplored. This journey is not a simple escape into the unknown but a deliberate movement toward understanding and exploring realities and possibilities that have thus far remained hidden or inaccessible.

By obstinately anchoring ourselves in what is pre-established, resisting what does not fit into our preconceived schemes, we restrict our capacity for development and adaptation. Acceptance gives us greater receptivity to experiences as they present themselves, allowing for more clarity and better-founded decisions. By freeing ourselves from the yoke of our desires and resistances, we are able to explore new alternatives, adopt different approaches, and find more creative and adaptive solutions.

Furthermore, acceptance gives us the possibility to transcend our limits and foster a profound internal transformation. We unleash our energy and potential to generate significant and tangible changes in our lives by ceasing resistance and embracing reality in its intrinsic essence. Acceptance becomes the threshold to a journey of self-discovery and authentic, lasting metamorphosis. The main challenge lies in shedding negativity and avoiding its projection onto objective reality, a key aspect in the practice of acceptance.

In areas such as marriage, health, or economic status, we possess the ability to react or act consciously. If our consciousness seeks to experience misfortune through drama, we renounce the present moment, which automatically leads us to suffering. Incorporating fatality into our life means rejecting existence in its present manifestation. The choice of the narrative of our life, with its twists and torments, is intrinsically personal and resides in our innermost being. However, in any circumstance, no matter how unfortunate or uncomfortable it may be, there always lies the possibility of settling into acceptance. Even if the current moment manifests in a form that is extremely ungrateful to be enjoyed, we can always choose to accept it. When we manage to accept the present moment, despite being adverse, we experience a sense of serenity that allows us to discern that situations that are impossible to enjoy are minimal compared to the vastness of the wonderful reality.

The exceptional reality can only be perceived in the ordinary of the accepted moment, never in the entirety of the life situation. We will always find in our path people or situations that do not fit our preferences. If we do not practice acceptance, we will live in constant disappointment and persistent frustration. By resisting and rejecting the present, we are repudiating reality and denying life itself. That resistance to the present, the rejection of the here and now, implies a kind of self-exile from reality. On the other hand, accepting the current moment, embracing it as it is, means allowing it to simply be, without adding anything, without taking anything away. In that precise moment when we manage to fully accept the present, we experience an expanded awareness and greater clarity, which provides us with a solid foundation for making decisions and seeking effective solutions.

In pursuit of finding solutions in the realm of life, it becomes essential for us to be fully conscious and vigilant, perceiving the current landscape with absolute clarity. Acceptance of the present moment frees us from resistance, providing us with the opportunity to experience serenity and mental sharpness. By opening ourselves up, we can direct our attention to what truly matters and take appropriate actions for growth and personal development. However, by merely collecting what we ourselves have thrown into the wind, by pursuing only our own desires and ambitions, we will never achieve more than what we have conceptualized. Only by mastering acceptance do we gain the opportunity to access something that transcends us, something beyond our limited individuality.

We do not have the capacity to conceptualize or imagine something grander than what existence dreams for us. We cannot aspire to something that surpasses what existence has reserved for us. Only by transcending the realm of conceptualization and learning to accept does catching transform into a power, not of individual ownership but universal. Do not seek to claim small corners of reality born from your own conceptualizations, but rather embrace what truly belongs to you: the entire universe. Accept the generosity of the cosmos, letting go of your narrow pretensions and opening yourself to the joy of the totality that existence offers you.

> If you do not expect the unexpected, you will not find it; for it is hard to be sought out and difficult.[128]

Catching is learning to take ownership of the phenomenon or event. Learning to take ownership of such an event implies making oneself accessible through dwelling in acceptance. The world is defined as the ethos, or "dwelling," the ontological space where gods and humans coexist. The dwelling is the first half, a divine creation, while humans, being entities molded by the gods, represent the myth or narrative. We are nothing but mere characters, beings inscribed in the narrative of the gods in this first half. It is not that the gods are a creation of human myths, but rather that we form part of the mythological construction of the gods. We are the result, product, or consequence of the gods' narrative. The second half is ours, and it is here where Sartre's thought comes into play when he states that human beings are what they make of what has been made of them. Genesis represents the divine half, the symbol; while the *arche* represents the human beginning, the second half, the concept. The appropriating event belongs to the first half, despite being buried by technique. *Arche* thinks beyond time, granting dominion, technique, and control. Genesis grants spiritual power but not manipulative power.

---

128. Heraclitus, in John Burnet, *Early Greek Philosophy*, 4th ed. (London: A. & C. Black, 1920), 133 (frag. 7 = DK B7).

Since power does not belong to us, but rather we belong to power, knowing how to take is not an individual power but emanates from the world. We dwell in the sacred by realizing that the first half is not at our disposal.

The gods populate the first half, but their presence manifests only when we have appropriated the second half. As long as we continue as self-convinced storytellers, we will persist in perfecting our ability to collect what we ourselves project, a loot devoid of transcendental meaning. By transmuting myth into philosophy, in an attempt to take ownership of the event through the rationality of concept, humans begin the task of collecting what they themselves project. From the perspective of the first half, we err in erecting ourselves as creators of myth, while in the second half, we consciously participate in the myth, being aware actors of a broader narrative. Only by detaching ourselves from yesterday, from what was, from the past, can we dwell in the sacredness of what is. The figure of the last God emerges in the horizon of the sacred.

Chapter 29

Tracing the origins of symbolic language

To recover the symbolic dimension of thought that certain philosophical turns have marginalized and distorted, the symbolic turn must return to the almost hidden past of its terms and original meanings in order to rescue its origin and essence from oblivion. Words, however, are not mere alphabetical sequences. A term is more than a group of letters or sounds. Every linguistic construct responds to an underlying motivation that gives rise to its manifestation. Therefore, if we truly wish to understand the words *sign* and *symbol*, which are the focus of our current study, we must first investigate how and why they began to be used from their very inception.

Therefore, this chapter delves into the study of semantic evolution within the Greco-Roman framework, focusing particularly on the etymology and historical development of the Greek terms *semeîon*, *tékmor*, and *symbolon*, all of which are precursors to modern semiotics, as Wenceslao Castañares skillfully analyzes in his famous work *History of semiotic thinking*.[129] These are fundamental concepts for understanding the birth of the scientific-rational thought with which, especially in the West, the world and the reality that structures it have been drawn, thought, and envisioned. In this context, the semiotic archaeology undertaken by the symbolic turn presents itself as a formal analysis of signs, rooted in philosophical thought. The importance of language in this process is unquestionable, acting

129. Wenceslao Castañares, *History of Semiotic Thought, Vol. 1: The Greco-Roman Antiquity* [*Historia del pensamiento semiótico. Vol. 1, La Antigüedad grecolatina*] (Madrid: Editorial Trotta, 2014).

as the medium through which scientific-philosophical thinkers shape their ideas. The absence of a precise language would be as debilitating for science as the lack of tools for an artist to express their art. Science, deprived of its linguistic medium, would lose its structure, just as art would fade without its physical manifestation.

Motivated by the need to express the notion of "meaning," of "wanting to say," as the act of attributing meaning, the Greeks created a wide range of words. In the rich lexicon of the Hellenes, certain terms emerge with notable prominence. Among these, *semeîon*, *tékmor*, and *symbolon* are those that, due to their implications and subsequent uses, demand a more detailed analysis.

In the conceptualization of signs as autonomous entities, we must recognize the influence of thinkers such as Hippocrates, Plato, and Aristotle. The understanding of the original meaning of their language arises from the effort to introduce ourselves into their minds and hearts to try to observe and understand the world through the words they chose. Although modern academic semiotics later formalized the idea of the *sign*, there were already notions and entities addressing this concept long before. For a full understanding of this subject, it is essential to go back and excavate the origins of these ideas, prior to the time of these philosophers and the academic disciplines they themselves inaugurated. To do so, it will be crucial to carry out an exhaustive inquiry into the primordial causes that laid the foundation for the introduction of a term into the lexicon and what its determining impulses were. To understand the need that motivated the creation of these terms, we must be word detectives and search for clues in history to access the meaning of each term in a given era and its origins.

The Greek terms *semeîon*, *tékmor*, and *symbolon* are intrinsically linked to the notion of a *sign*. Simplifying, we will say that *semeîon* denotes a sign, *tékmor* a proof, and *symbolon* a symbol. However, to understand the depth of their respective meanings, we must delve into their historical evolution across different contexts. In the field of semiotics, there is an evident distinction between the academic analysis of how words and signs acquire their meaning and the inherent interaction between these elements and their meanings.

This differentiation has roots that extend far before the era of formal academic studies. From our perspective, it is necessary to recognize the existence of a pre-academic era, a historical phase in which, despite the lack of a systematic approach, reflective thoughts were already being manifested and words and signs were used in communication.

As we will see later, in contemporary semiotic thought, *sign* and *symbol* have crystal-clear and defined meanings. However, in texts preceding the works of Plato and Aristotle, these terms were employed in a less rigorous and precise manner, with more diffuse and general contours, but no less important. We witness how words, like ideas, evolve, transitioning from a more fluid and broad semantic state to a more restricted and specific one. It is worth noting that the semantic genealogy of *semeîon* and *symbolon*, although sometimes converging, has followed distinct paths.

Originally, both words were used to refer to what represents or means something, but over time, both their use and meaning underwent significant changes. This happens naturally due to the very nature of the sign, whose signifier carries historical weight. Words emerge as a response to the need to express a specific idea. In this analysis, we aim to understand what needs drove the ancients to use these terms, as well as discern the subtle differences between them and the contexts in which they were employed. Following Heidegger's reflection, the primordial nature of a term reflects a more authentic connection with the object or concept it refers to. Therefore, our semiotic-archaeological study leads us to seek the origin of the term *symbol*, investigating the oldest writings that have reached us to this day.

(1) *Semeîon* - The genealogy of the terms from the *sem-* family

In a meticulous analysis of the etymology of words derived from the *sem-* prefix, the term *semeîon*, despite its evident prominence in contemporary discourse, does not rise as the primordial representative of this lexical lineage. In an earlier era, *sêma*, which translates as "meaning," emerged alongside the verb *semaínein*, referring to the process of "signifying," preceding *semeîon* and other derivatives that we will explore later in greater depth.

(1.1) *Sêma* – "sign or tomb"

The term *sêma* has been interpreted in many ways throughout time. Before the rigorous analysis of Plato and Aristotle, this term had a nebulous and imprecise definition, but it was no less rich for that. In Homer's work, the word unfolds with multiple meanings, being interpreted as "sign, signal, or indication," depending on the reality being conveyed. But it could also mean "tomb or mound," and it is precisely in this sense that it appears recurrently in *The Iliad* and *The Odyssey*, both works written in the 8th century BCE as part of what we now know as the Epic Cycle of Hellenic literature, typically composed in hexameter verses or alternatively in prose. These works capture the essence of the Hellenic oral tradition and stand as pillars in the study of ancient mythology and morality, reflecting the worldview and ideals of their time. What is important for our study, however, is that in them we find almost equally the two meanings of *sêma* as "tomb" and "sign," whether natural or conventional, thereby consolidating the multiple dimensions of this term.

This multiple meaning of the term should not be understood as confusion, and thus as something negative. On the contrary, etymology shows us often unexpected links between words and concepts. Moreover, in this specific case, the term *sêma* referred to a column marking the burial place of a person. Over time, this designation extended to the mound or burial mound that served the same identifying function. This connotation leads us to the semantic triangulation between the concepts of tomb, mound, and sign. In signaling, the accumulation of stones is required, thus forming a mound that operates as an indicator of the underlying presence of remains. The certainty of the deceased's presence is guaranteed only by this stone sign. Linguistic richness manifests in that the term *sêma* denotes both "tomb" and "sign" or "signal." Such duality extends to the term *symbol*, which refers to the joining of parts, akin to the mound that brings together stones. This etymological play allows us to reflect on the union of diversity into a singularity.

The same term *sêma* also appears in the work of Hesiod with the same etymological variations. In *Works and Days*, Hesiod mentions the cry of the crane, described as if it were a "sign" of something coming:

> Mark, when you hear the voice of the crane who cries year by year from the clouds above, for she gives the signal (*sêma*) for ploughing and shows the season of rainy winter; but she vexes the heart of the man who has no oxen.[130]

On the other hand, in *Theogony*, there is a passage that stands out for corroborating the previously mentioned duality of *sêma* in its reference to a tomb and a sign. Similarly to Homer's works, Hesiod's *Theogony* represents a pillar in the study of Greek mythology and offers a fascinating worldview and narrative structure of antiquity. It reflects the beliefs and imagination of an era defined by its epic tales and rich oral tradition. If we examine the heading of Hesiod's *Theogony*, we see that *theo* translates as "god," while *gonia*, derived from *genos*, means "origin or genesis," leading us to understand *Theogony* means "the origin of the Gods." In the following passage, it narrates how Cronos expels the stone he had mistakenly swallowed, thinking it was one of his descendants, namely Zeus. Later, the same Zeus places this stone at the foot of Mount Parnassus, thus instituting a "landmark for future generations" or "monument for posterity" (*sem'émen eksopíso*).

> Swiftly the strength and shining limbs
> of our king grew, and in the course of a year,
> tricked by Gaia's cunning advice,
> great, crooked-counselling Kronos disgorged his children
> defeated by the skill and strength of his son.

130. Hesiod, *Works and Days*, in *The Homeric Hymns and Homerica*, trans. Hugh G. Evelyn-White, Loeb Classical Library (London: William Heinemann; New York: Macmillan Co., 1914), 37.

First he vomited out the stone which he'd swallowed last.
Zeus set it down in the wide-wayed earth,
in holy Delphi, in the vales of Mount Parnassus,
to serve as a sign hereafter, a wonder for mortal men and women.[131]

In the dawn of Greek literature, specifically in the works of Homer and Hesiod, the term *semeîon* does not yet appear with the prominence it would later achieve, especially from the 6th century BCE onward, when writers like Aeschylus, Aesop, and Anaxagoras begin to incorporate the word more regularly in their works. In this context, however, the word *sêma* evolves, acquiring connotations different from those previously known.

The tragic work *The Seven Against Thebes* (Ἑπτὰ ἐπὶ Θῆβας), created by the playwright Aeschylus, dated to 467 BCE is part of a broader tetralogy that includes the tragedies *Laius* and *Oedipus*, as well as a satyr play known as *The Sphinx*. There, we find an illustrative example in which *sêma* is used to describe the heraldic markings on the shields of war:

> Hermes rightly brought them together: they will meet in battle as two enemies, just like the warlike gods on their two shields. For Hippomedon's armour proudly shows a fire-belching Typhon, whereas Hyperbios has Father Zeus erect on both his feet, a flaming lightning bolt gripped in his fist. And no one has yet seen a conquered Zeus. It is true one cannot always count on the goodwill of the gods, but nonetheless we are with the conquerors in that fight, and they are with the conquered, if Zeus is more ferocious in a war than Typhon. So, the insignia these warriors bear may well decide the outcome of the clash when they both meet, and our Hyperbios may find in Zeus depicted on his shield a fortunate defense. And now Hermes, god of chance, has

131. Hesiod, *Theogony*, in *Myths of the Greek and Roman Gods*, ed. Roberto Nickel (Toronto: Ryerson University, n.d.), vv. 450–500.

> brought both men together, as is appropriate, for these two men will meet in battle as two enemies, just like the warlike gods on their two shields. For Hippomedon's armour proudly shows a fire-belching Typhon, whereas Hyperbios has Father Zeus erect on both his feet, a flaming lightning bolt gripped in his fist. And no onehas yet seen a conquered Zeus. It is true one cannot always count on the goodwill of the gods, but nonetheless we are with the conquerors in that fight, and they are with the conquered, if Zeus is more ferocious in a war than Typhon. So the insignia these warriors bear may well decide the outcome of the clash when they both meet, and our Hyperbios may find in Zeus depicted on his shield a fortunate defence.[132]

> No. He is a man who will either die and give his country back what she paid to raise him, or he will seize two warriors and the city on the shield and with those spoils adorn his father's home. Now, tell me all about another braggart, and give me every detail of his boasting.[133]

As we mentioned earlier in Homer, we identify the recurring appearance of the terms *sêma* and *semaínō*, both with a broad semantic range and poorly defined boundaries. In its use, *sêma* unfolds as an indication, whether divine, natural, or human. An illustrative example of this would be when reference is made to the lightning emitted by Zeus, flashes that, within the context of Hellenic tradition, are interpreted as omens, whether favorable or unfavorable, of something to come:

> ἀλλὰ Ζεὺς ἔτρεψε παραίσια σήματα φαίνων.

> but Zeus turned them back, showing forth portents that crossed them. (*The Iliad*, IV, 381)

132. Aeschylus, *Seven Against Thebes*, trans. Ian Johnston (Nanaimo, BC: Vancouver Island University, 2013), vv. 505–520, p.23.
133. Ibid., vv. 475–480, p.21

Ζεὺς δέ σφιν Κρονίδης ἐνδέξια σήματα φαίνων

And Zeus, son of Kronos, lightens upon their right hand, showing them. (*The Iliad*, IX, 236)

Similarly, it also refers to the written signs on a tablet when it says:

πέμπε δέ μιν Λυκίηνδε, πόρεν δ' ὅ γε σήματα λυγρὰ

but sent him away to Lykia, and handed him murderous symbols. (*The Iliad*, VI, 168)

Sometimes it refers to the mark made on a token for casting lots, as when it writes:

ὣς ἔφαθ', οἳ δὲ κλῆρον ἐσημήναντο ἕκαστος, ἐν δ' ἔβαλον κυνέῃ Ἀγαμέμνονος Ἀτρεΐδαο.

So he spoke, and each of them marked a lot as his own one lot.
They threw them in the helmet of Atreus' son, Agamemnon.
(*The Iliad*, VII, 175–176)

γνῶ δὲ κλήρου σῆμα ἰδών, γήθησε δὲ θυμῷ.

and he saw his mark on the lot, and knew it, and his heart
was gladdened. (*The Iliad*, VII, 189)

In *The Odyssey*, *sêma* is sometimes used to denote a secret sign or a mark that helps identify an individual, like the scar that Odysseus carries, a legacy of an unfortunate encounter with a boar:

εἰ δ' ἄγε δή, καὶ σῆμα ἀριφραδὲς ἄλλο τι δείξω,

Come now, I will show you something else, a sign, a very clear one.

ὄφρα μ' [7ἐῢ γνῶτον πιστωθῆτόν τ' ἐνὶ θυμῷ,

So that you may know me well and trust me with all your heart.

οὐλήν, τήν ποτέ με σῦς ἤλασε λευκῷ ὀδόντι

A scar, the one that a pig once gave me with a white tusk.

Παρνησόνδ' ἐλθόντα σὺν υἱάσιν Αὐτολύκοιο.

When I went to Parnassus with the sons of Autolycus.
(*The Odyssey*, XXI, 217–220)

This sign was essential for Euriclea, the loyal servant, to be able to identify Ulysses without a doubt.

τὴν δ' ἀπαμειβόμενος προσέφη πολύμητις 'Οδυσσεύς:

Then resourceful Odysseus answered her and spoke:

ὦ γρηῦ, οὕτω φασὶν ὅσοι ἴδον ὀφθαλμοῖσιν

"O aged woman, so say all those who have looked upon us

ἡμέας ἀμφοτέρους, μάλα εἰκέλω ἀλλήλοιϊν

with their own eyes, that we two are much alike,

ἔμμεναι, ὡς σύ περ αὐτὴ ἐπιφρονέουσ' ἀγορεύεις.

even as thou thyself dost wisely declare."

ὣς ἄρ' ἔφη, γρηῢς δὲ λέβηθ' ἕλε παμφανόωντα

So he spoke, and the old woman took the gleaming basin,

τῷ πόδας ἐξαπένιζεν, ὕδωρ δ' ἐνεχεύατο πολλὸν

wherewith she washed his feet, and poured much water therein.

(*The Odyssey*, XIX, 386 ss.)

Likewise, when Ulysses points to a distinctive mark carved on the marital bed, he uses this detail as a means to reveal his true identity to Penelope:

ῥεῖα μετοχλίσσειεν, ἐπεὶ μέγα σῆμα τέτυκται

He could move it easily, since a great sign has been constructed.

ἐν λέχει ἀσκητῷ: τὸ δ'' ἐγὼ κάμον οὐδέ τις ἄλλος.

In the clever bed. I, and no one else, made it.

θάμνος ἔφυ τανύφυλλος ἐλαίης ἕρκεος ἐντός,

Inside the wall grew a bush with long olive leaves,

(*The Odyssey*, XXIII, 188 ss.)

Centuries later, specifically in the 2nd century CE, we find an example of the term *semeîon* in the work *Stromata* by Clement of Alexandria, in this case, understood as a "sign" that should be attributed to the gods:

> […] pleasant also it is to know a clear token of ill or good amid all the signs that the deathless ones have given to mortal men.[134]

134. Hesiod, *The Melampodia*, frag. 4.1 (Clement of Alexandria, Stromateis VI 2, 26), in *The Homeric Hymns and Homerica*, trans. Hugh G. Evelyn-White (London: William Heinemann; New York: The Macmillan Co., 1914), 269.

(1.2) *Sêmántor* – "He who gives orders"

Sêma often refers to the signs of command made by military leaders, such as in:

> τοῖσιν ἕκαστος ἀνὴρ σημαινέτω οἷσί περ ἄρχει,
>
> let each man who is their leader give orders to these men. (*The Iliad*, II, 805)
>
> σημαίνει φυλάκεσσι καὶ 'Ιδομενῆος ὀπάων
>
> commands the pickets, and with him the follower of Idomeneus (*The Iliad*, X, 58)

Similarly, the individual who fulfills the function of giving directives, whether a chief, leader, or guide, is identified as *sêmántor*:

> ἵππω δευέσθην σημάντορος: αἶψα γὰρ εὗρεν
>
> The horses had been without a charioteer for a long time, for soon he found one. (*The Iliad*, VIII, 127)
>
> ὥς τ' ἐπιτειλαμένῳ σημάντορι πάντα πιθέσθαι.
>
> And to obey fully a master who gives orders. (*The Odyssey*, XVII, 21)

Analogously, the term *sêmántôr* is applied to Zeus, described as the supreme chief, leader, and mentor of all other deities in Hesiod's *The Shield of Heracles* and *Fragments*, as well as later in the 5th century CE in the texts of the Byzantine historian Lydus and the *Oxyrhynchus Papyri* respectively:

> To him was born, embracing the son of Cronos, lord of the dark clouds, and the other, Iphicles, of Amphitryon, the

> spearman, two distinct sons, the one from the union with a mortal man, but the other from the union with Zeus, leader of all the gods.[135]

> After all had settled in Italy as shown, those who adopted the local customs were called Latins, and those who had the customs of the Greeks were called Greeks, taking the names of the brothers Latinus, the one recently mentioned by us, and Greek, as Hesiod says in the Catalogues: "Agrio and Latinus," and again: "And in the palaces of the illustrious Deucalion, a maiden, Pandora, in love united to Zeus father, lord of all the gods, gave birth to Greek, a steadfast fighter."[136]

> A very distinct offspring: the one, mixed with a mortal man; the other, with Zeus Cronion, guide of all the gods.[137]

(1.3) *Semeîon* – "Indicative sign, indication, or proof"

Through various literary contexts, both *semeîon* and *semaíno* evolve into a narrower and more delineated meaning. Aeschylus, when using the term *semeîon*, introduces a rich polysemy in its usage. In specific contexts, he aligns it closely with what, in a later period, would be conceptualized as "symbol," such as when he refers to Poseidon or Neptune's trident as *semeîon theou* or "sign of a god."

> Chorus Leader: "What divinity do I still invoke?"
> Danaus: "I see here a trident, sign of a god."

135. Hesíodo (*Hesiod*), *Escudo de Heracles* [*Shield of Heracles*], en *Obras y fragmentos* [*Works and Fragments*], trad. Aurelio Pérez Jiménez y Alfonso Martínez Díez (Madrid: Editorial Gredos, 1978), 178, vv. 54–56. Translation mine.

136. Ibid., *Catálogo de las mujeres* [*Catalogue of Women or Ehoiai*], frag. 5 (Lido, *De mensibus* I 13), 213–214. Translation mine.

137. Ibid., *Fragmentos* [*Fragments*], frag. 195 (*Papiros de Oxirrinco* 2355 y 2494 A; *Escudo de Heracles* 1–56), 288. Translation mine.

> Chorus Leader: "Since it has guided us well, let it receive us well in this land."[138]

In other instances, the term takes on a different nuance, suggesting the idea of "indication," as can be interpreted in the work *Agamemnon* (Ἀγαμέμνων), the first play of the famous trilogy *The Oresteia*, by Aeschylus, presented in 458 BCE.

> It is plain. Their opening act is the signal [*sêmeion* pl.] of a plan to set up a tyranny in the polis.?"[139]

Semeîon also means "proof," as suggested in *Prometheus Bound*, 842 (Προμηθεὺς Δεσμώτης), a tragedy traditionally attributed to Aeschylus. This multiplicity of meanings that Aeschylus gives to *semeîon* is not merely a stylistic matter, but rather represents the complexity of ancient thought and its symbolic expression.

> These, then, are the tokens to you of my understanding, to show that it discerns more than has been made manifest.[140]

The tragedy *Antigone* (Ἀντιγόνη), a seminal work by Sophocles based on the myth of Antigone, places us within the context of the Theban legend, resuming the narrative right where Aeschylus's *The Seven Against Thebes* concludes. The significance of *Antigone* lies in its position within the Theban cycle and in how it articulates themes of loyalty, justice, and the conflict between human and divine laws. With his narrative skill, Sophocles tells a story that, while ancient

---

138. Esquilo (Aeschylus), *Los suplicantes* [*The Suppliants*], en *Tragedias* [*Tragedies*] (Madrid: Librodot.com, n.d.), v. 218. Translation mine.

139. Aeschylus, *Agamemnon*, in *Aeschylus*, Volume II: *The Libation Bearers, The Eumenides, Fragments*, trans. Herbert Weir Smyth, revised by Gregory Crane, Graeme Bird, Gregory Nagy, and Casey Dué (Cambridge, MA: Harvard University Press, 1926), v.1355, p.l.

140. Aeschylus, *Prometheus Bound*, line 842, in *Aeschylus*, Volume II: *Persians, Seven Against Thebes, Suppliants, Prometheus Bound*, trans. Herbert Weir Smyth (Cambridge, MA: Harvard University Press, 1926).

in origin, resonates with ethical and moral questions that remain relevant today. Sophocles, like Aeschylus, handles *semeîon* with a subtlety that allows for multiple interpretations. We find that, in *Antigone* 257, he uses the term *semeîon* to denote "indication," and this word choice carries investigative connotations:

> Was none, nor any sign who did this tiling.[141]

Sophocles gives the term *semeîon* the meaning of "proof" in his tragedy *Oedipus Rex*, with a more firm and definitive certainty. In its origins, it was simply known as *Oedipus* (Οἰδίπους), a name even used by Aristotle in his *Poetics*. According to scholars, the addition of "Tyrant" to its title was an effort to distinguish it from another Sophoclean work, *Oedipus at Colonus*. It is worth noting that, at that time, the term *tyrant* did not inherently carry a pejorative connotation; rather, it referred to a ruler lacking dynastic legitimacy.

> JOCASTA
>
> Then thou mayst ease thy conscience on that score.
> Listen and I'll convince thee that no man
> Hath scot or lot in the prophetic art.
> Here is the proof in brief. An oracle.[142]

Beyond Attic tragedy, Heraclitus and Parmenides also introduce us to a universe of "signs," whose careful observation allows us to uncover the essence of reality. A reflection of this is found specifically in the philosophical statement *fysis criptesai filei* or "nature likes to hide itself," which underscores nature's tendency to veil its mysteries. This is evident in the opening lines of Fragment 8 of Parmenides' poem, where the goddess says:

---

141. Sophocles, *Antigone*, translated by Robert Whitelaw, with introduction and notes by J. Churton Collins (Oxford: Clarendon Press, 1906).

142. Sophocles, *Oedipus the King*, trans. F. Storr, in *Sophocles*. Vol. 1: *Oedipus the King, Oedipus at Colonus, Antigone* (London: William Heinemann, 1912) v.710, p. 67.

Μόνος δ' ἔτι μῦθος ὁδοῖο
λείπεται ὡς ἔστιν· ταύτῃ δ' ἐπὶ σήματ' ἔασι
πολλὰ μάλ', ὡς ἀγένητον ἐὸν καὶ ἀνώλεθρόν ἐστιν,
ἐστι γὰρ οὐλομελὲς καὶ ἀτρεμὲς ἠδ' ἀτέλεστον·
οὐδέ ποτ' ἦν οὐδ' ἔσται, ἐπεὶ νῦν ἔστιν ὁμοῦ πᾶν,
ἕν, συνεχές [...]

One path only is left for us to
speak of, namely, that It is.
In it are very many tokens that what is,
is uncreated and indestructible, alone, complete,
immovable and without end.
Nor was it ever, nor will it be;
for now it is, all at once, a continuous one.[143]

Here, the goddess warns of the existence of multiple signs (σήματα) that, for an individual fortunate and prepared enough like Parmenides, serve as a window into the understanding of reality in its purest and most undistorted state. These signs offer the insightful philosopher a unique opportunity to transcend superficial perceptions and delve into the essence of what truly is.

In this semantic transition, it is essential to highlight the contribution of Heraclitus, whose enigmatic Fragment 93 (D-K) continues to generate analysis and scholarly discussions to this day:

ὁ ἄναξ οὗ τὸ μαντεῖόν ἐστι τὸ ἐν Δελφοῖς, οὔτε λέγει οὔτε κρύπτει ἀλλὰ σημαίνει.

And just as the Lord, whose oracle is at Delphi, neither speaks (οὔτε λέγει) nor hides (οὔτε κρύπτει), but manifests through signs (*allá semaínei*). The Lord whose oracle is at Delphi

143. Parmenides, *On Nature*, in *Parmenides: On Nature*, trans. Leonardo Tarán (Princeton, NJ: Princeton University Press, 1965), frag. 8.

> neither reveals (οὔτε λέγει) nor conceals (οὔτε κρύπτει), but gives a sign (*allá semaínei*).[144]

The key to deciphering the essential through universal knowledge lies in a deeper understanding of how entities communicate about themselves, thus enlightening us about our own essence. Heraclitus' famous fragment 93 is crucial for understanding this point. It introduces us to the oracle of Delphi, which, represented by Apollo, does not express its message directly or secretly but rather points to it through symbols. This hermeneutic method is fundamental for interpreting Heraclitus and any discourse or reality, as argued by Alcmaeon of Croton and Xenophanes when they defend the idea that, in the absence of divine knowledge, humans must guide themselves by signs.

When Heraclitus refers to Apollo, he does not mention him explicitly but describes him unequivocally, applying the same method of indication. As a figure of knowledge and oracle, Apollo teaches us that the path to illumination is not found in what is manifest nor in what is hidden. The "unsaid" and the "not hidden" in his approach suggest that reality is neither completely inaccessible nor fully explicit; both are limited and erroneous perspectives. In science, for example, there is often a pursuit of clear and direct knowledge of things, but the essence and existence of phenomena are often left unexplored, with only the phenomena themselves being explained. On the other hand, when we approach the absolute, direct and literal accessibility becomes impossible, as difference is an essential component of reality. Heraclitus proposes analogy as a means to understand the relationship between the sign and its meaning, between the observable and its intrinsic reality. This vision of dialectics and analogy is central to his thought. Finally, it is noteworthy that Heraclitus does not directly mention Apollo by name, reflecting his approach of indicating rather than openly declaring. Sometimes, silence is the best of signs. This methodology

144. Heraclitus, *The Texts of Early Greek Philosophy: The Complete Fragments and Selected Testimonies of the Major Presocratics*, ed. Daniel W. Graham, Part 1 (New York: Cambridge University Press, 2010), 177 (frag. 93 = DK B93).

extends to how we understand reality—not through exact names or transparent visions, but through properties, relationships, and essences. Thus, just as we understand an indivisible point through its circumference, we access the ultimate substance of nature through its external manifestations.

The divine never communicates clearly nor hides completely, but rather offers signs. For what is shown by the divine does not require information, and if nothing is shown, it cannot be known. What it does is show itself through signs or by providing clues. The divine does not give all the information nor hide it entirely; instead, it offers hints so that the message can be understood.

(1.4) *Semaíno* – "generation of signs or signals"

The Greek term *semaíno* should not be merely reduced to "mean" as it is often misunderstood in rather negligent translations; its meaning leans toward the generation of "signs or signals." What Heraclitus actually meant in fragment 93 is that the oracle does not speak or hide completely, but rather communicates through signs, signals, or indications. It would be something like a riddle game where what is communicated must be interpreted through certain clues given. *Semaíno* thus consists of generating signals that suggest an underlying reality. This signaling process involves two entities: the object being pointed at and the signal itself. This dynamic highlights a notion frequently proclaimed in Greek thought: the potential clarity of human language and the enigmatic nature of divine language, which requires exegesis. However, even in this specialization, absolute clarity remains an unattainable chimera.

In the aforementioned fragment, Heraclitus presents the dynamism of the term *semaíno*, which means both to point out and to indicate. To indicate, in this context, operates on two levels: to show while hiding and to hide while showing. In Christianity, the figure of Jesus exemplifies this duality because Jesus embodies the revelation, and he simultaneously conceals the Father. The mistake occurs when Jesus is seen as the ultimate term without recognizing the transcendence to the Father, or when the Father is sought without Jesus. In relation to *alétheia,* which etymologically refers to the discovery or revelation of what is hidden, the divine message is characterized by an esoteric nature, as it is neither fully delivered in its reason for being nor fully withheld from human understanding, but instead communicated through signs and symbols that require deciphering.

> Then, the disciples approached him and said, "Why do you speak to them in parables?" He answered them, "Because it has been given to you to know the mysteries of the kingdom of heaven, but to them it has not been given. For whoever has, to him, more will be given, and he will have abundance; but whoever does not have, even what he has will be taken away from him. Therefore, I speak to them in parables, because seeing they do not see, and hearing they do not hear, nor do they understand. And in them the prophecy of Isaiah is fulfilled, which says:
>
> "Hearing you will hear and shall not understand,
> And seeing you will see and not perceive;
> For the hearts of this people have grown dull.
> Their ears are hard of hearing, and their eyes they have closed;
> Lest they should see with their eyes and hear with their ears,
> Lest they should understand with their hearts and turn,
> So that I should heal them."
> But blessed are your eyes, for they see; and your ears, for they hear. For assuredly, I say to you that many prophets and righteous men desired to see what you see and did not see it, and to hear what you hear and did not hear it.
>
> (Matthew, 13:10–17)

(1.5) *Semaínein* – "to point out, indicate, or to mean"

Within Heraclitus' thought, the oracle of Delphi is not dedicated merely to showing or hiding; rather, its action is more precisely defined as *semaínein,* meaning "to point out or to indicate." This analysis reinforces the understanding of the term in question and, in turn, illuminates the meaning of the associated verbs. After deliberations, the perspective has solidified that *semaínein* acquires a more concrete meaning when examined in light of the verbs that precede it: *légo* and *krýpto*. "Neither reveals (οὔτε λέγει) nor conceals (οὔτε κρύπτει), but gives a sign (*allá semaínei*)." We are left with the three key terms by which Heraclitus explains how the oracle communicates: *légo*, *krýpto*, and *semaínein*. When addressing *légo*, commonly linked to expression or *lógos*, we must not overlook its more archaic connotations, which imply "to select, choose, enumerate, or unveil," which stands in contrast to *krýpto*, meaning "to hide." The etymology of *légo* traces back to the Greek *logon*, which encompasses the notions of word, reason, and discourse. Thus, *légo* refers to a *logos*, understood as the articulated expression that is shown or unveiled. In contrast, *kripte sai* translates as the act of hiding or concealing. Therefore, *légo* is related to "speaking or showing something," *krýpto* means "to hide," and *semaínein* denotes "to point out" or "to give clues." These juxtaposed ideas invite us to contemplate the dualism inherent in language: the simultaneous capacity to reveal and to conceal meaning. Language has the ability to reveal and conceal simultaneously, and when we express ourselves, we can show one part while hiding another. This approach to Heraclitus' vocabulary offers a deeper insight into his thinking, where the word is a tool for both revealing and selecting what remains in the shadow.

The sacred does not openly divulge its foundations nor conceal them to the point of inaccessibility; rather, it requests a hermeneutics that unravels veiled truths, alluded to in the word *alétheia*, which points to a truth that can be discovered through strategies of selection and ordering. *Alétheia* is commonly translated as unveiling or uncovering. However, this concept acquires a dialectical complexity in the style of Heraclitus that goes beyond a simple contradiction. The "neither... nor..., but..." that Heraclitus employs must be interpreted as "and... and..., that is to say..." because "giving signs" means "revealing" and "concealing" simultaneously. That is, to point out involves both revelation and concealment. The interpretative error lies in the assertion that it neither shows nor hides. The proper exegesis leads us to understand that the oracle of Delphi both shows and hides, while also indicating. Indication arises in showing through concealment and concealing in showing. To point out, therefore, is a process where revelation and concealment intertwine: it conceals in the act of showing and shows in the act of concealing. Thus, the act of emitting signs encompasses both concealment and manifestation. Concrete truths, including human beliefs, transmit their truths while disguising and covering them in the very act of communicating them; this is coherent, as the logic lies precisely in this paradox, being antagonistic to irrationality and, simultaneously, identical to it.

Consider a hypothetical statement that declares all Chileans to be liars. If, following this statement, I, identifying myself as Chilean, uphold this assertion, a paradox arises regarding the truth or falsity of my claim. By asserting that I lie, I paradoxically anchor my statement in truth. Conversely, if I lie by saying that Chileans lie, by my own admission, I am being honest. Here lies an essential dialectic: truth is immersed in contradiction. We are not referring to the divinity itself but to the divinity manifested in language. The spoken divinity is fragile, not because of God's fragility but because of the language's fragility. Therefore, the paradox arises in the linguistic manifestation of God, not in God Himself. It is not God who limits but language. Humans relate to the God of the word, and it is this word that both shows and hides.

The divine can only be apprehended through the word because "nothing exists outside the text," as Jacques Derrida maintains. This statement underscores the primacy of language in our understanding of the world; according to him, our only way to approach reality is through text. Derrida argues that what cannot be articulated, what escapes our capacity to enunciate, belongs to the realm of "the impossible." This realm of the impossible, while unattainable in linguistic terms, exerts constant pressure toward the possibility of being symbolized, of being transformed into text. However, the divinity that is shown in language simultaneously hides in it. The human being faces the challenge of interpreting, as the word encodes the divine without fully showing or hiding it. Essentially, the word is a symbolic gesture toward the divine. This reflection leads us to the heart of hermeneutics, the art of interpretation. Although this field extends to multiple linguistic manifestations, such as poetry, its application is more precise in the analysis of sacred texts like the following:

श्रीभगवानुवाच
अभयं सत्त्वसंशुद्धिर्ज्ञानयोगव्यवस्थितिः ।
दानं दमश्च यज्ञश्च स्वाध्यायस्तप आर्जवम् ॥

śrī-bhagavān uvāca
abhayaṁ sattva-saṁśuddhir
jñāna-yoga-vyavasthitiḥ
dānaṁ damaś ca yajñaś ca
svādhyāyas tapa ārjavam

Śrī Bhagavān said: Fearlessness, purity of heart, steadfastness in Yoga and knowledge, alms-giving, control of the senses, sacrifice, study of scriptures, austerity and straightforwardness.

(Bhagavad Gita, 16.1)

अनुद्वेगकरं वाक्यं सत्यं प्रियहितं च यत् ।
स्वाध्यायाभ्यसनं चैव वाङ्मयं तप उच्यते ॥

anudvega-karaṁ vākyaṁ
satyaṁ priya-hitaṁ ca yat
svādhyāyābhyasanaṁ caiva
vāṅ-mayaṁ tapa ucyate

Austerity of speech consists in speaking words that are truthful, pleasing, beneficial, and not agitating to others, and also in regularly reciting Vedic literature.

(Bhagavad Gita, 17.15)

ऋतं च स्वाध्यायप्रवचने च । सत्यं च स्वाध्यायप्रवचने च । तपश्च स्वाध्यायप्रवचने च । दमश्च स्वाध्यायप्रवचने च । शमश्च स्वाध्यायप्रवचने च । अग्नयश्च स्वाध्यायप्रवचने च । अग्निहोत्रं च स्वाध्यायप्रवचने च । अतिथयश्च स्वाध्यायप्रवचने च । मानुषं च स्वाध्यायप्रवचने च । प्रजा च स्वाध्यायप्रवचने च । प्रजनश्च स्वाध्यायप्रवचने च । प्रजातिश्च स्वाध्यायप्रवचने च ॥
सत्यमिति सत्यवचा राथीतरः । तप इति तपोनित्यः पौरुशिष्टिः । स्वाध्यायप्रवचने एवेति नाको मौद्गल्यः । तद्धि तपस्तद्धि तपः ॥

ṛtaṁ ca svādhyāya-pravacane ca. satyaṁ ca svādhyāya-pravacane ca. tapaś ca svādhyāya-pravacane ca. damaś ca svādhyāya-pravacane ca. śamaś ca svādhyāya-pravacane ca. agnayaś ca svādhyāya-pravacane ca. agnihotraṁ ca. svādhyāya-pravacane ca. atithayaś ca svādhyāya-pravacane ca. mānuṣaṁ ca svādhyāya-pravacane ca. prajā ca svādhyāya-pravacane ca. prajanaś ca svādhyāya-pravacane ca. prajātiś ca svādhyāya-pravacane ca. satyam iti satya-vacā rāthītaraḥ. tapa iti tapo-nityaḥ pauruśiṣṭiḥ. svādhyāya-pravacane eveti nāko maudgalyaḥ [...] *taddhi tapas taddhi tapaḥ.*

The right, as well as study and teaching; the true, as well as study and teaching; penance, as well as study and teaching; restraint, as well as study and teaching; peace, as well as study and teaching; the [sacrificial] fires, as well as study and teaching; offering to the fires, as well as study and teaching; [entertaining] guests, as well as study and teaching; [seeking the welfare of] humanity, as well as study and teaching; the offspring, as well as study and teaching; begetting, as well as study and teaching; propagation of the race, as well as study and teaching [...]. That, verily, is penance, yes, that is penance.
(*Taittirīya Upanishad*, 1.9.1–2c)

כִּי עֶזְרָא הֵכִין לְבָבוֹ לִדְרוֹשׁ אֶת־תּוֹרַת יְהוָה וְלַעֲשֹׂת וּלְלַמֵּד בְּיִשְׂרָאֵל חֹק וּמִשְׁפָּט׃
(עזרא ז׳, י׳)

Because Ezra had prepared his heart to inquire into the law of the Lord, to observe it, and to teach in Israel His statutes and judgments.

(Ezra, 7:10)

> All Scripture is inspired by God and is useful for teaching, for reproof, for correction, for training in righteousness.
>
> (2 Timothy, 3:16)

From here comes the concept of hermeneutics, as the exegesis or interpretation of the messages of Zeus by Hermes. Hermeneutics, a term derived from the Greek *hermeneutiké tekhne* (ἑρμηνευτικὴ τέχνη), is defined as the art of interpreting, explaining, and translating. This field is primarily concerned with written and verbal communication and, to a lesser degree, with non-verbal communication. In its modern configuration, it focuses on the concept of understanding, particularly with regard to texts of substantial importance.

The existence of hermeneutics as a discipline is justified by the complexities inherent in language, which often give rise to divergent or even contradictory interpretations of the meaning of texts. Under the influence of Wilhelm Dilthey, its main proponent in the contemporary era, hermeneutics aims to achieve a deeper understanding of an author than the author themselves may have been able to attain. Due to the genius of the author, the text leaves its own imprint once it is abandoned to the possible interpretation of others. It is dedicated to revealing the deep, hidden, or non-obvious meanings present in discourse through careful and rigorous analysis, an exegesis that investigates reason and its connection to meaning.

While enlightening, the analysis we have carried out so far does not encompass the entire semantic spectrum, as the genealogy of the *sem-* terms coexists with that of the *tekm-* terms, which are closely linked by an intrinsic relationship.

(2) *Tékmor* - The genealogy of the *tekm-* family of terms

Tékmar or *tékmor*, *tek-mérion*, and *tekmaíno* are expressions that, although conceptually distinct from the *semeîon* and *semaíno* family, reveal themselves as mutually explanatory. A full understanding of each of them presupposes and requires the correlation with its counterpart, forming a mosaic where each piece acquires meaning in relation to the other.

(2.1) *Tékmor* or *tékmar* "test, term, end, or goal."

On one occasion, we find the term *tékmar* in *The Iliad* with the sense of "test":

> τέκμωρ: οὐ γὰρ ἐμὸν παλινάγρετον οὐδ' ἀπατηλὸν
>
> I can give, and nothing I do shall be vain nor revocable. (*The Iliad* I, 526)

Generally, however, it means "term, end, or goal," as in the citations below:

> σήμερον: ὕστερον αὖτε μαχήσοντ' εἰς ὅ κε τέκμωρ
>
> now; they shall fight again hereafter, till we witness the finish. (*The Iliad*, VII, 30)
>
> νῶϊ δ' ἐγὼ Σθένελός τε μαχησόμεθ' εἰς ὅ κε τέκμωρ
>
> still we two, Sthenelos and I, will fight till we witness. (*The Iliad*, IX, 48)
>
> οἴκαδ' ἀποπλείειν, ἐπεὶ οὐκέτι δήετε τέκμωρ
>
> home again, since no longer shall you find any term set. (*The Iliad*, IX, 418)
>
> τρὶς μὲν ὀρέξατ' ἰών, τὸ δὲ τέτρατον ἵκετο τέκμωρ
>
> He took three long strides forward, and in the fourth came to his goal. (*The Iliad*, XIII, 20)

In our terminology, we call "term" the concept that, although it is revealed at the end, was already latent at the beginning. It is essential to understand the relationship between "term" and *tekmo*, the latter being a related term derived from "termination." In Roman mythology, the god Terminus presided over territorial boundaries, overseeing the boundary markers. These markers, called *terminus* in Latin, were objects of his guardianship. Reverence for these boundaries was shown through sacrificial ceremonies that sanctified each boundary stone. Every February 23, the *Terminalia* was celebrated, a festival in honor of Terminus, where landowners would gather to commemorate and venerate the borders of their properties.

Therefore, *tekmo* and *terminus* are synonyms, both connected to completing, finishing, defining, or delimiting. One cannot understand an idea unless it is defined or delimited. If our boss asks us to bring them "that" without specifying what it refers to, we will not know how to fulfill the request. We can only know what we are referring to by delimiting or defining the thing. In English, the term is "to delimit" or "to set boundaries"; in Hebrew, it is *lehagdir*, meaning "to raise a *gader*," which refers to a grille, fence, or wall.

In this etymological context, darkness prevents us from distinguishing where something begins and where it ends. In other words, obscurity hinders the defining or delimiting of objects. The Bible also, from the beginning in Genesis, establishes the importance of light in creating a conceptual and objective reality. It says:

בְּרֵאשִׁית בָּרָא אֱלֹהִים אֵת הַשָּׁמַיִם וְאֵת הָאָרֶץ:
וְהָאָרֶץ הָיְתָה תֹהוּ וָבֹהוּ וְחֹשֶׁךְ עַל־פְּנֵי תְהוֹם וְרוּחַ אֱלֹהִים מְרַחֶפֶת עַל־פְּנֵי
הַמָּיִם: וַיֹּאמֶר אֱלֹהִים יְהִי אוֹר וַיְהִי־אוֹר:
וַיַּרְא אֱלֹהִים אֶת־הָאוֹר כִּי־טוֹב וַיַּבְדֵּל אֱלֹהִים בֵּין הָאוֹר וּבֵין הַחֹשֶׁךְ:
(בראשית א', א'–ד')

In the beginning God created the heavens and the earth. And the earth was without form and void; and darkness was on the face of the deep. And the spirit of God moved over the surface of the waters. And God said, Let there be light: and there was light. And God saw the light, that it was good: and God divided the light from the darkness.

(Genesis, 1:1–4)

The same meaning emerges in the New Testament, where we find:

> In the beginning was the Word, and the Word was with God, and the Word was God. He was in the beginning with God. All things were made by Him, and without him was not anything made that was made. In him was life, and the life was the light of men. The light shines in the darkness, and the darkness did not overcome it.
>
> (John, 1:1-5)

(2.2) *Tekmérion* – "signs or symptoms"

In the 6th and 5th centuries B.C., across the Greek colonies stretching from Magna Graecia and Sicily to the Ionian coast of Asia Minor and the island of Cos, an unprecedented event took place in the history of medicine: its evolution into a technique (*tékhnē iatrikē, ars medica*) rooted in a scientific understanding of natural processes (*physiología*). Medicine, which had once been intertwined with mysticism, now began to base its understanding on how the human body functions, thereby becoming a science.

Alcmeon of Crotona's brief exposition of his physiological approach to health and disease marks the first record of such a transformation; however, it will be the "Hippocratic medicine" that will soon inherit and spread this Hellenistic legacy as an invaluable heritage. In ancient medical practice, the term *tékmar* took on a refined form and function as it evolved into *tekmérion*. This was necessary to distinguish it from the connotations it had in other contexts, marking a deliberate departure from practices of divination and bringing it closer to a more empirical and rational approach to medicine.

In the Homeric epic, we begin to see a clear distinction between the roles of the physician and the priest. While the priest immersed himself in the mystery of the divine through supplication, the physician, on the other hand, worked in the realm of the observable, empirical, and concrete. In this context, *tekmérion* began to signify an indication or sign of a diagnostic nature, a mark of certainty in the treatment of ailments, a distinguishing feature of a practice that favored evidence and observation over esoteric conjectures. Thus, the word *tekmérion* began to be used to refer to the signs or symptoms that help diagnose and treat diseases, based more on what can be observed than on mystical beliefs, as we can see in the following citations:

> ἰητρὸς γὰρ ἀνὴρ πολλῶν ἀντάξιος ἄλλων
>
> A healer is a man worth many men in his knowledge. (*The Iliad*, XI, 514)
>
> ἰούς τ' ἐκτάμνειν ἐπί τ' ἤπια φάρμακα πάσσειν.
>
> of cutting out arrows and putting kindly medicines on wounds. (*The Iliad* XI, 515)

(2.3) *Tekmaíno* – "interpreted sign or symbol"

Despite their proximity in the semantic spectrum, the terms *semaíno* and *tekmaíno* present substantial differences in their interpretation. *Semaíno* implies a more direct, immediate, and comprehensible connection between the sign and its meaning. For example, the sound of a kettle boiling water is a clear and unambiguous indicator that the water has reached boiling point. No exhaustive analysis is required to understand that the rumbling of the clouds potentially heralds the arrival of rain. In contrast, *tekmaíno* refers to a more complex hermeneutic of signs, where the meaning is not immediate but emerges through reflective and meticulous analysis. In medicine, the importance of such signs is pragmatic, as doctors interpret symptoms to diagnose diseases like influenza, asthma, or measles, which are not immediately visible.

(2.4) *Tekmaíretai* – "set the term, limit, resolve a problem, or divine will"

In Homeric literature, *tekmaíretai* takes on a nuance of demarcation or restriction, being used in the sense of "set the term or limit." This sense coexists with another, that of providing a "solution or remedy" to a problem, a concept that we also find in both *The Iliad* and *The Odyssey*.

> τοῖο μὲν Αὐτομέδων δουρικλυτὸς εὕρετο τέκμωρ:
>
> But at this spear-famed Automedon saw what he must do. (*The Iliad*, XVI, 472)
>
> ὡς δὴ δήθ' ἐνὶ νήσῳ ἐρύκεαι, οὐδέ τι τέκμωρ
>
> You've been held back on the island so long now and can't find [a solution]. (*The Odyssey*, IV, 373)
>
> ὡς δὴ δήθ' ἐνὶ νήσῳ ἐρύκομαι, οὐδέ τι τέκμωρ
>
> I've been held back on the island so long now and can't find [a solution]. (*The Odyssey*, IV, 466)

Hesiod, on the other hand, uses the term *tekmaíretai* to refer to the divine will of Zeus as definitive and indisputable.

> Zeus never decrees cruel war against them.[145]
>
> But for those who practice violence and cruel deeds far-seeing Zeus, the son of Cronos, ordains a punishment.[146]

145. Hesiod, *Works and Days*, in *The Homeric Hymns and Homerica*, trans. Hugh G. Evelyn-White, Loeb Classical Library (London: William Heinemann; New York: Macmillan Co., 1914), v. 229, p.21.
146. Ibid., vv. 238–239, p.21.

However, over time, *tékmar* evolves into a notion of "sign, signal, or indication." It is notable how Aristotle in *Rhetoric*, associates *tékmar* with *péras* (πέρας), equating them to the idea of "a limit or conclusion," a linguistic connection that has puzzled scholars for ages:

> ὃ γὰρ τέκμαρ καὶ πέρας ταὐτόν ἐστι κατὰ τὴν ἀρχαίαν γλῶτταν. ἔστι δὲ τῶν σημείων τὸ μὲν ὡς τὸ καθ' ἕκαστον πρὸς τὸ καθόλου, οἷον εἴ τις εἴποιεν σημεῖον εἶναι ὅτι οἱ σοφοὶ δίκαιοι· Σωκράτης γὰρ σοφὸς ἦν καὶ δίκαιος· τοῦτο...
>
> An example of signs [*sēmeia*] related as the particular to the universal is if someone were to state that since Socrates was wise and just, it is a sign that the wise are just.[147]

This variety of uses shows how terms can evolve and expand in meaning, reflecting the complexity of human experience and perception. The interpretation of these terms is essential for understanding the thought and culture of ancient Greece. In general, it is impossible to understand a culture without understanding its language. For a clearer understanding of the multiple meanings of *tékmar*, we recommend the fascinating work by M. Detienne and J. P. Vernant, titled *The Weaving of Intelligence*, where both authors present a way of interpreting Greek culture and thought based on structural anthropology, historical sociology, and modern philology.

(2.5) *Tekmaíresthai* – "to conjecture or to recognize signs"

The Greek term *tekmaíresthai* appears in the ancient maritime context and translates as "to conjecture or to recognize signs." This word encapsulates the ability to deduce, infer, or interpret indications. In this sense, *tekmaíresthai* was used to describe how sailors, by observing the stars or the behavior of the sea, would draw conclusions about where to navigate. As Aristotle explains, this idea parallels the

---

147. Aristotle, *On Rhetoric: A Theory of Civic Discourse*, I, 1357b 9, trans. George A. Kennedy, 2nd ed. (New York: Oxford University Press, 2007), 58.

relationship between *peîrar* (limits) and *tékmar* (goal or signal). That is, both terms are interrelated because understanding where we are located and where we are heading are connected. Detienne and Vernant, in their analysis, shed light on how Heraclitus used *semaínein* (to signify), suggesting that meaning goes beyond the simple identification of signs. Understanding something is not just about seeing the signs but comprehending the true message and authentic meaning of those signs.

(2.6) *Tekmaíromai* – "to announce or to predict"

The Odyssey uses the term *tekmaíromai* to mean "to announce" (VII, 317) or "to predict" an unfortunate event (XI, 112), as well as to "indicate" a path or direction (X, 563).

> πομπὴν δ' ἐς τόδ' ἐγὼ τεκμαίρομαι, ὄφρ' ἐῢ εἰδῇς,
>
> So, you may well know it, I decree this time for your escort. (*The Odyssey*, VII, 317)
>
> εἰ δέ κε σίνηαι, τότε τοι τεκμαίρομ' ὄλεθρον,
>
> but if you harm them, I predict destruction for you then. (*The Odyssey*, XI, 112)
>
> εἰ δέ κε σίνηαι, τότε τοι τεκμαίρομ' ὄλεθρον,
>
> but if you harm them, I predict destruction for you then, (*The Odyssey*, XII, 139)
>
> ἔρχεσθ': ἄλλην δ' ἧμιν ὁδὸν τεκμήρατο Κίρκη,
>
> but Circe has ordained a different journey (*The Odyssey*, X, 563)

From a linguistic perspective, the roots of these terms in the *sem-*

family imply a more direct process of signification, whereas *tekmaíno* introduces an additional layer of interpretation. It is intriguing to consider how these terms have evolved: *semaíno* is associated with the concept of "sign," while *tekmaíno* has developed into the idea of a "symbol," each with its own role in human understanding. Hermeneutics proposes that comprehension is not an isolated act but part of a cyclical process, where that which we seek already forms part of our horizon of understanding. This is a notion that Heidegger referred to as "ontological pre-understanding." This means that we cannot question the nature of being without already possessing some degree of understanding about it.

(3) *Sýmbolon* – Exploring its Evolution

In the extensive corpus of Hellenic terminology, the concept of *sýmbolon* stands out for its profound influence and multiple interpretations, resembling the Latin term *signum*, another key pillar in the semantic arsenal of classical languages. The prominence of a term is measured by its wide adoption and dispersion, as well as its broad range of applications. *Symbállo*, in its origins as a verb, encapsulated ideas of "to gather, join, or to bring together." Over time, its semantic spectrum was enriched to include concepts like "to throw one thing against another, to engage in combat, to change, to converse, to agree, or to interpret." It is from this archaic notion of "to unite or to bring together" that the most authentic interpretation of *sýmbolon* seems to emanate.

We observe in the works of writers from the late 6th and early 5th centuries BCE, such as Aeschylus, the use of this term in the context of a conventional sign. An example of this can be found in his tragedy *Agamemnon*, where the light of torches is interpreted as an announcement of the arrival of a messenger with news. This application of the term emphasizes its semantic evolution, adapting to contexts where objects or actions acquire a symbolic and communicative meaning beyond their literal function:

> Watchman: "I pray to the gods for the release from these labors: a watch that has already lasted a whole year, in which, lying on the roof of the palace of the Atreidae, like a dog, I see the rounds of the nightly constellations and those that bring winter and summer to mortals, shining lords that stand out in the sky [the stars when they set and rise]. Now, I watch for the sign of a torch, the flash of fire that brings news of Troy and the news of its conquest."
> Watchman: Release from this weary task of mine has been my cry unto the gods throughout my long year's watch, wherein, couchant upon the palace roof of the Atreidae, upon my bended arm, like a hound, I have learned to know aright the conclave of the stars of night, yea those radiant potentates conspicuous in the firmament, bringers of winter and summer unto mankind [the constellations, what time they wane and rise].[148]

The reflection on the term *symbol* becomes clearer when examining its use in works such as Plato's *Symposium*, where it addresses the original androgynous being, and more specifically, in Aristotle's analysis in *Peri Hermeneias*, where the concept of "symbol" is established as a sign of a conventional nature, essentially a cultural artifact. The English word *table*, as well as its translations into Spanish (*mesa*) or Hebrew (*shulchan*), are conventional representations of an object, not inherent to its essence but socially agreed upon. Aristotle thus introduces the idea that linguistic signs are collective agreements, established by humans to designate a range of entities and concepts.

Sýmbolon is also understood as an agreed-upon sign that serves to quickly convey news, which, curiously, is simultaneously a reliable proof of the truth of the interpretation of the sign (*tékmar toiouton sýmbolon*). As we see below, the term was used to communicate that Troy had been conquered:

148. Aeschylus, *Agamemnon*, in *Aeschylus*, Volume II: *Agamemnon, Libation-Bearers, Eumenides, Fragments*, trans. Herbert Weir Smyth (Cambridge, MA: Harvard University Press, 1926), vv. 1–20, p.7.

> Such are the torch-bearers I have arranged—in succession one to the other completing the course ; and victor is he who ran both first and last. This is the warrant and the token I give thee, the message of my lord from Troy to me.[149]

In another tragic author like Euripides, we also find it used as a secretly agreed-upon sign:

> Here my husband still alive, we might have recognized each other, by having recourse to tokens which ourselves alone would know. But now this may not be, nor is there any chance of his escape.[150]

It is interesting to observe how, moving forward in time to our era, Plutarch, in his work *Consolation to his wife*, references the mystical symbols present in the orgiastic Dionysian rites. This use of the word *sýmbolon* is connected to its meaning as a conventional sign:

> Κα ὶμὴν ἂτῶν ἄλλων ἀκούεις, ο ἳ πείθουσι πολλοὺς λέγοντες ὡς οὐδὲν οὐδαμ ῇτ ᾡδιαλυθέντι κακὸν οὐδ ὲ λυπηρόν ἐστιν, οἶδ' ὅτι κωλύει σε πιστεύειν ὁπάτριος λόγος κα ὶτ ὰ μυστικ ὰσύμβολα τῶν περ ὶτὸν Διόνυσον ὀργιασμῶν, ἃσύνισμεν ἀλλήλοις ο ἱ κοινωνοῦντες. ὡς οὖν ἄφθαρτον οὖσαν τὴν ψυχὴν διανοο ῦταὐτ ὸταῖς

> You have often heard the assertion made—and the majority find it convincing—that the departed suffer no evil or distress whatever. You will not credit such assertions, I know, because of our ancestral doctrines and the mystic symbols of the Dionysiac initiations with which we have our intimate and shared bond.[151]

149. Ibid., vv. 310–315, p.31.

150. Euripides, *Helen*, trans. E. P. Coleridge, in The Internet Classics Archive, ed. Daniel C. Stevenson (Cambridge, MA: MIT Classics Archive, n.d.), vv. 290–291

151. Plutarch, *Consolation to His Wife*, in *Plutarch's Wisdom on Grief*, trans. W. C. Helmbold (n.p.: Plutarch Society, 1959), 611D 8, p.21.

This nuance of *sýmbolon* as a conventional sign remained prevalent during the classical era, thus showing the rich and diverse evolution of its meaning over time. However, the word was also applied in contexts where it represented non-conventional signs. For example, Anaxagoras, in his fragment D-K 19, uses the term to describe the rainbow as a "symbol" in relation to the storm:

> We call rainbow the reflexion of the sun in the clouds. Now it is a sign of storm; for the water that flows round the cloud causes wind or pours down in rain.[152]

A particularly fascinating aspect of the term *sýmbolon* is revealed in its function as a mechanism of identification. Imagine a situation where two individuals divide an object into two distinct fragments, whether friends or business partners. Each retains one of these parts as a tangible proof of their previously established relationship or agreement. Later, they validate and reaffirm their bond or pact by reuniting the two halves. In this context, *sýmbolon* assumes the meaning of an emblem of identity or, in certain cases, of an esoteric sign. This use of the term encapsulates the essence of connection and mutual understanding, transcending its mere literal function to acquire a symbolic character deeply rooted in human interactions.

Within the broad spectrum of experiences that constitute our existence, the terms *semeion*, *tekmairon*, and *sýmbolon* have found application in a variety of contexts. Over time, they have appeared in disciplines such as navigation, medicine, astronomy, philosophy, and prophecy, yet always preserving their essential function: to indicate, symbolize, or define something precisely. Let us examine some of these.

---

152. Anaxagoras, *The Texts of Early Greek Philosophy: The Complete Fragments and Selected Testimonies of the Major Presocratics*, ed. Daniel W. Graham, Part 1 (New York: Cambridge University Press, 2010), 261 (frag. 19 = DK 59 A91)

Semeîon, *tékmor*, and *symbolon* in navigation

Sailors do not see their destination from the outset of their journey; instead, they are guided by stars that shine in the vastness of the sky. It is clear that these stars are not the port they aspire to reach but indicators that guide them toward it. Thus, the sign is not in itself the object of arrival, but its role is crucial in navigation toward the goal. In other words, when in the middle of the ocean, although the stars do not constitute their destination, they serve as signs to find the correct path. Therefore, the concepts of *semeion* and *tekmairon* have been used interchangeably and in multiple domains. These words refer to what serves as a sign or an indicator that helps to understand or find something else, but that is not the final objective. Their use has been flexible and sometimes arbitrary, as these words have been explored in a broad and ambiguous spectrum, where precision and absolute consensus on their specific application to a single reality were still developing.

In ancient Greece, mastery of the sea was a fundamental pillar for their cultural and civilizational development. The Greeks, masters of navigation, established a *thalassocracy*, that is, a maritime empire based on an efficient colonization system. Furthermore, they transformed ships into crucial tools of military power. However, navigation, far from being a safe practice, was imbued with an aura of religiosity and superstition, given the vast dangers it presented.

Significant technological and scientific advances characterized this domain. A prominent milestone in its evolution was the incorporation of iron in shipbuilding. This material allowed for the use of nails and axes, which in turn facilitated the adoption of the "first frames" construction method. In this process, the skeleton of the ship was built first, then covered with planking.

Additionally, scientific advancements played a crucial role in the success of maritime journeys and expeditions. From the 6th century BCE onward, the first navigation guidelines were established, and the first maps were created. These maps were essential, providing valuable information about the Mediterranean coasts and prevailing winds, crucial elements for route planning and safety at sea.

Precisely defining and outlining entities is fundamental for understanding them. If *tékmor* represents the boundaries that separate the dark from the light, it is because of its inherent ability to illuminate. The term "conceive" carries in its root the action of "giving birth," and from this etymological process emerges the notion of "concept." Thus, terminus, *tékmor*, and "concept" are intertwined in a semantic fabric of luminosity.

> In the context of navigation, *tékmor* means the end of the journey; the point on the horizon which serves to orientate the course of the ship. In the elementary astronomy which the art of the pilot would seem to imply this same word denotes the position of the stars by which the course of the ship must be determined.[153]

A sailor never embarks on a journey without a defined destination; no ship sets sail without a set direction. This principle alludes to the notion of "term" as the site or goal that determines the end of a journey. Even before beginning their journey, the sailor fully knows the point where they will conclude. Terminus is the endpoint of arrival that is intrinsically present in the beginning or the starting point. The sailor, when raising the anchor, implicitly carries their destination in the compass; thus, the course is set in advance, as the port they are heading to already forms part of the initial act of departure; it is integrated into the pre-trip planning.

The main contribution of Hesychius of Alexandria, a prominent and notable Greek grammarian of Alexandria, possibly active in the 5th century CE, was the creation of an exceptional dictionary focusing on rare and little-known Greek terms. This work, of great value, has come down to us in a single copy dating from the 15th century CE and represents an invaluable resource for understanding

153. Marcel Detienne and Jean-Pierre Vernant, *Cunning Intelligence in Greek Culture and Society*, trans. Janet Lloyd (Chicago: University of Chicago Press, 1978), 288.

the Greek lexicon and its evolution over the centuries. In this context of signs and inferences, Hesychius, in his *Lexikon* (*alpha* 7911), uses the phrase *ástrois semeioûsthai*, meaning "signs of the stars," a critical process for navigation of the time. Similarly, in the encyclopedic work *Suda*, we find the expression *ástrois tekmaíresthai*. Although it could be interpreted as a stellar sum, its more accurate sense would be that of a synthetic understanding of the sky, a sort of celestial cartography implicit in the celestial bodies.

Apollonius of Rhodes, the prominent Greek poet born in Alexandria (295–215 BCE), is primarily known for his epic poem *Argonautica*. This narrative, focusing on the feats of Jason and the Argonauts, is a standout example of epic poetry in ancient Greece. For Apollonius of Rhodes, conjecture is vital; he also associates *peírata* and *tékmor* to refer to how sailors, discerning signs, can chart a safe route through the rocks:

> O aged sire, now hast thou come to the end of the toils of our sea-journeying and hast told us the token, trusting to which we shall make our way to Pontus through the hateful rocks; but whether, when we have escaped them, we shall have a return back again to Hellas, this too would we gladly learn from thee.[154]

Understanding these signs, both in ancient navigation and modern hermeneutics, is indispensable for the journey through the sea of uncertainty to the shore of understanding.

Semeîon, *tékmor*, and *symbolon* in divination

We find the term *tékmor* in the lexicon of such disparate fields as divination, astronomy, and navigation; it also designated divine signs, which express a celestial will (*boulé*) and, therefore, indicate an unalterable resolution. Detienne and Vernant have found the

154. Apollonius Rhodius, *The Argonautica*, trans. R. C. Seaton (London: William Heinemann; New York: G. P. Putnam's Sons, 1912), book II, vv. 411–15, p.131.

key to unraveling the enigma of *tékmor* in the cosmogony outlined by the Spartan poet Alcmán in the 7th century BCE, who stands out as a luminary in the choral lyric poetry. This author is the most ancient within the famous canon of the nine lyric poets codified by the scholars of Alexandria, a group that includes distinguished figures such as Sappho, Alcaeus, and Anacreon, among others. His work, immersed in the sphere of *mousikê*, encompassed the composition of hymns and odes where the young Spartan girls, integrated into the choruses of *parthenias*, celebrated with songs and dances the festive cycles in an intertwined devotion to religion and performative art.

In his choral poetry, Alcmán grants to the goddess and marine nymph named Thetis (Θέτις) a creative role, accompanied by Tékmor (sign) and Póros (way, path, journey), who together dispel the darkness, personified by Skótos (darkness).

> Within the expanse of the sea where they exercise their powers Guidemark and Path, Têkmôr and Póros, are the terms which define the activity of an intelligence entirely directed towards escaping from the aporie of a world dominated by confusion.[155]

For their part, Detienne and Vernant illuminate the function of these mythological beings in the narrative and do so with the following elucidation:

> Póros, which also belongs to the semantic family of *perâo*, "to cross," designates the stratagem, the trick that Metis invents to open a path; *tékmor* on the other hand—which means not only the end one desires to reach but also the plan or remedy for a difficult situation—is a notion constructed at the confluence of three complementary domains: navigation, astronomy, and divination. [...] But these two planes are

155. Marcel Detienne and Jean-Pierre Vernant, *Cunning Intelligence in Greek Culture and* Society, trans. Janet Lloyd (Chicago: University of Chicago Press, 1978), 288.

> inseparable from a third: for all the mythical tradition, of which the epic of the Argonauts is a narrative culmination, navigating according to the fixed points of orientation in the sky also means trusting the signs sent by the gods, revealed through the mediation of a prophet.[156]

The term *symbol,* derived from the Greek *sýmbolos* and often used in the plural as *sýmboloi,* acquires a specific meaning in the field of mantics, different from its other previously discussed uses. *Mantiké,* derived from *mainomai*—which implies a connection to ecstasy or divine possession—refers to knowledge or art related to divination. In ancient Greece, as in other cultures, two forms of divination were recognized: one technical or taught (*entechnós*, *techniké*) and the other natural or spontaneous (*ateknós*, *adidaktón*). The first focuses on interpreting external signs and operates by induction and conjecture; the second, on the other hand, involves interpreting divine messages revealed in dreams or in possession states, such as those experienced in oracles. Both forms played a crucial role in the Greek understanding of symbols as vehicles of divine knowledge and mystery. Although historians such as Philochorus, Chrysippus, Sphero, and Posidonius devoted efforts to elaborate treaties on *mantiké* (*Perìmantiké*), unfortunately, these writings have not survived to this day. However, through the works of other authors, such as Plutarch, Cicero, and Diogenes Laertius, we have been able to glimpse the essential content of these beliefs, which were deeply intertwined with the religious practices of the time.

In ancient times, it was about understanding and predicting through wisdom and experience what was not certain or evident. The work of "conjecturing" or *tekmaíresthai*, was a kind of celestial hermeneutics, a forecast of the probable, intrinsically linked to the mythological figure of Metis. Unlike the certain knowledge attributed to Thetis, the domain of Metis is that of possibilities, a terrain of hypotheses in the face of certainty, that is characteristic of the unpredictable future. It is not the knowledge that allows us to

156. Ibid.

affirm the simple and clear, such as 2 + 2 equals 4; such certainty transcends conjecture to rest in the realm of the axiomatic. The possessors of Metis are distinguished by their cunning, their ability to devise strategies, find new routes, and solve puzzles that escape common understanding.

Tékmar shares with *mêchos* a significant psychological burden, referring to the ingenious resolution of difficult conflicts. This type of insight is associated with practitioners of certain skills: shipbuilders, hunters, fishermen, pilots, strategists, doctors, and sophists. Among them, the figures of the doctor and the sophist, the latter often associated with the political sphere, are of particular interest.

The centrality of divination in ancient religious practices is evident when considering that, etymologically, it encompasses everything divine, thus covering both the gods and divination itself. The latter was especially vital in the religious beliefs of ancient Greeks and, similarly, in the Jewish religion during the period of ancient Rome. In these ancient cultures, divination and primitive medicine shared several intersections. Both disciplines, in their conjunction, laid the foundations for the development of sciences in the Christian era.

Unlike the Romans, Greek interest leaned more toward natural divination than artificial divination, possibly due to a more rationalistic view of the world. This more scientific perspective regarded mantic signs not as miracles or divine messages, but as natural phenomena subject to explainable laws. With philosophers like Plato and Aristotle, the concept of the sign became more refined, evolving into a means through which humans agreed to identify objects or ideas, a crucial sign of identification for communication and mutual understanding. Most philosophical thinkers, with the notable exception of the Stoics, exhibited a general attitude of reserve, if not skepticism or rejection, toward the acceptance of supernatural phenomena. In contrast to Rome, in Greek states, the practice of divination was not formally institutionalized or regulated. However, this does not deny the existence of a tradition that linked certain natural phenomena with sacred places such as Dodona or Delphi, which were pilgrimage centers for the Greek world.

Out of this context arises the reflection on the need to discern between purely natural phenomena and those that, although disguised as natural, were, in reality, divine manifestations. The need for this discrimination led to the formation of a specific and differentiated lexicon. In this regard, Artemidorus, in his work *Oneirocritica* (Book III, Chapter 28), references Melampus, a renowned diviner with legendary status in classical Greece, as the author of a treatise titled *Perí teráton kaì semeîon* (On Prodigies and Signs). In this text, the term *térata* is used to refer to extraordinary, astonishing, or even monstrous events, interpreted as signs sent by the gods to warn or guide humanity. The importance of this treatise lies in its approach to classifying and understanding these phenomena from a perspective that seeks to transcend mere superficial observation, delving into the complexity of their nature and meaning.

In the ancient philosophical tradition, *semeîon* was identified as a symbol of natural origin, while *teratom* was considered a sign of supernatural character. Initially, these terms did not have such precise demarcation, likely due to the early stage of development in the practice of divination, where prodigies seemed to manifest everywhere. Over time, a clearer distinction was developed between prodigies and the common, ordinary occurrences of nature. The diviners of the Homeric period, for example, based their prophecies on a range of phenomena, some truly exceptional, as described in *The Odyssey*:

> τοῖσιν δ' αὐτίκ' ἔπειτα θεοὶ τέραα προὔφαινον:
>
> Then the gods soon showed them portents. (*The Odyssey*, XII, 394)

In this passage, Ulysses' companions make the grave mistake of sacrificing the sacred cattle belonging to Helios. Despite Ulysses' warnings, his efforts prove fruitless, as the cows have already been sacrificed. In response, the gods unleash a series of terrifying omens: the skins of the cows move on their own, and the meat, whether raw or roasted, emits sounds similar to mooing. Furthermore, this act of sacrilege does not go unnoticed by Zeus, who, as punishment, intervenes to further delay Ulysses' long-awaited return home to Ithaca. On the other hand, we also see other everyday phenomena as thunder (*The Odyssey*, XX, 100-120).

φήμην τίς μοι φάσθω ἐγειρομένων ἀνθρώπων

may one of the waking men speak a word of omen to me

ἔνδοθεν, ἔκτοσθεν δὲ Διὸς τέρας ἄλλο φανήτω.

from inside, and may a portent, a different one, of Zeus appear outside.

ὣς ἔφατ' εὐχόμενος: τοῦ δ' ἔκλυε μητίετα Ζεύς,

So said he in prayer, and Zeus, the contriver, heard him,

αὐτίκα δ' ἐβρόντησεν ἀπ' αἰγλήεντος 'Ολύμπου,

then thundered at once from radiant Olympus,

ὑψόθεν ἐκ νεφέων: γήθησε δὲ δῖος 'Οδυσσεύς.

from the clouds on high, and divine Odysseus rejoiced.

φήμην δ' ἐξ οἴκοιο γυνὴ προέηκεν ἀλετρὶς

A miller woman sent a word of omen from a house.

πλησίον, ἔνθ' ἄρα οἱ μύλαι εἵατο ποιμένι λαῶν,

nearby, where the mills sat for the shepherd of people,

τῇσιν δώδεκα πᾶσαι ἐπερρώοντο γυναῖκες

with which twelve women in all worked hard

ἄλφιτα τεύχουσαι καὶ ἀλείατα, μυελὸν ἀνδρῶν.

to make barley and wheat flour, the marrow of men.

αἱ μὲν ἄρ' ἄλλαι εὗδον, ἐπεὶ κατὰ πυρὸν ἄλεσσαν,

The rest were sleeping, since they'd ground their wheat.

ἡ δὲ μί' οὔ πω παύετ', ἀφαυροτάτη δὲ τέτυκτο:

She was the only one who hadn't stopped yet and was the weakest.

ἥ ῥα μύλην στήσασα ἔπος φάτο, σῆμα ἄνακτι:

She stopped her mill and spoke a word, a sign to her master:

Ζεῦ πάτερ, ὅς τε θεοῖσι καὶ ἀνθρώποισιν ἀνάσσεις,

"Father Zeus, who are lord over gods and men,

ἦ μεγάλ' ἐβρόντησας ἀπ' οὐρανοῦ ἀστερόεντος,

yes, you thundered loudly from the starry heaven,

οὐδέ ποθι νέφος ἐστί: τέρας νύ τεῳ τόδε φαίνεις.

but there's no cloud anywhere. You show this as a portent to someone.

κρῆνον νῦν καὶ ἐμοὶ δειλῇ ἔπος, ὅττι κεν εἴπω:

Now make the word that I would say come true, for even wretched me.

μνηστῆρες πύματόν τε καὶ ὕστατον ἤματι τῷδε

May the suitors this day, for the last and final time,

ἐν μεγάροις 'Οδυσῆος ἑλοίατο δαῖτ' ἐρατεινήν,

take their lovely dinner in the palace of Odysseus,

οἳ δή μοι καμάτῳ θυμαλγέϊ: γούνατ' ἔλυσαν

those who undid my knees with heart-grieving toil

ἄλφιτα τευχούσῃ: νῦν ὕστατα δειπνήσειαν.

making barley meal. May they now dine their last!"

ὣς ἄρ' ἔφη, χαῖρεν δὲ κλεηδόνι δῖος 'Οδυσσεὺς

So said she, and divine Odysseus rejoiced at her omen

(*The Odyssey*, XX, 100–120)

However, not all events, susceptible to being interpreted as oracular or divinatory signs, retained this extraordinary character. For example, while the 3rd-century BCE historian Philochorus used the term *sýmboloi* with some ambiguity, Aristophanes and Xenophon, on the other hand, used this terminology more precisely, referring to chance encounters interpreted as messages from the gods, thus showing the evolution in the understanding and classification of such phenomena over time. In an excerpt from *The Birds*, Aristophanes condenses the events that the ancient Greeks interpreted as both positive and negative omens. This passage synthesizes the Hellenistic view of reading signs in everyday phenomena, reflecting the interaction between humans and the divine in their quest to understand the world:

> For, after first going to birds [seeking auguries] you thus turn to everything, to merchant-voyage, and to getting of property, and marriage of a husband. And you think all things a bird [omen] that decide about divination: an ominous utterance is for you a bird, and a sneeze you call a bird, a meeting a bird, a sound a bird, a servant a bird, an ass a bird. Are we not plainly for you a prophetic Apollo?[157]

People interpreted the appearance and activities of birds as divine signs. Even today, it is common to hear expressions like "it's a bird of ill omen." In ancient Greece, the word *aornos* or *averno* was used to refer to the underworld. *Aornos*, which translates as "without birds," designated a place that birds would not approach, and *averno*, derived from the Greek *a*, meaning "without," and *ornis*, meaning "bird," carries a similar connotation. The concept of *averno*, therefore, was associated with the absence of birds. For the ancients, this absence symbolized a space where the prediction of the future was impossible or a place devoid of a future. Both Mediterranean and Northern European cultures considered birds as divine messengers and attributed to them the ability to foretell future events, whether beneficial or harmful, through their presence. Traditionally, migratory birds were seen as embodiments of souls or spirits.

The practice of augury, observing birds to predict events, is a tradition rooted in ancient civilizations that maintained a deeper connection with nature. The flight of birds symbolized the connection between heaven and earth. In the Greek language, a single word could mean both a portent and a celestial message. In Celtic culture, birds were generally considered messengers or helpers of the gods and the afterlife. For example, the swan in Ireland, the crane or heron in Gaul, and the goose in Britain, while the raven played this role in Germanic traditions.

The environment described in the original text is particularly illustrative: the random events interpreted by experts as divine

157. Aristophanes, *The Birds*, trans. W. C. Green (Cambridge: J. Hall & Son; London: Whittaker & Co., Simpkin, Marshall & Co.; and G. Bell & Sons, 1874), lines 715–721, p. 26.

manifestations are often seen as signs that the gods convey through birds. Consequently, much of deductive divination is classified, in a sense, as *oionomancy*, meaning the practice of predicting the future through the observation of bird behavior. In this context, the term *sýmboloi* is specifically applied to unexpected encounters, whether with people, animals, or objects. In his philosophy, Heidegger conceptualizes the fortuitous event as the *ereignis* or "event." In a way—and as we will later see in more detail—it is an encounter with ourselves or our being. Sometimes, even spontaneously spoken words are considered *sýmboloi*, which in Roman culture would be equivalent to *omina*.

In the same way, the Greek distinction between *kledón*—which more closely aligns with the Roman *omina*—and *sýmboloi* is notable, as evidenced in the works of Aeschylus in his *Prometheus Bound*:

> I classified the many forms of divination and was the first to discern the part of each dream that is to occur in reality. I made known to them the sounds that contain omens of difficult interpretation and the prophecies contained in encounters on the roads. I precisely defined the flight of predatory birds: which are favorable by nature and which are sinister; what kind of life each one has, what their hatreds, loves, and companions are, the smoothness of their entrails, and what color their bile must be for it to be pleasing to the gods, and the varied beauty of the liver lobe.[158]

Cleromancy, a form of divination based on unsystematic rules, represents a crucial aspect of mantics. In works such as *Memorabilia* and *Apology of Socrates* by Xenophon, *sýmboloi* is used in the sense previously mentioned.

In *Memorabilia, Memories of Socrates* (Ἀπομνημονεύματα Σωκράτους), we read:

158. Aeschylus, *Prometheus Bound*, trans. Herbert Weir Smyth, Ph.D., vol. 1 of Aeschylus, with an English Translation by Herbert Weir Smyth, Ph.D., (Cambridge, MA: Harvard University Press, 1926), vv. 485–494.

[1.1.1] Πολλάκις ἐθαύμασα τίσι ποτὲ λόγοις Ἀθηναίους ἔπεισαν οἱ γραψάμενοι Σωκράτην ὡς ἄξιος εἴη θανάτου τῆι πόλει. ἡ μὲν γὰρ γραφὴ κατ' αὐτοῦ τοιάδε τις ἦν· ἀδικεῖ Σωκράτης οὓς μὲν ἡ πόλις νομίζει θεοὺς οὐ νομίζων, ἕτερα δὲ καινὰ δαιμόνια εἰσφέρων· ἀδικεῖ δὲ καὶ τοὺς νέους διαφθείρων.

[1.1.1] I have often wondered by what arguments those who drew up the indictment against Socrates could persuade the Athenians that his life was forfeit to the state. The indictment against him was to this effect: Socrates is guilty of rejecting the gods acknowledged by the state and of bringing in strange deities; he is also guilty of corrupting the youth.

[1.1.2] Πρῶτον μὲν οὖν, ὡς οὐκ ἐνόμιζεν οὓς ἡ πόλις νομίζει θεούς, ποίωι ποτ' ἐχρήσαντο τεκμηρίωι; θύων τε γὰρ φανερὸς ἦν πολλάκις μὲν οἴκοι, πολλάκις δὲ ἐπὶ τῶν κοινῶν τῆς πόλεως βωμῶν, καὶ μαντικῆι χρώμενος οὐκ ἀφανὴς ἦν. διετεθρύλητο γὰρ ὡς φαίη Σωκράτης τὸ δαιμόνιον ἑαυτῶι σημαίνειν· ὅθεν δὴ καὶ μάλιστά μοι δοκοῦσιν αὐτὸν αἰτιάσασθαι καινὰ δαιμόνια εἰσφέρειν.

[1.1.2] First then, that he rejected the gods acknowledged by the state—what evidence did they produce of that? He offered sacrifices constantly, and made no secret of it, now in his home, now at the altars of the state temples, and he made use of divination with as little secrecy. Indeed it had become notorious that Socrates claimed to be guided by "the deity"; it was out of this claim, I think, that the charge of bringing in strange deities arose.[159]

And in the *Apology of Socrates*, we read:

159. Xenophon, *Memorabilia*, Xenophon in Seven Volumes, 4, trans. E.C. Marchant (Cambridge, MA: Harvard University Press; London: William Heinemann, Ltd., 1923), vv. 1.1.1–1.1.2, p.3.

[11] Ἀλλ' ἐγώ, ὦ ἄνδρες,τοῦτο μὲν πρῶτον θαυμάζω Μελήτου, ὅτωι ποτὲ γνοὺς λέγει ὡς ἐγὼ οὓς ἡ πόλις νομίζει θεοὺς οὐ νομίζω· ἐπεὶ θύοντά γέ με ἐν ταῖς κοιναῖς ἑορταῖς καὶ ἐπὶ τῶν δημοσίων βωμῶν καὶ οἱ ἄλλοι οἱ παρατυγχάνοντες ἑώρων καὶ αὐτὸς Μέλητος,εἰ ἐβούλετο.

[11] But I, oh men, first marvel at Meletus, for once he says that I do not believe in the gods that the city believes, when, in fact, both those present and Meletus himself, if he wanted to, could have seen me when I made sacrifices at the city's festivals and at the public altars.

[12] καινά γε μὴν δαιμόνια πῶς ἂν ἐγὼ εἰσφέροιμι λέγων ὅτι θεοῦ μοι φωνὴ φαίνεται σημαίνουσα ὅ τι χρὴ ποιεῖν; καὶ γὰρ οἱ φθόγγοις οἰωνῶν καὶ οἱ φήμαις ἀνθρώπων χρώμενοι φωναῖς δήπου τεκμαίρονται. βροντὰς δὲ ἀμφιλέξει τις ἢ μὴ φωνεῖν ἢ μὴ μέγιστον οἰωνιστήριον εἶναι; ἡ δὲ Πυθοῖ ἐν τῶι τρίποδι ἱέρεια οὐ καὶ αὐτὴ φωνῆι τὰ παρὰ τοῦ θεοῦ διαγγέλλει;

[12] And as for new divinities, how could I introduce them by saying that a divine voice appears to me to tell me what I should do? For even those who use the cries of birds and the words of men rely on voices to support their conjectures. Would anyone argue that thunder is a voice or a very important omen? And the priestess at Delphi, sitting on her tripod, does she not also announce the oracles of the god through the voice?

[13] ἀλλὰ μέντοι καὶ τὸ προειδέναι γε τὸν θεὸν τὸ μέλλον καὶ τὸ προσημαίνειν ὧι βούλεται, καὶ τοῦτο,ὥσπερ ἐγώ φημι,οὕτω πάντες καὶ λέγουσι καὶ νομίζουσιν.ἀλλ' οἱ μὲν οἰωνούς τε καὶ φήμας καὶ συμβόλους τε καὶ μάντεις ὀνομάζουσι τοὺς προσημαίνοντας εἶναι, ἐγὼ δὲ τοῦτο δαιμόνιον καλῶ, καὶ οἶμαι οὕτως ὀνομάζων καὶ ἀληθέστερα καὶ ὁσιώτερα λέγειν τῶν τοῖς ὄρνισιν ἀνατιθέντων τὴν τῶν θεῶν δύναμιν. ὡς

γε μὴν οὐ ψεύδομαι κατὰ τοῦ θεοῦ καὶ τοῦτ᾽ ἔχω τεκμήριον· καὶ γὰρ τῶν φίλων πολλοῖς δὴ ἐξαγγείλας τὰ τοῦ θεοῦ συμβουλεύματα οὐδεπώποτε ψευσάμενος ἐφάνην.

[13] It is true that everyone knows and believes that the divinity knows the future and announces it to whomever it wishes, just as I say. But while they call auguries, voices, random encounters, and soothsayers those who give warnings, I call this divine genius, and I think that by calling it this way, I am speaking more truthfully and more piously than those who attribute to the birds the power that the gods possess. And this is the proof that I do not lie against the divinity: having announced to many of my friends the divine warnings, I have never been found to have been wrong.[160]

In both, the author defends Socrates from the serious accusation of impiety, arguing that he made frequent sacrifices and practiced divination. The accusation of introducing new gods is based on a misunderstanding of Socratic belief in receiving divine signs for personal interpretation. Xenophon continues in *Memorabilia* with a statement that reinforces this view:

[1.1.3] ὁ δ᾽ οὐδὲν καινότερον εἰσέφερε τῶν ἄλλων, ὅσοι μαντικὴν νομίζοντες οἰωνοῖς τε χρῶνται καὶ φήμαις καὶ συμβόλοις καὶ θυσίαις. οὗτοί τε γὰρ ὑπολαμβάνουσιν οὐ τοὺς ὄρνιθας οὐδὲ τοὺς ἀπαντῶντας εἰδέναι τὰ συμφέροντα τοῖς μαντευομένοις, ἀλλὰ τοὺς θεοὺς διὰ τούτων

[1.1.3] He was no more bringing in anything strange than are other believers in divination, who rely on augury, oracles, coincidences and sacrifices. For these men's belief is not that the birds or the folk met by accident know what profits the

160. Plato, *Apology*, Plato in Twelve Volumes, Vol. 1, trans. Harold North Fowler, intro. W.R.M. Lamb (Cambridge, MA: Harvard University Press; London: William Heinemann Ltd., 1966), vv. 11–13.

inquirer, but that they are the instruments by which the gods make this known; and that was Socrates' belief too.

> [1.1.4] ἀλλ' οἱ μὲν πλεῖστοί φασιν ὑπό τε τῶν ὀρνίθων καὶ τῶν ἀπαντώντων ἀποτρέπεσθαί τε καὶ προτρέπεσθαι· Σωκράτης δ' ὥσπερ ἐγίγνωσκεν, οὕτως ἔλεγε· τὸ δαιμόνιον γὰρ ἔφη σημαίνειν. καὶ πολλοῖς τῶν συνόντων προηγόρευε τὰ μὲν ποιεῖν, τὰ δὲ μὴ ποιεῖν, ὡς τοῦ δαιμονίου προσημαίνοντος· καὶ τοῖς μὲν πειθομένοις αὐτῶι συνέφερε, τοῖς δὲ μὴ πειθομένοις μετέμελε.
>
> [1.1.4] Only, whereas most men say that the birds or the folk they meet dissuade or encourage them, Socrates said what he meant: for he said that the deity gave him a sign. Many of his companions were counselled by him to do this or not to do that in accordance with the warnings of the deity: and those who followed his advice prospered, and those who rejected it had cause for regret.[161]

In his analysis, Xenophon highlights three fundamental types of signs in inductive divination, a practice also attributed to Philocorus: the observation of birds (*oionioi*), unforeseen events (*sýmboloi*), and the examination of the entrails of sacrificed animals (*thysíai*). Considering the etymological background discussed earlier, the use of *sýmboloi* in this framework may seem unexpected. However, there are reasonable interpretations for this terminological choice. These random incidents were apparently related to Demeter in her search for Persephone, who was abducted by Hades, leading the goddess to pay particular attention to any type of encounter. The meaning of "encounter" linked to *sýmboloi* aligns with the verb *symballein*, which means "to gather, join, or bring together." Divination, unlike science, does nothing more than establish conventional and artificial connections between signs and what they represent, similar to the

161. Xenophon, *Memorabilia*, Xenophon in Seven Volumes, 4, trans. E.C. Marchant (Cambridge, MA: Harvard University Press; London: William Heinemann, Ltd., 1923), vv.1.1.3–1.1.4, pp.3–5.

relationships formed between words and their meanings. The array of symbols used in ancient divination can be interpreted as an elaborate language akin to human language.

The Greeks posited that the gods had the autonomy to choose different symbols, thus establishing what could be called the grammar of their symbolic language. This knowledge, they believed, was later shared with the first diviners—figures such as Melampus, Tiresias, Amphiaraus, Mopsus, and Calchas—who were considered pioneers of national mantics. Mantic, perceived as teachable and scientific, was based on unchanging divine rules. With the teachings of Plato and Aristotle, the concept of *symbol* began to evolve, acquiring the connotation of a random event and being used in the exchange between gods and humans. Only those humans immersed in the meaning of these symbolic languages could interpret these messages. Thus, the symbol gradually transformed into the language of the gods, accessible only to those with the ability to perform a hermeneutics of the divine message.

Semeîon, *tékmor*, and *symbolon* in medicine

To understand the use of these terms in the context of medicine, we must briefly recount the origin of this discipline. In ancient Greece, the sick attributed their ailments to the punishment of the gods and went to the Temple of Epidaurus to purify themselves and receive treatment from Asclepius, the god of medicine. These sanctuaries, strategically located in mountainous areas or hills near hot spring sources, attracted crowds of patients who were attended by individuals who combined the roles of priest and nurse, embodying Asclepius and overseeing miraculous events. In clinical facilities that were merely walls used as dormitories, healing methods based on the use of water, herbs, baths, purifications, massages, frictions, and a combination of suggestion, including both ritual exorcisms and prayers and sacrifices, were carried out, seeking spiritual perfection. This form of medicine, with its magical and superstitious approach, dominated Greek medical practice until around the 5th century BCE.

Empedocles – The philosopher and physician from Agrigento, Sicily.

Empedocles (495–423 BCE) was born in Agrigento, on the coast of Sicily, present-day Italy, and was a philosopher whose discoveries and reflections would promote the emergence of a science of nature, especially medicine. He was the one who proposed the existence of four primary elements that constituted the essence of nature (*phýsis*): earth, air, fire, and water. Known as the "theory of the four elements," it integrated the perspectives of the *arche*, or "principle," of Thales of Miletus (water), Heraclitus of Ephesus (fire), Anaximenes of Miletus (air), and Xenophanes of Colophon (earth). He maintained that these elements coexist in various combinations in earthly entities and, when combined, give rise to all the manifestations of the world. According to his view, these elements were influenced by two opposing cosmic forces that explained the dynamism of the world: love, responsible for union and attraction, and hatred, responsible for separation and repulsion. In line with this perspective, Empedocles considered the human being as a combination of these four elements, thus reflecting the analogy between the microcosm and the macrocosm, that is, *phýsis*. Nature was conceived as a blend of energy and physical forms, including bodies in solid, liquid, and gaseous states. Similarly, the human being was composed of the four primary elements: water was associated with urine and tears, earth with muscles and bones, air with blood, and fire with the body's internal heat.

Cyclical patterns govern the cosmos and represent the totality of all its components. Since the human body is constituted by the same four elements present in the cosmos, it is possible to explore the cosmos through the knowledge of our own body. Consequently, the analogical method emerges as the most suitable approach to understanding *phýsis*, since through particular realities, one can access the understanding of the totality. This perspective sparked Empedocles' interest in understanding the functioning of the human body. He defined health as balance and illness as a consequence of the imbalance of the four fundamental elements and believed in the human capacity to intervene and modify the course of an illness.

Being both a physician and philosopher, Empedocles fused his cosmological concepts with his medical approach, shaping the doctrine of the four elements. In this theory, treatment focused on restoring an adequate balance of elements by controlling two sets of antagonistic qualities: heat and cold, moisture and dryness, which determined the nature of the elements. Fire was associated with heat and dryness; air, with heat and moisture; water, with cold and moisture; and earth, with cold and dryness. For example, if an individual had a fever, it was considered necessary to increase cold; if they experienced chills, they were thought to need more heat. It is evident that these theories lacked solid physiological foundations, and it was difficult for medical practice based on them to have positive effects.

Alcmeon – The philosopher and physician from Crotona, Italy

Alcmeon was a Pythagorean philosopher from the 6th century BCE who was born in Crotona, a city in the Italian peninsula. He focused on the field of medicine and replaced the principle of analogy with an approach based on observation and experimentation. He participated in the first medical school, established in the city of Cnidos around the year 700 BCE, where the practice of closely observing patients originated. This approach marked the beginning of secular medicine, which sought to be based on logical reasoning, separating itself from miraculous practices. Illness began to be conceived as a disorder unrelated to religious phenomena, laying the foundations for medicine based on reason and science. Alcmeon's theory of health marked a break with the ritual healing methods predominant in Greek medicine at the time, such as prayers (*eukhé*) to healing deities like Asclepius and dances or healing rituals dedicated to the god Dionysus.

Alcmeon's doctrines, presented in his work *On Nature* toward the end of the 6th century BCE, deliberately omit the debate over the principle of origin so heavily discussed by the presocratic *physiólogoi*, and are particularly enlightening in their examination of knowledge. Alcmeón proposes that all forms of life share sensory perception, while analytical understanding is presented as an exclusively human faculty that synthesizes experience and recognizes itself as a cognitive process. However, perhaps the most striking aspect of his view in relation to our inquiry is his perspective on human epistemology. Alcmeon asserts that:

> Concerning things unseen and things mortal the gods see clearly, but so far as men may conjecture (*tekmaíresthai*).[162]

The main objective of therapeutics was to restore the internal balance of the body, promoting eucrasia (a state of harmony) and isonomy (balance). Disease was conceived as a disturbance in these balances, and therapeutics focused on restoring the order disrupted by illness. Its therapeutic approach was based on the principle of curing through opposites: each excess or imbalance was counteracted with treatments possessing qualities opposite to those responsible for the disease. Historical records of medicine assign a decisive value to the work of Alcmeon, considering him the starting point of classical and technical medicine, marking his contribution as the fundamental break from symbolic medicine. Alcmeon paved the way for medical practice based on the observation of signs, the formulation of hypotheses, and validation through testing and evidence.

The Cnidian School of Health in Classical Greece

Following the line of Alcmeon of Croton, magical medicine began to disappear, giving rise to secular medicine. This evolution unfolded through various medical schools in places such as Cyrene, Rhodes, Cnidus, and Cos, each with particular nuances based on different philosophies. A theoretical rupture can be observed, marked by attempts to integrate knowledge about the human body and diseases into a broader explanation of the world. Between the 6th and 5th

162. Alcmaeon of Croton, in *The Presocratic Philosophers: A Critical History with a Selection of Texts*, by G. S. Kirk and J. E. Raven (Cambridge: Cambridge University Press, 1957), 285 (frag. DK B1).

centuries BCE, medicine transformed into a technical knowledge (*téchne*), systematizable in a series of rules and principles, grounded in the rational understanding of human nature (*phýsis*).

One of the first schools, which emerged on the coast of Cnidus in Asia Minor and later established itself in Italy, focused primarily on disease as an independent entity. This school did not emphasize the general state of patients; its interest lay in pathology as an object of study. Relying almost exclusively on empiricism, the doctors of this school observed the symptoms of the sick and the reactions caused by various plants, recording this information in their clinical notes. In the presence of a patient, they compared the symptoms with successful prior cases and applied similar treatments, without seeking explanations beyond or developing a theoretical framework. They had no clear understanding of the disease or why certain treatments worked while others did not; their approach was based on the observations collected by the doctors of the school. The importance of detailed diagnosis was emphasized, similar to the work of a detective gathering clues. However, their excessive focus on diagnosis led to a chaotic accumulation of clinical signs that prevented the generalization of disease characteristics and the determination of effective treatments.

The Hippocratic School of Health in Cos

Hippocrates (460–377 BCE) was born on the island of Cos, modern-day Greece. Tradition claims he descended from a line of physician-priests, although he was clearly influenced by Empedocles and Alcmeon of Croton. He is called the father of modern medicine because he developed a rational system based on observation and experience, repeating observations until he identified the distinguishing signs of each syndrome. He is credited with the leap from magical to scientific medicine. In addition to founding rational medicine, he was the precursor to medical ethics. His legacy includes the famous Hippocratic Oath, recited today by medical graduates upon completing their studies. Although he never met Socrates, being his contemporary, he was aware of the ethical principles spread throughout ancient Greece. For Hippocrates, the concept of the good stood as the fundamental and universal foundation of ethics, thus being the ultimate goal of humanity.

Hippocrates' followers also sought to identify in the individual what made him unique and irreplaceable, expressing the idea that "there are no diseases, only patients." From a philosophical perspective, a classification of the natural order (*phýsis*) is established, with the good being order and the bad being disorder (chaos). Health prevails when there is physical order (*physiologia*), while disease arises from a lack of balance or disorder.

The Hippocratic followers believed they had found the key to explaining the organism. The Greek physician proposed the theory of the four humors, linking these humors to the elements air, fire, earth, and water, which had been previously identified by the philosopher Empedocles as fundamental components of all existence. The four elements were adapted in organisms as humors, which are the physiological equivalents of the four elements of nature. The balance and imbalance in the amounts of these substances in an organism determined its health. Each of these humors expressed specific physical characteristics, following the prevailing thought of the time that sought to describe reality based on everyday, easily identifiable properties. Black bile was associated with the element earth, characterized by coldness and dryness; yellow bile was linked to the element fire, with warmth and dryness; blood was associated with the element air, with warmth and moisture; and finally, phlegm was connected to the element water, representing coldness and moisture. Medical treatments aimed at restoring the balance of the humors and included practices like bloodletting, the use of emetics, enemas, and other methods.

In addition to his theoretical approach, Hippocratism was distinguished by its practical focus on clinical care and meticulous observations on the progression of symptoms. The Hippocratic physician was conceived as a collaborator with nature, striving not to interfere violently with it. He avoided interventions that could force or harm the natural functioning of the organism. He described disease in terms of its phases: onset, increase, climax, and resolution. Each phase exhibited specific symptoms that, when properly interpreted by the doctor, facilitated the selection of the correct treatment. The critical moment occurred in the climax or acme when the disease reached its peak, a crisis or "cooking" phase took place, and the confrontation between the inherent healing forces of nature and the destructive forces of the disease was resolved.

Metaphysical theorists, immersed in their reflections, often speculate on the symbolic nature of disease without interacting with its tangible manifestation in the patient. They dive into abstraction in an effort to understand the hidden, neglecting the clues provided by visible manifestations. This tendency refers to philosophers who spend their time theorizing and inventing concepts that do not contribute to the patient's healing process. The Hippocratic perspective, however, embraces both the phenomenology of symptoms and theoretical speculation on the nature of the ailment, avoiding extremes by integrating observation with speculation, deviating from the one-sidedness of other schools.

In the treatise *On Ancient Medicine*, the Hippocratic author positions himself with a skill, a *téchne*, that distinguishes him from both abstract philosophical knowledge rooted in deductive principles and the rudimentary praxis of the Cnidians. He used these terms to refer to signs and to describe a type of skill or technique in medicine that was different from pure philosophy and the more basic methods of other doctors of his time.

The term *tekmérion* can be traced back to texts by figures like Aeschylus and Aesop from the 6th century BCE and reaches greater systematization in the works of the *Corpus Hippocraticum*, where *tekmérion* is invoked more frequently. The precision in the application of the concept of *tekmérion* is a testament to the consolidation of medicine as a distinguished and meticulous discipline.

The distinction between the practices of early medicine and those of divination emerges as a cornerstone in Hippocratic writings. This bifurcation is evident in the treatise *Prorrhetic II*, whose main purpose is to challenge the irrationality of precise predictions, described as "magnificent and wonderful" in the first chapter. Its focus is on demonstrating the scientific basis of prognoses derived from a thorough understanding of the human body. The author presents himself as a rationalist, equipped both with common sense and with profound knowledge of the subject. In his words, which criticize absurd popular predictions, the author declares his intention:

> I, for my part, will not make divinations (*manteúsômai*) of that sort; I write down the signs (*semeîa dè grapho*) by which one should form conjectures (*tekmaíresthai*) concerning which of the patients will recover or die, and which will do so speedily or slowly.[163]

The concept of *logismós* presented in *On Ancient Medicine* embodies structured logic, a discernment that goes beyond mere "conjecturing" or "operating through signs" (*tekmaíresthai*) as suggested in the *Prognostics II* text. This approach constitutes a significant methodological leap: it deviates from the principles applied analogically or deductively, perceived as dogmatic by the physicians of Cos, toward a meticulous scrutiny and interpretation of symptoms based on emerging rules of practice and experience.

In the medical tradition inaugurated by Hippocrates, a fundamental innovation in the paradigm of medical thought can be observed: the adoption of a semiotic approach to interpreting diseases. This methodology, characterized by its use of signs and symbols, represents a significant advancement in understanding human afflictions. The adoption of this semiotic approach enabled more detailed observation and deeper analysis of symptoms, thus paving the way for the development of accurate diagnoses and the application of effective treatments.

This new medical methodology is framed within the semiotic domain: discerning between a sign as a mere omen and another in its role as concrete evidence. While the omen points to a possibility, the evidence establishes an axiom; while the indication suggests an option, the confirmation establishes a fact. In the realm

163. Hippocrates, *Prorrhetic II*, in *Prognostic and Prorrhetic I–II*, trans. W. H. S. Jones (Cambridge, MA: Harvard University Press, 1923), II 1, 305.

of Hippocratic medicine, a critical distinction is made between two categories of signs: those that merely hint at an eventuality, resembling omens, and those that provide verification comparable to evidence. This conceptual duality was essential in the praxis of Hippocratic physicians.

Semiotic Medicine

In the realm of ancient medicine, the term *hékaston* is introduced to refer to an event that has not yet been definitively correlated with the systematic set of pathology. This word is used to refer to observations in patients whose relationship with specific diseases had not yet been clearly determined. Such an approach was akin to having a piece of a puzzle without knowing its exact position. This evolution in medical thinking marked a transition to a more scientific approach, where the interpretation of signs and symbols became a cornerstone for diagnosing and understanding pathologies.

An isolated event that has not yet been determined will not be integrated into the diagnostic framework of a pathology due to uncertainty about its causal relationship with the disease in question. Consider a sneeze: it might suggest a respiratory infection, a cold, or perhaps indicate an allergic reaction. Only certain phenomena under observation—still classified as *hékaston*—can rise to the category of *semeîon*, visible indications (*tàphainómena*) that hint at the presence of unperceived elements (*tà ádêla* or "something unseen"), which may potentially be interconnected. The term *hêkaston* was used to refer to those phenomena that, while perceptible, remained veiled in mystery due to the lack of comprehensive understanding. By deepening their observations and analyses, these physicians could transform an *hêkaston*, this initial enigma, into a *semeîon*. This process of transitioning from merely observed to significantly interpreted involved advancing from an initial state of ambiguity toward a stage of greater conceptual clarity.

The Hippocratic methodology shaped a semiotic approach through a dialectical procedure that begins with the *hékaston* given in observation. This moment is recognized as the incipient scientific experience, which is transmuted into *semeîon* through an inferential logical-conceptual process (*logismós*). The subsequent transition to *tekmérion* marks a culmination: the sealing of a cycle of understanding and the ability to act upon various *hékasta*. Thus, the *semeîon* becomes an indication, and the *tekmérion* the definitive proof.

In Hippocratic methodology, the process began with careful observation of clinical events unfolding in four distinct stages. First, the attentive observation (*sképtomai*) of reality, orchestrated by the norm of analogy. Then, the physicians determined whether what they observed constituted a *semeîon*, interpreted as an initial indicator, or a *tekmérion*, which was considered a more definitive proof. Based on these observations, they formulated hypotheses to explain the meaning of the *semeîon*. Sometimes, they conducted experiments to verify the validity of their hypotheses. Hippocratic texts clearly distinguish between *semeîon* and *tekmérion*: while *semeîon* is considered a sign that may suggest the presence of a disease, *tekmérion* is established as a more conclusive and specific proof of it. This step-by-step approach demonstrates how ancient physicians gradually advanced from simple observation to reaching firm and well-founded conclusions about various diseases.

There is a plurality of fragments within Hippocratic writings that illuminate the semantic differentiation between the terms *semeîon* and *tekmérion*. While *semeîon* refers to a sign that may potentially be interpreted as a symptomatic indication of a pathology, *tekmérion* ascends to the category of evidence or proof, practically irrefutable, of that condition. As illustrated by the final compilation in *The Prognosis*, where the author synthesizes:

> It is also necessary promptly to recognize the assaults of the endemic diseases, and not to pass over the constitution of the season. However, one must clearly realize about sure signs (*tekmérion*) and about symptoms (*semeîon*) generally, that in every year and in every land bad signs (*semaínei*) indicate something bad, and good signs something favourable, since the symptoms (*aletheonta semeîa*) described

> above prove to have the same significance in Libya, in Delos, and in Scythia.[164]

Faced with realities that remain hidden from direct perception, there are those that manifest through mediators. We identify a type of causality revealed through its consequences. A similar notion can be found in Vedantic epistemology, particularly in its tools of cognition, known as *pramāṇas*. Among these, *pratyakṣa* ("what is evident") stands out, associated with knowledge derived from sensory experience. *Pratyakṣa* holds that we first obtain data through the senses and, through deliberation, come to understand it. Likewise, *anumāna*, or "inference," uses logic to draw conclusions from accepted premises. Medicine, as a field of knowledge, adopts this strategy by studying the cause from the effect, as the physician does not come into direct contact with the disease itself — conditions like colds, asthma, or the plague are entities indetectable to the senses due to a lack of observable qualities. However, the patient is present, and the underlying pathologies can be deduced through the symptoms presented. This process of deducing the underlying cause through signs is an essential method of medical semiotics. In short, the symptom functions as the indicative sign of the disease.

The Hippocratics considered themselves scientists and despised philosophers, whom they saw as closer to poetry and literature, as they lacked rigor in their speculation. On the other hand, doctors had concrete evidence for what they claimed because they had scientific contact and experience with human beings. These proofs allowed them to validate each of their assertions. The demarcation of medicine as an autonomous discipline from philosophy did not arise from a divergent objective but from the search for truthful knowledge about nature. In the Hippocratic tradition, understanding human nature emerges from meticulous observation and practical experience. This methodology contrasts with philosophy, whose domain lies in deep reflection and theoretical construction. Talking

164. Hippocrates, *Prognostic*, in *Hippocrates*, Vol. II, trans. W. H. S. Jones (London: William Heinemann; Cambridge, MA: Harvard University Press, 1923), v.25, p.55.

about the Hippocratic epistemological methodology is, therefore, referring to their distinctive technique of approaching the truth. This technique can be interpreted as symbolic: doctors, through the analysis of symptoms and physical signs, decipher the complex language of health and disease. This interpretation allows doctors to discover and understand the underlying realities of the human being, similar to how an astute reader understands the text beyond the printed words. Therefore, although the Hippocratics rejected philosophical speculation, their methodology reveals a rich range of implicit meanings in corporeality, which in turn illuminates fundamental aspects of the human condition.

Semeîon, *tékmor*, and *symbolon* in philosophy and the development of knowledge

Alcmeon of Croton stated, as we have said, that "Concerning things unseen and things mortal the gods see clearly, but so far as men may conjecture (*tekmaíresthai*)."[165] This observation finds a parallel in the reflection of Saint Thomas Aquinas (1225–1274 CE), who postulated that the evidence of God is an inherent truth to the divinity itself, but this is not presented with the same clarity to human understanding. Therefore, its knowledge occurs in an ascending manner and starts with the being, as seen in the criticism of Anselm and his ontological argument. Both thoughts, separated by millennia, highlight a common element in the human intellectual journey: the absolute truth is the domain of the divine, while humans face the constant challenge of deciphering signs to attain an understanding of their world.

The principle of analogy, as postulated by Empedocles, rests upon the notion of *phýsis* as a pre-established cosmic order regulated by laws that dictate an inevitable cyclical sequence and, in its essence, refers to a primordial foundation or *arche*. This foundation could be a unique entity—water, air, or the *ápeiron* of the early Ionian thinkers—

165. Alcmaeon of Croton, *in The Presocratic Philosophers: A Critical History with a Selection of Texts*, by G. S. Kirk and J. E. Raven (Cambridge: Cambridge University Press, 1957), 285 (frag. DK B1).

or a synthesis of the four classical elements. This *arche* is what gives meaning to the cosmos in its magnitude as well as to the individual entities that comprise it. Every observable entity contains within itself the reason for its existence, its original principle. Therefore, to penetrate knowledge of *phýsis*, the analogical approach is revealed as the most accurate, as understanding individual entities facilitates, by extension, understanding the integral cosmic order. Empedocles holds a theory that positions the human being as a "microcosm," that is, a small-scale representation of *phýsis*. This proposal is based on the premise that "the similar knows the similar"; the emanations that flow from objects penetrate the pores of the human being until they find a correspondence with like elements present within us. Empedocles articulates this concept when he states:

> For it is with earth that we see Earth, and Water with water; by air we see bright Air, by fire destroying Fire. By love do we see Love, and Hate by grievous hate.[166]

Empedocles argues that the cosmos is a reflection of the divine, just as humanity, in turn, reflects the cosmos. In this way, human existence acts as a manifestation of the cosmic order and, reciprocally, the cosmos becomes a sign of the divine. Alcmeon of Croton argued that human knowledge is anchored in the interpretation of signs, assigning symbolism an indispensable role in our understanding of the world. In the absence of humanity, the meaning of symbols would fade, losing its resonance. Alcmeon's proposal is not merely a sensory theory based on opposites; it is, rather, a prelude to the medical knowledge as conceived by the Hippocratics, who would take it to its most refined expression, reasoning through signs, assumptions, and empirical evidence. This approach integrates semiotic tools as diverse as icons and indices in the nomenclature that Charles Sanders Peirce would establish twenty-five centuries later, with their corresponding interpretive norms, the first requiring

166. Empedocles, in *Early Greek Philosophy*, 3rd ed., by John Burnet (London: A & C Black, n.d.), 159 (frag. DK 109).

inventiveness, while the second is based on experience. As we will see in more detail later, in the 1860s, Peirce began his reflections on the field he himself called "semeiotics," a term that refers to the philosophical study of signs. His ideas arose parallel to the development of his system of three categories. Throughout the 20th century, semiotics became an umbrella term under which various schools in the study of signs were included, among them Ferdinand de Saussure's semiology. The latter, originating in linguistics, developed independently.

Peirce coined the concept of *semiosis* (or *semeiosis*), defining it as a process involving the interaction of three entities: a sign, its object, and its interpretant. This triadic process, according to Peirce, is irreducible to binary interactions. For him, this relationship was crucial for understanding "logic as formal semiotics," referring here to logic in a philosophical sense. Over time, he divided this field into three branches: (1) speculative grammar, or stechiology, which examines the fundamental elements of *semiosis* and the ways in which signs can signify, including the classification of signs, objects, and interpretants and their combinations; (2) logical critique, focused on modes of inference; and (3) speculative rhetoric, which contemplates the philosophical theory of inquiry, integrating its version of pragmatism. The contemporary scientific method must assign a precise role to each of these within the investigative process.

Regarding the impact of Hippocratic praxis on philosophy, its influence seems particularly palpable in Socratic approaches to confronting dilemmas and unraveling problems. In the realm of philosophical foundations, the shared concern was more a reflection on human essence than an exhaustive exploration of the cosmos, at least in the way the ancient naturalists conceived it. The central thesis holds that, since the human being is the entity most intimately known to us, it is through understanding them that we can grasp reality as a whole. In terms of methodology, its firm inclination toward induction and its view of knowledge as a technical skill, or *téchne*, resonated with the medical approach. These precepts were considered important enough to be inscribed in the Oracle of Delphi through the maxim: *gnōthi sauton* (Γνῶθι σαυτόν), or "know thyself."

According to Heidegger, it is through the study of *Dasein*, whose ontological supremacy is indisputable, that we can come to understand being in its entirety. In this line, Socrates emerges as a genuine clinician of the psyche, for his diligence toward the moral health of his disciples was as fervent as his care for their physical well-being, positioning himself primarily as the "doctor of the soul." Indeed, his maieutic method is analogous to obstetrics, facilitating the birth of truth, albeit not without the pains of labor. Observing Socrates, Plato, and Aristotle, we realize that medical practice begins its journey in the realm of the perceptible and moves toward the metaphysical, a transition that could be characterized as a symbolic transfiguration. There is a dialectical progression that rises from the concrete to the abstract, from the phenomenal reality to the hidden essence. In Plato's discourse, dialectics is elevated as the royal road of thought, a transition of logos that takes us from one concept to another in an ascending search for truth.

On the other hand, the dogmatic and sectarian confuses the symbol with its referent, becoming trapped in immobility and stagnating on the surface. In the twilight of his life, Socrates tells Criton, "we owe a rooster to Asclepius. Please, don't forget to pay the debt.!"[167] This symbolic debt to the god Asclepius, patron of healing and venerated in sacred sites like Epidaurus, reflects the ancestral bond between medicine and the divine. The lineage of Hippocrates, according to tradition, traces back to this deity. The interdependence between different areas of knowledge highlights an essential principle: knowledge is built cumulatively and spans multiple disciplines. From medicine to philosophy, each specialty contributes key pieces to the comprehensive understanding of human nature. This process, in which diverse fields intertwine, enriches our perception of being and existence. In this context, historical study, beyond being a mere collection of data, becomes an enriching narrative. This narrative allows us to explore and understand the intricate realities of human life. While medicine focuses on healing the body, history

---

167. Plato, *Phaedo*, in *Plato in Twelve Volumes*, vol. 1, trans. Harold North Fowler, intro. W. R. M. Lamb (Cambridge, MA: Harvard University Press; London: William Heinemann Ltd., 1966), v.118a.

and philosophy delve into the soul, providing insights on how to live ethically and make conscious political decisions.

In conclusion, inquiry into ancient medicine and history transcends the purely academic realm and becomes a bridge to the traditions and accumulated knowledge that have shaped our civilization. These areas of knowledge invite us to value the teachings of the past, applying them to illuminate and improve our future. We must consider that Socrates, along with the empirical-medical approach, catalyzes the transition toward a teleological vision of nature and the human being, culminating in Aristotle's biological perspective of the cosmos. This dialectical praxis, employed by Socrates, Plato, and Aristotle, stands out for its rigor and its capacity to transmute the empirical into the philosophical. While seemingly circumstantial, the confluence of philosophy and medicine is of considerable significance and presents itself as a juncture rather than a constant.

Despite the respect that Plato assigns to medicine in the excerpt from *Phaedrus* (270b-d), his stance reveals layers of greater depth and subtlety. Plato, in this passage, draws a parallel comparing medicine to rhetoric. It is not surprising, therefore, that, at this juncture, he critiques rhetoric as an art that touches the soul but, unfortunately, is distorted by "but those whom you have heard, who write treatises on the art of speech nowadays, are deceivers and conceal the nature of the soul, though they know it very well" (271c)[168]. In his dialogue *Gorgias*, and more precisely from passage 464a, Plato assigns rhetoric an ambiguous position. While on the one hand, he distinguishes it from medicine—granting medicine a degree of legitimacy—on the other hand, he likens it to gastronomy. The latter, in Plato's words (*Gorgias*, 465a), fades as a genuine art, as it is not *téchne*, since, according to his terms, "I do not call 'art' what is irrational" (*álogon pragma*).[169]

168. Plato. *Phaedrus*, in *Plato in Twelve Volumes*, Vol. 9, trans. Harold N. Fowler (Cambridge, MA: Harvard University Press; London: William Heinemann Ltd., 1925), 271c.

169. Plato. *Gorgias*, in *Plato in Twelve Volumes*, Vol. 3, trans. W.R.M. Lamb (Cambridge, MA: Harvard University Press; London: William Heinemann Ltd., 1967), 465a.

In Platonic thought, the essence of art lies in the lucid and calculated imitation of nature, or, what is the same, in the use of reason to reflect it. Therefore, those disciplines that do not employ reason to emulate nature do not meet the standard of art. By disregarding the use of numerical categories and measures, navigation and gastronomy do not satisfy this artistic criterion because, in Plato's view, art is mediated by rationality. And for him, rationality is identified with mathematical reason; reason is equivalent to the idea, the idea to the form, and the form, in turn, is interpreted as geometry. However, this peaceful disposition is merely superficial. In *Philebus* (56b), Plato expressly strips certain practices, including medicine, strategy, and navigation, of scientific status due to their disconnection from number, measure, and weight. Plato, in his exploration of rhetoric and medicine, makes use of arguments that require immersion in his philosophical framework to be fully understood.

However, we must not overlook the additional arguments that link both disciplines. Medicine and rhetoric have historically been considered domains of those possessing *metis*, or "practical cunning." The navigator, the sophist, the doctor, and the politician operate in spheres marked by flux and transformation. Both illness and rhetoric resemble entities as unpredictable and challenging as the ocean or molten metal: addressing them requires anticipating the fleeting opportunity to navigate these changing forces. Furthermore, this relationship explains why the stratagems employed by deities, humans, and certain creatures are categorized as *sophismata*, or "deceptions."

This historical connection, among various reasons, underpins the rejection of speculative knowledge of conjecture in favor of the certainty of *episteme*, firm, secure, and true knowledge. Aristotle, whose lineage includes a doctor, adopts a position that diverges from his predecessor, Plato. His ethical philosophy, and more precisely his interpretation of prudence, aligns more closely with medical praxis—a realm that confronts tangible reality—than with Plato's idealism of unchanging forms. According to Aristotle, ethical virtue lies in a middle ground, defined not from an impersonal geometric perspective but from the individuality of the subject in question (*Nicomachean Ethics* II, 6, 1106a, 29–33). This resonates more with medical practice, rooted in tangible knowledge of reality, than with Plato's eternal and static principles. It is exemplified in the differentiated nutrition between an established athlete and a novice, emphasizing the uniqueness of each situation.

Moreover, Aristotle rescues conjectural knowledge, which Plato dismissed, recognizing its validity in specific contexts such as rhetoric, where reasoning maintains its value even without empirical certainty. Although devoid of absolute certainty, it remains an exercise in rationality. The dynamic interaction between philosophy, medicine, and rhetoric, as explored by classical thinkers like Socrates, Plato, and Aristotle, has relevance to this day. Delving deeper into this topic, it is fascinating to consider how these ancient notions could be recontextualized to address contemporary ethical and pragmatic issues. On the one hand, Aristotle's teleological perspective, which interprets every aspect of nature and humanity as part of a larger purpose, offers valuable insights for modern debates on sustainability and environmental ethics. Such a vision could promote a more integrated and goal-oriented approach to resource management and environmental conservation.

On the other hand, Plato's observations on rhetoric, criticized for deviating from true art despite its potential to impact the soul, echo in our era, where information is frequently manipulated. The urgency for authentic and transparent dialogue becomes imperative in a world plagued by false information and deceptive advertising. In turn, Aristotle, with his appreciation for conjectural knowledge and medical practice, invites us to reflect on the importance of adaptability and critical thinking in an age marked by uncertainty and constant change. In a context where absolute certainty is rare, the ability to adapt to changing situations and make informed decisions is crucial. Moreover, Aristotle's notion that ethics must be contextual and based on individuality is especially pertinent to modern ethical dilemmas. There are various areas where ethical decisions must consider universal principles and also the particularities and complexities of each case. The reflections of these philosophers on the synergy between different disciplines offer a perspective of their time and provide a valuable framework for tackling the ethical, philosophical, and practical challenges that arise in our time.

The distinction between conjectural knowledge and verified knowledge is personified in the mythological figures of Metis and Tethys. Thus, the concept of *semeion* arises from Metis, who embodies wisdom in its most probabilistic form, not absolute. Metis embodies pragmatic and probabilistic wisdom, that cunning and adaptable faculty that feeds on observation and experience. While it lacks absolute certainty, its sharpness lies in the ability to forge predictions based on a multitude of past experiences. This mode of knowledge is akin to the work of a chef or a navigator, who, confronted with the urgency of changing circumstances, must rely on their skill and cunning to make critical decisions. They do not have an infallible manual or a detailed itinerary to guide each step, but their mastery is revealed in their ability to adapt dynamically to emerging challenges. In contrast, Tethys represents certainty, which is the inevitable companion of the mathematician, whose calculations produce invariable results. But a military strategist, unlike a mathematician, cannot guarantee victory in all battles, as their art is based on variables and conjectures. Each confrontation is a unique entity, requiring the strategist to have the capacity for adaptation and tactical insight that recognizes and responds to the uniqueness of each military situation. A general faces the uncertainty of conflict, where not all battles are won with the same formula. Here, wisdom lies not in rigidity but in flexibility and the ability to navigate the unpredictable terrain of conflict. This filial relationship between *semeion* and *metis* suggests that empirical knowledge, rooted in experience and inference, is indeed descended from an intelligence that thrives in prediction and adaptation rather than immutable certainty.

The frequent application of medical analogies in this and other discourses is not merely incidental. Historically, however, philosophical and scientific development has tended to align more with the Platonic view than with the Aristotelian one. It is important not to lose sight of the fact that, over time, medicine has found new pathways to influence thought. Significantly, modern philosophical empiricism owes more to the pragmatic methodology of Hellenistic medicine than to the abstract speculation of ancient philosophy.

Historically, the domains of science and philosophy have tended to emulate the constancy of Tethys, in their search for definitive and axiomatic truths. This approach is characterized by a tendency toward immutable principles, reflecting a longing for absolute certainty in knowledge. In contrast, medicine, with its inherent nature of fluidity and adaptation to the ever-changing needs of patients, resonates more with the essence of Metis. In contemporary times, we observe an evolution in scientific and philosophical perspectives, one that increasingly leans toward this flexibility and pragmatism, reminiscent of the methodical approach of Hellenistic medicine. These current trends mark a significant shift away from traditional rigidity, embracing instead a more dynamic and adaptable paradigm in the pursuit of knowledge and truth.

In our expositional effort, we have attempted to illustrate how *semeion* and *téchne* are tools for discerning realities that do not reveal themselves directly but indirectly, through intermediaries. The condition of the navigator, as well as that of the cook, the doctor, the astronomer, the soothsayer, and the prophet, has been analyzed in the context of indicative signs; signs that, rather than presenting the symbol immediately, announce it through their own manifestations. Let us visualize *semeion* and *téchne* as analogous elements to the clues in a detective investigation, whose purpose is not explicitly revealing the solution but guiding toward it through a deductive process. This methodology finds parallels in various professions: a chef interpreting the subtle indicators of taste and texture, a doctor diagnosing from symptoms not always evident, or an astronomer deciphering the mysteries of the cosmos through celestial signs. In each of these examples, sharp perception and inferential reasoning are crucial for transcending the apparent surface and gaining a deeper understanding of hidden or not immediately perceptible realities.

Exploring the Transcendental through the Symbol

In a way, Hippocrates realized that thinking leads nowhere but in circles. Philosophers advance rapidly but often without reaching a definitive destination in their quest for truth. It is crucial to understand this thoroughly, for without such understanding, the practice of meditation—which, as we will see later, is the true medicine for our egoic illness—remains inaccessible. Meditation, in this context, is antithetical to philosophy, as it is not based on the act of thinking. Philosophy distinguishes itself from science and religion through its perpetual interrogative nature; it does not seek definitive answers but is dedicated to the art of questioning. When analyzing philosophical answers, one realizes that they are merely superficial, devoid of essential content. The conclusions of philosophy, far from being definitive, open doors to new enigmas. Instead of experimenting with reality, philosophy confines itself to reflection and theoretical speculation.

On the other hand, both science and religion reach concrete answers, not merely through thought but through experimentation. This experimental process is fundamental because, while thought serves as scaffolding, the experiments generate definitive answers. In science, experimentation is characterized by its objective nature; the scientist, armed with instruments and methods, remains distant from the phenomenon studied. In contrast, in the realm of religion, experimentation takes on a subjective and profound character, where the experimenter participates actively and becomes the center of the experiment. This religious experimentation manifests as a total transformation of the individual.

Speculation about concepts such as paradise, enlightenment, or divinity, devoid of direct experience, proves fruitless. The mere memorization of sacred scriptures and the projection of an image of devotion do not equate to authentic religious experience, which is, at its core, a profound and transformative direct experience in which the individual is not only the observer but also the laboratory and the object of study, leading to an experience of change and inner recognition. Religious experience, in this sense, transcends the mere experiment to become an authentic experience. At the same time, it is crucial to remember that while we think about God, the soul, enlightenment, or the otherworldly reality, we may generate the illusion of knowledge, an inherently deceptive representation that has little to do with the authentic religious experience. The notion of knowing "about" God is a futile epistemological endeavor and, as such, subverts the essence of wisdom itself.

True knowledge of God transcends the ordinary conceptual framework; it is not about "knowing about" but about "knowing" God. In this subtle yet profound distinction lies the genesis of theological philosophy: an exploration that recognizes its own conceptual limits in the pursuit of the divine. In its attempt to articulate the ineffable, philosophy reveals itself as a continuous dialogue with the unknown, an effort to illuminate the shadows that surround the ultimate truths of existence. The notion of "knowing about" God is paradoxically distant. The conceptual approach to divinity intrinsically distances us from knowing God. In reality, it is possible to experience God directly, but knowing "about" God is a contradiction in itself, just as true self-understanding and the apprehension of love transcend mere knowledge "about" these.

Different religious organizations do not worship God Himself but the God of language. The God of language for the Hebrews differs from that of the Muslims or the Christians. When language tries to appropriate God, it always fails because it will never be able to do so perfectly.

The experience of meditation, for example, cannot be encapsulated in an objective description. The inherent risk of accumulating superficial knowledge "about" or "concerning" oneself, love, God, enlightenment, or meditation lies in becoming a scholar without direct experience. True knowledge of these aspects brings lasting happiness, while mere theoretical understanding is intrinsically hollow. It is essential to recognize that the challenges of life are not speculative but existential, and as such, they are not resolved through deliberation but through experience. Reflection distances us from tangible reality, while experience immerses us in the very being of existence. The further we distance ourselves from lived experience, the less able we are to face and resolve the dilemmas of life.

When transferring our reflection to the meditative realm, we encounter the individual who focuses solely on signs, neglecting the revelation itself. Alternatively, some devote themselves to the search for a divine entity, which, devoid of personification and not evidenced in the sensible realm, ignores the clues that might indicate its presence. Aspiration lies in achieving a balance where immediate experience, stripped of the subject-experimenter, intertwines with intellectual documentation in ideal congruence. Our goal is to decode, through semiotics, the Hippocratic methodology. This methodology constitutes the hermeneutic key that fully decodes the Hippocratic approach.

This principle is unequivocally articulated in the *Īśāvāsya Upanishad*, within the triad of its twelfth, thirteenth, and fourteenth aphorisms:

अन्धं तमः प्रविशन्ति येऽसम्भूतिमुपासते ।
ततो भूय इव ते तमो य उ सम्भूत्याꣳ रताः ॥

andhaṁ tamaḥ praviśanti
ye 'sambhūtim upāsate
tato bhūya iva te tamo
ya u sambhūtyāṁ ratāḥ

Those who worship the manifested enter the region of darkness; even worse happens to the worshippers of the unmanifested.

(*Īśāvāsya Upanishad*, Mantra 12)

अन्यदेवाहुः सम्भवादन्यदाहुरसम्भवात् ।
इति शुश्रुम धीराणां ये नस्तद्विचचक्षिरे ॥

anyad evāhuḥ sambhavād
anyad āhur asambhavāt
iti śuśruma dhīrāṇāṁ
ye nas tad vicacakṣire

It is stated that different results are obtained from the manifested and the unmanifested. All this has been heard from the lips of the sages, who have imparted it to us.

(*Īśāvāsya Upanishad*, Mantra 13)

सम्भूतिं च विनाशं च यस्तद्वेदोभयꣳसह ।
विनाशेन मृत्युं तीर्त्वा सम्भूत्याऽमृतमश्नुते ॥

sambhūtiṁ ca vināśaṁ ca
yas tad vedobhayaṁ saha
vināśena mṛtyuṁ tīrtvā
sambhūtyā 'mṛtam aśnute

One who worships God in his personal and impersonal aspects simultaneously transcends death through the worship of the manifested and realizes immortality through the worship of the unmanifested.

(*Īśāvāsya Upanishad*, Mantra 14)

This journey through the vast and multifaceted history of the symbol has led us to a point of deep reflection on its meaning and its impact on the human spectrum of knowledge and experience. More than just a tool for communication, the symbol has revealed itself to us as a portal that connects us with realities that transcend the tangible and the everyday. In the history of human thought, symbols have served as bridges between the known and the unknown, the material and the spiritual, the human and the divine. From ancient divination practices and religious rituals to complex philosophical theories and modern scientific advancements, the symbol has been a constant companion to humanity, offering us a way to interpret and make sense of our world. The evolution of the concept of the symbol reflects a parallel evolution in our understanding of the universe and of ourselves.

In antiquity, symbols were seen as direct connections with the divine or mystical realms. Ancient diviners and sages saw themselves as interpreters of these signs and as intermediaries between the earthly and celestial worlds. With the advent of rational philosophical thought, personified by figures such as Plato and Aristotle, the "symbol" began to be understood in a more abstract and metaphorical way. It was no longer just a messenger of the gods, but a representation of deeper ideas, a way to explore and explain concepts that were beyond direct comprehension.

In the modern era, with the influence of thinkers like Descartes and the rise of the scientific method, the perception of the "symbol" has continued to evolve. Descartes viewed the symbol as deceptive as the senses. This has led the symbol to become more secular, but no less significant. In science, for example, symbols are used to represent complex formulas and theories that describe the laws of the universe.

Despite this evolution, the essential core of the symbol remains unchanged. It continues to be a means of connecting the known with the unknown, the concrete with the abstract. At the heart of religious, artistic, philosophical, or scientific experience, the symbol is still a powerful tool that allows us to explore and express the deepest truths of our existence. The symbol is a testament to the unceasing human search for understanding and meaning. As we have seen in this initial approach to the etymological history of the term, the symbol has proven to be an indispensable part of our ongoing exploration of the world we live in and the universe surrounding us. Ultimately, it teaches us that, in our search for knowledge, we often find that the most meaningful answers are not found in the clarity of concrete evidence or in logical-discursive abstraction, but in the deep contemplation of the symbols that connect all aspects of our reality. However, although religions are all conceptual phenomena, genuine religion—that which arises from true religious and direct experience—does indeed belong to the symbolic dimension. There is no doubt that true religious experience, in its most refined expression, will always be symbolic.

BIBLIOGRAPHY SECTION IV

- Agamben, Giorgio. *What Is the Contemporary?* In *What Is an Apparatus? and Other Essays.* Translated by David Kishik and Stefan Pedatella. Stanford, CA: Stanford University Press, 2009.
- Aeschylus. *Agamemnon.* In *Aeschylus, Volume II: The Libation Bearers, The Eumenides, Fragments.* Translated by Herbert Weir Smyth, revised by Gregory Crane, Graeme Bird, Gregory Nagy, and Casey Dué. Cambridge, MA: Harvard University Press, 1926.
- Aeschylus. *Prometheus Bound.* In *Aeschylus, Volume II: Persians, Seven Against Thebes, Suppliants, Prometheus Bound.* Translated by Herbert Weir Smyth. Cambridge, MA: Harvard University Press, 1926.
- Aeschylus. *Seven Against Thebes.* Translated by Ian Johnston. Nanaimo, BC: Vancouver Island University, 2013.
- Aeschylus. *The Suppliants.* In *Tragedies.* Madrid: Librodot.com, n.d.
- Apollonius Rhodius. *The Argonautica.* Translated by R. C. Seaton. Loeb Classical Library 1. London: William Heinemann; New York: G. P. Putnam's Sons, 1912.
- Aristophanes. *The Birds.* Translated by W. C. Green. Cambridge: J. Hall & Son; London: Whittaker & Co.; Simpkin, Marshall & Co.; and G. Bell & Sons, 1874.
- Aristotle. *Nicomachean Ethics.* Translated by H. Rackham. Vol. 19 of *Aristotle,* edited by H. Rackham. Loeb Classical Library. Cambridge, MA: Harvard University Press, 1934.
- Aristotle. *On Rhetoric: A Theory of Civic Discourse.* Translated with introduction, notes, and appendices by George A. Kennedy. 2nd ed. New York: Oxford University Press, 2007.
- Burnet, John. *Early Greek Philosophy.* 3rd ed. London: A & C Black, 1920.
- Castañares, Wenceslao. *History of Semiotic Thought, Vol. 1: The Greco-Roman Antiquity (Historia del pensamiento semiótico. Vol. 1, La Antigüedad grecolatina).* Madrid: Editorial Trotta, 2014.

- Cassirer, Ernst. *The Philosophy of Symbolic Forms, Volume 1: Language.* Translated by Ralph Manheim. New Haven: Yale University Press, 1955.
- Descartes, René. *A Discourse on the Method.* Translated by Ian Maclean. Oxford: Oxford University Press, 2006.
- Detienne, Marcel, and Jean-Pierre Vernant. *Cunning Intelligence in Greek Culture and Society.* Translated by Janet Lloyd. Chicago: University of Chicago Press, 1978.
- Eliade, Mircea. *Images and Symbols: Studies in Religious Symbolism.* Translated by Philip Mairet. London: Harvill Press, 1961.
- Eliade, Mircea. *Tratado de historia de las religiones [Treatise on the History of Religions].* 2 vols. Madrid: Ediciones Cristiandad, 1974.
- Engels, Frederick. *Origin of the Family, Private Property, and the State.* Translated by Alick West. Leopard Books India, 2015.
- Euripides. *Helen.* Translated by E. P. Coleridge. In *The Internet Classics Archive,* edited by Daniel C. Stevenson. Cambridge, MA: MIT Classics Archive.
- Graham, Daniel W. *The Texts of Early Greek Philosophy: The Complete Fragments and Selected Testimonies of the Major Presocratics.* Part 1. New York: Cambridge University Press, 2010.
- Heraclitus. *Fragments.* In *Early Greek Philosophy,* by John Burnet. 3rd ed. London: A & C Black, 1920.
- Hesiod. *Theogony.* In *Myths of the Greek and Roman Gods,* edited by Roberto Nickel. Toronto: Ryerson University, n.d.
- Hesiod. *Works and Days.* In *The Homeric Hymns and Homerica.* Translated by Hugh G. Evelyn-White. Loeb Classical Library. London: William Heinemann; New York: Macmillan Co., 1914.
- Hesiod. *Fragments (The Melampodia, Shield of Heracles, Catalogue of Women).* In *The Homeric Hymns and Homerica.* Translated by Hugh G. Evelyn-White. London: William Heinemann; New York: Macmillan Co., 1914.
- Hippocrates. *Hippocrates, Vol. II.* Translated by W. H. S. Jones. Loeb Classical Library 148. London: William Heinemann; Cambridge, MA: Harvard University Press, 1923.
- Jung, C. G. *Man and His Symbols.* Edited by M.-L. von Franz. New York: Doubleday & Company, 1964.

- Jung, C. G. *Memories, Dreams, Reflections.* Recorded and edited by Aniela Jaffé. Translated by Richard and Clara Winston. Revised ed. New York: Vintage Books, 1989.
- Jung, C. G. *Psychological Types.* Vol. 6 of *The Collected Works of C. G. Jung.* Revised by R. F. C. Hull. Translated by H. G. Baynes. Princeton, NJ: Princeton University Press, 1971.
- Jung, C. G. *Psychology and Religion: West and East.* Translated by R. F. C. Hull. *The Collected Works of C. G. Jung,* vol. 11. Princeton, NJ: Princeton University Press, 1958.
- Kirk, G. S., and J. E. Raven. *The Presocratic Philosophers: A Critical History with a Selection of Texts.* Cambridge: Cambridge University Press, 1957.
- Marx, Karl, and Friedrich Engels. *The Communist Manifesto.* Translated by Samuel Moore. Introduction by David Harvey. London: Pluto Press, 2008.
- Nietzsche, Friedrich. *The Will to Power.* Translated by Walter Kaufmann and R. J. Hollingdale. New York: Vintage Books, 1968.
- Nietzsche, Friedrich. *The Use and Abuse of History for Life.* Translated by Adrian Collins. 2nd rev. ed. Indianapolis: The Bobbs-Merrill Company, 1957.
- Parmenides. *Parmenides: On Nature.* Translation and commentary by Leonardo Tarán. Princeton, NJ: Princeton University Press, 1965.
- Pinkus, Lucio. *La dimensione simbolica: aspetti psicodinamici [The Symbolic Dimension: Psychodynamic Aspects].* Rome: Astrolabio, 1985.
- Plato. *Apology.* In *Plato in Twelve Volumes,* Vol. 1. Translated by Harold North Fowler. Introduction by W. R. M. Lamb. Cambridge, MA: Harvard University Press; London: William Heinemann Ltd., 1966.
- Plato. *Gorgias.* In *Plato in Twelve Volumes,* Vol. 3. Translated by W. R. M. Lamb. Cambridge, MA: Harvard University Press; London: William Heinemann Ltd., 1967.
- Plato. *Phaedo.* In *Plato in Twelve Volumes,* Vol. 1. Translated by Harold North Fowler. Introduction by W. R. M. Lamb. Cambridge, MA: Harvard University Press; London: William Heinemann Ltd., 1966.

- Plato. *Phaedrus.* In *Plato in Twelve Volumes,* Vol. 9. Translated by Harold N. Fowler. Cambridge, MA: Harvard University Press; London: William Heinemann Ltd., 1925.
- Plutarch. *Consolation to His Wife.* In *Plutarch's Wisdom on Grief,* translated by W. C. Helmbold. Plutarch Society, 1959.
- Ricoeur, Paul. *Freud and Philosophy: An Essay on Interpretation.* Translated by Denis Savage. New Haven: Yale University Press, 1970.
- Rilke, Rainer Maria. "Poem to Nike." Translated by Walter Kaufmann. In *Twenty German Poets: A Bilingual Collection.* New York: Random House, 1962.
- Sartre, Jean-Paul. *Existentialism Is a Humanism.* Translated by Carol Macomber. Edited by John Kulka. New Haven: Yale University Press, 2007.
- Sophocles. *Antigone.* Translated by Robert Whitelaw. With introduction and notes by J. Churton Collins. Oxford: Clarendon Press, 1906.
- Sophocles. *Oedipus the King, Oedipus at Colonus, Antigone.* Translated by F. Storr. London: William Heinemann; New York: The Macmillan Co., 1912.
- Wittgenstein, Ludwig. *Tractatus Logico-Philosophicus.* Translated by D. F. Pears and B. F. McGuinness. With an introduction by Bertrand Russell. London: Routledge Classics, 2001.
- Xenophon. *Memorabilia.* In *Xenophon in Seven Volumes,* Vol. 4. Translated by E. C. Marchant. Cambridge, MA: Harvard University Press; London: William Heinemann, 1923.

Appendices

Prabhuji

H.H. Avadhūta Bhaktivedānta Yogācārya
Śrī Ramakrishnananda Bābājī Mahārāja

About Prabhuji

Prabhuji is a realized master, a universalist Advaita mystic, and an authorized representative of Hinduism. His profound religious dedication is expressed through his artistic work as a writer and painter. In recognition of his spiritual attainment, his guru has conferred upon him the title of *avadhūta*. He has developed the Retroprogressive Path, an original contribution rooted in the inclusive principles of *Sanātana Dharma*, an ancient tradition to which he maintains a formal and constant adherence.

His solid background includes a doctorate in *Vaiṣṇava* philosophy, awarded by the prestigious Jiva Institute of Vedic Studies in Vrindavan, India, and a doctorate in Yogic philosophy earned at Yoga-Samskrutham University. These doctorates reaffirm his commitment to traditional teachings and his connection to the spiritual roots of the Hindu religion.

Prabhuji has dedicated more than fifty years to the exploration and practice of different religions, philosophies, paths of liberation, and spiritual disciplines. He has absorbed the teachings of great masters, shamans, priests, machis, shifus, roshis, shaykhs, daoshis, yogis, pastors, swamis, rabbis, kabbalists, monks, gurus, philosophers, sages, and saints whom he personally visited during his years of searching. He has lived in many places and traveled the world, thirsting for Truth.

In 2011, with the blessings of his Gurudeva, Prabhuji adopted the path of a secluded *bhajanānandī* and withdrew from society to lead the contemplative life of a hermit. Since then, he has been living as an independent Christian-Marian Hindu religious hermit. His days have been spent in solitude, praying, writing, painting, and meditating in silence and contemplation. His *iṣṭa-devatā*, or "chosen deity," is Lord Yeshua, understood from the traditional Hindu perspective as the *avatāra*, the "incarnate God" in whom he centers his devotion. Unlike the interpretation of Western Christianity, his connection with Yeshua arises from the Semitic roots of the historical Jesus, within the original Hebrew horizon of his revelation.

Prabhuji is the sole disciple of H.D.G. Avadhūta Śrī Brahmānanda Bābājī Mahārāja, who in turn is one of the closest and most intimate disciples of H.D.G. Avadhūta Śrī Mastarāma Bābājī Mahārāja.

Prabhuji was appointed as the successor of the lineage by his master, who conferred upon him the responsibility of continuing the sacred *paramparā* of *avadhūtas*, officially appointing him as guru and ordering him to serve as Ācārya successor under the name H.H. Avadhūta Bhaktivedānta Yogācārya Śrī Ramakrishnananda Bābājī Mahārāja.

Prabhuji is also a disciple of H.D.G. Bhakti-kavi Atulānanda Ācārya Mahārāja, who is a direct disciple of H.D.G. A.C. Bhaktivedānta Swami Prabhupāda. We could say that Gurudeva Atulānanda affectionately assumed the role of guide during his initial stage of learning, and because he was Prabhuji's first guru, he is considered a fundamental part of his evolutionary process. For his part, Guru Mahārāja was Prabhuji's second and last guru and provided him with guidance during his advanced stage. Gurudeva acted as the primary educator at the dawn of his spiritual path, while Guru Mahārāja exercised with great diligence the role of master at the highest level, accompanying him until his realization.

Prabhuji's Hinduism is broad, universal, and pluralistic. Living up to his title of *avadhūta*, his lively and fresh teachings are not confined by any philosophy or religion, even his own. His teachings promote critical thinking and invite us to question our own convictions. The essence of his syncretic vision, the Retroprogressive Path, is self-awareness and the recognition of consciousness. For him, awakening at the level of consciousness, or the transcendence of the egoic phenomenon, is the next step in humanity's evolution.

Prabhuji was born on March 21, 1958, in Santiago, the capital of the Republic of Chile. When he was eight years old, he had a mystical experience that motivated his search for the Truth, or the Ultimate Reality. This transformed his life into an authentic inner and outer pilgrimage. He has completely devoted his life to deepening the early transformative experience that marked the beginning of his process of retroevolution.

From an early age, his father, Yosef Har-Zion ZT"L, and his mother, Frida Lazcano ZT"L, expressed a constant and unconditional love, independent of academic performance or achievements. Prabhuji's paternal grandfather was a distinguished senior officer in the Chilean police, who raised his father Yosef under a strict discipline. Marked by this, Yosef decided to raise his own children in an environment defined by freedom. Prabhuji and his sister were their parents' most cherished endeavors, guided by their trust in life itself as the compass for their choices.

In this context, Prabhuji grew up without experiencing any sense of urgency, demand, or external pressure. From a very young age, he noticed that the educational system prevented him from devoting himself to what truly mattered: learning about himself. At the age of eleven, he decided to stop attending conventional school and devote himself to autodidactic learning. When he chose to leave school in pursuit of his inner quest, his family responded with profound respect and acceptance. Yosef fully supported his son's interests, encouraging him at every step of his search for Truth.

From the age of ten onward, his father shared with him the wisdom of Hebrew spirituality and Western philosophy, fostering an environment of daily discussions that often extended late into the night. In essence, Prabhuji embodied the ideal of freedom and unconditional love that his parents had striven to cultivate within their home.

From a very young age and on his own initiative, Prabhuji began to practice karate and to study Eastern philosophy and religions in a self-taught manner. During his adolescence, no one interfered with his decisions. At the age of 15, he established a deep, intimate, and long friendship with the famous Uruguayan writer and poet Blanca Luz Brum, who was his neighbor on Merced Street in Santiago, Chile. He traveled throughout Chile in search of wise and interesting people from whom he could learn. In southern Chile, he met *machis* who taught him about the rich Mapuche spirituality and shamanism.

In June 1975, at the young age of 17, he earned his first certification as a Yoga Teacher under H.H. Śrī Brahmānanda Sarasvatī (Rāmamurti S. Mishra, M.D.), the founder of the World Yoga University, the Yoga Society of NY, and the Ananda Ashram.

At the age of 18, Prabhuji embraced the monastic discipline through long stays in various ashrams of different Hindu currents (*Gauḍīya* Vaishnavas, Advaita Vedanta, etc.) in Chile and Israel. There, he underwent rigorous training within the Hindu religion. Immersed in the strict observance of religious life, he received a systematic education, following traditional methods of monastic teaching. His training included the in-depth study of sacred scriptures, the practice of austerities, the fulfillment of strict vows, and participation in prescribed rituals, all under the guidance of masters or gurus. Through this intensive discipline, he internalized the fundamental principles of Hindu monastic life, adopting its values, codes of conduct, and contemplative practices. This allowed him to learn the theory and also to incorporate the ideals that characterize the spirituality of Hinduism.

Over the years, Prabhuji became a recognized authority on Eastern wisdom. He is known for his erudition on the *Vaidika* and *Tāntrika* aspects of Hinduism and all branches of yoga (*jñāna*, *karma*, *bhakti*, *haṭha*, *rāja*, *kuṇḍalinī*, *tantra*, *mantra*, and others). He has an inclusive attitude toward all religions and is intimately familiar with Judaism, Christianity, Buddhism, Islam, Sufism, Taoism, Sikhism, Jainism, Shintoism, Bahaism, Shamanism, and the Mapuche religion, among others.

During his stay in the Middle East, his esteemed friend and scholar, Kamil Shchadi, imparted to him profound knowledge about the Druze faith. He also benefited from his closeness to the revered and wise Salach Abbas, who helped him to reach a thorough understanding of Islam and Sufism. He studied Theravada Buddhism personally from the Venerable W. Medhananda Thero of Sri Lanka. He delved deeper into Christian theology with H.H. Monsignor Iván Larraín Eyzaguirre at the Veracruz Church in Santiago de Chile and with Mr. Héctor Luis Muñoz, who holds a degree in theology from the Universidad Católica de la Santísima

Concepción, Chile. His profound studies, his masters' blessings, his research into the sacred scriptures, and his vast teaching experience have earned him international recognition in the field of religion and spirituality.

Prabhuji's curiosity for Western thought led him to venture into the field of philosophy in all its different branches. He specialized in Transcendental Phenomenology and the Phenomenology of Religion. He had the privilege of studying intensively for several years with his uncle Jorge Balazs, philosopher, researcher, and author, who wrote *The world upside-down* under his pen name Gyuri Akos. Prabhuji pursued private studies in mythology and philosophy for four years (1984–1987) under Dr. Meira Laneado of Bar-Ilan University. He studied privately for many years with Dr. Jonathan Ramos, a renowned philosopher, historian, and university professor graduated from the Universidad Católica de Salta, Argentina. He also studied with Dr. Alejandro Cavallazzi Sánchez, who holds an undergraduate degree in philosophy from the Universidad Panamericana, a master's degree in philosophy from the Universidad Iberoamericana, and a doctorate in philosophy from the Universidad Nacional Autónoma de México (UNAM). He also studied privately with Santiago Sánchez Borboa, who holds a PhD in Philosophy from the University of Arizona, USA.

Prabhuji's spiritual quest led him to study with masters from different traditions and to travel far from his native Chile, to places as distant as Israel, Brazil, India, and the United States. He is fluent in Spanish, Hebrew, Portuguese, and English. During his stay in Israel, he furthered his Hebrew and Aramaic studies in order to broaden his knowledge of the sacred scriptures. He studied other languages intensively, such as Sanskrit with Dr. Naga Kanya Kumari Garipathi, from Osmania University in Hyderabad (India); Pali at the Oxford Center for Buddhist Studies; and Latin and Ancient Greek with Professor Ariel Lazcano and later with Javier Alvarez, who holds a degree in Classical Philology from the University of Seville.

Two great masters contributed to Prabhuji's retroprogressive process. In 1976, he met his first guru, H.D.G Bhakti-kavi Atulānanda Ācārya Swami, whom he called Gurudeva. In those days, Gurudeva was a young *brahmacārī* who held the position of president of the ISKCON temple at Eyzaguirre 2404, Puente Alto, Santiago, Chile. Years later, he gave Prabhuji his first initiation, Brahminical initiation, and finally, Prabhuji formally accepted the sacraments of the holy order of *sannyāsa*, becoming a monk of the Brahma Gauḍīya Saṁpradāya. Gurudeva connected him to the devotion to Kṛṣṇa. He imparted to him the wisdom of bhakti yoga and instructed him in the practice of the *māhā-mantra* and the study of the holy scriptures.

In 1996, Prabhuji met his second guru, H.D.G. Avadhūta Śrī Brahmānanda Bābājī Mahārāja, in Rishikesh, India. Guru Mahārāja, as Prabhuji would call him, revealed that his own master, H.D.G. Avadhūta Śrī Mastarāma Bābājī Mahārāja, had told him years before he died that a person would come from the West and request to be his disciple. He commanded him to accept only that particular seeker. When he asked how he would identify this person, Mastarāma Bābājī replied, "You will recognize him by his eyes. You must accept him because he will be the continuation of the lineage." From his first meeting with young Prabhuji, Guru Mahārāja recognized him and officially initiated him as his disciple. For Prabhuji, this initiation marked the beginning of the most intense and mature stage of his retroprogressive process. Under the guidance of Guru Mahārāja, he studied Advaita Vedanta and deepened his meditation. Since his guru was a great devotee of Śrī Rāmakṛṣṇa Paramahaṁsa and Śāradā Devī, Prabhuji desired to be initiated into this disciplic lineage. He sought initiation from Swami Swahananda (1921–2012), minister and spiritual leader of the Vedanta Society of Southern California from 1976 to 2012. Swami Swahananda was a disciple of Swami Vijñānānanda, a direct disciple of Rāmakṛṣṇa. In 2008, Swami Swahananda initiated him, granting him both *dīkṣā* and the blessings of Śrī Rāmakṛṣṇa and the Divine Mother.

Guru Mahārāja guided Prabhuji until he officially bestowed upon him the sacraments of the sacred order of *avadhūtas*. In March 2011, H.D.G. Avadhūta Śrī Brahmānanda Bābājī Mahārāja ordered Prabhuji, on behalf of his own master, to accept the responsibility of continuing the lineage of *avadhūtas*. With this title, Prabhuji is the official representative of the line of this disciplic succession for the present generation.

Besides his *dikṣā-gurus*, Prabhuji studied with important spiritual and religious personalities, such as H.H. Swami Yajñavālkyānanda, H.H. Swami Dayānanda Sarasvatī, H.H. Swami Viṣṇu Devānanda Sarasvatī, H.H. Swami Jyotirmayānanda Sarasvatī, H.H. Swami Kṛṣṇānanda Sarasvatī from the Divine Life Society, H.H. Ma Yoga Śakti, H.H. Swami Pratyagbodhānanda, H.H. Swami Mahādevānanda, H.H. Swami Swahānanda of the Ramakrishna Mission, H.H. Swami Adhyātmānanda, H.H. Swami Svarūpanānda, and H.H. Swami Viditātmānanda of the Arsha Vidya Gurukulam, while the wisdom of tantra was awakened in Prabhuji by H.G. Mātājī Rīnā Śarmā in India.

In Vrindavan, he studied the bhakti yoga path in depth with H.H. Narahari Dāsa Bābājī Mahārāja, disciple of H.H. Nityānanda Dāsa Bābājī Mahārāja of Vraja. He also studied bhakti yoga with various disciples of His Divine Grace A.C. Bhaktivedānta Swami Prabhupāda: H.H. Kapīndra Swami, H.H. Paramadvaiti Mahārāja, H.H. Jagajīvana Dāsa, H.H. Tamāla Kṛṣṇa Gosvāmī, H.H. Bhagavān Dāsa Mahārāja, and H.H. Kīrtanānanda Swami, among others.

In 1980, Prabhuji received the blessings of H.G. Mother Krishnabai, the famous disciple of H.D.G. Swami Rāmdās. In 1984, he learned and began to practice Maharishi Mahesh Yogi's Transcendental Meditation technique. In 1988, he took the *kriyā-yoga* course on Paramahaṁsa Yogānanda. After two years, he was officially initiated into the technique of *kriyā-yoga* by the Self-Realization Fellowship. In 1982 he received *dikṣā* from H.H. Kīrtanānanda Swami, disciple of Śrīla Prabhupāda, who also gave him his second initiation in 1991 and *sannyāsa* initiation in 1993.

Prabhuji wanted to confirm the sacraments of the holy order of *sannyāsa* also within the Advaita Vedanta lineage. His *sannyāsa-dīkṣā* was confirmed on August 11, 1995, by H.H. Swami Jyotirmayānanda Sarasvatī, founder of the Yoga Research Foundation and disciple of H.H. Swami Śivānanda Sarasvatī of Rishikesh.

Prabhuji has been honored with various titles and diplomas by many leaders of prestigious religious and spiritual institutions in India. He was given the honorable title Kṛṣṇa Bhakta by H.H. Swami Viṣṇu Devānanda (the only title of Bhakti Yoga given by Swami Viṣṇu), disciple of H.H. Swami Śivānanda Sarasvatī and the founder of the Sivananda Organization. He was given the title Bhaktivedānta by H.H. B.A. Paramadvaiti Mahārāja, the founder of Vrinda. He was given the title Yogācārya by H.H. Swami Viṣṇu Devānanda, the Paramanand Institute of Yoga Sciences and Research of Indore, India, the International Yoga Federation, the Indian Association of Yoga, and the Śrī Shankarananda Yogashram of Mysore, India. He received the respectable title Śrī Śrī Rādhā Śyam Sunder Pāda-Padma Bhakta Śiromaṇi directly from H.H. Satyanārāyaṇa Dāsa Bābājī Mahant of the Chatu Vaiṣṇava Saṁpradāya.

Prabhuji dedicated more than forty years to studying hatha yoga with prestigious masters of classical and traditional yoga, such as H.H. Bapuji, H.H. Swami Viṣṇu Devānanda Sarasvatī, H.H. Swami Jyotirmayānanda Sarasvatī, H.H. Swami Satchidānanda Sarasvatī, H.H. Swami Vignānānanda Sarasvatī, and Śrī Madana-mohana.

He attended several systematic hatha yoga teacher training courses at prestigious institutions until he achieved the level of Master Ācārya. He has completed studies at the following institutions: World Yoga University, the Sivananda Yoga Vedanta, the Ananda Ashram, the Yoga Research Foundation, the Integral Yoga Academy, the Patanjala Yoga Kendra, the Ma Yoga Shakti International Mission, the Prana Yoga Organization, the Rishikesh Yoga Peeth, the Swami Sivananda Yoga Research Center, and the Swami Sivananda Yogasana Research Center.

Prabhuji is a member of the Indian Association of Yoga, Yoga Alliance ERYT 500 and YACEP, the International Association of Yoga Therapists, and the International Yoga Federation. In 2014, the International Yoga Federation honored him with the position of Honorary Member of the World Yoga Council.

His interest in the complex anatomy of the human body led him to study chiropractic at the prestigious Institute of Health of the Back and Extremities in Tel Aviv, Israel. In 1993, he received a diploma from Dr. Sheinerman, the founder and director of the institute. Later, he earned a massage therapy diploma at the Academy of Western Galilee. The knowledge he acquired in this field deepened his understanding of hatha yoga and contributed to the creation of his own method.

Retroprogressive Yoga is the result of Prabhuji's efforts to improve his practice and teaching methods. It is a system based especially on the teachings of his gurus and the sacred scriptures. Prabhuji has systematized various traditional yoga techniques to create a methodology suitable for Western audiences. Retroprogressive Yoga aspires to the experience of our authentic nature, promoting balance, health, and flexibility through proper diet, cleansing techniques, preparations (*āyojanas*), sequences (*vinyāsas*), postures (*āsanas*), breathing exercises (*prāṇayama*), relaxation (*śavāsana*), meditation (*dhyāna*), and exercises with locks (*bandhas*) and seals (*mudras*) to direct and empower *prāṇa*.

Since his childhood and throughout his life, Prabhuji has been an enthusiastic admirer, student, and practitioner of classic karate-do. From the age of 13, he studied different styles in Chile, such as kenpo with Sensei Arturo Petit and kung-fu, but specialized in the most traditional Japanese style of shotokan. He received the rank of black belt (third dan) from Shihan Kenneth Funakoshi (ninth dan). He also learned from Sensei Takahashi (seventh dan) and Sensei Masataka Mori (ninth dan). Additionally, he practiced shorin ryu style with Sensei Enrique Daniel Welcher (seventh dan), who granted him the rank of black belt (second dan). Through karate-do, he delved into Buddhism and gained additional knowledge about the physics of motion. He is a member of Funakoshi's Shotokan Karate Association.

Prabhuji grew up in an artistic environment and his love of painting began to develop in his childhood. His father, the renowned Chilean painter Yosef Har-Zion ZT"L, motivated him to devote himself to art. He learned painting from both his father and the famous Chilean painter Marcelo Cuevas. Prabhuji's abstract paintings reflect the depths of the spirit.

Since he was a young boy, Prabhuji has been especially drawn to postal stamps, postcards, mailboxes, postal transportation systems, and all mail-related activities. He has taken every opportunity to visit post offices in different cities and countries. He has delved into the study of philately, the field of collecting, sorting, and studying postage stamps. This passion led him to become a professional philatelist, a stamp distributor authorized by the American Philatelic Society, and a member of the following societies: the Royal Philatelic Society London, the Royal Philatelic Society of Victoria, the United States Stamp Society, the Great Britain Philatelic Society, the American Philatelic Society, the Society of Israel Philatelists, the Society for Hungarian Philately, the National Philatelic Society UK, the Fort Orange Stamp Club, the American Stamp Dealers Association, the US Philatelic Classics Society, Filabras - Associação dos Filatelistas Brasileiros, and the Collectors Club of NYC.

Based on his extensive knowledge of philately, theology, and Eastern philosophy, Prabhuji created "Meditative Philately" or "Philatelic Yoga," a spiritual practice that uses philately as the basis for practicing attention, concentration, observation, and meditation. It is inspired by the ancient Hindu mandala meditation and it can lead the practitioner to elevated states of consciousness, deep relaxation, and concentration that fosters the recognition of consciousness. Prabhuji wrote his thesis on this new type of yoga, "Meditative Philately," attracting the interest of the Indian academic community due to its innovative way of connecting meditation with different hobbies and activities. For this thesis, he was honored with a PhD in Yogic Philosophy from Yoga-Samskrutham University.

For more than 20 years, Prabhuji lived in Israel, where he furthered his studies of Judaism. One of his main teachers and sources of inspiration was Rabbi Shalom Dov Lifshitz ZT"L, whom he met in 1997. This great saint guided him for several years along the intricate paths of the Torah and Hassidism. He personally taught him Tanakh, Talmud, Midrash, Shulchan Aruch, Mishneh Torah, Tanya, Kabbalah and Zohar. The two developed a very close relationship. Prabhuji also studied the Talmud with Rabbi Raphael Rapaport Shlit"a (Ponovich), Hassidism with Rabbi Israel

Lifshitz Shlit"a, and the Torah with Rabbi Daniel Sandler Shlit"a. Prabhuji is a great devotee of Rabbi Mordechai Eliyahu ZT"L, who personally blessed him.

Prabhuji visited the United States in 2000 and during his stay in New York, he realized that it was the most appropriate place to found a religious organization. He was particularly attracted by the pluralism and respectful attitude of American society toward freedom of religion. He was impressed by the deep respect of both the public and the government for religious minorities. After consulting his masters and requesting their blessings, Prabhuji relocated to the United States. In 2003, the Prabhuji Mission was born, a Hindu church aimed at preserving Prabhuji's universal and pluralistic vision of Hinduism and his "Retroprogressive Path."

Although he did not seek to attract followers, for 15 years (1995–2010), Prabhuji considered the requests of a few people who approached him asking to become his monastic disciples. Those who chose to see him as their spiritual master voluntarily accepted vows of poverty and life-long dedication to spiritual practice (*sadhāna*), religious devotion (*bhakti*), and selfless service (*seva*). Although he no longer accepts new disciples, he continues to guide the small group of monastic disciples of the contemplative Ramakrishnananda Monastic Order that he founded.

In 2011, Prabhuji founded the Avadhutashram (monastery) in the Catskills Mountains in upstate New York, USA. The Avadhutashram is his hermitage, the residence of the monastic disciples of the Ramakrishnananda Order, and the headquarters of the Prabhuji Mission. He operates various humanitarian projects, inspired in his experience that "serving the part is serving the Whole." The ashram organizes humanitarian projects such as the Prabhuji Food Distribution Program and the Prabhuji Toy Distribution Program.

According to Prabhuji, the quest for the Self is individual, solitary, personal, private, and intimate. It is not a collective endeavor to be undertaken through organized, institutional, or communitarian religiosity. Nowadays, he disagrees with spirituality practiced in a social, communal, or collective manner. Therefore, he does not proselytize or preach, nor does he try to persuade, convince, or make anyone change their perspective, philosophy, or religion. His message does not promote collective spirituality, but individual inner search.

Prabhuji has delegated the choice to his disciples between keeping his teachings exclusively within the monastic order or spreading his message to the public. Upon the explicit request of his disciples, he has agreed to have his books published and his lectures disseminated, as long as this does not compromise his privacy and his life as a hermit.

In 2022, Prabhuji founded the Retroprogressive Institute. Here, his most senior disciples can systematically share his teachings and message through video conferences. The institute offers support and help for a deeper understanding of his teachings.

In 2025, he established the Retroprogressive Yoga Academy, where he personally transmits his yoga method to disciples and students without departing from his hermitic life. That same year, he founded the Retroprogressive Karate Academy, through which he shares his knowledge of the martial arts as a path toward the expansion of consciousness.

Prabhuji is a respected member of the American Philosophical Association, the American Association of Philosophy Teachers, the American Association of University Professors, the Southwestern Philosophical Society, the Authors Guild, the National Writers Union, PEN America, the International Writers Association, the National Association of Independent Writers and Editors, the National Writers Association, the Alliance Independent Authors, and the Independent Book Publishers Association.

Prabhuji's vast literary contribution includes books in Spanish, English, and Hebrew, such as *Kundalini Yoga: The Power is in you, What is, as it is, Bhakti Yoga: The Path of Love, Tantra: Liberation in the World, Experimenting with the Truth, Advaita Vedanta: Being the Self, Yoga: Union with reality*, commentaries on the *Īśāvāsya Upanishad* and the *Diamond Sūtra, I am that I am, The Symbolic Turn, Being, Questioning your Answers: Philosophy as a Question, Beyond Answers: Philosophy in the Eternal Search, Phenomenology of the Sacred: Foundations for a Retroprogressive Phenomenology, Discovering the Last God*, and *Mapuche Spirituality*.

The term *Prabhuji*
by Swami Ramananda

Several years ago, some disciples, followers and friends of His Holiness Avadhūta Bhaktivedānta Yogācārya Śrī Ramakrishnananda Bābājī Mahārāja, opted to refer to him as Prabhuji. In this article, I would like to clarify the deep meaning of this Sanskrit term. The word *prabhu* in Sanskrit means "a master, lord or a king" and it is applied in the scriptures to God and to the Guru.

Like many words in the Sanskrit language, the word is actually made of some components, and understanding its etymology will lead us to discover its various meanings. The word *prabhu* is a combination of the root *bhu* which means "to become, to exist, to be, to live" and the prefix *pra*, which can mean "forth, or forward" and which then, when attached to *bhu* would mean "one who causes to exist, who gives life, from whom life emanates, that which sustains or maintains."

The prefix *pra* can also mean "very much, or supremacy," and then when attached to the root *bhu* would mean "to be the master, to rule over."

The suffix *jī* is an honorific title in Hindi and other Indian languages. It is added after the names of Gods and esteemed personalities to show respect and reverence.

As manifestations of the Divine, great *ṛṣis*, or 'seers' and gurus are also called *prabhus*. For example, the sage Nārada is addressing the *ṛṣi* Vyasadeva as *prabhu*:

जिज्ञासितमधीतं च ब्रह्म यत्तत्सनातनम् ।
तथापि शोचस्यात्मानमकृतार्थ इव प्रभो ॥

jijñāsitam adhītaṁ ca
brahma yat tat sanātanam
tathāpi śocasy ātmānam
akṛtārtha iva prabho

You have fully delineated the subject of impersonal Brahman as well as the knowledge derived therefrom. Why should you be despondent in spite of all this, thinking that you are undone, my dear master (*prabhu*)?

(*Bhāgavata Purana*, 1.5.4)

Mahārāja Parīkṣit addresses Śukadeva as *prabhu* when he approaches the sage to seek spiritual guidance, thus accepting him as his guru.

यच्छ्रोतव्यमथो जप्यं यत्कर्तव्यं नृभिः प्रभो ।
स्मर्तव्यं भजनीयं वा ब्रूहि यद्वा विपर्ययम् ॥

yac chrotavyam atho japyaṁ
yat kartavyaṁ nṛbhiḥ prabho
smartavyaṁ bhajanīyaṁ vā
brūhi yad vā viparyayam

O prabhu, please let me know what a man should hear, chant, remember and worship, and also what he should not do. Please explain all this to me.

(*Bhāgavata Purana*, 1.19.38)

The term *avadhūta*

This is an excerpt from the book *Sannyāsa Darśana* by Swami Niranjanānanda Sarasvatī, a disciple of Paramahaṁsa Swami Satyānanda.

Stages of *sannyāsāvadhūta*

"The *avadhūta* represents the pinnacle of spiritual evolution; none is superior to him. *Avadhūta* means 'one who is immortal' (*akṣara*) and who has totally discarded worldly ties. He is really Brahman itself. He has realized he is pure intelligence and is not concerned about the six frailties of human birth, namely: sorrow, delusion, old age, death, hunger, and thirst. He has shaken off all bondage of the experimental world and roams freely like a child, a madman or one possessed by spirits.

He may be with or without clothes. He wears no distinctive emblem of any order. He has no desire to sleep, beg, or bathe. He views his body as a corpse and subsists on the food that comes to him from all classes. He does not interpret the *śāstras* or the Vedas. For him, nothing is righteous or unrighteous, holy or unholy.

He is free from karma. The karmas of this life and past lives are all burned out, and due to the absence of *kartṛtva* (the doer) and *bhoktṛtva* (the desire for enjoyment), no future karmas are created. Only the *prārabdha-karmas* (unalterable) that have already begun to operate will affect his body, helping to sustain it, but his mind will remain unaffected. He will live in this world until the *prārabdha-karmas* are extinguished, and then his body will fall. Then he is said to attain *videhamukti* (the state beyond body consciousness).

Such a liberated soul never returns to the embodied state. He is not born again; he is immortal. He has achieved the final aim of being born in this world."

The *Bṛhad-avadhūta Upanishad* reads as follows: "The *avadhūta* is so called because he is immortal; he is the greatest; he has discarded worldly ties, and he is alluded to in the meaning of the sentence 'Thou art That.'"

His Divine Grace Śrīla Bhakti Ballabh Tīrtha Mahārāja in his article entitled "*Pariṣads*: Śrīla Vamśi das Bābājī" wrote: "He was a Paramahaṁsa Vaiṣṇava who acted in the manner of an *avadhūta*. The word *avadhūta* refers to one who has shaken off from himself all worldly feelings and obligations. He does not care for social conventions, especially the *varṇāśrama-dharma*, that is, he is quite eccentric in his behavior. Nityānanda Prabhu is often characterized as an *avadhūta*."

From the foreword to Dattātreya's *Avadhūta-gītā*, translated and annotated by Swami Aśokānanda: "The *Avadhūta-gītā* is a Vedanta text representing extreme Advaita or non-dualism. It is attributed to Dattātreya, who is looked upon as an Incarnation of God. Unfortunately, we possess no historical data concerning when or where he was born, how long he lived, or how he arrived at the knowledge disclosed in the text.

Avadhūta means a liberated soul, one who has 'passed away from' or 'shaken off' all worldly attachments and cares and has attained a spiritual state equivalent to the existence of God. Although *avadhūta* naturally implies renunciation, it includes an additional and even higher state that is neither attachment nor detachment, but is beyond both. An *avadhūta* feels no need to observe any rules, whether secular or religious. He seeks nothing and avoids nothing. He has neither knowledge nor ignorance. Having realized that he is the infinite Self, he lives in that vivid realization."

Swami Vivekānanda, one of the greatest advaitins of all times, often quoted this *Gītā*. He once said, "Men like the one who wrote this song keep religion alive. They have experienced. They care for nothing, and feel nothing done to the body; they don't care for heat, cold, danger, or anything else. They sit still, enjoying the bliss of the

Ātman, and even if embers burn their bodies, they do not feel them."

The *Avadhūta Upanishad* is number 79 in the *Muktikā* canon of Upanishads. It is a *Sannyāsa Upanishad* associated with the Black (Kṛṣṇa) Yajur-veda: "One who has transcended the *varṇāśrama* system and has always established in himself, that yogi, who is above the *varṇāśrama* divisions, is called *avadhūta*." (*Avadhūta Upanishad*, 2).

The *Brahma-nirvāṇa Tantra* book describes how to identify *avadhūtas* of the following types:

- *Bramhāvadhūta*: An *avadhūta* by birth, who appears in any cast of society and is completely indifferent to the world or worldly matters.
- *Śaivāvadhūta*: *Avadhūtas* who have taken to the renounced order of life or *sannyāsa*, often with long matted hair (*jaṭa*), or who dress in the manner of Shaivites and spend almost all of their time in trance *samādhi*, or meditation.
- *Virāvadhūta*: This person looks like a *sadhū* who has put red-colored sandal paste on his body and wears saffron-colored clothes. His hair is very well grown and is normally furling in the wind. They wear around their necks a *rudrākṣa-mālā* or a chain of bones. They carry a wooden stick, or *daṇḍa*, in their hand, and additionally always carry an axe (*paraśu*) or an *ḍamaru* (small drum) with them.
- *Kulāvadhūta*: These people are supposed to have taken the Kaul *Saṁpradāya* initiation. It is very difficult to recognize these people as they do not wear any outward signs that can identify them from others. The specialty of these people is that they stay and live like normal people. They may show themselves in the form of kings or family men.

The *Nātha Saṁpradāya* is a form of *Avadhūta-pantha* (sect). In this *Saṁpradāya*, Guru and yoga are of extreme importance. Therefore, the most important book of this *Saṁpradāya* is the *Avadhūta-gītā*. Śrī Gorakṣanāth is considered the highest form of the *avadhūta* state.

The nature of *avadhūta* is the subject of the *Avadhūta-gītā*, traditionally attributed to Dattātreya.

According to Bipin Joshi, the main characteristics of an *avadhūta* are: "He who is a sinless philosopher and has cast off the shackles of ignorance (*ajñāna*). He who lives in a stateless state and relishes the experience all the time. He revels in this blissful state, unperturbed by the material world. In this unique state, the *avadhūta* is neither awake nor in deep sleep; there is no sign of life or death. It is a state defying all descriptions. It is the state of infinite bliss, which a finite language is incapable of describing. It can only be intuited purely by our intellect. A state that is neither truth nor non-truth, neither existence nor nonexistence. He who has realized his identity with the imperishable, who possesses incomparable excellence, who has shaken off the bonds of *saṁsāra* and never deviates from his goal. That thou art (*tat tvam asi*), and other upanishadic statements, are ever present in the mind of such an enlightened soul. That sage who is rooted in the plenary experience of 'Verily, I am Brahman (*ahaṁ Brahmāsmi*)', 'All this is Brahman (*sarvaṁ khalvidaṁ brahma*)', and that '...there is no plurality, I and God are one and the same...', etc. Supported by the personal experience of such Vedic statements, he moves freely in a state of total bliss. Such a person is a renunciant, liberated, *avadhūta*, yogi, paramahamsa, *brāhmaṇa*."

From Wikipedia, the free encyclopedia:

Avadhūta is a Sanskrit term used in Indian religions to refer to mystics or antinomian saints who are beyond ego-consciousness, duality, and common worldly concerns, and act without consideration of standard social etiquette. Such personalities "roam free as a child on the face of the Earth." An *avadhūta* does not identify with his mind or body or 'names and forms' (Sanskrit: *nāma-rūpa*). Such a person is considered pure consciousness (Sanskrit: *caitanya*) in human form.

Avadhūtas play a significant role in the history, origins, and rejuvenation of a number of traditions such as yoga, Advaita Vedanta, Buddhist, and bhakti *paraṁparās* even as they are released from standard observances. *Avadhūtas* are the voice of the *avadhūti*, the channel that resolves the dichotomy of *Vāmācāra* and *Dakṣiṇācāra* or "left and right-handed traditions." An *avadhūta* may or may not continue to practice religious rites as long as they are free from sectarian ritual observance and affiliation. The Monier Williams Sanskrit dictionary defines the term *avadhūta* as follows: "अवधूत / अव-धूत — one who has shaken off from himself worldly feelings and obligations."

From *Hinduism, an alphabetical guide* by Roshen Dalal

Avadhūta: A term for a liberated soul, one who has renounced the world. Totally beyond all that is, an *avadhūta* follows no rules, no fixed practices, and has no need to follow conventional norms. There are several texts dealing with the life and nature of an *avadhūta*. In the *Avadhūta Upanishad*, the Ṛṣi Dattātreya describes the nature of the *avadhūta*. Such a person is immortal, has discarded all worldly ties, and is always full of bliss. One of its verses states: "Let thought contemplate Viṣṇu, or let it be dissolved in the bliss of Brahman. I, the witness, do nothing, nor do I cause anything to be done." (v.28)

The *Turīyātīta Avadhūta Upanishad* contains a description of the *avadhūta* who has reached the state of consciousness beyond the *turīya*. In this state, a person is pure, detached and totally free. An *avadhūta* who has reached this level does not chant mantras or practice rituals, wears no caste marks, and is finished with all religious and secular duties. He wears no clothes and eats whatever comes his way. He wanders alone, observing silence, and is totally absorbed in non-duality. The *Avadhūta-gītā* has similar descriptions.

The *Uddhava-gītā*, which is part of the *Bhāgavata Purana*, describes an *avadhūta* who learned from all aspects of life and was at home anywhere in the world. The term *avadhūta* can be applied to any liberated person, but it also refers specifically to a *sannyāsa* sect.

Avadhūta Upanishad

Avadhūta Upanishad is a small Upanishad consisting of about 32 mantras. It falls under the category of the *Sannyāsa Upanishads* and is a part of Kṛṣṇa Yajurveda. The *Avadhūta Upanishad* takes the form of a dialogue between Dattātreya and Ṛṣi Saṁkṛti.

One day Ṛṣi Saṁkṛti asks Dattātreya the following questions: "Who is an *avadhūta*?; What is his state?; What are the signs of the *avadhūta*?; How does he live?"

The following are the answers given by the compassionate Dattātreya.

Who is an *avadhūta*?

The *avadhūta* is so called because he is beyond any decay; he lives freely according to his will, he destroys the bondage of worldly desires, and his only goal is That thou Art (*tat tvam asi*).

The *avadhūta* goes far beyond all the castes (such as *brāhmaṇa*, *vaiśya*, *kṣatrya*, and *śūdra*) and *Āśramas* (such as *brāmhacaryā*, *gṛhastha*, *vānaprastha*, and *sannyāsa*). He is the highest Yogi who is established in a constant state of self-realization.

What is his state?

An *avadhūta* always enjoys supreme bliss. The divine joy represents his head, happiness is his right wing, ecstasy represents his left wing, and bliss is his very nature. The life of an *avadhūta* shows extreme detachment.

What are the signs of *avadhūta*? How does he live?

An *avadhūta* lives according to his own will. He may wear clothes or go naked. For him, there is no difference between *dharma* or *adharma*, sacrifice or non-sacrifice, because he is beyond these aspects. He performs inner sacrifice and that forms their *aśvamedha-yajña.* He is a great yogi who remains unaffected even when engaged in worldly objects. He remains pure.

The ocean accepts water from all the rivers but remains unchanged. Similarly, an *avadhūta* is unaffected by worldly objects. He is always at peace and (like the ocean), all his desires are absorbed in this supreme peace.

For an *avadhūta* there is no birth or death, no bondage or liberation. He may have performed various actions for the sake of liberation, but they become history once he becomes an *avadhūta*. He is always satisfied. Others wander to fulfill their desires. But an *avadhūta*, being already satisfied, does not run after any desire. Others perform various rituals for the sake of heaven, but an *avadhūta* is already established in the omnipresent state and hence needs no rituals.

Other qualified teachers spend time teaching the scriptures (Vedas) but *avadhūta* goes beyond those activities, because he has no actions. He doesn't have any desire to sleep, beg (*bhikṣa*), bathe, or clean.

An *avadhūta* is always free from doubt, and since he is always in union with the supreme reality, he does not even need to meditate. Meditation is for those people who are not yet one with God, but an *avadhūta* is always in the state of union and therefore does not need to meditate.

Those who are after *karmas* (actions) are filled with *vāsanās*. These *vāsanās* haunt them even when they finish their *prārabdha-karma*. Ordinary men meditate because they wish to fulfill their desires. However, an *avadhūta* always stays away from that trap. His mind is beyond mental destruction and *samādhi*. Mental destruction as well as *samādhi* are possibly modifications of the mind. The *avadhūta* is already eternal and hence, there is nothing to attain for him.

Following worldly duties is like an arrow released from a bow, i.e. it cannot be stopped from giving good or bad fruits causing a cycle of action-reaction. However, an *avadhūta* is not a doer at any level and is not engaged in any action.

Having attained such a stage of detachment, an *avadhūta* remains unaffected even if he follows a way of life as prescribed by the scriptures. Even if he engages in *actions* such as worshipping God, bathing, begging, etc., he remains unattached to them. He lives as a witness and therefore does not perform any action.

An *avadhūta* can clearly see Brahman before his eyes. He is free from ignorance or *māyā*. He has no actions left to be performed and nothing left to achieve. He is totally satisfied and there is no one else with whom he can be compared.

नलिनी नालिनी नासे गन्धः सौरभ उच्च्यते ।
घ्राणोऽवधूतो मुख्यास्यं विपणो वाग्रसविद्रसः ॥

nalinī nālinī nāse
gandhaḥ saurabha ucyate
ghrāṇo 'vadhūto mukhyāsyaṁ
vipaṇo vāg rasavid rasaḥ

> The two doors called Nalinī and Nālinī are to be known as the two nostrils, and the city named Saurabha represents the aroma. The companion spoken of as *avadhūta* is the sense of smell. The door called Mukhyā is the mouth, and Vipaṇa is the faculty of speech. Rasajña is the sense of taste.
>
> (*Bhāgavata Purana*, 4.29.11)

Purport of H.D.G. A.C. Bhaktivedanta Swami Prabhupada:

The word *avadhūta* means "most free." A person is not under the rules and regulations of any injunction when he has attained the stage of *avadhūta*. In other words, he can act as he likes. This stage of *avadhūta* is exactly like air, which does not care for any obstruction. In the Bhagavad Gita (6.34) it is said:

चञ्चलं हि मनः कृष्ण प्रमाथि बलवद्दृढम् ।
तस्याहं निग्रहं मन्ये वायोरिव सुदुष्करम् ॥

cañcalaṁ hi manaḥ kṛṣṇa
pramāthi balavad dṛḍham
tasyāhaṁ nigrahaṁ manye
vāyor iva suduṣkaram

> The mind is restless, turbulent, obstinate, and very strong, O Kṛṣṇa, and to subdue it is, it seems to me, more difficult than controlling the wind.
>
> (Bhagavad Gita, 6.34)

Just as air or wind cannot be stopped by anyone, the two nostrils, situated in one place, enjoy the sense of smell without impediment. With the tongue, the mouth continuously tastes all kinds of tasty foods.

अक्षरत्वाद्वरेण्यत्वाद्धूतसंसारबन्धनात् ।
तत्त्वमस्यर्थसिद्धत्वात् अवधूतोऽभिधीयते ॥

akṣaratvād vareṇyatvād
dhūta-saṁsāra-bandhanāt
tat tvam asy-artha siddhatvāt
avadhūto 'bhidhīyate

Since he is immutable (*akṣara*), the most excellent (*varenya*), since he has removed the worldly attachments (*dhūta-samsāra-bandanāt*) and he has realized the meaning of *tat tvam asi* (That thou art), he is called *avadhūta.*

(*Kulārṇava Tantra*, 17.24)

From Yogapedia: What does *avadhūta* mean?

Avadhūta is a Sanskrit term used to refer to a person who has reached a stage in their spiritual development in which they are beyond worldly concerns. People who have reached the stage of *avadhūta* may act without considering common social etiquette or their own ego. This term is often used in the cases of mystics or saints.

Advanced yoga practitioners may find inspiration in the idea of reaching this stage through further sustained meditation and asana practice.

Avadhūta is often associated with some sort of eccentric and spontaneous behavior from a holy person. This comes partly from the fact that mystics who have achieved this level of spiritual enlightenment may forget wearing clothes or other normal social behavior.

About the Prabhuji Mission

Prabhuji Mission is a Hindu religious, spiritual, and charitable organization founded by H.H. Avadhūta Bhaktivedānta Yogācārya Śrī Ramakrishnananda Bābājī Mahārāja. Its purpose is to preserve the "Retroprogressive Path," which reflects Prabhuji's vision of *Sanātana-dharma* and advocates for the global awakening of consciousness as the radical solution to humanity's problems.

Apart from imparting religious and spiritual teachings, the organization carries out extensive philanthropic work in the USA, based on the principles of karma yoga, selfless work performed with dedication to God.

Prabhuji Mission was established in 2003 in the USA as a Hindu church aimed at preserving its founder's universal and pluralistic vision of Hinduism.

The Prabhuji Mission operates a Hindu temple called Śrī Śrī Bhagavān Yeshua Jagat Jananī Miriam Premānanda Mandir, which offers worship and religious ceremonies to parishioners.

The extensive library of the Retroprogressive Institute provides its teachers with abundant study materials to research the various theologies and philosophies explored by Prabhuji in his books and lectures.

The Avadhutashram monastery educates monastic disciples on various aspects of Prabhuji's approach to Hinduism and offers them the opportunity to express devotion to God through devotional service by selflessly contributing their skills and training to the Mission's programs.

The Mission publishes and distributes Prabhuji's books and lectures and operates humanitarian projects such as the "Prabhuji Food Distribution Program," a weekly event in which dozens of families in need from Upstate New York receive fresh and nutritious food and the "Prabhuji Toy Distribution Program," which provides the less privileged kids with abundance of Christmas gifts.

Avadhutashram
Round Top, New York, USA

About the Avadhutashram

The Avadhutashram (monastery) was founded by Prabhuji. It is the headquarters of the Prabhuji Mission and the hermitage of H.H. Avadhūta Bhaktivedānta Yogācārya Śrī Ramakrishnananda Bābājī Mahārāja and his monastic disciples of the Ramakrishnananda Contemplative Monastic Order.

The ideals of the Avadhutashram are love and selfless service, based on the universal vision that God is in everything and everyone. Its mission is to distribute spiritual books and organize humanitarian projects such as the Prabhuji Food Distribution Program and the Prabhuji Toy Distribution Program.

The Avadhutashram is not commercial and operates without soliciting donations. Its activities are funded by Prabhuji's Gifts, a non-profit company founded by Prabhuji, which sells esoteric items from different traditions that he himself has used for spiritual practices during his evolutionary process. Its mission is to preserve and disseminate traditional religious, mystical, and ancestral crafts.

The Retroprogressive Path

The Retroprogressive Path does not require you to be part of a group or a member of an organization, institution, society, congregation, club, or exclusive community. Living in a temple, monastery, or *āśram* is not mandatory, because it is not about a change of residence, but of consciousness. It does not urge you to believe, but to doubt. It does not demand you to accept something, but to explore, investigate, examine, inquire, and question everything. It does not suggest being what you should be but being what you really are.

The Retroprogressive Path supports freedom of expression but not proselytizing. This route does not promise answers to our questions but induces us to question our answers. It does not promise to be what we are not or to attain what we have not already achieved. It is a retro-evolutionary path of self-discovery that leads us from what we think we are to what we really are. It is not the only way, nor the best, the simplest, or the most direct. It is an involutionary process par excellence that shows what is obvious and undeniable but usually goes unnoticed: that which is simple, innocent, and natural. It is a path that begins and ends in you.

The Retroprogressive Path is a continuous revelation that expands eternally. It delves into consciousness from an ontological perspective, transcending all religion and spiritual paths. It is the discovery of diversity as a unique and inclusive reality. It is the encounter of consciousness with itself, aware of itself and its own reality. In fact, this path is a simple invitation to dance in the now, to love the present moment, and to celebrate our authenticity. It is an unconditional proposal to stop living as a victim of circumstance and to live as a passionate adventurer. It is a call to return to the place we have never left, without offering us anything we do not already possess or teaching us anything we do not already know. It is a call for an inner revolution and to enter the fire of life that only consumes dreams, illusions, and fantasies but does not touch what we are. It does not help us reach our desired goal, but instead prepares us for the unexpected miracle.

This path was nurtured over a lifetime dedicated to the search for Truth. It is a grateful offering to existence for what I have received. But remember, do not look for me. Look for yourself. It is not me you need, because you are the only one who really matters. This life is just a wonderful parenthesis in eternity to know and love. What you yearn for lies in you, here and now, as what you really are.

Your unconditional well-wisher,
Prabhuji

Prabhuji today

Prabhuji has retired from public life

Prabhuji is the sole disciple of H.D.G. Avadhūta Śrī Brahmānanda Bābājī Mahārāja, who is himself one of the closest and most intimate disciples of H.D.G. Avadhūta Śrī Mastarāma Bābājī Mahārāja.

Guru Mahārāja guided Prabhuji until he officially bestowed upon him the sacraments of the sacred order of *avadhūtas*. Prabhuji was appointed as the successor of the lineage by his master, who conferred upon him the responsibility of continuing the line of disciplic succession of *avadhūtas*, or the sacred *paramparā*, officially designating him as guru and commanding him to serve as the successor Ācārya under the name H.H. Avadhūta Bhaktivedānta Yogācārya Śrī Ramakrishnananda Bābājī Mahārāja.

Prabhuji is also a disciple of H.D.G. Bhakti-kavi Atulānanda Ācārya Mahārāja, who is a direct disciple of H.D.G. A.C. Bhaktivedānta Swami Prabhupāda.

In 2011, with the blessings of his Gurudeva, he adopted the path of a secluded *bhajanānandī* and withdrew from society to lead the contemplative life of a hermit. Since then, he has been living as an independent Christian-Marian Hindu religious hermit. His days have been spent in solitude, praying, writing, painting, and meditating in silence and contemplation.

He no longer participates in *sat-saṅgs*, lectures, gatherings, meetings, retreats, seminars, study groups, or courses. We ask everyone to respect his privacy and do not try to contact him by any means for gatherings, meetings, interviews, blessings, *śaktipāta*, initiations, or personal visits.

Prabhuji's teachings

As an *avadhūta* and a realized master, Prabhuji has always appreciated the essence and wisdom of a wide variety of religious practices from around the world. Although many see him as an enlightened being, Prabhuji has no intention of presenting himself as a public figure, preacher, propagator of beliefs, promoter of philosophies, guide, coach, content creator, influencer, preceptor, mentor, counselor, consultant, monitor, tutor, teacher, instructor, educator, enlightener, pedagogue, evangelist, rabbi, *posek halacha*, healer, therapist, satsangist, pointer, psychic, leader, medium, savior, New Age guru, or authority of any kind, whether spiritual or material. According to Prabhuji, the quest for the Self is individual, solitary, personal, private, and intimate. It is not a collective endeavor to be undertaken through organized, institutional, or community religiosity. Since 2011, Prabhuji has disagreed with spirituality practiced in a social, communal, or collective manner. Therefore, he does not proselytize or preach, nor does he try to persuade, convince, or make anyone change their perspective, philosophy, or religion. Many may find his insights valuable and apply them partially or fully to their own development, but Prabhuji's teachings should not be interpreted as personal advice, direction, counseling, instruction, guidance, tutoring, self-help methods, or techniques for spiritual, physical, emotional, or psychological development. The proposed teachings do not aspire to be definitive solutions for life's spiritual, material, financial, psychological, emotional, romantic, family, social, or physical problems. Prabhuji does not promise miracles, mystical experiences, astral journeys, healings of any kind, connections with spirits, angels or extraterrestrials, astral travel to other planets, supernatural powers, or spiritual salvation.

Service and glorification of the guru are fundamental spiritual principles in Hinduism. The Prabhuji Mission, as a traditional Hindu church, practices the millenary *guru-bhakti* tradition of reverence to the master.

Some disciples and friends of the Prabhuji Mission, on their own initiative, help to preserve Prabhuji's legacy and his interfaith teachings for future generations by disseminating his books, videos of his internal talks, and websites.

The sacred way

Some time ago, on the sacred journey toward transcendence, Prabhuji reaffirmed his resolve not to disturb those who showed no interest in joining him on this path. This decision is not simple detachment, but instead, a deliberate choice to preserve the essence of this migratory route: a commitment to authenticity and deepening self-inquiry. Such a decision, far from being an abandonment, is a respectful recognition of individual autonomy and divergent destinies and aspirations. On this journey, choosing fellow travelers is not a mere whim, but an exercise in critical discernment and alignment with those whose vision intertwines with our own in the search for our home within our own house.

Public services

Even though the monastery does not accept new residents, volunteers, donations, collaborations, or sponsorships, the public is invited to participate in daily religious services and devotional festivals at the Śrī Śrī Bhagavān Yeshua Jagat Jananī Miriam Premānanda Mandir.

Titles by Prabhuji

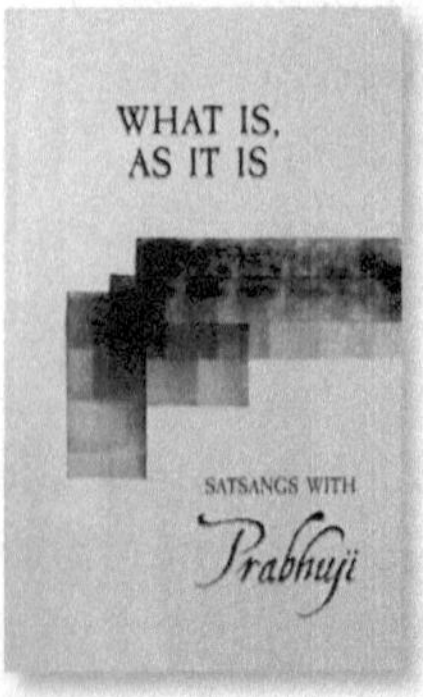

What is, as it is: Satsangs with Prabhuji (English)
ISBN-13: 978-1-945894-26-8

Lo que es, tal como es: *Sat-saṅgas* con Prabhuji (Spanish)
ISBN-13: 978-1-945894-27-5
Russian: ISBN-13: 978-1-945894-18-3
Hebrew: ISBN-13: 978-1-945894-24-4

Kundalini Yoga: The Power is in you (English)
ISBN-13: 978-1-945894-30-5

***Kuṇḍalinī-yoga*: El poder está en ti (Spanish)**
ISBN-13: 978-1-945894-31-2

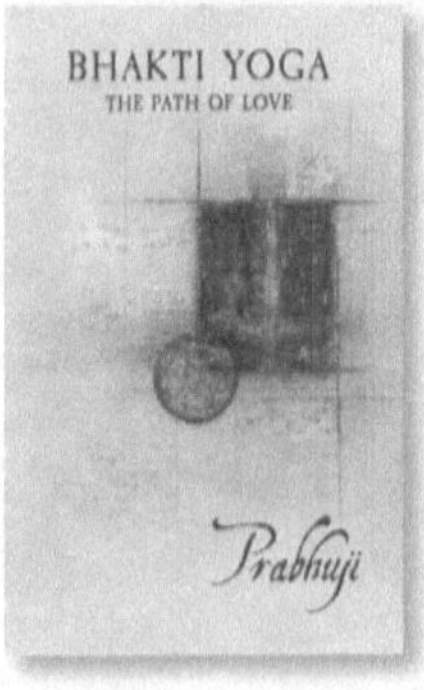

Bhakti Yoga: The Path of Love (English)
ISBN-13: 978-1-945894-28-2

***Bhakti-yoga*: El sendero del amor (Spanish)**
ISBN-13: 978-1-945894-29-9

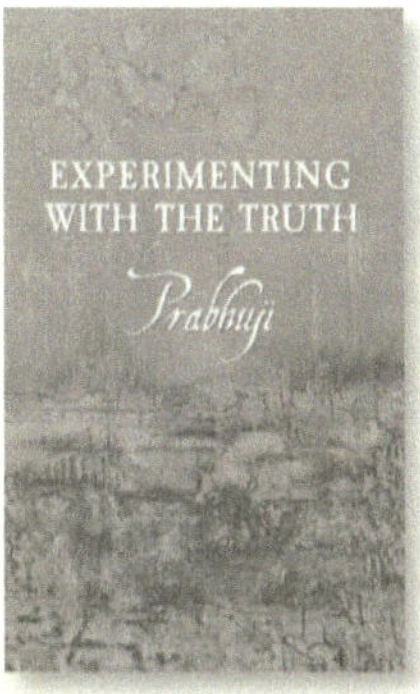

Experimenting with the Truth (English)
ISBN-13: 978-1-945894-32-9

Experimentando con la Verdad (Spanish)
ISBN-13: 978-1-945894-33-6

Hebrew
ISBN-13: 978-1-945894-93-0

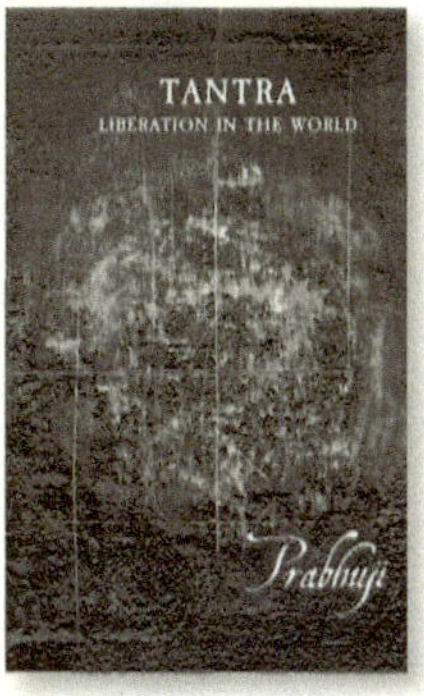

Tantra: Liberation in the World (English)
ISBN-13: 978-1-945894-36-7

Tantra: La liberación en el mundo (Spanish)
ISBN-13: 978-1-945894-37-4

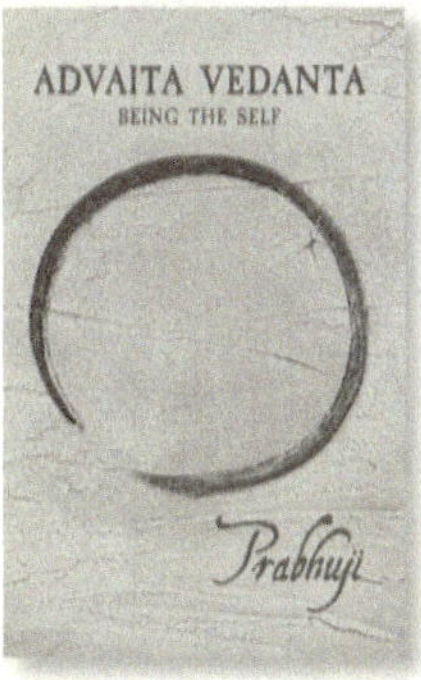

Advaita Vedanta: Being the Self (English)
ISBN-13: 978-1-945894-34-3

***Advaita Vedānta*: Ser el Ser (Spanish)**
ISBN-13: 978-1-945894-35-0

Beyond Answers: Philosophy in the Eternal Search (English)
ISBN-13: 978-1-945894-91-6

Más allá de las respuestas: La filosofía en la búsqueda eterna (Spanish)
ISBN-13: 978-1-945894-88-6

Discovering the Last God (English)
ISBN-13: 978-1-945894-71-8

Descubriendo el Último Dios (Spanish)
ISBN-13: 978-1-945894-89-3

Questioning your Answers: Philosophy as a Question (English)
ISBN-13: 978-1-945894-80-0

Cuestionando tus respuestas: La filosofía como pregunta (Spanish)
ISBN-13: 978-1-945894-77-0

Īśāvāsya Upanishad
commented by Prabhuji
(English)
ISBN-13: 978-1-945894-38-1

Īśāvāsya Upaniṣad
comentado por Prabhuji
(Spanish)
ISBN-13: 978-1-945894-40-4

The Diamond Sūtra
commented by Prabhuji
(English)
ISBN-13: 978-1-945894-51-0

El Sūtra del Diamante
comentado por Prabhuji
(Spanish)
ISBN-13: 978-1-945894-54-1

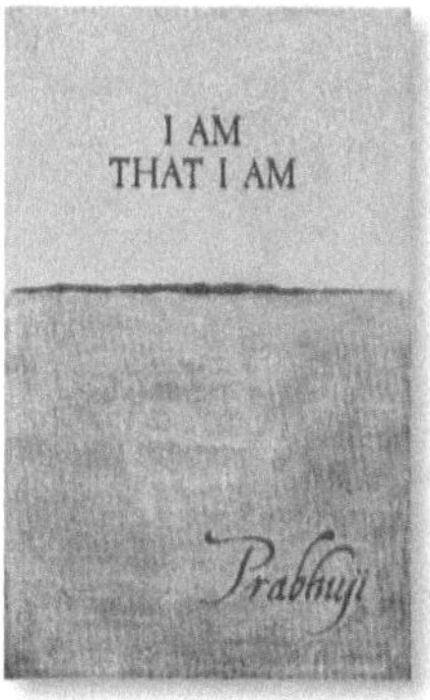

I am that I am
(English)
ISBN-13: 978-1-945894-78-7

Soy el que soy
(Spanish)
ISBN-13: 978-1-945894-48-0

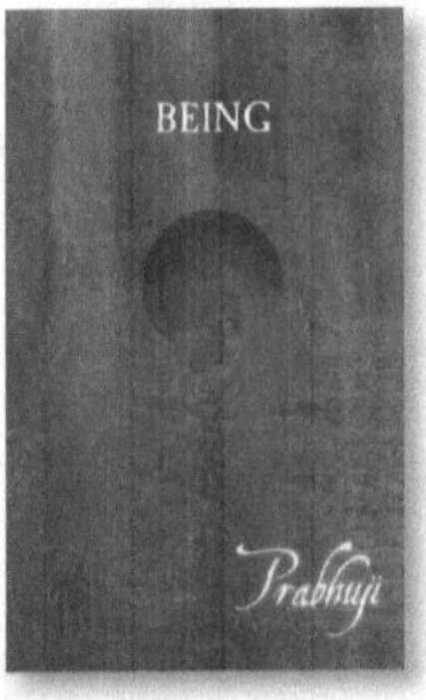

Being (English)
Vol I: 978-1-945894-73-2
Vol II: 978-1-945894-74-9
Vol III: 978-1-945894-55-8
Ser (Spanish)
Vol I: 978-1-945894-70-1
Vol II: 978-1-945894-94-7
Vol III: 978-1-945894-56-5

The Symbolic Turn (English)
ISBN-13: 978-1-945894-62-6

El giro simbólico (Spanish)
ISBN-13: 978-1-945894-59-6

Phenomenology of the Sacred: Foundations for a Retroprogressive Phenomenology (English)
ISBN-13: 978-1-945894-68-8

La fenomenología de lo sagrado: Fundamentos para una Fenomenología Retroprogresiva (Spanish)
ISBN-13: 978-1-945894-65-7

Mapuche Spirituality
(English)
ISBN-13: 978-1-945894-92-3

La espiritualidad mapuche
(Spanish)
ISBN-13: 978-1-945894-95-4

www.ingramcontent.com/pod-product-compliance
Lightning Source LLC
Chambersburg PA
CBHW021129230426
43667CB00005B/72
* 9 7 8 1 9 4 5 8 9 4 6 1 9 *